S

THEATRE COMPANIES
OF THE WORLD

THEATRE
COMPANIES
OF THE
WORLD

Africa, Asia, Australia and New Zealand,
Canada, Eastern Europe, Latin America,
The Middle East, Scandinavia

Edited by
COLBY H. KULLMAN
and
WILLIAM C. YOUNG

GREENWOOD PRESS
New York · Westport, Connecticut · London

Library of Congress Cataloging-in-Publication Data

Main entry under title:

Theatre companies of the world.

Bibliography: p.
Includes index.

Contents: v. 1 Africa, Asia, Australia and New Zealand,
Canada, Eastern Europe, Latin America, The Middle East,
Scandinavia — v. 2 United States of America, Western Europe
(excluding Scandinavia)

1. Theater—Handbooks, manuals, etc.   I. Kullman,
Colby, H.   II. Young, William C., 1928–   .
PN2052.T48   1986   792'.09   84–539
ISBN 0-313-21456-5 (set)
ISBN 0-313-25667-5 (lib. bdg. : v. 1 : alk paper)
ISBN 0-313-25668-3 (lib. bdg. : v. 2 : alk paper)

Library of Congress Catalog Card Number: 84–539
ISBN 0-313-21456-5 (set)
ISBN 0-313-25667-5 (v. 1)
ISBN 0-313-25668-3 (v. 2)

First published in 1986

Greenwood Press, Inc.
88 Post Road West
Westport, Connecticut 06881

Printed in the United States of America

The paper used in this book complies with the
Permanent Paper Standard issued by the National
Information Standards Organization (Z39.48–1984).

10 9 8 7 6 5 4 3 2 1

TO

Joan McCabe Moore
in Appreciation for Her Encouragement
and Her Assistance

AND TO THE MEMORY OF
William C. Young
WITH LOVE

Contents

Preface

Argentina's Comedia Nacional Argentina, Australia's Melbourne Theatre Company, Canada's Stratford Festival, East Germany's Berliner Ensemble, France's La Comédie Française, Great Britain's Royal Shakespeare Company, Indonesia's Giri Harja, Israel's Habima, Italy's Teatro di Eduardo, Korea's National Theatre Company, Nigeria's Ogunde Theatre Company, Poland's Jerzy Grotowski's Laboratory Theatre, the Soviet Union's Moscow Art Theatre, Sweden's Royal Dramatic Theatre, and the United States of America's Guthrie Theater—these are a few of the great theatre companies of the world that represent a proud tradition of excellence in every aspect of performance: producing; directing; acting; scenery, lighting, and sound; choreography, dancing, and mime; costume and makeup. They sponsor classical and modern plays by foreign and national playwrights. As companies, they are distinguished by what Rustom Bharucha calls "an indefinable cohesion, a certain tone and style of acting, a spirit that unites actors, directors, designers, technicians, and crew in a meaningful synthesis" ["Anatomy of a Regional Theatre," *Theater* (Summer 1979), 10–20]. A performance resulting from such collaboration is often so intense that the audience is aware of only one thing—the performance itself.

Not all the troupes included in *Theatre Companies of the World* represent a concept of theatre companies as it might be defined in the West: a permanent group of actors and actresses, under contract for a specified period each year, who perform a season of plays that includes nonmusical productions. The 1960 Masks, Wole Soyinka's first theatre company formed in the year of Nigerian Independence, consisted of part-time actors from the cities of Lagos and Ibadan. Ketu H. Katrak reports that one group usually rehearsed in a jolting landrover while traveling the hundred miles to meet the other group. There were no regular contracts. Indonesian drama, like much of Southeast Asian drama, is a rich theatrical expression that includes singing, dancing, puppetry, and the martial arts along with improvised theatre. Nonmusical productions do not exist. Consequently, as Kathy Foley writes, the distinction between drama and dance blurs since much of the performance portrays a character and/or event. Schools of drama thrive in Japan where theatrical experiences are extremely diverse, with traditional theatre companies performing Nō, Kyōgen, Kabuki, and Bunraku puppet theatre and modern companies doing everything from conventional Western plays to daring new forms of antiestablishment drama. Andrew T. Tsubaki explains that the Nō theatre of Japan allows the head of each of the five Nō schools to function in a producing capacity in order to permit its varied groups to perform separately under its protection. In India, historical circumstances and economic conditions have conspired to prevent the establishment of an equivalent to the Royal Shakesepare Company, a Guthrie Theater Company, or a Stratford Festival. In fact, as Farley Richmond points out, India has not produced a great theatre company with a home of its own; yet thousands of theatre organizations, many with long and impressive histories, exist. Originally family affairs, companies began to earn their bread by touring and performing plays in regional languages rather than in Sanskrit, the classical language. This regionalism predominates today with major theatrical centers in Calcutta, Bombay, Delhi, and the state of Kerala.

Decisions as to what companies to include or exclude were made by a group of nine area editors who have in some way displayed a specialized knowledge of the theatrical tradition of a specific geographical area. Since its founding in 1967, George Woodyard's *Latin American Theatre Review* has successfully represented the theatrical arts in Latin America; Robert Page's *Theatre Australia* reigned for years as ''Australia's magazine for the performing arts.'' As director of the International Theatre Studies Center and chairperson of the East Asian Languages and Cultures Department at the University of Kansas, Andrew T. Tsubaki has been instrumental in bringing the best of the Asian theatre companies to this country to perform. He has toured the Far East on numerous occasions, studying various traditions of drama, dance, and song. A fellow of the Royal Society of Arts (Great Britain), a UNESCO consultant on the promotion and presentation of the performing arts in Africa, and a member of the Executive Committee of the International Federation for Theatre Research, Joel A. Adedeji has promoted African theatre around the world, touring most frequently with his Nigerian Showcase Ensemble production of *A Flash in the Sun*. Edward J. Czerwinski and Carla Waal have published extensively on the theatre of Eastern Europe and Scandinavia, respectively, frequently traveling abroad in order to work with primary materials. Leon M. Aufdemberge, John Brockington, and Jill N. Brantley have achieved a specialized knowledge of the theatrical arts in Western Europe, Canada, and the United States of America through the study of dramatic literature, the production of plays, and travels at home and abroad.

At the outset, each area editor was asked to select the important theatre companies in the assigned area by considering significant factors such as international reputation, historical importance, innovative technology, theatre tradition, and experimental drama. Once companies were chosen, the area editors contacted potential contributors who had access to primary information and often a specialized knowledge of a particular theatre group. For example, Kazimierz Braun, author of six books on Eastern European and world drama, co-authored many of the articles on the theatre companies of Bulgaria; Emanuel Levy, author of *The Habima—Israel's National Theatre, 1917–1977: A Study of Cultural Nationalism*, wrote the article on the Habima; Lise-Lone Marker, co-author of *The Scandinavian Theatre: A Short History*, composed the essay on the Danish Royal Theatre; Michael Mullin, author of *Macbeth Onstage* and *Theatre at Stratford-upon-Avon, 1879–1978*, put together the piece on the Royal Shakespeare Company; Raymond Stanley, Australian correspondent to *Screen International* (London) and *The Stage and Television Today* (London), authored the article on the Melbourne Theatre Company; and Surapone Virulrak, author of *Likey, A Popular Theatre in Thailand*, wrote the articles on the theatre companies of Thailand. The area editors often selected particular companies and wrote the articles themselves. All of the articles are signed by their authors whose credentials may be found in the "About the Contributors" section of this volume.

Contributors were asked to supply the following information in a clearly organized narrative essay: (1) the name and address of the company; (2) a general statement explaining the company's significance; (3) a brief history of the company, usually mentioning the date of the founding, the names of the founders, important dates and personalities in the history of the company, and outstanding productions; (4) the achievements of certain playwrights who may have been associated with the company; (5) a philosophy or special purpose that might unify the company's approach to production; (6) the number of stages included in the company's facilities and their seating capacity, participation in tours or festivals, sources of funding, size of company and staff, and any unusual feature of the organization and administration; and (7) the future plans of the company.

Only the most significant companies from the United States of America have been included because this area will be covered more fully in *American Theatre Companies*, edited by Weldon B. Durham, also to be published by Greenwood Press.

The vagaries of obtaining information from all over the world necessitated the inclusion of some material that does not follow the established format. For example, Peter J. Chelkowski's "Iran" describes the existing ritual Islamic drama and evaluates the theatre groups present in Iran before the 1978 revolution put an end to their endeavors; and Farley Richmond's essay on India lays out the historical background against which the modern theatre of India may be seen, presents the general characteristics of contemporary theatre in selected regions of the country, and cites unique theatre organizations and individuals. In a very few cases, theatre companies are listed that are now defunct. Most often, such troupes played a significant role in the history of the theatre in a particular country. Costa Rica's Harlequin Theatre (Teatro Arlequín), 1956–1978, established a strong base for later developments of dramatic art in the country, performing more than one hundred titles from a national and universal repertory; Mexico's Poetry Aloud (Poesía en Voz Alta), 1956–1963, expanded the panorama of refined theatre in Mexico, creating a wide variety of different paths a production could assume; and Nigeria's the 1960 Masks, 1960–1963, brought together the best Nigerian actors to produce uniquely African dramas, combining Yoruba dramatic elements like dance, mime, and song, along with a highly poetic English language idiom.

The rationale behind the placement of materials reflects continental and national boundaries with two exceptions which are based on ethnic considerations: Puerto Rico is included in Latin America and East Germany in Western Europe. The major areas are listed alphabetically: Africa, Asia, Australia and New Zealand, Canada, Eastern Europe, Latin America, the Middle East, Scandinavia, the United States of America, and Western Europe (excluding Scandinavia). If more than one nation exists within an area, then the nations included are listed in alphabetical order. The companies follow, arranged alphabetically according to their English names, with the vernacular names given in parentheses in the headings. An exception has been made in the case of Japan where the theatre companies are listed alphabetically under one of four subject headings: (1) Nō and Kyōgen Theatre; (2) Bunraku Puppet Theatre, Kabuki, and Other Commercial Theatre; (3) Shingeki, the New Theatre of Japan; and (4) the Post-Shingeki Theatre Movement in Japan. On occasion, the translations of the names of theatre companies are curious: Brazil's Asdrúbal Trouxe o Trombone becomes Asdrúbal Brought the Trombone; France's Grenier de Toulouse, the Attic of Toulouse; Japan's Kaze no Ko, the Child of the Wind; and Mexico's Poesía en Voz Alta, Poetry Aloud.

Section or country introductions provide an overall view of theatre development in an area. A general bibliography at the end of the volume provides sources for further information, and a comprehensive index provides access to material not provided in separate entries. Plays cited in the text are given in translation with the vernacular title following in parentheses.

Theatre Companies of the World is designed as a general reference guide for the layman and the scholar.

Colby H. Kullman
The University of Mississippi

Acknowledgments

In 1978 Marilyn Brownstein, acquisitions editor at Greenwood Press, approached Andrew T. Tsubaki, director of the International Theatre Studies Center at the University of Kansas, with the idea for a reference book devoted to theatre companies of the world. As a result of Professor Tsubaki's recommendations, William C. Young was asked to serve as editor-in-chief of the project, a position that he was pleased to accept with his former research assistant, Colby H. Kullman, serving as co-editor-in-chief. Before his death in 1979, Professor Young provided a focus and scope for the project, enlisted the aid of seven of the nine area editors, and established guidelines for the articles. Without his initial inspiration and guidance, *Theatre Companies of the World* would not exist.

After Professor Young's death, Marilyn Brownstein, James T. Sabin, and the staff at Greenwood Press provided the encouragement necessary to revitalize the project. Their enthusiastic support has provided energy and stability throughout.

The area editors deserve special acknowledgment for their professional expertise and hard work: Joel A. Adedeji (Africa), Andrew T. Tsubaki (Asia), Leon M. Aufdemberge (Western Europe, excluding Scandinavia), Jill N. Brantley (United States of America), John Brockington (Canada), Edward J. Czerwinski (Eastern Europe), Robert Page (Australia and New Zealand), Carla Waal (Scandinavia), and George Woodyard (Latin America).

Thanks are due Andrew T. Tsubaki, Carla Waal, and George Woodyard for making themselves available for consultation on matters related to every aspect of this reference book. Their advice has been an invaluable aid in the completion of *Theatre Companies of the World*.

Joan McCabe Moore has given generously of her editing, proofreading, and typing skills. At a time when textual problems seemed overwhelming, her rational, organized, and steady labors managed to bring order out of chaos. Peggy G. French, Lisa Lee Anne McCartney, Sally Clark Johnson, and Barbara Phillips also assisted in the preparation of the final manuscript.

Lance Reppert, reference librarian at Lawrence Public Library, served as consultant for the bibliographical materials; and Thelma Reinhard Morreale, professor emeritus at Baker University, gave much helpful advice garnered from her lifetime of experience as a teacher of theatre arts. Andrew Colby Maye, Geraldo de Sousa, Hester Williams, George Worth, and Jane van Meter helped with various translation problems. Maureen Melino helped with matters involving contracts with area editors and contributors. The expertise of Cynthia Harris, Arlene Belzer, and the Editorial and Production Departments of Greenwood Press have been an invaluable aid to the completion of *Theatre Companies of the World.*

The area editors and I would like to thank the many people who have assisted and supported our research involving theatre companies of the world. Among them are Gretl Aicher, Hartwig Albiro, William Allan, Lilian Andreone, Salvatore Arico, Erik Aschengreen, G. Douglas Atkins, Jean Atkins, Leslie Auerbach, Norbert Baensch, Susan Baker, Nicholas Bakolas, Daniel Barrett, Christel Benner, Beverly Ann Benson, David M. Bergeron, James Beyer, Kathleen Collins Beyer, Uta Bitterli, Jacques Blanc, Gerhard Blasche, Josette Borja, James Brantley, Catherine Brook, Richard Bryant, Ionna Butzos, Mario Cadalora, Errico Centofanti, Susan Cooper, Mary R. Davidson, Armande Delcampe, Maria Lidia Dias, Gergana Doynova, Ingrid Dubberke, Denise Duhamel, José Echegaray, Barbara Elling, Ritva-Liisa Elomaa, Ann Mari Engel, Spyros Evangelatos, Luciano Fabiani, Raphael Fernandez, Eduardo de Filippo, Isabelle Filippo, Günther Fleckenstein, Mary Kathleen Foley, Jean E. Gagen, Peter Georgaras, Joel J. Gold, David Goodman, Judith S. Gottlieb, Gayle Graves, Giorgio Guazzatti, Grazyna Hartwig, Giles Havergal, Josephine Hayford, Jean-Pierre Henin, Anita Herzfeld, Niels Ingwersen, Germana Kampa, Sarah H. Kerr, Paul Schindler Klemens, Gerhard Knoop, Verena Knorr, Yasuharu Kobayashi, Philip C. Kolin, Joyce Schalla Kullman, Russell Peabody Kullman, Jacob Landau, Rudi Lekens, Eric Lindqvist, Byron Lippert, Fredric M. Litto, Peggy Marks, Bernhard Mauer, Andrew Colby Maye, Fred Maye, Deidre McQuillan, Mary Lou Means, Susan Medak, Rina Mendelsohn, Ruth Mikkelson, Donna Miles, Constance Minichelli, Kenkichi Miyata, James Moutzouros, Carolyn Ely Neuringer, Charles Neuringer, Vera Noll, Christina Nygren, Mary O'Neill, Gianna Sommi Panofsky, Olga Pavlatow, Janine Pefley, Amalia Pelled, Moira Piekalkiewicz, Christine Räia, Carlo Repetti, Duncan Ross, Jean-Louis Roux, Harvey Sawler, Guillermo Schmidhuber de la Mora, Anne Selby, Riitta Seppälä, Joan Sargent Sherwood, Nicle Simon-Vermot, Lilian Six, Frida Somers-Hatley, Beruria Stroke, Mario Susko, Ralph E. Taylor, Joachim Tenschert, Hans Ullberg, Jane Van Meter, Esther C. Waal, Laura H. Weaver, Bess Weinstein, Jennie Weinstein, Timothy A. Whitcomb, Jytte Wiingaard, Christine Wilkinson, Charles Wittenberg, Katarzyna Zawadzka, and Wolfgang Zimmermann and staff members of the Confederation Centre of the Arts, the Finnish Centre of the International Theatre Institute, Interpress Publishers (Warsaw, Poland), the Israel Centre of the International Theatre Institute, the Lawrence Public Library, the National Theatre Society Limited, the Norwegian International Theatre Institute, the Slavic Cultural Center, the Swedish Information Service, the Swedish International Theatre Institute Centre, and the University of Kansas Libraries, the University of Mississippi Library, and the various centers of the International Theatre Institute.

C.H.K.

AFRICA

Joel A. Adedeji, Area Editor

Introduction

Theatre companies have been established in Africa in response to a number of stimuli, ranging from individual commercial interests and artistic instincts to political considerations and logistics. More specifically, theatrical developments in Africa reflect the vicissitudes of that continent's political background and cultural evolution. By their nature and means, these vicissitudes have in turn contributed to the evanescent existence of most of the theatre companies.

The colonial history of Africa is a good index to the chequered fortunes of the theatre companies. It also affords an exciting insight into the peculiar circumstances that have characterized their shape and form. In all, two types of theatre companies have been identified: the private and the public.

The private theatre company is run as a private enterprise. It is managed by an individual or a group (body corporate) whose capital forms the stock that enables the company to operate. Since such a company is not usually governed and regulated by a licensing act of government, individual differences and business acumen come into play and, sometimes, become the basis of the company's viability. As a result, Africa's companies have experienced a number of trial-and-error experiments, some of which have been adventurous and even hazardous, simply in order to survive.

In contrast, the public theatre company is established by an act of government with a subsidy in perpetuity and is designed for the benefit and services of the people at large. The company is managed by a board or council set up by the government and charged with the responsibility that governs its artistic and business operations. Although it is not run as a profit-making venture, it is maintained as a service unit with a functional attribute that sustains its viability.

JOEL A. ADEDEJI

Ghana

GOMIDO THEATRE COMPANY
Accra, Ghana, West Africa

The Gomido Theatre Company was founded in April 1971 in the city of Accra, Ghana, with eight enthusiasts as foundation members. The originator of the founding concept, Wisdom Aglonoo, had envisioned a professionally oriented company that would give regular performances. But since they lacked basic amenities such as costumes, traditional musical instruments, and equipment, the founding members wisely decided to do radio and television plays in order to earn some money to purchase supplies. Another useful decision they made was to affiliate with the Arts Council of Ghana so that they could receive artistic and technical aid. The company was soon invited to put on radio and television shows. The shows that were well received by the general viewing public were "Kpe du do," "Hiame holo," "Nuvowo fe dzofe," "Nye fofovava," and "Sroda." The company was able to realize its financial objectives.

At this stage in its life, the Gomido Theatre Company was all set for a stage production. Its total membership had risen to twenty. The first stage playscript to be produced was *Vimasetonu* by Wisdom Aglonoo. As an affiliate company of the Arts Council, it requested artistic and technical aid. The council was very helpful, and as a result, a unique, integrated African art form for the stage was born—an art form that incorporated dance, music, mime, acting, and active audience participation. The uniqueness of the presentation is partially realized when the group of musicians and dancers are regarded as an organic part of the main audience. The relationship that needs to be established between the performers and the audience must first be established between the actors on one side and the musicians and dancers on the other. This interrelationship is spiritual. *Vimasetonu* was performed in Ewe. Language was no barrier because of the directorial emphasis and the company's superb acting.

The company has been successful because of its bold, determined approach to its basic problems of transportation and lack of convenient and adequate rehearsal space. Its first rehearsal place was at the Modern School of Commerce at Mamprobi. The company's use of the facility here was short-lived. Serious problems arose soon afterwards, and the company had to move to the open space of Aglonoo's residence. In spite of the regular monthly rent that the company paid, the landlord issued a "quit-order" after only a few months in residence. The company again moved from there to the premises of the Otu Blohum Secondary School. Because of arbitrary increases in rent, the company was compelled to move out again to its present base—the premises of the Datus International School at Obose Okai (a section in the city of Accra) where it enjoys rent-free facilities.

As a seasoned company, the Gomido Theatre Company takes part in the yearly Regional Arts Festival, organized by the Arts Council. In all, the company has taken part in four such festivals. All this is possible because of the company's effective administration. It has a Management Council made up of representatives of finance, disciplinary, and steering committees. Membership in the company now stands at twenty-six, with ten full-time and sixteen part-time members.

The company's repertory encompasses the following plays, all written by Wisdom Aglonoo for radio, television, and stage: *Vimasetonu, Gbeto nye ku, Tsanebu, Tugbenkuga, Kpe du do, Hiame holo, Nuvowo fe dzofe, Nye fofovava, Sroda, Kokloxo mekpea nu na koklo o, Adzoblauswo, Fiadeke mefa o,* and *Duko dekawo ko mienye.* In its productions, the company uses stock names, such as Sena, Agbedefu, Sefenya, Novienyo, Katsekpo, Wotomenyo, Malofa, Naomi, Kumedzro, Nanegbe, Tonyeko, Akofa, Dzifa, and Agbaglo. These personalities have so charmed the Ewe community that people prefer to address them in private life by their stock names. The company has so far appeared eleven times on radio and fifty-four times on television. It is currently touring the Volta Region of Ghana with a repertory of stage plays.

The Gomido Theatre Company is committed to serving as a community workshop for the youth, in order to realize the following objectives: (1) to satisfy an ethical need in particular and the country's need in general, that is, to project the performing arts heritage of the Ewe, an ethnic group in Ghana, as a significant contribution to the country's artistic performances; (2) to create an entertainment forum for the community; (3) to raise the level of artistic taste and appreciation of the community, as well as standards for the drama and theatre; (4) to provide opportunities for interested persons to participate, either as full-time or part-time members, in a professional artistic endeavor; (5) to create a living "nonwritten textbook" for the community; and (6) to be the integrated African theatre pacesetter for the community and dedicate itself to establishing a model of excellence.

For its policy considerations, the company has set up a Management Council, charged with translating its preestablished philosophy, planning viable touring programs, dealing with finance and budgeting, and upholding the company's image. The council's financial considerations are to formulate a budget and adhere to it. It has to approve all expenditures in respect of purchases, stipends, and salaries, and to make a decision on a minimum income goal.

The company's image is of vital importance to the Management Council. In order to ensure the proper image, the council serves as a link between the company and the community. The council also sees that the company maintains the community's respect by making a judicious selection and casting of plays.

Wisdom Aglonoo, founding father of the Gomido Theatre Company, hails from a family of traditional musicians. His father, Agbezudor Aglonoo, is an accomplished composer, drummer, and dancer. At the age of four, Wisdom was already singing. He became a dancer at the age of six and occasionally played the supporting drums in his father's dance ensemble. Wisdom entered elementary school a fully fledged musician of the oral tradition. He quickly acquired a taste for educational theatre and appeared in almost all his school's dramatic performances. As a young and gifted pupil-teacher, Wisdom founded a dance ensemble at Akatsi in the Volta Region in 1959 and put on regular performances to entertain the community.

The period that followed saw Wisdom in the city of Accra, where he founded the Gomido Theatre Company in April 1971. He composes the songs, writes the drama, and choreographs all the dances for his plays. Aglonoo's artistic endeavors rightly caught the eyes of Ghana's cultural leaders. Consequently, he was invited as a guest artist to the National Arts Festival, which was held in Kumasi in 1973, to perform the Libation Pouring Ritual. Thereafter, he was invited as a special guest artist to the Anlo Hogbetsotso Festival for four consecutive years, to perform the Libation Pouring Ritual. He has so far written thirteen plays for the company: four stage, six television, and three radio plays.

In order to continue to function effectively as the sole financial backbone of the theatre company, Wisdom Aglonoo kept his job with the VALCO (Volta Aluminum Company) of Ghana, where he was held in very high esteem for his versatility and artistic endeavors. He recently left the VALCO establishment and has since become a full-time producer/director/actor of his theatre company.

ALLEN W. W. TAMAKLOE

JAGUA JOKERS THEATRE COMPANY
Accra, Ghana, West Africa

Theatre companies in Ghana are exemplified in the operations of the Concert Party. A Concert Party is a professional organization composed of a central core of actors and musicians (band-set). The company is formed when the core of the actors invites the band-set or vice versa. The company is an association of individuals bound together with a common purpose. The company is usually formed through the initiative of a single leader, who normally becomes the artistic director and manager. The leader gives the company some permanence and security, while the other members pool their artistic, technical, and management resources.

Because of the rugged nature of operations in Ghana characterized by the sheer force of survival, the dozens of theatre companies in existence exhibit no neat patterns or systems. The structure and mode of operations of the Jagua

Jokers Theatre Company present an exciting model. Formed in 1954 by Mr. Bampoe and two other friends, the Hammond Brothers, the Jagua Jokers Company was first composed of the trio (the Jokers) and the guitar-band which Bampoe owned and named the Jagua. As a professional group, the company is run by an Executive Committee, which includes Bampoe as secretary, a chairman, and a treasurer. The Executive Committee, the governing board of the company, is comprised of its main financiers and principal actors. Other actors and musicians are hired and paid wages according to agreed terms. After the running costs of production and other stock expenses are paid out, whatever amount is left in the balance sheet belongs to the Executive Committee. The artists are paid monthly wages.

The company's income is highly dependent on the promotional efforts of the Executive Committee, which plans the touring schedules and contracts other engagements on radio and television. The company's operations are sometimes arranged by a private promoter who pays the company an agreed sum of money for an engagement. The private promoter pays for the hired minibus in which the troupe is transported as well as for hiring the place of performance, including the necessary police permits and other costs. He takes charge of the box office and collects all gate receipts. The profitability of this venture is dependent on the private promoter's own organizing ability, public relations, and industry. In spite of the risks, such promoters make a lot of profit. But for the company, the system is a means of an assured income in view of the usual privations they encounter.

JOEL A. ADEDEJI

Guinea

BALLETS AFRICAN AND THE JOLIBA
National Theatre of Guinea
Conakry, Guinea, West Africa

There are two theatre companies in the Republic of Guinea: the Ballets African and the Joliba. Both are public theatre companies because they are state-owned and -operated. Established to perform on commissions, both companies have cultural and educational objectives. While the Ballets African has been designed to promote the image of the country abroad, the Joliba operates to translate the enlightenment program of the government in theatrical terms.

Artists are recruited from the grass-roots level, and final employment is regarded as a mark of distinction. The theatre workers and artists are paid titular wages with gradations that relate more to administrative and technical responsibilities than to artistic talents and applications. Distinctions are marked by promotions, and preferment is widely acclaimed.

The National Theatre of Guinea in Conakry is the base of the companies where all commissioned and command performances take place.

JOEL A. ADEDEJI

Kenya

DONOVAN MAULE THEATRE
P.O. Box 2333
Nairobi, Kenya, East Africa

Since achieving independence in 1963, this former British colony has continued with a tradition that consigns the theatre as a European heritage. The country's imposing National Theatre located in Nairobi still bears the emblem and credentials of the British colonial administration which first established and maintained it in order to give a "home-away-from-home" premise to the British touring companies. Against the background of this legacy of colonialism the Donovan Maule Theatre has been established as a model of British colonial enterprise.

Beginning as a little studio theatre in 1948 and a private property of Donovan and Mollie Maule, by 1958 the "Donovan Maule" had become a growing concern. Moving into its new premises on Parliament Road, Nairobi (adjacent to the Kenyan Parliament Building), the Donovan Maule Theatre maintains a professional company that presents plays throughout the year. Its affiliated company in London is the Theatre Arts Society's Wyndham's Theatre on Charing Cross Road. This arrangement brings the theatre into a circuit orbit for touring purposes and other forms of exchange.

Annabel Maule is the current managing director of the theatre, having taken over from her parents in 1971. As a private enterprise the theatre company is run strictly for profit and is highly sustained and promoted by the Kenyan tourist industry.

JOEL A. ADEDEJI

Nigeria

DURO LADIPO NATIONAL THEATRE COMPANY
Ibadan, Nigeria, West Africa

Established by Chief Duro Ladipo in 1963, the Duro Ladipo National Theatre Company has managed to survive many vicissitudes, including the death of its founder and managing director. The nucleus of the company was based on Chief Duro Ladipo and his wives. He then recruited the services of a number of talented and trusted artists, who joined him (some of them with their wives) and were trained in the arts and allied areas, which included technical and management skills. As a kind of cooperative society, the company has thrived in spite of desertions and mishaps. When profits are declared, they are shared according to an agreed system of distribution and a savings scheme in favor of the company.

The company operates through touring schedules and runs a circuit system within the Yoruba-speaking areas and communities of Nigeria. Its income is augmented by a regular contract with the Nigerian Television Authority and through foreign travels (which include commissions and other contractual engagements).

JOEL A. ADEDEJI

THE 1960 MASKS AND BEYOND
(defunct)

Wole Soyinka's contribution to Nigerian drama has gone beyond his achievement as a playwright, from the printed page to the boards of a stage. Playing a significant role in the development of a professional English-language theatre in Nigeria, he recognized very early in his career that production of his own plays and those of other Nigerian dramatists in English was contingent upon the availability of a trained company. In fact, Soyinka's own artistic development parallels the beginnings and development of a professional English-language theatre in his country.

When Soyinka returned to Nigeria after spending an exciting year (1959–

1960) as playreader for the Royal Court Theatre in London, he established "The 1960 Masks." As Karen Morell in *In Person: Achebe, Awoonor, and Soyinka* (1975) reports, the experience of the London dramatic scene was so inspirational that "the first thing he wanted to do when [he] got back to Nigeria was to get [his] own company together." Soyinka discusses the "many ways in which this could be done":

I could move towards trying to establish a fully professional theatre from the very beginning, but there were many factors which militated against this: lack of money, and then there was the training problem because this was in January 1960, and I wanted the company to be ready—say, in October 1960—when we would stage a production for the Independence Celebration. . . . So I rejected what was my main intention, my real ambition, which was to start a company from scratch: young, semiprofessional people and go through the process of training and so on. We had to make do instead with those who'd had enormous acting experience. This meant both on the radio, on the stage, and it meant I wanted those who could use already the English language because I wrote in English, those who could use it and be very comfortable in it. . . . And that is how the 1960 Masks was born. [Morell, p. 95]

When Soyinka submitted his play, *A Dance of the Forests*, for the independence celebrations in 1960, he must have recognized that the theatre groups in existence were mainly amateurish and imitative of European and Shakespearean drama. For instance, the University College of Ibadan's Dramatic Society, functioning under the leadership of Geoffrey Axworthy and Martin Banham, was involved in producing Western drama using conventional stagecraft and acting techniques. Since *A Dance of the Forests* was a new kind of play, a unique combination of Yoruba dramatic elements of mime, song, and dance, along with highly poetic English language and idiom, Soyinka needed actors well versed in both traditions: fluent in the English language and equally at home with Yoruba language and culture.

Soyinka drew together the best actors he could find to constitute his new company. Some well-known names in *A Dance of the Forests* were Yemi Lijadu as Demoke; Olga Adeniyi-Jones as Rola; Afolabi Ajayi as Ogun; and Soyinka himself as Forest Father. The 1960 Masks also performed two other Soyinka plays—a radio play, *Camwood on the Leaves* (not published until 1973), and an extract of *The Strong Breed*, included as part of the film *Culture in Transition*—with actors well known on the Nigerian television and stage scene: Yemi Lijadu, Betty Okotie, Ralph Opara, and Segun Olusola, among others. This company also successfully produced works by other playwrights—*Song of a Goat* by J. P. Clark of Nigeria; *Dear Parent and Ogre* by Sarif Easmon of Sierra Leone; and *You in Your Small Corner* by Barry Reckord.

Since the 1960 Masks was not composed of professional actors who could devote their full time and energies to theatre, it was not the kind of theatre Soyinka wanted. These part-time actors had other jobs, such as civil service; hence, they could participate in theatre activities only on a weekend basis.

The company had to face the added difficulties of commuting between Ibadan and Lagos, separated by a hundred miles, since Soyinka included the best actors he could find in these two cities. The dramatist graphically describes the inconveniences of rehearsing on bumpy Nigerian roads: "Very often we'd do preliminary rehearsals in a jolting landrover while going to meet the other group. We would rehearse in Lagos this week; the next weekend would be in Ibadan" (Morell, p. 95). Given the limited time available to these actors because of their other commitments, rehearsals mostly took place on weekends: "We'd rehearse all day Saturday," remarks Soyinka in the same interview, "go to the nightclub all night, drink, dance, do a bit of rehearsing also in the nightclubs. . . . It was a kind of community theatre with a very strong sense of professionalism."

The word "professional" when used in the context of Nigerian theatre in the 1960s has different implications from its Western context. For the 1960 Masks professionalism meant a personal sense of commitment and responsibility to members of the group rather than a contractual agreement to a theatre company run by an external body unrelated to the actors except by a financial relationship. The actors in the 1960 Masks did not make a living from their work in the theatre.

Since the 1960 Masks used part-time actors, located in different cities, the company did not fulfill Soyinka's goal of establishing a full professional theatre company. Even in 1962, when commenting about his current plans to Lewis Nkosi (a conversation recorded by Dennis Duerden and Pieterse Cosmo, editors, in the 1972 *African Writers Talking*, pp. 169–180), Soyinka remarked:

The sooner we can get a professional theatre going the better. I would like to be able to work full-time in the theatre. I find I'm as much interested in producing and in acting as I am in writing, and with a professional theatre I find I can live a very fulfilled existence.

This "professional" theatre was established in 1963—the Orisun Theatre, described by Soyinka as "the first English-language professional theater in Nigeria." In fact, Orisun was a "foster-child" of the 1960 Masks and grew out of the original parent body. Members of the original group "understood from the beginning," comments Soyinka in the Morell interview, "that they were there to encourage a new, younger group of fully professional actors and actresses."

Soyinka wanted to form a company whose members were fully committed to theatre primarily because he wanted them to enact very open, caustic political sketches. Heretofore, Soyinka had been careful not to jeopardize the government jobs held by the actors of the 1960 Masks. Now, in 1963, one may hypothesize that the dramatist himself more acutely felt the need to criticize the government. In 1960, in the afterglow of independence, the nation was in a celebratory mood; by 1963 the climate was beginning to darken.

The major political revues produced by the Orisun Theatre were *The (New) Republican* in March 1964 and *Before the Blackout* in March 1965. In *Critical Perspectives on Wole Soyinka* (1980), edited by James Gibbs, the latter notes in his Introduction that during the performance of these two satirical revues "the actors guarded the stage doors against hired thugs'' (p. 10). The state viewed the biting political content of these sketches as potentially threatening and disruptive.

Soyinka was primarily interested in these revues as stage productions with immediate impact rather than as texts. *The (New) Republican*, in fact, has never been published—its purpose was served entirely in the actual production. *Before the Blackout*, although published by Orisun Acting Editions without a date, contains several prefatory comments on the disadvantage of selecting particular satiric sketches for publication. The criterion for the printed page is the efficacy of dialogue, whereas "mime sometimes proves the most effective way to make a pungent and immediate statement on stage." Since the significance of the sketches is embodied precisely in their topicality, Soyinka exhorts producers to "feel free to adapt [these sketches] where necessary for the contemporary event and to alter entire sequences to relate the action closely to whatever is happening *now*."

Apart from the political revues, another prominent event for this company was "The Orisun Repertory Theatre Season" which opened in August 1964 in Lagos and in Ibadan. In this new kind of dramatic venture, Orisun actors participated with the Duro Ladipo and Kola Ogunmola Folk Opera companies, and with university-based groups. This kind of joint theatre activity was undertaken by different theatre companies coexisting at a particular time. The repertory collectively presented an exciting program of contemporary Nigerian drama in English and Yoruba: Soyinka's *The Lion and the Jewel* and *The Trials of Brother Jero*; Ogunmola's *The Palm-Wine Drinkard*; and Lapido's *Oba Koso* and *Oba Waja*.

The Orisun Theatre's problem became one of survival after 1967 when the federal government of Nigeria imprisoned Soyinka and detained him for nearly two years. In the Morell interview, Soyinka comments on how "an assistant of his who was very keen to keep the company going at all costs . . . took a regular slot on television and actually began producing a one-act play every fortnight for television. Now this was absolutely insane. They were not equipped for that sort of speed. . . . So, naturally, standards fell to pieces." Soyinka describes how, when he came out of prison and saw their first television performance, he called the television station, broke their contract, and disbanded the group. The company had broken up just before the civil war anyway because of the political turmoil. "Many people, Igbo members," remarks the playwright, "had fled back to the East, others had left, everything was really in pieces. It was just a matter of keeping a small core of the group going."

This was the "core" that Soyinka took with him to the University of Ibadan where he was named head of the Department of Theatre Arts in 1967. Since the late 1960s Soyinka's involvement with theatre groups has been mainly with university-based companies, comprised of students and of professional actors from the general community. Some of the actors who have remained with Soyinka since the early 1960s and who have worked with the various companies with which the playwright has been involved at different times are Tunji Oyelana, Femi Fatoba, Jimi Johnson, Jimi Solanke, Betty Okotie, and Wale Ogunyemi.

At the University of Ibadan in the early 1970s Soyinka amalgamated the Orisun actors with "the new student company which he was forming," as he comments in the Morell interview, "and so built a new semi-professional troupe attached to the University." In 1970 he brought this Unibadan Acting Company to the Playwright's Workshop Conference at the Eugene O'Neill Theatre in Waterford, Connecticut, for a production of his drama *Madmen and Specialists*. He also directed other plays with this company in Ibadan. When he moved to the University of Ife in 1976, he formed the University of Ife Theatre Company from an existing community theatre along with a professional unit.

The history of English-language professional theatre in Nigeria is integrally related to Soyinka's dramatic career. There is a clear correspondence between the timing of his plays, the prevalent political climate, and the stage of development of a professional theatre in the English language. Soyinka's involvement with different theatre companies over the years, and the kinds of drama each group has produced, closely reflect the social needs and political moods of that time. For instance, in 1982, he wrote and produced directly satirical agit-prop sketches entitled *Priority Projects* with the Unife Guerrilla Theatre. Most recently, in 1983, in timely response to the Nigerian election rigging, Soyinka brought out a record disc entitled "Unlimited Liability Company," featuring Tunji Oyelana and the Benders. The dramatist, who once described himself as a "frustrated musician," wrote the lyrics and set them to music. This newest venture reflects his past experience in writing political songs for the theatre throughout his career in general, and in the political revues, such as *Before the Blackout*, in particular. Lyrics such as "Ethike Revolution" and "I Love My Country," on the record disc, pungently criticize President Shehu Shagari's ironic declaration of leading an "ethical revolution" in Nigeria while blatantly arranging his return to power.

Soyinka's contribution to Nigerian drama is to be recognized not only as that of a major dramatist of the twentieth century but equally as that of a man-of-theatre, actor-manager, an inspiring director with a fine sense of stagecraft, and an exciting use of space on stage. His indefatigable efforts to professionalize theatre activity over the past twenty years demonstrate his commitment to Nigerian theatre.

KETU H. KATRAK

OGUNDE THEATRE
Lagos, Nigeria, West Africa

The Ogunde Theatre was formed in 1944 in Lagos, Nigeria. This, the leading and oldest indigenous theatre company in Nigeria, was founded by Hubert Dehinbo Ogunde as an amateur dramatic society group composed of a number of people with similar interest in the theatre. The group called itself the African Music Research Party, for one of its aims was the preservation of African music and dances. Ogunde retained the name of the group when in 1946 he formally launched the first professional theatre company in the history of modern Nigerian theatre.

Ogunde and his group first attained public attention in 1944 with the production of the Native Air Opera, *The Garden of Eden and the Throne of God*. This production set Ogunde apart from contemporary composers of Native Air Operas, like David, Dawodu, Layeni, and Onimole, whose works, from all accounts, were devoid of dramatic action and realism. Ogunde, by including dramatic action and realism in his first opera, directed attention from a pure musical form to the composite business of the theatre. The production of *The Garden of Eden* is a landmark in the history and development of modern Nigerian theatre because it represents the beginning of contemporary theatre in Nigeria.

In 1945 Ogunde changed the name of his company to the Ogunde Theatre Party but held fast to the original aims of the African Music Research Party. Later in the fifties the Ogunde Concert Party was founded. Ogunde modeled the style of this theatre on the Western variety theatres. It is a measure of the man's originality that it was with this much misunderstood form that he created yet another revolution in Yoruba theatre, moving it away from a musical form to that of speech. It was during this phase of his career that he gave his actors the freedom to speak their lines rather than sing them. This was a tremendous innovation, for the major characteristic of Ogunde's operas, and indeed of all Yoruba operas up to this point, was that they had no dialogue. When he introduced dialogue, he did away with the usual practice of publishing his works at the time of production. It was also in the fifties that the theatre of Ogunde became bilingual with the actors performing either in Yoruba, when within the Yoruba linguistic area, or in pidgin English, when outside Yoruba-speaking areas of Nigeria. This company's bilingualism, among many other factors, marks this company as a unique one among Nigerian theatre troupes.

In the sixties, Hubert Ogunde abandoned the concert medium, doing away with many of its features, such as his use of Western musical instruments such as the saxophone and trumpet. He returned once more to his roots to make use of traditional literature and music, changing the name of his company to its former one of the Ogunde Theatre Company and dropping the word party from the title to remove any possible connection with any political party.

It is very difficult to be specific about the great variety of dramatic genres in the Ogunde Theatre because the dividing line between any two is very fine indeed. But what is clear is that Ogunde's theatre, and indeed all Yoruba theatre, is didactic, its aim being to instruct, to inform, and to entertain. And the Ogunde Theatre Company has entertained and given pleasure to millions of people within and without the country since its inception some thirty-five years ago. In fact, it is the only theatre company that tours the whole length and breadth of Nigeria, recruiting its members from all over the country. It is indeed truly national in character.

Since 1948 the Ogunde Theatre has been on tour of Nigeria's neighboring African states: Benin, Togo, Ghana, and the Ivory Coast. In 1967 Ogunde founded his dance company when he was invited by the Nigerian government to perform in the Nigerian pavilion at the Expo '67 in Montreal. The same year he took this new company on a tour of the United States, where the dance company was well received at the Apollo Theatre in Harlem. Later, in 1969, the company was one of the guest troupes invited to perform at the prestigious Llangollen International Musical Eisteddfod in Wales.

The theatre of Ogunde has often been at the center of controversy. This is not surprising. Out of a repertory of about fifty-one pieces, nine have strong political themes, and most were written during the colonial rule; for as his theatre involved itself in the renaissance of cultural consciousness in the forties, so it involved itself with the nationalist movement for independence and by so doing clashed often with the law. For instance, his historical opera, *Worse Than Crime*, which had its premiere in 1945, boldly stated that "Slavery in any shape or form is worse than crime." The colonial government rightly interpreted the opera to mean that "Colonialism in any shape or form is worse than crime." After the performance, Ogunde and another member of his company were questioned by the police and detained. Fortunately for Ogunde, by that time he had resigned from the police force.

Not only was his opera, *Strike and Hunger*, banned in Jos in 1946, but he was also fined £125 (N250) for staging it. The same year he luckily escaped the wrath of the law with *Tiger's Empire*, another important opera, which contains his most vicious attack on colonial rule. In 1950 he was discouraged from touring the northern parts of the country with *Bread and Bullet*. He was banned from the former Western Region in 1964 for staging *Yoruba Ronu* (*Yoruba, Think*). The ban was not lifted until the military takeover in 1966. Meanwhile, he retaliated by staging *Otito Koro* (*Truth Is Bitter*). It is ironical that the theatre that risked its very existence in its fight for freedom from colonial rule should suffer the same harassment and banishment at the hands of the very politicians by whose sides it so bravely and fearlessly fought for the people.

Ogunde now has many entertainment companies: the Ogunde Theatre, which is the oldest and most famous; the Ogunde Record Company, formed in 1947; the Ogunde Concert Party, founded in 1948 specifically for tours along the west coast of Africa; the Ogunde Dance Company, formed for productions solely outside Africa; and the Ogunde Film Company. While all of these companies are interrelated, each has its individual functions. In 1978 Ogunde incorporated his multifarious companies into two separate enterprises: the Ogunde Enterprise Nigeria Limited (OEN) in which are merged all the various offshoots of the Ogunde Theatre; and the Ogunde Pictures Company (OPC) which was formed for the specific purpose of producing directors and producers for the motion picture industry in Nigeria and of distributing motion picture films.

However much Ogunde expands as an entertainment entrepreneur, his drama company, the Ogunde Theatre, will remain the central focus of his vast empire. The history of the Ogunde Theatre is a phenomenon. Other companies have either emulated his many styles or merely built upon them. It is considered supreme among the Nigerian theatre troupes, which at present number over one hundred, and its leader is revered as the father of them all.

EBUN CLARK

UNIBADAN PERFORMING COMPANY
University of Ibadan
Ibadan, Nigeria, West Africa

The University of Ibadan set the pace for theatrical development in Nigeria first by establishing a School of Drama in 1963 and later by launching a theatre company as a profit-making venture within its Consultancy Services Organization. The Unibadan Performing Company, which was established in 1979, actually began operations in 1968 when it was known as the School of Drama Acting Company. Largely under the leadership of the head of the Department of Theatre Arts (who was also its director), the company operated as a traveling theatre. Known as the Unibadan Masques, it performed a repertory of plays in the English language. Through a university decision, it became an independent body in 1979 under the auspices of the Consultancy Services with a subvention and Board of Management charged with running the company as a profitable business concern.

Performers are recruited into the company through advertisement and audition. The bulk of the artists are graduates of the university's professional program. Their conditions of service are determined by the board, which also has the right of "hire and fire." The company's day-to-day operation is supervised by a managing director, who also contracts with play directors for stage, radio, and television productions. The wages and salaries, which are distributed monthly, do not necessarily reflect the company's monthly returns but are guided by a rationale that ensures the company's survival.

JOEL A. ADEDEJI

Senegal

DANIEL SORANO THEATRE—NATIONAL THEATRE
Boulevard de la République
Dakar, Republic of Senegal, West Africa

The Daniel Sorano Theatre is the national theatre of Senegal and houses the National Theatre Company which performs plays written in the French theatrical tradition. The colonial experience has left a scar on the theatre's artistic and administrative layout.

The theatre company is resident in Dakar and maintains occasional touring schedules. But it is firmly established in the Comédie-Française tradition. With its varied repertory representing the best in French and Francophone drama, the company, which is a nonprofit-making organization, is subsidized by the state. It has also become the training camp for Senegal's best theatre artists and practitioners.

Maurice Sona Senghor is the managing director of the theatre, and Alioune Diop is the administrator. The theatre maintains the services of a large body of salaried workers including artists, technicians, and crews.

JOEL A. ADEDEJI

Uganda

THEATRE LIMITED, UGANDA
Uganda National Cultural Centre, National Theatre
P.O. Box 3187, Kampala, Uganda

The British colonial administration built an Arts Theatre in the center of Kampala in 1959. At independence in 1962, the theatre was named the Uganda National Theatre. In 1968 the late Robert Serumaga began his theatrical experiment under the auspices of the National Theatre, which provided him with a much needed base (under a rental agreement) for the operations of his Theatre Limited, a private profit-oriented theatre company.

Theatre Limited began in September 1968 as a committee company with a Board of Directors and fifteen members. Sponsored productions by multinational corporations helped the company to overcome its teething problems. Robert Serumaga's business acumen combined with his artistic talents and dedication pulled the company through its experimental phase. In 1973 Theatre Limited was registered as the Abafume Theatre Company. Serumaga became both its artistic director and manager. With a staff strength of about twenty (including artists, technical and crew workers), he worked out a system that kept the company economically viable. The company developed a cooperative system which enabled the artists to bind themselves together as a team with a common purpose. The profit motive did not minimize attempts toward excellence, which, in turn, became the yardstick of the company's promotion and sponsorship. With a repertory of plays and a touring schedule, the Abafume Theatre Company began to claim the attention of many theatre lovers, especially with its improvisational plays, which utilized the resources of total theatre.

Political events following the 1971 military takeover in Uganda disrupted the company's operations and life-style. When it became difficult to secure regular salaries and wages for his workers, Serumaga heedlessly involved himself in the politics of survival, which eventually, and unfortunately, consumed him. His death in 1979 brought a sad end to an experiment that had opened far-reaching possibilities.

JOEL A. ADEDEJI

Union of South Africa

GIBSON KENTE INDEPENDENT THEATRE COMPANY
c/o Donaldson Community Centre, Orlando East
Soweto, Johannesburg, Union of South Africa

Gibson Kente is the first black South African to whom the theatre represented a serious business concern. His development as a theatre artist and impresario began in 1959, under the Union of South African Artists (Union Artists), a trade union organization seeking to patronize and service the interests of black artists. The Union Artists, however, was funded and administered by whites and operated from Dorkay House in Johannesburg. The organization supported "a multiplicity of projects," including sponsorship of professional commercial productions. Kente's association with this organization influenced his auspicious decision to make the theatre a commercial activity. In 1966 he began to fight a protracted battle with the Union Artists to free himself and his theatre projects from their management, especially after production of his play, *Sikalo*, launched him into the orbit of theatre business.

In October 1967 Gibson Kente's own company, the first independent theatre company of Soweto, was registered under the Companies Act. Soweto, a derivative from *South-Western Native Townships*, with a population of over 1 million, is the largest of the township settlements on the outskirts of Johannesburg. It is inhabited by a concentration of proletarian black Africans working in industries and mines in Johannesburg and became a flourishing urban center for popular theatre. Kente's entrepreneurship began between 1967 and 1970, when his three successful musical plays, *Sikalo*, *Lifa*, and *Zwi*, turned him into a big businessman in Soweto and in the other newly created townships on the outskirts of industrial centers in South Africa. The popularity of Kente's productions rested on their affinity, in both form and attribute, to *King Kong*, a successful musical showcase, which stormed South Africa in 1959 under the auspices of the Union Artists.

Gibson Kente's touring circuit is estimated to include over one hundred venues throughout the country, usually with two or three performances at each. The so-called township theatres are actually municipally owned halls and community centers.

By 1970 Kente's "theatrical organization employed up to three large companies of actors, actresses, and musicians, and administrative and technical others" (Robert Mshengu Kavanagh's edition of *South African People's Plays* [London: Heinemann Educational Books, 1981], p. xxiii). He operated a number of vehicles for touring throughout South Africa. Despite reverses in 1971, he was still able to pay the manager of his theatre organization (his wife) a salary of R500 a month. He was paying his average regular actor R50 a week, and most of the experienced actors and actresses earned up to R100 a week, especially for the boom years between 1973 and 1976.

Kente's involvement with the political struggle in South Africa became apparent in 1973, when he began to produce protest plays, such as *How Long, I Believe*, and *Too Late*. He was arrested in 1976, while filming his most popular play, *How Long*. He was released a year later and has since been running his theatre with "uncontentious musicals." Kente dabbled in protest plays more from a desire to make money by appealing to the nationalistic sentiments of the surging black masses than to back an avowed commitment to Black Consciousness movements. *How Long* (1973) was a great popular success and, like most of Kente's popular productions, was based on improvisations—"non-literary, non-intellectual" with "unarticulated areas of communication" (Kavanagh, p. xxiii). His decision to script the play and film it in 1976 brought him into the clutches of the Publications Control Board under Section 12 of Act 26 of 1963.

Gibson Kente, a successful theatre businessman, is also a playmaker, director, choreographer, and musician. His theatre provides an exciting experience in developing African cultural consciousness. His ensemble method of production, business acumen, and political sagacity have made his theatre one of the most successfully run theatre organizations in black Africa—much like that of Chief Hubert Ogunde of Nigeria.

JOEL A. ADEDEJI

UNION OF SOUTH AFRICAN ARTISTS
Dorkay House, 6b Eloff Street Extension
Johannesburg, 2000, South Africa

During World War II, many black entertainers from South Africa joined the South African Army, mainly as porters to do menial tasks. It was during this period that white promoters discovered the rich talent of black actors and singers. Soon after the war, Ike Brookes put together a touring extravaganza of black actors and singers called *Zonk*. During the 1950s and 1960s black and white men collaborated to exploit black theatrical talent. In 1959 *Shebeen*, a musical written by British-born South African stage personality Bill Brewer, opened in Cape Town with a mixed cast of Africans and Cape Coloreds. The story of the play takes place in the then notorious Colored area in Cape Town known as

District Six. This play was soon followed by another musical, *Mkhumbani*, with the book by Alan Paton and music by the late Todd Matshikiza, a teacher, composer, and radio personality. Mkhumbani is the Zulu name for the African township of Cato Manor in Durban. The cast was entirely black.

After these early successes, the ground was now ready for bigger and better organized productions, but it was also clear that the job could only be done by a well-organized body. In the late 1950s Father Trevor Huddleston, Ezekiel Mphahlele, Ian Bernhardt, and other blacks and whites established the Union of South African Artists to promote theatre and to protect the blacks against exploitation by white recording companies. The Union of South African Artists had two other wings: Union Artists, a promotional body, and the African Music and Drama Association (AMDA); and the Edward Joseph Foundation. Whites and Africans served on the boards of directors of these bodies. The writer and actor Dan Poho filled the positions of manager of Union Artists and secretary general of the Union of South African Artists.

The year 1960 saw the birth of the Union's smash hit, all-African jazz opera, *King Kong*, with Miriam Makeba as the leading lady. The story was based on the life of a young Zulu man, Ezekiel Dlamini, who became involved in the underground black gang world. He died while serving a term of imprisonment. The book was by white lawyer Harry Bloom, the music by Todd Matshikiza, and the lyrics by British-born Pat Williams and Ralf Trewhela. The late Leon Gluckman, prominent white producer and director, directed the production; "Spike" Stanley Glasser directed the music; Britisher Arnold Dover choreographed the dances; Arthur Goldreich designed the costumes; and the late Mackay Davashe led the orchestra. The cast was composed of the cream of Johannesburg's actors, actresses, singers, dancers, and instrumentalists. Among them were Hugh Masekela, Jonas Gwangwa, Caiphus Semenya, and Letta Mbulo, all of whom are now in the United States where they have been very successful in the entertainment world. Running for over six months at London's Princess Theatre on Shaftsbury Avenue, *King Kong* also toured major cities of England and Scotland.

White and black audiences saw the play together every night. Seeing *King Kong* and possessing the record of its music became prestigious among the white people of South Africa. The cast was invited to white homes for parties, although it was illegal for black people to drink the white man's liquor and for white people to entertain black people. White workers and organizers were on first-name terms with blacks for the first time in South African history.

King Kong was quickly followed by other major productions like Eugene O'Neill's *The Emperor Jones*; Rabindranath Tagore's *King of the Dark Chamber*, featuring international New York stars Surya Kumari and dancer Bhaskar, and directed by Krishna Shah; Athol Fugard's *The Blood Knot*; and a triple bill of plays by Bob Leshoai and students of the African Music and Drama Association (*Morati of the Bataung*, *No Place to Hide*, and *U-Ntombinde, the Tall Maiden*, a Zulu traditional folk tale). Athol Fugard has conducted workshops and written and produced other African plays with black casts—such as *No Good Friday*.

An important project by the Union was the Schools Theatre Project started by Bob Leshoai and run by Basil Somhlahlo, after Leshoai's departure for Zambia in 1963. Partly sponsored by the Coca-Cola Bottling Company, the program went straight to all primary and secondary schools across the Transvaal. Its main funds came from the Congress for Cultural Freedom based in Paris. The program was such a success that in subsequent years white schools in Johannesburg welcomed performances in their school halls. The casts were paid professionals and the directors were either volunteers or teachers of AMDA. Some of the important plays were by white writers because it was difficult to find suitable children's plays by black writers. James Ambrose Brown of the Johannesburg *Sunday Times* wrote plays for the Union. Other productions included improvised plays by AMDA students.

The Union spread its work to Durban in 1963, founding the Durban Theatre Academy. In the same year it also tried to establish a branch in Cape Town by staging another musical based on the life of the Colored people of that city. The book was by Harry Bloom and the music by "Spike" Stanley Glasser. Because of the misrepresentation of Colored life by these two men, the play, *Mr. Paljas*, was a disastrous flop, which wrecked the chances of a Union Artists branch in Cape Town.

The earlier successes of the Union began to dwindle early in 1963 and, though another partially successful musical hit the boards, things really never shaped up properly for the Union. Alan Paton and New York-based director Krishna Shah came up with *Sponono*, based on the life of boys at Diep Kloof Reformatory, where Alan Paton was once principal. Financed by Mary Frank, *Sponono* went to the Cort Theatre on Broadway in New York in 1964, but it closed within fourteen days as white Americans regarded it as a cheap imitation of *West Side Story* and the blacks as a revolting and unpalatable Uncle Tom play. While it still struggled limply along for a while, the Union was unable to recover from this financial disaster.

The Union has ceased to function for other reasons besides the New York financial disaster of 1964. The most important reason was the birth of a black theatre tradition in Soweto, the African township outside metropolitan Johannesburg. While *King Kong* was riding on the crest of the wave of success, the whites at Union Artists scorned the idea of blacks writing and directing plays. The breakthrough came in 1962 with Ben Masinga's improvised musical *Back in Your Own Backyard*, which was based on township life. This was soon followed by Gibson Kente's improvised musicals, *Manana the Jazz Prophet*, *Sikalo*, *Lifa*, and *Zwi*. Kente has now established himself as South Africa's leading black musical comedy writer and director. Drawing large audiences, his musical, *How Long*, tells the grim story of the past problems of black people in South Africa. It is for this reason that it drew crowds. Following his visits to

British and American theatres, Kente introduced elements of commercialism and sheer entertainment into his productions at the expense of a revolutionary theatre of education for change in South Africa. These new African musicals play before many thousand black people and schoolchildren in the countryside and urban areas for long seasons at popular prices. They also have brought to light many new talents far superior to those of some veterans of *King Kong* and *Sponono*.

The second reason why the Union's activities have ceased is that white theatre houses have now opened their doors to black audiences. Therefore, the need to create a separate black theatre no longer exists. In addition, the radical blacks, who scorn the "privilege" of attending shows in the white theatres, have established several independent commercial traveling theatre companies, which take plays into South Africa's towns and rural areas. This new trend has also stimulated dramatic writings among the black people of South Africa on themes relevant to their own lives.

Before the Union became nonexistent, it established the Phoenix Players consisting of black actors and actresses. Most of their plays were by Athol Fugard, such as *Hello and Goodbye*, *Boesman and Lena*, and *People Are Living There*. In 1974 Fugard took two of his plays to London with a two-man black cast consisting of John Kani and Winston Ntshona from Port Elizabeth. The shows, *Sizwe Bansi Is Dead* and *The Island*, are improvisations by the two actors dealing with South Africa's current political situation as it adversely affects its black citizens. The plays scored great successes and received rave reviews in the English press. In writing about the themes of the two plays in *Plays and Players* (March 1974), Jonathan Hammonds says:

Though there have been plenty of books, films and documents in the past 20 years outlining or illuminating different areas of repression and distortion in South African life caused by apartheid, the recent season of plays by or involving Athol Fugard at the Royal Court provides the first sustained attempt to show British theatre audiences the terrible effects of the regime in human terms, reaching into the most personal areas of life.

Ian E. Bernhardt, one of the founders of the Union of South African Artists, is still in Johannesburg. He runs his own marketing business, and also acts as advisor and sometimes manager to black musical groups, such as the famous female trio, Joy, composed of Felicity Marion, Anneline Malebo, and Thoko Ndlozi. He can be contacted at P.O. Box 10466, Johannesburg, 2000, South Africa.

BENJAMIN LETHOLOA LESHOAI

ASIA

Andrew T. Tsubaki, Area Editor

Introduction

Rich traditions of practicing theatre thrive throughout Asia. The oldest of these forms goes back to at least the seventeenth century with the *Gagaku* and *Bugaku* of Japan. At the same time modern theatre has been gradually introduced to the Asian world and now maintains its own activities. This coexistence of traditional and modern theatre has continued for several decades in many Asian countries. In the West there is a certain reluctance to repeat what has been done in the past for such "repetitions" are often thought uncreative, boring, and stifling. A presentation of classical drama in an authentic manner may be called a museum piece, suggesting that it is lifeless or that it bears very little value for today's life. The situation in Asia is not quite that way, although there are some individuals who would also voice negative opinions about the value of traditional theatre forms. The majority of Asians, however, are quite content to let these forms survive. Staging classical works in a traditional manner is not only respected but is also profitable enough for productions to exist in a thoroughly meaningful manner.

Still viable traditional theatre exists in Asia while nothing of the sort is realized in the West. It is interesting to note, however, that many exciting experiments of Western theatre originating from such geniuses as W. B. Yeats, Bertolt Brecht, Peter Brook, and Jerzy Grotowsky, were inspired by these Asian traditional theatre practices. Moreover, a number of significant productions using English dialogue but with authentic detail in movement, costumes, make-up, and other elements of staging have been mounted in the last two decades at a dozen or so universities in the United States of America. The laborious work of leaders in this area, who have covered theatre activities from India to Japan, has had the valuable result of introducing unfamiliar yet fascinating Asian genres and techniques to Western performers and audiences.

The coexistence of traditional theatre and modern theatre in Asia parallels the way of life of Asians. Modern life styles, clearly based on the Western way, are necessary to survive in today's world. Asian countries have paid the West costly tuition fees to learn how to survive and do well in this competitive world, and some of them have learned well enough to stay abreast of the West in the development of technology and acquisition of modern social mores. And yet, Asian peoples are reluctant to become thoroughly Westernized. It is almost as if their instinct guides them to retain the essential aspects of their traditions as the roots of their survival. Traditional theatre activities help people to see where they are from and what their life is about. From primitive folk theatre forms performed in a village square in India to the sophisticated form of Nō theatre in Japan, traditional theatre forms appeal to the part of the body which still requires nourishment from one's own tradition, despite all the modern education and exposure to the new way of life. In the West one makes special efforts to retain any vanishing traditions while in Asia traditional theatre is very much in the minds of people as a part of their daily lives.

The majority of Asian theatre productions, regardless of whether they are traditional or modern, are staged by companies that are organized on a semi-permanent basis. In other words it is a clearly established troupe which produces a production, not a group of actors gathered together for a production on a temporary basis. The members of a troupe enjoy privileges and discharge responsibilities. They train and perform together. In traditional theatre such loyalty is a necessity since each form of theatre has its own identifiable style. Members of the troupe have to try their best to acquire the techniques of the style. It is inconceivable for an actor to switch from one theatre form to another in his or her lifetime, since acquiring the techniques is a lifetime's work. In some cases, when only limited possibilities for performance exist, it is not unusual to see a genre actually represented by a single company.

Most major Asian countries are covered in this reference work, with two notable exceptions: the People's Republic of China and the Philippines. Some aspects of modern theatre in the People's Republic of China are covered in the section on Taiwan. When the preliminary plan was laid out for this project, the door to the People's Republic of China was still closed. The Cultural Revolution and the ensuing confusion revealed only discouraging pictures. Last minute efforts to get some material did not bring satisfactory results so the idea of including the country had to be abandoned. The situation in the Philippines was also difficult due in part to recent political unrest. Repeated attempts to establish proper connections for an article contributor failed.

Despite these uncovered regions, much valuable information about the theatre activities of this huge area is presented along with explanations of rather complicated situations. I am indebted to many capable contributors who generously helped to bring this worthy project into reality.

ANDREW T. TSUBAKI

India

India has thousands of theatre organizations, many of which have long and impressive histories. Yet few of the organizations satisfy the definition of "company" established in this work. In other words, India has not produced the equivalent of a Royal Shakespeare Company, a Minnesota Theatre Company, or a Stratford Shakespeare Festival. To a great extent historical circumstances and economic conditions have conspired to prevent this from happening. This brief essay lays out the historical background against which the modern theatre may be seen, presents the general characteristics of contemporary theatre in selected regions of the country, and cites unique theatre organizations and individuals. It is not meant to be comprehensive; there is far too much unexplored territory to make that possible.

HISTORICAL BACKGROUND

India is a country with a long history of theatre. Theatre existed on the subcontinent as early as the first century B.C. and perhaps even earlier. The notion of what a theatre organization should consist of is carefully laid out in the *Natyasastra*, the oldest and certainly the most complete dramaturgical text of the ancient world. According to this authoritative work, companies were originally family affairs. The mythological origin of theatre assigns leadership of the first company to Bharata, the supposed author of the *Natyasastra* and the eldest member of a priestly family. His company consisted of his actor-sons (one hundred in all!) who gained their knowledge from their father who learned the art directly from Brahma, the god-creator. Therefore, ancient theatre was regarded as a sacred act since it descended directly from God to man and extended from generation to generation through family lineages. Women were admitted to this closed circle when another deity pointed out that women made exceptional dancers and ought to be incorporated into play productions.

Well beyond the classical period of the fifth century A.D., theatre was patronized by the ruling classes. Because of historical events far too complex to discuss here, troupes of actors left the safe haven of court life and began to earn their bread by touring and performing plays in the regional languages, rather than in Sanskrit, the classical language. Despite the enormous fragmentation that might have occurred, the company structure remained virtually intact, except that members of different subcastes assumed specific responsibilities in the performance of plays. How strict the prohibitions and restrictions were may only be imagined since historical records are missing or vague on this point. The living tradition of classical theatre came to an end around the tenth century A.D.

Up to the fifteenth century, a relatively dark period ensued in the evolution of Indian theatre. Then, suddenly, for a variety of reasons, theatre was resurrected throughout the length and breadth of the country, taking on various shapes and characteristics, according to the differing needs and tastes of the rural population that supported it. Some pockets of the North played host to Nautanki, some to Ramlila and Raslila, others to Maach, to name but a few of the forms that emerged in this region. Some areas of the South created Kathakali and Krishnanattam; others produced Therukoothu and Yakshagana; in others Kuchipudi and Vithi Natakam were born. The West saw the emergence of Tamasha and Bhavai. The East developed Jatra and Ankiya Nat. So many theatre forms were born between the fifteenth and the eighteenth centuries that it is virtually impossible to determine how many were created, much less to discuss the features of the company structure of even one form. The field is rich and has often baffled enthusiastic researchers. The picture that emerges is a panorama of traditional theatre forms, some of which have preserved the essence of their original form and structure even to the extent that only members of hereditary castes may perform them in orthodox surroundings. Others have so modified their composition that their former structure is hardly recognizable underneath the veil of contemporary revisions.

These then are the layers on which the modern Indian theatre is built: Underneath, an antiquated classical tradition, overwhelming in its literary accomplishments, of symbolic and ritual significance, dating back to the *Natyasastra* for its rules and regulations; and over that a rich and varied multiplicity of theatre forms in every region of the country, some of which have kept their essence intact and others which have responded to the pressures of change. Those who perform modern theatre may not always have a working knowledge of the characteristics of the classical or regional traditional theatre, but they are aware of its impressive history and what they produce contrasts markedly with the theatre of the past and, to an extent, absorbs and uses elements of it.

Not unexpectedly, modern Indian theatre owes its origin and development to the growth of India's cities in the eighteenth and nineteenth centuries. Calcutta, Madras, and Bombay, the three cradles of modern Indian civilization, were founded and nurtured as a result of the British presence. To satisfy the demand of British soldiers, merchants, and bureaucrats for a taste of home, English theatre was imported wholesale into India. Proscenium arch stages built on London models became the center of urban theatrical activity. English plays were seen and later adapted and imitated in Indian languages. Lord Macaulay's famous remark of 1835 that "We must at present do our best to form a class who may be interpreters between us and the millions whom we govern—a class of persons Indian in blood and colour, but English in tastes, in opinions, in morals, and in intellect," soon became a reality. Between 1850 and 1875 modern Indian theatre was born—urban in setting, housed in proscenium arch stages, geared to appeal to the tastes of a small but growing middle class. It is a theatre written and performed in the language of the region, using staging and production techniques similar to those found abroad and performed by a generous mix of individuals of different castes, races, religions, occupations, and social classes. By the late nineteenth century, this theatre, so British in its original design, was to serve the ends of the independence movement by spreading sedition in the guise of historical and mythological tales. It had its own uniquely Indian characteristics. Songs and dances, so popular with Indian audiences, were grafted wholesale onto dialogue dramas. This was a theatre of painted scenery, wings and drops, and declamatory acting, a theatre in which stars and company managers ruled the stage as completely as they did in the United States. Famous companies arose and declined in the late nineteenth century—the Victoria Theatre Company of Delhi, the New Alfred Theatrical Company, the Old Parsi Theatrical Company, the Corinthian Company, and the Alexandra Company of Bombay, to name but a few.

NINETEENTH-CENTURY DERIVATIVES

Derivatives of these nineteenth-century companies may still be seen today in some areas of South India. Two examples are striking in their tenacity: Manohar's National Theatres of Madras and Kalanilaya Vistavision Dramascope of Trivandrum. Both organizations emphasize the use of extensive and elaborate scene changes. *Ottakoothar*, a drama about a historical personality produced by the National in 1980, boasted fifty-three scene changes in the space of two hours, all executed with wings and drops on cue from the stage manager's whistle. It had spectacular effects such as explosions producing fire and smoke followed by scenic revelations, swords flying across the stage, floods, beheadings, and many other complicated tricks executed with perfect seriousness. Costs for creating these marvelous illusions, luxuries of a bygone era, soared to well above $4,000 (Rs. 50,000). In order to keep a company of sixty-seven individuals satisfied, the National demands and receives nearly $350 (Rs. 3,000) per performance to astound enthusiastic patrons in Madras and smaller towns and cities in the state of Tamil Nadu and on tour to Bombay, Bangalore, New Delhi, Singapore, and Kuala Lampur.

The National was begun in 1954 under the guidance of R. S. Manohar, a highly organized, tasteful, and shrewd actor-manager who usually performs the leading male roles in all his productions. His company includes a staff of dedicated and professional theatre workers. Perhaps nowhere in the world are the vestiges of nineteenth-century staging better preserved than they are in Manohar's National Theatre.

Closely akin to the style and manner of Manohar's company is the Kalanilaya Vistavision Dramascope Company of Trivandrum, Kerala. One of the most fascinating features of this organization is the temporary home it constructs for its members when on tour. A special theatre building is erected of bamboo, thatch, and rope, which seats well over a thousand patrons. The impressive structure also contains separate living quarters for women, men, and families; dressing rooms; scene storage; facilities for building and painting scenery; costume storage; covered walkways for patrons; snack bars; toilets; as well as a huge backstage space; a raised proscenium stage with traps and fly space; rigging for sliding wings; and innumerable staging effects to astound the spectators.

Actors of the Kalanilaya agree to a yearly contract and spend the nine-month season playing extended stints in several localities of the state and perform before urban and rural audiences alike.

Besides multiple scene changes (thirty-six in its 1980 production of *Ragam Thanam Pallavi*), the Kalanilaya boasts of scenes enacted on film, integrated with segments of the stage play. The gimmick serves as an extension of the nineteenth-century idea of using novel devices to appeal to audience taste. The central office of the Kalanilaya is located in the city of Trivandrum where bookings are made. A tour manager and a member of the family that founded the company travel with the troupe to handle the box office and the multiple demands of a large company of 115 actors and technicians. Like the National, the Kalanilaya performs a repertory of plays derived from historical and mythological sources. The taste of Kerala audiences demands that the plays be a generous blend of spicy and, at times, even racy dialogue, provocative dances, slapstick farce, emotional and tearful sentimentality, combined with heavy doses of surprising and miraculous scenic effects.

TWENTIETH-CENTURY PRECURSORS

Although these vestiges of the nineteenth century are intriguing, they are not characteristic of the modern Indian theatre movement. Modern Indian theatre has developed plays that center on the plight of individuals and families, on social and political events. It is little wonder that Indian theatre in the early twentieth century was influenced by the works of Shaw, Ibsen, and Chekhov. Political events in India, and in particular the demise of colonialism and the struggle for India's independence, which finally occurred in 1947, also served as a major dramatic theme during the first few decades of this century.

One of the most significant theatre operations to emerge during the thirties and forties was the Indian People's Theatre Association (IPTA). In its heyday IPTA established regional centers in all the major urban areas of the country. Some of the most famous names in the performing arts were initially associated with the IPTA; Ravi Shankar, Mulk Raj Anand, Romesh Thapar, and Khwaja Ahmad Abbas are perhaps the best known.

IPTA's first play production to attract national attention was *Rich Harvest*

(*Nabanna*), produced on a shoestring in Calcutta in 1944. The play is a probing view of the terrible Bengal famine of 1943–1944. With the simplest of means Sombhu Mitra, then a young and promising director, brought home to urban audiences the plight of Bengal's helpless peasants. Tripti Mitra's moving portrayal of a starving woman launched her career as one of India's most prominent and finest contemporary actresses. The play attracted many thousands of spectators to the theatre because of its timeliness, honesty, and raw appeal.

But because of its connections with the Communist party, IPTA soon frightened off its best talent, most of whom, for good reason, feared that the theatre might simply become a tool of politicians. Although IPTA served to raise the consciousness of urban audiences for sensitive social issues, it was not to exert a lasting influence on the direction of the modern theatre. Today it continues to function in several urban centers with the help of devoted followers, but it has become an anachronism.

CONTEMPORARY DEVELOPMENTS

With this brief historical setting before us, let us examine the characteristics of contemporary theatre with particular reference to the composition of theatre companies.

Some areas of the country are regarded as more theatre-minded than others. Any Indian who is asked what area of the country has the most active modern theatre movement would probably mention Calcutta first. Indeed, there are an estimated three thousand registered theatre organizations in the city alone. Bombay is said to have about five hundred groups and the state of Maharashtra, in which Bombay is located, around two thousand organizations. Far less active, Madras and Delhi have little more than fifty theatre organizations each, and the whole state of Kerala may have no more than fifty active organizations.

It must be remembered that these are only estimates and not actual tabulations and that the cities represented constitute only a portion of the total urban base. The survey does not include theatre organizations in such populous cities as Bangalore, Pune, Ahmedabad, Lucknow, Patna, and Allahabad. Undoubtedly, if these cities were included in the survey, the total number of contemporary groups might range between four and five thousand. Even though this figure is impressive, it must be remembered that urban areas comprise only 20 percent of India's enormous population of 650 million people. Thus, modern theatre is a product of a minority of India's people.

India has a small but active commercial theatre, a very large and extremely active amateur theatre, and a limited but enterprising experimental theatre. Circumstances, which we shall deal with as we come to them, have prevented commercial theatre from being as extensive as those who participate in theatre might wish it to be. As indicated earlier, India has no company that enjoys the national and international reputation of the Royal Shakespeare Company and the Stratford Festival. Moreover, unlike many forms of folk theatre, the performance of a modern production does not last all night. It is usually contained within the span of two and one-half to three hours. Reflecting the slower pace of life there, even modern Western plays are slowed down somewhat so that they also take that long to unfold. Since the circumstances that guide the theatre differ from one region and one city to another, we shall examine the spectrum of theatre in each area separately.

CALCUTTA

Calcutta has the oldest and perhaps the most active tradition of theatre partly because very early in the colonial period the British established the city as a center of trade and commerce in the Far East. The first proscenium arch stage dates from 1756. It figured prominently in the battle between forces of the local Nawab and the English soldiers before the fort was seized and the Black Hole of Calcutta incident took place. Numerous theatre structures followed swiftly in the wake of the Playhouse. Some of the more famous are the Calcutta Theatre, the Chowringhee Theatre, the Sans Souci, and the Royal Opera House.

Today Calcutta has one of India's most vigorous commercial theatre enterprises. Commercial theatre is centered in the north side of the city, in the heart of the Bengali-speaking area. Within the radius of a few city blocks are five important theatre structures where the major commercial fare is presented.

The Star, constructed in 1883, is the oldest of the commercial houses. Once the home of companies headed by famous actors like Girish Chandra Ghosh and Sisir Bhaduri, the Star now contracts actors and technical personnel to mount a single new production each season. R. M. Kankaria, the proprietor-manager of the house, sorts through various ideas for plays, hires writers to develop different segments of the dialogue, includes his chief actors in the planning and staging of the play, and relies on his stage technicians to pull together effective scenery and properties from the Star's enormous stock, some of which dates back to its origin. Actors have contracts with the management for a run of the play unless either party gives a twenty-one day notice. Actors earn a decent living performing five or six shows a week. Nevertheless, on their days off, many of them supplement their income by acting in other productions elsewhere in the city or by making films, by serving as talent on radio and television programs, and by making commercials for Calcutta's advertising business.

A company of ninety-five actors and technicians works for the Star's manager to keep the productions running and the house functioning afternoons and evenings. It is estimated that mounting a production may run between $2,750 (Rs. 22,000) and $12,500 (Rs. 100,000), depending on whether the play is a single set social drama or a historical play requiring elaborate costumes and music. Salaries for musicians invariably swell the cost of a production budget considerably. Running costs per show are estimated at $475 (Rs. 3,000) a day with possible box office returns of $1,750 (Rs. 14,000) per month, above expenses. Groups that wish to rent the Star when it is dark (and many do because they believe that achieving a critical success at the Star insures continued commercial success at other theatres) pay the highest rental charge for any theatre in the city—$175 (Rs. 1,400) per show. Few groups can afford this luxury.

The objective of the Star's management is to cover expenses and turn as handsome a profit as possible. Ultimately, the motive of all concerned is to realize a decent living from the theatre. For this reason the fare that is offered has some of the same earmarks as that at Madras's National. Multiscene changes are devised to appeal to the spectators' taste for variety. Plays deal with modern issues that usually concern family life. The plots are filled with sentiment and humor, spiced with a hint of promiscuity, and performed by attractive actors and actresses, many of whom have made a name for themselves in the film industry. The productions have some of the characteristics of the fare dished up by commercial television in the United States. Yet the management of the Star prides itself on producing works that are above the base interests of audiences that frequent other commercial houses in the city. For example, in the summer of 1980, Shyamaprasad Mancha's *Lajrakiro* was advertised in the local newspapers as "A super hit drama with extra blow hot dance by sweet sixteen!" On the same evening, Circarena's *Samrat-O-Sundari*, then in its 450th performance, offered provocative dances performed by its two female stars (both local cabaret artists), a car chase, and a wreck resulting in an explosion on stage. Despite the gimmicks of this particular production, the Circarena Theatre is worth mentioning since it is India's only major arena theatre building and is modeled on Washington, D.C.'s Arena Stage.

Circarena has a 20-foot disk stage which rotates and functions on a hydraulic lift. The demand for scene changes is so great in India that the stage often sinks into the basement with the dimming of the stage lights so that scene changes can be made. In order to keep a play moving, transition scenes are played on the 4-foot wide acting area around the circumference of the disk. Revolving disks like that of the Circarena are a descendant of an idea brought to Calcutta in the 1930s by a theatre artist who had seen similar stages in New York. Most of the major proscenium theatre houses in Calcutta now have a revolving disk. In this respect, they differ from all the other theatre buildings elsewhere in India.

The commercial theatre in Calcutta is also unique in that it functions virtually without the benefit of stage directors. The leading actors of a production usually provide whatever stage directions are necessary, while the production manager and his staff of technicians work out details concerning settings, lighting, and properties.

Worlds apart from the commercial theatre is the so-called other theatre of South Calcutta. The philosophy of the organizations of the "other theatre" is to produce a high-quality product that is serious in content and slick and challenging in production detail. For years actors, directors, and theatre technicians of the "other theatre" have been struggling to survive with a bare minimum of financial compensation for their efforts. For this reason the "other theatre" must be considered amateur. Yet many of the artists resent being categorized as amateurs. They pride themselves on their "professional" standards and accomplishments. Indeed, critics in India and abroad who have seen the work of the groups concerned rightly claim that it is as fine as the best work to be seen in the professional theatre in the Western world, comparing favorably with that of London's National, the companies in Stratford, England, and Ontario, Canada, and similar organizations on the European continent.

Many of the groups have a long and notable history. Bohurupee, originated and once headed by the talented director Sombhu Mitra and now managed by a team of distinguished actor-directors, has made many notable contributions to the Calcutta theatre since 1948. Some of the finest examples of Bohurupee's work are Rabindranath Tagore's *Red Oleanders* and *King of the Dark Chamber*, as well as *A Doll's House*, *An Enemy of the People*, and *Oedipus Rex*, to name but a few of the thirty-odd works produced by the group since it began. Bohurupee prides itself on producing plays that challenge the intellect as well as the emotions of its audiences. The People's Little Theatre, which originated in 1969, places major emphasis on plays with strong themes. The organization is headed by Utpal Dutt, who is rightly regarded as one of the most outstanding actors, directors, and playwrights of the modern Indian theatre. Dutt is something of a celebrity in India for his controversial support of Communist causes.

Nandikar, founded by Ajitesh Banerjee and now run by Rudra Prasad Sen Gupta, has produced a wide array of translations and adaptations of Western plays, the best of which includes Bertolt Brecht's *The Threepenny Opera*, Jean Anouilh's *Antigone*, Luigi Pirandello's *Six Characters in Search of an Author*, Brecht's *The Good Woman of Setzuan*, and Arthur Miller's *Death of a Salesman*. It recently presented a popular original work entitled *Football*. The play is a commentary on the violence of the younger generation and the web of social circumstances that they find themselves caught up in.

Productions and groups representing the "other theatre" movement are generally to be seen in South Calcutta, in newer and more luxurious theatres like the Academy of Fine Arts. It is said that the audiences for the plays of the "other theatre" are more cosmopolitan than those of the commercial theatre and that many of the individuals who attend the plays are college educated and hold white-collar jobs. A casual observation of the audience of any of the groups indicates that a good percentage of the audience is young, perhaps college age, and that they can afford the relatively high price of a theatre ticket which ranges from $1.25 (Rs. 10) to 20 cents (Rs. 2) per production compared with the cost of a movie ticket which ranges from 55 cents (Rs. 5) to 18 cents (90 pice).

Despite years of persistent struggle and a consistently high production standard, none of Calcutta's "other theatres" has been able to establish itself on a commercial basis. Many factors, especially economic pressures, have prevented this from happening. Like similar theatre organizations in other Indian cities, the groups must rent a theatre building in order to produce a play. Only one group in Calcutta, the Theatre Centre, owns its own building, which is located on the ground floor of a private dwelling in the residential section of South Calcutta and seats barely a hundred patrons.

As a result of the high land prices and soaring value of commercial property in urban India, theatre rentals have risen dramatically in recent years. Easily a quarter of a production budget is earmarked for renting space for performance. Hence, a group must continually move from one theatre to another in order to survive. This means that scenery must be struck, crated, and stored between performances, which contributes to the total performance cost. Complicating the problem still further is the fact that the cost of constructing scenery has risen considerably in recent years, as it seems to have done everywhere in the world. It is estimated that an average production of one of Calcutta's theatre groups costs between $2,750 (Rs. 22,000) and $3,750 (Rs. 30,000) to mount.

Newspaper advertising also adds considerably to the total cost of production. A 3-centimeter column ad in the local Bengali papers costs approximately $18.75 (Rs. 150) per day to run. Because of frequent shifts and changes from one theatre to another, groups are obliged to alert potential patrons when and where a show will be playing every week.

The great hardships caused by such economic pressures have literally led theatre groups to take to the road. In order for a group to put aside income for future productions, to defray the transportation expenses of its members during rehearsals, and to provide the actors with a small but enticing subsidiary income for their theatre work, it accepts bookings in smaller towns and cities outside Calcutta, producing what are referred to as "call" shows. Typically, if a theatre organization has a reputation for excellence and its latest production in Calcutta has met with some degree of success, organizers outside the city communicate with the director and request that he bring the company (actors, settings, costumes, properties, lights, and all) to their town or city to perform the play for a relatively high set fee, plus transportation expenses.

Since the "other theatre" depends on the dedication of individuals who hold down permanent jobs, the troupe is obliged to leave Calcutta on weekends or to accept bookings late in the evening on weekdays. Since Calcutta is connected with many large urban centers by rail, theoretically the troupe can depart for a "call" engagement after office hours, play a late evening show in a distant town, and return to the city by the early morning train, in time for company members to shower, change, and get to their offices in time for work.

With the hardships that touring obviously causes and the rewards that it offers, none of the groups has made the jump from the status of amateur to that of professional. Despite this situation, some prominent members of the "other theatre," like Ajitesh Banerjee, Sombhu Mitra, Utpal Dutt, and Tripti Mitra, to name but a few, do make a living working in the theatre. They do so by piecing together engagements in group plays with other acting and directing assignments, film appearances, and work in advertising. A few actors have even sold their service to producers of Jatra. Jatra is a tremendously popular form of traditional theatre. One prominent actor-director confided that he could earn enough from one season performing Jatra to sustain himself and his family for an entire year. This allowed him to continue to work in the "other theatre," his real love.

Experimental theatre in Calcutta is an extension of the amateur theatre movement, and yet its philosophy and pattern of activity are quite distinct. Badal Sircar, regarded as one of India's finest serious playwrights, has stated the philosophy of the experimental theatre in his book, *The Third Theatre* (Calcutta: Badal Sircar, 1978). Sircar argues that because of economic restrictions the "other theatre" cannot experiment and grow but is forced to rely on safe formulas that cater to the taste of the middle class. Sircar has proposed that theatre organizations should abandon the notion that they require a theatre building in order to produce plays. Satabdi, Sircar's theatre group, develops productions that have few frills. Satabdi may be seen every Friday of the year performing in "found" spaces, which cost relatively little or nothing to use; have no stage, no lighting instruments, no scenery (only properties and selected scene pieces); require little or no advertising; cost the audience the remarkably low admission fee of 10 cents (R. 1); and in which patrons are admitted free if they cannot afford to pay. Given this philosophy, it is no wonder that Sircar has no respect for or intention of forming a commercial theatre. He abhors the idea that theatre should be bound to economic considerations for its survival.

Sircar's philosophy and that of numerous Western theoreticians, namely Jerzy Grotowski, Julian Beck, and Richard Schechner, have inspired the creation of yet another branch of experimental theatre in Calcutta. This is typified by the work of the Living Theatre of Khardah. Young actors who hold jobs in the city meet regularly after work and produce events that they themselves have created from their own life experiences. They operate the Living Theatre in the suburban community of Khardah, an hour away from the city by train. The group functions democratically, with all members having an equal voice and vote in the creative product and affairs of the organization. Local critics regard the Living Theatre of Khardah as one of the best of many similar organizations operating on the outskirts of Calcutta. Its work has a liberal dose of chanted sounds and physical movement, akin to acrobatics and dance. Its 1980 production of *I, You and We* was performed in a tiny grade school room which held no more than twenty patrons. The simple light bulb on an extension cord was borrowed from a shopkeeper next door. No scenery was used, and yet the actors provided a compelling presentation that lasted about an hour. Because of their sincerity and dedication and level of work, Jerzy Grotowski gave a few of the actors financial assistance to participate in his mountain retreat in 1980–1981. Like the work of Sircar, it is not the intention of the Living Theatre and groups like it to form a commercial enterprise or to function in any way like the "other theatre" or the commercial theatres. Their aim is to return to the roots of theatre in the human community and to seek the ritual origins of the theatre art.

Theatre Groups

BOHURUPEE
c/o Mr. Amar Ganguly
Song and Drama Division
20 Garia Hat Road
Calcutta, India

LIVING THEATRE
c/o Mr. Sushil Smrity Kunja
Adarshapally, Khardah
Dist. 24, Parganas
West Bengal, India

NANDIKAR
c/o Mr. Rudra Prasad Sen Gupta
47/1, Shambazar Street
Calcutta, India 700004

PEOPLE'S LITTLE THEATRE
c/o Mr. Utpal Dutt
"Kallol," 140, Netaji Road
Calcutta 40, India

SATABDI
c/o Mr. Badal Sircar
1A, Peary Row
Calcutta, India 700001

STAR THEATRE
c/o Mr. R. M. Kankaria
Shree Ranjit Pictures, 87 Dharamtalla Street
Calcutta 13, India

THEATRE CENTRE
c/o Mr. Tarun Roy
31-A Chakraberia Rd. (South)
Calcutta, India 700025

BOMBAY

Apart from Calcutta, Bombay has the most active modern theatre movement
in India. Even during the heavy monsoon rains (which occur between June and

September, regarded as the slump season for theatre activity), many plays may be seen throughout the city.

Bombay's theatre business more nearly resembles that of Calcutta's "other theatre": At the head of a typical theatre organization is invariably a dynamic director, without whom the group would flounder. Directors are surrounded by a small core of dedicated members, many of whom have been involved in the affairs of their group for years. Around the periphery of this core are less active, often transient, fledgling members whose loyalty has not yet been tested by years of faithful service.

In contrast to Calcutta, which has a predominantly Bengali-speaking population, Bombay has several large population groups that speak different languages. The largest of these is the Marathi-speaking community, and likewise the most active theatre tradition in the city is the Marathi theatre. There are also active theatre organizations in Gujarati, Hindi, English, and some South Indian languages.

Bombay's theatre must contend with some of the same problems as those experienced by similar groups in Calcutta. Theatre buildings are not in the hands of the theatre organizations but are owned by individual landowners, trusts, or the government. Several dozen theatre buildings are sprinkled from the northern suburbs to the commercial heart of the city in the South. The pattern of constructing theatre buildings has responded to the needs of an ever-expanding population which has steadily moved northward since the early twentieth century. Most of the buildings are conveniently located near the main transportation arteries—the eastern and western railway lines and the highly efficient BEST bus system.

Although the city seems to have many theatre buildings, in fact there is fierce competition among the theatre organizations for bookings. So much rivalry exists that forty-five of the leading Marathi theatre producing organizations have formed the Marathi Professional Drama Producers Guild, one of the main missions of which has been to bring order and some degree of control over the bookings of the most popular theatre buildings. Collectively, it has managed to assure that guild members get 60 percent of the available bookings each month in popular halls like Shivaji Mandir, Natya Mandir, Gadkari Rangayatan, and Balagandharva Natya Mandir (Pune), as well as unofficial acceptance of the system from government-run halls like Ravindra Natya Mandir and Mumbai Maratha Sahitya Sangh, which are forbidden from entering into such agreements owing to government regulations. Pressure from the guild has also helped to keep the rental charges down somewhat from what they are in Calcutta. Through its efforts the guild has managed to hold down the cost of newspaper advertising to some extent.

Despite the guild's best efforts, none of the theatre organizations in Bombay has been able to earn enough from box office receipts to pay a permanent company of actors. "Call" shows outside the city have also become a way of life for the theatre groups of Bombay in order to meet the escalating costs of production and to provide the much needed capital for producing future seasons of plays. In 1980 a tragic road accident in which eight members of a touring theatre company were killed prompted newspaper critics to focus public attention on the fact that most Bombay companies must tour in order to survive. Some individuals do manage to piece together a living wage from numerous activities in theatre, films, and advertising. But no one has been able to create the conditions in which an entire company can survive.

In terms of the content of the plays, Bombay's amateur groups produce a variety fare, ranging from sentimental comedies to tragedies and including satires and farces. They also rely on original works written by nationally recognized authors such as Vijay Tendulkar and Satish Alekar, as well as the work of locally popular writers like Jaswant Dalvi. Some groups also depend on translations and adaptations of the works of Shakespeare, George Bernard Shaw, Harold Pinter, Tennessee Williams, Arthur Miller, Edward Albee, Bertolt Brecht, Jean Genet, and Jean Anouilh.

Small and enterprising experimental groups perform in either the Chabildas School Hall or the Prithvi Theatre. The Chabildas School Hall is located near the crowded Dadar Railway Station. During the day the hall serves the needs of schoolchildren, and at night the entire facility is transformed into an intimate proscenium theatre seating about three hundred. The facilities must be completely struck every evening after the last show in order to ready it for the use of the school the next day. Avishkar, a small experimental group run by Arvind Desh-pande, a sincere and talented actor-director, holds the lease on the space. During the evenings that the group is not performing its own productions, it rents out the space to other groups for the nominal charge of $5.00 (Rs. 40).

In attempting to meet the crying need for experimental space, Shashi Kapoor, a well-known movie actor and son of Prithvi Raj Kapoor, the indefatigable stage and screen star, and his English wife opened a thrust stage facility seating about 250 persons in Juhu, a popular beachfront resort in North Bombay. Since it opened its doors in 1979, hundreds of amateur and experimental groups have produced plays in the facility, even though it is somewhat out of the way for most theatre patrons.

In contrast to experimental theatre groups in Calcutta, those in Bombay have not attempted to break away from the prevailing system. Rather, they have tried to work within its framework but on a smaller, more conservative scale. Their productions are somewhat radical in content and generally traditional in their manner of production.

Among Bombay's most active amateur theatre organizations are the Goa Hindu Association, Abhishek, and Anatranga, all of whose plays are performed in Marathi; the Indian National Theatre which produces works in Marathi and Gujurati; the Theatre Unit which prides itself on producing Hindi plays; and the Theatre Group, which is one of India's oldest and best English-language theatre organizations.

The Indian National Theatre (INT) deserves special mention in that it has a long history of active work beginning in 1944. The INT obtains substantial financial support from the national government to help support the salary of its office personnel. The organization conducts workshops for adult actors and children. It has production units for Gujarati and Marathi plays, as well as a popular program of children's theatre. Its Research Centre for the Performing Folk Arts probes rural forms of theatre, music, and dance in the states of Gujarat and Maharashtra for inspiration and ideas.

Among Bombay's active theatre personalities are many individuals who have achieved national prominence. Some of the best known are P. L. Despande, Jabbar Patel, Arvind Deshpande, Damoo Kinkre, Vijaya Mehta, Kamlakar Sontakke, Kamlakar Sarang, Dina Pathak, Mansukh Joshi, Daji Bhatavadekar, Adi Marzban, Alyque Padamsee, and Pearl Padamsee.

Theatre Groups

ABHISHEK
c/o Mr. Kamlakar Sarang
36, Lady Jamshedji Road (1st Cross Road)
Mahim, Bombay, India 400016

ANATRANGA
c/o Mr. Kamlakar Sarang
36, Lady Jamshedji Road (1st Cross Road)
Mahim, Bombay, India 400016

AVISHKAR
c/o Mr. Arvind Deshpande
3144 Madhavi Sahariwas, Mogal Line
Mahim, Bombay, India 400016

GOA HINDU ASSOCIATION
c/o Mr. Damoo Kenkre
23, Kala Nagar
Bandra (East), Bombay, India 51

INDIAN NATIONAL THEATRE
19/21 Bombay Mutual Chambers (2d Floor)
19 Hamam Street
Bombay, India 400023

THEATRE GROUP
c/o Mr. Alyque Padamsee
Lintas
Nariman Point, Bombay, India 1

THEATRE UNIT
c/o Mr. Satyadev Dubey
Lintas
Nariman Point, Bombay, India 1

MADRAS

Other than the commercial efforts of the Manohar's National Theatre which produces nineteenth-century theatre, theatre organizations in Madras may be classified as amateur. A few individuals are compensated financially for their efforts, but none of the groups has managed to form a company of paid actors.

Theatre people in Madras face unique circumstances which deserve special consideration. In order to get female talent for their productions, most of the local directors must pay an actress a set fee per show. Social pressures have dissuaded the majority of middle-class women from participating in theatre. Unless the family's financial state is such that a woman has no other alternative, she will not act in plays. The situation is similar in other parts of the South as well.

It is said that a woman may make a decent living by acting in several productions a month. While this is a tremendous advantage for the few women who perform, it proves to be something of a nightmare for the directors who must plan complicated rehearsal schedules around the performance bookings of the female artists, plus coordinate the schedules of individuals who hold down steady jobs during the day.

Amateur theatre organizations in Madras are also unique in that the content of the plays and their success with the public are dictated by the whims of the Association and Federation of City Sabhas. Sabhas are commercial bodies that sell a subscription to a broad membership for monthly programs of music, dance, and drama. Today Madras City is said to have nearly one hundred active sabhas, each with thousands of members. In the late 1950s the sabhas, who up to that point were in the business of sponsoring music and dance programs, began to sponsor plays. Initially, it seemed like a tremendous boon for most amateur theatre organizations, since the sabhas assumed the burden of marketing their work. Sabhas also offered a ready market for play productions. However, before long the amateur theatre realized that the tail could wag the dog. The sabhas, through their strong central administration, could dictate the type of plays they chose to sponsor, and not infrequently included plays that appealed only to the lowest common denominator of the audience. Local critics are quick to complain of the trite, safe fare that characterizes the majority of Madras theatre today.

Experimental theatre, like that found in Bombay and Calcutta, and even serious theatre like that of the "other theatre" have no role in a system in which all the emphasis is placed on making money and pleasing the audience. Few individuals have the power and audience sympathy to dictate terms to the sabhas. Cho S.

Ramaswamy is an exception. Cho is one of the most colorful figures of the modern Indian theatre. A bald-headed man with a striking personality, Cho is the editor of *Tughlak*, a popular weekly. He is author of twenty-two plays, most of which are thinly veiled satires of government corruption. Cho has managed to manipulate the sabha system to his advantage. His popularity is so wide that a feature article on him appeared in the May 30, 1980, edition of *Asia Week*, an Asian version of *Time* magazine.

The Association and Federation of City Sabhas normally invites Cho to write and produce a play for its member groups. If he agrees, he usually secludes himself for several days and writes a work which he rehearses and in which he frequently acts the lead. His organization, the Viveka Fine Arts Club, the only group he allows to perform his plays, demands a handsome fee of $175 (Rs. 1,400) per show from the sabhas. Most of his plays have run at least one hundred performances, and some have played over four hundred performances. Even with his high success rate, Cho cannot make a full-time living from theatre, and he and his group must play "call" shows in the provinces in order to survive.

Despite its positive initial contributions to the sustaining of amateur theatre in Madras, the sabha system is partially responsible for the demise of all but one of the commercial companies. Some famous older groups, such as the TKS Brothers, the Seva Stage, and the Rajamanickam Company, folded because they had high overhead and a small audience base and thus needed the sabhas to survive. When low-overhead amateur organizations entered the market, the commercial theatre could not compete. The sabha system is firmly entrenched in the theatre life of the city and does not appear to be willing to let go.

Theatre Groups

MANOHAR'S NATIONAL THEATRE
c/o Mr. R. S. Manohar
"Suraji," 18, Sri Ram Colony
Madras, India 600018

VIVEKA FINE ARTS CLUB
10 Prithivi Avenue
Madras, India 18

KERALA

As noted earlier, the state of Kerala contains the vestiges of nineteenth-century theatre, as well as a wide range of traditional theatre forms. Kerala also has two very interesting commercial theatre companies with affiliations to different branches of the Communist party. The Kerala People's Art Club (KPAC) is older than the Kalidasa Kalakendra, which is a splinter organization founded when the

Marxist-oriented leaders split with the pro-Soviet leadership. KPAC was founded in 1950 and has produced some highly controversial works ever since, including *You Made Me a Communist*, a scathing satire on the politics of the ruling Congress party. The work ran for two thousand nights.

Today the KPAC operates out of its rural headquarters in the village of Kayamgulam. Picturesque living quarters, including a rehearsal space and a shed protecting a bus used in its tours, are situated on a small plot of rich paddy land near the Arabian Sea coast. During the monsoon months the actors and technicians gather to rehearse the latest work of Thoppil Bhasi, the well-known Kerala playwright and director. The twenty-five members of the group receive an equal share in the profits of their lucrative tours throughout the state and the nation. A percentage of the profits is also contributed to the Communist party of India (CPI) to further its work. The productions of the KPAC are serious and reveal a high level of talent. All of them are geared to reflect the CPI's latest philosophy. In its 1980 production of *Keep Your Head and Hands Inside the Bus*, for example, Bhasi demonstrates that strikes and public disturbances are counterproductive and only disrupt the lives of the helpless common people. The play proposes that those with like-minded ideas (meaning the CPI [Marxists]) ought to work in harmony with the CPI to bring about social change through democratic means.

Since its founding, the KPAC has produced twenty-two works, some of which enjoyed runs of over a thousand nights, often playing to crowds of between five and ten thousand spectators.

The Kalidasa Kalakendra is a branch of the CPI (Marxist). Its headquarters are located in the port city of Quilon, where an office, rehearsal hall, living quarters, and shed with a bus are situated on a small plot of land. The group was founded in 1960 and has produced nineteen different productions which have run an average of three hundred shows each. The dynamic head of the organization is O. Madhavan, who, with his wife, a popular local actress, keeps the organization running. Madhavan recently was elected head of the local village council and now spreads his political views through democratic means, as well as through the theatre.

Kerala boasts of other popular organizations which run commercial ventures and tour widely throughout the state. Among the best of these is the Kottayam-based Viswakerala Kalasamithi, headed by N. N. Pillai, the popular playwright-director-actor. Another popular organization is based in Calicut and is run by K. T. Mohamed, a famous author-director. The plays of both individuals have strong political overtones, if they do not directly rubber-stamp the philosophies of the left-wing political parties in the state.

Kerala does not have an active experimental theatre. One of the few individuals to pioneer experimental theatre in the state is Kavalam Narayana Panikkar of Trivandrum, whose Thiruvarang drama group was founded in 1964. The organization valiantly fights an uphill battle to bring daring experiments to the attention of urban audiences. But the lethargy that exists in the sprawling urban centers of Kerala does not help to promote a positive environment in which experimental theatre can thrive. In recent years, the plays of G. Shankaran Pillai have added strength to the proposition that experimental theatre in the Malayalam language makes exciting theatre fare.

Theatre Groups

KALIDASA KALAKENDRA
c/o Mr. O. Madhavan
Quilon 1, Kerala, India

KALANILAYAN VISTAVISION DRAMASCOPE
c/o Mr. Vijya Kumar
Pooja Pura
Trivandrum-12, Kerala, India

KERALA PEOPLE'S ART CLUB
Kayamgulam 690502, Kerala, India

THIRUVARANG
c/o Mr. Kavalam Narayana Panikkar
Vasantham
Peroorkada, Trivandrum, India 5

VISWAKERALA KALASAMITHI
c/o Mr. N. N. Pillai
Kottayam, Kerala, India

DELHI

The ancient city of Delhi is India's third largest metropolitan center. New Delhi, its sister city, is the seat of a powerful government with a vast bureaucracy. It would stand to reason that Delhi should also be a center for theatre, but in fact Delhi is not a theatre city at all. Despite the best efforts of many theatre organizations and the establishment of the National School of Drama (NSD), an entirely government-funded training institution which rightly boasts of being the best place in India to study theatre, the city has produced only one commercial theatre group, the Naya Theatre. This organization is run by Habib Tanvir, a bright and talented director and former member of Parliament who performs widely outside the city in order to pay his actors their meager wages.

Delhi's amateur theatre organizations can usually find enough patrons to fill the house for only five shows. And yet some of the most beautiful theatre facilities have been constructed in the city in the last ten years. The Sri Ram Centre,

Kamani Auditorium, the Little Theatre Group Auditorium, and the Gandhi Memorial Theatre have joined the ranks of older theatre facilities, such as the All India Fine Arts and Crafts Theatre, Sapru House, and the Triveni Auditorium. Coupled with the interesting outdoor theatre and the small experimental room of the NSD, Delhi theatre is primarily concentrated within the radius of a few city blocks. Although public transportation in the city has improved remarkably in the last few years, the theatres are not conveniently located near channels of public access. Indeed, Delhi is like Los Angeles in that it is spread out for miles and miles in all directions. Potential audiences are more concerned with making their way home after work than seeing a play.

Although Delhi does not inspire the enthusiasm of most theatre artists, it has attracted some of the best directorial talent in the country. Ebrahim Alkazi, one of India's finest directors and former leader of the NSD, for many years has brought high-quality work to the capital, as well as attracted some of the world's leading theatre personalities to lecture, demonstrate, direct, and teach at the NSD. B. V. Karanth, who succeeded to the directorship of the school, continues to sustain the high level of the institution and is recognized as one of India's brightest and most talented directors of the younger generation. Other young and talented directors include B. M. Shah, Bansi Kaul, and M. K. Raina; seasoned older talent includes Shila Bhatia, Habib Tanvir, Joy Michael, and Rajinder Nath, who have continually kept the standards of Delhi theatre high, despite the lethargy of Delhi audiences.

Theatre Groups

NATIONAL SCHOOL OF DRAMA
Bhrakambra Road
New Delhi, India 110001

NAYA THEATRE
c/o Mr. Habib Tanvir
L-15, D.D.A. Staff Quarters
Ber Sarai, New Delhi, India 29

SRI RAM CENTRE FOR ART AND CULTURE
c/o Mr. Rajinder Nath
4 College Road
New Delhi, India 110001

CONCLUSIONS

India has an abundance of highly capable and enthusiastic theatre personnel. This essay is a tribute to the perseverance of individuals to survive the remarkably complicated problems caused by historical circumstances, economic conditions, the vicissitudes of audiences, and the political climate. While India has not produced a theatre company with its own permanent home, it has been the haven of dedicated and creative artists, some of whom may one day realize their dreams and aspirations after undergoing their long and terrible ordeal by fire.

FARLEY RICHMOND

Indonesia

INTRODUCTION

The Indonesian archipelago, consisting of over thirteen thousand islands, stretches for three thousand miles across the Pacific, the Indian Ocean, and the South China Sea, descending in an arc from the Malay Peninsula and reaching to Papua, New Guinea. People live on six thousand of these islands, the major of which are Sumatra, Java, Bali, Lombok, Sumbawa, Timor, Flores, Kalimantan (Borneo), Sulawesi (the Celebes), the Moluccas, and Irian Jaya (the western part of New Guinea). Except for Irian Jaya, the inhabitants of these islands are largely of Malay extraction, but they belong to many different groups, speaking twenty-five major languages and numerous dialects. The area has experienced the impact of successive culture flows along the trade routes: Hinduism predominated from about A.D. 100 to the fifteenth century when Muslim influence began to spread. Western influence began during the colonial period, initiated by the Portuguese in 1522, and continued for over three hundred years under the Dutch, but even today is largely confined to urban centers. Japanese occupation for three years during World War II was followed by independence, declared in 1945. After a protracted war with the Dutch, the Republic of Indonesia, with its concept of one nation bound by one language, Indonesian, was fully established by 1950. Through the following decades, marked by experiments in socialism and technological development, the country has sought to modernize while retaining its diverse cultural heritage.

At present the population numbers over 130 million people. The Muslim religion, practiced by 90 percent of the inhabitants, is often highly modified by indigenous beliefs. Most people (80 percent) live in rural areas and are engaged primarily in agricultural activities. Eighty million of the people live on the relatively small island of Java, where the primary groups are the Javanese in the

---

Unless otherwise indicated, foreign terms used in the articles on Indonesia have been given in Indonesian rather than the local languages.

east and central areas and the Sundanese to the west. The traditional cultural and political preeminence of Java in the archipelago continues to the present.

The only large group that has remained Hindu is the Balinese. To the small island of Bali, Javanese of the Majapait Dynasty fled in the second half of the fifteenth century to avoid the encroaching Islam. As a result, Bali is a storehouse of Hindu-Javanese culture, much of which is recorded in *lontar* (palm leaf books). The Balinese avoided strong Western influence even after the Dutch completed their occupation of the island in 1906. Tourism, which has accelerated in the last decades, has perhaps had greater impact on the economics and, hence, the life of the Balinese.

Indonesia, like much of Southeast Asia, is rich in theatrical expression. Dance is found virtually everywhere; improvised theatre, often coupled with singing, dancing, and martial arts (*pencak silat*), appears on many of the islands. Some of the better known variants of the rough, improvised theatre forms are *mak jong* and *randai* in Sumatra, *lenong* in Jakarta, *longser* and *topeng banjet* in Sunda, *keto-prak* in Central Java, *ludruk* in East Java, *arja* in Bali, and *mamanda* in Kaliman-tan. Various forms of puppetry, often showing the influence of Javanese forms, exist in Sumatra, Kalimantan, Sulawesi, and, recently, as far east as Irian Jaya. But largely because of historical conditions—Hindu Bali's tradition of sacred dance that remains as a vital part of religious practice and Java's cultivation of the arts under the refining influence of the feudal courts—the artistic standards and profes-sionalism in theatre are most highly developed in Bali, Java, and Sunda.

The essential impulses behind the varied forms of Indonesian drama recur from place to place. Drama is almost always found in conjunction with dance, music, and song. The distinction between actor and dancer blurs since much of the dance portrays a character and/or event. This is especially true of Bali, Java, and Sunda, where the way in which a dancer performs the various movements of a classical dance reveals the type of character represented. The major character types include women, refined knights, proud knights, strong warriors, and a variety of giants. Slight nuances in the movement of each of these types will disclose even more subtle personality traits to the viewer attuned to the conven-tions of the dance.

As the canons of dance are well defined, so too are many of the stories. A dance, which to the outsider may appear as pure dance, may, like the *legong* of Bali or the *bedaya* of Central Java, actually be the enactment of a well-known story. The most frequently presented stories in Java, Sunda, and Bali are those drawn from the Mahabharata, Ramayana, and Arjuna Sastra Bahu cycles. The Mahabharata stories tell of the five Pandawa brothers who, after building up the prosperous kingdom of Amarta where truth and justice reign, are cheated of their realm by their one hundred Kurawa cousins. This eventually leads to the bloody Bharatayudha, the great war. All are ultimately losers in this battle of brother against brother, as the Pandawa recognize after having destroyed the Kurawa. Their friends, their brothers, and their children are dead; their kingdom is in chaos; and their will to live is gone.

Other story sources are less frequently presented but important. The Ramayana tells of how the young Rama is denied his kingly birthright and exiled to the forest where his wife is kidnapped by the king of Alengka, Rahwana. After a great war, in which Rahwana and his cohorts die, she is restored to her husband. Arjuna Sastra Bahu stories tell how he fought and subdued Rahwana in the period preceding the Ramayana.

Besides Hindu derived tales, local legends and Muslim stories are also represented in some theatre forms. Important tales tell of Amir Hamzah, the uncle of the prophet Mohammed, and of Panji, a prince of East Java, or of many other members of royal houses that have created kingdoms in Bali, Java, or Sunda. The audience is usually aware of the stories behind the performances before viewing them.

Another consistent feature of Indonesian entertainment is a clown figure, who often acts as a servant to the more serious characters. This type of character usually has license to improvise freely about current events and is considered representative of the voice of the common people.

A final connecting link is that much of the dramatic art stems from the *wayang* tradition. *Wayang* uses a *dalang* (storyteller) in connection with a *gamelan* (orchestra, composed primarily of metallophones) to tell a *lakon* (story) drawn from various epic sources.

There are many forms of *wayang*, with one genre usually distinguished from another by the combination of the medium it uses and the epic it relates. The most common mediums are leather (*kulit*) shadow puppets, round wooden puppets (*golek*), flat wooden puppets (*klitik*), dancers (*orang*, literally "person"), or dancers with masks (*topeng*). Stories from indigenous variations on the Hindu epics are designated *purwa* (original, the oldest) stories in Java. Stories may also stem from Muslim tales and others come from Javanese chronicles (*babad*).

Medium and story combined result in a specific performance genre. Thus, *wayang kulit purwa*, *wayang golek purwa*, and *wayang orang purwa* all use Hindu-derived tales, but the first is performed with leather puppets, the second with round wooden puppets, and the third with dancers. *Wayang gedog*, *wayang cepak*, and *topeng babakan*, on the other hand, may all tell Panji stories, but the first uses shadow puppets, the second round wooden puppets, and the third a masked dancer. Each time the medium or the story material alters, the genre is apt to be called by a different name.

Although the names change, forms found within a language area, be it Bali, Java, or Sunda, often share important features. There is usually a division of oral elements into dialogue, narration, and mood songs that highlight the actions of the drama. Within an area, the formulaic principles for the construction of a plot, stock phrases of dialogue, narrative passages, and mood songs are often much the same, although the medium and epic it relates vary from one form to another.

The Indonesian motto, "unity in diversity," seems aptly applied to the *wayang*. While it is always different, similar features reappear at its core from form to form and place to place. Though not the sole source of dramatic material, it dominates the traditional theatre and continues to affect the more modern entertainment that has evolved in the last one hundred years.

Major theatre companies can essentially be classed as traditional or modern. Here traditional is used to mean arising from the environs in which the arts have always been cultivated, the villages and courts, and using the traditionally evolved genre to entertain audiences that are comprised largely of traditionally oriented people. Traditional companies will usually be called upon to perform for specific occasions. These may be village or court festivals or celebrations in connection with life-cycle rites. Performances are not normally held in a set place but are commissioned by an individual or group to come to the site of the celebration. The patron normally pays all the fees, while the remainder of the audience is not charged.

By modern is meant companies arising from urban environments and adapting traditional genres or devising new ones to appeal to audiences that are undergoing the culture change city life brings. These companies normally perform on a set schedule, in a permanent location, and admission is charged.

Among the traditional groups are those that are essentially loose, village groupings; court groupings; and organized, professional companies hired to perform a traditional genre in which they specialize.

The area of Indonesia where the village groupings have earned the greatest international acclaim is Bali. Throughout this island there are groups of performers of highest artistry who are maintaining and reviving the older genres of dance-drama, even as they create new forms for themselves and for tourists. Peliatan-Teges in Gianyur District is only one example of how these villages are functioning as companies, where company is taken in the broad sense of the term: a place where performance is cultivated, perfected, and executed by a group.

The courts are also a traditional focal point of performance; in former times, permanent companies were supported by the courts. Although the political power of the courts has waned and most performers are now hired for specific occasions rather than kept on a permanent payroll, the courts still retain influence over the performing arts. The palace of Yogyakarta's bureau of performance, Krida Mardawa (Movement and Voice), is particularly important in this respect to the present day.

Although the courts and the villages, where the performances are often carried on with ultimate artistry, are the seed-beds of the arts in Indonesia, most performing companies are of the type that specialize in a particular genre and are hired by a host to perform at a feast. The popular genres vary from one area to the next, but some of the most important ones include the following.

In Sunda, the most popular entertainment is *wayang golek purwa*, which tells the stories derived from the Hindu epics with three-dimensional wooden puppets. The most popular troupe is probably Giri Harja (Mountain of Abundance), located near Bandung. Groups led by Amung Sutarya of Bandung and Cecep Supriadi of Karawang are also of major stature.

Cirebon, a northern coastal city that lies on the border of Central Java and Sunda, boasts a variety of important genres. Among these is *wayang kulit purwa*, a shadow puppet play using Hindu-derived tales, which is performed in a style distinctive to the area rather than following the model of Surakarta in Central Java which has now come to predominate in many parts of Indonesia. A major company performing this Cirebon genre is that led by Warih Priadi. A second form of puppet theatre found in East Cirebon and favored along the northern coast of Central Java is *wayang cepak*. This form uses round wooden puppets to tell a repertory drawn from local legends and Muslim tales. Dalang Aliwijaya and his group, Sinar Binangkit (Ray of Accomplishment) of Cirebon, are noted performers of this form. A third art, found only in Cirebon, is *topeng babakan*, in which a masked dancer performs characters drawn from the Panji stories. Major troupes are found in the village of Slangit, where Sujana is the best known dancer of Panji Asmara (Panji the Brilliant), and in Palimanan, where a female dancer named Suji leads a troupe.

Central and East Java are rich in all types of genres, with the *wayang kulit purwa* being the most popular traditional genre. Leather puppets cast shadows on a lighted screen to recreate tales derived from the Hindu epics. Major exponents of this form are Panut of East Java, known for his poetic language, and Nartosabdho of Semarang, whose innovative use of music and clowns has earned him enormous fame. Other important *dalang* in this form include Aman Suroto of Surakarta and Timbul Adiprajitno of Yogyakarta.

In Bali *wayang kulit* and *topeng* are only two among many popular genres. *Wayang kulit*, the shadow play of Bali, uses less stylized puppets than are found in Java, and the orchestral accompaniment, generally four xylophone-like instruments, is less complicated than the larger Javanese *gamelan*. No *dalang* in Bali commands the same kind of fees or superstar status that some of the Javanese and Sundanese *dalang* enjoy, but such artistry is rich in its own right. *Topeng*, the masked dance, usually takes the form of *topeng pajegan*, in which a single dancer assumes all the roles, or *topeng panca*, in which several dancers form an ad hoc group to improvise a performance. There are many talented performers in this genre. Mandra of Bantuan village and Ida Bagus Anom of Mas are only two such performers, according to Elizabeth Young, an anthropologist studying this genre.

The companies that fall into the modern classification are more consistent with the concept of a company as a set group that performs in a certain place on a regular schedule. Many such companies have appeared in urban centers over the last century. Few thrive as consistently as do the traditional forms, confronted by the challenge of the mass media, especially film and television, and the need to please an audience that is undergoing significant social change.

Important companies falling into this modern category include such groups as Ngesti Pandowo (Unity of the Pandowo) of Semarang and Sri Wedari of Surakarta. Both groups perform in the traditional genre of *wayang orang*, a dance-drama form modeled after the Javanese *wayang kulit purwa*, invented by the palaces. These companies are both modifying the form by shortening the hours of performance and adapting story material to suit the new tastes of their urban audiences in Central Java.

Ketoprak, a spoken drama which is accompanied by *gamelan* music and usually tells stories drawn from local legends through improvised dialogue based on a scenario, is a form found in Central Javanese cities. Ketoprak Mataram (Ketoprak of Mataram) and Sapta Mandala (Seventh World), both companies found in Yogyakarta, are significant troupes.

The *ludruk* and *sandiwara* forms have been created in the last century and are found in East Java. The *ludruk* is well known for its use of female impersonators, while the *sandiwara* is a spoken drama in which dialogue is largely improvised from a preplanned scenario. Both forms often depart from traditional story cycles for their material. A major *sandiwara* company is Sri Mulat in Surabaya.

Also among modern companies are those groups emerging from educational institutions. Rather than appealing to a largely proletarian audience as do *ketoprak, ludruk, sandiwara*, and, to an extent, even *wayang orang*, they respond to the tastes of the modern, educated elite. As this class grows, so do their audiences.

Some of these modern companies come from institutions such as the government conservatories of traditional music and dance academies that are located in Denpasar, Yogyakarta, Surakarta, Bandung, and other major cities. While preserving and perpetuating the traditional performing arts, these institutions are also creating new genres such as *sendratari*, a dance-drama that employs traditional dance but largely eliminates the dialogue characteristic of older styles of dance-drama. This form is an excellent vehicle for these companies when they perform in areas of the country using a different regional language or when they tour abroad. Sekolah Menengah Karawitan Indonesia (High School of Traditional Music), formerly called KOKAR (Konservatori Karawitan—"Conservatory of Traditional Music") and ASTI (Akademi Seni Tari Indonesia—"Indonesian Academy of Dance") in Bali are companies representative of the performing groups developed in the government schools during the last generation.

A final modern theatre form is spoken, modern drama, which is concentrated in such centers of modern intellectual life as Jakarta and Yogyakarta. A central figure in the modern drama movement that has flourished in the last ten years is W. S. Rendra, who led the Bengkel Teatre (Workshop/Theatre) from 1968 until it disbanded in 1979. Rendra's work has been characterized by social and political protest. Such works as *Kisah Perjuangan Suku Naga* (*The Struggle of the Naga People*) in 1975 and *SEKDA* (*District Administrator*) in 1977 combined elements from traditional genres, such as *gamelan* music, and movement technique and story structure from Javanese *wayang*, with *tai chi* and techniques borrowed from Western theatre practice to make striking statements about social injustice and corruption.

Rendra's group spawned some of the other small theatre companies, helping to make modern drama in Indonesian language a genre of growing importance. Groups such as Putu Wijaya's Teatre Mandiri (Independent Theatre) and Arifin C. Nur's Teatre Kecil (Little Theatre) have been important, as has been the company led by Ikranagara, Teatre Saja (formerly Teatre Siapa Saja or Anyone's Theatre). All these companies have performed frequently in the Jakarta arts center, Taman Ismail Marzuki. The creative way in which performers are mixing traditional and Western elements is a striking feature of current modern drama productions. Sanggar Karuna Kerti (Karuna Kerti Studio), a group led by Pasek Tempo of Bali, is representative of this trend to meld the old with the new.

The groups described in the following articles represent only a small number of the many creative, distinctive companies in the Indonesian archipelago.

KATHY FOLEY

HARMONIOUS FEELING
(Ki Nartosabdho and Condong Raos)
Jalan Anggrek VII/10
Semarang, Jawa Tengah, Indonesia

Nartosabdho is one of the foremost *dalang* (storytellers) of the *wayang kulit* (shadow play) theatre of Central Java. Since 1969 he has led his own *gamelan* orchestra, Condong Raos, which travels with him and provides highly polished accompaniment for his performance of stories derived from the Mahabharata or Ramayana, which are ordinarily performed all night in connection with *slametan* (feasts) held for weddings, circumcisions, and other special occasions. As *dalang*, he is the dominant figure, and the history of the group is largely the history of this individual.

Nartosabdho was born on August 25, 1925, in Wedi, a small town in the Klaten region of Central Java. He was the youngest of eight children in a poor family and was known in his youth as Sunarto. Left fatherless at an early age, he helped to finance his own elementary school education (which included painting, Javanese dance, and *gamelan*) by carving and selling wooden masks. He later left home to wander about Java with various traveling folk theatre companies. Sunarto played drum with about ten of these companies during the Japanese occupation (1942 to 1945). He remained with each group one to five months before traveling on; it was an extremely unstable period for the young musician.

In 1945 he played drum with the Sri Wandowo *ketoprak* (improvised, spoken drama) group in Klaten. At that time, the directors of a *wayang orang* (dance-drama) company called Ngesti Pandowo (*Unity of the Pandowo*) heard his drumming and, recognizing a fine musical talent, asked Sunarto to join their company. On August 10, 1945, Sunarto became a member of Ngesti Pandowo and thus began what he calls his "evolutionizing" of the music for the Javanese *gamelan*. In recognition of his exceptional talent, the manager of Ngesti Pandowo gave him, what for the Javanese is an important sign of recognition, a new name— Nartosabdho.

It was during his first year with Ngesti Pandowo that he composed *gamelan* pieces with a waltz tempo (pieces such as "Sang Lelana" (*The Wanderer*), "Aku Ngimpi" (*I Dream*), and "Sampur Ijo" (*Green Dance Scarf*) which he composed for dance. He caused a stir among the group's musicians and has remained a controversial but dominant composer until the present. His critics, mostly of the *priyayi* (educated elite) class, have charged him with overstepping the boundaries of traditional Javanese modal and rhythmic systems. Nevertheless, his tunes are extremely catchy, and their popularity has spread quickly across Java, particularly among the common people.

Nartosabdho's education as a *dalang* for *wayang kulit* began in Wedi with the *dalang* Pujo Sumarto. Since childhood he also observed countless other *wayang kulit* performances, educating himself in the art of puppetry. He learned a great deal while working with Ngesti Pandowo, for *wayang orang* and *wayang kulit* have a number of elements in common. Both dramatize the same repertory, utilize the same *gamelan* pieces, and require a *dalang* who narrates, sings, and plays percussion instruments. However, the *dalang*'s role is much greater in *wayang kulit*, since he must also operate the puppets and perform all dialogue. In the early 1950s Nartosabdho amazed his audiences and fellow performers by simultaneously filling the roles of drummer and *wayang orang dalang* at Ngesti Pandowo. He then went on to develop as a full-fledged *dalang* in the more prestigious genre of *wayang kulit* in the late 1950s.

His first major public performance as a *wayang kulit dalang* was in 1955, with the story *Kresna Duta* (*Kresna as Ambassador*), at a night fair being held in the city of Yogyakarta to celebrate the two hundredth birthday of the city's founding. In 1958 Nartosabdho was called for the first time to perform a *wayang kulit* in Jakarta for a broadcast at the national radio station, Radio Republik Indonesia (RRI), which would be heard across Indonesia. Previously, he had been mainly known as a musician; from this time on, he gained a reputation as a *dalang*.

For the *dalang*, the two most important *gamelan* musicians are the *gender* (metallophone) player, who provides constant accompaniment for the *dalang*'s voice, and the drummer, who accompanies the action and relays signals from the *dalang* to the other musicians. In the early years, when Nartosabdho was hired to perform *wayang kulit*, he always took along these two essential musicians, Wiryo as drummer and Slamet as *gender* player. In 1969 he formed his own *gamelan* group, Condong Raos, retaining Slamet as his *gender* player and making Srimoro his drummer. The group is extremely compact and well known for its ability to play at breakneck speed and come to a sudden halt. Under Nartosabdho's influence, female singers have been given greater recognition than they had before for their important role in *gamelan* accompaniment.

The best known female singers with Condong Raos are Ngatirah, Supami, Maryati, Suryati, and Tantinah, who are featured on many of the Nartosabdho commercial cassette recordings. Well over fifty complete *wayang kulit* performances have been recorded since 1973.

Nartosabdho's innovations in the *wayang kulit* tradition can also be seen as more "evolutionary" than revolutionary. He has carried on the tradition of Surakarta style *sabetan* (puppet manipulation), vocal style, and musical accompaniment, with the addition of compositions that reflect the musical influence of other parts of Java—including Semarang, Yogyakarta, Banyumas, Surabaya, Banyuwangi, Jakarta, and Sunda—as well as the island of Bali, and even the West. He introduced humorous, yet realistic, touches such as the use of a bicycle puppet. Of more importance is his bringing the servants (including the humorous clown-servants) into greater relief, thus enabling the *wayang kulit* to communicate more directly to the common people with fresh life and humor. Traditionally, in the first section of the *wayang kulit* performance, lasting from about 9:00 P.M. to midnight, there is an avoidance of humor. The female servants, Limbuk and Cangik, merely appear, say a few lines, and otherwise act as silent escorts for their royal mistresses. Nartosabdho spotlighted these female clown-servants and accompanied their appearance with *gending dolanan* (playful, non-serious pieces). Other ladies-in-waiting traditionally imitated the serious and refined movements of the *serimpi*, a female court dance. Nartosabdho changed their dancing to imitate *gambyong*, a livelier and flirtatious female dance, popular outside the court tradition. The musical accompaniment was also changed from long, serious pieces to shorter, more spirited ones.

Nartosabdho has transcended the rigid boundaries between the traditions of the two rival cities Yogyakarta and Surakarta. He has made occasional use of Yogyakarta–style musical pieces and has adopted the Yogyakarta practice of including the clown-servant scene *gara-gara* in every performance. This is part of the middle section of the *wayang kulit*, which, according to the Surakarta tradition, occurs only when a great warrior is extremely troubled. The heat of his meditating body is so intense that it causes turmoil in nature (*gara-gara*). The male clown-servants appear, accompanying their master, and joke among themselves.

Often playing one or two times a week and traveling to major cities such as Surabaya, Surakarta, and Yogyakarta, Nartosabdho is now the most popular *dalang* in Java. Four times he has played at President Suharto's request in the presidential palace in Jakarta—an honor bestowed upon the greatest of Indonesian performing artists.

Nartosabdho sees neither *wayang kulit* nor Javanese *gamelan* music as merely entertainment, but as arts that cannot be separated from religion and mysticism. In addition to this integration with the sacred, there is a strong educational element in these arts. The term *education* is taken in a much fuller sense than that with which the Westerner is familiar, for it includes education in proper behavior, spirituality, literature, and aesthetics. This education is intended for all strata of society. Nartosabdho's innovations, as well as his ability to give life and energy to his performances, allow him to communicate particularly well with the masses.

With an eye toward the future, Nartosabdho feels it is not possible to predict creative innovations in the arts, his own notwithstanding. For example, he does not rule out the possibility of *wayang kulit* being successfully performed in Indonesian, the national language, although Javanese, the regional language, is the richer and, in his opinion, the more appropriate for *wayang kulit*. Thus far, Nartosabdho and Condong Raos have been actively participating in bringing about artistic changes. While some people still question the aesthetic value of these changes, Nartosabdho and Condong Raos continue to be powerful forces in the development and perpetuation of the rich and ancient tradition of *wayang kulit*.

PEGGY ANN CHOY and
R. ANDERSON SUTTON

K.H.P. KRIDA MARDAWA
Kraton Yogyakarta
Yogyakarta, Indonesia

K.H.P. Krida Mardawa (Bureau of the Arts), located in the Palace of Yogyakarta, is the bureau that administers all art activities of the court, foremost of which are music, dance, and drama. Although Krida Mardawa has existed under that title only since 1942, it continues a long tradition. Its history is essentially the history of arts in the palace, Kraton Ngayogyakarta Hadiningrat, which has been the center of classical Yogyanese dance, dance-drama, shadow puppet theatre, and music since its founding in 1755.

Sultan Hamengku Buwana I, who first ruled the sultanate from 1755 to 1792, is credited with creating the Yogyanese style of court dance. At least in the case of female style dance, this probably represented a modification of the dance existing in the preceding Javanese kingdom of Mataram. In particular, the dance forms *bedhaya* and *srimpi* are said to have originated in Mataram. Both are highly formal, abstract dances, slow and fluid, for groups of female dancers, and are considered to be the epitome of court dance, an elegant statement of the aesthetic and philosophical values of the Javanese courts. Today, new *bedhaya* and *srimpi* compositions are taught and performed as part of the classical repertory.

The court of Sultan Hamengku Buwana I was famous for its disciplined militarism, and many of the dances created at that time were inspired by the battle practices, tournaments, and pageantry of the palace army. The most famous of these dances is "Beksan Lawung" (Lawung Dance) in which various soldier types are portrayed, from the restrained and majestic to the rough and boisterous. The dances focus on strictly disciplined fighting skills, often using daggers or lances, and all are executed in exacting dance techniques. These dances are a popular part of the classical repertory.

Shadow puppet theatre, *wayang kulit*, was being performed in Java as early as A.D. 1000 and has traditionally been patronized by the rulers of Java. Most of the stories come from the Mahabharata epic which contains a wealth of both dramatic entertainment and spiritual teaching. During the reign of the first Yogyanese sultan, all-night performances were a weekly event in the palace. *Wayang kulit* is still popular today, but performances sponsored by Krida Mardawa are infrequent, usually only one per year. Palace musicians, however, often play for *wayang kulit* performances outside the court.

The influence of the shadow puppet theatre upon dance has been far-reaching, molding ideas of characterization and dramatic form, and providing vast resources of story material for dance-drama. Sultan Hamengku Buwana I initiated the dance-drama form known as *wayang orang*, the danced enactment of stories from the shadow puppet theatre. The first such performance told the story *Gondowerdoyo*. In this century, *wayang orang* became the highlight of palace art and is the source for much of today's performing repertory.

The earliest written notation of musical compositions, dance sequences, and dance-drama scenarios comes from the time of Sultan Hamengku Buwana V (1823–1855). One of the present concerns of Krida Mardawa is the reconstruction of music and dance works based on modern transcriptions of the old notation. Old *bedhaya* compositions are often included in the radio concerts broadcast from the palace once every thirty-five days.

The golden age of court dance began in the early 1920s and continued until the late 1930s, during the reign of Sultan Hamengku Buwana VIII (1921–1939). Dance, as a royally favored art, was accorded great respect, and talented dancers in the service of the palace enjoyed both high rank and generous material rewards. The many sons of the sultan were required to study dance for its training in the subtle refinements of court etiquette and the proper princely demeanor. Furthermore, it was felt that the intense role-identification involved in *wayang orang* also provided material for an in-depth study of human character types and their interaction.

During this time, *wayang orang* dance-drama enlarged to spectacular proportions. A single story sometimes covered three or four days of continuous performing, from 6:00 A.M. to 11:00 P.M., involving hundreds of dancers and musicians who had been in rehearsal for over a year. Twelve such colossal presentations were staged, including *Jaya Semedhi* (*Arjuna as Ascete*), *Samba Sebit* (*The Death of Samba*), *Ciptoning Mintaraga-Arjuna Wiwaha* (*The Meditation and Marriage of Arjuna*), *Sri Suwela*, and *Pregiwa-Pregiwati*. Dance techniques and costumes became elaborate and specific, again taking their models from the detailed stylizations of the shadow puppets. At the same time, standardizations began to appear in the choice of music used to accompany specific characters and scenes.

In addition to these colossal presentations, an extensive repertory of excerpts was developed. These free-standing works are basically of two kinds: fragments, which present a one- to three-hour abridged version of the story; and *beksan petilan*, which show the confrontation and decisive duel between two major characters. Present-day dance-drama works produced by Krida Mardawa use these shorter forms exclusively.

Historically, palace personnel and family members were also active in developing music and dance outside the court, the results of which, in turn, influenced palace activities. In particular, the solo female dance form, *golek*, which is standard repertory today, was first created outside the palace and later adopted and made into a court dance in the 1920s.

The great flowering of court music and dance, which occurred during the golden age, was due not only to the support of the sultan, but also to the exceptional talents of choreographer K.R.T. Purbaningrat, dancers K.R.T. Brongtodiningrat and R. W. Indramardawa, composer K.R.T. Wiroguno, and designer K.R.T. Joyodipuro.

The modern era of palace art began with the reign of Sultan Hamengku Buwana IX in 1940. A major reorganization of court bureaucracy in 1942 resulted in the establishment of Krida Mardawa as an independent bureau of the arts directed by B.P.H. Pujokusumo. Also at this time, a new dance form was created based on the movements and characters of *wayang golek*, wooden puppets that tell the Amir Hamzah stories. This dance style, most often choreographed as *beksan petilan*, is popular and is being actively developed.

In the democratic interest of making the palace arts available to the entire populace, Krida Mardawa, by order of the sultan, established four schools outside the palace in 1950 which taught dance, *gamelan* music, singing, and shadow puppetry. At that time, directly following World War II and the Indonesian Revolution, no performances were given in the court. Of the four schools, the one for shadow puppetry, Habiranda, now functions as an independent organization.

Dance was taught by Bebadan Among Beksa (Institute for the Classical Dance), a group composed of palace dance teachers. They were active in teaching court dance techniques and staged official performances on the occasions of the sultan's birthday and the respective anniversaries of his accession to the throne and the founding of the Yogyakarta Sultanate. Works were presented in the style of the court, but differing in that female dancers were allowed to perform alongside male dancers.

An offshoot of the school is the Yayasan Siswa Among Beksa (Among Beksa Student Foundation), which was founded as a student group in 1952 by B.P.H. Yudonegoro. This group, dedicated to the preservation of classical dance, is now under the direction of R. M. Dinusatomo and functions as a separate entity; yet its ties to the court are still close, and the director of Krida Mardawa sits on its advisory board.

In 1973 Krida Mardawa resumed dance activities inside the palace, simultaneously opening them to the general public. Krida Mardawa maintains a permanent teaching staff; however, there are no full-time performers in the palace service as in former times, and dancers are specially invited for each performance.

In 1978 Krida Mardawa produced several concerts at the Jakarta Festival, which included performances of traditional arts from all areas of Indonesia. A group of eighty dancers and musicians presented five large dance works and a music concert. Included were "Srimpi Renggowati" ("Romance of Renggowati"), dating from the reign of Sultan Hamengku Buwana V, and "Beksan Lawung Ageng" (Major Lance Dance) and "Beksan Sekar Medura" (Soldiers Toasting Dance), two of the male group dances from the time of Sultan Hamengku Buwana I. *Arjuna Wiwaha* (*Marriage of Arjuna*), a story that tells of the meditation of Arjuna on Mount Indrakila, of the temptations he successfully overcomes, and of the enemy giant he is thereby enabled to defeat, was presented in both the abstract poetic *bedaya* form and in the more narrative *wayang orang*. R.L. Sasminta Mardawa, who served as choreographer for both works, is one of the foremost classical Yogyanese choreographers and teachers of the present day. In addition to his role as teacher and director with Krida Mardawa, he has his own performing group, Mardawa Budaya, and a dance school, Pamulangan Beksa Ngayugyakarta (School of Yogyanese Dance).

Performances by Krida Mardawa in Yogyakarta are usually held in connection with the sultan's birthday, the traditional festivities surrounding Islamic holidays, and for special guests of the sultan and the national government. Performers are drawn from among the best classical Yogyanese dancers.

In the past, the palace has staged theatrical productions in the truly grand manner with the best sets of *gamelan* instruments, exquisitely crafted leather shadow puppets and wooden puppets, and elegant handmade costumes. In the modesty of the present era, the palace grounds still retain a special atmosphere, and dancers coming to a rehearsal in traditional Javanese dress have a different bearing and demeanor than at other times. There is deep loyalty to and respect for the palace traditions—the careful etiquette of humility, the sensitivity to one's surroundings, and the classical elegance of the music and dance. Performing for Krida Mardawa carries a traditional element of prestige which is not diminished by the fact that the palace is no longer a seat of governing power in modern Indonesia. Under the directorship of B.P.H. Puger, Krida Mardawa hopes to increase its performing activities inside the palace and to continue its projects of reconstructing old works for public performance.

JAN HOSTETLER

HIGH SCHOOL OF TRADITIONAL MUSIC
(SMKI—Sekolah Menengah Karawitan Indonesia) and
INDONESIAN ACADEMY OF DANCE
(ASTI—Akademi Seni Tari Indonesia)
Denpasar, Bali, Indonesia

SMKI—still generally called KOKAR (Konservatori Karawitan—Conservatory of Traditional Music), its name until 1978—began in 1961 in Denpasar, the capital city of Bali. The success of KOKAR in the training of dancers and musicians led to the establishment of ASTI, the college of dance, in 1967. The curriculum in both schools is primarily devoted to performance courses in music and dance. At KOKAR students study the melodies and movements of *tari lepas*, dances choreographed independently of classical dance-drama forms, as well as the more intricate, precise structure of *topeng*, the mask dance form; *legong keraton*, classical female dances; and *arja*, an operatic dance form which is several centuries old. At ASTI, students continue with studies of classical Balinese music and dance and also prepare for teaching certification. As a natural outgrowth of the performance studies curricula, both KOKAR and ASTI have an excellent performing company comprised of the most talented of their many students.

Most students have training in dance and music before enrollment at KOKAR. The more than two hundred KOKAR students come from throughout Bali, and, as KOKAR frequently tours Bali, its reputation has spread throughout the island. Many children with talent now leave their villages and further their studies at KOKAR, seeking to become professional dancers and teachers, a profession that has become economically possible only in the last decade. The large tourist industry in Bali has caused an increase in demand for the services of dance companies to perform on a regular basis, primarily in the tourist areas of Sanur Beach and Kuta Beach.

I Wayan Beratha is on the music faculty at KOKAR and is also resident choreographer of the performing group. Wayan Beratha is from a family of musicians and had an active career teaching music and dance to *gamelan* groups throughout Bali before KOKAR began. He was born in 1924 and had traditional training in music and dance in his village and with famous master teachers. In 1962 he introduced the new dance-drama form of *sendratari* to Bali, with the performance of *Jayaprana* at KOKAR. *Sendratari* uses plots from the epics of Ramayana and Mahabharata, as well as Balinese legends. The dialogue is spoken for the dancers who enact the events by a *dalang*, a person trained in the classical art of *wayang kulit*. The large *gamelan gong gede* accompanies the play, and female singers are included in imitation of Javanese dance-dramas. Since *sendratari* is usually two to three hours in length, whereas classical dance-drama forms may last six or seven hours, *sendratari* might be considered modern ''condensed'' versions of the traditional dance-dramas. Wayan Beratha's *Ramayana*, choreographed in 1965, has inspired dozens of imitations. He followed this beloved *sendratari* with *Rajapala*, the Balinese tale of a hunter who captures an angel, in 1966; *Arjuna Wiwaha* (*Arjuna's Wedding*), the legend of the nymphs tempting Arjuna during his meditation; and *Nara Kesuma*, the tale of the uncle of the Pandawas, which won at the *sendratari* festival in Bali in 1978. The KOKAR dance company also performs dance-dramas of *topeng*, *arja*, *legong keraton*, as well as *tari lepas*. KOKAR's company has toured throughout Indonesia, represented Bali in the International Ramayana Festival in 1971, and performs for the foreign dignitaries visiting Bali at the governor's mansion in Denpasar. Its most extensive international tour was in 1965 to China, North Korea, the Philippines, and Japan, sponsored by the Indonesian State Department.

The performing group at ASTI could almost be considered two separate performing organizations. It teaches and performs dance-drama forms that are rarely seen in the village, including *gambuh*, the nearly one-thousand-year-old dance-drama form based on the Panji legend of East Java; *wayang wong*, based on stories from the Ramayana; and *parwa*, which uses stories of the Mahabharata. ASTI also performs *topeng*, *arja*, *legong keraton*, and *tari lepas*, as well as having the most extensive repertory of new choreography in Bali. Thus, both the newest and the oldest Balinese dances are performed by ASTI, which has the largest and most widely varied repertory in Bali.

I Wayan Dibia is the resident choreographer at ASTI. He was born in 1948 in Singapadu, which has the most famous *barong* group in Bali. (*Barong* may be performed as a sacred solo dance or in the context of a secular dance-drama.) He studied dance as a child, attended KOKAR in Denpasar, and graduated with an advanced degree in dance from ASTI in Yogyakarta, Java. Since joining the dance faculty in 1974, Wayan Dibia has choreographed more than sixteen major, new dance-dramas, as well as a new *cak* using 125 ASTI students as the chorus of dancers, who chant the accompaniment of the story of Sugriwa and Subali. Wayan Dibia's most notable *sendratari* include: *Sampik Enthai*, a variation of the Romeo and Juliet story premiered by ASTI in Singapore in 1977; *Sayembrama Drupati (The Wedding Contest of Drupati)*, telling of the Pandawas success in the contest for the hand of Princess Drupati; *Sang Kaca*, a Balinese morality play about the *karma* of evil deeds; and *Banjir Darah di Badung (Blood Bath in Badung)*, the dramatic reenactment of the ritual suicides of the kings of Bali in 1906. Wayan Dibia has also experimented with the invention and use of percussion instruments and dialogue spoken directly by the dancers in his productions of *Sakuntala* and *Cupak*. Wayan Dibia and his wife, Ni Made Wiratini (also on the faculty of ASTI), also rehearse and stage classical dance-dramas in cooperation with old master teachers. ASTI performed *gambuh* at temple ceremonies in Singapadu in 1978, at Besakih in 1979 during the Eka Dasa Rudra ceremony held once every hundred years, and at the Panji Festival in Java in 1978. In 1982 I Made Bandem led the ASTI *gambuh* troupe on tour to Japan. In 1983 as the new director of ASTI he led a tour of *Calon Arang* to the U.S.

The performing companies of KOKAR and ASTI have a reputation of performing excellence throughout Bali, and both groups command the highest performance fee. The student performers receive a small honorarium each time they perform, while a large portion of the fee is used to purchase costumes, masks, props, and scenery. The costumes are often borrowed by individual dancers and smaller performing groups lacking funds to purchase new costumes. The performing groups of KOKAR and ASTI have promoted the growth of dance in Bali during the past two decades. The establishment and continued financial support of KOKAR and ASTI by the Indonesian Ministry of Education demonstrates the commitment of the Indonesian government to the performing arts in Bali, which are viewed as living national treasures.*

MARIANNE ARIYANTO

MOUNTAIN OF GOOD FORTUNE
(Giri Harja)
Jelekong
Ciparay
Bandung, West Java, Indonesia

The most popular exponents of Sundanese *wayang golek purwa*, a theatre form that uses up to ninety three-dimensional, wooden rod puppets about 2 to 3 feet in height to present stories derived from the Mahabharata, Ramayana, and Arjuna Sastra Bahu cycles, are the members of the Sunarya family located in a small village, 15 kilometers outside of Bandung, the capital of West Java. The performances of this company are immensely popular throughout the Sundanese language area in the highlands of West Java. A single *dalang* (storyteller) manipulates all the *golek* (puppets), speaks all the dialogue, gives narration, and interpolates mood songs (*kakawen*) highlighting the action of the play in poetic language. This virtuoso performer is accompanied by a *gamelan* (orchestra), composed of nine to fifteen musicians who provide music, sound effects, and incidental singing, as well as a female singer. Her singing between scenes allows the *dalang* short rests in the all-night performance, which takes place outside on a temporarily raised stage. Companies are usually hired by a family to play in connection with a wedding or circumcision. Anyone is free to attend the performance, and the flock of food sellers that the event draws creates a carnival atmosphere.

The Sunarya troupe is known by the name Giri Harja (Mountain of Good Fortune) and is noted for its boisterous playing. The history of the company begins with Dalang Johari who played widely from the 1920s to the 1940s. But Giri Harja's rise to prominence has come only since 1955 under Johari's son, A. Sunarya. He has had a major impact on the development of *wayang golek purwa* in the last twenty-five years.

---

*EDITOR'S NOTE: Rachel Cooper, a dance ethnologist currently writing a thesis at UCLA on ASTI, reports that KOKAR and ASTI have undertaken major projects in the last two years. KOKAR sponsored a festival of women *dalang* (puppet-masters) in November-December 1981 and a festival of child *dalang* in 1982. ASTI recently held a festival at Kuta Beach, the most popular tourist area on the island. The event was aimed at upgrading the performing arts in that area where catering to tourism has caused major modifications. A new *cak* by Dibia was performed. Another project which was undertaken in 1981 was the revitalization of *janger*, a form that has lost popularity in recent years. Two individuals who have been important in these projects are I Nyoman Sumandhi of KOKAR and I Made Bandem, who took over as director of ASTI in 1982. Both studied at Wesleyan University in Connecticut, Sumandhi earning an M.A. and Bandem a Ph.D. degree.

Sunarya began to perform *wayang* in 1928 when he was ten years old. He had attended three years of formal schooling by this time, but his true education had been, and throughout his life would remain, the study of the *wayang*. Born into the family of a *dalang*, he already had a grounding in the art from play with the puppets in his childhood and information shared by his father in leisure moments. Only after following along with his father's *gamelan* for a year— acting as an assistant, passing puppets to his father, or playing one of the less complicated musical instruments—did he first perform in public.

Many *dalang* are taught in this way. They begin playing a few scenes in their father's performance, and, as they advance in expertise and age, graduate to full-length performances. When they are ready to perform as *dalang* in their own right, they will be initiated in a *tawajuh* ceremony by the *dalang* who has taught them. In this rite the student receives the teacher's seal of approval on his learning, and the spiritual power of the teacher helps reinforce the student, bringing God's blessing on his future career.

Sunarya's rise to popularity has come only since the 1950s. Many attribute the prodigious reputation he enjoys to the power he has gained through meditation, burning incense, and other practices associated with the syncretic form of Islam mixed with traditional belief (*adat*), which is practiced in the villages of West Java. Many people seek his aid in blessing holy water which they believe will help cure illness or bring some other benefit, be it a promotion in a job or an end to marital problems. These powers, it is believed, allow Sunarya to bring a blessing upon the family that commissions his performance, as well as giving him the capability of keeping his audience entertained throughout the night-long play (*lakon*). In 1978 Sunarya performed at the Wayang Festival in Jakarta and in 1983 he toured to Belgium.

Sunarya is the center of Giri Harja, but he relies heavily on Momod, the leader of the *gamelan* musicians, who joined Giri Harja in 1950. Momod acts as the business manager, in addition to enlivening Sunarya's performances with his constant patter. Throughout the action of the play, he constantly interjects comments and may even talk directly with certain humorous puppets. His glib wit adds to the presentation.

Many other members of the *gamelan* are relatives of Sunarya, as are many of the female singers who have worked with his troupe. The obvious enjoyment that the whole troupe takes in performing adds a dimension that makes their style prized. Giri Harja has become famous through all of Sunda. Sunarya, or one of his sons who have become *dalang*, is often hired to play in villages as far as one hundred miles away.

Sunarya is noted for certain innovations in *wayang golek purwa*, some of which have had impact throughout Sunda. One characteristic, confined to Sunarya and his sons, is his preference for the clown-servant Dawala. He presents this tall puppet with a penis-shaped nose as a quixotic character, upright and dedicated to his father and his country. Most other *dalang* deemphasize Dawala in favor of his more rambunctious brother, Cepot.

Of greater general impact is Sunarya's use of many giants. Giant invaders from over the seas have long been a staple of *wayang golek purwa*. Instead of the few giants formerly used in performances, Sunarya may have fifteen of these characters, usually bizarre and twisted puppets that he has carved himself, appearing in a battle. The proliferation of these giants, who are not bound by the same conventions as the epic characters of the stories, makes for many innovative and comic moments.

Sunarya has also had influence on the kinds of stories that are played. In recent years there has been a great increase in the number of new stories in *wayang golek purwa*. Although still about the traditional characters, they recount events never mentioned in the older *wayang* versions of the epics. Sunarya has added to this trend by creating many new plots. These may focus on the clown-servants or tell of how the spirit of Rahwana, the lustful king of the Ramayana, finds another incarnation and threatens the Pandawas, the heroes of the Mahabharata, in a later generation. Although he has contributed new material to the repertory, he has also helped popularize less well-known stories of the traditional cycles by recording versions of the little known Ramayana stories and tales about the ancestors of the Pandawas. Cassettes of these plays have been sold all over Sunda.

Many of the Sunarya's innovations have been adopted by other *dalang*. It seems inevitable that his effect will be lasting since his fame and stature have brought him many students.

Of the three hundred students that Sunarya claims, the most notable are members of his immediate family. Sunarya's younger brother, Lili Adi Sunarya, leads a separate troupe, Mekar Budaya (Flower of Culture). He has performed since 1951 and from 1956 to 1962 served in the Army as a *dalang*, entertaining Sundanese troops stationed everywhere in Indonesia.

In recent years Sunarya's sons, Ade Kosasih and Asep Sunandar, have gained great fame. Ade Kosasih, at present probably the highest paid *dalang* in Sunda, took up the family profession in 1966 after attending junior high school. In his thirties, he is already known for his ability to explore the philosophical implications of a story in a manner uncommon for a *dalang* of his age. Stories he has created are well known from his many cassette recordings, which are marketed commercially. Many months he is booked solid, playing an eight-hour performance every night.

Quickly rising in popularity is Asep Sunandar, who made his debut in 1970 at age seventeen. Asep brings the puppets to life with his manipulation technique as they perform Sundanese classical dance or fight in battles. His sense of comic timing makes him a master of playing the popular clown-servants. Since 1981 he has increasingly incorporated trick puppets into his shows. Ogres that split into pieces in battle are his favorites.

The younger sons of Sunarya, Ugan and Iden, are just embarking on the family profession and often play for a few hours before their father or older brothers perform. Sunarya himself, for health reasons, takes fewer bookings than formerly. Most of these are for exorcisms, which, according to tradition, are necessary to release certain individuals who have been born in certain ways or broken some taboo from the threat of Kala, a monstrous god who brings bad luck on his victims.

Even though his sons are currently more active as performers, Sunarya, as the father and teacher, remains the main figure of the company. He hopes, with government aid, to establish a school for *dalang* so that he can share his knowledge with an even larger number of students. The mark of A. Sunarya and Giri Harja on *wayang golek purwa* is sure to endure for some time to come.

KATHY FOLEY

PANJI THE BRILLIANT
(Panji Asmara)
Slangit
Klangenan
Cirebon, West Java, Indonesia

Situated near the boundary of Central and West Java, the city of Cirebon is a focal point of cultural and historical importance. Once a great kingdom (it still boasts three palaces), it was a center and source for traditional West Javanese art forms. Although the palaces no longer retain a strong influence on artistic development, the particularly famous masked dance-drama forms of this region continue to flourish in the surrounding villages. These include two basic types: *wayang orang*, a popular theatrical form found throughout the island of Java (although usually performed without masks in Central Java), which depicts stories from the Hindu epics of the Ramayana and Mahabharata, and *topeng babakan* (literally, "masked acts"), which is unique to the Cirebon area. *Topeng babakan* is loosely based on a story from the Panji cycle, which tells of a refined Javanese hero, but it is more concerned with the characterization of a series of masks than the story line, which remains secondary to the theatrical experience. The emphasis is on the skill and interpretation of the dancer/actor. A prominent and very popular group of this style is Panji Asmara, from the small and rather remote village of Slangit (accessible only by pedicab or private motorcycle), headed by Sujana Arja, a performer of outstanding artistry.

A *topeng babakan* performance is usually held from morning to afternoon (about 9:00 A.M. to 3:00 P.M.) on a variety of occasions. Panji Asmara normally performs at such traditional events as weddings, circumcision ceremonies, birthdays, a Javanese ceremony called *memitu*, which marks the seventh month of pregnancy, a "descent to the ground" ceremony for a baby making his first contact with the earth or for the harvest of the fields to honor the rice goddess, Dewi Sri. They may be hired by a sugar factory or a fishing company, to help ensure a good harvest or catch for the year, and have even performed on fishing boats sitting in Cirebon's harbor. The group habitually performs at an official government ceremony in Cirebon on Indonesia's Independence Day, August 17.

The group received its official name from the Department of Education and Culture in 1963 and has since performed nationally and internationally. In 1972 it performed at the presidential palace in Bogor and in 1978 at the Jakarta Festival. In 1978 Sujana and Bulus, the clown specialist of Panji Asmara, were featured by the Asia Society in presentation of West Javanese dance, which toured the United States. In April 1979 Sujana and Bulus were part of a group of Cirebon dancers, which included two of Sujana's older brothers and his younger sister, that was sent to represent Indonesia in an Asian arts festival at the Hong Kong Arts Center. In 1981 Sujana taught at the Institute for Arts (IKI) in Bandung.

Like many things in Indonesia, the traditional arts in Cirebon are a family affair—a heritage passed from one generation to another. Sujana's father was a noted dancer who taught all of his nine children to dance and used them in his performing group. Four of these children, now all grown, are still dancing, and three have functioning groups. These include a group led by Sujana, who is the fifth-born and in his late forties. His younger sister, Keni, has her own very popular group and frequently collaborates with Sujana for major performances. Her teenage daughter is already an accomplished performer.

A *topeng babakan* performance generally consists of a soloist who dances a range of masked characters, supported by one or more clowns and accompanied by a *gamelan* orchestra of approximately twelve musicians. The central dancer, called a *dalang*, uses five different masks. The *bodor* (clown) dances one major mask role and often adds several other comic characters throughout the performance, adopting a different mask for each. The *bodor* may comment on current events, from the village to international level, or spoof the *dalang*'s style. In a Harpoesque attempt to imitate Sujana, Bulus might slap on a headdress sideways and make a show of entangling himself in his sarong. A beautiful dancer himself, he has a genius for exaggerating certain movements to a hilarious degree. Bulus creates an intimate atmosphere with the audience and *gamelan* players with whom he may have a continuing repartee.

The performance begins with the mask of Panji, the most refined character in the cosmology, and develops to a wild and coarse character, Klana. The dancer enters from the *gamelan* and sits next to the trunk containing the masks, meditating while the musicians begin to play. Presently he rises and does a very slow, subtle dance, sometimes hardly seeming to move, donning the mask in the course of the movement. The *gamelan* clangs raucously, accompanied by the shouts from the musicians who almost seem to be trying to startle the dreamy figure in front of them. The Panji mask is white with simple lines—elongated eyes, a long, slanting nose, and a small mouth. According to the story, this is Prince Inu Kertapati who is on his way to the neighboring kingdom of Bawarna to attend the wedding of his cousin, the princess. The character represents the Javanese ideal of refinement amidst a chaotic world, as well as the first stage of human development—an infant just beginning to test his senses, curious but cautious in the puzzling world in which he finds himself.

The second mask is called Samba or Pamindo, which literally means number two. It is light blue and has more ornamentation than the Panji mask. This is Prince Kuda Panolih of Bawarna, who is preparing for his older sister's wedding. This character represents adolescence, and depicts the playful and nimble qualities of this age. The *bodor* will usually make his first appearance during this dance, wearing a comic female mask and teasing the *dalang* and audience.

The third mask, Rumyang, is usually bright pink and is an extension of the Samba character. The movement becomes more flirtatious and lively, and this androgynous character spends much time in self-beautifying. Rumyang depicts the period of the late teens and early twenties, when youth is still searching and not yet settled down. Rumyang is changeable and eager to explore the world. In some villages this dance is performed last, perhaps symbolizing the return to youthfulness in old age.

The fourth mask is Tumenggung, a noble warrior. The mask's name is a high Javanese title, sometimes used for prime minister characters. In the story, this is the bridegroom, Tumenggung Manganggraja. The mask is a light reddish-brown, with eyes looking ahead, a straight nose, and a dashing moustache. The movements danced are strong and sure, and a mature, confident personality emerges. In order to claim his bride, Tumenggung must defeat the giant king Jingga Anom, who has been troubling Bawarna. The mask of Jingga Anom is grotesquely played by the *bodor*. He is arrogant with his red face, bulging eyes, and wild hair. During the battle with Tumenggung, who naturally defeats him, he often breaks character. Conveniently, as he is about to be killed, he raises some trivial question or complains about Tumenggung's fighting method. After his death as Jingga Anom, the actor Bulus may rise and amble off, informing the audience with a mischievous grin, "Jingga Anom dies . . . but Bulus lives again!"

The last mask, Klana, represents a strange and coarse king from "across the seas." His face is red with popping eyes, a large nose, and protruding teeth. His fierce expression contrasts with the foolish one of Jingga Anom. He is an example of what no Javanese wants to be—a person out of control of his emotions and consumed by his desires and greed. The movements of this dance are strong, fast, and powerful, accentuated by much arrogant laughter and threatening postures, giving Sujana admirable opportunity to amaze his audience with his strength, speed, and exact articulation. On this wild note, the performance ends, leaving the viewer to ponder the ages and aspects of man he may have glimpsed and to resume his life in the calm evening hours.

A *topeng babakan dalang* keeps maturing and developing his skills over a lifetime. A dancer like Sujana, in his forties, has just arrived at the peak performing years that extend through a performer's fifties. In this period a dancer's maturity and feeling, as well as his or her dexterity and technical skill, make the dancer more satisfying to watch. Many performers dance into their sixties, and some are septuagenarians. A *dalang* may be a man or a woman, since the sex of the character is defined by the mask rather than corresponding to the sex of the performer. Two other very exciting performers in this field are women in their mid-sixties.

Topeng babakan dalang usually stress that they do not particularly identify with any one character, and that it is important to be impartial so as to enter each personality completely. Sujana says he often fasts before a performance. He considers it important to be hungry so as to create a kind of vacuum into which to draw the audience and give people good and calm feelings. He states that a dancer in this tradition must take care to keep his or her spirit good and strong and guard against evil feelings.

Occasionally, two *dalang* will split a performance, alternating in the roles. Sometimes two or more *topeng babakan* groups will be hired to dance at the same time. The two dancers, or sometimes four, and their *gamelan* enter into a sort of competition. Identical mask characters dance simultaneously. This old practice is called *kupu tarung* (battling butterflies) and adds to the excitement of a performance, as well as expressing an extra dimension of the psyche—alter-ego-like, the spiritual twin exists perhaps in another universe or perhaps within the self.

DEENA BURTON

PELIATAN-TEGES
(Peliatan-Teges)
Ubud
Gianyar, Bali, Indonesia

Performing groups in Bali are an integral part of the Hindu-Bali culture. Dance and drama are not only the popular entertainments of small villages but also serve as a required ritual in many temple ceremonies. Thus, there are performing groups throughout Bali, although most performers must earn their livelihood through another profession. While the performers are not professionals, in the usual monetary meaning of the term, the high standards of performing companies have enabled this small island to produce performances that have entranced audiences throughout the world. Peliatan village in the Gianyar region of Bali has a long history as a center of excellent dance companies.

John Coast brought the dance company and *gamelan* orchestral accompaniment of Peliatan to America in the 1950s and chronicled that tour in his book, *Dancers of Bali* (New York: Putnam, 1953). The child stars of that original group have retired, but the *gamelan* continues with new dancers performing the same type of repertory: *Baris*, a male solo dance which is a secularized version of the sacred warriors' dance performed in two lines (*baris* means line or row); *Oleg Tamulilingan* (*Bumblebee Sips Honey*), a dance abstractly depicting the courtship of a male and female bumblebee choreographed by the late I Maria of Tabanan; *Kebyar Trompong* (*Lightning Style Playing the Trompong*), a solo male dance also choreographed by I Maria more than thirty years ago in which the dancer also plays the *trompong* (a musical instrument) while dancing; *Gabor*, a dance of welcome adapted from the sacred dance of the same name; and *Taruna Jaya* (*Adolescence Dance*), a virtuoso solo dance choreographed by Gede Manik of Singaradja, which depicts the turbulent mood changes of adolescence. These dances are classified as *tari lepas*, short dances choreographed independently of dance-drama forms, in which the dancer is freer to improvise and interpret than in classical dance forms. The Peliatan group's repertory is completed by the shortened version of the classical dance for young girls, *Legong Keraton Lasem* (*Palace Dance of Lasem*), which is loosely based on the story of the King of Lasem's abduction of Lankesari from the epic Panji legend.

The group, under the musical direction of I Wayan Gandera, is frequently chartered to perform for tourists at the small hotel of Anak Agung Gede Mandera, a member of Balinese royalty and patron of the arts. Anak Agung Mandera has also been prominent in the preservation of the classical *legong keraton*, a dance form more than one hundred years old and formerly the favorite of royalty. In 1971 the *Semar Pegulingan* orchestra of Anak Agung Mandera was loaned to the *gamelan* organization at Teges, which is part of greater Peliatan village. Musicians I Wayan Gerindum, I Made Lebah, and master dance-teacher Sang Ayu Ketut Muklun worked to restage the five dances of *legong keraton* indigenous to the Peliatan area in the original versions. The five dances are *Lasem*; *Kuntul* (*White Crane*), which abstractly portrays two white cranes in the rice field; *Kuntir* (*Subali-Sugriwa*), the battle between Sugriwa and Subali as children; *Pelayon* (*Dance to the Tune Pelayon*), a dance of almost one hour without specific plot; and *Semarandana* (*Legend of Semara*), the love story of Bhatari Ratih and Bhatara Semara. All of the dances have similar musical melodies and dance movements, and the dancers use the same costuming for all of these *legong* forms. The Teges company is undisputed as the most active group of *legong keraton* in Bali. In recognition of that fact, the group received a large grant from the Ford Foundation.

The growth in popularity of these classical revivals continues. With funding from the Ford grant in October 1978 another *Semar Pegulingan* orchestra was purchased, and Anak Agung Mandera has sponsored the newest group, headed by musician Made Lebah and sharing rehearsal space with Wayan Gandera's *gamelan*. Several of the musicians are members of more than one *gamelan*, in these three groups which are closely interrelated. Anak Agung Mandera is the sponsor of all the groups, and Wayan Gandera is the son of Made Lebah. Many of the *tari lepas* dancers of Peliatan are invited to perform in concert at Teges. Thus, the local talents are shared, and excellent standards of performance are evident in all the groups.

The Teges group toured Europe in 1974, performed in Iran in 1976, has frequently performed at the Werdi Budaya Art Center in Denpasar, Bali, and in 1978 represented Bali at the Jakarta Festival. A group from Peliatan toured the United States and Mexico in 1981. While all three groups are primarily interested in preserving Balinese dance, creative innovation also thrives. Sardono Kusumo, a Javanese dancer from Taman Ismail Mazuki College faculty, has choreographed three new dances in the Balinese style at Teges since 1974. I Ketut Tutur, the teacher of many outstanding young male dancers in the Peliatan area, has created a new *baris* dance, with a choreographed battle between two young warriors in the Peliatan group.

Thus, the village of Peliatan remains a strong center of dance in Bali. Village companies in Bali often form, become famous, and later splinter or disband, sometimes in a matter of a few short years. Under the direction of Anak Agung Madera, Peliatan has not only continued its fame throughout several decades, but also its talent and interest have produced two new companies within the last decade. Peliatan will undoubtedly continue to remain a flourishing center of performance in the future.

MARIANNE ARIYANTO

RAY OF ACCOMPLISHMENT
(Sinar Binangkit)
Dalang Aliwijaya
Curug, Karang Sumbung
Cirebon, West Java, Indonesia

Sinar Binangkit (Ray of Accomplishment) is the *gamelan* orchestra, and, by association, the group of performers that accompany Aliwijaya, the foremost *dalang* (storyteller) of *wayang cepak* in Cirebon, an area that lies on the border of Sunda and Java. *Wayang cepak* uses three-dimensional wooden puppets to perform stories drawn from history and legend. The group performs an average of nineteen times a month, usually outdoors, on a raised, temporary stage in celebration of a *selamatan* (ritual feast) for a wedding, circumcision, or other important occasion. Performances last about eight hours and may be held at night or during the day.

Wayang cepak employs seventy puppets ranging from 1 1/2 to 2 feet in height and attired in traditional Javanese court dress. Unlike *wayang purwa*, a theatre form in which each puppet represents a set character from the Ramayana or Mahabharata, *wayang cepak* puppets represent types of characters—a refined prince, a brave warrior, and so on—and the same puppet will be used to represent a different character from one story to the next.

In the performance the *dalang* assumes the major role—speaking all the dialogue, supplying the narration, and singing mood songs that highlight the action of the play—while the *gamelan* enlivens the performance with its shimmering tunes. Although the instruments are similar to those found throughout Java, the style of playing them in Cirebon is generally more lively than in other areas, partially because of the use of metal plates (*beri*) and a large drum (*bedug*) for percussive effects, to which are added the spirited calls of the players. Fifteen musicians habitually perform in Sinar Binangkit, in addition to one or two female singers. The singers will often be one or more of Aliwijaya's four wives. Jaera Punia is one of his wives who is a noted performer. She, like other singers of Cirebon, is noted for her ability to make the lyrics of her song fit the action of the scene being played. Her tonal quality, too, will add to the effect. If a character in the play is about to part from a lover, the song of Jaera Punia will entwine plaintively with the wail of the flute.

Aliwijaya owns four sets of puppets and *gamelan*, three sets of *wayang cepak*, and one of *wayang kulit*, which he uses to perform the story of Kala for exorcisms. He keeps the equipment in the different households he maintains for his different wives. When he is hired for a performance, he sends the equipment located nearest to the site ahead of him. This facilitates performances on the many occasions when he plays all night in one village and must begin another presentation at 9:00 A.M. the next day in a distant place.

For Aliwijaya and his family, art has been an enduring tradition. He is now in his fifties and has been playing *wayang* since the 1930s. He learned the art from his father, Sajum, who had learned from his father before him. Aliwijaya says that he is the twenty-third generation of his family to perform *wayang cepak*.

The form itself was supposedly developed in 1584 by the Sunan of Kudus so that *wayang*, which could only be played at night in the shadow puppet form, could be presented during the day to teach the Muslim religion. This association of *wayang* and religion is still strong in the northern coastal area where *wayang cepak* flourishes. Religious influence is clear in the repertory Aliwijaya plays, which tells of the triumph of Islam in Arabia, or is drawn from the chronicles (*babad*) of the Javanese cities of Demak, Japara, or Cirebon itself, centering on Muslim heroes.

Since the structure of the performance is set by tradition and dialogue is improvised in a formulaic manner with only the plots changing, Aliwijaya commands a large repertory. He can play over one hundred of the stories from the Menak cycle, which deal with the exploits of Amir Hamzah, the uncle of the prophet Mohammed, who was a defender of the Islamic faith. Although ostensibly set in Arabia, the tales adhere more clearly to Javanese custom and story patterns than to Arab history. Amir Hamzah is portrayed as the king of Arabia, already a Muslim, although Mohammed has yet to be born, and, hence, the religion could not yet have been conceived. His constant battles with greedy kings from overseas kingdoms coincide with the normal pattern of Javanese *wayang*.

Even more frequently than Menak stories, Aliwijaya will be asked to play *babad* Cirebon, which chronicle the area where he lives and is hired. Many of the stories focus on leaders like Sunan Gunung Jati, who converted the area to Islam, founded the royal house, and carried the religion into the interior of Java. Officials of the Department of Education and Culture point out the irony that the same material played by Aliwijaya and the twelve other *wayang cepak dalang* of Cirebon is recorded in books that are locked away in the palace, since the events they deal with are considered too fraught with spiritual power to allow them to be read. Yet the *dalang* play these same stories almost daily.

The values presented by Aliwijaya seem largely to bolster traditional social and religious beliefs of this area, where the influence of the palace tradition and religion is perhaps the strongest in West Java. Aliwijaya explains that he has followed faithfully what he learned from his father and would be afraid to alter the way of playing the *wayang*. Because he never attended school or learned to read and write, he feels all his knowledge has come from the *wayang* and says he has taught his art to his ten students in the same traditional way.

Yet there have been changes in Aliwijaya's lifetime, and his performances reflect a widening of the world that independence has brought to Indonesia's traditional artists. *Wayang* has become a channel of government propaganda, and Aliwijaya agrees that it is appropriate to put references to family planning and other development programs into the dialogue of the clown puppets. Under the auspices of the Department of Education and Culture, the group has traveled widely in Java, performing in Bandung, the capital of West Java, and in Jakarta at Wayang Festivals in 1978, 1983, and on other occasions. The group's artistry is much appreciated. The precise choreography of the puppets' movements, accompanied by the lively style of *gamelan*, turns battle scenes into balletic delights. The energetic dance of the Klana-type puppet reveals the aggressive, emotionally uncontrolled character represented and reflects a beauty of movement that caused the masked Klana dance of Cirebon to be imitated throughout West Java. But since the language used in the performance of *wayang cepak* is a dialect spoken only in the Cirebon area, the true audience of this company remains the people of Cirebon, who see their heritage reflected in its performances.

KATHY FOLEY

SRI WEDARI DANCE-DRAMA COMPANY
(Wayang Orang Sri Wedari)
Taman Sri Wedari
Jalan Brigjen, Slamet Riyadi
Surakarta, Jawa Tengah, Indonesia

Sri Wedari is a major exponent of *wayang orang*, a Javanese performance genre combining dancer/actors who enact the story with a *dalang* (storyteller) and *gamelan* orchestra to tell tales derived largely from the Mahabharata and Ramayana epics. The company, which has a long and illustrious history, plays seven times a week, with performers from its group of one hundred enacting a different story each night.

The name of the company is taken from the park in which it performs. In 1899 the royal court of Surakarta, then ruled by H.H. Paku Buwana X, officially opened a public park called Taman Sri Wedari. For nearly twenty years, the park entertained various traveling *wayang orang* companies, until in 1918 the

Sri Cahya Mulya (Beautiful Light of Well-being) company, owned by Lie Wat Gien, was invited to give weekly performances at the park. By this time, the building Panti Matoyo had been built within the park for occasional dance and *wayang orang* performances. The stage was raised, with a place on the side (stage left) for musicians of the *gamelan* orchestra. The audience was protected by only a tent at first. Several years later, a tile roof was added, making the audience hall more permanent. It was at this time, about 1920, that Lie Wat Gien's company was replaced by a new one, owned and directed by R. M. Sastrotanoyo, which came to be known as Wayang Orang Sri Wedari.

His group played to paying audiences every Saturday night and Sunday afternoon and, during special festivals, every night of the week. Profits from each performance went into the palace treasury, from which the performers received a fixed salary. They were considered servants of the court (*abdi dalem*), and many were given honorary court titles. The players—dancer/actors and musicians—lived together in Kebunan, a compound behind the park, in financial security, and with royal recognition.

Most of the stories performed were taken from the repertory of *wayang purwa*, the Javanese shadow puppet tradition based on the Ramayana and the Mahabharata epics. While shadow plays last all night, the plays performed by the *wayang orang* at Sri Wedari, and indeed by most other *wayang orang* companies, last only three to six hours. Because of the formulaic means of constructing a *wayang* story, the performance time can be expanded or contracted without eliminating the basic elements required of the genre.

In the early 1930s the Sri Wedari company began to feature certain dancer/actors, a practice that persisted for nearly two decades. Those who attended performances in the 1930s still remember Harjowugu in the role of the heroic warrior Gathutkaca, Sastrodirun in the role of the clown-servant Pétruk, Lebdowibakso as the refined King Kresna, and Resowibakso as the ogre Cakil. It was during the 1930s also that roles of very refined male characters, such as Arjuna, began to be played by females—notably Madhyorini and Tumini. Performances usually took place two or three times a week.

During the 1940s the company continued to play, despite the turmoil brought about by the Japanese occupation (1942 to 1945) and the revolution against the Dutch (1945 to 1949). In some periods it could play only during daylight hours, but the company kept going and swelled its ranks with new performers, some of whom are still active today. Cokrowibakso and Nolowibakso joined as clown-servants (Semar and Garèng, respectively); Patmosurono took over as Kresna; Ronowibakso (popularly known as Surono) joined in 1941; and Harjowibakso (popularly known as Rusman) in 1942. The last two men played a variety of male roles, including Gathutkaca, for which Rusman is still famous. Three outstanding women also joined soon afterward: Sitorini, who played refined male roles, and two who played coquettish female roles, Sarworini and Darsi. (Darsi soon became Rusman's wife.) Dancers were taught by the palace dancer R. Ng. Wignyohambekso, under the direction of Wiryopradoto.

At the end of the 1940s, there were many changes at Sri Wedari. The court had lost much of its power, prestige, and wealth and could no longer support or manage the *wayang orang* company. Governmental power in 1949 came unequivocally into the hands of the new Republic of Indonesia, and the local city government (of Surakarta) took over the functions of the court previous to the revolution, vis à vis the *wayang orang* company at Sri Wedari. The performers became government employees with fixed salaries, and profits from performances became city revenue. During the early 1950s, Tumini returned after years of retirement, followed by new females, such as Ratmi and Wahyuni, and a new comedian, Ranto, who took over as Pétruk on the death of Sastrodirun in 1958. An important addition was the clown-servant character Bagong, who at Sri Wedari had been played first by Suradi in 1956. At about this time, the company moved to a large new building within the park which had been under construction for several years. It resembled, more so than the first building, the Western idea of a proscenium theatre, with an orchestra pit in front of the stage and machinery for changing painted backdrops.

In 1950 the company came under the artistic direction of Tohiran, an energetic and insightful man who stressed versatility. He created a policy whereby performers had to shift roles frequently and young members were trained to be able to take on many roles, limited only by their body types and the character of their speaking voices. The company also began to play nearly every night of the week. The players were so accustomed to performing that they needed only to be reminded of the outline of each scene as they made their entrance and were able to fill in details as they performed. This practice persists to the present in the most professional *wayang orang* companies and is a remarkable example of the power of oral tradition. During the 1950s Tohiran was aided in his role as director by Martodiarjo and in the 1960s by Warnowibakso, both experienced dancer/ actors. In order to attract a sufficiently large audience every night, new stories were devised—employing the same characters as the older *wayang purwa* stories, but often with stress on the light and the humorous.

Throughout his rule (1949 to 1965), Sukarno called on Sri Wedari *wayang orang* players to perform for his own and his foreign guests' entertainment. The Indonesian mission to the New York World's Fair in 1964 included Rusman and Surono. Since Suharto has come to power, the national government has given financial support in the form of grants and subsidy to Sri Wedari, but performers are no longer asked to come to the president's palace to perform.

Tohiran resigned in 1968. Since then the directorship has been held by a number of people, the most recent being Martoyo, who has been director only since mid-1978. He chooses what story is to be performed and who is to play which role; during the performance he advises the performers of what must occur in each scene. Yet most people acknowledge Surono as the director. Because of his long years of experience with Sri Wedari, he is able to provide continuity in the philosophy of the company, and Martoyo's decisions are heavily based on consultation with Surono and, to a lesser extent, with Rusman.

As a professional company, Sri Wedari has always sought, at least in part, to please the audience; yet, while entertaining, it consciously presents something it considers beautiful and instructive. In the early twentieth century it was easier to please Javanese audiences with standard *wayang purwa* stories than it is now. The audiences are too often disappointingly small, and the directors are looking for ways to appeal to a larger sector of the population. The length of performances has been shortened from about five hours (the norm as recently as 1974) to about three and one-half hours (1979). Long verbal exchanges that are neither humorous nor advance the plot have been curtailed, as have been long dance sequences. Surono estimates the current repertory at Sri Wedari to be about five hundred stories based on the Mahabharata and Ramayana; of these about one hundred are popular and repeated fairly often to draw larger crowds. The most publicized recent change in policy, however, is the inclusion of stories from Javanese historical legends, often performed in the popular *ketoprak* (improvised, spoken drama) genre. The company at Sri Wedari performs these stories not as *ketoprak*, but as *wayang orang*, with the stylized speech, singing, dance, and gestures typical of *wayang orang*. These stories are performed nearly every Wednesday night, with the famous Darsi, Rusman, and Surono taking major roles to ensure a substantial audience. These performances, in contrast to those based on the standard repertory, are rehearsed at least once. They are demanding of the dancer/ actors as they are more complex in choreography and require the performers to assume new roles, playing characters who are not so well known as those in the Mahabharata and Ramayana.

Despite such changes, the Sri Wedari company is encountering stiff competition from films and TV, which offer the residents of Surakarta more exotic forms of entertainment. The performers are well aware that they stand on the side of Javanese tradition, and they present a regional art to a population that is increasingly conscious of its national identity and increasingly wary of Javanese art as something "old fashioned." In the face of very low wages and dwindling audiences, the future at Sri Wedari may be a bleak one, but the performers— currently about sixty dancer/actors and forty musicians—are committed to pre- serving Javanese regional culture in all its richness for present and future gen- erations. They are willing to bend with the times, altering format and expanding repertory, while maintaining all the basic elements that have made *wayang orang* an important Javanese art form.

R. ANDERSON SUTTON

STUDIO KARUNA KERTI
(Sanggar Karuna Kerti)
Banjar Kawan, Tampak Siring
Gianyar, Bali, Indonesia

The leader of Sanggar Karuna Kerti is I Made Pasek Tempo, born in 1927 and a living encyclopedia of the arts of Bali. He is an actor, puppeteer, director, dancer, choreographer, singer, musician, and scholar of ancient literature. Pasek Tempo has been teaching and performing with this group across Bali since 1953. Prominent members of this troupe at present are Made Wati (Pasek Tempo's daughter), an actress, singer, and dancer, and Swindra, a puppet maker. As in most Balinese troupes, the group has a family structure. Children and adults of the village study with the group. When they are thought to be ready, they join in performances. They have presented primarily masked drama (*arja*) and other dance performances.

Recently, a number of new influences have been incorporated. In 1974 Sardono, a Javanese dancer, organized a European tour of Balinese dancers in which Pasek Tempo and some of his group took active part, especially in the newly arranged *kecak* dance, *Cak Tarian Rina* (*Monkey Chant Battle Dance*), with the village group of Teges. After this tour, Pasek Tempo and some of his group members worked with Julie Taymor, an American dramatist, in creating a drama with masks and puppets, entitled *Tirai* (*Curtain*), to tour Indonesia. The theme was the confrontation of East and West. Again in 1978 Pasek Tempo and his group collaborated with several other artists from Bali—Ikranagara, Wayan Dibia, and Abu Bakar—in creating a performance combining drama, masks, shadow puppets, scroll drama, and dance. The production was entitled *Rimba Tiwikrama* (*The Great Anger of the Forest*), and the theme was the despoiling of nature as a negative effect of modernization in Bali. The present projects of the Sanggar Karuna Kerti are a version of the *Rimba Tiwikrama*, done completely with shadow puppets, and a traditional masked drama performed entirely by women—an innovation. Pasek Tempo toured Europe once more in 1981.

The aim of Sanggar Karuna Kerti is to create new performances in the tradition of Bali. In the traditional way, the group has cooperative ownership of its practice hall, orchestra, and costumes. It has been reluctant to receive monetary payment from students; instead, students offer a form of mutual aid. Recently, Sanggar Karuna Kerti has received some government assistance.

KAY IKRANAGARA

UNITY OF THE PANDOWO DANCE-DRAMA CO.
(Wayang Orang Ngesti Pandowo)
Gedung Rakyat Indonesia Semarang (GRIS)
Jalan Pemuda No. 116
Semarang, Jawa Tengah, Indonesia

Ngesti Pandowo is a company of 105 active members, performing stories derived from the Mahabharata and Ramayana in *wayang orang* style, seven times a week. Dancer/actors perform the drama to the accompaniment of a *gamelan* orchestra, with narrative passages and mood songs provided by a *dalang* (storyteller).

The Ngesti Pandowo company was officially founded on July 1, 1937, in Madiun, a town in East Java. Sastrosabdho, the owner and director of this new company, had formerly played with Tan Tiam Ping's Sedyo Wandono (*Longing for Beautiful*) *the wayang orang* company, which disbanded in 1937. Members of the defunct Sedyo Wandono joined forces with some members of the Sri Widodo company, owned and directed by Kartodiwiryo, a dancer from Surakarta who had been Sastrosabdho's teacher. When this second group disbanded, Kartodiwiryo, along with his young son, Kusni, joined the new Ngesti Pandowo, bringing the costumes and properties from his previous company.

In keeping with the company name, which suggests identification with the five Pandowo brothers of the Mahabharata epic, there were five leaders involved in decision-making. In addition to Sastrosabdho, his brother-in-law Sastrosudirjo acted as manager. Others involved were the dancer/actors Kusni and Darsosabdho and a representative from the *gamelan* orchestra. Unlike many *wayang orang* companies, Ngesti Pandowo has always stressed group decision-making and performer versatility. Only a few roles in this theatre of set characters have had fixed personnel. These include the refined king, Kresna, played by Harjomartoyo and others after him; and the clown-servants, played by Darmosurono as Semar, Darsosabdho as Garèng, and Sastrosabdho himself as Pétruk. The other actors were required to perform a variety of roles; for example, Kusni was able to play both refined and strong male roles, although these two types of role require very different vocal and movement styles.

Many of the sixty performers in the company at its outset had been trained in the court city of Surakarta, by teachers such as Wiryopradoto and Kartodiwiryo; even today the company's dance and music are essentially Surakarta style. Nevertheless, the group decided to play first in East Java, where it would have less competition and a less critical audience than it might encounter in Surakarta. It opened at a night fair in Madiun and drew good audiences for nearly a month, after which it traveled from town to town, remaining in the East Javanese area for five years. In 1939 the group began to use females to play refined male roles, following the Surakarta practice; yet it has always had males occasionally take these roles. In 1942, when the Japanese began their occupation of Indonesia, the Ngesti Pandowo company was in Kediri. It was permitted—indeed encouraged—to continue performing, though for the first six months only during daylight hours.

After its initial success in East Java and its five years of experience together, the group felt ready to return to Surakarta to perform amidst stiff competition from other *wayang orang* companies. Throughout most of the Japanese occupation (1942 to 1945) and the revolution against the Dutch (1945 to 1949), the Ngesti Pandowo company was based in Surakarta, first in the north square in front of the royal palace and then in a rented building near the market Pasar Pon. An important event in the company's history occurred in 1945, when, in the small town of Klaten, about 30 kilometers outside Surakarta, several of the leaders were impressed by the drumming of a young man named Sunarto, who was accompanying a *ketoprak* (improvised, spoken drama) performance. He was asked to join Ngesti Pandowo, where he was given the name Nartosabdho and soon became the controversially innovative leader of Ngesti Pandowo's *gamelan* musicians, though not without opposition from some of the older members.

Many of the members of Ngesti Pandowo were active as guerrillas in the revolution against the Dutch. Shortly before the revolution ended in 1949, the owner, Sastrosabdho, was caught by the Dutch and threatened with imprisonment if he did not take his entire company out of Surakarta to Semarang, on the north coast, where the Dutch had firm control and the people were in want of Javanese entertainment. While the company did not wish to acquiesce, the offer of security in Semarang and the release of their owner was sufficient to cause the members to move to Semarang, where they have remained to the present.

Soon after their move, the Dutch were ousted, and the Semarang city government under the new Republic of Indonesia provided them with land for housing and a permanent building for performance (the Gedung Rakyat Indonesia Semarang), with proscenium stage and orchestra pit. They have exclusive right to rent the building, and they pay a nominal fee. Ngesti Pandowo has always been a private organization, earning its money directly from the box office. The company funds not only pay salaries to active members, but also pensions to those who wish to retire at age fifty, and schooling costs for performers' children. The children are not forced to make performance their profession, but they are required to gain facility as either musicians or dancer/actors, so they can join the company if they wish. Many of them join, giving the company a significant percentage of young members and making Ngesti Pandowo very much a family enterprise. The intimacy of the performer families, who live and work together, is apparent to audiences in the occasional jokes they throw at each other between the lines of the story and the sense of enjoyment they convey while performing together night after night, seven times a week.

Since its first performances in Semarang, Ngesti Pandowo has been known for its innovative productions. The directors often created new stories, based on the *wayang purwa* repertory (that is, the Ramayana and Mahabharata epics), with the heroes turning into ogres as one of their new dramatic twists. Ngesti Pandowo soon gained recognition for costumes, colorful lighting, props, and scenery, which were elaborate in comparison with those of other *wayang orang* companies. Above all, the musical arrangements and compositions of Nartosabdho, used for scenes with the clown-servants, sometimes represented radical alterations of traditional Javanese musical principles. They were controversial, particularly among the educated elite, but they gained popularity among the masses.

In 1954 Ngesti Pandowo added a fourth clown-servant, Bagong, played by Senen. The combination of the clown-servants and Nartosabdho's music, in addition to the excellence of many of the dancer/actors in more serious roles, brought Ngesti Pandowo into great demand. The entire company often traveled to other Javanese towns and cities, playing at special night fairs, such as the city of Yogyakarta's bicentennial celebration in 1955. During the era of President Sukarno (1949 to 1967), members of Ngesti Pandowo were frequently called to perform at the presidential palace in Jakarta. Well-known performers included, in addition to the men mentioned previously, versatile female dancer/actors, such as Rusmini, Suwarni, Linggarsih, and Tumpuk.

There was little change in personnel or management until after 1966, when the owner, Sastrosabdho, died. Sastrosudirjo took over as owner and remained manager at the same time; Jayasugito, who had been with the company since 1938, filled in as Pétruk. Nartosabdho was fast demonstrating his excellence as both musician and *wayang kulit dalang* (shadow puppeteer) independent of Ngesti Pandowo, and relinquished his Ngesti Pandowo responsibilities to Sriyono, the present musical director. Kusni was frequently involved in artistic tours outside the country and officially retired in 1970, turning his duties over to Sastrosabdho's stepson, Sunarjo, the current artistic director. It is he who assigns roles and outlines the stories, usually the afternoon before the performance. Dancer/actors who cannot perform on a certain day must let him know before noon so that he can either find someone else or adjust the staging to accommodate the story.

It is the owner, Sastrosudirjo, who determines which story is to be performed, and since 1976 he has included *ketoprak* stories and original Ngesti Pandowo stories with the standard repertory in hopes of drawing larger crowds. The company has taken steps to meet the demands of modern audiences, for whom motion pictures and television are popular and accessible entertainment media. Ngesti Pandowo has added a measure of sophistication to its lighting techniques, using projected slide images and slide overlays for special effects since 1973. Within the last several years, it has trimmed performance time to about three hours (8:30 to 11:30 P.M.) The audiences consist of a good percentage of young people, who are equally at home in Indonesian, the national language, and in Javanese, used for Javanese *wayang orang*. However, there seems at present little chance that the group might substitute Indonesian for Javanese, for Javanese is, in the opinion of the directors, far richer and more appropriate for *wayang orang*. The only change in language has been the elimination of much of the *Kawi*—old Javanese poetic language, which very few Javanese understand today. Long speaking parts in general have also been condensed, as have dance sequences.

Sastrosudirjo feels that the basic philosophical content of *wayang orang*, as presented at Ngesti Pandowo, is no different from that of the far more ancient *wayang kulit* (shadow puppet) tradition. In both types of *wayang*, one finds Javanese values and aesthetics in all their richness. The Ngesti Pandowo company is committed to carrying on a regional art form, which, with continuing flexibility to changes, will not lose its relevance in modern Javanese society.

PEGGY ANN CHOY and
R. ANDERSON SUTTON

Japan

INTRODUCTION

Japanese theatre is extremely diverse. In time it ranges from the seventh-century importation of Bugaku dance (from India, China, and Korea), as the oldest existing dramatic form, to a variety of thoroughly experimental forms in the 1980s. The magnificent courtly and archaic dance of Bugaku is accompanied by Gagaku music. From the beginning both forms were patronized by aristocrats of the Imperial Court; thus, even today, they are regularly presented together by members of the Imperial Orchestra. Passes to performances are available by request from the Kunaichō Shikibu Shikigakubu (Department of Ceremonies in the Imperial Household Agency). Some ancient Shinto shrines also present Bugaku and Gagaku on festive occasions, but such performances are only held annually and are difficult to attend without advance planning.

Nō and Kyōgen, the most rigidly formalized and conventionalized of theatre forms, were established in the fourteenth century and are presented today in their own unique environment. In addition, other theatre forms have gained in popularity. Under a tent, one of the most daring forms of new antiestablishment plays is challenging the limits of the audiences' imagination and, in a huge theatre, such favorites of the West as musicals and the most predictable of melodramas unfold their unchanging plots.

The preservation of classical theatre forms with their traditional production style intact is a uniquely Asian rather than a solely Japanese phenomenon. The intense effort to adhere to tradition and to maintain high artistic integrity is, however, characteristically Japanese. Moreover, the number of participating artists in these forms and the stability of these genres, as independent art forms free from governmental subsidy, are remarkable when compared with similar forms in other Asian countries.

The rich diversity within the Japanese traditional theatre forms is most impressive. In addition to the forms already mentioned, Kabuki and Bunraku puppet theatre are also significant. Both forms originated in the seventeenth century, patronized by the then rising merchant class. This contrasts with the Imperial

Court patronage of Bugaku dance and Gagaku music and with warrior-class support of Nō and Kyōgen.

Japan's traditional theatre forms must be seen in terms of the country's entire theatrical activities. Western readers tend to pay too much attention to the uniqueness of traditional theatre and sometimes overlook the existence of a thriving modern theatre.

Despite drastic differences between traditional and modern theatre, most of the producing theatre organizations share one major element—the troupe-oriented system. The idea of making a fresh company for each production as on Broadway has been tried but has not caught on with Japanese modern theatre. This is not necessarily the result of the strong bonds among the troupe members, since companies, particularly modern theatre groups, tend to break up and to form new companies. In traditional theatre the training and discipline are so intense that strong ties develop between the leader and supporting troupe members. Actually, the relationship is that of a master and his disciples. Breaking one's association with the company could mean the end of one's career.

In general, these companies seem to do best as a tightly knit team rather than as a group of strong but individual artists who get together temporarily. The make-up of the company is sometimes very clearcut, particularly in the case of modern theatre, Kabuki, and Bunraku. But the practice of the Nō and Kyōgen theatre is rather unique and cannot be explained simply.

NŌ AND KYŌGEN THEATRE

There are five Nō schools (*ryū*) and two Kyōgen. Four of the Nō schools (Kanze, Hōshō, Komparu, and Kongō) originated with four families active from the beginning of the Nō, which was known as Sarugaku, while the fifth, Kita, was added in 1618. Each school has outgrown its original scale and contains members who do not belong to the family. The art of the school, however, has been transmitted through generations from one head of the school to the next within the core family. The head of such a family has assumed leadership of the school.

As the size of a school grew, it could no longer function as a single producing organization. It had to allow divisions within itself to promote sufficient activities among the professional members of the school. For example, the Kanze school has been the largest from its early days, but today it has 681 members who are professional Nō artists (Nōgaku Kyōkai members), among whom 145 enjoy the governmental designation of "Intangible Cultural Asset" (Jūyō Mukei Bunkazai). In many cases the production of Nō plays is organized and presented by each division within the school, with certain members of the school being retained as permanent division members. On artistic and organizational matters, each division submits itself to the authority of the head of the school. Thus, there are many productions of Nō plays, each clearly identified by school as well as group.

Kyōgen today has two schools: Okura and Izumi. In the beginning there was a third school, Sagi, but it terminated in the early twentieth century. By the sixteenth century, however, the oldest and largest school, Okura, was established. Izumi was founded at the beginning of the eighteenth century.

Unlike the Nō play which requires the participation of principal characters and musicians, in addition to secondary character(s), the Kyōgen play can generally be performed by two or three actors. Hence, it is quite possible for a family to constitute the entire membership of a troupe, or at least the core of the troupe. Even the style of Kyōgen reflects this basic nature, and within the same school, different families tend to show their own individualized styles, each clearly distinctive.

Basically, there are two ways for Kyōgen actors to participate in a Nō program. In its wider sense the term *Nō* denotes a program containing both Nō and Kyōgen plays. Nō in its narrower sense means simply a Nō play, which is essentially lyrical, presenting chanting accompanied by instrumental music, while the dance and movement are utilized to illustrate the content of the chanting and dialogue. The theme is serious and frequently tragic. A Nō program contains one or more Kyōgen plays, depending upon scope. Kyōgen is a dialogue-oriented play, relying upon regular mimetic movement interspersed with short dances and chanting. It usually deals with a humorous situation frequently presenting a biting satire against contemporary authority figures.

The actor of Kyōgen has another function aside from play performance. He also appears either singularly or as a member of a small group within a Nō play. In this case, he is called an Ai-Kyōgen because he appears in a section called an ''ai'' or in-between. In this capacity, a Kyōgen actor appears as a local person who provides an explanation of the situation in an archaic vernacular common to the fifteenth century. Some Nō plays have developed a method employing Ai-Kyōgen as supporting characters who are much more significantly integrated into the plot, contributing far more than simply information about the play.

The main character (including his or her companion) and stage assistants (*kōken*) belong to the five schools of principal actors (*shite*). The number of the veteran professionals is cited in this work under separate headings of each school (*ryū*). The Nō program requires the participation of other professionals as well. They are the secondary actors (*waki*), twenty from each of three schools, namely, Takayasu-ryū, Fukuō-ryū, and Hōshō-ryū. In addition, there are musicians specializing in one of four instruments: forty-five in the flute, sixty in the small hand drum, fifty in the large hand drum, and forty in the stick drum. The Kyōgen actors also take significant parts in both Nō and Kyōgen plays.

The production style of the Nō play is formalized and distilled to essential elements of movement backed by dance and choral chanting with accompanying music. A certain amount of prior study would be helpful to increase one's appreciation of this form. The style of the Kyōgen play is, on the other hand, reasonably clearcut with mimetic movements and gestures supported by dialogues. In both cases, prior knowledge of at least the plot of each play should be obtained to enhance one's appreciation.

The most formal Nō program today consists of *Okina* (*The Old Man*), the oldest Nō play in the repertoire of 240, followed by 5 plays, each of them representing categories of the Nō (God, Man, Woman, Frenzied People, and Concluding Pieces). Such a full program takes a whole day to perform; hence, it is limited to special ceremonious performances on holidays and other special occasions. The usual program presented on weekdays tends to be two Nō plays, with a Kyōgen play sandwiched between, and on weekends, three Nō plays and two Kyōgen. A Kyōgen play is normally presented in this sandwiched manner unless a Kyōgen troupe is holding its special all-Kyōgen program, which has recently become quite popular among young people. A Nō program that presents Nō and Kyōgen in an alternating manner reflects the wisdom of the ancient originator of this method, reinforcing the program with totally opposite elements.

Nō programs are usually presented in the Nō theatre where the unique arrangement of the stage and the auditorium area is set by ancient convention. About 20 feet square, most stages today are kept indoors, sheltered by an outer architectural shell, but still covered by the roof, held by the four pillars marking the four corners of the stage. The stage proper is surrounded by the audience on the front and on one side by a long corridor. On the extension stage left sits a group of eight chorus members, facing the audience on the stage right side, while on the extension up stage, three or four musicians sit facing straight toward the audience in front. The long corridor connects with the stage at the point of up right and with the mirror room on the other end. This room is furnished with a wall mirror in which actors can observe themselves when they don their masks. In addition, all characters and musicians make entrances from this room.

Polished Japanese cypress wood is used for the entire stage. Decoration is kept at a minimum, reflecting major characteristics of the Nō and Kyōgen, that is, elimination of the excess in reality and the expression of the essence of the being. The only permanent decor is an old pine tree painted on the backboard; a few bamboos on the side board; three live, small pine trees along the corridor spaced at a proper distance; and a five-colored, vertically striped drape at the corridor entranceway. Some plays require one or two so-called structured pieces, which are basically an outline of a gate, a boat, a hut, and so forth, made of bamboo pieces and wrapped with strips of white and/or red tape. In the case of one particular play, *Dōjōji*, a large bell is woven. It is completely wrapped with purple damask and hung from the center of the stage roof. These pieces help to suggest rather symbolically an environment in which the main character appears.

The use of masks is one of the significant characteristics of Nō and Kyōgen. In Nō the masks are mostly employed by the principal character (*shite*), who is frequently the ghost of a man or a woman, or a supernatural being. Sometimes accompanying characters (*tsure*) may also wear masks. The secondary character (*waki*) never wears a mask, since he is a live person, frequently a priest who is making his pilgrimage. He is, in a sense, an intermediary who brings the world of the dead or supernatural to the present world of the audience.

The masks worn in Kyōgen plays are those of exaggeration. Their use is limited to the human characters of gross attributes, supernatural beings, beastly characters, and the spirits of certain creatures, such as a mushroom or a crab. Both Nō and Kyōgen masks are carved out of cypress wood with utmost artistry and treasured as valuable artifacts.

The essential qualities of the masks were so firmly set by the mid-seventeenth century that even when a new mask is made it usually follows the features of the famous mask of the same kind. In other words, copies have been made, but a truly original work has not been made for centuries. Such is the nature of the masks and of the Nō and Kyōgen theatre.

The availability of the Nō stage was eased somewhat when each of the three major schools in Tokyo had its own theatre built after World War II. It is not unusual, however, to find certain groups of Nō performers renting available stages when their school does not own a theatre or when their own theatre is not available. If a group rents a theatre, it tends to use the same stage when the program takes place regularly. In main cities, such as Tokyo and Kyoto, a number of performances take place throughout the year, except in July and August.

The addresses of the main Nō stages mentioned in the following pages are listed below. "Nōgakudō" means Nō stage or Nō theatre.

In Tokyo:

1. Ginza Nōgakudō (capacity: 120), 6-5-15, Ginza, Chuō-ku, Tokyo (Nōgakudō Bldg. 8F).

2. Hōshō Nōgakudō (capacity: 501), 1-5-9, Hongō, Bunkyo-ku, Tokyo.

3. Kanze Nōgakudō (capacity: 540), 1-16-4, Shōtō, Shibuya-ku, Tokyo.

4. Kita Roppeita Kinen Nōgakudō (capacity: 350), 4-6-9, Kami-Osaki, Shinagawa-ku, Tokyo.

5. Kokuritsu Nōgakudō (capacity: 591), 4-18-1, Sendagaya, Shibuya-ku, Tokyo. To supplement Kokuritsu Gekijo (the National Theatre) in Chiyoda-ku, Tokyo, a National Nō Theatre was built, in September 1983. It is more than a theatre for performance as its plan calls for the training of future professionals in the field as well as for providing research staff and facilities.

6. Kunaichō Shikibu Shikigakubu (the Department of Ceremonies in the Imperial Household Agency), (capacity: 150), Kōkyo-nai, Chiyoda-ku, Tokyo.

7. Tessenkai Butai (capacity: 150), 4-21-29, Minami Aoyama, Minato-ku, Tokyo.

8. Umewaka Nōgaku Gakuin Kaikan Butai (capacity: 308), 2-6-14, Higashi-Nakano, Nakano-ku, Tokyo.

9. Yarai Nōgakudō, (capacity: 250), 60, Yarai-cho, Shinjuku-ku, Tokyo.

In Kyoto and Nara:

1. Knogō Nōgakudō (capacity: 500), Shijō Agaru, Muromachi-dōri, Nakagyō-ku, Kyoto.

2. Kyoto Kanze Kaikan (capacity: 510), 44, Enshōji, Okazaki, Sakyō-ku, Kyoto.

3. Nara Komparu Nōgakudō (capacity: 250), 14, Horen Minami-machi, Nara.

In Osaka:

Osaka Nōgaku Kaikan (capacity: 532), 2-3-17, Nakazaki-Nishi, Kita-ku, Osaka.

In Nagoya:

Atsuta Jingū Nōgakuden (capacity: 500) 1, Shinmiyazaka-cho, Atsuta-ku, Nagoya.

All Japanese names appearing in this section (excluding contributors) are listed in the traditional Japanese way, with family name first and given name second, unless the name contains a Westernized portion.

ANDREW T. TSUBAKI

Five Nō Schools

Hōshō-ryū

Hōshō-ryū began with Ren'ami, brother of Zeami, the second head of the Kanze school. The sixteenth head of the Hōshō school, Kuro Tomoharu (1837–1917), with the first Umewaka Minoru and Sakurama Bamba, were called three great masters of the Meiji era (1868–1911). The present head is the eighteenth, Hōshō Fusai (1920–). Second only to the Kanze school, the Hōshō school retains 149 members of Nōgaku Kyōkai (including thirty-one holders of the title of Intangible Cultural Asset).

The performance activities of this school were based earlier in Kanazawa, situated in the midpart of the main island facing the Japan Sea; presently, its foundation is in Tokyo, and it has been quite active in a wide range of activities. The current repertoire of this school numbers 180 plays. The performance activities are presented through the following production series:

1. Hōshō-kai: Organized by the head of Hōshō school, this series is performed on the second Sunday of each month in the Hōshō Nō Stage in Tokyo, which reopened in June 1979 after extensive rebuilding. They have two additional performances, one in the spring and one in the fall.

2. Goun-kai: This series takes on the characteristics of studio performances, reflecting the result of study by young veteran performers of the school. It is performed on the third Saturday of each month.

3. Hōshō Sēnen-Nō: This series is presented by the youthful performers of the Hōshō school on Wednesdays of even numbered months.

4. Hōshō-ryū Fujin-Nō: This is a performance presented by the female performers of the Hōshō school in February of each year.

5. Nagoya Hōshō Jōshiki-Nō: Three times a year, the Nagoya branch of the Hōshō school presents this production at the Atsuta Shrine Nō Stage.

6. Fukui Nōgaku-kai Kanshō-Nō: Three times a year, the Fukui branch of the Hōshō school presents performances at the Fukui Nō Stage.

Kanze-ryū

The beginning of the Kanze school is traced to the father and son artists, Kannami (1333–1384) and Zeami (1363–1443), who are credited with perfecting the art of Nō theatre. Currently, the school is represented by the twenty-fifth Kanze Motomasa (1930–) and holds the greatest influence among the five Nō schools. It has 681 members of Nōgaku Kyōkai (including 145 holders of the title of Intangible Cultural Asset). Various branches of this school hold regular performing activities in such cities as Tokyo, Kyoto, Osaka, Kobe, Nagoya, and on Kyūshu Island. Because of the school's large membership, it holds not only formal performances of the Kanze school but also a number of productions individually, according to the various groups within the school and under the tutorship of various leading masters. The current repertoire of the Kanze school is 210 plays.

1. Kanze-kai Teiki-nō: This most important series of Nō performances of the Kanze school is organized by the head of the school, Motomasa. The performance was presented on the stage for sixty-some years in Omagari in Tokyo but was moved to Shōtō in Tokyo in 1972 after the Omagari stage was disassembled because of congestion in the area. Performances are held the first Sunday of each month.

2. Kanze-kai Yanō: This series of performances is organized by the veteran performers of the Kanze-ryū school, who make up a group called the Kanze-kai Yanō Dōjin-kai and perform on the second Thursday of odd months.

3. Kenkyū-kai: This series is sponsored by the group of disciples who are taught directly by Motomasa. The performances are held the fourth Thursday of each month.

4. Tessen-kai: Organized by the eighth Kanze Tetsunojō (1931– , head of the cadet family of the Kanze school), the Tessen-kai perform on the second Friday of each month at the Hōshō Stage in Tokyo. In addition to the regular performances, they add two to three productions of a special nature.

5. Umewaka-kai: This is a series of regular performances, organized by the Umewaka family, which has a history of a few hundred years. Currently, the family is headed by Umewaka Rokunojo (1948–). Their performances take place on the third Sunday of each month at the Umewaka Nō Stage. In addition, there are two performances annually at the Umewaka-kai Kyoto branch.

6. Umewaka-Kennō-kai: Organized by the thirteenth Umewaka Manzaburo (1908–), this series of Nō performances is on the third Thursday of every month at the Kanze Nō Stage in Tokyo.

7. Tokyo Baiyū-kai: First organized by Umewaka Naoyoshi (1911–1972), who was the brother of Manzaburo, after Naoyoshi's death this series was taken over by his son, Noriyoshi. They perform on the second Wednesday of odd months at the Kanze Nō Stage in Tokyo.

8. Kyūkō-kai: Under the guidance of Kanze Yoshiyuki (1935–), this series is performed on the second Sunday of each month in Yarai Nō Stage in Tokyo. In addition, the group holds other regular performances in several cities of Japan.

9. Kyoto Kanze-kai: Organized by the Kanze-kai in Kyoto, this series is performed on the fourth Sunday of each month at the Kanze Nō Stage of Kyoto. As the second largest Kanze association, the group also presents a number of performances in Kyoto sponsored by various masters of the Kanze school.

10. Osaka Kanze-kai: Sponsored by the Osaka branch of Kanze-kai, this series is performed four times a year—in March, June, September, and December—at the Osaka

Nō Stage. Here also are produced several independent performance series, which are put together by various masters of the Kanze school.

11. Kōbe Kanze-kai: Like the others, the series is sponsored by the Kōbe branch of the Kanze school. They perform in January, May, June, July, and December at the Nō stage of Minatogawa Shrine in Kōbe.

12. Nagoya Kanze-kai: This group has two series of performances sponsored by the Nagoya branch of the Kanze school. One series takes place in odd numbered months, while the other takes place four times in even numbered months at the Atsuta Shrine Nō Stage in Nagoya.

In addition, various regular performances take place once or twice a year, each sponsored by various masters of the Nō school. Recently, it has been popular to have takigi-Nō (a Nō performance under the torchlight) in the courtyards of temples and shrines on the temporary stage, during the season from spring to fall.

Kita-ryū

This school was added to the old four in 1618 with the permission of the Shogun, Tokugawa Hidetada. The head of the Kita clan then was Kita Shichidayu. Kita-kai was the association established in 1892 to back the activities of the fourteenth head of the Kita school, Kita Rokuheita (1874–1971). Holding 190 plays in their repertoire, this school distinguishes itself by including newly written plays in its repertoire. There are about ten such works. Currently, Kita Minoru (1900–), the fifteenth head of the school, leads its fifty-odd members of the Nōgaku Kyōkai, including eighteen Intangible Cultural Assets. All the performances organized by this association are staged at the Kita Rokuheita Memorial Nō Stage in Tokyo.

1. Kita Rei-kai: Totaling ten performances annually, this series is performed on the second Sunday in the months of January and December and on the fourth Sunday for the months of February, March, May, June, July, August, September, and October. They present three to four Nō and some Kyōgen plays.

2. Kita Bekkai: Offered twice a year in April and November, this series involves three to four Nō and some Kyōgen plays.

3. Sēnen Kita-kai: Twice annually, in April or May and December, four Nō and some Kyōgen plays are presented by young performers in the Sēnen Kita-kai program.

4. Kasui-kai: Once between February and April, and then again in September, three Nō and some Kyōgen plays are performed by the young veterans in the Kasui-kai program.

5. Nō ni Shitashimu-kai: This series is unique in that most newly written Nō plays are performed here. These plays, choreographed by Kita Minoru, usually include two Nō plays in which Kita Minoru and a member from Kasui-kai will take parts. Some Kyōgen accompanies the Nō plays.

In addition to the above, there are two worthy series of performances by other members of the school. Awaya Kyōdai Nō is staged by four Awaya brothers and their children, led by Awaya Shintaro. They perform twice annually in

March and October. There is also Tomoeda-kai, which presents the father and son performers, Tomoeda Kikuo and Akiyo.

Komparu-ryū

This school of Nō performers has been in existence since the fourteenth century. Born in 1920 and living in Tokyo, Nobutaka is the head of the Komparu clan. He is seventy-ninth generation. The troupe has about eighty members of the Nōgaku Kyōkai (including eight holders of the title of Intangible Cultural Asset). Performing about 160 plays, the troupe presents the fewest number of plays among the five schools. It has reached this number after reviving some major plays in recent years. Although the troupe has a Nō stage in Nara, it has none in Tokyo, and so it performs there by borrowing stages belonging to other schools. The following are the major performances presented by this school:

1. Komparu-kai: Several Tuesdays of March, April, May, June, September, and October are chosen to present this performance by the veteran performers of the Komparu school. In Tokyo there are five productions each year in the Hōshō Nō Stage. In addition, there are four performances in Nara and one in Osaka. They present two Nō plays and one Kyōgen play.

2. Sanshunkai-shōkai: This is a new group developed from Sanshunkai which maintained a high standard with the three performers: Komparu Nobutaka, Honda Hideo, and Umemura Heishirō. After the death of Hideo and Heishirō, Yasuki (the son of Nobutaka), Mitsuhiro (the son of Hideo), and Yokoyama Shinichi, three veterans of the younger generation, renewed the original performance series. They perform twice annually in May and November in Yarai Nō Stage of Tokyo, presenting three Nō plays and one Kyōgen.

3. Sakurama-kai: This series of performances stars Sakurama Kintaro in the Kanze Nō Stage of Tokyo and is performed four times annually in April, June, October, and November. The program consists of two Nō plays and one Kyōgen play.

4. Hōshun-kai: This series of performances presented by female Nō performers of the Komparu school is guided by Komparu Nobutaka. Completing twenty years of activity in 1981, this group plays four or five times annually on Thursdays in April, June, September, and November at Umewaka Nō Stage in Tokyo, presenting two Nō plays and one Kyōgen play.

Other significant performances by the veteran performers of this school include the programs by Sakurama Michio's group, by Komparu Yasuaki and his patron's, by Komparu Kinzō's, and by "Wadachi," the group led by Honda Mitsuhiro and Seo Kikuji.

Kongō-ryū

The death of Kongō Ukyō in 1936 terminated the Kongō family of Sakado which had continued since the fourteenth century. Kongō Iwao (1886–1951), the son of Kinnosuke, the Nō performer in Kyoto, was recommended by the heads of four other schools and became the first head of the Kongō school with the new family line. Presently, the second Iwao of the Kongō family (1924–)

heads the school. It has eighty members of the Nōgaku Kyōkai (including six holders of the title of the Intangible Cultural Asset) and performs mainly at the Kongō Nō Stage in Kyoto. It retains about 200 plays in its repertoire. Major performances are as follows:

1. Kongō Teikinō: This group meets in its own Kongō Nō Stage in Kyoto nine times a year (January, February, April, May, June, September, October, November, and December) and presents three Nō plays and one Kyōgen. It meets on the fourth Saturday in April and October, the second Sunday in December, and the fourth Sunday in the other months.

2. Tokyo Kongō-kai: Begun in 1938, the Tokyo Kongō-kai performs on the second Saturday of March and September in Tokyo (recently at the Kita Nō Stage) and presents two Nō plays and one Kyōgen.

3. Kongō Sēnen-kai: Composed of younger veteran players who perform four times a year (May, June, July, and August), the Kongō Sēnen-kai presents two or three Nō plays at the Kongō Nō Stage in Kyoto.

4. and 5. Hōshun-kai and Teshima Nō no kai: In the spring and fall, these two groups give performances by professionals such as Teshima Michiharu, Teshima Kunzo, Teshima Keizaburo, and Teshima Kazuyoshi.

There is also a Nō program sponsored by the patrons of the Hirotas, which stars Hirota Kaiichi, Hirota Taizo, and Hirota Sachiminoru.

Other Important Performances of Nō Theatre

There are several Nō theatre events of a special nature. They are presented frequently with the cooperation of all five schools, breaking away from the usual presentation by performers of a single school. Some of these events have considerable value and, hence, are included here.

1. Shiki-Nō: The performance of the formal or full-scale program is staged infrequently because of its time demand. The modern tendency is to have only three Nō plays in a program, but once a year this full-scale, grand program is staged in February, concurrently in Tokyo and Osaka, with the cooperation of the five schools. In Tokyo the Hōshō Stage is used and in Osaka the Nōgaku-Kaikan. The performance begins with *Okina*, the oldest Nō play, followed by one from each of the five groups of Nō plays, performed by each of the five schools. Four Kyōgen plays will be presented between each two Nō plays. The performance stretches from 10:00 A.M. to 7:00 P.M. but is broken into two parts, the first half beginning at 10:00 A.M. and the second at 3:30 P.M. The house is cleared after the first half of the performance so that a new audience will view the second. The sponsor of the program is the Nōgaku Kyōkai.

2. Hayashika-Kyōgikai-Nō: This is also an event in which all five schools participate. There are three performances a year on the fourth Wednesday in February, May, and September, organized by the Hayashika-Kyōgikai (the Association of Nō Musicians)

and presented at the Kanze Nō Stage in Tokyo. Each program consists of several pieces of dance music, one Nō play, and one Kyōgen play.

3. Ginza Teiki-Nō: At the Ginza Nō Stage which was opened in 1979, one Nō and one Kyōgen are played in the even numbered months by the five schools in rotation.

4. Nō o Shiru Kai (A Performance to Get to Know Nō): Four performances are presented annually in the months of January, April, July, and October at the Kita Roppeita Memoril Nō Stage in Tokyo. The organizer is Nakamori Shōzō, a veteran performer of the Kanze school. He has been promoting the better understanding and wider acceptance of Nō for a number of years, basing his activities at the Kamakura Nō Stage.

5. Takigi-Nō: Staging Nō performances under the torch (*takigi*) light has recently become popular throughout Japan. A temporary stage in the courtyards of temples and shrines is set up during the season from spring to fall. The major events of this type are seen in eastern Japan, namely at the Zōjōji of Tokyo in April; at the Kawasaki Daishi of Kawasaki and the Naritazan Shinshōji of Chiba in May; at the Hi-e-jinjya, the Gokokuji, the Sensōji of Tokyo, and the Samukawa-jinjya of Kanagawa in August; and at the Daitōgū of Kamakura in September. In western Japan, the performance takes place at the Heian-Jingū of Kyoto and the Uji-jinjya of Uji in July; at the Ikutama-jinjya of Osaka in August; and at the Gokoku-jinjya of Hiroshima in October.

Two Kyōgen Schools

In Kyōgen, two major schools exist: Okura-ryū, established in the fifteenth century; and Izumi-ryū, founded in the beginning of the eighteenth century. Until about 1910, a third school, Sagi-ryū, existed. The Okura school served the Tokugawa Shogunate while the Izumi school served a branch of the Tokugawa family in Owari. Presently, Okura Yatarō (1912–) is head of the Okura school. About seventy performers belong to this school, which has about 180 plays in its repertoire. Izumi Motohide (1925–), the eldest son of Miyake Tōkuro (1902–), heads the Izumi school. With approximately thirty performers, the school has about 250 Kyōgen plays in its repertoire.

The Kyōgen performers participate in a Nō play by taking roles of Ai-Kyōgen. In addition, they perform an independent play (humorous plays), presented between two Nō plays. Various Kyōgen families present their own series of all Kyōgen programs several times a year. Among the important Kyōgen performances are the following:

1. Okura-kai: In September of each year, the head of Okura-ryū sponsors a great production of Kyōgen in the Hōshō Nō Stage in Tokyo. The program contains four Kyōgen plays.

2. Okura-kai Ginza: The members of the Okura school perform four times a year, in February, April, July, and November, staging two Kyōgen plays each in the Ginza Nō Stage of Tokyo.

3. Shigeyama Kyōgen-kai: This important series of performances is organized by the Shigeyama family (a clan belonging to the Okura-ryū) who stage four Kyōgen plays for two consecutive days in January and October, in the Kanze Nō Stage of Kyoto.

4. Zenchiku Kyōgen no kai: Every June, the Zenchiku family (a clan of the Okura school) organizes a program of five Kyōgen plays in the Umewaka Nō Stage in Tokyo.

5. Izumi-kai: The head of the Izumi school organizes its performance of Kyōgen in May, September, and November, presenting three Kyōgen plays in the Hōshō Nō Stage.

6. Nomura Kyōgen no kai: The Nomura Manzō clan (a member of the Izumi school) presents five performances annually, in January, March, July, November, and December, in the Hōshō Nō Stage of Tokyo. Each time they perform three Kyōgen plays, and occasionally they invite Kyōgen performers of the Okura school.

7. Kyōgen Shin-no-kai: Represented by Yamamoto Norinao, Zenchiku Jūrō, and Nomura Mannosuke, this performance provides a stage for young veteran performers of both schools. The plays are performed in October in the Umewaka Nō Stage.

There are other important performance series, such as the Citizen's Kyōgen Performances in Kyoto, which produce Kyōgen performances in February, May, and December. Two other Kyōgen productions are staged in Kyoto. Also in Osaka in December, the series called Kuratake-kai presents four Kyōgen plays by the mixed members of the Okura and Zenchiku clan of the Okura school in the Osaka Nō Stage.

YASUHARU KOBAYASHI,
TAMOTSU MATSUDA, and
ANDREW T. TSUBAKI

BUNRAKU PUPPET THEATRE, KABUKI, AND OTHER COMMERCIAL THEATRE

In contrast to the patronage the warrior class gave to Nō and Kyōgen, Bunraku and Kabuki grew with the support of the merchant class, which became increasingly wealthy but lacked political power. The warrior class was able to maintain its feudalistic rule over the general public through the establishment of the Tokugawa Shogunate, whose reign spanned from 1603 to 1868 when the modernization of Japan began. Prior to the ascent of Yeyasu to the first Shogunate of Tokugawa, Kabuki and the early form of puppet theatre evolved. Before the Tokugawa reestablished the authority of the warrior class, several heads of the warring clans in medieval Japan eliminated one another, leaving only one at the top. Thus, relative calm was brought to the daily lives of the general public, who in turn became interested in developing their own entertainment. When they saw these performing art forms coming their way, they gladly accepted them.

An early form of puppet theatre in Japan, which involved essentially hand puppets, was a crude one. It came to Japan from the Asian continent as early as the eighth century. In its developed form, it successfully combined Jōruri chanting of the fifteenth century and the three-stringed instrument known as *shamisen*, whose original form, *jabisen*, arrived in Japan in the sixteenth century. This theatre form not only combined effectively the varied and yet useful elements of other art forms to strengthen itself, but also continued to improve through the seventeenth and into the eighteenth century, dominating the theatre scene of the general public.

While Kabuki was struggling to establish its identity as a mature performing art form, as late as the mid-seventeenth century, the puppet theatre (known formally as Ningyō Jōruri—the doll theatre with Jōruri-style chanting) was benefited enormously by the superbly talented playwright, Chikamatsu Monzaemon (1653–1724). Ironically, Chikamatsu began his career with Kabuki but switched to the puppet theatre as a result of the lowly position of the playwright in the Kabuki world. After his death, the puppet theatre invented a method of manipulating an over 3-foot tall puppet with three men, thus, adding the capability of intricate expression on the puppet's face as well as elaborate body movements, particularly with the puppet's hands and arms.

After the mid-eighteenth century, Kabuki finally caught up with the puppet theatre in popularity, having benefited by borrowing heavily from the solidly written plays and clever blocking of the puppet theatre and having added its own innovation in stage devices and vastly improved acting. Meanwhile, the puppet theatre managed to remain a viable form of theatre through these years, despite its slow decline. In 1871 Daizō, the fourth Bunraku-ken, opened in Osaka, and his theatre was named Bunraku-za; the name of "Bunraku" began to be used to represent the form itself.

Both Bunraku and Kabuki developed separate troupes and theatres in the Kyoto/Osaka area and Edo (today's Tokyo) from its early days. While Kabuki managed to foster two separate styles of acting, one from each area, Bunraku has not taken that path. In the early nineteenth century, the activities of Edo puppet theatre declined. Throughout these years the center of Bunraku has been Osaka, although it has regularly toured to Tokyo.

The beginning of Kabuki in Kyoto was an eye-catching event. A simple prayer and folk dances by an all-girl troupe, led by Okuni, seem to have ignited the passion for a more attractive, free form of entertainment that differed from Nō and Kyōgen. The form was to be known as Kabuki. The term originally meant to be different, unbalanced, abnormal, which was in contrast to the formal and reserved Nō theatre. These girls' troupes began presenting a loosely structured dance-drama portraying a young warrior (played by a beautiful woman) visiting the entertainment quarter and being entertained by dancing girls. Soon young boys' troupes developed, doing similar performances; both were banned for their immoral activities, the girls in 1629 and the boys in 1652. This oppressive censorship taken by the Shogunate indicates the enormous attraction Kabuki generated in those days.

After repeated petitions from the Kabuki personnel, the Shogunate allowed Kabuki to be reopened in 1653 with the stern condition that no actor was to leave his forelock unshaven. Women's participation in Kabuki as actresses had been completely banned earlier. Thus, having the Kabuki destined to rely on actors to portray female characters, the custom actually became one of the major characteristics of Kabuki known as *onnagata* (female impersonation). The unshaven forelock was a commonly practiced convention of young men at pre-adulthood, a symbol of charm in a youthful actor. The Kabuki world responded by having all actors shave the forelock but did not terminate its use of young boys. More importantly, the Kabuki world had to find a more serious way to develop an art form that did not rely so completely on the sex appeal of women or young boys. The content of production had to change from a fluffy musical dance show to a drama in its truest sense.

Along with the puppet theatre, Kabuki had been played widely all over Japan; after 1653, as the serious attempt for the survival of this genre began and as the need for *onnagata* actors increased, the Kyoto/Osaka area became quite adept at bringing up superb *onnagata*. The Edo Kabuki, on the other hand, reflecting the rather coarse but macho tendency of Edo people, succeeded in developing the acting style of strong male characters.

While the Kyoto/Osaka Kabuki excelled in the detailed and refined portrayal of a softer mood dealing with the entertainment quarter populated by the beautiful woman and the genteel man, the Edo Kabuki produced the bravado style with enormous exaggeration not only in action and gestures but also in vocalization, costumes, and make-up. By the mid-eighteenth century, Kabuki had established itself firmly in all aspects of production: acting, playwriting, theatre building, stage facilities, and the system of transmitting the acting tradition.

What Kabuki accomplished is no small matter. In the words of Kawatake Shigetoshi:

Kabuki offered but also absorbed the useful elements of their art. Furthermore, it combined the considerable amount of Ningyo Jōruri characteristics into Kabuki. It was able to develop complex musical plays and dance drama. In a word we can say that the Kabuki updated and popularized a variety of performing art forms of earlier and contemporary times. It crystalized itself into a total theatre form which is based on the amalgamation of complex and diverse elements. [*Nihon Engeki Zenshi*, p. 225]

Chikamatsu Monzaemon made a great contribution in playwriting for both Kabuki and Bunraku in the early stages; the Kawatake Mokuami (1816–1893) also provided a significant amount of worthwhile plays immediately before Kabuki was confronted with the drastically changing world after the Meiji Restoration in 1868. The degree of change in Japan was quite thorough in every phase of life. Kabuki had undergone many significant changes to cope with the new way of life: new theatre buildings, new facilities including night-time performance, and even a changed manner of acting, which was less exaggerated and more true to life.

A number of attempts were made to modernize Kabuki; each time Kabuki only spun off from such an attempt, allowing it to form itself into a mode somewhat akin to Kabuki in acting style but more modern in the dramatization of plots that dealt with situations new to people. These spin-off activities reached a significant stage up to the immediate postwar years; today these forms are barely active. They are known as Shimpa (New School) and Shinkokugeki (New National Theatre).

In addition, there are several theatre troupes whose main purpose is to provide profitable, live entertainment through theatre to the public. In a way they can be compared with those large-scale Broadway productions whose raison d'être is to make money by entertaining the public. Despite the newness of their plays, the manner in which they present them tends to be rather quaint in comparison with that of Shingeki (New Theatre) or of post-Shingeki theatre. Nonetheless, plays staged by these commercial companies are quite popular among certain audiences. Most of the companies are owned by the Tōhō. The following sections present information dealing with theatre companies and theatre facilities for Bunraku, Kabuki, and other commercial theatres.

For the following portion of individualized troupe activities, Fujita Hiroshi provided useful information. Mr. Fujita is president of Engeki Shuppansha and editor of *Engekikai* (*The World of Theatre*). He is the author of *Onnagata no Keizu* (*The Lineage of Onnagata*), *Engeki Nempō* (*Annual Report on Theatre*), *Ganjiro no Saigetsu* (*The Years of Ganjiro*), and other books.

Bunraku

BUNRAKU KYŌKAI
(The Bunraku Association)
1, Higashiyagura-cho, Minami-ku, Osaka 542, Japan

Theatres

ASAHI-ZA
(seating capacity—1,000)
1, Higashiyagura-cho, Minami-ku, Osaka 542, Japan

Performances in January, April, July, and October.

KOKURITSU BUNRAKU GEKIJŌ
(The National Bunraku Theatre, seating capacity—730)
1-12-15, Nihonbashi, Minami-ku, Osaka 542, Japan

KOKURITSU GEKIJO
(The Small Hall of the National Theatre, seating capacity—618)
4-1, Hayabusa-cho, Chiyoda-ku, Tokyo 102, Japan

Performances in February, May, September, and December.

As was pointed out earlier, the theatre named Bunraku-za was built in Osaka by the fourth Bunraku-ken in September 1871. This new theatre was opened to counter the threat imposed by the opening of Hikoroku-za in the spring of the same year by the rival puppet theatre company of the same name. After centuries of illustrious activities of Ningyō Jōruri, the puppet theatre was in intense competition once again, but this time it involved only these two remaining companies in Osaka. The long, slow decline of the puppet theatre was arrested. Actually, the increased popularity of the Bunraku troupe was such that it reached a new peak under the management of the sixth Bunraku-ken, Taizō. But this same Taizō failed miserably in an outside business venture and had to sell the entire contents of the theatre, along with the building and the troupe itself to the Shōchiku Gōmei (the Shōchiku Company) in 1909.

At that time a record shows there were thirty-eight chanters, fifty-one *shamisen* players, and twenty-four puppeteers. These figures provide an interesting base for measuring the relative strength of the present Bunraku Kyōkai, which is now the sole Bunraku puppet theatre with a national and international reputation, excluding several other local puppet theatre companies that operate more at the folk art level. According to a report of the National Theatre, as of October 1980 the employees of the Bunraku Kyōkai included twenty-four chanters, eighteen *shamisen* players, and thirty-two puppeteers.

Since the National Theatre put its training program into practice for Bunraku, a number of young professionals have joined the company. Obviously, a grave shortage in the number of chanters and *shamisen* players remains, but a definite increase in young professionals and in young audience members is a healthy sign of recovery.

Bunraku has become so popular in the past few years that tickets for all performances are sold very quickly. Such a recovery seemed unthinkable when one looks back on the days of the struggle of the Shōchiku Company to maintain performance activities after World War II. In 1948 awakening labor unionism influenced the Bunraku artists. The Shōchiku Company suffered from two divided groups of the artists, one against and the other for the company. Despite such a difficult time, the Shōchiku Company managed to build a new theatre, Bunraku-za, in the middle of the old theatre and commercial area of Osaka, known as Dōtombori in 1956.

The Bunraku is the only professional theatre company that receives an annual subsidy from the government's Ministry of Education. The subsidy was given at first to defray part of the loss of the Shōchiku Company suffered after the war and later to aid the Bunraku Kyōkai, founded in 1963 combining the two dissenting groups. The Shōchiku Company yielded its ownership of Bunraku to the Bunraku Kyōkai, which assumed the management of all phases of the operation of the theatre company.

The Bunraku-za, renovated in 1963 and given the new name of Asahi-za, owned still by the Shōchiku Company, has been the base of the Bunraku Kyōkai. When it tours Tokyo, the Small Hall of the National Theatre is regularly used. Performances are divided equally, four months each between the two cities. Having opened in April 1984, the National Bunraku Theatre is a thoroughly new building located further south of the Asahi-za in Osaka. The portion of Bunraku performances to be presented in the new theatre is not clear at this time, but it is expected to help a great deal of Bunraku and other performing arts in Osaka.

The repertory of Bunraku leaned heavily on classical pieces, frequently sharing a number of famous favorites with Kabuki and yet retaining its uniqueness. Combining three groups of artists who work in complete unison, the company demonstrates magnificent team work by fusing technique and artistic imagination, both executed at their highest level.

For further information on its activities, see "Shōchiku."

Kabuki

SHŌCHIKU KABUSHIKI GAISHA
(The Shōchiku Jointstock Corporation)
1-13-5 Chuō-ku, Tokyo 104, Japan

Theatres

KABUKI-ZA
(seating capacity—2,066)
4-12-15, Ginza, Chuō-ku, Tokyo 104, Japan

KOKURITSU GEKIJO
(The National Theatre, seating capacity—1,850)
4-1 Hayabusa-chō, Chiyoda-ku, Tokyo 102, Japan

SHINBASHI EMBUJO
(seating capacity—1,428)
6-18-2 Ginza, Chuō-ku, Tokyo 104, Japan

SUNSHINE GEKIJO
(seating capacity—832)
3-1-4 Higashi Ikebukuro, Toshima-ku, Tokyo 170, Japan

Kabuki actors are employed by a single company, Shōchiku Kabushiki Gaisha (hereafter referred to as the Shōchiku). Kabuki actors move a great deal from one troupe to another, such shifts being the norm rather than the exception in this unique theatre world. This reflects partially the large number of "star" actors involved in the trade and also the enormous amount of money spent to run the business.

The complex organization of the Kabuki becomes easier to understand once one accepts a simple fact: the Kabuki theatre troupe is actually made up of several groups, each headed by a few name actors as leaders and performing independently of each other, even though all are the employees of Shōchiku. The Shōchiku has several theatre buildings available to the productions through their ownership or exclusive lease arrangement. The theatres most frequently used by Kabuki are listed above. The Shōchiku owns other theatres outside Tokyo which the Kabuki may utilize when one of the groups is on tour.

The National Theatre, which opened in 1966, became a producer of Kabuki productions, leasing a troupe of Kabuki actors from the Shōchiku to stage classical Kabuki plays in their totality. This is in contrast to the usual pattern of the Kabuki program of having several famous acts from different plays. When Kabuki is presented in the National Theatre, there is a single evening performance, instead of the usual double bill of separate matinee and evening programs as presented in all other Kabuki productions by the Shōchiku.

The Shinbashi Embujo is leased by the Shōchiku, while the Sunshine Gekijo is a new building opened in 1978. The Shōchiku runs its program.

The Kabuki-za, the home base of the Kabuki theatre, has been run by the Shōchiku since 1913. It was built in 1889 as one of several new theatres breaking away from the old style facilities. With a seating capacity of 2,066, it was decorated with a Western-style brick wall and a chandelier in the middle of the auditorium illuminating it with electricity to daytime brightness. But in 1911, a daringly Westernized theatre building was opened as the Teikoku Gekijo (the Imperial Theatre) just across from the Imperial Palace moat. This theatre helped revolutionize the attitude of the theatre audience and their theatregoing habits. The modernization of the theatre was truly taking a good hold in every aspect of theatre, finally breaking away from the habits of the archaic Edo period.

Feeling threatened by the Imperial Theatre, the Kabuki-za decided to extensively remodel its exterior with the decor of the ornate, traditional architectural characteristics of the Momoyama period (1583–1602). This style can still be seen in the present-day Kabuki-za. It was burned in 1921, and during the rebuilding, Tokyo suffered the 1923 earthquake. The concrete structure of the rebuilt theatre was eventually what we see in today's Kabuki-za, but the building suffered fire damage caused by bombing during World War II.

The Shōchiku was the product of the twin brothers Shirai Matsujiro (1877–1951) and Otani Takejiro (1877–1969). After a modest success in theatre management in Kyoto, the brothers founded the Shōchiku Gōmeisha in 1902. In 1909, as mentioned in the Bunraku entry, they bought out the Bunraku-za and its operation. Beginning in 1912 they hired Kabuki actors, luring them away from their companies; and they finally managed to put themselves in a position to be asked to run the Kabuki-za in 1913. After buying four theatres in Tokyo and Kyoto/Osaka, they added a movie company. In 1929 they expanded the company, not only by having its branch of land and entertainment operation joined with the main company but also by acquiring the management right of the Imperial Theatre, thus placing all Kabuki actors under their control. After another expansion, which joined the Kabuki-za and two other theatres in Tokyo to the company in 1931, they unified the total operation in 1937 and founded the Shōchiku Kabushiki Gaisha, placing Otani as the president and Shirai as the chairman of the board.

Today, the Shōchiku ranks with the Tōhō as the two largest theatrical producing companies in Japan. Lately it has been diversifying its operations by entering into the so-called leisure industry. It contributed to the success of the Bunraku by maintaining it through the financially difficult time after the war, and it has helped the Kabuki by preserving its high artistic standard, which is now internationally recognized. Despite these great accomplishments, the Shōchiku has received some serious criticism for its efforts to make theatre a commercial commodity and an object of tourist attraction, as well as its wish to retain the daily double bill system at the risk of overworked actors and shortages in rehearsal time.

The names and leaders of several groups of Kabuki actors belonging to the Shōchiku are as follows.

Kikugoro Gekidan—After the death of Onoe Kikugoro VI in 1949, Onoe Baiko, Onoe Shōroku, and Ichimura Uzaemon swore their unity as a group for their betterment in the future. Today the weight of activities is shifting to their sons' generation. This group celebrated the thirtieth anniversary of the unity in 1978, which was an extremely rare occasion since all the other groups have lost their united front. At that time Onoe Baiko reportedly said, "I feel we somehow managed to get here. We hope our younger generation will take over from now on." His son, Kikugoro VII, responded, "We are in a severe situation which is different from that of my father's. For him and others to inherit the art of the Kikugoro VI was the primary concern, but for us it is now the matter of whether or not we can maintain the Kabuki itself."

Nakamura Kichiemon Gekidan—Since the death of Kichiemon I in 1954, the group has not performed particularly under the banner of the Kichiemon Group. Rather, it maintains cooperation among Nakamura Utaemon, Nakamura Kanzaburo, Matsumoto Kōshiro, and the present Kichiemon.

Ichikawa Ennosuke is a unique actor whose vitality is creating an energetic, spectacular trend for Kabuki productions. He makes a point of presenting his performance with an easily understandable story line. A charismatic figure, he is establishing a brand of Kabuki that has become widely accepted. His brother, Danshiro, provides strong support for him.

Shōgyō Engeki (Commercial Theatre)

While the term *shōgyō engeki* could include the activities of Kabuki in the sense that it is produced on a commercial basis, we have chosen to handle the Kabuki separately as a traditional form established with a clear distinction of its own. The troupes presented here as commercial companies are more varied than the Kabuki. Only two of the most significant troupes are discussed here: Tōhō Kabushiki Gaisha and Zenshin-za Engeki Eiga Kenkyūjo.

TŌHŌ KABUSHIKI GAISHA
(The Tōhō Jointstock Corporation)
1-2-1, Yūraku-chō, Chiyoda-ku, Tokyo 100, Japan

Theatres

TOKYO TAKARAZUKA GEKIJO
(seating capacity—3,000)
1-1-3, Yūraku-chō, Chiyoda-ku, Tokyo 100, Japan

TEIKOKU GEKIJO
(rebuilt in 1966, seating capacity—1,926)
3-1-1, Marunouchi, Chiyoda-ku, Tokyo 100, Japan

GEIJITSU-ZA
(seating capacity—710)
1-2-1, Yūraku-chō, Chiyoda-ku, Tokyo 100, Japan

Tōhō Kabushiki Gaisha (hereafter referred to as the Tōhō) is one of the two most powerful theatre companies in today's Japan, the Shōchiku being the other. The founder, Kobayashi Ichizo (1873–1957), came to Tokyo in 1932 with a design to build a theatre where his successful venture of Takarazuka Shōjo Kageki (Takarazuka Girls' Musical Company) of Hyōgo-ken (outside of Osaka) could be performed. After building a movie theatre in the following year, he went on to add another theatre, Tokyo Takarazuka Gekijo, in 1934. Erecting a few more theatres, including Geijitsu-za (the Art Theatre), Kobayashi proceeded to construct an amusement center in the Yūrakuchō area, right outside Ginza.

In addition to the Takarazuka Shōjo Kageki, the Tōhō hired almost forty actors and actresses after 1935 to organize a theatre troupe, including youthful Kabuki actors Nakamura Kanzaburo and Ichikawa Ebizo, giving a scare to the Shōchiku. The troupe, however, suffered from a weak performance record and was eventually dissolved in 1939.

Another troupe headed by a comedian, Furukawa Roppa, played a series of works written by Kikuta Kazuo and established a rather strong company catering particularly to the general public. The foundation laid by this successful attempt is still very much intact and continues to provide popular plays. In Geijitsu-za an original play has been played for two-month periods in the evening slot.

The new Teikoku Gekijo (the Imperial Theatre) has provided many popular musicals, marking a record in a long run with *Fiddler on the Roof* with Morishige Hisaya, a famous comedian. Ichikawa Somegoro, who recently assumed the name of Kōshiro IX, as a son of Matumoto Kōshiro VIII, has been a popular star in musicals such as *Man of La Mancha* and *The King and I*. He retains his credibility as a Kabuki actor and occasionally performs in that capacity.

The Tōhō began a program called "Tōhō Kabuki" in 1955 with big name movie stars, such as Hasegawa Kazuo and Yamada Isuzu, to provide a popular version of Kabuki with new plays. While the program is still viable, its offerings have become infrequent, no more than once or twice a year. In 1961 the Tōhō hired several Shōchiku name Kabuki actors, including Matsumoto Kōshiro VIII and Nakamura Matagoro II, to produce classical Kabuki, but this venture was short-lived. Today, when such a performance takes place, a number of Kabuki actors are hired especially to mount a production.

Just as the Shōchiku was active in moviemaking, the Tōhō also had its fair share beginning in 1936. The movie company joined with the Tōhō in 1943, but a labor strike began in 1946 and dragged on for about five years, leaving the company in desperate shape. The Tōhō recalled Kobayashi, who had retired earlier as president as a result of the purge directed against him for his wartime activities. He helped to revive the company's fortunes. Even so, the general weakening of the movie industry in Japan has taken its toll on the Tōhō, as it has on the Shōchiku in the last twenty years or so, and the company's participation in this area has decreased significantly.

Zenshin-za

ZENSHIN-ZA ENGEKI EIGA KENKYŪJO
(March Forward Theatre Research Center for Theatre and Film)
2546, Kichijōji, Musashino-shi, Tokyo, Japan

This company is the only one of its kind, founded on idealistic principles in 1931 by the Kabuki actors Kawarasaki Chōjūrō and Nakamura Gan'emon. The company's goals are based on three principles: Any matters will be discussed by all; each will hold equal right and duty; salary for each will be determined by the general meeting. In other words, it aimed to destroy the feudalistic system in the theatre company and to promote a democratic management of the company.

Through a series of financial and artistic difficulties, the company toiled to accomplish its goals. It presented a Kabuki play, *Kanjincho*, in 1935, and it also began to make films with success. In 1937 it built the Research Center in Kichijōji where members began to live together. After the war years, the company concentrated on providing healthy theatre for youth. It toured schools, factories, and offices all over Japan, and it marked over six hundred performances of Shakespeare's *The Merchant of Venice*.

In 1949, all members of the company and some members of their families, numbering seventy-five in all, joined the Japanese Communist Party. This move somewhat restricted their ability to visit schools, but they energetically continued their tour activities and they added three more films.

Since 1953 Zenshin-za has also performed in established commercial theatres for a long run in an urban center. In 1958 the company returned to Tokyo to perform. At its thirtieth anniversary in 1961, it was invited to visit the People's Republic of China; seventy members participated in this tour.

The Zenshin-za stages both classical works of Kabuki, giving them a modern interpretation, and many original plays for audiences throughout Japan. At the end of a year's hectic production schedule in 1980, the company performed in the Kabuki-za in December after a long absence from it. The following year it celebrated its fiftieth anniversary.

It is remarkable that such a company as the Zenshin-za came to be organized among Kabuki actors. But it is even more impressive that it has survived for a half-century in good health and with as much zeal as it had at its start.

ANDREW T. TSUBAKI

SHINGEKI, THE NEW THEATRE OF JAPAN

Modern Japanese theatre was born and developed as a reaction against traditional theatre forms during the modernization of Japanese society following the Meiji Restoration in 1868. Through this endeavor Japan was transformed from a feudal society during the 260-year isolation period to a new and Westernized society. Traditional theatre forms such as Nō (a highly lyrical and symbolic form of drama that originated in the fourteenth century) and Kabuki (a relatively realistic form, known for its larger-than-life mode of expression, dating from the seventeenth century), soon became outdated and unrealistic, unable to respond directly to the needs of the general public.

Some tried to innovate the traditional theatre in order to survive. The New School Theatre (Shimpa) and the New National Theatre (Shinkoku-geki) appeared in answer to the need to modernize Kabuki. This effort was not sufficient. Against this background, a new theatre movement, based completely on a different tradition, was started by several courageous intellectuals, strongly influenced by European dramaturgy and production conventions. "Shin-geki," meaning "new theatre," became the only dramatic form that truly reflected the life and progressive mentality of young people and intellectuals living in this transitional period.

In the early years of Shingeki development, two prominent groups emerged. One of them was the Literature and Art Society (Bungei Kyōkai, 1906–1913), founded by two professors, Tsubouchi Shōyō (1859–1935) and Shimamura Hōgetsu (1871–1918), at Waseda University in Tokyo. Tsubouchi Shōyō was a translator of the complete works of Shakespeare, while Shimamura Hōgetsu was noted for his education at Oxford University and the University of Berlin. In 1911 they presented their first production by staging *Hamlet* in Tsubouchi's translation in Tokyo. After the dissolution of this society, Shimamura organized the Art Theatre (Geijutsu-za, 1913–1919). Its opening production was Ibsen's *A Doll's House* (1914). It is said that the phrase "Shingeki" first appeared in public in connection with this production.

About the same time, Osanai Kaoru (1881–1928), a novelist and director, and Ichikawa Sadanji II (1880–1940), a Kabuki actor, founded the Free Theatre (Jiyū Gekijō, 1909–1914). Named after A. Antoine's Théâtre Libre in France, this company was modeled on the Stage Society founded in 1899 in England. Their first performance starred many Kabuki actors and was a presentation of Ibsen's *John Gabriel Borkman* (1909). The plays they presented later consisted of the works of Anton Chekhov, Maxim Gorky, and Gerhart Hauptmann.

While the Tsubouchi group tried to eliminate all inadequate elements of the traditional theatre by training amateurs as their actors and actresses, Osanai's group relied upon a group of adventuresome Kabuki actors, including those who specialized in female impersonation, to stage mostly European plays. Although both collapsed while halfway through their attempts to establish New Theatre in Japan, their performances of Western drama made a strong impact upon the audiences.

In 1923 Tokyo and most of its surrounding area was devastated by a great earthquake. As a result, Hijikata Yoshi (1898–1959) discontinued his study of theatre in Germany, returning to Tokyo, where he built his own playhouse named Tsukiji Little Theatre (Tsukiji Shō-gekijō, 1924–1945) at Tsukiji in Tokyo, near the Kabuki-za. This wooden, Gothic-Romanesque playhouse with 468 seats was Japan's first structure built exclusively for staging Western plays. It has a stage equipped with a permanent sky dome (kuppelhorizont). On the wall above the front entrance, a picture of grapes was painted to suggest the Greek god, Bacchus, to tie the theatre with the Western theatre tradition.

Hijikata wisely enlisted Osanai as the leader of six (including himself) principal members of the acting company of the same name. With completion of the theatre in 1924, the company embarked on the most significant and energetic venture of the new theatre movement of Japan. A number of young apprentices later became founders, directors, and leading actors and actresses of many new troupes in the next generations of the new theatre activities. In this respect, the Tsukiji Little Theatre can be regarded as the true starting point of the New Theatre movement in Japan.

Among these apprentices were Senda Koreya, founder of the Actors' Theatre (Haiyū-za, 1944–), and Tamura Akiko, founder of the Tsukiji Theatre (Tsukiji-za, 1932–1936). Among the remaining members were those who organized the Troupe Tsukiji Theatre (Gekidan Tsukiji Gekijō, 1929–1930) after Hijikata seceded from the troupe to found the New Tsukiji Troupe (Shin-Tsukiji Gekidan, 1929–1940). Also included were Sugimura Haruko, who was to become the leading actress of the Literary Theatre (Bungaku-za, 1937–); Yamamoto Yasue, the founder of the Grape Society (Budō no Kai, 1948–1964); and Takizawa Osamu and Uno Jūkichi, the founders of the People's Art Theatre (Minshū Geijutsu Gekijō, 1947–1949). This was to be revived as the People's Art Theatre (Gekidan Mingei, 1950–) after dissolution of the earlier troupe.

Osanai Kaoru established the Tsukiji Little Theatre's policy of developing Japan's modern theatre foundation on the Western theatre tradition. As a result, the company staged mainly translated dramas: of the 117 plays performed only 27 were Japanese. Despite initial weakness, he presented all of these with an energy that was to become phenomenal. The repertoire of this troupe eventually included Chekhov's *The Cherry Orchard*, Ibsen's *Ghosts*, August Strindberg's *Miss Julie*, and Eugene O'Neill's *Beyond the Horizon*.

Starting about this period, the theatre movement in Japan began to be influenced by radical ideology, leading to the formation of several proletarian theatre companies, such as the New Cooperative Drama Group (Shinkyō Gekidan, 1934–1940). With the rise of militarism, however, the governmental suppression of leftist theatre movements intensified and finally resulted in the police ordering their members either to disband or to face imprisonment. Because of differences in ideologies and attitudes among the members toward the national cultural policy and of suppression by the government, many troupes disbanded. The exception to this general trend was the Literary Theatre, which had never adopted any radical political ideology, and, as a result, was allowed to remain active through World War II.

When we look back on the new theatre movement in Japan, we cannot find any essential difference in its activities between the prewar and postwar periods. After the end of World War II, the primary objective of the movement was to rebuild the troupes and their repertories in order to continue their performances. The popularity of the mass media, such as motion pictures and television, gained at an amazing pace. The increasing demands of movies and television provided the opportunity for actors to earn a decent living, and yet created a schism between the haves and the have-nots. Some of the popular starring actors, who were busy making money in the mass media, began to neglect their obligations to stage work, causing considerable trouble within the troupes.

The gravest shake-up to the troupes came in the 1960s when the worldwide antiestablishment movement swept through the modern Japanese theatre world as well, prompting the emergence of many and diverse troupes, collectively identified as *angura* (underground) theatre. This group has been severely critical of the New Theatre for its conservative approach and for its pursuit of financial security. (A group of these new troupes and their activities are described separately in the following section.)

The new theatre movement today is attacked from both sides—the traditional theatre and the *angura* theatre—because of its failure to become a significant and mature theatre; yet it is too large and well established to disappear overnight. To some critics its creative force seems to have been spent. It is not succeeding in relating meaningfully with new Japan. Meanwhile, the tendency to mix directors and actors from different genres has been gaining to such an extent that the dividing lines among these genres of Japanese theatre are becoming less important. The fact remains, however, that the world of Japanese theatre still consists of three clearly identifiable forms: traditional theatre, new theatre, and *angura* theatre.

It will be observed that the companies mentioned below sometimes have several theatres listed for the stages they use for their productions. The situation in Japan is such that only a handful of modern theatre companies can afford to own their own theatre buildings. Most of the performances take place in rented theatres. However, each company tends to have its favorite theatre or a set of theatres for its use. Thus, it is possible to indicate which theatre is used by what company. For reference convenience, the theatres are listed in alphabetical order.

ANDREW T. TSUBAKI and
KENKICHI MIYATA

ABE STUDIO
(Abe Sutajio)
Yamate Mansion 19-5
Udagawa-cho, Shibuya-ku
Tokyo 151, Japan

Established on January 11, 1973, the Abe Studio performs in repertory the plays of its leader, Abe Kōbō: *The Man Who Turned into a Stick* (*Bō ni Natta Otoko*), *The Crime of Mr. S. Karuma* (*Esu Karuma-shi no Hanzai*), *Wē: New Slave Hunting* (*Wē: Shin Dorei-gari*), *Underwater City* (*Suichū Toshi*), and *Image Exhibition* (*Imeiji no Tenran-kai*). Influenced in his early days by Luigi Pirandello, the Italian dramatist, Abe is the leading proponent of absurdist theatre in Japan. The Abe Studio, however, is not always successful in presenting the author's true intent because of the immaturity of the actors in the troupe. Itō Yūhei (actor) and Yamaguchi Karin (actress) are the company's core members. Productions are staged in the Seibu Theatre (Seibu Gekijō) with 478 seats, Shibuya Parco, 9th floor, 15-1 Udagawa-cho, Shibuya-ku, Tokyo.

ACTORS' THEATRE
(Haiyū-za)
4-9-2 Roppongi, Minato-ku
Tokyo 106, Japan

The Actors' Theatre was established on February 10, 1944, by Senda Koreya, who is an actor, director, and translator of works by Konstantin Stanislavsky and Bertolt Brecht. Senda withdrew from the Tsukiji Little Theatre in 1926 and has been contributing toward the establishment of a modern art of actors by using Stanislavsky's *Building a Character* as a guide. In 1949 he founded the Research Institute of Actors' Theatre, a three-year program of instruction. During the following eighteen years (until 1967), he trained 623 artists at this institute, which terminated its existence when the theatre department was established at the Tōhō Gakuen. Meanwhile, following the pattern set by the Moscow Art Theatre, he built several satellite theatre troupes around the Actors' Theatre: Sēnen-za, Sanki-kai, Haishō, Shinjin-kai, Dōjin-kai, and Nakama.

Senda Koreya continues to be the representative of the Actors' Theatre which includes in its repertory Shakespeare's *Hamlet*, *Macbeth*, and *Romeo and Juliet*; Ibsen's *A Doll's House*, *Hedda Gabler*, and *The Wild Duck*; Chekhov's *The*

Cherry Orchard, *The Sea Gull*, and *The Three Sisters*; Harold Pinter's *The Caretaker*; and Seiich Yashiro's *The Fate of the Castaways* (*Hyōryū-min no Hate*). Core members of the company are Tōno Eijirō (actor and director), Kishi Teruko (actress and director), Matsumoto Kappei (actor), and Nagai Tomowo (actor). The Actors' Theatre owns its 302-seat theatre in Tokyo.

The Actors' Theatre built its own theatre at the present site in 1954 with the help of company members who donated a certain percentage of their earnings toward the construction. The theatre was the first of its kind devoted to the production of Shingeki since the Tsukiji Little Theatre which was destroyed by an air raid during World War II.

CHILD OF THE WIND
(Kaze no Ko)
4-21-19 Kitazawa, Setagaya-ku
Tokyo 155, Japan

Established on July 1, 1950, the Child of the Wind was a product of cultural movements for children. As early as 1958, it began nationwide touring performances in an effort to establish itself as a professional theatre troupe for children. There are almost eighty members in the troupe, which is divided into seven groups, each group taking a different production on tour and spending 180 days performing throughout Japan, as well as in various parts of the world. The productions strive to attract children's attention without relying on any particular spoken language. The troupe's concern is to encourage children to become independent of outside influence, to see with their own eyes, and to think in their own words.

Playwright Tada Tōru officially represents the company, whose repertory includes *Three Pigs* (*Sanbiki no Kobuta*) and *Happy Hans* (*Yōki na Hans*). The company owns its own studio theatre which seats two hundred.

LITERARY THEATRE
(Bungaku-za)
10 Shinano-machi, Shinjuku-ku
Tokyo 160, Japan

Established on September 6, 1937, the Literary Theatre was the sole theatre troupe allowed to be active during World War II. Devoted to the cause of developing theatre as spiritual entertainment for the intellect, the company took a nonpolitical stand, which made it unique as the other troupes had intense leftist inclinations. The Literary Theatre is the oldest surviving troupe which consistently strives to present enjoyable productions of artistic and literary value. During the politically unsettled days of the 1960s, some of the troupe members joined other artists to tour the People's Republic of China, an event that marked the Literary Theatre's first involvement in a political situation. Since then, it has gone through several painful moves that split the company. Fortunately, the core of the company remains intact and continues to thrive.

Representative Tatsuoka Shin is helped by the core members Sugimura Haruko (actress), Mitsuda Ken (actor), Kitamura Kazuo (actor), Araki Michiko (actress), and Nagaoka Teruko (actress and director). Their repertory includes the following plays: Morimoto Kaoru's *A Woman's Life* (*Onna no Isshō*), Tennessee Williams' *A Streetcar Named Desire*, Anton Chekhov's *The Three Sisters* and *Uncle Vanya*; and Arnold Wesker's *The Kitchen*. The troupe performs in three theatres: the Atelier of the Literary Theatre (Bungaku-za Atorie) with 150 seats; the Toyoko Theatre (Toyoko Gekijō) with 1,002 seats, Tokyu Department Store, 9th Floor, 2-24 Dōgen-zaka, Shibuya-ku, Tokyo, Japan; the Mitsukoshi Theatre (Mitsukoshi Gekijō) with 550 seats; and Mitsukoshi Department Store, 1-7-4 Muromachi, Nihonbashi, Chūo-ku, Tokyo, Japan.

THE PLEIADES: MODERN THEATRE INSTITUTE
(Gendai Engeki Kyōkai: Subaru)
2-29-10 Hon-komagome, Bunkyō-ku
Tokyo 113, Japan

Founded on January 1, 1976, the Pleiades: Modern Theatre Institute established a repertory with productions of T. S. Eliot's *The Cocktail Party*, Tennessee Williams' *A Streetcar Named Desire*, and Neil Simon's *Barefoot in the Park*. Under the leadership of Fukuda Tsuneari, who was a good friend of the famous novelist Mishima Yukio, this institute and its attached troupe, Subaru, have engaged in diverse activities, which include repertory productions as well as a Research Institute for Modern Drama (Gendai Engeki Kenkyūsho), and a theatre school, the Institute of United Arts (Sōgō Geijutsu Gakuin), which involves a three-year course of study. Since the institute owns its own theatre building, the Three Hundred People Theatre, it can impose tight control over its various programs.

Represented by the playwright and director Fukuda Tsuneari, the company lists Uchida Minoru (actor), Kume Akira (actor), Koike Asao (actor), and Kōzuki Sachiko (actress) as its core members.

PUPPET THEATRE PUK (LA PUPA KLUDO)
(Ningyō Gekidan Pūku)
2-12-3 Yoyogi, Shibuya-ku
Tokyo 151, Japan

Established on November 25, 1929, by Kawajiri Tōji (1908–1932), Puppet Theatre Puk now performs over six hundred times annually before over three hundred thousand people. Since it joined Union Internationale de la Marionnette (UNIMA) in 1958, it has engaged in international activities through its direct contact with artists of the puppet theatre in forty-eight countries and through its nearly 160 performances in ten countries. On the basis of its over half-century of activities, Puk strives for innovative and useful creation in the art of puppet theatre. Its appeal is to children and adults who love puppet theatre and who are concerned for peace and democracy.

Under the leadership of Kawajiri Taiji, Puk performs in its repertory Molière's *Amphitryon*, Camille Saint-Saëns' *The Carnival of Animals*, Kawajiri Taiji's *The Golden Key—The Adventures of Pinocchio*, *Peter and the Wolf* based on the work by Sergei Prokoviev, and *The Pied Piper of Hamlin* based on the work by Robert Browning. Among the company's many prestigious awards are the Art Festival Prize of the Education Ministry (1961), the Japanese Play Institute Prize (1966), the Excellent Juvenile Play Prize of Tokyo Metropolis (1976), and the Special Prize of the fourth International Puppet Festival in Pece (1976).

Puk operates its own 106-seat theatre, the Puk Puppet Theatre (Pūkū Ningyō Gekijō), in Tokyo. Attached to the theatre are a school (Puk Puppet Academy) and television studio (Studio NOVA).

THEATRE ECHO
(Teatoru Ekō)
1-18-18 Ebisu, Shibuya-ku
Tokyo 150, Japan

Skilled in staging comedies, since its founding on September 1, 1951 (reorganized in 1956), Theatre Echo has strengthened its activities by the addition of Inoue Hisashi, a playwright who specializes in comedies. Included in the troupe's repertory are Tanaka Chikao's *Mother* (*Ofukuro*), Inoue Hisashi's *The Oddly Translated Bible* (*Chin-yaku Seisho*), Kino Toru's *The Man of Men* (*Otoko no naka no Otoko*), and Neil Simon's *The Prisoner of Second Avenue* (*Nibangai no Shūjin*).

Representative Wada Fumio is supported by core members Kino Toru (playwright and director), Kumakura Kazuo (actor and director), Kaji Tetsuya (actor), and Shima Mieko (actress). Theatre Echo performs in two Tokyo theatres: the Theatre Echo (Teaturo Ekō), owned by the troupe, with 71 seats; and the Kinokuniya Hall (Kinokuniya Hōru), with 426 seats, 1-801 Tsunohazu, Shinjuku-ku, Tokyo.

THEATRE FOUR SEASONS
(Gekidan Shiki)
4-5-17 Yoyogi, Shibuya-ku
Tokyo 151, Japan

The Theatre Four Seasons was established on July 14, 1953. The leader of this group, Asari Keita, pursues the ideal established by playwright Katō Michio (1918–1953), who was strongly influenced by French literature. Rejecting the main trend of Shingeki, which relies heavily upon the art of acting and the training method of realism represented by the works of Ibsen, Asari has sought to establish a modern Japanese theatre following the pattern of French theatre.

Core members Kusaka Takeshi (actor), Fujino Setsuko (actress), and Hamahata Kenkichi (actor) perform in the company's repertory which includes Jean Anouilh's *L'Alouette* and *Antigone*, Jean Giraudoux's *Ondine*, Chekhov's *The Cherry Orchard* and *The Sea Gull*, Michael Bennett's *A Chorus Line*, and Bernard Pomerance's *The Elephant Man*.

The troupe's productions are staged in one of two theatres: the Seibu Theatre (Seibu Gekijō); and the Nissei Theatre (Nissei Gekijō), with 1,356 seats, 1-12 Yūraku-chō, Chiyoda-ku, Tokyo.

PEOPLE'S ART THEATRE
(Gekidan Mingei)
2-3-4 Minami-Aoyama
Minato-ku, Tokyo 107, Japan

The People's Art Theatre was founded on April 3, 1950, by Takizawa Osamu and Uno Jūkichi. Considered one of the three major Shingeki companies of Japan (with the Actor's Theatre and the Literary Theatre), the troupe was the first company to take its productions on the road in order to popularize the new theatre among the masses. The scope of its activities has been quite extensive, and the troupe has produced talented actors and playwrights. The goal of this company is to establish realistic theatre founded on harmonious and ever-improving ensemble acting, which relates directly to the life of the masses.

Takizawa Osamu, actor and director, is the representative of the troupe, whose repertory includes Fujimura Tōson's *Before the Dawn* (*Yoake-mae*); Maxim Gorky's *The Lower Depths*; Anton Chekhov's *The Sea Gull*, *The Cherry Orchard*, and *The Three Sisters*; Samuel Beckett's *Waiting for Godot*; Tennessee Williams' *Cat on a Hot Tin Roof*; and Arthur Miller's *Death of a Salesman*.

Uno Jūkichi (actor and director), Kitabayashi Tanie (actress), Naraoka Tomoko (actress), Wakasugi Mitsuo (director), and Watanabe Hiroko (director) comprise the company's core membership.

The People's Art Theatre performs in the following theatres: the Tōyoko Theatre (Tōyoko Gekijō); the Mitsukoshi Theatre (Mitsukoshi Gekijō); the Sabo Assembly Hall (Sabo Kaikan Hōru), with 800 seats, 2-7 Hirakawa-chō, Chiyodo-ku, Tokyo; and the Seibu Theatre (Seibu Gekijō).

ANDREW T. TSUBAKI and
KENKICHI MIYATA

THE POST-SHINGEKI THEATRE MOVEMENT IN JAPAN

During the 1960s a number of young theatre troupes emerged in Japan, significantly altering the paradigm of modern theatre in that country. The most important of these were the Black Tent Theatre 68/71, the Situation Theatre, and the Waseda Little Theatre. A fourth troupe that deserves mention is Tenjō Sajiki. Together these companies successfully established a new genre of modern Japanese theatre known generally, though not necessarily felicitously, as *angura* or underground theatre.

In order to understand the significance of this new genre, a brief review of the orthodoxy against which it rebelled will be useful. Japanese orthodox modern theatre, known as Shingeki, began to develop in the first decade of the twentieth century. At the time, the dominant mode of Japanese theatre was Kabuki, a highly stylized form whose very name implies a distortion of reality. Shingeki as envisioned by its greatest early theorist, Osanai Kaoru (1881–1928), would rebel against Kabuki and attempt to establish in Japan a realistic theatre along European lines. The favorite playwright of this new theatre was to be Ibsen, and its ideal, Stanislavsky's Moscow Art Theatre.

Nothing describes Shingeki's relationship to traditional Japanese theatre more succinctly than comments made by Osanai in 1926:

Above all, the enemy we must fight against in our effort to establish *the national* theatre we hold as our ideal is the traditional theatre, that is *kabuki* drama. . . . We must first wage war on this *tradition*. We must destroy *kabuki patterns*. By divorcing ourselves from *tradition* and ignoring *kabuki patterns*, we must create completely separately *our own theatre art*, new and free. [*Osanai Kaoru zenshū*, vol. 6 (Kyoto: Rinsen shoten, 1975), pp. 459–60. Emphasis is in original.]

Shingeki thus originated as a realistic theatre in fierce opposition to the stylized traditions of Kabuki.

There were, of course, divisions within the Shingeki movement. "Literary" playwrights like Kishida Kunio (1890–1954) were interested in a psychological realism and in the meticulous portrayal of a carefully defined environment; "political" playwrights like Kubo Sakae (1901–1958), on the other hand, sought to portray "reality" in terms of man's social, economic, and political relationships and deprecated the style of the literary playwrights as "drawing room realism."

In the postwar period, these divisions became less important, and a consensus was achieved. This consensus in the Shingeki movement constitutes the orthodox paradigm for Japanese modern theatre. Those who had come out of the political theatre tradition became less ideological and came to acknowledge the achievements of the literary theatre in the accurate delineation of character and environment. Those aligned with the literary faction, on the other hand, came to acknowledge the theatre's mission in society as an "enlightening" force and admitted the relevance of social concerns. Together, the three major theatre companies of the postwar period, the Actors' Theatre (Haiyū-za), the People's Art Theatre (Gekidan Mingei), and the Literary Theatre (Bungaku-za), despite differences in emphasis, joined together to continue Osanai's efforts to establish a realistic theatre in Japan based on the European model.

The first tenet of Shingeki, that is, of orthodox Japanese modern theatre, is

therefore the commitment to realism. This commitment has had important ram-
ifications. First, Shingeki has been a textually based theatre, the play being seen
as the foundation of the theatre's efforts to accurately portray reality. In this
textually based theatre, the actor has been conceived as an individual who strives
to faithfully recreate the text on stage, and the director guides him toward this
end. The audience "reads" the text through the actors' performance, and its
relationship to the theatre is that of educated to educator. In other words, theatre
presents great ideas and examples of world culture to an audience that is almost
entirely passive. Finally, Shingeki's commitment to realism has affected its
attitudes toward the physical environment of the theatre. Theatre buildings have
had to shut out the unrefined reality of the streets so that a truer reality might
be accurately mounted on the stage. This has meant an almost exclusive commitment to the proscenium stage.

To those brought up in the Western theatre tradition, all of this will seem
perfectly obvious, but it must not be forgotten that a realistic theatre of this type
was a foreign import for which no ready-made audience or support system existed
in Japan. Even today it has been estimated that the total audience that spontaneously buys tickets to modern theatre performances in Tokyo, a city of close
to 12 million, may be as small as ten thousand. The remainder of the spectators
arrive at the theatre in preorganized groups.

The first problem Shingeki companies faced after the war—as indeed they did
before—was therefore survival. The way they solved this problem added two
more characteristics to the paradigm of orthodox modern theatre in Japan. The
first of these was "the company system" (*gekidan-sei*), that is, the organization
of theatres into companies or troupes supported by their actors who contribute
a fixed percentage of their income from extratheatrical work in film, radio, and
television to support the troupe. The most remarkable example of the success
of this system is the Actors' Theatre which, in 1953, sent its entire troupe of
actors out to work full time in films and radio. The actors contributed a full 65
percent of their income to the troupe, and in a year enough money was earned
to finance a theatre building, the first in postwar Japan devoted solely to modern
theatre. The structure was completed on April 20, 1954.

Today the company system continues to dominate Shingeki. Actors contribute
an average of 25 percent of their outside earnings to the troupe. Actors are not
salaried but are paid by the performance on a sliding scale according to seniority,
although some companies do guarantee actors payment for a minimum number
of performances, usually one hundred, even when they do not appear on stage.
No actors are able to support themselves through work in the theatre alone, so
virtually everyone, with the exception of a handful of managers, works outside
the theatre proper for his or her living.

The second characteristic of the Shingeki paradigm that emerged from the
struggle for survival was the creation of "audience organizations" established
to guarantee a stable economic base for modern theatre productions. The most

important such organization has been the Workers' Theatre Council (Rōen), which organizes audiences through labor unions and which, according to some observers, was responsible in large part for the survival of modern theatre in Japan in the postwar period.

One aspect of the Workers' Theatre Council and of the postwar Shingeki movement that played an important part in alienating the younger generation was their relationship with the Japanese Communist Party (JCP). The Workers' Theatre Council has historically served the JCP, implementing its cultural policies in the area of theatre. The relationship has been symbiotic. In effect, the self-assigned educative function of Shingeki and its need for audiences have coincided with the cultural policies and organizing capabilities of the JCP and have led to a *modus vivendi* by which the Workers' Theatre Council provides, in return for prepackaged cultural programs, guaranteed audiences for Shingeki productions through JCP-controlled or -influenced unions.

Paradoxically, the involvement of the Japanese Communist Party in the post-war modern theatre movement made it more conservative and discouraged ex-perimentation. It added a political dogmatism to what was already an artistic orthodoxy. It was this condition, in fact, that precipitated the emergence of a countermovement in the theatre.

The turning point was 1960. Playwrights Kubo Sakae and Miyoshi Jūrō both died in 1958, and in the same year the Moscow Art Theatre, which Osanai Kaoru and others had idealized, performed for the first time in Japan: in effect, the older generation was passing, and the theatre they had sought to emulate was no longer an unattainable ideal. Above all, it was the political disagreements growing out of the massive demonstrations opposing renewal of the United States-Japan Mutual Security Treaty that, in 1960, prepared student amateurs and the younger generation of Shingeki actors to challenge the consensus, the orthodox paradigm, that their elders had achieved.

To sum up a very complex issue briefly, the national debate over the 1960 renewal of the Mutual Security Treaty concerned whether or not Japan should in effect ally itself with the West by continuing to allow U.S. military bases on Japanese soil. From the younger generation's point of view, the alternative proposed by the old left, principally the JCP, merely substituted an alliance with the Soviet Union for the alliance with the U.S. The student activists, who found the prospect of an alliance with the Soviet bloc at least as repugnant as the existing relationships with the West, envisioned a neutral and nonaligned position for Japan.

In the area of theatre, the subservience of the Shingeki establishment to the JCP old left line alienated important segments of the younger generation of theatre practitioners. It is primarily these people who, beginning very shortly after the unsuccessful conclusion of the demonstrations and the renewal of the Security Treaty in June 1960, commenced to reconsider and eventually reject in a systematic fashion all of the elements of the paradigm of orthodox modern theatre in Japan. They then proceeded to build a theatre which, like their political ideals, sought to be a truly original, autonomous contemporary Japanese stage art.

BLACK TENT THEATRE 68/71
(Kuro, or kokushoku tento roku-hachi nana-ichi)
Nakamura-Minami 1-9
Nerima-ku, Tokyo, Japan

The Black Tent Theatre (BTT) 68/71 is the best example of this syndrome. It has been the most vocal in its rejection of the Shingeki paradigm, and its theoreticians, Tsuno Kairarō (1938–) and Saeki Ryūkō, (1941–) have been largely responsible for articulating the critique of Shingeki shared by the entire movement.

BTT 68/71 grew out of the confluence of two important streams in postwar Japanese modern theatre: amateur student theatre and the Shingeki movement itself. The Waseda Theatre Study Group (Waseda engeki kenkyūkai) and the Tokyo University Theatre Study Group (Tōkyō daigaku engeki kenkyūkai) were two of the student theatre clubs that actively participated in the 1960 demonstrations and that became thoroughly alienated from the Shingeki establishment. In the autumn of 1960, the Waseda group produced Jean-Paul Sartre's *Dirty Hands*, a play concerning youth's problematic relationship to an entrenched and bureaucratic Communist party. The following January, members of the group organized a theatrical presentation on behalf of those arrested during the June demonstrations. Both of these productions demonstrated the group's critical attitude toward the old left and their desire to deal with their historical situation through the medium of the theatre.

In 1962 members of the Tokyo University Theatre Study Group, who had produced Sartre's *The Condemned of Altona* in the fall of 1961 and who shared many of the concerns and attitudes of the Waseda group, joined their Waseda contemporaries in the Independent Theatre (Dokuritsu gekijō), a semiprofessional troupe founded by members of the Waseda group upon their graduation. In 1966 the Independent Theatre was reorganized as the June Theatre (Rokugatsu gekijō), named in commemoration of the June 1960 demonstrations. In addition to Tsuno and Saeki, the members of the June Theatre that became affiliated with BTT 68/71 included playwright Yamamoto Kiyokazu, actor Muramatsu Katsumi, actress Inaba Ryōko, and critic Fujimoto Kazuko.

In 1968 the June Theatre became allied with the Freedom Theatre (Jiyū gekijō), which represented an entirely different stream in modern theatre history, and the following year the two formally merged into what was eventually to become the Black Tent Theatre. The members of the Freedom Theatre, including playwright Satoh Makoto and actress Arai Jun, were several years younger than the members of the June Theatre and came, not from the student theatre clubs at the country's most prestigious universities, but directly out of the Shingeki movement itself.

They were graduates of the Actors' Theatre Training Academy (Haiyū-za yō-seijō), the theatre conservatory established by the Actors' Theatre troupe immediately after the war, and represented the orthodox modern theatre movement's own carefully trained offspring.

The formal merger of the June Theatre and the Freedom Theatre in 1969 therefore represented a marriage of the intellectually astute, politically committed student theatre of 1960 and the best professional training the Shingeki movement could afford. With these resources the newly established troupe launched a concerted, systematic, and highly self-conscious attack on the orthodox paradigm of Japanese modern theatre.

The first volley was fired in June 1969, when the group published its "Communication Plan No. 1," which attacked every major tenet of the Shingeki paradigm. It first rejected Shingeki's narrow commitment to realism. In contrast, its own performances would be much more far-reaching:

Beginning with traditional dramatic presentation, they will avalanche from songs, dances, one-liners, agit-prop, promotions, readings, record concerts, film screenings, standup comedy, slapstick, Noh and Kyōgen, through lectures and panel discussions, to demonstrations, carnivals, parties, and mass meetings. [Quoted in *Concerned Theatre Japan*, vol. I, no. 3, p. 15.]

It rejected the notion of the passive audience and vowed independence of the proscenium stage, the Workers' Theatre Council, the old left, the "company system"—in fact, the entire economic and intellectual structure of the postwar Shingeki movement.

The enormous black tent that the troupe designed and began using in 1970 gave concrete form to its rebellion. It was truly a "plastic vessel" that could mold itself to the rich variety of performances the troupe proposed. Its vinylized canvas walls, far from shutting out the reality of the streets, allowed the troupe to maintain an organic relationship with them.

Covering an area of 250 square meters and able to accommodate as many as eight hundred people, including standing room, the black tent also made it possible for this non-Shingeki troupe to perform outside of Tokyo and reach a national audience. Until the 1960s and the anti-Shingeki movement's rejection of realism, it had been virtually impossible for a modern theatre troupe to perform outside of Tokyo. In order to do so, the troupe, which would require a rental hall with a proscenium stage, had to rely upon the Workers' Theatre Council to guarantee the audiences that would make the performances economically feasible. Because of its relationship with the JCP and its own fiscal conservatism, however, the Workers' Theatre Council was unwilling to book tours by experimental troupes. The tent theatre, which was born out of the rejection of realism and the proscenium stage, freed the troupe from this entire system of dependencies. Since realism was not the aim, the proscenium stage was no longer a necessity; since the proscenium stage was not required, there was no need to rent expensive halls that only the Workers' Theatre Council could fill; and since it was no longer necessary to cater to the tastes of the Workers' Theatre Council, the new theatre was freed to perform exactly what it pleased.

In the years since 1970, BTT 68/71 has performed throughout Japan and Okinawa. Members of the troupe travel to each locale in advance of the tour to make arrangements with student groups, labor unions, local theatres, and the like to handle ticket sales and promotion. In addition to guaranteeing the troupe's independence, this system also fulfills the political need to maintain direct and immediate contact with an audience that, far from being the passive recipient of the theatre, is directly involved in the process of making it possible.

The productions that BTT 68/71 has staged in its tent theatre have covered the entire gamut described in its 1969 manifesto and have gone beyond it. The group's most prolific playwright, and perhaps the most profound dramatist working in Japan today, has been Satoh Makoto. Unlike the other troupes described below, which rely almost entirely upon a single playwright, however, BTT 68/71 regularly produces the work of other writers affiliated with the company, particularly Yamamoto Kiyokazu and Katō Tadashi.

In addition to its major tent productions, which tour the country for four to six weeks each spring and fall, BTT 68/71 also stages smaller studio productions as part of its Red Cabaret. In 1978 the troupe established a workshop in the Nerima ward of Tokyo. The large, two-storied structure of galvanized sheet metal serves as the troupe's headquarters and rehearsal space, and it is here that the Cabaret productions premier. Unlike the tent productions, which are highly sophisticated theatrical extravaganzas, the Red Cabaret productions are designed to be performed by a small number of actors using a minimum of props and sets. Red Cabaret productions also travel throughout Japan and have been staged in such diverse places as public parks, university campuses, and Tokyo's German Cultural Center. Among recent productions have been Bertolt Brecht's *The Measures Taken* directed by Satoh; a tribute to Federico García Lorca's traveling university-theatre, La Barraca, conceived and directed by Tsuno; an original play by Kāto; and a collage of the work of the poet-visionary Miyazawa Kenji created by the actors themselves.

BTT 68/71 has also been involved in theatre education and publishing. Each year the group runs seminars open to the public lasting ten to fifteen weeks on topics ranging from circus techniques to basic acting. From 1969 to 1973 the troupe published quarterly magazines in Japanese and English, *Dōjidai engeki* (Contemporary Theatre) and *Concerned Theatre Japan*. These magazines remain primary sources of information about BTT 68/71 and about the entire post-Shingeki movement during this period. Currently, the troupe publishes a newsletter in English and an organ called "Steering Committee Report" (*Hyōgikai tsūshin*) in Japanese.

As to the future, BTT 68/71, which has a permanent membership of about thirty, will remain one of the seminal forces in Japanese contemporary theatre. Satoh, Yamamoto, and Katō, who are in their mid-forties, can be expected to continue producing significant dramatic literature. Increasing emphasis on Asian theatre and classical acting technique will also infuse the troupe with new energy. In recent years BTT actors have gone to study in India and the Philippines, and renditions of such classical works of Asian literature as *Pilgrimage to the West* (*Hsi-yu chi*), the sixteenth-century Chinese picaresque novel which was performed as the 1980 tent production, have displayed the fruits of their efforts. The 1980 production of the Nō play *Dōjōji*, which combined the original Nō choreography with Korean folk dance and the poetry of Korean dissident poet Kim Chi-ha, is also worth noting in this regard.

SITUATION THEATRE
(Jokyō gekijō)
Narita-Nishi 2-19
Suginami-ku, Tokyo, Japan

The Situation Theatre grew out of the same conditions and in much the same way as the Black Tent Theatre. In many ways it has been the pacesetter for the entire underground theatre movement, and its leader, Kara Jūrō (1940–), is clearly one of the seminal imaginations in all of postwar Japanese theatre.

Like the Black Tent Theatre, the Situation Theatre grew out of student theatre. During his undergraduate days at Meiji University in Tokyo, Kara had been active in the student Experimental Theatre (Jikken gekijō). The experience of 1960 had been of no little importance to him and the other students in the group, and in 1961 Kara played the leading role in a play written by members of the group, *To Friends Returning Home* (*Kikyō suru tomo e*), concerning the problems faced by a youth who takes the spirit of democracy born of the 1960 demonstrations home to the conservatism of his native village.

Like the students in the Tokyo and Waseda University theatre study groups, Kara was also deeply influenced by Sartre and his ''theatre of situations.'' Indeed, the name of Kara's troupe derives from this source. The Situation Theatre, which Kara founded with other graduates of Meiji University in 1963, staged the French playwright's *Respectful Prostitute* as its first production with Kara himself in the role of the senator.

Sartre's existentialist influence on Kara is evident not only in his plays but also in the operating strategy of the troupe as a whole. On March 6, 1965, the Situation Theatre performed its first ''metaphysical street theatre'' in the Ginza section of Tokyo. The following October, the troupe performed Kara's *Petticoat Osen: A Tale of Forgetfulness* (*Koshimaki osen bokyaku hen*) in the ruins of the prewar concert hall at Toyamagahara in Tokyo. Although it lasted just three days and attracted only about seventy people, this production is often cited as the starting point for the entire post-Shingeki movement. Kara's creative use of his environment, the relationship of tension he was able to create between his text and the physical reminders of Japan's recent past, set a precedent for an entire generation of theatre artists. In subsequent productions, Kara and his troupe have used public toilets, railroad stations, and even lily ponds (from the waters of which the cast make their entrances and exits) as the setting for his plays.

More than anything else, the appearance of the Situation Theatre's red tent in the precincts of the Hanazono Shrine in the bustling Shinjuku section of Tokyo on August 5, 1967, established Kara and his troupe as leaders of the post-Shingeki theatre movement. Prominent artists and intellectuals like designer Yokoo Tadanori and Sade scholar Shibusawa Tatsuhiko had early recognized the importance of Kara's work, but general recognition did not come until the troupe's appearance in the very center of the metropolis. Not only did Kara's red tent antedate other tent theatres, including the Black Tent Theatre, but it also anticipated the uproar that overwhelmed Shinjuku Station, the second busiest rail hub in Japan, the following summer. Kara Jūrō, the Situation Theatre, and their red tent became a symbol of youthful resistance to the trends of urbanization and modernization represented by Shinjuku. It was for this reason that director Oshima Nagisa featured them in his film *Diary of a Shinjuku Thief (Shinjuku dorobō nikki*, 1968).

Kara is the most prolific of Japan's younger playwrights. He was awarded the Kishida Prize for Playwrighting for his *Virgin Mask (Shōjo kamen)* in 1969. In 1978 he was awarded the sixth Izumi Kyōka Prize for his literary achievements, and by 1980 his "complete works" had been published in six volumes. In 1983 he won the coveted Akutagawa Prize for literature. The vitality of Kara's language, his refusal to compromise with "reality," and his ability to give form to the subliminal fantasies of the Japanese people have made him the most popular and marketable of Japan's playwrights, young or old. The intrusion of a fantasy dimension, usually out of the past and generally concerning the more unsavory aspects of Japanese history, into the predictable world of everyday urban existence has been the consistent hallmark of Kara's plays.

Kara's theory of acting, his "theory of privileged entities" (*tokkenteki nikutai ron*), has also been of great significance for the entire post-Shingeki generation. Diametrically opposed to the Shingeki conception, Kara's theatre is actor-centered. The actor's physical presence in any given space is what defines the theatrical enterprise, not the text of the play. Indeed, the way Kara has directed his work has tended to make the already difficult plays almost incomprehensible, further focusing the audience's attention on the actors.

Those actors, six or eight identifiable personalities supported by a fluid group of perhaps a dozen others, have engaged in an active process of self-mythologization, the creation of an alternate, public persona that shows through and dominates the role the actor is ostensibly playing. Perhaps the best example of this is Yotsuya Shimon, who revived the Kabuki tradition of *onnagata* female impersonation in the Situation Theatre and created one of the most enthralling female personalities to grace the post-Shingeki stage. Unfortunately, the rate of attrition from the Situation Theatre has been great. Yotsuya left the troupe in 1971, and by the early 1980s Kara had lost all of his veteran actors except Ri Reisen, his wife. (Yotsuya reappeared on the Situation Theatre stage in 1984, but it is unclear how long the association will last.) This phenomenon has significantly affected the character of the troupe, which has become increasingly a vehicle for Kara's individual genius.

That genius has been restricted neither to the theatre nor to Japan. In 1976 Kara directed the feature film *The Sea of Genkai: Portrait in Chivalry (Ninkyō gaiden genkai nada)*. He has given vocal recitals, edited magazines, and written a novel and numerous short stories. In 1972 the Situation Theatre staged its first performances outside Japan, in Seoul, Korea. The following year, Kara and his troupe performed in Bangladesh, and in 1974 the troupe spent a month touring Palestinian refugee camps in Syria and Lebanon.

Although Kara and Ri Reisen visited New York in 1978, the closest the Situation Theatre has come to performing in the West was its 1980 trip to Brazil. The troupe's frequent trips to the Third World, performing Kara's plays in Korean, Arabic, and the like, represent the most radical expression of the underground theatre movement's general rejection of the West as its model and ideal. Unlike Terayama Shūji, with whom Kara is sometimes compared, whose frequent trips to Europe have made him and his troupe as well or better known on that continent as in Japan, Kara has used his overseas adventures as yet another means of provoking the complacent Japanese, who have come to consider themselves "honorary Europeans."

In every respect, the Situation Theatre departs radically from the orthodox paradigm of Japanese modern theatre. Even the organization of the troupe around the charismatic personality of Kara Jūrō, a pattern of organization more appropriate to the premodern period when actors were considered pariahs and survived through their sacerdotal charisma, flies in the face of the modern, rationally organized Shingeki company. The future of the Situation Theatre will depend upon Kara's ability to maintain his charisma and continue his provocative career.

WASEDA LITTLE THEATRE
(Waseda shōgeki jō)
3-3-25-712 Zoshigaya
Toshima-ku, Tokyo, Japan

The Waseda Little Theatre has its roots in student theatre at Waseda University, where its leader Suzuki Tadashi (1939–) was a contemporary of the students in the Waseda Theatre Study Group who went on to form the Black Tent Theatre. While at Waseda, Suzuki and the others who formed the Waseda Little Theatre belonged to a university theatre club called the Waseda Free Stage (Waseda jiyū butai) that had been in existence since 1951 and that had produced a significant number of active theatre artists, including playwrights Fukuda Yoshiyuki, Fujita Asaya, and Akihama Satoshi.

The Waseda Free Stage did not react to the events of 1960 with the same immediacy as the university's Theatre Study Group. In the spring of 1960, when the nation was already convulsed with debate and demonstration against the projected renewal of the Mutual Security Treaty in June, the Waseda Free Stage produced Gorky's *The Lower Depths*, a play that had first been produced in Japan in 1910 and that epitomized the realistic ideal of the Shingeki movement. Arthur Miller's *Death of a Salesman*, a play premiered by the People's Theatre troupe in 1954, was the group's fall 1960 production; and the following spring it presented Chekhov's *The Three Sisters*, a play first staged in Japan in 1925. The group was not completely out of step with the times, however, and in the fall of 1961 it presented Sartre's *The Flies*, joining the other student groups in their interest in the French existentialist. The last three productions were directed by the youthful Suzuki Tadashi.

In December 1961 the leading members of the Waseda Free Stage moved out of the university and dropped the word "Waseda" from the name of their troupe, now calling themselves simply the Free Stage. The leading members of the group at this time were Suzuki, actor Ono Kei, and playwright Betsuyaku Minoru.

As its first production, the newly established Free Stage troupe produced Betsuyaku's *The Elephant* on April 3–8, 1962, another cardinal date in the development of the underground theatre movement. *The Elephant* ostensibly concerns a victim of the Hiroshima blast and his struggle to keep his rapidly fading experience alive. Its message was much more immediate to the students of 1960, however, for they saw reflected in it time's corrosive process eating away at their own intense historical experience, their commitment, and their resolve.

At least as important as the play's message was its language. Using a style inspired in part by the absurdist playwrights of Europe, Betsuyaku created a new Japanese stage language in *The Elephant* whose power was in inverse proportion to its deceptive simplicity. Betsuyaku's linguistic influence has been profound throughout the entire post-Shingeki movement.

After a period of inactivity, the Free Stage moved to the second floor of a coffee shop near Waseda University in 1966 and changed its name to the Waseda Little Theatre. In May, the group produced Betsuyaku's *Gate* (*Mon*), directed by Suzuki and featuring Ono, in their newly converted theatre space, and until his departure in August 1969, Betsuyaku remained the featured playwright of the group. In 1968 Betsuyaku became the first playwright of the post-Shingeki movement to receive the Kishida Prize for Playwriting for his *Little Match Girl* (*Matchi-uri no shōjo*).

The Waseda Little Theatre did not limit itself entirely to Betsuyaku's work. In April 1966 the troupe produced Satoh Makoto's *My Beatles or the Funeral* (*Atashi no biitoruzu arui wa soshiki*), which Satoh later rewrote simply as *My Beatles*, and in 1969 it staged Kara's *Virgin Mask*, the play for which Kara was awarded the Kishida Prize. This production record gives the Waseda Little Theatre and Suzuki, who directed all the plays, the unique distinction of having staged seminal works by all three of the underground theatre's most important playwrights.

In April 1969 the Waseda Little Theatre produced *On the Dramatic Passions*

I (*Gekiteki naru mono o megutte I*), a collage of dramatic scenes organized by Suzuki from works ranging from nineteenth-century Kabuki to *Waiting for Godot*. The work starred Shiraishi Kayoko, who had joined the troupe in 1966 and who has since become its principal actress. *On the Dramatic Passions I* was followed by *On the Dramatic Passions II* and *III* in 1970.

These productions and Betsuyaku's departure from the group marked a new stage in the troupe's development. Organizationally, power was becoming increasingly concentrated in Suzuki's hands, a process that was enhanced by the departure of six of the group's veteran actors led by Sekiguchi Ei in 1971. At the same time, Suzuki's growing interest in acting technique and classical Japanese theatre were turning the troupe away from the minimalist approach of Betsuyaku to the banquet of world theatre. *On the Dramatic Passions I, II,* and *III* reclaimed the wealth of the theatre history, including both Western and Japanese traditions, to which modern Japanese theatre could by the late 1960s lay claim. The collage technique challenged the actors of the troupe to come up with a new acting synthesis; it created a dialectical encounter between the actors' bodies and the most challenging material in world drama literature. In the final analysis, the classical Japanese material was the most interesting and challenging, and the material taken from modern theatre came to serve as a bridge by the avenue of which the classics could be approached. Suzuki became increasingly engrossed with the possibilities of classical Japanese theatre. A truly fruitful feedback relationship developed between him and his actors, eventually becoming systematized into a series of training exercises that theatre scholar James Brandon has dubbed "the Suzuki Method."

The powerful new acting synthesis being developed by actress Shiraishi and the rest of the Waseda Little Theatre's acting ensemble rapidly attracted widespread attention. Partially as a reaction against the tyranny of the Stanislavsky system in the Shingeki movement, actor training and discipline had been deemphasized in the post-Shingeki movement. The Waseda Little Theatre under Suzuki was the only troupe developing a systematic program of actor training out of the dialectical encounter between modern actors and classical Japanese material. In addition to the general interest this aroused, three specific groups began to take an active interest in Suzuki's work: classical theatre actors such as the late Nō paragon Kanze Hisao, who had been searching for years for a means to make the classical theatre tradition more immediate and meaningful in the modern world; Japanese intellectuals who were excited by the bridges the troupe was creating between the Japanese and Western traditions; and Western theatre people, who perceived the Waseda Little Theatre's new acting synthesis as a means by which they too might take advantage of the riches of the Oriental theatre heritage.

The Waseda Little Theatre's first trip abroad came in 1972, when members of the troupe participated in the Théâtres des Nations Festival in Paris. This was followed by appearances at Nancy, Paris, and Amsterdam in 1973. Most recently the troupe was scheduled to appear with Robert Wilson in the art festival of the

Los Angeles Olympic games in 1984, but the production was cancelled for lack of funds.

Back in Japan, intellectuals connected with the Iwanami Publishing Company, the country's most influential publisher of scholarly books, began to take an increasing interest in the troupe's work. The troupe's productions of Greek tragedies at Iwanami Hall in central Tokyo (*The Trojan Women* in 1974 and *The Bacchae* in 1978) demonstrated both the power of the troupe's highly disciplined acting ensemble and its acceptance by the highest echelons of the Japanese intellectual and scholarly communities.

In 1976 the troupe left its Tokyo coffee shop theatre and, partly through the inspiration of European groups like Jerzy Grotowski's Laboratory Theatre in Wrocław, Poland, and Eugenio Barba's Odin Teatret in Holstebro, Denmark, both provincial cities far from the centers of culture and power, moved to Toga-mura, a small farming village in Toyama Prefecture, eight hours by train and bus from Tokyo. Using a converted thatched-roof farm house, the troupe began a five-year period of intensive training and rehearsal that lasted until 1980. Despite the time and expense required to attend their performances, the Waseda Little Theatre's Toyama productions were consistently packed. During this period, the troupe also appeared in Tokyo, but their base remained in Toyama.

In 1980 the Waseda Little Theatre opened an atelier theatre in Tokyo, thus reestablishing its base in the capital. Presently, the troupe works in Tokyo most of the year, its actors holding jobs during the day and rehearsing from 6:00 to 10:00 nightly. The troupe's major annual production, however, is still performed each summer at the Toyama theatre, which, with an addition designed by architect Isozaki Arata and a thirty-room hostel, completed in June 1982, is becoming a major theatre center.

Suzuki Tadashi's personal reputation as a teacher, director, and theorist has spread throughout the world. He has conducted acting seminars throughout Europe and America, and is currently teaching for a period each year at the Juilliard School in New York. Suzuki has also taught at the University of Wisconsin, Milwaukee, where in 1981 he directed a production of Euripides' *The Bacchae* with a cast of Japanese and American actors trained in his acting system. Despite the fact that each actor spoke his lines in his native language, thus making it impossible for the American audience to understand the dialogue, the production was extremely well received, a tribute to the actors and to Suzuki's direction.

Beginning in 1982, the Waseda Little Theatre initiated a Japan Performing Arts Center (Kokusai butai geijutsu kenkyūjō) at its Toyama headquarters. The center gives six months of intensive training in Suzuki's acting method annually to thirty actors, half from Japan and half from abroad, who are expected to live at the Toga-mura theatre. In 1982 the troupe began sponsoring an annual international theatre festival, using its facilities in Toyama.

As of September 1984, the Waseda Little Theatre changed its name to SCOT (Suzuki Company of Toga).

TENJŌ SAJIKI
Moto-Azabu 3-12-43
Minato-ku, Tokyo, Japan

All three of the theatre companies discussed so far emerged from student theatre. All three were motivated to a greater or lesser extent by the political experience of 1960, and all three consciously set out to create in Japan an autonomous contemporary theatre independent of European models. In every respect, Tenjō Sajiki differs from the other groups, and although deserving of mention, it falls outside the mainstream of the post-Shingeki movement.

More than any other comparable theatre, Tenjō Sajiki is the creation of one man: Terayama Shūji. Born in 1935, Terayama is four years older than Suzuki, five years older than Kara, and eight years older than Satoh Makoto. Although the gap may not seem significant, it represents a major difference in generation and perspective. Whereas in 1960 both Kara and Suzuki were university students caught up in student politics and amateur theatre, Terayama had already dropped out of Waseda University for health reasons and was having his first play produced by a professional Shingeki troupe. The play, *Blood Sleeps Standing Up* (*Chi wa tatta mama nemutte iru*), was produced by the Shiki company, which had distinguished itself during the 1950s by producing French avant-garde playwrights like Giraudoux and Anouilh. (Today the Shiki company is the most highly commercialized of Japan's modern theatre companies with a $7.5 million annual budget.)

The difference in age also means a disparity in the experience of World War II. Terayama was ten years old the year the war ended and thus has vivid memories of the war years. The prime movers of the post-Shingeki mainstream, on the other hand, have no such memories, having been at most five or six in 1945. Their memories are of the postwar years, particularly of the desolation left by the saturation bombing of Tokyo, and their plays reflect this difference.

Another significant difference between Terayama and virtually all the other theatre artists discussed so far is the fact that unlike them he was raised in the provinces, not in Tokyo. Terayama was born and raised in Aomori Prefecture in northeastern Japan. In addition to being poor and underdeveloped, the northeastern region is one of the areas where indigenous Japanese religion has remained the most alive. Aomori Prefecture is the site of Mount Osore, a center of shamanistic religious practice. Terayama climbed this mountain in 1962, and it, its cult, and the northeastern region in general have played an important role in his work.

Two more things that separate Terayama from his younger contemporaries are his personal deprivation as a child and his poor health. Terayama's father, who was a member of the so-called Thought Police before the war, died of alcoholism in the Celebes in 1946. His mother Hatsu went to work on American bases after Japan's defeat, and Terayama was forced to live alone from the age of nine. In 1955, while attending Waseda University, he became seriously ill with nephritis, a kidney ailment, and spent most of the next three years in the hospital. During this time he read such writers as Lautreamont, Antonin Artaud, and the Japanese Gothic novelist Izumi Kyōka. On May 9, 1983, Terayama's illness finally claimed his life.

Terayama's loneliness as a child, the influence of the Northeast, a sense of alienation from the advanced culture of Tokyo, and his years of illness seem to have contributed to the development of an exceedingly active imagination. He began writing poetry very early and in 1954 was awarded a poetry prize by the influential poetry journal, *Tanka kenkyū*. His first book of poems, *For Me the Month of May* (*Ware ni gogatsu o*), was published in 1957, and he has been widely recognized as master of the thirty-one-syllable *tanka* form of Japanese poetry.

All of these factors characterize Terayama's work and distinguish him from others in the post-Shingeki theatre movement. Where the catalyst for their theatre was the political experience of the demonstrations in 1960, that experience was less important to Terayama than his personal experience of loneliness, alienation, and illness. Unlike the others, for whom theatre was and has been the first and primary commitment, moreover, Terayama began his career as a poet, and it is out of his poetry and his poetic imagination that his theatre grew. Finally, Terayama's idea of the theatre and the actual activities of the Tenjō Sajiki troupe are closer to a European model, specifically the French avant-garde, than any other post-Shingeki troupe.

Tenjō Sajiki, Terayama's troupe, was founded in 1967. Terayama claimed that the troupe emerged from a series of lectures he had been giving on university campuses around the country, in which he recommended running away from home, the theme of one of his books (*Iede no susume*). According to Terayama, as a result of these lectures, he found his apartment filled with runaways, and having nothing better to do with them he began to cast them in plays he had written. Tenjō Sajiki grew out of this activity. Terayama continued to use amateurs in his plays, a practice that militated against the development of a strong acting ensemble and reinforced the impression that the troupe is fundamentally a vehicle for his unique and mercurial poetic imagination.

That imagination was both fertile and fearless. Under Terayama's direction the Tenjō Sajiki troupe performed happenings, street theatre, and audience participation theatre, not only ignoring the Shingeki paradigm but lavishly demonstrating that it was the most obdurately avant-garde troupe in Japan.

Opinion on the merit of these experiments is divided. Devotees see Terayama and Tenjō Sajiki as trailblazers, pioneering new theatrical forms and methods in Japan. Certainly, no one has been more radical, more antagonistic to bourgeois sensibilities, or more voluntaristic in his experiments than Terayama. His 1970 production, *The Man-Powered Airplane, Solomon* (*Jinriki hikōki soromon*), for example, provided those who bought tickets with a map of Tokyo marked with a variety of times and places. The audience was free to attend the performances in any order they pleased, no one being able to see the entire play and everyone's experience of it necessarily differing. Spectacular as these experiments have been, however, many critics believe that because of their very hit-and-run nature, they have been less significant than the sustained efforts of the Situation and Black Tent theatres to produce theatre outside theatre buildings.

The same division of opinion exists regarding Tenjō Sajiki's frequent tours abroad. Terayama Shuji was more willing to deal with the West and to participate in European and American theatre festivals than any other comparable Japanese theatre figure. He personally traveled abroad every year since 1967, and Tenjō Sajiki has participated almost annually in theatre festivals from Experimenta 3 in Germany in 1969 to the Shiraz Festival at Persepolis in 1973 and a tour of European capitals in 1979. In each case, the troupe has received wide acclaim. Critics like Kan Takayuki, however, believe that in the final analysis the highly disciplined and systematic approach of Suzuki Tadashi and the Waseda Little Theatre, which makes available to Western audiences and actors the richness of the Japanese theatre heritage, will ultimately be more significant than the notoriety generated by what he calls Terayama's "scandalous" style.

It is perhaps inevitable that the activities of an artist as relentless in his pursuit of novelty as Teryama Shūji should generate this kind of debate. His untimely death has already led to the dissolution of Tenjō Sajiki as a functioning theatre company.

CONCLUSIONS

The Shingeki movement began by rejecting the Kabuki tradition of stylization in the theatre. The idea of Osanai Kaoru and others in the early Shingeki movement was to create a contemporary Japanese theatre modeled after the rational, realistic theatre of Europe.

Around 1960 a movement began in Japanese theatre that rejected the idea that realism was the *sine qua non* of a meaningful modern theatre. The fact that all of the troupes discussed in this article have made extensive use of classical theatre language, acting technique, stagecraft, and theory should not come as a surprise. It might be suggested that the greatest contribution the post-Shingeki troupes have made to theatre history in Japan has been to recapture the power and potential of the native theatre tradition within the context of a thoroughly modern theatre movement. Ironically, it may be by reaffirming tradition in this way, rather than by waging war upon it, that the young troupes discussed here may yet create in Japan the new national theatre of which Osanai Kaoru dreamed.

DAVID G. GOODMAN

Korea

INTRODUCTION

Prior to the birth of the modern theatre in Korea, there were three major forms of traditional theatre: the mask dance drama, the puppet theatre, and the *pansori* (traditional opera).

The mask dance drama is characterized by the use of masks and the accompaniment of dancing and singing. Its stinging satire exposed the corruption of society through comic parody and vulgar jest, expressing disgust for the ruling class, disdain for depraved Buddhist monks, and contempt for immorality in domestic life.

The birth of modern Korean theatre took place in 1908 when Yi Inchik produced the first modern drama in Wonkaksa Theatre. The form of Western theatre was introduced and developed during the 1920s and 1930s via Japan. Through the new theatre movement, the plays of Gogol, Ibsen, Chekhov, and many other Western playwrights were produced. Parallel to the Western plays, the original Korean plays and the melodramas were quite popular during this period.

With the end of World War II, a new phase of modern Korean theatre began. In 1950 the government established the National Theatre, and this theatre's resident company presented many remarkable productions.

In the early 1960s the so-called Little Theatre movement was established mainly by young college graduates. They produced the experimental and avant-garde plays of Ionesco, Beckett, Albee, and others. The domination of Western play production, however, hampered the development of original Korean plays. Accordingly, efforts were made to encourage Korean playwrights to write good original plays.

A great reform took place in the 1970s, paralleling Korea's economic development. The new National Theatre was constructed in 1971; the Sejong Cultural Center was completed in 1978; and the Korean Culture and Arts Foundation built its main and small theatres in 1981. With the availability of new theatres, many theatre groups were organized. Although there were only about ten theatre groups in the 1960s, there are presently thirty-seven registered theatre groups. In the 1970s various theatre artists began to recognize afresh the value of traditional theatre. Eventually, traditional theatre returned to the Korean stage.

HO SOON KIM

BRIDGE DRAMA TROUPE
(Kuktan Kagyo)
371 Shinsoo-dong, Mapo-ku
Seoul, Korea

The Bridge Drama Troupe was founded in May 1965 with the ambitious goal of searching out audiences wherever possible, whether in hospitals, prisons, churches, schools, or the countryside, through the "bridge" of drama.

Under the directorship of Chintae Kim and, after 1966, Seung-kyoo Lee, the group developed a repertory consisting mainly of musicals and comedies, and including shadow plays and dramas of a religious nature. The group has received assistance from American missionary Mrs. Margaret Martin Moore. An evangelical flavor is present in productions such as *The Prince of Peace*, a story of Jesus Christ, which proved to be one of the troupe's most popular productions. The group has managed, however, to maintain a balance between the evangelical and artistic in its productions. The troupe's tremendous appeal is through its successful combination of social, religious, and artistic elements.

Some of the group's other productions have been Max Frisch's *Biedermann and the Firebugs* (1970), *The Fantastiks* (1973), Keum-sam Lee's *The Touring Company* (1975), Dubose Hayward's *Porgy and Bess* (1976), Shakespeare's *The Taming of the Shrew* (1977) and *As You Like It* (1980), and Lillian Hellman's *The Little Foxes* (1981). *The Touring Company* received the award for the Best Drama of 1975 from the *Hankook Daily Newspaper* and another award from the 1977 Korean Drama Festival. *The Trial of Abelman* by Keum-sam Lee received the Ministry of Culture and Information Award. *The Hurricane* (*Taepoong*) by Bockun Chung received the same award the following year at the 1978 Korean Drama Festival.

In addition to their constant travels within Korea, the group has performed in several East Asian countries: Taiwan, Japan, Hong Kong, and the Philippines in 1976 with productions of *The Wedding Day* by Yongjin Oh and *The Prince of Peace*.

HO SOON KIM

DONG NANG REPERTORY COMPANY
The Korea Drama Center
8-19 Yejang-dong, Choong-ku
Seoul 100, Korea

The Dong Nang Repertory Company was founded in 1962 by Chi Jin Yoo, with the assistance of the Rockefeller Foundation and private donations. Originally founded as the Drama Center, the company assumed the name of Dong Nang, the artistic name of the founder Chi Jin Yoo, after his death in 1975. Yoo was succeeded in the directorship of the company by his son, Duk-Hyung Yoo, who received his theatre training in the United States at Yale University. He is the present managing director of the Dong Nang Repertory Company.

Under the directorship of Duk-Hyung Yoo, the company has produced numerous experimental productions. The company's primary objective is to search for the universal in the particular. Thus, its dramas explore the emotions and thoughts of the Korean people in order to discover universal traits of humanity. Although its immediate appeal is to Korean audiences, the company seeks to illuminate aspects of the human condition common to all mankind.

In its pursuit of such objectives, the company has transcended conventional Korean dramatic forms and has attempted to express indigenous motifs of traditional Korean stage art in highly abstract forms. The key to the successful realization of this abstraction is "composite art," a blend of stage possibilities, that is, sounds, colors, rhythms, shapes, and words, which provide the audience with a "total experience" surpassing that of conventional dramatic forms.

Drawing from contemporary Western theatrical experiment and practice, the company has produced a number of outstanding productions which have received both national and international recognition. *Jilsoe (Choboon)*, written by Tae-Sok Oh and directed by Duk-Hyung Yoo, was performed in 1973 and won three awards for best direction of the year from Hankook, Seoul, and Dong-A daily newspapers. The play was performed again in New York's Café La Mama with an American cast, and in 1975 it received the Grand Prize of Art and Culture from the *Chung-Ang Daily Newspaper*. Another production, *The Cycle (Tae)*, written by Tae-Sok Oh and directed by Min-Soo Ahn, won the award for the best production of 1974 from the *Hankook Daily Newspaper*.

The company toured Europe and the United States in 1977 with productions of *Hamlet (Prince Hamyol)* and *The Cycle*. The company's staging of *Hamlet* was a Korean version adapted and directed by Min-Soo Ahn. The production demonstrated clearly the company's goal of expressing traditional Korean stage art through contemporary Western theatrical practices.

The Dong Nang Repertory Company has made an outstanding contribution to the development of the theatre arts in Korea. The quality of the resident repertory company and its attached drama school makes this company the most promising theatre group in Korea.

HO SOON KIM

EXPERIMENTAL THEATRE GROUP
(Shilhom Kukchang)
114 Wonso-dong, Chongno-ku
Seoul, Korea

The Experimental Theatre Group was organized by a group of college students and graduates in October 1960 under the direction of Kim Uikyong. Its express purpose was to create an experimental production group for the Korean stage. The group combines its theatrical activities with academic programs, such as seminars and playwriting workshops, and until 1975 published the theatre journal *Our Stage*.

The company came to the forefront of Korean drama in the 1960s when it pioneered the Little Theatre, or "nonprofessional theatre," movement. The first production of the Experimental Theatre Group opened in November 1960 with Ionesco's *The Lesson*, directed by Kyu Huh. The group went on to win critical acclaim with the following productions: *The Wedding Day*, written by Yong Jin Oh and directed by Yongsae Noh, received the Dong-A Dramatic Award for 1960; *King Lear*, directed by Kyu Huh, received the Dong-A Dramatic Award for 1965; *Judas Before the Cock Crows*, written by Tae-Sok Oh and directed by Kyu Huh, received the Grand Prize of Korean Culture Award for the Best Play of 1969; *Equus* (1975), written by Peter Shaffer and directed by Yong-Yul Kim; *Ireland*, written by Athol Fugard, directed by Go-Jin Yoon, and awarded the Dong-A Dramatic Award for 1978; *Death of a Salesman* (1980) by Arthur Miller; and *A Wild Ox* (1981) by Moonyul Lee.

The company has also been recognized for the individual excellence of cast members such as Soon-Choe Lee, Nak-Hoon Lee, Hyun-Kyong Oh, Tong-Hoon Kim, and Un-Kye Yo. The company has benefited from the talent of directors such as Ho Kyu, Yong-Sal Na, Kihn Lee, and Yong-Yul Kim.

The Experimental Theatre Group is managed collectively by its members and has made special efforts to recruit subscribers. Although collectively operated, the group owed much to the guidance of manager Ui-Kyong Kim during the 1960s, when the group launched an ambitious campaign under his direction to increase the number of subscribers.

Under the present management of Tong-Hoon Kim, the Experimental Theatre Group has maintained an innovative approach to drama and continues to enjoy popularity, particularly with the college student audience in Korea.

HO SOON KIM

MIN-JUNG THEATRICAL COMPANY

(Min-Jung Kukchang)

88 Hanyang-ro 2 ka, Yongsan-ku

Seoul, Korea

The Min-Jung Theatrical Company was formed on January 29, 1963, under the leadership of playwright Gunsam Lee. Except for a five-year hiatus of activity from 1969 to 1974, the company has produced delightful comedies which have drawn large audiences. The company seeks to reach and to establish an intimacy with its audience. If one judges from the popularity of the group's productions, it has been largely successful in achieving its goal.

Min-Jung's first production, Fèlcien Marceaux's *The Egg*, opened in May

1963 to a sold-out house. In 1964 its production of *The Rabbit and the Hunter* by Choyol Park received the Dong-A Dramatic Award.

Productions since the resumption of the group's performances in 1974 have included *The Hunting Society* (1975) by Gunsam Lee, *Grief* (*Taehan*, 1976) by Chaehyun Lee, Shakespeare's *The Merchant of Venice* (1976), *A Taste of Honey* (1977) by Shelagh Delaney, *Race with the Dead* (1977) by Onyung Lee, *Cadenza* (1978) by Hyun-hwa Lee, *Metamorphosis* (1981) by Franz Kafka, and *A Taste of Honey* once again (1982).

The company encourages new talent and operates workshops for aspiring writers and actors. It regularly stages those works selected by nationwide script-writing competitions sponsored each spring in Korea by several newspapers. The company aspires to join the ranks of professional theatre in Korea. Under the ambitious guidance of director Jinsoo Chung, the company appears to be nearing that goal.

HO SOON KIM

MODERN THEATRE GROUP
(Hyundae Kukchang)
Hyondae Building, 4th Floor, 64-1, Haewha-dong Chongno-ku
Seoul, Korea

The dramatic philosophy of this group is that drama should be both entertaining and appealing as it attempts to inform and move its audience. The group seeks to entertain audiences of all ages and deplores the presently limited composition of the theatre audience in Korea, which consists mainly of college-age students. The group has thus staged a wide variety of plays designed to draw adults, youths, and children to the theatre and, despite criticism from dramatic quarters regarding its somewhat commercially oriented approach, has succeeded in attracting large audiences to its productions. Besides expanding the appeal of Korean theatre, the Modern Theatre Group's efforts represent the first attempt to develop professional theatre in Korea on a commercial scale approaching that of Western productions such as those found on Broadway.

Since the group's formation in 1976, its productions for adult audiences have included Eugene Ionesco's *Macbett* (1976); Leonard Gersh's *Butterflies Are Free* (1977); *Padam, Padam, Padam* written by Seung-Kyoo Park and based on the life of singer Jacqueline Francois; *Anna Christie* (1977) by Eugene O'Neill; *Death of a Salesman* (1978) by Arthur Miller; *Gone with the Wind* (1978) by Margaret Mitchell; *The Long Tunnel* (1978) by Chae Hyun Lee, which received the Presidential Award in Direction and Design at the Korean Drama Festival of 1978; *Jesus Christ, Superstar* (1980) by Tim Rice and Andrew Lloyd Webber; and *The Sound of Music* (1981) by Oscar Hammerstein II and Richard Rodgers.

Productions geared for youths or teenagers and college-age students have included Shakespeare's *Hamlet* (1977), Schiller's *Maid of Orleans* (1977), and

Romeo and Juliet (1978). Children's theatre productions have included *Treasure Island* (1977), a dramatization of the book by Robert Louis Stevenson; *The Dog of Flanders* (1978) by Lady Ouida; *Snow White* (1978), staged from the Grimm Brothers' story; and *Peter Pan* (1979) by Sir James M. Barrie, which was performed at the Sejong Cultural Center in Seoul in honor of Children's Year and played to capacity audiences. The phenomenal success of *Peter Pan* resulted in two encore performances of the production later that year.

HO SOON KIM

NATIONAL THEATRE COMPANY
(Kuknip Kuktan)
14-67 Changchoong-dong, Choong-ku
Seoul, Korea

Founded in 1950, the National Theatre has made pioneering contributions to Korean drama and constitutes the dramatic company with the longest tradition in Korea. The company existed as two separate repertory companies, the Association of New Dramas (Shinhyop) and the Association of Dramatic Art (Kukhyesul Hyophae), until 1962, when the groups were reorganized and combined under the general management of Chin Park. The National Theatre represents one of the few groups that continued performances during the Korean War, and it was the leading theatrical group in the nation, until the appearance of amateur and membership drama groups in the early 1960s. As the only government-subsidized theatre group in the country, the company is housed in the National Theatre building, erected in 1973. The main theatre seats 1,518 spectators, while the smaller theatre seats 344.

The theatre's productions have included the following plays: *Warrior Wonsul* (*Wonsul-long*, 1950) by Chijin Yoo; *The Forest Fire* (*Sanpul*, 1962) by Pomsak Cha; *The Martyr* (*Soonkyocha*, 1964) by Ungook Kim; *Admiral Yi Soonshin* (*Yi Soonshin*, 1966) by Myongsoon Shin; *Change of the Season* (*Whanchul-ki*, 1968) by Tae-Sok Oh; *The Great Wall of Namhan* (*Namhan Sansong*, 1974) by Ui-Kyong Kim, a play that won the award for the best play of the year 1974 from the *Hankook Daily Newspaper*; *Princess Naknang* (*Doong Doong Naknang Doong*, 1980) by Inhoon Choi; and *King Seajong* (1981) by Chaehyun Lee.

The company possesses a strong cast consisting of such well-known Korean actors as Tongwon Kim, Minho Chang, Sunghee Paek, Hyochae Lee, and Moosong Chun. Talented directors, such as Haerang Lee, Chin Park, Chin-soon Lee, and Kyu Huh, have directed plays for the National Theatre.

The company's dramatic goal has been to establish a native Korean theatrical tradition by combining elements from traditional and modern drama. Although this approach brought innovative results during the early years of the company, recent productions have been characterized by a lack of originality and a stifling adherence to tradition which have seriously limited the company's role in current Korean drama.

HO SOON KIM

SANHA THEATRE GROUP
(Kuktan Sanha)
266-10 Chungneung-dong, Sungbook-ku
Seoul, Korea

Despite the general efforts of Korean theatrical groups to bring original Korean works to the stage, foreign plays still dominate the Korean dramatic scene today. The Sanha Theatre Group, however, has been particularly successful in producing original Korean plays. The company has staged many of the original works of Korean playwright Pomsak Cha, who has also acted as managing director of the group since its formation in 1963. The productions of the Sanha Group shared naturalistic or realistic approach to drama, reflecting essentially the artistic philosophy of Cha and that of director Pyo Chaesoon.

The company's productions of Cha's works have included the following plays: *The House with the Blue Roof* (1964), *The Tropical Fish* (1966), *The Forest Fire* (1966), and *The Castle of Roses* (1968), which won the March 1 Dramatic Award. The group's other outstanding productions include *Mannerhouse*(1965) by Thomas Wolfe, *Slave Register* (1973) by Taesung Yoon, *The Bell* (1978) by Tae-Sok Oh, *Phaedra* (1980) by Jean Racine, and *Juno and the Paycock* (1981) by Sean O'Casey.

The group's productions of original Korean works represent significant contributions to the development of native Korean drama. The group was disbanded in 1984.

HO SOON KIM

THEATRE LIBRE
(Chayoo Kukchang)
303-24 Kwanghi-dong 2 Ka, Choong-ku
Seoul, Korea

The Théâtre Libre was organized in May 1966 under the leadership of the present managing director, Pyong Boc Lee. The company's repertory consists largely of foreign plays, reflecting the foreign training of Lee and the company's dramatic director, Chong-Ok Kim, both of whom studied in France. Director Kim's preference for light comedy and lively, fast-paced action has resulted in the predominance of comedy in the company's repertory. The group's approach to drama is thus characterized by a lightness and avoidance of excessive melancholy or direct realism.

The company's representative productions have included: *Misere et Nobless* by Scarpetta, which won the Dong-A Dramatic Award of 1967; *Requiem pour une Nonne* (*Requiem for a Nun*), written by Albert Camus from the book by William Faulkner, which was awarded the *Hankuk Daily Newspaper*'s Drama and Film Award for 1970; *Where Shall We Meet Again?* (1971) by Inhoon Choi; *The Ballad of a Sad Café* by Edward Albee, based on a story by Carson McCullers, which received the *Hankuk Daily Newspaper*'s Drama and Film Award for 1972; *The Barber of Seville* by Beaumarchais, which won the Dong-A Award for 1973; *What I Wish to Be* by Woochon Park, which attempted ensemble improvisation and won the Dong-A Award and the Grand Prix of the *Hankook Daily Newspaper* for 1979; and *The Elephant Man* (1980) by Bernard Pomerance.

The Théâtre Libre also established the Café Theatre in April 1969, which serves as a tearoom by day and a theatre seating about one hundred spectators by night. The Café welcomes the talents of unknown playwrights and directors and has succeeded in popularizing theatre under circumstances relatively more free and relaxed than those of traditional theatre. Although the Théâtre Libre has been generally criticized for its preference for foreign plays, it must be credited for being one of the few companies in Korea providing light, enjoyable drama.

HO SOON KIM

Taiwan

INTRODUCTION

Theatre in Taiwan can roughly be classified into three categories: (1) Kuo-chü or the National Classical Drama, which is better known to the West as Peking Opera, (2) Ti-fang hsi or local drama, and (3) Hua-chü or modern drama. The first two have a long history, while the third was imported a little before the turn of the century from the West and has remained basically a theatre molded upon Western realistic theatre in form, with Chinese stories as its content. In the following articles, only one representative troupe or production company is selected from each category. The selection is based upon their history, achievement, and popularity today. In Taiwan local theatre is represented by various kinds of opera, puppet theatre, and shadow plays. Of these, Taiwanese opera, or Ko-tsai-hsi, is presented most frequently and is, therefore, included here.

Taiwan has several Kuo-chü, or National Classical Drama, troupes with a history of over fifteen years. Of these troupes, the majority belong to the armed forces. The private and regional troupes of this category perform only on special occasions like national holidays and festivals, though some of them have a very long history and a good reputation. The most active Kuo-chü companies are as follows (dates indicate the time of their establishment): the Ta-p'eng Kuo-chü Company (1950), the Hai-kuang Kuo-chü Company (1954), the Lu-kuang Kuo-chü Company (1958), the Kuo-chü Troupe of the Fu-hsing Drama School (1957), and the Ming-to Kuo-chü Company (1961). The Drama School specifically trains talents for the classical Chinese theatre; the other four companies also have training programs, although they are production-oriented.

The Ta-p'eng, Hai-kuang, Lu-kuang, and Ming-to companies belong to the Chinese armed forces, though they also perform for the general public regularly and many of their actors and actresses are civilians. Financially, they are supported by the armed forces; theatrically, they are national troupes of the people of Taiwan.

Besides entertaining the army and the civilians, all four troupes and the Fu-hsing Troupe have contributed greatly to the survival or revival and the spread of Peking Opera. There is now no purely commercial theatre company of this theatre because its audience is rather small and the best talents of its members have been recruited by the five groups mentioned above.

Of all these troupes of classical Chinese theatre, the Ta-p'eng Kuo-chü Company is undoubtedly the most outstanding, for not only its longer history among them but also its greater contribution to and influence on the development of this theatre in Taiwan during the last thirty years or so.

In the Taipei area alone, there are about one hundred Ti-fang hsi (local drama groups, of which the Ming-kuang troupe is representative). In Central and Southern Taiwan and north of Taipei, many troupes are based in medium-sized towns and tour surrounding villages and towns. Being a traditional theatre, versions of plays and styles of performance and singing vary from area to area and troupe to troupe.

The modern Chinese theatre is better known in China as Hua-chü because the plays of this theatre use vernacular Chinese or the prose of everyday speech (*pai hua*), whereas the traditional Chinese theatre uses mostly classical language (*wen-yen*) and singing. This theatre was first imported from the West by the missionaries, who began presenting Hua-chü dramas in their schools around 1907. Plays by Shakespeare and Molière were among the earliest to be translated into Chinese and staged in Shanghai and other big cities of China. But if the Wen-ming hsi (a kind of Hua-chü with the rather vague difference that it usually did not have fully written scripts but scenarios) is included, the bud of China's modern theatre could go back to the *Ugly Story of Officialdom* produced by the St. John College in Shanghai in 1889. Both the Hua-chü and Wen-ming hsi were called Hsin-chü or New Drama, but the Wen-ming hsi disappeared gradually around the 1930s when more and more Western masterpieces were translated into Chinese and China's own playwrights began to mature. At this time more and more well-organized troupes and drama clubs rose to strengthen the movement. Then after 1937, partly because of the rise of movies (and later television) and partly because of other social factors, the professional and nonprofessional troupes of the New Drama, both private and government-supported, began to decline in both quantity and quality. But in recent years, this New Drama has started to grow again, trying not merely to copy the Western but to combine the art of both the Western and traditional Chinese theatre. Today, there are still many small groups, but none of them is purely commercial.

In Taiwan productions of modern theatre were staged as early as 1924. When the central government of China moved to the island in 1949, theatre activities were encouraged. In addition to some army theatre troupes which came to the island with the government, new theatre groups were organized, such as the China Experimental Theatre Company (1949), the Twentieth Century Theatre Club, the Free Theatre Group, the Avant-garde Theatre, and the Oriental Theatre Group. However, it is generally agreed that in Taiwan the movement initiated by the late Professor Li Man-kuei in 1960 has been the most significant. She founded the Chinese Drama Exhibition Committee and the Three Unities Dramatic Group in 1962, the latter ceasing to function some years ago. Although the committee does not have its own actors, playwrights, or directors, it has encouraged and helped organize theatre activities, chiefly in the universities and colleges, and it holds drama contests every year. As a result of her effort and those of her followers, the World Drama Exhibition (started in 1967) and the Youth Drama Exhibition (started in 1968) have continued to stage famous plays of Western masters and modern plays of Chinese playwrights. It has formed a strong current and very likely will remain the mainstream and strength of the Chinese theatre in the future.

Among the existing young theatre groups, the most representative and promising ones seem to be the Theatre Group of the Deaf, the Chen-shan-mei Drama Group, and the Experimental Theatre Group of the T'ien Educational Center, which became independent and the most active Lan-ling Theatre Workshop in 1980. All these young groups are experimental in nature. But the oldest and still most active troupe of the New Drama is undoubtedly the Drama Troupe of the Art Division of the Chinese Armed Forces.

MEI-SHU HWANG

DRAMA TROUPE OF THE ART DIVISION OF THE CHINESE ARMED FORCES
(I-Shu Kung-Tso-Tsung-Tui Hwa-Chü-Tui)
No. 667 Ch'eng-te Road
Taipei, Taiwan

The forerunners of the Drama Troupe of the Art Division of the Chinese Armed Forces go as far back as the Sino-Japanese War during the 1930s. There were once three troupes in the Military Art Division headed by Hsiao Yü, Tung Hsin-ming, and Wu Chien-sheng, respectively. These three groups were combined into two on July 1, 1965, with T'an Hui and Kao Ch'ien as the executive directors. On October 1, 1969, at a time when more effort was being devoted to making movies and television programs, these two groups were consolidated under the directorship of Ms. T'an Hui. There have been no further organizational changes since, but the directorship has passed from Ms. T'an to Tai Hua-min, Sun P'u-sheng, Chu Lei, and now Ping Chen-Kang. Important playwrights, directors, actors, actresses, and designers who worked, or have been working, for the troupe include Ting Yi, Wang Sheng-shan, Chu Pai-shui, Chih Ch'ien-hsieh, Wu Feng, Ma Chi, Chang Yung-hsiang, Chang Pin-yü, T'ang Shao-hua, Ts'ao Chien, Kao Ch'ien, P'eng Hsing-ts'ai, Ch'ien Lu, Lu Chih, Ko Hsiang-t'ing, Fu Pi-hui, Teng Yü-ping, and Lang Hsiung.

Although organizationally the troupe belongs to the armed forces, many of its artists are civilians, and it produces plays not only for the army and the general public, but also for overseas Chinese. Its principal policy has been "education through entertainment," which is a tradition of Chinese theatre. It views its dual functions as helping to maintain high morale in the army and the society and developing modern drama and theatre in China. For this purpose a training program was set up in 1976, which became the Kuo-kuang Experimental Drama School in 1980 and is still under the directorship of the Art Division. Since 1950, it has produced more than one hundred full-length plays and more than two hundred one-act plays, all written by its own playwrights. The following were considered to be the more successful: *Heroes of the Ming Dynasty (Ta-ming ying-lieh-ch'uan)* (1950), *Cheng Cheng-kung* (1951, 1953; the hero is better known in the West as Koxinga, and after its premiere in 1951 the play toured the Philippines, Vietnam, Thailand, and Korea), *Ko Tzu-yi* (1962), *The Bright October (Yang-ch'un shih-yüeh)* (1965, awarded the best playwriting and leading roles), *Tradition (Ch'uan-t'ung)* (1966, awarded the best production of the year), *Silkworms in Spring (Ch'un-ts'an)* (1968, best playwriting award of the year), *The Native (Ku-hsiang-jen)* (1970), *The Flower Age (Chin-hsiu nien-hua)* (1971), *Spring in the Plum Garden (Mei-yüan ch'un hui)* (1976), *Reunion Ten Years after Commencement (Shih-nien chih-yüeh)* (1980), *The Same Homesickness in Five Places (Yi-yeh-hsiang-hsin wu-ch'u-t'ung)* (1981), and *The Family (Che-yi-chia)* (1982). Since its founding, the troupe has given more than two thousand performances.

MEI-SHU HWANG

MING-KUANG WANG FAMILY THREE SISTERS' TROUPE
(Ming-Kuang Wang-Chia San Chieh-Mei T'uan)
Yung-ho Chen, Ta Hsin Street, Lane 22, Alley 1, Number 2
Taipei, Taiwan

The Ming-kuang Troupe, like many other traditional troupes of local opera in Taiwanese dialect, consists of a core of actors and actresses belonging to one family and headed by a manager who is father to some of the performers. Including the performers not belonging to the Wang family and musicians, the total troupe size varies from thirteen to fourteen members to a performing group of about twenty for important occasions. The troupe currently performs three-day stints at temples for special folk religious celebrations, such as birthdays of folk Buddhist and Taoist gods and goddesses. Each day before the performers begin acting a play, they enact lesser gods and goddesses or saints in ritualistic honor of the temple's deity. Then they present two plays: the afternoon play is usually the enactment of a Chinese historical legend, a performance that contains martial dance and acrobatic feats; the evening play is one with modern themes, though still in classical costume, arranged by the troupe's storyteller-managers. Musically, the troupe combines Taiwanese folksong, popular music, and music from the repertoires of Chinese Nan-kuan or southern music and the Pei-kuan or northern music traditions common to Peking Opera.

The troupe was founded in 1935 by Wang Ting at Chia-yi, a town in Central Taiwan, and began by performing at the temples in and around Chia-yi. Later, they moved to the northern city of Taipei in search of greater opportunities.

Even after the move, although urban musical styles were learned, the connections with folk and nonurban popular music were not broken. In order to appeal to other migrants from the south, the hometown of Chia-yi is still often mentioned in association with the troupe.

The best years for Wang Ting and his troupe were when they were performing in indoor theatres in the 1940s and early 1950s. During this time, the troupe consisted of about forty members, and since there were so many available actors, each performer played only one role type. The audience for such indoor performances was ticket-purchasing, unlike the temple audiences for the outdoor street performances. The troupe became so popular that it was asked to perform in Singapore for overseas Taiwanese families. But the years of relative prosperity and success for Taiwanese opera in general and this troupe in particular did not last long into the 1960s. Now the troupe is once again largely subsidized by temples in the city of Taipei and in surrounding suburbs. Since there are fewer troupe members, some of the actors have to play more than one character in a particular play. However, the high standard of performance of the Wang troupe has not suffered. As late as 1973, the troupe won the contest of local opera troupes sponsored by the government through the Local Drama Association.

Wang Ting, the founder of the troupe, is the bearer of the traditional stories the troupe enacts and the dominant musical styles they use. He is also the creator and arranger of new plots. Although he used to perform the old man roles in such plays as *Split Open the Mountain to Save Mother* (*P'i Shan Chiu-mu*), a traditional play about a boy who saves his mother, Wang is now primarily a musician and manager. During performances, he plays the Chinese musical instruments *ching-hu*, the *hu-chin*, and the *sona*; to accompany popular music, he also plays the Western saxophone. As family head and troupe manager, he decides where and when the troupe will perform.

Wang Ting's oldest daughter, Wang Hsiu-yüeh, born during the indoor theatre period, was acting by the time she was ten years old. She now plays the scholarly young hero in most of the troupe's plays and excels in acting the major role in such popular plays as *Liang Shan-po and Chu Ying-t'ai* (*Liang Shan-po yü Chu Ying-t'ai*), a tragic romance about a girl who, disguising herself as a male in order to get an education, falls in love with a fellow student, but a marriage arranged by her parents prevents her from marrying her lover. Wang Hsiu-yüeh was so successful in the young hero roles that she performed for a while for the television performances of Taiwanese opera. The second daughter, Wang Ch'iu-lien, often plays the young heroes in historical legends and is particularly adept at martial dance. The third daughter, Wang Ch'iu-chu, also plays acrobatic roles. She performs characters such as the child-god hero No-cha and minor clown roles. Having been taught by their father, all three daughters sing the seven-word phrase songs and the crying songs or laments characteristic of traditional Taiwanese opera. In their combination of singing and acrobatic skills, they are fulfilling the aims of their father, who believes that a performer should be equally skilled in both of these arts.

Ch'en Ts'ung-ming, who began acting in the troupe of his father but later joined the Wang troupe, is the present play arranger for the troupe. That is, preceding each performance he assigns roles and reviews the plot of the story to be acted out. He is most talented as an actor of acrobatic roles, such as that of the legendary Sun Wu-k'ung, the monkey from the *Hsi-you Chi*, a story cycle widely known in popular novel form. Ch'en also plays the standard clown role and is recognized for his spontaneous wit. For Taiwanese opera movies, he has instructed other actors and actresses in acrobatics, and he has been a director of revised Taiwanese opera for television. He also has the genius for devising new plots for the troupe's evening performances.

The great versatility of these troupe members and other talented actors and musicians has made this troupe extremely popular with temple audiences. It is, therefore, not only representative but also outstanding among the traditional Taiwanese opera troupes in the Republic of China.

PATRICIA HASELTINE

TA-P'ENG NATIONAL THEATRE COMPANY
(Ta-P'eng Kuo-Chü-Tui)
No. 11, Alley 9, Lane 5, Chiu-ch'uan Street
Taipei, Taiwan

The Ta-p'eng Kuo-chü Company was established on May 1, 1950, largely through the effort of General Wang Shu-ming, the deputy commander-in-chief of the Chinese Air Force at the time. Like many Chinese soldiers, Wang himself is a great lover of the classical Chinese theatre. The troupe then recruited most of the best Peking Opera actors and actresses, such as Chiang Hsin-ping, Ha Yüan-chang, Sun Yüan-pin, Sun Yüan-p'o, Ma Yung-hsiang, Wang Ming-chao, Tai Ch'i-hsia, Wang Chen-tsu, Tuan Ch'eng-jun, and Chao Yu-ch'ing.

Beginning in September 1955, Ta-p'eng started a training program, and seven students were admitted—three girls and four boys, including the now most famous Hsu Lu, who is in various ways comparable to Mei Lan-fang. This program was later expanded into a training school for the art. Its training basically follows the traditional system; that is, each boy or girl is trained for one character type. A girl may be trained to portray a male character and a boy to portray a female character. The troupe is now under the leadership of Hsu Ch'u-nan and still has the best actors of each character type among all the troupes. For instance, it has Ha Yüan-chang for the *lao-sheng* (old male characters with no facial painting), Sun Yüan-pin for the *wu-sheng* (military male characters), Yen Lan-ching for the *tan* (female characters), Sun Yüan-p'o for the *ching* (male characters with facial painting), and Wang Ming-chao for the *ch'ou* (comic characters). Its training program has produced most of the best actors and actresses of the younger generation—to name just a few: *hsiao-sheng* type—Sun Li-hung, Kao Hui-lan; *wu-sheng* type—Chen Yü-hsia; *tan* type—Hsu Lu, Yen Lan-ching, Chiang Chu-hua, Kuo Hsiao-chuang, Niu Fang-yu; *lao-tan* type—Pai Tz'u-ai; *ching* type—K'ang Ping-ch'uan; and *ch'ou* type—Hsia Yüan-cheng.

The troupe tours the island for the armed forces and the general public all the year round (the Hai-kuang, Lu-kuang, and Ming-to troupes operate under the same policy). It has been noted for its productions of plays with large casts, such as the complete *Restoration of Peace in Heaven* (*An T'ien Hui*), the complete *Heavenly Maiden Scattering Flowers* (*T'ien-nü San-hua*), and the complete *Wild Goose Pass* (*Yen-men Kuan*). The troupe also has the richest collection of Peking Opera scripts. However, with the exception of the annual Classical Drama Contest, in which new scripts are encouraged, the regular performances are as a rule composed largely of scenes from familiar old plays. The same play may be produced by different troupes several times in a season. This seems very natural to the Chinese lovers of this theatre as it is actor-oriented; that is, customarily, people go there to see the actors and the acting, not the story. It is, therefore, very difficult to name any particular productions as representatives of its success. It may be mentioned, however, that in 1981, with the cooperation of Tze-yün Wei, John Hu, and Mei-shu Hwang who shared the directorship and adaptation of Eugene Ionesco's *The Chairs*, the troupe made a significant experiment in staging the absurdist play in the Peking Opera style—the first experiment of this kind in the long history of this classical theatre of China. The production received very good reaction from the general public and critics, including Ionesco himself.

The troupe also tours abroad. For instance, the first and second North American tours in 1973 and 1974, respectively, contained actors and actresses from this company. Its most significant tour abroad was its worldwide tour from September 1957 to February 1958, including England, Ireland, France, Spain, Morocco, Belgium, Italy, the Philippines, Thailand, Vietnam, Korea, and Japan. It presented 124 performances, including 33 in London, 18 in Paris, and 15 in Madrid. Of the 18 scenes or plays they presented, the best liked were *Heavenly Maiden Scattering Flowers*, *Chin-shan Temple* (a scene from *The White Snake—Pai-she Ch'uan*), *The Jade Bracelet* (*Shih Yü-cho*—a comic scene from a long play, emphasizing delicate movements and pantomiming), *The Crossroad Inn* (*San-cha K'ou*—also included in the 1974 North American tour), and *The Fisherman's Revenge* (*Ta-yü Sha-chia*).

MEI-SHU HWANG

Thailand

INTRODUCTION

More than one thousand professional theatre companies entertain a Thai population of forty-five million. These theatres can be classified into six major genres: masked pantomime, dance-drama, folk musical comedy (*likay*), shadow play, puppet theatre, and modern spoken drama. The masked pantomime (*khon*) and the dance-drama (*lakhon rum*) are considered classic and are well preserved by the National Theatre under government patronage. The folk musical comedy, the shadow play, and the puppet theatre are regarded as undignified and live solely on popular support. The spoken drama, also without government support, is actively performed on television, but spoken drama stage productions stopped a long time ago.

Thai theatre can also be divided into four regional theatres, by the four Thai dialect regions—north, northeast, central, and south. Each region contains one or two important forms of theatre except for the central region, where a wide variety of art forms thrive as a result of the prosperity of this socially and politically prominent region. Because the central dialect is the national language, its theatre can be understood throughout the country, whereas the regional forms are accepted only by the dialect speakers.

Thailand is an agricultural country in which most social activities conform to an agrarian cycle. The busiest season is the summer, from March to May, when the majority of farmers and peasants are free from work. The slowest season is the monsoon, from August to October, when the rain is a serious deterrent. Because of the tropical environment, theatre activities generally take place at night when the temperatures are cooler.

The production is commonly hired for a single performance period. There are three performance periods in a day: the daytime performance is from 10:00 A.M. to 4:00 P.M. nonstop; the first half-night performance is from 9:00 P.M. to midnight; and the second-half is from midnight to 6:00 A.M. The full-night performance occurs in areas where transportation is inconvenient. Few performances run for consecutive days; most are one-period productions.

A performance may be offered free-of-charge or by the sale of tickets. The free-of-charge production is more common to the Thai audience, offered to them by the community elite, generally on auspicious occasions as a token of generosity. The pay-to-see production occurs when a theatre company, during the slow season, performs to earn a living or when a fund-raising performance is underwritten by an organization. The audiences of some pay-to-see productions are required to pay an entrance fee to stand and watch at the outer ring, as well as a seating fee for a chair closer to the stage.

Although Thailand has numerous theatre activities, it has few theatre buildings. The only active operating theatre building today is the National Theatre where the National Company constantly performs *khon* and *lakhon rum*. The others can be seen on temporary stages at various feasts and fairs, usually taking place at community centers such as temple grounds, at marketplaces, or at the main compounds of well-to-do families. Therefore, a theatre company in Thailand is generally a traveling troupe, performing from place to place. In order to contact a company or to know its schedule, one has to go to its central office. A company sends its troupe out for a certain production, to return to its home station after performing.

The Bangkok Bicentennial took place in 1982, significantly increasing the frequency of each company's performances. The bicentennial celebration was year-long and involved every social segment of society.

The selection of the following representative theatre companies of Thailand is based upon their popularity, quality, and uniqueness.

SURAPONE VIRULRAK

SOMSAK PHAKDEE COMPANY
(Khana Somsak Phakdee)
471 Prachasongkroa Road
Din Dang
Bangkok, Thailand

The Somsak Phakdee Company presents *likay*, a folk musical comedy of the central region of Thailand, which is made up of large portions of spoken dialogue, interspersed with songs and dances, and accompanied by traditional musical ensemble *pi-pat*, which consists mainly of a variety of percussion instruments. Western instruments such as drum sets and congas are sometimes added. Stories are taken from classic literature, historical legends, novels, and original creations. A typical story is an adventurous romantic comedy of a hero or a heroine, undergoing all kinds of suffering before a happy reunion. Dialogue, song lyric, and story line are improvised by the actors throughout a performance. Dance and music are derived from a classical dance-drama, *lakhon rum*. Modern songs and Western disco dances occur occasionally as parts of the play. There is no off-stage chorus. Narration is used to describe an actor's background and to clarify the complication of a story. The scenery is a standard of wing and drop

6 meters wide and 3.5 meters high. The stage is 6 meters deep, with a multi-purpose bench in the center. A music stage of 3 by 4 meters is placed stage right of the acting area. The stage is either a raised platform or a matted floor on the ground. Costumes are varied in pattern. The remnants of court costumes of the late nineteenth century are used for a play based upon classic literature. Modern-style costumes are generally used in a play dealing with contemporary stories. The actor dresses in sash on top of knee-length trousers and white knee socks; jewelry; embroidered short- or long-sleeved shirt; bandana, head gear, earrings, belt, and necklaces heavily decorated with jewels. The actress dresses in a long flowing blouse with a tiara and jewelry. Shoes are prohibited on stage.

In a *likay* performance, the audience, comprised mostly of women, expects to see young and handsome actors adorned in beautiful costumes, a fast-moving story, and comic devices. If the performance appeals to them, they will show their appreciation by offering leis and monetary gifts, especially to leading actors. The actress generally receives less attention from the audience.

Somsak Phakdee is the most famous professional *likay* company in Thailand today. Those who read Thai newspapers would recognize this name as it is often mentioned. The company actively performed for more than fifteen years under the name of Saw. Phakdee, before changing it to Somsak Phakdee in 1975 when Tieng Phakdee, the owner-manager, passed his career on to his son, Somsak Phakdee. Tieng Phakdee, however, is still the manager. Before moving to Bangkok in 1975, the company was located in Rachaburi Province.

Consisting of fifty people (thirty-five actors and actresses, ten musicians, and five technicians), the company owns a bus, full-scale *pi-pat* instruments, scenery, sound equipment, and over fifty costumes.

The performance fee of this company is 10,000 baht, or $500, for a half-night performance (plus transportation fee). The company prefers not to perform during the day because the actors would then be too tired to perform later at night. Since the company is very famous, contracts for performances must be made six months in advance. The company has no interest in noncontract, pay-to-see performances because it is booked throughout most of the year. The company owns a daily radio and a weekly television program. In the near future, it plans to open a branch called Monrak Phakdee, which will be managed by a cousin of Tieng Phakdee. The two companies will then join for extravagant productions.

Somsak Phakdee, the star of the company and also the most famous star of Thai theatre today, is twenty-three years old. Starting his career at the age of fourteen, he became a very famous star in 1975. Thus, the company was named for him. In the same year, he was invited to the National Theatre, to receive an honorary certificate for his superb performance. Such recognition is extremely rare. Thereafter, he began to appear regularly on radio and television. He invites movie stars and comedians to join his television program, making his name and company ever more popular. Sometimes he is personally invited to give two or three performances in one night, which he dislikes and tries to avoid.

Somsak Phakdee, despite his popularity, still wants to improve his acting ability. He recently hired a poet to tutor him and his colleagues in the poetic art and to help create poetry. A very creative artist, he designed a new style of *likay* costume that became widely accepted and has now replaced the traditional style used for more than a half-century. He also enlarged the size of the stage from 6 meters, a conventional width, to 12 meters to give a sense of panoramic view.

The repertoire of this company is not particularly interesting because the main attraction is Phakdee himself. Basically, the story line is a romantic comedy in which Phakdee, the hero of every play, undergoes all kinds of suffering before a happy reunion with his lover. The most famous story by this company for television production is an excerpt from a work of classic literature entitled *Khun Chang Khun Phan* (*Master Chang and Master Phan*), a triangle love plot leading to a tragic ending, the execution of the heroine.

SURAPONE VIRULRAK

THONGBAI ROUNGNON COMPANY
(Khana Thongbai Roungnon)
193 Lanluang Road
Bangkok, Thailand

The Thongbai Roungnon Company is over sixty years old and is probably the oldest theatre company in Thailand. The original name of this company was Phoon Roungnon, until Phoon's death in 1976 at the age of ninety-three. Thongbai then took over the business, naming the company for himself. He is fifty-four years old and is well versed in acting, singing, dancing, and playing many kinds of musical instruments. He also performs in other forms of theatre such as *likay* and *nang talung* (shadow play).

The Thongbai Roungnon Company is distinguished for its productions of *lakhon chatree*, a dance-drama of the central region which is based on classical dramatic literature. The cast is female, except for the clowns. A narrator delivers a poetic line for an actress to sing, and then the chorus repeats it. Several pairs of bamboo clappers and drums are used during the singing, and the traditional ensemble *pi-pat* is used for the dance. Songs, dances, stage directions, and costumes are very similar to a classical dance-drama, *lakhon rum*, but less refined. The 4 by 4 meter stage is situated on the ground, with a music stage of about the same size on the stage right. A bench is placed in the upper center stage for multiple uses. The scenery is a piece of 3 by 4 meter backdrop with two doors on both ends for entrances and exits. Many performances do not use scenery.

Lakhon chatree is commonly used in religious functions of animistic Buddhism, Brahmanism, and animism. There are *lakhon chatree* performances every day in many famous temples and shrines in Central Thailand. A person pays for the performance when he wants to fulfill his vow after he has received an answer to his prayers. *Lakhon chatree* is most often performed during the day. This theatre is famous for its music. The loudness and various fast rhythmic patterns of drum beating maintain audience attention.

In the Thongbai Roungnon Company, the number of members varies because Thongbai includes everyone in the Thongbai family in his accounting, which totals nearly a hundred people. Actors and musicians—both young and old—are included. This idea is acceptable because it is the tradition of this family that every female is trained to be a dancer and every male a musician; furthermore, some are trained in both fields, such as Thongbai. Thus, every family member is a company member. But a *lakhon chatree* performance usually requires only ten to fifteen actors and actresses and eight to ten musicians. These performers are recruited from among family members. Therefore, many of them have to earn their living by other professions. This does not mean the performance quality is decreased. The National Theatre still recognizes this company and invites it to perform each year. Boonsri Roungnon, a senior member of the family, is a teacher at the National School of Dancing. She still performs for the company.

The repertoire of this company is a vast collection of classical dramatic literature of which *Chaiyachet* is the most popular story. The word *chai* means glory, and thus, a performance of *Chaiyachet* serves to glorify a feast or fair. The story is about the adventure of Prince Chaiyachet and the princess who bore him a son. The baby is abducted and replaced with a wooden block by a jealous queen. The princess is finally exiled to return to her city amidst great sorrow. The prince, after learning the truth, follows her. He has many adventures before a happy reunion is realized.

The production fee for a half-night performance is around 3,000 to 5,000 baht or $150 to $250, depending upon the size of the cast required in each play. Transportation costs are added to this fee. The music can be hired separately, and the costumes may be rented. The company is also an agent for all types of theatre.

SURAPONE VIRULRAK

WAT SAWANG AROM COMPANY
(Khana Wat Sawang Arom)
Tambon Tone-Po
Amper Muang
Changwat Singhburi, Thailand

The Wat Sawang Arom Company performs *nang yai*, the grand silhouette play, a unique form of theatre in which shadow puppet technique is mingled with classical dance form on a grandiose scale.

In the *nang yai* performance, the male puppeteers hold the large, nonarticulated puppets over their heads and post them in front of a large, white screen on the audience side. When a sense of distance is needed, the puppets are posted backstage. Each puppet is moved slightly when its part is narrated by two male narrators who stand on opposite ends of the screen. But during the musical intervention, the puppeteers hold their puppets over their heads and dance in front of the screen on the bare dirt ground that serves as their stage. The dances depict the characters and moods of the puppets; for example, the puppeteer dances softly for a refined character such as Sita, or he leaps and swirls for a restless character like Hanuman, when he becomes angry. These dances are similar to the styles used in the *khon* masked dance-drama.

Besides the syncreticism of the shadow form and the dance form which distinguishes itself from other kinds of theatre, the grandiose scale of a *nang yai* performance is also extraordinary. The intricately fretted cowhide puppets are of varying sizes. The smaller size, usually the single figure puppet, is about 1.2 meters high; the larger size, normally the group compositions, which may include buildings and trees, is around 2 meters high. In some performances more than two hundred puppets are required, and as many as ten puppeteers perform at the same time. Since the puppets are big, they require a screen as large as 4 meters high and 12 meters wide. This is a white, translucent, cotton screen, backlighted by coconut fire, creating a neon-like, smokeless flame. Tied with four posts, of which two in the center are 6 meters apart, this screen becomes the main performing area, whereas the white, less translucent sheets on both ends serve as the antestage. The bottom line of the screen is 1.2 meters above the ground, and the bottom space is covered with thick cloth to protect the source of light from view of the audience.

As the above description indicates, the audience does not see the shadow of the puppets or the dancer-puppeteers because the source of light comes from behind the screen and they are in front of it. Nor does the audience see the puppets and the dancer-puppeteers themselves because there is no source of light from the audience's side. Therefore, what the audience actually sees are the silhouettes of the puppets and of the dancer-puppeteers. Given the grandiose scale of the performance, this form of theatre, *nang yai*, should be identified as "the grand silhouette play."

Music is another indispensable ingredient of *nang yai*, for it is used to accompany singing and dancing. The musical ensemble, *pi-pat* as it is called, consists of a *ranad ek* (melodic wooden xylophone), a *ranad thum* (bass wooden xylophone), a *pi* (oboe), two *kong wong* (a set of circular gongs), a *tapone* (small barrel drum), a pair of *klong thad* (large barrel drum), a pair of *ching* (cymbals), and a *grong* (bamboo post and sticks which serve as clappers).

Nang yai can be performed during the day or at night. The gold and colored printed puppets are used for day performance, whereas the black puppets are used at night. The day-style puppets were designated for royal ceremonies and now are museum pieces.

The Wat Sawang Arom Company has more than 350 opaque puppets in its collection, which belongs to Cha-on Supanakorn, the manager of the company. Some of these puppets are more than 150 years old and very well preserved. The company is composed of twenty-four men: ten puppeteers, four narrators, and ten musicians. The youngest is the fifty-four-year-old manager, and the eldest is the eighty-four-year-old narrator-teacher of the troupe.

The company asks for 6,000 baht or $300 for a half-night performance (plus transportation fee) and 4,000 baht or $200 for two hours of a full-scale demonstration (plus transportation fee).

The only story this company performs is Ramakien, the Thai version of Ramayana, which is divided into many episodes. Their most famous episode is "Suk Yai," the great battle in which Totsakan, or Ravana, the demon king, engages in battle with Pra Ram or Rama, the incarnation of Lord Vishnu. Totsakan uses all his mightiest power but is finally defeated.

These episodes are memorized from classic literature. However, narrators have the right to shorten, lengthen, or adjust the script, especially in the dialogue section, to suit each performance. Thai language (central dialect) is used throughout.

Nang yai has nearly become an extinct form of theatre, for only two companies are performing it. There is a movement, however, to train and encourage a new generation to pursue this art.

SURAPONE VIRULRAK

AUSTRALIA AND NEW ZEALAND

Robert Page, Area Editor

Introduction

It has taken almost until Australia's bicentenary—marked, significantly, from the arrival of the first convicts eighteen years after Captain Cook had claimed the continent for Great Britain in 1770—to be able to report a healthy, thriving, and richly diverse theatre in Australia. The consolidation of the profession represented by the establishment of major state companies (which form the body of the theatres surveyed in this profile) has only come about in the past two decades. Preceding them, a few false starts notwithstanding, theatre was chasmically divided between the commercial houses and the amateur groups.

Now there is a spectrum: the amateur theatre remains strong, student theatre has burgeoned, and fringe companies have sprung up everywhere. Theatre restaurants and cafe theatres present everything from melodramas to the most outré postpunk acts. Away from state capitals, regional theatre has become a major force with companies germinating in a number of country centers, some bringing mainstream theatre to the locals and others developing work out of the heart of the region. In the major conurbations not only are there the prestigious state companies, but also a number of what may be termed first, second, and third city companies. The commercial theatre may be in a period of uneven fortune, but it continues to mount blockbuster imports, even though it also turns to subsidized companies to satisfy the voracious needs of its touring venues.

The country's theatre was slow to develop largely because of Australia's beginnings as a British colony—with all the problems of discovering a distinct national identity and the difficulties of achieving a degree of self-confidence bound up with that status. Theatre in Australia goes back to the first fleet, when the convicts, in celebration of George III's birthday on June 4, 1789, were allowed "humbly to excite a smile" with a production of George Farquhar's *The Recruiting Officer*. With it that tradition was begun of Australia hanging on the apron strings of an English repertoire. This practice was not severely and effectively questioned until 170 years later, even though the country became a nation in its own right in 1901. What was also to have continuing significance about that production was its amateur status and the rough, rudely ebullient manner of its performance: the hallmark of one aspect of the tradition in Australia.

In the nineteenth century local plays were not unknown on the country's stages, but by and large audiences were trained to think of superior plays and performers as emanating from across the seas. George Selth Coppin, a major builder of theatres on the eastern seaboard, was an English low comedian who in the antipodes became a leading entrepreneur until his death in 1906. But it was an American, J. C. Williamson, who topped the actor-manager (as was nineteenth-century practice) stakes. He arrived in 1874 with a play prophetically entitled *Struck Oil*, and the company he formed in his own name rose to such power and ubiquity that it became known simply as The Firm, outliving him to become the longest established theatre chain in the world. As it turned out, the new nationalism of the 1970s helped bring about its demise when, in 1977, its name and theatres were sold.

Another factor that defeated it was the sheer scale of the continent. Its size—as big as America, yet with a population scattered across it less than that of New York—is a major problem at a time of dizzily escalating costs. Nonetheless, a number of leaner and less real-estate-oriented entrepreneurial companies have stepped into the breach (the J. C. Williamson name remains attached to a production company, although the Michael Edgley [International] organization is now the most powerful). This ensures that Australia maintains its diet of plays like *A Chorus Line*, *Annie*, *Evita*, and revivals of *Oklahoma!* It is also true that a degree of discrimination and sophistication is becoming evident in contemporary audiences; huge publicity and extravagant staging are no longer sure-fire at the box office.

When the commercial theatre was bringing in the tried and tested pick of the crop from Broadway and the West End, often complete with well-seasoned players, it is not surprising that embryonic talents and local theatres paled by comparison. Undeterred, some tried. After World War I, the playwright Louis Esson, influenced by William Butler Yeats and the Abbey Theatre movement, aimed to emulate them with a small theatre devoted to establishing a serious national drama. Esson's Pioneer Players faded within two years, but a torch had been lit. In the 1930s a host of little theatres grew up. In major capitals a chain of New Theatres were set up by the left, some of which still exist, presenting agit-prop and street theatre in addition to stage plays. The Independent Theatre, crucible for many leading talents, was established in Sydney; the Little Theatre in Melbourne; Twelfth Night in Brisbane; and Patch Theatre in Perth. In these playhouses local dramatists had the chance to gain a hearing.

The next step forward came with another tug on the old colonial apron strings. In 1954, to commemorate the queen's visit, it was felt that a continuing memorial to the event was appropriate: the result was the Australian Elizabethan Theatre Trust (AETT). With a brief to foster the performing arts, it represented the first commitment of government aid to the arts. The initial step, however, was to appoint the inevitable Englishman to be its first director and to import the inevitable English production (with Ralph Richardson and Sybil Thorndike in the leads) as its first offering.

In the same year the AETT was founded, another Englishman, John Sumner, was invited by Melbourne University to begin the Union Theatre Repertory Company (UTRC). Its program of the classics, major contemporary plays, and some Australian plays was to set the pattern for others in its wake. The first move had been made toward state companies, for the UTRC was to move off campus and become the mighty Melbourne Theatre Company.

Back in the fifties, however, hopes were pinned on national companies—for the opera, the ballet, and the theatre. In the Australian Opera and the Australian Ballet, the envisioned ideal of technically superb and lavishly funded enterprises was eventually realized. But, for the theatre, the dream steadfastly refused to become a reality. At first, however, with the Trust Players and a modern classic of Australian drama, *Summer of the Seventeenth Doll*, which had popped up at the UTRC from the pen of an actor there, Ray Lawler, it seemed that the national drama had been born overnight—albeit after a lengthy gestation period. The play itself went on to gain the ultimate accolade of a West End run and even a limited airing on Broadway. Lawler emigrated with the play, for the belief persisted that success in Australia counted as nothing against recognition in the cultural "real worlds" of the United Kingdom and America. Despite early hits and even an eleventh-hour success with *The One Day of the Year*, it soon became obvious that theatre needed to put down roots in communities if it was to build a solid following. The Trust Players crashed in 1961.

Also in the fifties, two more localized ventures began, which, as it turned out, were much closer auguries of the future. One, the Ensemble in Sydney, founded by an American actor, Hayes Gordon, was based not surprisingly on U.S. models—the Group Theatre and the Actors' Studio. The other, Emerald Hill in Melbourne, followed European ideas—Littlewood's Stratford East, the Berliner Ensemble, and Vilar's Théâtre National Populaire. The Ensemble, Australia's first theatre-in-the-round, was to endure, but Emerald Hill, the "right theatre in the wrong place at the wrong time," lived only until the mid-sixties, although it closed needing only $4,000 to $5,000 to survive. Sadly, subsidy in those days was not generally available.

Although the Trust Players collapsed in 1961, its parent organization, the Australian Elizabethan Theatre Trust (AETT), had shifted its thinking by 1960 toward the development of a number of state capital companies. In Melbourne the Union Theatre Repertory Company was already up and running (Melbourne Theatre Company, or MTC); in Perth there was a large amateur company, which had built itself a substantial theatre, the Playhouse, in 1956 (National Theatre); and for Sydney it was felt that the Independent, the Ensemble, or the Trust Players could provide the basis for a state company.

History does not always follow foreseen courses, and the Sydney initiative came from elsewhere. In 1958 the National Institute of Dramatic Art had been established along the lines of the United Kingdom's Royal Academy of Dramatic

Art. Its requirement for a new theatre, together with the need for a company for its graduates to work in, resulted in the foundation of the Old Tote in 1963 (so named because of the old totalisator building near Randwick Racecourse which was its first venue).

It took a little longer in other states: the South Australian Theatre Company, based in Adelaide, was formed in 1965; the Queensland Theatre Company in Brisbane in 1969; and the Tasmanian Theatre Company in Hobart's historic Theatre Royal, beginning productions in 1973. Most followed the established, essentially English repertory pattern of the first state theatre company, the MTC. Indeed, before the collapse of the Old Tote and its replacement by the Sydney Theatre Company (STC), all five state companies were run by British directors. Even now, only two, the STC, under Richard Wherrett (ex-Nimrod), and the State Theatre Company of South Australia, headed by the internationally known Jim Sharman (*Hair*, *Superstar*, and *Rocky Horror*), have Australian-born artistic directors.

Unquestionably, the state companies are the flagships of the Australian theatre fleet, but as with all flagships, they tend to be top heavy, expensive to keep afloat, and rarely in the front line. Their captains tend to be of an older guard, whose records are as solid as their imaginations have become stodgy. Seasons— to change the metaphor—tend to be a stew of pop classics for the meat; farces, thrillers, and the odd musical for sauce; and a few indigenous plays thrown in for local flavor. Interestingly, the two Australian directors are proving to have sufficient breadth of vision, energy, and commitment to allow the kind of continual reappraisal and rejuvenation these hefty companies need to avoid churning out well-dressed, middle-brow entertainment which is so acceptable to their cosily middle-class audiences.

If the establishment of the AETT allowed national companies to develop, it was the establishment of the Australian Council for the Arts (later simply the Australia Council) which consolidated the position of the state companies. Australia is a federation and has no single focus equitable with London or New York, but Sydney and Melbourne are the largest cities, and their companies received the bulk of the new central government funding. State governments also began to fund the arts and established ministries and cultural affairs departments to disburse their subsidies. With money from government flowing, it became possible to build and support substantial modern theatres and arts venues: the Old Tote and now the Sydney Theatre Company have the Opera House as a home, while the South Australian Company performs in the huge Adelaide Festival Centre complex. Homes along similar lines are presently nearing completion for the Melbourne and Queensland Theatre companies.

Yet the government subsidies that allowed the growth of these monolithic companies also flowed into a new breed of aggressively Australian companies, which developed in the late sixties and early seventies. Being innovative and politically and socially concerned, it took the election of a Labour government in 1972 to gain the kind of subsidies that would allow them to become fully professional. A new approach to theatre and drama went hand-in-hand, with the ascendancy of the companies matching that of a new wave of indigenous playwrights. They developed in converted warehouses, where the enforced intimacy and open staging were as confrontational as the subject matter. Modern Australia was under the microscope. If *The Doll* had been virtually the first time the accent had been heard on stage, now the warts-and-all vernacular had arrived, too.

Politically, the theatre was given its dynamism not only by the rise of the Labour party gaining power after twenty-three years of conservative government, but also by the opposition to the Vietnam War and the worldwide shift to pop culture, and the youth/feminist/antiracist movements.

The most important of these alternative companies were the Australian Performing Group (APG) and the Nimrod, both started in 1970. The APG grew out of the radical experiment to found a New York Café La Mama in Melbourne, soon gathering to itself actors and writers. Young bloods arrived from the universities, and the enterprise moved into an old Pram Factory, retaining the name for its theatre. In Sydney a vaudeville-based play, *The Legend of King O'Malley*, exploded out of an alternative Old Tote season to a national tour. As a result, its director and actors, disgruntled with the major company, set up an alternative company in an old stable in the red light district.

Other capitals followed suit as the new wave became a tide: in Brisbane, La Boite was founded; in Perth, the Hole in the Wall; in Adelaide, Troupe and the Stage Company. And in Sydney and Melbourne other groups sprang up (and some faded): in Sydney, the Stables Company, Griffin, King O'Malley Company, and Marian Street; and in Melbourne, Hoopla (later Playbox) and Anthill.

These companies, beginning as they did with a mix of acerbic, sinewy "supernaturalism"—identifying the new Australia—and the rough song and dance, vaudeville-based shows and documentaries (tapping a rich heritage of Australia which stretches back to the nineteenth-century music hall via tent shows and the Tivoli circuits), have themselves become establishment. The radicals of yesterday have become the middle class of today, and the headiness of the seventies has yielded to the bleak realities of recession and monetarism in the eighties, so the companies have tempered their repertoires. It is not insignificant that the new head of the state company in Sydney is from the Nimrod.

As the theatre in the eighties settles into this "age of uncertainty" and the belt-tightening increases, seasons are becoming ever more commercial. There is little sign of a third new wave or of a strong avant-garde, though "fringe" and "special interest" companies—women's groups, writers' theatres, and regional companies—are emerging. The state and second companies are looking to transfers for an increasing part of each new season's productions. Consequently, old divisions between the commercial and subsidized companies are beginning to blur. Concomitantly, there has been a slight swing away, yet again, from local writers. The fortunes of indigenous writers are provedly tied to the vicissitudes of subvention: the government giveth and the government taketh away.

Nonetheless, it is no longer necessary for writers to go overseas if they want to make a career for themselves, and some of Australia's best playwrights are established in a way not thought possible twenty years ago. They are going beyond the fervent nationalism of a decade ago, and now, without apology, they set their plays in other parts of the world and consider major social and political upheavals of the modern age. The booming film industry has also proved a fillip to local writers.

With several plays, from *The Doll* onward, touring overseas, some in their original productions, two international agencies have been set up—the World Theatre Exchange (another AETT initiative) and the Cladan Institute for Cultural Exchange. The new confidence in things Australian—the "cultural cringe" was once a common phrase—is demonstrated by the establishment of a major publishing house, Currency Press, dedicated to putting indigenous plays in print. In addition, the country supported a national magazine of the performing arts, *Theatre Australia*, which went into the major libraries of the world and had a substantial circulation at home.

New Zealand experienced in microcosm much the same pattern of development as Australia. In the nineteenth and twentieth centuries, theatre was dominated by English, American—and Australian!—tours. As they went into decline, the amateur movement became predominant but had little concern for developing a national drama. Again, it was not until the late 1960s and early 1970s, with the factor of government funding through the establishment of the Arts Council, that a strong local professional theatre, presenting the work of New Zealand writers, developed. There were the same initial attempts to found a national company, which then fragmented into community-based theatres. The drama has gone through the stage of aggressive naturalism to a more mature and wider view. Just as Australia's David Williamson has gained several West End (and one Broadway) productions of his plays, so New Zealand's Roger Hall has gained international acclaim for his plays, *Glide Time* (or *Flexitime*) and *Middle Age Spread*.

Of the many companies in New Zealand, it has only been possible to examine the two major ones in this survey, the Downstage in Wellington and the Mercury Theatre Company, Auckland. The importance of the others should not be ignored. Theatre Corporate is an ensemble working in a converted warehouse in Auckland; Centrepoint did the same thing in Palmerston North but intriguingly operates as a *serious* theatre restaurant; Circa, Wellington's second company, is operated cooperatively; the Court Theatre in Christchurch's Arts Centre has two auditoriums playing modern and classical works; and the Fortune, Dunedin, is the only professional company in the southern half of the South Island.

Australia supports a breadth of theatre activity out of proportion to its size—in respect to population. In the seventies, a burgeoning, in terms of both quantity and quality, occurred which put its theatre on a par with that of the rest of the "Western" world and signaled a new confidence in itself, its writers, and its practitioners. This excellence, so lately gained, can never now be lost.

ROBERT PAGE

AUSTRALIAN PERFORMING GROUP
The Pram Factory
Carlton, Melbourne, Victoria, Australia

The Australian Performing Group emerged in Melbourne during the late 1960s. It began as a loosely knit cell of actors, directors, and writers, who came together out of a common impulse to explore new and neglected forms of theatre, to investigate the nature of performance, and to work in an atmosphere free from the alleged stylistic encumbrances of conventional professional theatre. The Australian Performing Group was, in fact, Australia's first alternative theatre company.

Its immediate origins reach back to Melbourne University, a consistently vigorous center of theatrical activity through the postwar period until the present. The sixties on that campus saw many productions of absurdist plays, along with works by Bertolt Brecht and John Arden (who visited in 1964), thus stimulating a broad curiosity in modernist drama and a skepticism toward the status quo.

In 1967 Betty Burstall acquired an old shirt factory in the nearby suburb of Carlton and agitated for its use as a theatre venue. She christened her building La Mama, after Ellen Stewart's theatre in New York, an enterprise that impressed her by both its work and environment. Initially, La Mama (Melbourne) was a hodge-podge locale for poets, singers, musicians, and actors. Within a year, theatre groups had formed in order to present plays in a less ad hoc fashion. The most substantial and enduring of these was to become the Australian Performing Group (APG).

Jack Hibberd's *Brain Rot: An Evening of Pathology and Violence, Love and Friendship*, first performed at Melbourne University in April 1968, is generally acknowledged as the seminal event in the history of the APG. The central members of this production (Graeme Blundell, Brian Davies, David Kendall, and Kerry Dwyer) promptly formed the La Mama Company, a year later changing its name to the Australian Performing Group.

The first eighteen months of work by the APG were noteworthy for their explanatory zeal and rabid eclecticism. Workshops, readings, group discussions, exercises, open and closed improvisations, all became staple activities. The key influences (in no particular order) were the theory and works of Brecht, Jerzy Grotowski and his book *Towards a Poor Theatre*, role theory and games psychology, Richard Schechner's *Public Domain* with its notions of ritualized communal theatre, articles from the *Tulane Drama Review*, in addition to sprinklings of Antontin Artaud, Konstantin Stanislavsky, and silent film comic techniques.

Around this time there appeared a new batch of Australian playwrights. John Romeril, Alex Buzo, and Barry Oakley, along with Jack Hibberd, were the writers principally associated or linked with the APG in its early years. Their plays, and those of Off-Off-Broadway writers, Brecht, and some contemporary English dramatists, were the chief dramaturgical fare.

As 1969 progressed, the APG started to discover and adopt individual stances and articulate its first policies. It saw itself then as a cooperative venture designed to provide a foundation for experiment in the performing arts and concerned with developing a uniquely Australian form of theatre. Animated by the Vietnam crisis and shifting community attitudes to Australian institutions and mores, the APG also depicted itself as a theatre of social and political concern, expressing this in events as diverse as street agit-prop and lunch hour plays in factories at the behest of trade unions. The most politically engaged had been bloodied in student protest movements and sought strenuously, at times practically, at times rhetorically, to mix-marry theatre and politics.

Until late 1969 the primary drives of the APG had been exploratory and almost totally experimental. These emphases diminished as the group became more urgently concerned with the establishment of a distinctive indigenous theatre, a theatre of broad cultural pertinence and tang.

This first period of the APG's history climaxed in its attendance at the Perth Festival in February 1970 with a full program of contemporary Australian plays, a singular event in Australian theatre history and one that presaged, even announced, new times for local writers, actors, and directors. The stage idiom of these productions was alarmingly Australian, the style was virile, physically aggressive, toughly comic, rather unpolished though refreshingly direct, and devoid of conventional artifice. The dominant substyle has been variously described as "supernaturalism" and "antipodean heterosexual," the latter to distinguish it from "fop theatre" and "cosmetic pseudo-Englishness," then held to be typical of Australian drama.

The works presented at the Perth Festival were *The Front Room Boys* and *Norm and Ahmed* (Alex Buzo), *The Man from Chicago* (John Romeril), and *White with Wire Wheels* and *Who?* (Jack Hibberd). On top of this formal program, political street theatre and impromptu open air events at recreational centers were performed.

The APG, along with a production of *The Boys in the Band* and interstate theatres, played a significant part in the relaxation of Australian theatre censorship laws. Several of the members were prosecuted in 1969 and 1970 on obscenity charges relating to the use of salacious words in public. The subsequent court cases and protests helped create the healthier and more liberal climate currently existing in Australia.

During the second half of 1970 the APG transported itself to new quarters, called the Pram Factory, in Carlton. It was felt that the chamber space of La Mama did not lend itself to large-cast and theatrically, physically expansive stagecraft. The other substyle, totally nonnaturalistic and more cartoonlike, had come to the front of the group's thinking.

Accordingly, the yearnings of the majority of the company were for a broader, more theatrically expressive and pungent kind of theatre, a theatre of bold pageantry, popular types, songs, crude comedy, and improvisational spontaneity, hopefully underpinned with social and political strictures. The relatively spacious hall of the Pram Factory enabled these aspirations to bear fruit in the highly successful egalitarian show called *Marvellous Melbourne*, the result of six months of historical research, workshops, writing, and rehearsal by writers, actors, and directors.

Although *Marvellous Melbourne* did not receive the national acclaim of its coeval *The Legend of King O'Malley*, nor the powerful trumpeting of the Port Jackson (a disparaging term for Sydney harking back to the first colonization) media machine, it has exerted a more lasting influence, both on several playwrights and on the development of a genre of popular theatre evolved by the APG.

During 1971 the APG was troubled by internal divisions, which led to a few resignations and departures, as well as reforms implementing a proper constitution, regular election of officeholders, and determination of the artistic program through group convocations.

The principal achievements of 1971 were the premieres of *Mrs. Thally F* (John Romeril), *The Feet of Daniel Mannix* (Barry Oakley), and *Don's Party* (David Williamson). Williamson was soon to become the most successful of the "new wave" playwrights, though in reality he had not been a part of the early experimental APG and La Mama fermentations, and really only emerged as a phenomenon in the early seventies. This is evident in his well-crafted, yet highly conventional realism, a realism untouched by modernist theatre idioms, and explains his hearty acceptance as part of the mainstream of Australian naturalism.

The international flowering of feminism had an immediate impact on the APG, and its women were the first in Australia to respond theatrically. Their feminist threnody, *Betty Can Jump*, was an enormous success and led eventually to the formation of a Women's Theatre Group. Thus, 1972 saw increased diversity and activity, which were partly an expression of proliferating energy and partly a response to increased government funding.

In 1973 there was further expansion of activities. A new small theatre space was opened featuring plays by Harold Pinter, John Romeril, and Jack Hibberd. These productions toured three states. Notable events were *The Bob and Joe Show*, *Beware of Imitations* (Barry Oakley), and *Dimboola* (Jack Hibberd). The APG had premiered this last play in 1969; this new production provoked a rash of long runs all over the country, rendering it the most popular of all Australian plays.

The next four years were remarkable chiefly for a wide range of community theatre tours (factories, community centers, schools, prisons, and so on): the premiere of *The Floating World* (John Romeril); a group-devised popular theatre piece, *The Hills Family Show*; and a four-week tour of New Zealand, exhibiting *The Les Darcy Show* and *One of Nature's Gentlemen* (Jack Hibberd); and *Mrs. Thally F* (John Romeril).

The APG's most energetic year, 1976, saw productions of plays by Peter Handke, David Hare, and Heathcote Williams; premieres of *A Toast to Melba* and *The Overcoat* (Jack Hibberd); and country and interstate tours of *The Hills Family Show* and *A Stretch of the Imagination* (a new production of Jack Hibberd's monodrama premiered by the APG in 1972).

Since 1976 the APG has diversified into circus, radio, and film. Its policies have been revised and now include a more active attitude to new overseas drama. The APG is a legally constituted and registered cooperative. Programming and management, having been streamlined, are in the hands of elected committees.

Circus Oz, a larrikin countercultural circus, was spawned by the APG. Now independent of the APG, it has proved a huge national and international success, taking England, Scotland, and Europe by storm in 1981.

In 1977 a small group of APG actors presented *Back to Bourke St.*, a show that took an affectionate, yet comic, look at Australia through a history of local popular song. This show was featured at the 1978 Adelaide Festival of Arts and has since had two successful seasons in Melbourne theatre restaurants. There are now several cabaret theatre restaurants in Melbourne, and their theatrical fare has largely been influenced and inspired by the comic traditions of the APG.

The year 1978 saw the APG sponsoring a film of the play *Dimboola*. While failing to achieve immediate box office success, it has since gained in popularity and is in danger of becoming a cult or sect masterpiece. If nothing else, it is a fine record of the skills and styles of many of the APG's most forthright actors.

These diversifications did not entail a neglect of local theatre. Over the late 1970s the APG continued to produce Romeril's political burlesques: *The Golden Holden*, *The Uranium Show*, and *Mickey's Moomba*. It also produced the work of a new absurdist playwright, Barry Dickins, with comedies like *The Foolshoe Hotel* and *The Rotten Teeth Show*.

In 1979 the APG premiered Stephen Sewell's *Traitors*, a play that has since been produced across Australia and in London. Sewell is now regarded as Australia's most febrile and taxing political playwright.

A year of soul-searching and self-scrutiny occurred for the APG in 1979. The risk-taking hit-and-miss approach to theatre had increasingly been producing too many misses, in contrast to previous years. It was decided to appoint an ensemble of actors to determine a program.

The APG was always an actors' and writers' theatre; its finest achievements emerged from a creative tension between these poles. The appointment of an ensemble of new actors was only a temporary solution to the waning powers of the old guard of actors and writers.

The years 1980 and 1981 can be seen as bridging years for the APG, yet on this bridge stood some memorable productions: *Cloud Nine* (Caryl Churchill), *Kate Kelly* (Frank Hatherly), *The Ken Wright Show* (Barry Dickins), *Steel City Sister* (Joy Wiedersatz), *The Two-Headed Calf* (Stanislaw Witkiewicz), and *Bold Tales* (Peewee King).*

JACK HIBBERD

*AREA EDITOR'S NOTE: In 1982 the APG fell to the executioner's axe, honed by recession, and disbanded.

DOWNSTAGE
P.O. Box 1503
Wellington, New Zealand

"Our job was to get the theatre out amongst people, and downstage was the area we should be working in rather than upstage," so said Martyn Sanderson, defining its philosophy and giving it a name. Harry Seresin created its ambience and gave it a home, a place where theatre was simply part of the business of living, eating, talking, and relaxing. Together with Tim Eliott, actor, and Peter Bland, writer, they founded Downstage.

Their ideas took shape toward the end of 1963. An inaugural meeting was held on May 15, 1964, at the end of which Downstage could count on the support of 110 members. The plans for incorporating the Downstage Theatre Society recognized explicitly that Bland, Eliott, and Sanderson should be written into it as artistic directors. Its first management committee was strong on academics, also including invaluable legal and business skills. New Zealand's leading playwright, Bruce Mason, was also a member.

For several months Downstage had neither a home nor an agreed philosophy, and in retrospect many have thought its first production (Ionesco's *Exit the King*, opened on August 14, 1964, in a large rented theatre) at odds with the theatre they now know. It was not entirely so, for Ionesco's crumbling world also imaged the decayed state of conventional theatre as Sanderson saw it. The most salutary consequence of the production, however, was a loss of NZ$300 and the recognition that "downstage" also meant small-scale, intimate, financially modest theatre, flexibly *un*committed to the rigid forms of a proscenium stage, as well as the social forms of foyer elegance and elitist rituals. The ghost of "professional" theatre on the old model of English provincial repertory, or a single national touring company like the defunct New Zealand Players, had at last been laid.

The old guard was still to be persuaded, and Downstage was still to make its point, but by 1964 sheer economics, changing social attitudes, the advent of television, and the decline of the large-cast, well-made play were all in its favor. Later that year Downstage found a home and, in the very act of doing so, defined its distinctive role.

The form it took was to prove an original and widely influential model for the emergent professional theatres in New Zealand economically, administratively, artistically, and socially. Only Canterbury and Auckland thereafter tried to follow the old pattern of large theatre and full-scale company. The first failed spectacularly within a few months of opening. Auckland's Mercury Theatre, drawing on New Zealand's largest population base, flourished, but its tradition of appointing directors from England, like its West End-style "Garrick" bar, its excessively large auditorium, and its more tenuous links with the community, give it a character quite different from that of any other theatre in New Zealand.

The Gateway (Tauranga), Four Seasons (Wanganui), Centrepoint (Palmerston

North), Court (Christchurch), and Fortune (Dunedin) have all been developed as small professional community theatres on the Downstage pattern.

Late in 1964, a series of members' evenings was held in the intimacy of Harry Seresin's Coffee Gallery, the kind of warm, friendly, and relaxed content which was hoped for the theatre itself. In November the society took over a bankrupt coffee bar called the Walkabout, threw out its Australian aboriginal motifs, renamed it the Downstage Theatre Café, and on November 21 opened to the public with dinner, Edward Albee's *The Zoo Story* (Bland and Sanderson), and informal dress.

For all the mutability of its fortunes since, Downstage at its best still aspires to that kind of experience: one in which the intimacy of casual conversation over a modest dinner grows naturally toward the sharing of a serious theatrical event, before the dinner table itself.

After Edward Albee's *The Zoo Story* came Miss Braddon's *Lady Audley's Secret* (for Christmas), Ben Jonson's *Bartholomew Fair*, Harold Pinter's *The Dumb Waiter*, Sławomir Mrożek's *Foursome*, E. A. Whitehead's *The Foursome*, Eugene Ionesco's *The Lessons*, Murray Schisgal's *The Tiger* and *The Typist*, Nicolai Gogol's *Diary of a Madman*, Pergolesi's opera *La Serva Padrona*, and Ibsen's *Hedda Gabler*. But the high points were a brilliant production by Sanderson of Samuel Beckett's *Happy Days* (another dismissive comment on the "old style"), with an equally brilliant performance by Pat Evison as Winnie and set by the painter Pat Hanly. A sensational *Oh What a Lovely War* by Charles Chilton and Theatre Workshops and a fiery version of Jean Genet's *The Maids* set the seal on Downstage's professional status within a year of its opening.

Bland's inclusion in the original team and Bruce Mason's supportive presence reflect the commitment Downstage has always had to producing its own writers. Bland came up first with *The Bed Settee*, to be followed by his impressive three-act play, *Father's Day*, and his hilarious short comedy, *George the Mad Ad Man*. His experience in acting and writing for a regular and well-known audience, intimate, relaxed, and responsive, completely vindicated the "downstage" philosophy. Bruce Mason's evocative one-man show, *The End of the Golden Weather*, was the first of many of his own scripts which he performed for Downstage: *To Russia with Love*, *Waters of Silence* (adapted from Vercours), *Counsels of the Wood*, *Not Christmas But Guy Fawkes*, and *Courting Blackbird*. His full-length plays, *Birds in the Wilderness* and *Awatea* (for Inia Te Wiata); Douglas Stewart's *The Golden Lover*; James K. Baxter's *Spots on the Leopard*; Warren Dibble's *Operation Pigstick*, *Lines to M*, and *Lord Dismiss Us*; E. S. Bowman's *Salve Regina*; Alistair Campbell's *When the Bough Breaks*; Owen Leeming's *The Quarry Game*; Robert Lord's *It Isn't Cricket*, *Meeting Place*, *Well Hung*, *Heroes and Butterflies*, and *Balance of Payments*; Joseph Musaphia's *Victims*, *Obstacles*, and *Mothers and Fathers*; and Roger Hall's *State of the Play* by no means exhaust the list of New Zealand plays which Downstage has performed and in most cases generated.

The idea that actors and audience should be involved in a common experience and learn from one another led to the founding of a critical house magazine, *ACT*. Bruce Mason was its first editor and established a policy of substantial reviewing of Downstage productions. He also initiated publication of New Zealand plays as lift-out sections. Although Downstage did not directly initiate the scheme, the theatre also gave hospitality and clerical help to a closely associated group, anxious to found a script advisory service and national agency for New Zealand playwrights. Later the group emerged entirely on its own as Playmarket, taking with it *ACT* (and its fortuitous acronym ACT), and the secretariat of the Association of Community Theatres.

But transformations are the very stock-in-trade of theatre, and Downstage itself was not immune. Sanderson and Eliott moved to Australia, and Bland to England. Seresin and the academics moved aside to let the second round of practitioners run their own show, by this time with the generous funding of the Arts Council. Sunny Amey returned from her position as personal assistant to Sir Laurence Olivier at the National Theatre in London to take over Downstage.

Momentous changes in its physical setting were also happening. The old Downstage Theatre Café held about eighty people at a squeeze; by the end of 1965 it had extended its lease to include the adjoining building, moved its auditorium through the wall, and doubled its capacity. In 1968 Downstage made a bid for NZ$150,000 donated by Mrs. Sheila Winn to the Arts Council to build a theatre for the people of Wellington. Raymond Boyce, former stage designer for the New Zealand Players, had joined the committee and, together with the architect Ronald Parker, made preliminary sketches for what was to become the Hannah Playhouse. These won over the Arts Council and with the clear understanding that the new Playhouse would be built to express the "downstage" philosophy and that Downstage itself would be its first and long-term theatre company, a trust was formed to buy the site and build the theatre. Downstage shifted to the Star Boating Club for three years, while the Hannah Playhouse was built to its own design. At the end of 1973 it returned to a brand new theatre building with an auditorium designed to permit flexible staging and a maximum audience of about two hundred, on the site of Downstage's first home, the old Walkabout Coffee Bar.

The physical lushness of the new Hannah Playhouse is a little at odds with the conditions under which Downstage evolved, but the principle of dinner and play continues, the flexibility of staging gives a sense of constant renewal, as play succeeds play, and the intimacy remains. The decision to keep the auditorium small recognizes the fundamental principles: first, the positive value for actors and audience alike of *full* houses, in contrast with the extremely negative effect of having the same number of people in a larger but half-empty auditorium; and, second, the night-by-night and week-by-week continuity of work for actors as the season finds its economic length in relation to demand, together with its consequences of regular access to theatre for people who want it and when they want it, instead of the intermittent, all-or-nothing presence of the touring companies which preceded Downstage.

Anthony Taylor, himself a playwright, now directs Downstage, and Raymond Boyce is an associate director (design). The company employs a staff of fifty and has a subscribing membership of over four thousand. It has a long-term lease on the Hannah Playhouse, owned and run by an independent Trust Board (on which the company is represented). The Downstage Theatre Company is no longer an incorporated society administered by its members, but one of three distinct groups, which also include the Downstage Theatre Society (the subscribing membership) and the Downstage Theatre Trust Board (business advisors). Each contributes three representatives to make up the Downstage Company Board, to which the director is immediately responsible. A director's absolute freedom to choose his program, it should be added, has never been questioned. The company has also developed a subsidiary group called Stagestruck, which takes theatre to schools, hospitals, prisons, and so on, and has developed productions with younger actors. One of those, Frank Wedekind's *Spring Awakening*, under the brilliant direction of Colin McColl, produced a theatrical experience of rare authenticity.

Although Downstage is now Wellington's establishment theatre, its own record would be incomplete without mention of its main rival, Circa, a professional theatre set up and run by actors nurtured in Downstage, notably Ray Henwood and actor-designer Grant Tilly. Each production is in effect mounted by a syndicate of those directly involved. By keeping its auditorium small (about eighty seats, like the first Downstage) and overhead down, it has offered continuous alternative theatre since early 1976 without claiming one cent from the Arts Council to do so. Its system maximizes returns to the actors, both monetarily and in personal satisfaction through choice of their plays. Its commitment to new drama, and especially New Zealand writing, paid off handsomely in New Zealand's biggest box office success of all time, Roger Hall's *Glide Time*. That play, which speaks to New Zealanders as no other has done, and its highly original auspices in Circa, testify ultimately to the fertility of the theatrical forms first evolved for Downstage, although their most vigorous expression is now to be found elsewhere.

DONALD F. MCKENZIE

MELBOURNE THEATRE COMPANY
Russell Street Theatre
19 Russell Street
Melbourne 3001, Australia

Australia's oldest and first professional repertory theatre began in a small way in August 1953. Its founder, Englishman John Sumner, who had worked as stage manager and director with a Scottish repertory company and H. M. Tennent's in London, was appointed manager of Melbourne University's theatre in 1952. As it was not in use for half the year, with the backing of the university authorities Sumner formed the Union Theatre Repertory Company (UTRC) to occupy the theatre during such periods.

From August 31, 1953, over a seven-month period, fifteen plays were staged. Many were good English "rep" vehicles: Noel Coward's *Blithe Spirit*, Terence Rattigan's *French Without Tears*, Wynyard Browne's *The Holly and the Ivy*, and Esther McCracken's *Quiet Weekend*. Interspersed were Jean Anouilh's *Colombe* (the opening production), George Bernard Shaw's *Pygmalion*, Jean Giraudoux's *Amphitryon 38*, Irwin Shaw's *The Gentle People*, Christopher Fry's *The Lady's Not for Burning*, and Oscar Wilde's *The Importance of Being Earnest*.

Cast lists of that first season now read like a "Who's Who of the Australian Theatre." They include Zoe Caldwell and Barry Humphries.

Sumner was at the helm of the company for a second season, by which time the Australian Elizabethan Theatre Trust had been formed and he was appointed general manager of its theatre in Sydney. Ray Lawler, who had joined the company during its second season, took over, following very much the format set by Sumner.

Back to direct one play, Sumner selected Lawler's unperformed *Summer of the Seventeenth Doll*, the first Australian play to be staged by the company. The *Doll* took Lawler and Sumner away from Melbourne—Lawler for a lengthy period overseas.

The UTRC's head now became Wal Cherry, who, as an undergraduate, had received much acclaim for his direction of university productions. Cherry's debut with the company was in February 1956 and, obviously ahead of his time, caused controversy with productions that included four Tennessee Williams plays. By the end of the sixth season, audiences had dwindled and the company was so far into the red it appeared problematical whether it could continue. The trust came to its financial aid, and August 1959 saw Sumner once more in charge for the UTRC's seventh season and looking after the trust's activities in Victoria.

In many ways Sumner's return season set a yardstick that has seldom been overshadowed and has not been reached as many times as it ought. Its highlight was Sumner's production of *Moby Dick-Rehearsed* by Orson Welles with Frank Thring.

By mid-1960 it was obvious the UTRC must be a permanent year-round affair. In August arrangements were made to occupy the Council of Adult Education's Russell Street Theatre in the city when not playing at the university. In 1966 Russell Street became the permanent home of the company, which early in that year became known as the Melbourne Theatre Company (MTC).

Since then, the MTC has expanded in all directions. Early in 1969 it mounted a production of *Henry IV, Part I*, in a courtyard of the newly opened gallery of the Victoria Arts Centre. There were seasons at both the larger Comedy and Princess theatres, and, with the demise of the rival St. Martin's Theatre Company in 1973, it played simultaneously at Russell Street and the St. Martin's.

In 1975 staging two so-called alternative theatre plays was attempted in an avant-garde theatre, but the all-round standard of the project was abysmal. In a second try in 1976 (this time in a theatre attached to the Victoria College of the Arts), performance results were much happier, although the audiences were sparse.

Then, in 1977, the company occupied the larger Athenaeum Theatre (for many years a motion picture theatre) for classical and modern classical plays, using Russell Street for productions of contemporary drama.

Besides its main theatre season, the MTC engages in other activities. It frequently mounts extensive country and interstate tours. A Saturday morning youth club has been extended to two weekday nights. There is a playreading service, and sometimes the company commissions plays and engages in workshop productions and what are now called "tributary" productions, a sort of compromise between the workshop and "alternative theatre."

Without subsidies the MTC could not survive. For 1977 the Australia Council provided A$650,000, the Victorian Government A$325,000, and other grants (the University of Melbourne, Melbourne City Council, and private funds) totaled A$15,000. Box office receipts amounted to A$1,353,118.

For many years the MTC was considered Australia's top company. Today the reputations of Adelaide's South Australian Theatre Company and Sydney's Nimrod are higher. Yet there are probably few actors and directors in the country who would not work at the MTC if invited and commitments permitted.

Company plays appear to be selected because they have appeared, a few seasons earlier, in the repertoires of the National or Royal Shakespeare companies in England. Melbourne is missing a number of good overseas plays because the MTC is the only company geared to stage them. It is now presenting several Australian plays, many, like most local plays, of poor quality.

The MTC has always been happiest staging plays by contemporary authors such as Edward Albee or stylish comedies like Ferenc Molnár's *The Play's the Thing*. By world standards its productions of the classics have seldom been entirely satisfactory. Probably Tyrone Guthrie's production of Shakespeare's *All's Well That Ends Well* in 1970 came off best, with George Farquhar's *The Beaux' Stratagem* and Sophocles' *Electra* by English visiting director Frank Hauser in 1978, also very highly regarded.

While local critics have been satisfied with MTC productions of Chekhov, these productions have left much to be desired. Shaw is a particular favorite of Sumner's, who has directed many of his plays. In an effort to play up the comedy for Melbourne audiences, Sumner has frequently marred these plays by introducing "funny business" instead of allowing Shaw to speak for himself.

The MTC record for Henrik Ibsen, William Congreve, Oscar Wilde, George Farquhar, and other classical writers has usually been little more than adequate. The acquisition of the Athenaeum promised a step up for classical productions and it was hoped all-around standards would be improved. But, with the exception of the two Hauser productions (*Beaux' Stratagem* and *Electra*), this has rarely occurred.

When the MTC was created, the objectives of the company were stated to be

(1) to provide for the production, representation, and performance of theatrical entertainments that are not generally offered to the public by commercial arrangements; (2) to educate theatregoers to a finer appreciation of the theatre by first-class presentations; (3) to present theatrical entertainments that seek both to educate and to entertain; (4) to give young artists interested in the work of the theatre a chance to become educated in that work by first-hand experience; (5) to encourage playwrights, give them an opportunity to become educated in the work of the theatre, and to present their work whenever possible; and (6) to encourage the talents and skills necessary or ancillary to the development and maintenance of first-class theatrical entertainment.

Whether the MTC has always lived up to these ideals is open to question. On several occasions it has staged attractions that would have been more happily presented by a commercial management. One cannot say its presentations have always been first-class, or that they always educate and entertain. It has certainly done justice to Australian plays. Just as Alan Hopgood's *And the Big Men Fly* was a milestone in 1963, John Power's *The Last of the Knucklemen* achieved a peak ten years later. David Williamson has always had a good showing at the MTC. But one wishes other new Australian plays might have been presented instead of some which possessed no worth whatsoever.

Too long now the MTC has been going through a "marking time" period, waiting to occupy the main drama theatre of the Victoria Arts Centre (VAC), and during that time endeavoring to build audiences, when at the same time it ought to be raising standards. For Sumner it must have been frustrating to see other companies, not nearly as long established, presented with almost perfect venues in which to mount their productions. The MTC has always had to compromise, first with the Union Theatre, then Russell Street, St. Martin's, and finally the Athenaeum. The VAC's drama theatre was originally due to open in the early seventies. Because of industrial strife, the opening date was often announced and postponed. Finally, the Center opened in 1983.

RAYMOND STANLEY

MERCURY THEATRE COMPANY
Auckland, New Zealand

In 1864 an Auckland newspaper thundered, "When will Auckland be able to support a theatre and a company of her own?" After insisting a theatre would keep the populace out of bars and "worse places," it ended more positively, "Our youth are growing up untouched and unhumanized by the great moral-inculcating lessons of drama." On May 1, 1968, a gala performance of James M. Barrie's *The Admirable Crichton* inaugurated the Mercury Theatre, Auckland's first permanent theatre with a resident professional company. Prior to the opening, a city councillor argued, "This was an important enterprise, if only to counteract some of the nauseating rubbish that's filtering into our drawing rooms by the medium of television."

Those 104 years had seen many attempts to establish professional theatre in a country where there was a thriving, generally British, tradition of amateur theatricals. In 1965 the newly formed Queen Elizabeth II Arts Council decided to establish regional professional theatres solidly based in four main cities. Regional theatre would succeed because it would have its roots in the community. Professor J. C. Reid was given the task of initiating the project in Auckland. At public meetings in 1966 he canvassed for an intimate theatre to act as a center for community stimulus and recreation, but first he had to find a home. The operation of the theatre would be subsidized by the Arts Council. The council would not assist with capital costs.

The old Playhouse Cinema, the city's first modern picture house established in 1910, was chosen, and the dream of intimacy vanished. It had seated 1,800. No act of conversion could make one forget its origins. The Auckland Theatre Trust, with Professor Reid as founder-chairman, was created to raise funds. They aimed for NZ$250,000 and achieved three-quarters of the sum. The Auckland City Council gave NZ$60,000. Since that day it has not given another single penny; it just remitted some of the taxes. The community was hesitant. They remembered the recent collapse of the Canterbury Theatre Trust, which died in 1967 with debts of NZ$20,000 after two years of operation. Arguments raged that theatre is people. "We are being asked to support another building." The conversion went ahead. The Mercury was born as a theatre containing 660 seats with a smaller studio seating 130. An acoustic false ceiling was added, but the Mercury's playing area has remained its single greatest disadvantage. Productions can be lost on a cavernous stage. Directors are often uneasy with the relationship between stage and audience. Above all, the size of the theatre and the financial stringencies under which it exists have forced on the theatre a policy of doing what it thinks might be popular, and hoping it is good.

The trust's next most important task was to appoint a founder-director. It recognized that the theatre's character would largely come from the director. Advertising was worldwide. From the ninety-eight applicants, Anthony Richardson of the Belgrade Theatre, Coventry, England, was appointed. He arrived in 1967 to name the theatre after the god of wit, but to remind Auckland that Mercury was also the god of commerce.

In his nine years as director Anthony Richardson was never able to forget "the unseen side of the play." From the start he had to maintain a "fully realistic financial attitude." The Canterbury Theatre's final disaster had been *The Entertainer*. Richardson, unfamiliar with both country and city, started by playing safe in the colonies. He also argued that he had chosen the Barrie play because it involved a servant who took over from the master, a theme relevant to New Zealand. If this was an oblique allusion to a hope that the Mercury would lead New Zealand in the struggle to shrug off the shackles of a largely British middle-class culture, Richardson could never commit himself to this endeavor.

Other plays in the first season were equally cautious. Bill Naughton's *Alfie* and Lionel Bart and Frank Norman's *Fings Ain't Wot They Used T'Be* were most successful. They were leavened by an obligatory Shakespeare and one gesture of daring, Brecht's *The Caucasian Chalk Circle*. The only works done in the studio were four experimental programs to prepare the audiences for the shock of Brecht.

Criticism of the first season as "safe," "stuffy," and "unadventurous" was predictable. More dangerous was the fact that with such a generalized program of school plays, serious drama, farce and musical, the Mercury, in cultivating all sections of the community, was putting its roots down nowhere. Richardson pointed to an operating surplus of NZ$181 and asked for time. Some were not prepared to grant it. But over the next few years, under the combined leadership of Reid and Richardson, the Mercury produced a progressively more interesting program. Reid was the academic New Zealander prepared to trust his fellow citizens' intelligence and urge Richardson to be more ambitious. By the end of 1970, he could point to the considerable success of Peter Weiss' *Marat/Sade*, Pirandello's *Henry IV*, and Peter Barnes' *The Ruling Class* as well as Shakespeare's *Othello* and *Hamlet*.

What he failed to see was that, if the frothier part of the West End was no longer the model for the Mercury's repertory, London still dominated Auckland's stage. The year in which Reid died, 1973, reveals this most clearly. There were productions of recent London successes: *Jumpers*, a new translation of *Le Misanthrope* from the National Theatre in London, and *Butley* from the West End. There were revivals of faded minor English classics: *Hay Fever* and *The Lady's Not for Burning*. There was a controversial play from the Royal Court, carefully advertised as "not for the squeamish," and Edward Bond's *Lear*. Inevitably, there were a Shakespeare, a musical, and a children's play. Finally, a new ingredient was added. As its sixty-second production to celebrate its fifth birthday, the Mercury performed a New Zealand play. James McNeish's *The Rocking Cave* was a well-made play by a well-known novelist about a well-loved subject: New Zealand's early pioneers. The risk was minimal and the reward considerable.

Later in the year a New Zealand musical, *Mr. King Hongi*, was performed with even greater success. Much is revealed by these first indigenous premieres: white settlers are the subject for serious drama, while Maori history can be turned into bouncy musicals. Evidently, a fair percentage of the population of the largest Polynesian city in the world was not considered ready for community stimulus.

Richardson left at the end of 1976. His successes had been considerable, but his policy shortsighted. For his first seven years, aided by ever-increasing grants, the theatre had run at a profit. The building was almost totally owned by the trust. He had offered and Auckland had accepted many interesting plays, but he had always glanced toward "home" to find them. He had been ready to seize on any London success, not always understanding why it had succeeded in a different environment. He had forgotten the rationale that lay behind regional theatre and neglected large parts of the community in which the Mercury was placed. It had become just another semiserious British repertory company imposing British middle-class cultural standards.

Few New Zealand plays had been attempted, nor had there been any effort to create an atmosphere in which they might have been written. Experiment had been forgotten, and the studio had been turned into a rehearsal room.

For his successor the trust turned inevitably to England. Ian Mullins of the Redgrave Theatre, Farnham, arrived in mid-1977. The interregnum had been uneasy. Plays had failed and inflation was galloping. The theatre had started to lose money regularly. At the end of 1977 Mullins reviewed the year's program. He saw the greatest successes were a New Zealand comedy, Roger Hall's *Glide Time*, and two musicals. The failures were a Brecht, a Shakespeare, and a product of the new Australian theatre, John Powers' *Last of the Knucklemen*.

For him the public had chosen. The studio had been renamed Mercury Two and the semiserious repertory relegated there. In Mercury One the program is as frothy as it was in 1968. Audiences are encouraged to attend through a massive commercial subscription scheme. Many are turning to Auckland's second professional theatre for what the Mercury originally promised. Theatre Corporate, which was founded in 1974, is both intimate and, in a classical way, adventurous. Unfortunately, neither theatre is actively fostering local playwrights, without whom Auckland's theatre will finally wither.

SEBASTIAN BLACK

NATIONAL THEATRE COMPANY
Perth, Western Australia, Australia

The National Theatre at the Playhouse was set up to provide Perth and, by touring, the rest of Western Australia with a resident theatre of at least semi-professional standard. Until its inception in 1956, Perth depended for its professional theatre upon companies touring either from the eastern states or overseas, usually England. Musicals were, for the most part, Broadway successes of some vintage, with an eastern states cast, not all of them the original performers. Legitimate theatre likewise consisted of West End successes, also of some years' standing, with English casts, or English leads with Sydney or Melbourne supporting casts. Overseas companies were rare, usually consisting of a "royal visit" by such companies as the Old Vic, with Sir Laurence Olivier in 1948, or the Stratford Memorial Theatre, with Anthony Quayle in 1953.

Amateur theatre in Perth, indeed throughout Western Australia, was strong and kept so by British immigrants. Classical and experimental drama, such as that of the absurdists, was the province of the state's then sole campus, the University of Western Australia, through the undergraduate University Dramatic Society and the Graduate Dramatic Society. Both had considerable guidance from staff members of the university's Department of English. The most serious and highest standard of legitimate theatre in the city was carried out at two amateur theatres: Patch and the Repertory. It was from the Repertory that the Playhouse grew and from which it drew many of its personnel. It had not been possible for any significant number of actors in Perth to practice their craft on a full-time basis. Those who managed to do so were heavily dependent upon radio drama (principally with the Australian Broadcasting Commission) and intermittent and casual appearances on stage.

The main impetus for the formation of the National Theatre came from the desire of the Repertory Club, Incorporated, to find a permanent theatre. Since 1933 the club had rented an old composing room from West Australian Newspapers, but there was no security of tenure. In 1953 a fifty-year lease was obtained for the site on which the Playhouse now stands. With the backing of the state government, A$80,000 was borrowed from the Colonial Mutual Life Assurance Society, Limited, and sufficient additional funds were raised by public subscriptions to have a 750-seat, proscenium-arch theatre, the Playhouse Theatre, built. It was opened by the state premier on August 22, 1956, with a production of *The Teahouse of the August Moon.*

Control of the theatre is in the hands of a Board of Management elected annually by member vote. Membership is open to the public, and, apart from the voting rights, the membership has usual booking and concession privileges. There are also concessions for students and pensioners. The board's policy is to provide as wide a range of theatre as possible, from musicals such as *Hello, Dolly!*, through light comedy and classical drama.

During its first two years, the theatre alternated between semiprofessional productions (the company was not bound by Equity) and amateur theatre on an unpaid basis, although the directors of the amateur productions were later paid. The decision was then made to set the theatre on a more professional basis, with a resident director and a company of actors under contract.

Although for the first few years no outside financial support was received, the National Theatre is now subsidized by the federal Australia Council and the State Western Australian Arts Council. As part of its ''charter,'' under these subsidies, the company has formed touring companies and toured the principal company (including special presentations for schools). It has also built up its youth theatre work, with a director especially appointed for the task. In addition, it has opened a small fifty-seat intimate theatre, the Greenroom, for the presentation of smaller and more experimental productions. In the financial year June 1978–June 1979, the National Theatre received a A$165,000 subsidy from the state government and A$215,000 from the Commonwealth.

The development of the National Theatre is best understood in light of the work of three directors, who guided the development and shaped the company through the sixties and seventies: Raymond Westwell, Edgar Metcalfe, and Aarne Neeme.

Raymond Westwell visited Australia with the Stratford Memorial Theatre Company in 1953. He returned to the Playhouse as resident director in November 1960, remaining until July 1961. He was responsible for setting up a company based on a three-week repertory system. Plays presented ranged from Hugh Williams' *The Grass Is Greener* to T. S. Eliot's *Murder in the Cathedral*. Westwell's groundwork was responsible for the first resident theatre company of a high professional standard in the state and was the basis on which later directors built.

Edgar Metcalfe came from England as director of the Playhouse in 1963 and served his first term until 1967. He extended both the size and range of the company, showing an uncanny ability to balance popular theatre with more serious and unusual works. In his first production, *The Cat and the Canary*, he showed an eye for period style, extended the range of musical offerings, and also presented pantomime in the best English tradition (as an actor he is an excellent and inventive "Dame"). He also presented with success such controversial works as Rolf Hochuth's *The Representative* and Peter Weiss' *Marat/Sade*. When all the Australian subsidiary companies toured the other states in the 1960s, his production of Jean-Paul Sartre's *Altóna* brought credit to the company.

Estonian-born Aarne Neeme came to Australia as a young child; hence, his cultural background is Australian. This was an important fact, as he was director of the Playhouse during the upsurge in Australian playwriting, which occurred in the 1970s. He was director of the theatre from June 1973 to December 1977. At this time, Perth's other professional theatre, the small, 130-seat, three-quarter-round Hole-in-the-Wall Theatre, also had an Australian director, John Milson. Both men, together with the National's assistant director, Terence Clarke, had their theatrical training and cultural roots in Australia. Between them they were responsible for presenting fourteen contemporary Australian plays in twelve months. A director of prodigious output, Aarne Neeme initiated a period of growth at the Playhouse which coincided with a flourishing of Australian drama.

Because of the effects of the general economic depression on arts funding, the Board of the National Theatre decided in 1978 to dispense with the concept of a permanent company and in the future to employ actors on a play-by-play basis. The usual arguments were advanced: lower overhead costs and less restrictions in the choice of plays due to a small restricted company, with the concomitant greater choice from a larger pool of performers.

Companies such as the Royal Shakespeare Company and the German state theatre companies have proved conclusively that strong ensemble companies produce the best theatre and nurture indigenous drama. Although the Playhouse spent a lot of money on public relations in 1978, fewer productions emanated from the theatre and were arguably of lower general standards than in previous years. The gap was filled in part by two imported plays presented back-to-back, which were no doubt successful for the entrepreneurs but hardly helped either the theatre or the local actors. With the return in 1977 to the policy of actively recruiting directors from England (the new director is Stephen Barry), it would seem that a reversion has been made to the situation of the 1950s, one that perhaps only enlightened government policy can reverse.

COLLIN O'BRIEN

NIMROD THEATRE COMPANY
Nimrod Theatre, 500 Elizabeth Street
Surry Hills, NSW 2010, Australia

Since its auspicious opening in December 1970, the Nimrod Theatre Company has consolidated its position as the most consistently fertile, exciting, and go-getting company in Australia. It has always been in the vanguard of the new theatrical odyssey.

That it was a major enterprise from its inception suggests a series of socio-political-theatrical events conspired by its founders at the birth of the venture. While the Old Tote, the major established company, was moving into menopausal conservatism, and the previous generation's stucco and velvet theatres were closing in Sydney, Nimrod proved that there was no essential wane of interest but rather that a new, uncatered, audience had emerged.

The boom babies had reached maturity and, in a time of material welfare and economic expansion, were swelling the universities and colleges. These unprecedented numbers of young people, experiencing the liberalizing effects of tertiary education, demanded to be heard. The febrile activity of hot-blooded young men and women, which reached its apogee in the worldwide student riots of 1968, was by no means over. Opposition to the Vietnam War was a cause célèbre; at the theatre over one-half million people flooded to *Hair*.

If the major theatrical cause for the founding of the Australian Performing Group in Melbourne was the success of the La Mama Theatre, for Sydney's Nimrod it was a play, Michael Boddy and Bob Ellis' *The Legend of King O'Malley*. The production, in the tiny Jane Street Theatre in 1970, established many precedents for the company. It was indigenously written, urgently topical (using O'Malley's opposition to conscription in World War I to comment on the Vietnam birthday-lottery system), vaudevillian in approach, boisterously ensemble in its acting style, and innovative in the actor/audience relationship it set.

Nimrod was the brainchild of the director of *O'Malley*, John Bell, and Ken Horler. Since their active days in undergraduate theatre together, these university wits had moved on to become, respectively, an associate of the Royal Shakespeare Company and a practicing barrister. The first venue they took over was a wedge-shaped warehouse, at the rough end of King's Cross (equitable with London's Soho). They converted its first floor into an auditorium where 140 people could huddle around a tiny, diamond-form playing space, not even a stage.

In the Globe-like atmosphere of this ''unurinalled fire trap,'' (having no gentleman's lavatory) as local writer Bob Ellis described it, the decision was taken to champion the local and the new, to continue and develop the ribald, gutsy, and hard-hitting theatricalism of *O'Malley*. Whereas the Australian Performing Group began with a commitment to the radicalist's testament, at Nimrod there has never been a readily identifiable political stance. Rather, its style has something of the cartoonist's approach—irreverence towards all, but immediate in appeal and eye-catching in directness.

The inaugural play, under this direction, proved his words no empty shibboleth by becoming a sell-out success. *Biggles* by Ron Blair, Marcus Cooney, and Michael Boddy (co-author of *O'Malley*) opened on December 2, 1970. Comic book in approach, it used its swashbuckling hero to parody the old school tie syndrome and satirize an Australian institution, the ubiquitous Returned Services Leagues (RSL) Clubs. The formula was repeated in other ebullient musical plays: Ron Blair's *Flash Jim Vaux* (opened April 28, 1971) and Ron Blair and Michael Boddy's *Hamlet on Ice* (December 8, 1971). *Flash Jim Vaux* is a chronology-warping chronicle of the eponymous character, whose major claim to fame rested on being thrice transported to the colony for incessant criminality, and *Hamlet on Ice* is an outrageous panto-burlesquing of the Bard.

Nimrod not only presented such coruscating entertainments, but in its first year it also ran boldly up its mast the several flags under which it was to continue. The characteristic "abrasive cynicism" of Australian drama was to be found in other writers it championed. The year 1971 saw a production of *The Removalists* by David Williamson, which went on to earn for author and theatre jointly the coveted George Devine Award in London. Nimrod productions of Williamson's plays helped to establish this socially acute and provocative writer as the country's most successful playwright to date and as the second Australian to have a play presented on Broadway (the first was Ray Lawler with *Summer of the Seventeenth Doll*).

It premiered plays by Alex Buzo, who had become an *enfant terrible* in the late sixties with the first use of the horror word "fuck" on the country's stage (*Norm and Ahmed*, 1968). Like Williamson, he is a witty satirical writer but tends more toward a Pinteresque theatre of terror than to his contemporary's social comedy. Examples are *Rooted* (1972) and *Tom* (1973), both produced by Nimrod.

The policy of presenting the works of local writers paid off. The theatre was seen as nationalistic, at a time when the country was thumbing its nose at inherited English traditions, and youthfully energetic, at a time when Australia was poised to throw off the yoke of twenty-three years of Menzies' paternalism. It was, in Restoration fashion, a theatre where a new society's social manners and sexual mores were being explored and exposed. Sydney had caught up with swinging London, and the Nimrod had established itself as the antipodean counterpart to the Royal Court Theatre in London.

Besides hoisting the flag for indigenous playwrights in that year, the company first showed its two other abiding areas of interest: the English classic and the modern great. For the classic, by and large, we may read Shakespeare, a passion of John Bell's, an actor and director no doubt influenced by his RSC days. Indeed, Nimrod's third production in that tiny space was *Measure for Measure*. Its third Shakespeare was a very creditable *Hamlet*, with Bell in the title role; the national television network put it on the air, bringing Nimrod into the country's living rooms. Since then, the company has been recognized as being of first significance in the production of Shakespeare in Australia. Mostly innovative in conception, often strongly out-front in presentation, and always strikingly bold in design, it has won numerous awards and generated heated contention among the critics. Of the modern classics, Samuel Beckett's *Endgame* (first presented January 27, 1971), in a double bill with his *Act Without Words*, was the first of a distinguished line from the pens of such major playwrights as Edward Albee, Peter Handke, David Hare, David Rudkin, Tom Stoppard, Sam Shepard, Tennessee Williams, and the "founding father" of modern drama, Anton Chekhov.

The little theatre in Kings Cross had been under threat within weeks of opening its doors. The city council debated the fire hazard it presented and the lack of adequate lavatories, with the company moving temporarily while improvements were made. Later, the Department of Main Roads made sinister noises about bulldozing the building to make way for a new highway. The company had in the meantime established an enormous reputation and had gained a third artistic director, Richard Wherrett, in 1973. The triumvirate decided to move. Masterminded by Ken Horler, and with over A$250,000 in public and private benefactions, a three-hundred-seat, open-stage theatre was created from an old Cerebos Salt Factory in Surry Hills, then a long way from Sydney's traditional theatre district. It was expanded again in 1976 when a second, totally flexible, one-hundred-seat capacity space was included.

The change of buildings reflects both the development of the company and the increasing affluence of its patrons. It began by appealing largely to relatively poor students, who now, seven years later, are the wealthy middle class. One of the criticisms that can be leveled against the theatre relates to this: namely, that it has often risked trivializing for the sake of being fashionable.

Certainly, some productions obscure serious import with a "trendy" veneer, but overall the change is rather one from rough-and-ready vitality to more slick and stylish presentation. New premises and increased subsidies have raised standards to new heights, so much so that Nimrod can now successfully transfer whole productions to the country's major venues and even to London's West End. Its reputation is now such that it is virtually alone among subsidized theatre companies in making touring financially viable, with some of the shows transferring to commercial circuits.

Of its recent successes, *The Elocution of Benjamin Franklin* by Steve J. Spears, directed by Richard Wherrett, is the most outstanding, having achieved both London and Broadway seasons. The portrait of a transvestite, flamboyantly camp in its young author's conception and wonderfully frenetic in Gordon Chater's execution, has been hailed the world over. Another one-man show, Ron Blair's *The Christian Brothers*, has had almost equal success in Australia. It combines fine character drawing with a shattering déjà vu for anyone who attended a religious school. Again Nimrod displayed its acute flair for casting in choosing the brilliant Peter Carroll for the sole part.

A new internationalism is apparent in the company, not only in its transfers but also its guest directors, such as Steve Berkoff, and in the work of a new breed of writers. The play *Inner Voices*, set in the Russia of Catherine the Great and centered around the piteous treatment of Ivan, the heir kept mute through boyhood, is the work of Louis Nowra. The great Brecht singer Robyn Archer, acclaimed at London's National Theatre, together with actor John Gaden, concocted a thirties German cabaret (entitled *Kold Komfort Kafee*), which packed two seasons in the small theatre in 1978.

Nimrod has had its own brand of actors but has never relied on an established company. Its continuity and style, though apparently very democratic in policymaking, has mainly resided with the triumvirate of directors—and it should be classified as a directors' theatre. The importance of its commitment to fostering indigenous writers cannot be overestimated, and its productions of classics place it among the front-runners of the world. For such a small group, with only a handful of administrative staff, to have molded a theatre company that has been noticed by international entrepreneurs is a measure of its astonishing success.

ROBERT PAGE

OLD TOTE THEATRE
University of New South Wales
High Street, Anzac Parade
Kensington, Sydney NSW 2033, Australia

It is a sign of the poverty of Australian theatre in the early sixties that the founding of the Old Tote Theatre Company should have assumed such importance. Set up in 1963 on the campus of the University of New South Wales, one of its chief aims was to provide a professional training ground for students from the then four-year-old National Institute of Dramatic Art (NIDA). Within ten years, it had become one of Australia's leading companies and was moving into the Sydney Opera House. Within another five years it was in the hands of a receiver. In many ways the gap left in 1978 by the demise of a company with assets of over A$1 million was smaller than the gap filled in 1963 by a company with a guarantee against less than A$10,000 and an old tin shed.

In 1963 there were no fully professional companies in Sydney which were "serious" or "art" theatres. After a couple of false starts with the Trust Players in 1959 and the (Sydney) University Union Repertory Theater Company in 1961, the "Tote" was established, with a policy of presenting both classics and modern plays and, after 1966, with a special "experimental" commitment to Australian plays. NIDA was housed in an old totalisator building, dating from the days when the campus of the University of New South Wales was a racetrack. Robert Quentin and Tom Brown, respectively the director and deputy director of NIDA, decided on an adjoining tin shed and the university agreed to provide A$6,000 to cover the cost of converting it into an intimate, 183-seat theatre. On February 2, 1963, it was opened with Robert Quentin's production of Chekhov's *The Cherry Orchard*.

During its first three years, the Tote quickly built a considerable reputation among Sydney theatregoers. The group was exciting and controversial, and did reliable productions of great plays little seen on the Sydney stage. Robert Quentin's productions of Chekhov and Tom Brown's *Hamlet*, with John Bell, were particularly successful. Most important financially, considering the difficulties of setting up a theatre in such a time in Sydney, was the outstanding popular success of John Clarke's production of *Who's Afraid of Virginia Woolf?*, which, with touring and return seasons, ran on and off for two years. Without this production it is unlikely the Tote would have come so far in so short a time.

From the beginning the Tote became involved in a number of subsidiary activities, which over the years have had as much influence as the main seasons. In late 1963 the Three Shilling Theatre was started as a lunch-hour theatre in the city. In 1964 *Virginia Woolf* toured in Brisbane and Canberra, and, in 1966, there was an Interstate Theatre Season, involving the state companies from Sydney, Melbourne, Adelaide, and Perth. In a country the size of the United States, with a population less than that of New York, such inner-city contact is as difficult as it is important. By 1978 it was an established custom, but in 1966 it was not a great success.

Possibly the most important subsidiary activity of the Tote was the annual experimental seasons of Australian plays at the tiny Jane Street Theatre, an old church also belonging to the university. From 1966 to 1977 a succession of new plays were given small but professional productions. Two of the most successful Australian plays ever were produced in these seasons: Michael Boddy and Bob Ellis' *The Legend of King O'Malley* (1970) and David Williamson's *Don's Party* (1972).

Apart from the first Jane Street season, 1966 was not a good year. The first of the often repeated criticisms that the Tote was declining into an uninteresting respectability was made. In 1967, however, two productions (Robin Lovejoy's *The School for Scandal* and Robert Quentin's *Hedda Gabler*) did a great deal to revive interest, and the company began the first of the expansionist moves which were to become its established way of injecting new excitement into the theatre and which eventually led to their disastrous collapse in 1978. The University of New South Wales Drama Foundation launched a fund to raise A$500,000 to build a new theatre on the campus to serve as an interim theatre. This became the Parade Theatre, which, far from being temporary, the company continued to use until 1978. Suggestions that they might move into the Sydney Opera House, when it was completed, stopped the plans for a new theatre in 1969. The appeal raised A$21,000, which was used to build a flytower on the Parade.

The deliberations about theatre buildings aroused some comment, but open and heated controversy flared at the beginning of 1969, when the newly founded government subsidizing body, the Australian Council for the Arts, announced a policy of concentrating funds on one leading company in each state. That the Tote became, overnight, New South Wales' "leading company" caused considerable resentment, especially among some of Sydney's older, established companies, which received little or no subsidy.

Thus "tapped on the shoulder," as the new artistic director Robin Lovejoy put it, the Tote set about trying to justify its position by expanding. Two companies were established; one toured while the other played in the Sydney venue, which after May 7, 1969, was the refurbished Parade Theatre. A successful production of Tom Stoppard's *Rosencrantz and Guildenstern Are Dead* was followed by a large-scale production of *Hamlet*, for which the company used yet another campus venue, the Science Theatre. The touring of four large productions to country towns and interstate was an ambitious project and was not repeated, but set a useful precedent for smaller touring ventures.

The year 1969 also saw the union of the Australian Theatre for Young People and the Old Tote Theatre Company, an association that continued until the end of both.

The halcyon years of the Old Tote were 1970–1972. Sir Tyrone Guthrie's huge production of *Oedipus*, in the Sir John Clancy Auditorium on campus, and the great popular success of *King O'Malley* set the company on its feet financially in 1970, and during the next three years it went from strength to strength. These were also years of unprecedented growth in Australian playwriting and theatrical activity in general. The Old Tote came to preside over the Sydney scene like a dowager duchess. Young directors such as John Bell, Richard Wherrett, and Rex Cramphorne worked briefly (and not always happily) for the company, while Robin Lovejoy ruled as artistic director until his retirement in 1974, with Bill Redmond taking over. ·

At the beginning of 1974 the company finally moved into the Opera House Drama Theatre, having played at one time or another in five different theatres on the campus. For a time the university had housed one of the largest drama complexes in the world, with the Tote, NIDA, the School of Drama, and the University of New South Wales Drama Foundation. The Tote still maintained a company at the Parade and also bought a large building in Alexandria to provide rehearsal and office space, as well as workshops and storage.

This expansion in the middle seventies was matched by an increasing feeling among critics and audiences that the Tote was growing conservative and failing in its original policy. It was compared unfavorably to young companies such as the Nimrod Theatre. Productions of plays by Ferenc Molnár, Arthur Wing Pinero, and Ben Travers were considered neither "classics" nor "the best of modern writing," and what seemed to be a slavish imitation of the latest theatrical trends in London was criticized in the growing cultural nationalism of Gough Whitlam's years as prime minister. Successful and exciting achievements, such as wooing Australia's Nobel Prize-winning author Patrick White back to the theatre, served only to emphasize the general staidness and lack of excitement which, in the public mind, came to characterize the work of the Old Tote.

Yet again, the company's reaction was to announce further plans for expansion. In 1977 it was announced that a third theatre would be brought into operation (at the recently opened Seymour Centre) for the purpose of "experimental"or innovative productions of new Australian plays and new work from overseas.

By this time, however, a serious financial crisis was looming. Although subscriptions had been taken for a new season, the plan was dropped. Repeated failures at the box office (with some successes but not enough); the cost of the building at Alexandria; the failure to appoint a single artistic director after Bill Redmond's retirement in 1977; and the feeling that the company was being run by a faceless, unaccountable Board of Directors eventually led the Australia Council (as the Australian Council for the Arts was now called) to announce that it would not continue to provide subsidy. The Tote went into liquidation, and plans were drawn to establish an official state company to replace the Old Tote.

The Old Tote Theatre made an enormous contribution to Sydney's theatrical life. In part, the company was lucky to be at the right place at the right time, but for most of its existence it struggled seriously and energetically to present good plays to a deprived public and to improve the standards of production in a theatrical environment it found mediocre and left considerably enriched.

JOHN MCCALLUM

QUEENSLAND THEATRE COMPANY
State Government Insurance Office Building
Brisbane, Queensland, Australia

The Queensland Theatre Company (QTC) is the first established professional company in Queensland—indeed, the first state theatre company in Australia. It was incorporated as a statutory body by an act of the Queensland State Parliament in April 1970 and, in the same year, commenced an ambitious program of providing theatre experience not only for metropolitan audiences, but also for the entire state. At its inception, the company was housed in what has become its permanent, if rented, Brisbane home, the 600-seat theatre, specially built in the State Government Insurance Office (SGIO) Building, in the heart of Brisbane. The company is subsidized for all its expensive operations by both state and commonwealth funding bodies to a total, in 1978, of A$650,000. As the state's first professional company, its initial and continuing policy has been to build surely the foundations of its repertoire, artists, and audience. The circumstances of its rapid creation by government fiat in order to cater to a perceived need in the community's cultural life have given it a largely pioneering and educational brief to which, under the artistic directorship of Alan Edwards, the company has speedily responded with usually successful results.

The company's philosophy and development are determined by the nature of the area served. Queensland, covering 667,000 square miles, is a sprawling, decentralized community deriving its livelihood from primary industries. The population outside the southeast area is concentrated in regional cities, spread up the long coastline as far north as Cape York Peninsula, 1,300 miles from the capital, and in the scattered farming and mining towns of the west. Because of this isolation and distance, the state's total population of only 2 million was and is comparatively unused to forms of live entertainment and theatrical experience. The QTC's firm policy is partly education, in accustoming audiences to this experience, and partly an assumption of the social responsibility for bringing professional theatre to all the isolated areas in its territory. Unlike many a publicly subsidized theatre company, QTC has never seen itself as merely a metropolitan operation content to bask in the security of catering to sophisticated capital city audiences. It takes seriously the implied imperative of subsidy: to service as broadly as possible the geographical area from which the funds are ultimately, by taxation, derived. Before the doors of the SGIO theatre opened in 1970, a team of actors was already on the 7,000-mile school circuit, and in the same year three of the four full-scale productions toured the state. Because of costs, the number of adult tours is now two small-cast shows per year, one each for the coastal and hinterland circuits of 5,000 miles each. The company also shows its work outside the state, with performances in Darwin, Canberra, Sydney, and northern New South Wales.

The scope of this daunting program is a predominant factor in a full assessment of the QTC's tasks and achievements. Many, however, judge the company mainly on its Brisbane seasons; consideration must be paid to this aspect before examining the extent of its other operations. As a metropolitan company offering eight new productions annually, QTC must fairly be measured against similar companies such as Sydney's now defunct Old Tote, Nimrod, the Melbourne Theatre Company, or the State Theatre Company of South Australia. Until 1974 when the amateur Twelfth Night Theatre went professional, QTC carried the burden of being the state's first and only professional company. Local standards of artistic comparison were, and indeed still are, set mainly by Brisbane's long-established amateur groups, of which Brisbane Repertory Theatre at La Boite maintains adventurous programs and offers some outstanding achievements. Conscious of its unique status and its subsidy dependence—in a state whose politicians have rarely been a byword for cultural adventurousness—QTC's programming tends to cater rather blandly to middle-of-the-road tastes, avoiding the experimental and the provocative. It blends the safe and solid fare of the established classics, contemporary successes of the commercial West End stage, and, more recently, Australian drama. A spectrum selected from, say, Shakespeare, Shaw, and Chekhov, plus farce, thrillers, and musicals, is offered yearly; Peter Shaffer's *Equus* has to date been the company's most popular success. The play selection is usually steady, balanced, and reminiscent of the virtues of provincial English repertory.

The six hundred-seat SGIO Theatre is partially a factor in this programming and, in order to overcome the limitations of its proscenium stage and large size, some productions have been created in more flexible venues such as La Boite. The theatre is considerably larger than comparable subsidized houses (for example, Nimrod's 300 and MTC's 450 seats), and the psychological and financial benefits of full houses are more urgently sought and, comparatively, more difficult to attain. Edwards and Joe MacColum, the associate artistic director, have worked diligently to build consistent audiences, and subscribers currently number four thousand. Full houses and sell-outs are not infrequent, with the company regularly playing to 1.7 percent of the metropolitan population, a creditable figure comparable to that of any similarly situated company.

Most of the shows have been directed by the house team of Alan Edwards, Joe MacColum, and Murray Foy (recently replaced as education officer by Lloyd Nickson), though a wider policy of importing guest directors is now being implemented. The company's teaching bias has nurtured many fine talents in Australian theatre, and artists from interstate companies work for limited periods with the resident ensemble. Notable imported "star" performers were Diane Cilento in *The Taming of the Shrew* (1975) and Warren Mitchell in *King Lear* (1978). QTC has shown a cautious, yet solid, approach to the display and nurture of contemporary Australian drama. Indeed, its inaugural venture was the premiere of a local musical, *A Rum Do!* In 1978 the Queensland Playwrights' Competition was instituted, the winning script (Beverley Mahoney's *Flightpath*) being produced as the initial play for the season. The current repertoire offers about three Australian plays annually, bringing QTC in line with the average practice for subsidized companies.

Reference has been made to the company's extensive touring activities; yet the two annual adult tours represent only a fraction of the QTC's commitment in this respect. As early as 1970, a school program was on the road, and primary and secondary school programs are mounted annually, each with more than one show. An indication of the scope of this project may be gathered by describing the school plans for 1979. The secondary school four-actor team toured for twenty-one weeks, playing an average of three fifty-minute shows per day in over one hundred schools. The primary school team performed thirty-six weeks in over three hundred schools. Both teams had circuits of over 7,000 miles. The content of this youth work has evolved from potted versions of Shakespeare to show isolated students some modicum of living experience of the then compulsorily studied Bard, to the development of locally scripted drama or poetry programs closely related to the experiences of children and young adults. Most successful has been the work of local writers sensitive to this reconsidered need: Michael Boddy, Richard Fotheringham, and Bille Brown. Each year, too, a statewide selection of high school students resides in Brisbane for an intensive course, Theatre Experience Week, which germinated, as a local follow-up, a new program, Theatre Techniques Week.

The company showed an early commitment to the concept of Theatre in Education (TIE) and in 1976, for example, a three-actor team flew a grueling 11,000-mile tour to schools in remote areas, usually only accessible by aircraft: Arnhem Land, Cape York, and some Pacific islands. The growth in the state of tertiary institutions catering to TIE, associated with dissatisfaction about the extent of the existing exploitation of TIE, led Murray Foy and Lloyd Nickson to rethink priorities in the community's needs and how the company could best service these. The outcome appeared in 1977 as Project Spearhead, a team of actor-teachers capable of going into schools to give a vocabulary of theatre skills and resources, which the pupils and teachers could learn to adapt for the articulation of their own concerns. Spearhead's work is not confined to the classroom. Its activities take in hospitals and old people's homes, and it has a particular concern in reaching minority language groups, aboriginal children, the deaf, and the disadvantaged. Actors are chosen for range and adaptability in skills and experience. Nickson's contributions to the concept of Spearhead's "learning through learning" were formed by his study in San Antonio, Texas, and with the National Theatre of the Deaf.

The company's initiatives in youth theatre derived from its conviction that its activities were not sufficiently decentralized; it had no wish simply to come and go in communities, leaving them unchanged by its passage. In 1977 a full-scale project was initiated to set up youth theatre in regional centers, resulting in the trial experiment of the Darling Downs Theatre. Forty young people from the Darling Downs (an agricultural area one-half the size of Tasmania and located west of Brisbane) were involved for five months in training in all aspects of theatre production, under professional guidance, with the ultimate aim of community involvement and pride in regional identity, expressed through the sharing of the creation of theatre. The results were highly encouraging, and the resulting performance, based on genesis myths, toured all the regional towns from which the young people were drawn. So far the policy of leaving behind in a community an autonomous, going theatrical concern has helped develop youth theatres in three regional centers.

In its short fourteen years of operation, QTC has attempted tasks in the community which many professional companies either would not have to face, would not care to face, or would consider to be outside their province. Despite its many areas of operation, growth has been responsibly extended and gratifyingly supported. The foundations are now laid for a company that need no longer be all things to all people, that can carve out with a sure hand its own territory in experimental theatre, that can make more use of alternative theatre venues and personnel, and that can develop a distinctive house style and artistic philosophy to compete with Nimrod or MTC. These are the expectations of a metropolitan audience. Yet, aided by the impending inception of competing professional companies in Queensland, when these goals are tackled, QTC will be able to add to its formidable accomplishments and the implementation of distinctive theatrical explorations and challenges and become an authoritative germinal force in Australian theatre.

VERONICA KELLY

CANADA

John Brockington, Area Editor

Introduction

The Canada Council, established by the government of Canada in 1957 to foster and promote the study, production, and enjoyment of works in the humanities and social sciences, is a principal source of support for many Canadian theatre companies. As an independent agency that reports annually to Parliament, it establishes policies and makes decisions within the guidelines set by the Canada Council Act. Assisting both individuals and organizations, the Canada Council gives fellowships, scholarships, and grants as well as prizes and special awards to persons in Canada for outstanding accomplishments in the theatrical arts. Functioning on national and provincial levels, it establishes grants to individual theatre companies throughout Canada; for example, in the spring of 1968, it supported the inaugural tour of the Stratford National Theatre of Canada. The council's recent efforts are designed to improve the quality of productions at the theatres it supports. Consequently, the financial support awarded each group is partially determined by the excellence of their productions. The Canada Council is dedicated to the development and presentation of new Canadian playwrights through readings, workshops, and productions.

Canadian theatre companies generally receive financing from federal, provincial, and municipal sources, with private donations and ticket sales accounting for only a portion of the revenue needed to keep the companies in operation. For example, the Shaw Festival was organized in 1962 but did not receive its first grants from the Canada Council until 1966. In 1965 it had received its first award from the Ontario Arts Council. Before that time, it survived through ticket sales as well as through the generosity of its actors, designers, directors, and patrons.

The four theatre companies chosen from the dozens of excellent companies operating throughout Canada are a representative selection: the Charlottetown Festival as the largest producer of original Canadian musicals; the Shaw Festival as a nonprofit theatrical organization devoted to the production of contemporary and classic plays as well as to the plays of George Bernard Shaw; the Stratford Festival as one of the world's most celebrated Shakespearean troupes; and the

Théâtre du Nouveau Monde as an excellent example of a professional, Canadian, French-speaking theatre company.

COLBY H. KULLMAN
(Notes from an interview with
John Brockington)

CHARLOTTETOWN FESTIVAL
Box 848, Charlottetown
Prince Edward Island, X1A 7L9, Canada

There is more to a theatre festival and national memorial than construction of a stage and concrete walls. Creativity and determination applied by many talented people have brought the Charlottetown Festival and its home, the Confederation Centre of the Arts, to the theatrical forefront in Canada.

The Confederation Complex is situated at the core of downtown Charlottetown, housing spacious convention facilities, one of Canada's major art galleries, Prince Edward Island's largest public library, and the Confederation Centre Theatre. The property immediately adjacent to the Centre Block is Province House, a Palladian-styled structure, where the fathers of Canadian Confederation first met in 1864.

The summer and fall of 1964, the centenary of that first important meeting, presented travelers and the Prince Edward Island public with an unbroken series of theatrical events, led by the Dominion Drama Festival in the new Confederation Centre complex. Queen Elizabeth II officially opened the building on October 6, 1964.

The following summer, a new phenomenon appeared in Charlottetown: a seven-week festival emerged, headlined by *Anne of Green Gables*, a musical based on the classic island novel by Lucy Maud Montgomery. Much to the amazement of Canada's theatrical pundits, a unique happening occurred each June. Under the artistic direction of one of Canada's leading choreographers, Alan Lund (the festival's artistic director since 1968), each season was headlined by the doyen of Canadian musicals, *Anne of Green Gables*. As the Charlottetown Festival's main attraction, *Anne* never fails to delight audiences. Add to that two national Canadian tours, engagements in London and New York City, and enormous popularity at Osaka, Japan, in 1970, and you have one of the country's most remarkable theatre legends. *Anne* has had a catalytic effect upon the theatrical scene, resulting in a variety of unmistakably Canadian enterprises that have brought the festival both national and international prominence.

Alan Lund's artistic sensibility unmistakenly identifies a festival production. With split-second timing, he has transformed a World War I battlefield into a gleaming Broadway stage in George Salverson's *The Legend of the Dumbbells*. He uses the talent of Canadian entertainers to the utmost, proving in Cliff Jones' rock-opera version of *Hamlet, Kronberg: 1582*, that country singers and rock production numbers can create new insights for Shakespeare enthusiasts. Cliff Jones' rewritten version of *Kronberg: 1582*, under the title of *Rockabye Hamlet*, opened on Broadway on February 17, 1976. Although the musical failed to impress critics, it nevertheless gained a number of aficionados during its short New York run.

Tens of thousands of people attend the festival every season, including major critics from across Canada and the United States. Initially, Charlottetown appeared a most unlikely and isolated home for Canadian musical theatre. Today, however, audiences in Toronto, Ottawa, Hamilton, and other urban centers have been able to sample touring productions from Charlottetown, such as *Anne*, *The Dumbbells*, *Mavor Moore*, *Johnny Belinda*, *By George!* (conceived by Alan Lund), and *Kronberg: 1582*.

Without growth, no theatre festival could hope to remain in the national vanguard. With that concept in mind, in 1977 festival producers began to create a second stage, drawing into focus actors, directors, musicians, and writers, who might not ordinarily enter the Charlottetown scene. Cedric Smith's *The Road to Charlottetown* (directed and choreographed by Alan Lund) opened on August 1, 1977, playing to sizable houses for five weeks of the ten-week festival schedule. It is a production based on the poems and writings of Prince Edward Island poet Milton Acron, one-time winner of the Canadian Governor General's Award for Literature. Audience acceptance indicated to producers that the second stage could be considered a positive addition to the summer festival.

On July 6, 1978, the second stage concept emerged in Charlottetown as STAGE 2, premiering a pair of unusual musicals at the MacKenzie Theatre Cabaret, Atlantic Canada's only licensed cabaret theatre. The MacKenzie Theatre is situated immediately opposite the Confederation Centre of the Arts, affording the festival added visibility in the core of Charlottetown and giving the city's night life needed stimulation. *Lies and Other Lyrics* featured two of Canada's better known performers, Brian McKay and Wanda Cannon, in a "whirlwind lyrical debate about love," which received critical support. The following night, a spirited musical comedy, *Eight to the Bar*, began nine weeks of sell-out houses, playing in repertory with Nancy Phillips' *Lies and Other Lyrics* (directed and choreographed by Alan Lund). STAGE 2 proved an integral part of summer entertainment in Canada's smallest province.

In 1979 artistic director Alan Lund and newly appointed executive producer Ron Francis produced a stimulating festival line-up. *Anne of Green Gables* returned to the main stage for its fifteenth consecutive season, joined by two additional full-scale musicals. As in previous seasons, musicals were staged six nights a week, with additional matinee performances of *Anne of Green Gables*, and internationally renowned artists were engaged for Sunday night concerts in the main theatre. Children's productions were staged during the afternoon in the center's Lecture Theatre, allowing parents to relax and enjoy the building's other amenities.

Musicals produced since 1981 include *Aimee!*, based on the life of evangelist Aimee Semple McPherson, with book and lyrics by Patrick Young and Bob Ashley, 1981; and the cabaret productions *Magcap* and *Cocktails for Two Hundred*, 1981. In 1982 *Skin Deep* was produced, with book and lyrics by Nika Rylski and music by Rosemary Radcliff. *Skin Deep* is about the backstage goings-on of a beauty pageant, where the audience actually picked the winner, thereby determining one of four surprise conclusions. *Singin' & Dancin' TONIGHT* was conceived by Alan Lund and went on a national tour early in 1983, returning in the summer of 1983 to play in repertory with *Anne of Green Gables* and a remount of *Johnny Belinda. Singin' & Dancin' TONIGHT* is a glittery revue, featuring the best in music and song from Canada's premiere composers, lyricists, and recording artists. This show was the feature entertainment at Rotary International's 1983 Convention at Toronto's Maple Leaf Gardens.

In 1980 the festival removed the reference to "Summer," which had previously been in its name (the Charlottetown Summer Festival), as the troupe had become a touring company that toured throughout the year.

The publicity files of the Charlottetown Festival are brimming with evidence that Canada's largest producer of original Canadian musicals is Confederation Centre. Both national and international critics and writers have followed the festival's development closely since its creation. The fact that this country's largest daily newspapers and most progressive magazines concern themselves with Charlottetown Festival happenings has added to the importance of theatre in this city.

The names associated with the festival are among Canada's most distinguished. Norman Campbell, composer of *Anne of Green Gables*, is regarded as one of the nation's leading television producers. Donald Barron, writer of *Anne*, is a successful actor, radio and television personality, comedian, and author. Wayne and Shuster, who appeared in repertory with *Anne* and *Laugh with Leacock* during its first season in 1965, remain Canada's best known team of comedians and comedy writers.

The writers, directors, and festival company are all Canadian, directly linked with the overall mandate of the Confederation Centre of the Arts. Memorial Hall, the central block of the complex, is the national memorial to the Confederation. Art Gallery and extension programs are generally Canadian in nature as well. There is a commitment to the Canadian context because people in all parts of the country support Confederation Centre and its programs through federal or provincial grants, together with earned revenues and donations from the corporate sector.

The creation of a distinctive contemporary architectural landmark fifteen years ago was an astounding alteration to the center of Charlottetown. More astounding still has been the Confederation Centre's impact on Canadian culture, the performing and visual arts. Today the center has a reputation for producing original musical theatre as yet unrivalled in this country.

JOHN BROCKINGTON
(With gratitude to Harvey Sawler,
Public Relations Consultant to the
Confederation Centre of the Arts)

SHAW FESTIVAL
Shaw Festival Theatre Foundation
Box 774, Niagara-on-the-Lake
Ontario, L0S 1J0, Canada

The inception of Niagara-on-the-Lake's Shaw Festival in 1962 marked the end of the long period when Shaw's plays were offered occasionally in Canada by touring companies or by determined local theatre groups. A nineteenth-century courthouse was converted into a theatre, where over two hundred Shaw enthusiasts endured excessive heat and cramped conditions to watch the opening performance of *Salute to Shaw*. A company of ten unpaid actors, under the direction of Maynard Burgess, presented *Don Juan in Hell* and *Candida*, for eight weekend performances between June 29 and August 11. As a result of the determined leadership of Brian Doherty, Q.C., retired lawyer and resident of Niagara-on-the-Lake, the Shaw Festival was founded. An idea had become a reality, and George Bernard Shaw and Niagara-on-the-Lake became synonymous.

Excited by the enthusiastic response to *Salute to Shaw*, Brian Doherty decided to create a fully professional Shaw Festival. To this end, in 1963 he established the theatre as a nonprofit organization with a board of directors. He also obtained the services of Andrew Allan as artistic director.

In the first of his three years at the festival, Allan began a program of expansion that was to characterize his tenure. With the money received from a pre-Toronto engagement of Mavor Moore's revue *Spring Thaw*, he increased the company to fourteen and the season to three weeks, with three Shavian plays. In 1964 he extended the season to four weeks with four Shavian plays, added two full-time designers to the staff, and increased the company to twenty-five.

Allan's last year as artistic director, 1965, was one of firsts. It was the year the festival first received a government grant from the Ontario Arts Council. It was the year a full-time company manager/publicity director was engaged. It was the year Doherty inaugurated a series of dramatic seminars, a practice repeated every year. It was also the first year a non-Shavian play, Sean O'Casey's *The Shadow of a Gunman*, was performed, thereby establishing the practice of producing plays by some of Shaw's contemporaries as well.

In 1966 the Canada Council made its first financial grant, and Barry Morse succeeded Andrew Allan as artistic director. Although the presence of his numerous other commitments dictated his brief stay, it did not prevent Morse from continuing his predecessor's program of expansion. His enthusiasm for the theatre, and particularly Shaw, infected all those in contact with him, and finally transformed the festival into a truly professional endeavor worthy of international attention.

Paxton Whitehead was appointed artistic director of the Shaw Festival in 1967, a year highlighted by an end-of-season tour, as part of a cooperative venture with the Manitoba Theatre Centre (MTC). Guest director Edward Gilbert, artistic director of the Manitoba Theatre Centre, took *Major Barbara* to the Royal Theatre, Montreal, for Expo '67, and then to MTC in Winnipeg.

In 1968 the English-language world premiere of Georges Feydeau's *La main passe*, retitled *The Chemmy Circle*, was in Niagara-on-the-Lake as part of the season. The following year, a postseason tour of Ottawa, with a production of *The Guardsman*, was undertaken, and an hour-long documentary, *The Summer Is for Shaw*, was produced by Toronto's CFTO-TV.

The year 1970 began with a preseason tour of *Candida* to Kingston and Ottawa. As part of the season in Niagara-on-the-Lake, Alan Bennett's *Forty Years On* was produced. The year's activities were now financed in part by federal, provincial, and municipal grants.

The tenth anniversary season, in 1971, began with the largest preseason tour undertaken by the festival. *The Philanderer* visited Kingston, Montreal, and Rochester, and Romain Weingarten's *Summer Days* was performed in Ottawa.

The pattern of growth had long since necessitated a new theatre. Dreams of a new Shaw Festival Theatre began as early as 1965, with many setbacks encountered and overcome before, in December 1969, Toronto architect Ron Thom was chosen. In 1971 Thom finalized his design, and, on April 17, 1972, founder Brian Doherty turned the first sod at the site chosen for the new theatre and building began.

Meanwhile, it was "business as usual" in the four-hundred-seat Court House Theatre. A preseason tour of *Misalliance* played in Ottawa, Rochester, Kingston, Montreal, and Washington, D.C., where the festival was honored by being the first foreign theatre company to appear in the new Eisenhower Theatre at the John F. Kennedy Center for the Performing Arts.

In January 1973 the Shaw Festival was invited to the Eisenhower Theatre for a return two-week engagement of *The Philanderer*. Thus began the activities of a fifteen-week season in this very special year, a year not without difficulties. A month before the opening of the new theatre, the stage and rehearsal halls were still unfinished, and there were no seats in the auditorium, no lighting, and no curtain. Whether the theatre would be ready was a matter of speculation. Yet, in spite of the problems, on June 12 the premier of Ontario, William Davis, performed the ribbon-cutting ceremony opening the new 830-seat Festival Theatre.

The inaugural week continued with a special round of afternoon concerts. Among the many dignitaries attending were Prime Minister Pierre Trudeau and his guest, Prime Minister Indira Gandhi of India; Premier William Davis; and Lieutenant-Governor Ross Macdonald of Ontario. On June 26, a special performance of *You Never Can Tell* was held in honor of Her Majesty Queen Elizabeth II and His Royal Highness, the Duke of Edinburgh.

The Shaw Festival had been considering expanding into a year-round center for the performing arts, and, in the fall of 1973, the first International Concert Series was introduced. In the spring of 1974, under the sponsorship of the Touring Office of the Canada Council, the Shaw Festival made its first tour of the Maritime Provinces, presenting George Bernard Shaw's *The Devil's Disciple*. Camerata, previously heard in concert during the winter of 1973–1974, returned to take up residency in Niagara-on-the-Lake. After the season ended, the company toured during September, October, and November. *Charley's Aunt* visited Ottawa, Boston, and Philadelphia, and *Too True to Be Good* was taken to Boston.

In 1975 longtime Shaw Festival associate Tony van Bridge was appointed acting artistic director while Paxton Whitehead was on sabbatical. In the fall of the year, *Caesar and Cleopatra* toured Ottawa and Philadelphia. *The Devil's Disciple* was specially remounted at the John F. Kennedy Center for the Performing Arts as part of the U.S. bicentennial celebration. Returning to the Shaw Festival in 1976, after a year's sabbatical, artistic director Paxton Whitehead headed a twenty-two-week season which was both exciting and an overwhelming success at the box office. Summer music featured Camerata, as well as Cleo Laine and John Dankworth.

The challenging presentation of the full-length version of *Man and Superman* highlighted the artistic productions of the 1977 season. This success was reflected in increased interest from the press, not only in Canada but also in New York and London, establishing firm international recognition of the Shaw Festival as the world's major center for Shavian productions.

In August 1977 Whitehead resigned as artistic director, having produced over a ten-year period twenty-two plays by Bernard Shaw and twelve plays by other playwrights, as well as appearing in more Shaw plays than any other actor of his generation. Richard Kirschner, executive director for the previous two years, took over as producer, combining the artistic and administrative direction of the Shaw Festival.

Shaw Festival 1979 saw Leslie Yeo as artistic director. The summer season included plays by Bernard Shaw (*You Never Can Tell*, *Village Wooing*, and *Captain Brassbound's Conversion*), plays about Bernard Shaw (Jerome Kilty's *Dear Liar* and Michael Voysey's *My Astonishing Self*), and plays by Shaw's contemporaries (Emlyn Williams' *The Corn Is Green* and Noel Coward's *Blithe Spirit*). Directors included Tony van Bridge, Scott Swan, Douglas Campbell, and Leslie Yeo; special attractions were Liona Boyd, Tony van Bridge, John Ciarney, Oscar Peterson, and Anna Russell.

In June 1978 Christopher Newton, from the Vancouver Playhouse Theatre, was appointed new artistic director and assumed his duties on January 1, 1980. The 1980 Shaw Festival saw productions of Shaw's *Misalliance*, Anton Chekhov's *The Cherry Orchard*, Georges Feydeau's *A Flea in Her Ear*, and Gyula Hernády's *The Grand Hunt* at the Festival Theatre; Shaw's *The Philanderer* and *Overruled*, Bertolt Brecht's *A Respectable Wedding*, and John Bruce Cowan's *Canuck* at the Court House Theatre; and Irving Berlin's *Puttin' on the Ritz* and Heath Lambert's *Gunga Heath* at the Royal Gorge Theatre. The 1981 Shaw Festival, its twentieth season, was highlighted by productions of Shaw's *Saint Joan*, *In Good King Charles' Golden Days*, and *Man of Destiny*; Nikolai Erdman's *The Suicide*; Will Evans and Valentine's *Tons of Money*; Arthur Wing Pinero's *The Magistrate*; and Robert David MacDonald's *Camille*. During the following summer season, the featured productions were Shaw's *Pygmalion*, *Too True to Be Good*, and *The Music-Cure*; Philip King's *See How They Run*; Edmond Rostand's *Cyrano de Bergerac*; and Simone Benmussa's *The Singular Life of Albert Nobbs* (based on the short story by George Moore).

Among the many awards won by the Shaw Festival are the following: the Ronson Award (1972) presented to Marsha Sibthorpe, lighting technician; the Ronson Award (1973) presented to Hilary Corbett, costume designer; the Ronson Award (1974) presented to Heath Lamberts, actor; the Ronson Award (1975) presented to Nancy Pankiw, scenic designer; the Ronson Award (1976) presented to Robin Craven, sound technician; the Loewen, Ondaatje, McCutcheon and Company Drama Award (1977) presented to Paxton Whitehead, artistic director; and the Loewen, Ondaatje, McCutcheon and Company Drama Award (1979) presented to Leslie Yeo, artistic director.

It was once asked, "Can Bernard Shaw find happiness in a small Ontario town?" Obviously, he has.

JOHN BROCKINGTON

STRATFORD FESTIVAL
Stratford, Ontario, N5A 6V2, Canada

Conceived in the mind of a local journalist and holding its first performance in a tent, the Stratford Festival has become one of the North American continent's most durable and exciting theatre ventures. Each year between June and October, over one-half million people flock to the small southwestern Ontario town of Stratford, a one-time railway switching center, that sits on the banks of a narrow ribbon of water named the Avon River. At first, the people came to see the plays of Shakespeare. Today, they come to see Shakespeare and a wide variety of other theatrical fare, covering the spectrum from Elizabethan classical to modern plays and musicals.

Backtracking slightly to the early 1950s, when 80 percent of the then 19,500 residents of Stratford depended on the railway for their livelihood, we find Tom Patterson, a local newspaperman, whose first exposure to classical theatre was as a soldier in Europe. He returned to his hometown obsessed with the idea of establishing a local theatre, devoted to presenting the plays of Shakespeare. Having assembled a committee of interested citizens, he contacted the celebrated English director, Tyrone Guthrie, who came to Canada to discuss the project and agreed to take part, provided a star and experienced theatre personnel were hired, and on condition that performances be held in a tent with an open stage.

Mostly because of lack of funds, the next twelve months were plagued with uncertainty. Volunteers worked around the clock to keep the venture moving. Actors continued to rehearse, an act of faith if ever there was one. Their optimism was transmitted to at least one contractor, who continued working far after being told that there was not enough money to pay him. At the last minute, an anonymous donor contributed a large sum of money, which alleviated the most pressing of the committee's financial worries; and on July 13, 1953, Alec Guinness made his first entrance in the title role of Richard III, performing in a giant circus tent on a revolutionary open stage.

It was typical of Guthrie's daring that, in choosing the opening repertoire, he brought together the popular *Richard III* with the unknown, rarely performed *All's Well That Ends Well*, again featuring Alec Guinness and Irene Worth. It was typical of Guthrie's long and rewarding relationship with Tanya Moiseiwitsch that, together, they were able to mold so resourceful a performing space, a stage architecture with a remarkable affinity for Shakespeare's own style.

All summer long tourists filled the tent to 98 percent capacity; the original five-week season was extended to six. At final count, some 68,000 people had traveled to Stratford to see the plays.

In 1954 Tyrone Guthrie turned the reins over to Cecil Clarke, who had come from England to assist him; and in 1955 Guthrie himself returned to steer the festival's artistic course through one more season. Michael Langham followed as artistic director and was succeeded in 1968 by Jean Gascon. Robin Phillips became artistic director in 1974. He has only recently been succeeded by John Hirsch. The season has been expanded from six to twenty-two weeks, and festival productions have toured from coast to coast in Canada and gone as far afield as the Chichester and Edinburgh festivals in England and Scotland; New York, Los Angeles, Chicago, and Minneapolis in the United States; Denmark, Holland, Poland, and Russia in Europe; and the Adelaide Festival in Australia.

In 1956 the tent was replaced with a permanent building retaining the pillared thrust stage that has become the festival's hallmark and served as the model for similar platforms in the United States and England. There is no necessity for scenery on the festival stage. Costumes and properties serve as the only dressing. A modern adaptation of the Elizabethan stage, it has a balcony, trapdoors, seven acting levels, and nine major entrances. Seating capacity in the auditorium is 2,262, with no spectator ever more than 65 feet from the stage. In 1975 revisions were completed to make the balcony mobile, thereby widening the scope for staging musicals and other works on the open platform.

Since 1956 the Avon Theatre has played an increasingly important role in the festival's operations. Bought by the festival in 1963 and refurbished to provide enlarged stage facilities and comfortable, attractive auditorium seating for 1,092 people, the Avon Theatre houses operettas, operas, and a variety of classical and modern plays.

In 1971 the festival opened another performing area. The Third Stage, housed in rented quarters overlooking the river, is a three-hundred-seat, open-space theatre, envisioned as a home for original theatre work in both music and drama.

Each successive artistic director has left his personal stamp on the festival. Tyrone Guthrie gave it a physical shape and style of production that were remarkably imaginative, highly theatrical, and always daring. Michael Langham expanded the festival's activities through major tours, smaller scale university workshop presentations, and the first collaboration with television (*Henry V* for

CTV) in 1967. A director of formidable intelligence, incisive wit, and theatrical brilliance, he gave the festival such landmark productions as the 1961 *Love's Labour's Lost*, with Zoe Caldwell, and *Coriolanus*, with Paul Scofield; the 1964 *King Lear*, with John Colicos; Gogol's *The Inspector General* in 1967; and Richard Brinsley Sheridan's *The School for Scandal* in 1970. Jean Gascon expanded the list of authors presented at the festival, introducing Stratford audiences to the exceptional riches of French theatre. His 1968 production of Molière's *Tartuffe*, starring William Hutt, exhibited what has been described as the elegant sophistication of French theatre encountering the unique exuberance of the New World and emerging as a very individualized, contemporary, and even Canadian Molière. Gascon brought startling theatricality to the work of such writers as the Elizabethan John Webster, thereby creating yet another outstanding production with *The Duchess of Malfi* in 1970.

Robin Phillips' tenure was characterized by exciting, innovative work that placed the festival in the front ranks of the English-speaking world's classical theatre companies. Serious critics and scholars have hailed his productions for their often astonishing clarity, coupled with a rare fidelity to the text and to the inner reality of character and situation. His remarkable output includes several productions that have won an incontrovertible place for themselves in theatre history: *Measure for Measure* in 1975 and 1976, *Richard III* in 1977, *The Winter's Tale* in 1978, and *As You Like It* in 1977 and 1978. Three of his lighter productions (Oscar Wilde's *The Importance of Being Earnest* in 1975 and 1976, Ferenc Molnár's *The Guardsman* in 1977, and Noel Coward's *Private Lives* in 1978) have won accolades from the public and a majority of reviewers. Such controversial productions as the 1976 *Antony and Cleopatra*, the 1978 *Macbeth*, and the 1979/80 *King Lear* have caused great diversity of critical opinion. The only consensus is in a general assessment of the productions as significant statements of an original mind, a mind intelligent and intuitive, sensitive to the nuance of the unspoken as well as the spoken word, and capable of imaginative leaps inward to new insights and outward to a wider vision.

Robin Phillips saw the festival's mandate in history as threefold: to provide audiences with the standards of quality they must be able to expect from a world-class classical theatre company; to provide training for the Canadian actors, playwrights, directors, designers, and theatre technicians of the future; and to expand the scope of the festival's activities, nationally and internationally, through the media of film and television.

A newly formed Young Company was the first step in the training program, with worthwhile results. Through cross-casting of productions at the three theatres, inexperienced performers had the opportunity to work with and learn from accomplished and talented actors of the calibre of Maggie Smith, Martha Henry, Jessica Tandy, Margaret Tyzack, Brian Bedford, William Hutt, Hume Cronyn, Douglas Rain, Peter Ustinov, and many others.

John Hirsch, Stratford's present artistic director, agrees that there is an urgent need to train actors to perform the great works of theatre. To this end, he has initiated the Shakespeare 3 Company, which made its debut at the Third Stage in 1982. Twelve talented young actors, with professional but not necessarily classical experience, and four senior actors, with extensive experience on the classical stage, undertook an intensive training and performance schedule over a period of nineteen weeks from April through August.

In the publicity materials of the company, Hirsch views the festival as both a "national treasure" and a "continental resource." He is dedicated to "a strong company doing understandable, accessible theatre" and is concerned that the festival help achieve a measure of Canadian self-actualization through the works presented on its stages.

Under his direction, the festival celebrated its thirtieth anniversary season in 1982 with ten productions on its three stages and a host of activities—concerts, film, a virtuoso performance series of one-man presentations, public lectures by theatre scholars, major exhibitions, and other programs designed to involve visitors as fully as possible in an exciting, exhilarating theatrical event.

In his first season as artistic director, Hirsch introduced the work of Friedrich Dürrenmatt to the festival repertory with a production of *The Visit*, directed by former artistic director Jean Gascon and starring William Hutt and Alexis Smith. In 1983 he added Friedrich Schiller to the list of authors performed at Stratford. The anniversary season also marked the Canadian premiere of a new work by Brian Friel, titled *Translations*.

The festival is heading into its third decade with the commitment and vigor that have already won it a place among the great English-speaking theatre companies.

ANNE SELBY

THEATRE DU NOUVEAU MONDE
84 Ouest Ste-Catherine
Montreal, Quebec H2X 9Z9, Canada

On October 9, 1951, Quebec's first truly professional French-speaking theatre company, Le Théâtre du Nouveau Monde (TNM), opened its premiere season with a production of Molière's classic comedy, *L'avare* (*The Miser*). Its first home, until 1957, was a hall beneath Gesù Church in Montreal. The people of Montreal received the company with great enthusiasm.

The dream that became Le Théâtre du Nouveau Monde was the vision of seven men: Jean Gascon, Jean-Louis Roux, Guy Hoffmann, André Gascon, Mark Drouin, Eloide Grandmont, and Georges Groulx. They appointed Jean Gascon first artistic director. The mandate of this group was stated in the program for the first season: the founders primarily wanted to enable actors in Montreal to work seriously in an atmosphere of stability. It was time, they felt, for a permanently based troupe, whose members could support themselves with stage work. Secondary objectives included presenting fully professional theatre, gaining public support through the performance of quality productions, and establishing a viable Canadian theatre with the cooperation of groups already in existence. They also hoped to produce their first Canadian play the following season and eventually to develop a theatre school for training professional actors within Canada. This was a demanding commitment for a fledgling company, struggling to survive without government subsidy in a makeshift theatre.

Despite great obstacles, TNM endured. Its first production of a Canadian play was *Une nuit d'amour* (*A Night of Love*) by André Langevin in the 1953–1954 season; the company made its international debut at the Paris International Festival in 1955, with a production of Molière's *Trois farces* (*Three Farces*). Taking classic French comedy to sophisticated Parisian audiences required courage, but the move justified itself when the comedy received critical acclaim. The reputation of Le Théâtre du Nouveau Monde as a company of national importance was assured by its international success.

The following year, many members of the company appeared at the Stratford Festival in Ontario, as French courtiers in Michael Langham's production of *Henry V*. They also presented *Trois farces* in French.

Lack of financing and the need for a more suitable and permanent home had been major problems for the company during this period. In 1957 the Gesù Theatre was abandoned for an old theatre formerly converted into a money house, the Orpheum, which, though not ideal, was an improvement. In 1958 the troupe made a grand tour, beginning in April in New York City and continuing on to Paris, Brussels, and other Belgian cities. The company returned to Canada to appear again at the Stratford Festival and then crossed Canada, giving eighty-two performances in twenty-three cities. During this tour, the TNM again presented Molière's *Three Farces* (*Trois farces*), as well as his *Imaginary Invalid* (*Le malade imaginaire*), and a Canadian play, Marcel Dubé's *Le temps des lilas*, in French, as well as an English version (*The Time of Lilacs*).

The company's first ten years were characterized by growing popularity, despite the lack of a permanent home theatre. Difficult times were to follow, however. With its tenth anniversary at hand, Gascon felt strongly that TNM must be able to pay its dedicated players a living wage, have a permanent theatre building, and expand its repertoire beyond Molière and Feydeau. TNM players were then subsisting on earnings from other sources, and Gascon privately vowed in 1961 that he would close down the company unless its financial needs were met. Certain 1961 projects actually were canceled, but adequate pledges of private and governmental support were received to keep operating. Despite Gascon's campaigning, however, it was not until 1967 that TNM was even able to obtain a promise of a suitable new address—space in the Place des Arts complex then under construction, before finally purchasing its own theatre building in 1971.

TNM had previously performed more than just Molière and Feydeau farces; until 1960, of a total of thirty-six productions, there had been eight French versions of English-language plays (such as *Le baladin du monde occidental* from Sean O'Casey's *The Playboy of the Western World*); there had also been several productions of Quebec playwrights. Despite the difficulty of finding suitable material, TNM had tried to produce one Canadian play per year by means of a provincially subsidized playwrights' competition, beginning with Andre Langevin's *L'oeuil du peuple* (*The Eye of the People*) in 1957. Nevertheless, there was to be a gradual expansion beyond such current divertissements as the musical *Irma La Douce*. Quebec society was changing; entertainment was no longer enough.

Of course, the ever-popular Molière productions continued— *Georges Dandin* and *Le medecin malgré lui* (*The Doctor in Spite of Himself*) in the 1962–1963 season—but over the next few seasons more politically oriented plays were also performed. One of the early examples of these was *L'ombre d'un franc-tireur* (*The Shadow of a Free-shooter*), from Sean O'Casey's *The Shadow of a Gunman*, in the 1960–1961 season. By the 1965–1966 season, this new political consciousness was an established element of TNM's philosophy. That season's offerings alternated Molière with French versions of Brecht's *The Threepenny Opera* (for which Gascon had obtained the rights after a five-year struggle) and of Arthur Miller's *The Crucible* (as *Les sorcières de Salem*, *The Sorcerers of Salem*). A French version of Barrie Stavis' *The Man Who Never Died*, Jean-Louis Roux's *On n'a pas tué Joe Hill* (*Nobody's Killed Joe Hill*), was perhaps the most direct attempt to reach working-class people.

In 1966 Jean Gascon resigned as artistic director. Financial problems were still unresolved, and the promised new home, the Port-Royal Theatre in Place des Arts, remained unfinished. Jean-Louis Roux, who left the company in 1963, returned to become Gascon's successor.

Roux did manage eventually to obtain a lease on the Port-Royal Theatre and, by curtailing budgets, overcame an operating deficit of $290,000 in the 1967–1968 season. On the other hand, Roux proposed a new seven-point philosophy. He maintained that the purposes of TNM should be: (1) to create a national theatre for the performance of works by national authors; (2) to develop educational activity; (3) to awaken the public conscience; (4) to develop a concern for diversity at its highest level; (5) to develop a true public service approach; (6) to maintain admission prices as low as possible; and (7) to put forth deep roots in the milieu in which TNM worked.

TNM continued to offer a diversity of attractions to theatregoers. In 1971, on its twentieth anniversary, the troupe presented *La Guerre, Yes Sir* (*War, Yes Sir!*, from the Roch Carrier novel) as well as the perennial *Tartuffe* by Molière. Plays by Quebec writers began to be produced regularly. A noteworthy innovation in this regard, *Theatre-midi*, an annual series of lunchtime performances of one-act plays by Quebec playwrights, was instituted in 1973. The first *Theatre-midi* production, *Joualez-moi d'amour* (*"Joualez" to Me of Love*) by Jean Barbeau, was an immediate hit, and two other satires by Barbeau, *Goglu* and *Knockout*, followed. The 1976 offerings, Francois Beaulieu's *Septième ciel* (*Seventh Heaven*) and Michel Tremblay's *Surprise, Surprise*, also were major hits. This program has been successful in drawing in working people who are not normally theatregoers.

The landmarks of recent seasons were, among other plays, *Eux, ou la prise du pouvoir (Them, or The Grip of Power)* by Eduardo Manet (with an admirable performance by Geneviève Bujold); *Les oranges sont vertes (The Oranges Are Green)* by Claude Gauvreau (the first genuine masterpiece of the Canadian theatre); *Citrouille (Pumpkin)* by Jean Barbeau (women's lib through healthy violence); *La nef des sorcières (The Ship of the Sorcerers*, seven colorful monologues with Luce Guilbeault as ''conductor''); *Le balcon (The Balcony)* by Jean Genet (the Revolution recuperated by its own image); *Les fées ont soif (The Fairies Are Thirsty)* by Denise Boucher (which resulted in a lawsuit against TNM on the account of ''blasphemous libel''); *L'impromptu d'Outremont (Impromptu Outremont)* by Michel Temblay (elitist culture as opposed to the so-called popular culture); and *Quelle vie? . . .* (a Quebec version of the famous Brian Clark's *Whose Life Is It Anyway?*). Paul Claudel, Jean Baptiste Racine, Eugene Ionesco, Carlo Goldoni, Roger Vitrac, and Pierre Carlet de Chamblain de Marivaux are still part of the bill of fare.

In that balance between the present and past, Le Théâtre du Nouveau Monde has perhaps found the solution between two ideals that are often antagonistic, yet vital to any cultural enterprise: tradition and progress; permanency and movement.

On October 9, 1981, Le Théâtre du Nouveau Monde celebrated its thirtieth anniversary.

JOHN BROCKINGTON

EASTERN EUROPE

Edward J. Czerwinski, Area Editor

Introduction

The only monolithic characteristic of Eastern Europe is that most of the countries comprising the area have a connection with the Soviet Union. Besides this historical imperative, few similarities exist. Even the languages are different, and few Eastern Europeans can understand one another, linguistically or socially. For example, the dominant language in the Soviet Union is Russian, but the native language of over 50 percent of the population (because today the Great Russians constitute merely the greatest minority) is Armenian, Estonian, Latvian, Ukrainian, and so on. Unfortunately, few minorities are given the opportunity to develop a culture stronger or greater than the Soviet Russian. Thus, we find outstanding directors and theatres in Estonia, Latvia, Lithuania, Georgia, and the Ukraine, but few companies are permitted to develop without interference.

The rest of Eastern Europe presents a different problem. Most Western critics familiar with the theatres in Eastern Europe would admit that some of the finest experimental work is being done in countries such as Poland, Romania, Hungary, Yugoslavia, and Czechoslovakia. Unfortunately, the political vicissitudes of each country dictate the amount of artistic freedom allowed. After martial-law was declared in Poland in December, 1981, artists became the main target of repression. Even artists in liberal Poland had trouble with the censor. Many artists, including theatre people, have been forced to leave Czechoslovakia or to retire to another profession. Some, like Václav Havel, have been imprisoned. The political climate seems always to be in a state of agitation. And yet the theatre thrives on the tension that politics invariably creates in each community. Thanks to government subsidies given to the arts in the Socialist countries, theatres continue to develop programs that are the envy of artists and companies in the West. Companies, such as Jerzy Grotowski's Laboratory Theatre, Józef Szajna's Teatr Studio, and Mira Trailović's Atelier 212, receive funds from their respective governments and take active part in the cultural life of the nation. In fact, most of the companies in this reference work probably could not have survived in the West. Socialism should be given credit for the present high state of the arts in most of these Eastern European countries, in spite of the censorship.

Because the present volume includes only companies that have existed for several years and have continued to develop artistic programs, several outstanding artists do not appear. Some directors and actors are not identified with any one company; thus their names are absent. One can cite scores of brilliant directors in this category: Adam Hanuszkiewicz, Izabella Cywińska, Jerzy Jarocki, Jerzy Grzegorzewski, Kazimierz Dejmek, Gustaw Holoubek, Zygmunt Hübner, Helmut Kajzar, Tadeusz Łomnicki, Maciej Prus, and Janusz Warmiński from Poland; Peter Fomenko, Ruben Agamirzjan, Karel Ird (Estonia), Voldemar Panso (Estonia), Mark Rozovskij, Anatolij Silin, Mixail Tumanišvili (Georgia), and Galina Volček from the Soviet Union; David Esrig, Radu Beligan, Dinu Cernescu, Liviu Ciulei, Radu Pencuilescu, and Lucian Pintilie from Romania; Ottó Adám, József Ruszt, and Gabor Zsámbéki from Hungary; Jaroslav Dudek, Václav Hudeček, Jan Kačer, Otomar Krejča, Miroslav Machaček, Evžen, Sokolovský, and Jaroslav Vostrý from Czechoslovakia; Krikor Azarjan, Vili Cankov, Leon Daniel, and Luben Grojs from Bulgaria; and Mile Korun (Slovenia), Kosta Spaić, and Georgij Paro from Yugoslavia. In addition, because of the political situation in Albania, no company has come to light that has developed a sequential repertory.

Certain omissions will undoubtedly occur. Student companies like the excellent Teatr STU from Kraków or the Theatre of the Eighth Day in Poznán have been excluded from this volume. Certain directors like Andrei Serban and Jonaš Jurašaš who started their careers in Eastern Europe have also been excluded, since they now work in the United States. Oddly enough, the reader will find that no two companies in Eastern Europe are alike: happily, artists in the Socialist world, like artists anywhere else, are determined to insinuate their own individuality in their work.

EDWARD J. CZERWINSKI

Bulgaria

ADRIANA BUDEVSKA THEATRE OF BURGAS
(Dramatičen Teatyr "Adriana Budevska," Burgas)
Stalin Boulevard, Burgas, Bulgaria

The Drama Theatre of Burgas was founded in 1919 by Anton Popov and Trayko Antonov. It is a theatre with a great tradition. Some of Bulgaria's greatest directors have been associated with it: Ivan Andrejčin, Stefan Kirov, Krystju Sarafov, Zlatina Nedeva, Georgi Kostov, Stefan Karalambov, Stefan Dobrev, Vili Tsankov, Anatas Mihajlov, Nikolaj Savov, and Krystju Dojnov. And yet it is difficult to define a clear artistic profile for this company. The emphasis has been on experimentation with regard to native Bulgarian drama, but on traditional fare with regard to foreign writers. Recently, the foreign plays have included works by Maxim Gorky, Anton Chekhov, Tennessee Williams, Friedrich Dürrenmatt, and Sławomir Mrożek. The repertory of Bulgarian works includes the names of the nation's best dramatists: Ivan Vazov, Anton Strašimirov, Yordan Yovkov, and Stojan L. Kostov.

The Drama Theatre of Burgas has also concentrated on laboratory productions. It contributed a number of works to the "poetic wave" in Bulgaria, better known as the "April Tendency" in literature. The following dramatists were given their first productions in this theatre: Ivan Pejchev, Ivan Radojev, Stefan Tsanev, and Nedjalko Yordanov.

The past thirty years have been extremely fruitful ones for the Burgas Theatre. Talented directors have contributed to the tradition of developing new native talent: Vili Tsankov, Leon Laniel, and Z. A. Andonov in the 1950s and 1960s; and Asen Šopov and Nedjalko Yordanov in the 1970s. During this period the company developed a "lyric" style. The emphasis was on simplicity in acting and scene design. This is not to say that the members of the ensemble projected bland personalities. On the contrary, the actors and directors were "politically sophisticated"—in the words of Aleko Minchev—and fought for artistic honesty "within the boundaries of a socialist framework." The style was a blend of Stanislavsky and Brecht; the productions were both lyrical and tendentious.

Stanislavsky is emphasized in the acting style and ensemble playing; Brecht is used as a model in dramaturgy.

Recent productions have emphasized this epic-lyric style, notably Williams' *A Streetcar Named Desire*, directed by Krassimir Spassov; Yordanov's *Unexplained Love*, directed by Yordanov; Tsanev's *Put on Your New Duds, Boys*, directed by Yordanov; Tsanev's *The Case Against the Bogomils*, directed by Krystju Dojnov; Sławomir Mrożek's *Tango*, directed by Jan Maciejewski; and Dale Wasserman's *One Flew Over the Cuckoo's Nest*, directed by Simeon Dimitrov.

The Drama Theatre of Burgas has introduced more native talent than any other theatre in Bulgaria. Among the dramatists who made their debut in the theatre are Krystju Sarafov, Asparuh Temelkov, Tseno Kandov, Stefan Karalambov, Dimitur Panov, Stefan Gudularov, Georgi Kalojančev, Stefan Getsov, Ivan Kondov, and Spas Djonev.

Greatly contributing to the Drama Theatre's rich tradition are the following scene designers: Vladimir Yordanov, Asen Mitev, Vera Macheva, Georgi Ivanov, Mladen Mladenov, and Todor Stanilov. The roster of directors includes Tačo Tanev, Nikolaj Fol, Metodi Andonov, Yulija Ognjanova, Nikolaj Ljustkanov, Nikolaj Savov, Dimitrina Gjurova, and Ivan Dobčev.

THOMAS STADTMILLER

DRAMA THEATRE "A TEAR AND LAUGHTER"
(Dramatičen Teatyr "sylza i smjax")
Slavjanska 5, Sofia, Bulgaria

Founded in 1967, "A Tear and Laughter" Theatre enjoyed great success, largely due to its managing director, Professor Filip Filipov, who died in 1983. At the time of his death, Filipov was also engaged as a director at the National Theatre.

The theatre was set up to explore social ideas by means of psychological analyses of motives of characters in the classics and contemporary plays. The present artistic director, Xristo Krychmarov, continues this approach to theatre, quite different from the realistic style seen in most traditional theatres in Bulgaria.

His staff of directors includes Nadezhda Sejkova, Krasimir Spasov, Dimityr Stojanov, Nikolaj Kolev, Stojko Genov, and Beljo Goranov. The company includes some of the best artists in Bulgaria, such as Stojcho Mazgalov, Ljuben Saev, Ljuben Kalinov, Lora Keranova, Kaja Chukova, Petyr Chernev, Lora Kremen, Yuri Yakovlev, Cvetana Maneva, Svetoslav Karbojkov, Ani Bakalova, Vasil Dimitrov, Marin Yanev, Venchislav Kisjov, Vylcho Kamarashev, and Bocho Vasilev.

Comparatively new, the theatre already has the respect of Sofia's artistic community. Although the repertory is a traditional one, the approach to each play is quite unique: the company strives for psychological depiction of characters. It is truly an actor's company.

Some of the more successful productions during the past few years include August Strindberg's *Miss Julie* (1981), directed by Rumen Chakyrov, with scene design by Veselin Kobachev, and costumes by Vesela Kircheva; Shakespeare's *Much Ado About Nothing* (1982), directed by Ljuben Grojs, with scene design by Veselin Kobachev; Ibsen's *John Gabriel Borkman* (1982), directed by Nadezhda Sejkova, with scene design by Angel Avramov; and Konstantin Iliev's *Nirvana* (1983), directed by Leon Daniel, with scene design by Angel Axrjanov, and costumes by Vesela Kircheva.

EDWARD J. CZERWINSKI and
ALEKO MINCHEV

DRAMA THEATRE OF PLOVDIV (N. O. MASALITINOV)
(Dramatičen Teatyr "Nikolaj Osipovič Masalitinov," Plovdiv)
Ul. Vasil Kolarov Nr. 34/38, Plovdiv, Bulgaria

When Bulgaria's famous writer, Ivan Vazov, wrote in the program on December 10, 1881, that "with the opening of the Drama Theatre of Plovdiv, the foundation of a true Bulgarian National Theatre has been laid," the nation echoed his sentiments. The founding of the theatre was a sign of national unity, a consolidation of the two separated parts of the nation.

The administration of the theatre consisted of three prominent artists: Stefan Popov, Ivan Popov, and Boris Pojarov. The repertory included both native and foreign plays: Ivan Vazov's *Ruska* and *Mihalaki Chorbadji*, Dobri Vojnikov's *Princess Raina*, and Vasil Drumev's *Ivanko*—contemporary Bulgarian writers. The foreign repertory included works by Shakespeare, Schiller, Hugo, Dumas, Voltaire, Turgenev, and Molière. Before World War II, the theatre had produced over five hundred plays by such Bulgarian dramatists as Vazov, Todorov, Yavorov, Strašimirov, Yovkov, Kostov, and Stoyanov; Russian and Soviet writers included Gogol, Gorky, Valentin Kataev, Aleksandr Korneičuk, Aleksandr Ostrovsky, Tolstoy, and Chekhov. Only during the past five years have American and Western plays appeared in the repertory. The most significant of these productions have been William Gibson's *Two for the Seesaw*, John Osborne's *Look Back in Anger*, and Murray Schisgal's *The Typist* and *The Tiger*.

The Plovdiv Theatre has an enviable record. It presents over four hundred performances yearly to an audience of over two hundred thousand people; the theatre is equipped with five stages—the Grand Stage, the Chamber Stage, the Youth House Stage, the Club Stage, and the Hall Stage. The company consists of forty-five actors and an equal number of technicians and administrative staff. The theatre was awarded the Highest Honor of the People's Republic of Bulgaria, the second theatre (the other, the Ivan Vazov Theatre) so distinguished.

As a result of its outstanding record in Bulgaria, the company has traveled extensively throughout Eastern Europe: Yugoslavia, Poland, the Soviet Union, and Romania. Credit should be given its creative management, especially its present artistic director, Bogomil Stoilov. But a company is only as good as its actors and, according to Stoilov, the Plovdiv Theatre has had its share of great acting talents: Elena Yordanova, Raina Petrova, Ljubomir Bobčevski, Elena Hranova, Vesa Kortenska, Georgi Fratev, Tsano Stojkov, Nadja Lolova, Dimitur Panov, Petur Slabakov, Lili Yosifova, Tsvetana Maneva, Pasa Berova, Zlatina Todeva, and Naum Šopov.

Past directors of the theatre are also cited as having contributed to the success of the company: Petur Dimitrov, Boyan Petrov, Dimitur Stratev, Georgi Mulevski, Svetoslav Genev, Nikola Ikonografov, Vladimir Polyanov, Hristo Hristov, Dimitur Punev, Nikola Petkov, Krikor Azarian, Krystaju Doynov, and Ljuben Groys. Among the younger generation of directors the following are considered the most talented: Panteley Panteleyev, Ivan Dobčev, and Nikolaj Lambrev. The following scene designers are held in high esteem: Vladimir Misin, Todor Bruskov, and Veselin Kovačev.

The company's most significant productions during 1979–1983 included Dimityr Dimov's *Irene* (*Irinia*, 1981), based on the novel by Atanas Bojadžiev, directed by Nikolaj Lamorev, with scene design by Svetoslav Genev; Dragomir Asenov's *The Award* (*Nagradata*, 1981), directed by Rumen Čakyrov, with scene design by Veslin Kovačev; Edvard Radzinski's *She in the Absence of Love and Death* (*Tja v otsystvie na ljubov i smyrt*, 1982), directed by Nikolaj Lambrev, with scene design by Zoja Genčeva; August Strindberg's *The Father* (1983), directed by Rumen Čakyrov, with scene design by Zoja Genčeva; and Kolyo Georgiev's *The Tuzluk's Story* (*Tuzluška istorija*, 1984), directed by Rumen Čakyrov, with scene design by Čajka Petruševa.

Perhaps the most significant aspect of the work of the Plovdiv Theatre is its development of native talent. During the past decade over fifty productions were devoted to new writers, including works by Stojan L. Kostov, Emilian Stanev, Dimityr Dimov, and Valeri Petrov.

KAZIMIERZ BRAUN and
THOMAS STADTMILLER

DRAMA THEATRE OF VARNA (STÓYAN BYCHVAROV)
(Dramatičen Teatyr "Stojan Byčvarov," Varna)
Ul. D. Kondov, Varna, Bulgaria

The Drama Theatre of Varna was founded and organized by the "Red Mayor" of Varna, D. Kondov. On February 13, 1921, the regional council of the Red Varna Commune voted to support the new theatre. It seemed only natural that the first artistic director of the theatre should be both a fine artist and a good Communist. The position was given to Stóyan Bychvarov; the theatre was later named in his honor.

Other great Bulgarian talents have been associated with this theatre, including Ivan Yanev, Yordan Čerkezov, Petko Atanassov, Nikolaj Fol, Nikola Ikonomov, Nikola Popov, Nikolaj Savov, Penka Damyanova, Ljubomir Kirilov, Georgi

Parusev, Źelko Mandadjev, Persiyan Mirčev, Alexander Hadjihristov, and Grishna Ostrovski. The present director of the theatre is Stančo Stančev.

Each of these directors and actors has influenced the philosophy of the Drama Theatre of Varna. The emphasis has always been on "epic theater," where the "human spirit could soar in space." In a personal interview, Ljubomir Tenev explained that the company has "always been concerned with the human condition. Although the style of acting is realistic, the actors are always instructed to reach out, to feel the blue of the sky. Man's courage, his hopes and aspirations as rendered by Shakespeare, is the guiding spirit of our theater."

Some of Bulgaria's best directors have worked in Varna: Stefan Kortenski, Vili Tsankov, Nikola Savov, Dimitrina Gjurova, Ljuben Grois, Cvetan Cvetkov, Andrej Koludov, and Boris Paskov. The roster of acting talent is equally impressive: Nikola Ganev, Ivan Yanev, Angel Todorov, Hristo Dinev, Vladimir Trendafilov, Atanas Kirčev, Roza Popova, Ideal Petrov, Veneta Slavčeva, Borislav Petrov, Nadja Stanislavska, Ana Felixova, Apostol Karamitev, Ivan Kandov, Boris Lukanov, Katja Čukova, Hindo Kasimov, Petur Zlatev, Ina Russeva, Vesko Tsanev, and Dafinka Danailova.

The most significant productions of the past decade include Milko Milkov's *The Other Truth About Saint George* (*Drugata istina za Sveti Georgi*, 1981), directed by Rusi Karabaliev, with scene design by Živko Dimitrov; Ivan Radoev's *The Buffalo* (*Bivolyt*, 1982), directed by Cvetan Cvetkov, with scene design by Rina Petrova; Anthony Shaffer's *The Private Eye* (1982), directed by Simeon Dimitrov, with scene design by Živko Dimitrov; Chekhov's *Three Sisters* (1983), directed by Cvetan Cvetkov, with scene design by Todor Stanilov; and Stanislav Stratiev's *The Maximalist* (*Maksimalistyt*, 1984), directed by Stančo Stančev, with scene design by Živko Dimitrov.

NATIONAL THEATRE "IVAN VAZOV"
(Naroden Teatyr "Ivan Vazov")
Levski 5, Sofia, Bulgaria

Founded in 1904, the National was initially a nonprofessional company called "A Tear and Laughter" Theatre. Ilia Milarov was its first managing director (its Intendant). From the very beginning, the company was greatly influenced by what Georgi Sayev in his study, *The Ivan Vazov National Theatre* (Centre for Publicity, Sofia, 1982), refers to as "the aesthetics of the Russian theatrical school with its demands for a realistic and generally accessible art." In 1984, the philosophy remains the same. Whatever the play—Russian (Alexey Arbuzov) or American (Tennessee Williams)—the acting style remains the same. Within this stricture, the National manages to be a showcase for good acting talent.

The theatre is one of the most popular in Bulgaria. The company has made more tours abroad than any other theatre in the country: the Soviet Union, the German Democratic Republic, Yugoslavia, Poland, Czechoslovakia, Austria, and Romania.

The Russian influence is widespread. After 1944 a number of Soviet directors were invited to work with the actors of the National, among them, Nikolaj Petrov, Boris Babochkin, Boris Livanov, Georgij Tovstonogov, Boris Zakhava, and Alexander Goncharov. Russian plays are a permanent part of the company's repertoire.

The company is composed of a number of distinguished actors: Stefan Danailov, Violetta Bahchevanova, Maria Stefanova, Georgetta Chakurova, Sava Hashumov, Venelin Pehlivanov, Vancha Doycheva, Kiril Kavadarkov, Velko Kunev, Yuri Angelov, Violetta Gindeva, Krassimira Petrova, Mihail Petrov; and guest artists, such as Kosta Tsovev, Tsvetana Maneva, Naoum Shopov, Todor Kolev, Yossif Surchadjiev, and Ilija Dovrev.

Special mention should be made of two actors considered to be the finest of recent years—Apostol Karamiev, who died in 1976, and Ljubomir Kabakchiev. One of the company's best recent productions was Luigi Pirandello's *Henry IV* (1970), directed by Encho Xalachev, with scene design by Atanas Velyanov, with Karamiev in the leading role. One of Kabakchiev's best performances was as Ivan in Dostoevsky's *The Brothers Karamazov* (1971), directed by Boris Livanov, the Soviet director, who also designed the production.

Undoubtedly, the theatre is an actor-oriented company, and plays are usually fashioned for particular talents. Some of the best examples in which the acting was outstanding, while the play was less than felicitous, include Vsevolod Vishnevsky's *The Optimistic Tragedy* (1981), directed by Encho Xalachev, with scene design by Mladen Mladenov; Ivan Vazov's *Under the Yoke* (*Pod igoto*, 1981), directed by Filip Filipov, with scene design by Stefan Savov; and Ivan Peychev's *Every Autumn Evening* (*Vsjaka esenna vecher*, 1983), directed by Asen Shopov, with scene design by Mladen Mladenov. Sometimes the wedding of play and acting brings excellent results, for example, Aristophanes' *Lysistrata* (1983), directed by Nikolaj Ljuckanov, with scene design by Georgi Ivanov; and Tennessee Williams' *Cat on a Hot Tin Roof*, (1982), directed by Encho Xalachev, with scene design by Atanas Velyanov.

The company's present managing and artistic director is Diko Fouchedjiev. The theatre has been honored by the Bulgarian government on a number of occasions, and its company includes more decorated artists than any other theatre in Bulgaria.

EDWARD J. CZERWINSKI and
ALEKO MINCHEV

NATIONAL YOUTH THEATRE "LJUDMILA ŽIVKOVA"
(Naroden Teatyr za Maldežta "Ljudmila Živkova")
Dondukov 36, Sofia, Bulgaria

Founded in 1944, the National Youth Theatre is principally a child- and youth-oriented company. Its first director was the well-known actor-director Peter Stoychev. The present artistic director is Vasil Popiliev. The directorial staff is equally impressive: Grisha Ostrovski, Gertruda Lukanova, Liljana Todorova, Nikolina Tomanova, Nikolaj Polyakov, and Andrej Avramov.

According to Sevelina Gyorova, in her study *The Bulgarian Dramatic Theatre* (State Publishing House, Septemvry, Sofia, 1979, p. 82), "the People's Youth Theatre was established to meet a growing spiritual need—to entertain and instruct Bulgarian youth, children, teenagers, and young people." Gradually the theatre was divided into two separate sections—for adults (Otdel za vyzrastni) and for children (Otdel za deca). The theatre is the first of its kind in Bulgaria, although an attempt was made in the thirties by Boris Borozanov, an actor from the National Theatre, to set up a children's theatre, in which the repertory consisted of fairy tales and children's literature. His work was resumed after the war by Liljana Todorova, who has had great success with such works as *The Three Musketeers* and Dimityr Dimitrov's *The Gay Musicians* (1981), with scene design by Mixail Mixailov, and with music by Aleksandyr Vladiregov.

The list of outstanding talents includes Yordanka Kuzmanova, Conka Miteva, Luna Davidova, Boris Arabov, Ginka Stancheva, Ljuba Alesieva, Nikolaj Binev, Stoil Popov, Dimityr Bujnozov, Vasil Mirchovski, Nadezhda Popalova, Vladimir Smirnov, and Domna Ganeva. Special mention should be made of one of the older actresses, Lora Kernanova, long a favorite with children.

The company has traveled abroad a number of times, namely to Greece, West Germany, the Soviet Union, Yugoslavia, Italy, and France. Its most successful productions during the past five years include, in the Children's Section, Stanislav Stratiev's *Don't Give Up* (*Ne padaj duxom*, 1981), directed by Nikolaj Poljakov, with scene design by Vjacheslav Parapanov, and music by Yuri Stupel; Rada Moskova's *Love for Three Oranges* (*Ljubovta kym trite portokala*, 1982), directed by Liljana Todorova, with scene design by Ekaterina Eneva, and music by Ljubomir Denev; and in the Adult Section, William Shakespeare's *Taming of the Shrew* (1980), directed by Nikolina Tomanova, with scene design by Ekaterina Eneva, and music by Petyr Cankov; Robert Patrick's *Kennedy's Children* (1981), directed by Nikolaj Poljakov, with scene design by Aleksandrina Ignatova; Ivo Andrić's *Conversation with Goya* (1982), directed by Miroslav Belović, with scene design by Vjacheslav Parapanov; and Peter Shaffer's *Amadeus* (1983), directed by Gertruda Lukanova, with scene design by Konstantin Radev.

EDWARD J. CZERWINSKI and
ALEKO MINCHEV

RUSÉ DRAMA THEATRE (SAVA OGNYANOV)
(Dramatičen Teatyr "Sava Ognyanov," Rusé)
Ul. Hristov Botev, Rusé, Bulgaria

The Rusé Drama Theatre (named in honor of Sava Ognyanov) is one of the oldest continuing ensembles in Bulgaria. Established on December 27, 1870, when its first production, Todor Hadjistančev's *The Honor of Ružitsa*, premiered, the Rusé has remained the center of professional theatre, the oldest artistic "collective" in the country. Founded by Hadjistančev, the Rusé has had a long list of eminent directors, including Vladimir Tenev, Boris Espe, Matyo Makedonski, and Tano Tanev, and more recently (after World War II), Iliya Kiselov, Petur Kjučjukov, Stefan Penčev, and the present artistic director, Atanas Bojadžiev.

The Rusé has always been the center of Bulgaria's theatrical scene, most notably at the end of the nineteenth century and during its peak years in the 1920s and 1930s. It continues to influence all phases of Bulgarian theatrical life.

The Rusé is not an experimental theatre; it relies heavily on the classics, both native and foreign. According to Aleko Minchev, the theatre "is revolutionary ideologically and realistic in its execution." In a way the Rusé prides itself on its experimental productions, most of which emphasize acting style and political statements. The productions tend to be tendentious in nature and content; the acting style ranges from realistic to stylized, depending on the social and political content of the play. The eclectic acting style was best illustrated in the following productions during the past five years: Valeri Petrov's *When the Roses Dance* (*Kogato rozite tancuvat*, 1980), directed by Ilija Atanasov, with scene design by Violeta Radkova; Emilijan Stanev's *The Legend of Sibin* (*Legenda za Sibin*, 1981), directed by Cvetan Cvetkov, with scene design by Todor Stanilov; Ben Jonson's *Volpone* (1981), directed by Ilija Atanasov, with scene design by Viktor Keculescu; Stanislav Stratiev's *The Suede Coat* (*Sako ot velur*, 1982), directed by Slavi Škarov, with scene design by Nejko Nejkov; and Yordan Radičkov's *The Baskets* (*Kosnici*, 1983), directed by Slavi Škarov, with scene design by Nejko Nejkov.

These Bulgarian works were perhaps the Rusé's best productions. On the other hand, foreign plays have usually been less successful: for example, Gorky's *The Lower Depths* (which is almost satirical in its realism) and Wojciech Bogusławski's *Cracoviennes and Mountaineers* (which is too heavy-handed in its emphasis on social content).

The company's strength ultimately lies in its fine directors and talented actors, some of whom, like the following, share a dual capacity: Roza Popova, Vladimir Tenev, Krystju Sarafov, Georgi Stamatov, Mara Toteva, Teodorina Stojčeva, and Penčo Georgiev (also an excellent scene designer). Others, like the following, are considered among Bulgaria's best directors: Nikolaj Fol, Leon Daniel, Lyubomir Sarlandjev, and Venelin Tsankov. The Rusé's roster also includes numerous distinguished actors, namely, Ivan Kondov, Nevena Koranova, Katja Zehireva, Spas Djonev, Nikolaj Benev, and people's artists Elena Stefanova, Vasil Popiliev, Kosjo Stanev, Konstantin Dimče, Minko Minkov, Božidar Manev, and Georgi Radomirov.

KAZIMIERZ BRAUN and
THOMAS STADTMILLER

"SOFIA" DRAMA THEATRE
(Dramatičen Teatyr "Sofia")
Vladimir Zaimov 23 A, Sofia, Bulgaria

Founded in 1966 as a showcase for poetry and concerts (*Estrada*), the theatre became the "Sofia" Drama Theatre in 1969. Its first managing director was an actor-director from the National, Andrej Čaprazov. Nikolina Tomonova took over as artistic director in 1969. The present artistic director is Koljo Georgiev.

Two of Bulgaria's best directors, Vili Cankov and Vasil Lukanov, are permanently connected with the company. They work with a roster of excellent talent, including Kosta Conev, Dosjo Dosev, Yordan Spirov, Tatjana Lolova, Isxak Finci, Nevena Mandadzheva, Bella Coneva, Doroteja Toncheva, Todor Kolev, Leda Taseva, Anton Gorchev, Stefan Iliev, Kiril Gospodinov, Rusi Chanev, Ilija Raev, and Rashko Mladenov.

Under Tomonova's leadership the theatre attracted a number of young talented actors from various theatres in the capital and from all over the country. The company drew the attention of the public with its repertory which included works never seen in Bulgaria, including Eugene O'Neill's *A Moon for the Misbegotten* and Shakespeare's *The Winter's Tale*.

The company continues to present works of new writers. Some of the best productions of the past five years include Harold Pinter's *The Birthday Party* (1981), directed by Pantelej Panteleev, with scene design by Georgi Ivanov; Richard Sheridan's *School for Scandal* (1981), directed by Margarita Mladenova, with scene design by Georgi Pozharov; William Shakespeare's *Hamlet* (1982), directed by Vili Cankov, with scene design by Valja Uzunova; Akosh Kertes' *Name's Day* (*Imen den*, 1983), directed by Ivan Dobchev, with scene design by Vjacheslav Parapanov; and Oscar Wilde's *A Florentine Tragedy* (1984), directed by Vili Cankov, with scene design by Georgi Ivanov.

EDWARD J. CZERWINSKI and
ALEKO MINCHEV

STATE SATIRICAL THEATRE
(Dyržaven Satiričen Teatyr)
Ul. Stefan Karakja 26, Sofia, Bulgaria

Established in 1957, the State Satirical Theatre has since its inception concentrated on satire and comedy. The satire is broad and general; the comedy is lighthearted; and its subjects are contemporary.

The profile of the Satirical Theatre was formed mainly by its administrative and artistic directors. They have dictated both artistic and political policy. Past directors have included Stefan Surchajiev, Boyan Danovski, Jelčo Mandayev, Metodi Andonov, Miroslav, Mindov and Nikolaj Savov. Stanislav Stratiev is the present artistic director, and Blagoy Hadjiyankov serves as administrative director.

The theatre's roster includes artists who are actors as well as directors; most have served in both capacities during the past ten years. Because of their unique abilities, these artists have helped shape an artistic policy for the company. The emphasis has been on human foibles rather than on political topics. In a theatre owned by the government, the emphasis seems well advised. The following artists are members of the actor-director ensemble: Boyan Danovski, Grisha

Ostrovski, Metodi Andonov, Nejčo Popov, Mladen Kiselov, Nevena Kokanova, Stoyanka Mutafova, Grigor Vačkov, Konstantin Kotsev, Nikola Anastasov, and Georgi Partsalev.

The most significant productions of the past decade were Stanislav Stratiev's *Roman Bath*, directed by Nejčo Popov; Yeži Stavinski's *The Hour of the Spade*, directed by Nikolaj Ljunkanov; Aleksandyr Vampilov's *Provincial Anecdotes*, directed by Asen Šopov; Stanislav Stratiev's *The Suede Coat*, directed by Mladen Kiselov; and Aleksandr Ostrovski's *The Wisest Is Still a Bit Simple*, directed by Mladen Kiselov.

In 1983 the Satirical scored great successes with István Örkény's *The Tot Family*, directed by Plamen Markov, with scene design by Radina Bliznakova; and Carlo Gozzi's *Princess Turandot*, directed by Vili Cankov, with scene design by Marija Nikolaeva. Its greatest success, however, was Stratiev's *The Suede Coat* (1976), which still played to full houses in 1984.

KAZIMIERZ BRAUN and
THOMAS STADTMILLER

THEATRE 199
(Teatyr 199)
Slavjanska 8, Sofia, Bulgaria

One of Bulgaria's most experimentally oriented theatres, Teatyr 199, was founded in 1965 under the direction of Nikolaj Savov. The present managing and artistic director is Kaja Zexireva. There are only two directors on the staff of this company—Nikolaj Savov and Boris Spirov—and no permanent actors. Artists are engaged for each production.

Theatre 199 was set up as a chamber theatre, principally to acquaint the public with foreign works and to reduce the distance between spectator and actor, a problem in most theatres in Sofia. As a result, a number of theatres have established chamber theatres and a number of writers have lately devoted their efforts to writing for these small spaces. It is not unusual to find coffee houses, foyers of theatres, and even bars converted to chamber theatres. None, however, has duplicated the artistic success of Theatre 199.

The company has had a number of outstanding productions during the past several years, including Albert Camus' *The Misunderstanding* (1980), directed by Stefka Proxaskova, with scene design by Stesoslav Genev; Valeri Petrov's *Theatre—My Love (Teatyr—Ljubov Moja*, 1981), directed by Mladen Kiselov, with scene design by Stefan Savov (an excellent play for two actresses); Boris Aprilov's *The Prairie (Prerija*, 1982), directed by Boris Spirov, with scene design by Rumjana Krushanova; John Merrill's *Sarah Bernhardt* (1983), directed by Nevena Miteva, with scene design by Todor Chobanov; and Stefan Canev's *Life—with Two Women (Životyt—tova sa dve ženi*, 1984), directed by Mladen Kiselov, with scene design by Stefan Savov.

Theatre 199 has influenced theatres all over Bulgaria. The company tours regularly throughout the country and has made several tours abroad, including Austria, Holland, Greece, and the German Democratic Republic.

EDWARD J. CZERWINSKI

THEATRE OF THE PEOPLE'S ARMY OF SOFIA
(Teatyr na Narodnata Armija)
Ul. Rakovski 98, Sofia, Bulgaria

Established in 1950, the Theatre of the People's Army of Sofia is clearly a politically oriented company. Almost every director of the theatre has come from the ranks of the Bulgarian Army: Colonel Dimitur Ugrinov, Colonel Tsano Ignev, Colonel Rangel Ignatov, and Colonel Stefan Tamakhkrjarov, the present artistic director. Only two of its directors have not come from the military: Alexander Girginov and Sasho Stoyanov.

From its inception the People's Army Theatre has emphasized plays with patriotic and military themes. It is perhaps the best example in any Socialist country of a cultural organization that adheres religiously to the tenets of Socialist Realism: to show the leading role of the Communist party, the positive role of the nation's people, and the subservience of the individual to the good of the masses. Within these strictures, the theatre has tried to employ Stanislavsky's methods in its acting style. It is not surprising that the bulk of the repertory consists of Soviet and Bulgarian "war-plays," such as Mikhail Bulgakov's *The Days of the Turbins*, directed by the Soviet director Lev Heifets in 1977; and Nikola Rusev's *From Earth to Heaven*, directed by Krikor Azarian in 1976.

The theatre has also concentrated on Chekhov, emphasizing his criticism of pre-Revolutionary Russian *pošlost'*—self-satisfied mediocrity. The world-weary characters of Chekhov's world were almost satirized in these productions: *The Cherry Orchard*, directed by Krikor Azarian in 1974; and *Ivanov*, directed by Ivan Dobčev in 1979.

During the past decade the directors of the company have experimented with foreign plays, always, of course, emphasizing the social aspect of the work, especially in Athol Fugard's *Sizwe Banzi Is Dead* (1976) and Edward Albee's *The Zoo Story* (1977), both directed by Azarian. The foreign plays have been a feature of the productions of the Chamber Club TPA.

During the past several years the theatre has invited a number of foreign directors to direct in the People's Army Theatre. These have included Andrzej Wajda (Poland) with Stanisława Przybyszewska's *Danton's Affair* in 1978 and Lev Heifets from the Soviet Union in 1977. Other Soviet directors have included B. Lvov-Anohin, L. V. Varpakhovski, and K. A. Zubov. Peter Kupke from East Germany and Ivan Petrovsky from Czechoslovakia have also directed plays in the theatre.

Bulgarian dramatists are also well represented in the repertory. The following are among the more significant productions of the past few years: Dragomir

Assenov's *The Gold Hideout*, directed by Krystjo Mirski (1974); Orlin Vasiliev's *Death Is for Death*, directed by Asen Šopov (1975); Rusi Vožanov's *The Happy One Comes*, directed by Asen Šopov (1978); Ion Drutse's *World of Worlds*, directed by Ivan Dobčev (1979); George Bernard Shaw's *The Devil's Disciple* (1982), directed by Leon Daniel, with scene design by Asen Mitev; and Neda Antonova's *And God Comes Down to Earth* (1984), directed by Enčo Xalačev, with scene design by Atanas Veljanov.

The company consists of fifty actors and directors. The following actors deserve special mention: Kiril Yanev (People's Artist), Ivan Kondov, Stefan Gudularov, Mara Penkova, Dimitur Straten, Stefan Danailov, Ilija Dobrev, Maria Simova, Petur Slabakov, Basil Mixajlov, Veselin Vasilev, Ivan Yančev, Naum Popov, Asen Angelov, and Violeta Doneva.

KAZIMIERZ BRAUN and
THOMAS STADTMILLER

Czechoslovakia

DRAMA CLUB
(Činoherni klub)
U. Ve Smečkach 26, Prague, Czechoslovakia

The Drama Club was founded by Ladislav Smoček, Jan Kačer, and Jaroslav Vostrý in 1965. They were subsequently joined by Alena Vostrá, one of Czechoslovakia's leading playwrights, and actors from the Bezruč Theatre in Ostrava, where Kačer had earlier been resident director. Located in the center of Prague, the Drama Club was inaugurated chiefly to put on new plays. The directors never professed any systematic or complex philosophy for this actor-oriented company. They deliberately avoided ideological and political statements. According to Vostrý, who adumbrated his views in *Divadelní noviny* (*Theatre News*) (12, 1968–69, p. 4) and in the theatre journal *Divadlo* (*Theatre*, 12, 1961, p. 26), the company wished to present "man in play" and "actors stretching to capture man's essence."

Smoček has had considerable success with the Drama Club. The theatre was inaugurated in 1965 with the production of his most famous play, *Picnic* (published in *Divadlo* in 1964). Subsequent productions included *The Maze* (1966), *The Strange Afternoon of Dr. Zvonko Burke* (1966), and *Cosmic Spring* (1970). *Cosmic Spring* is generally considered to be the swan-song of the absurdist movement in Czechoslovakia.

Besides Smoček, the Drama Club can boast of another outstanding talent, Alena Vostrá. Unfortunately, because of the Soviet invasion of Czechoslovakia which virtually brought the arts to a standstill, Vostrá had only two plays produced: *Eeny, Meeny, Miney Mo* (1966) and *On Knife's Edge* (1968). Both plays were written with the actors in the company in mind and with its policy to permit "personal creativity." The husband-wife team defined the policy of the Drama Club in the program notes to *On Knife's Edge*: "We have here a comedy to a certain degree virtually tailor-made for certain actors. . . . It expects actors to perform not only with their souls but also with their bodies. . . . Its staging is unthinkable outside the context of the theater in which it was premiered."

A good example of the results of the Drama Club's philosophic position is Pavel Landovský, the brilliant Czech actor who, following the lead of the Vostrýs, wrote a play for himself, which was produced by the company on the eve of the cultural crackdown. *Rooms by the Hour* (1969) managed to be published in *Divadlo* in 1969, shortly before complete censorship was imposed on all theatre companies in Czechoslovakia. Unfortunately, the past decade has witnessed the repression of the arts in the entire country.

Nonetheless, the Drama Club continues to develop. It has staged the largest number of Czech plays among the "small theatre" group, even though its physical quarters are the most restrictive among Prague's small theatres. Seating approximately 220, the theatre is quite shallow; the three-sided balcony permits a limited view of the cramped stage. With no fly-space the stage measures 15 feet deep and 24 feet wide. There are virtually no dressing rooms or offstage space. Because of these limitations, the theatre boasts an intimacy that has become its chief virtue. An immediate rapport with the audience is established; every gesture and facial expression is calculated to create a low-key performance. Even with such closeness, physical contact with the audience is eschewed and the traditional fourth wall remains intact. But because of the intimate space, indirect contact or awareness of each other's presence is unavoidable.

The repertoire of the Drama Club emphasizes, according to Jaroslav Vostrý, the "encounters of individual human possibilities with actuality." The themes of most of these plays touch upon questions of human freedom and responsibility, of the individual's relationship to society. The plays of Smoček, Vostrá, and Landovský explore these themes. Other plays in the repertoire lend themselves to such an interpretation: Pinter's *The Birthday Party*, Dostoevsky's *Crime and Punishment*, and Chekhov's *The Cherry Orchard*. These plays also offer the actor a unique opportunity to develop his character to fit the text, to grow into his role. According to Vostrý, "the discovery of the actor's possibilities is . . . the discovery of the 'possibilities' of man—and, after all, that's what theater art is concerned with foremost." (*Divadelní noviny*, 12, 1968–69, p. 4.)

The Drama Club is perhaps the least "engaged" theatre in Czechoslovakia. It is rather "extremely responsive to what it views as the complex interpersonal realities of human behavior underlying that world and to the embodiment of those realities by means of actors whose distinctly personal creativity is nurtured and given priority in the total production process." (Jarka M. Burian, "Art and Relevance: The Small Theatres of Prague, 1958–1970," *Educational Theatre Journal* [23, Oct. 1971], p. 246.)

The present artistic director is Míka Zdeněk. The directorial staff includes Ladislav Smoček, and Ivo Krobot. The present dramaturges are Jiří Daněk and Vladimír Procházka.

Pavel Landovský, one of the Drama Club's best actor-dramatists, left the group in 1978 and has continued writing and working at the Burg Theatre in Vienna.

The most successful productions during the past several years include Alexandr

Ostrovsky's *The Storm* (1980), directed by Ivo Krobot; Gogol's *The Players* (1982), directed by Ladislav Smoček, with scene design by Smoček; Bohumil Hrabal's *The Gentle Barbarian* (*Něžný barbar*, 1982), directed by Krobot; István Örkény's *The Tot Family* (1983), directed by Krobot; and Alfred de Musset's *Marianne's Caprices* (1984), directed by Krobot.

Since 1983, the Drama Club has been performing in the Klicperovo Theatre in the Kobilisy section of Prague, while their old space is being renovated. During this period, the company toured the provinces.

EDWARD J. CZERWINSKI

NATIONAL THEATRE
(Národní Divadlo)
Ostrovní 1
Prague 11230, Czechoslovakia

Founded in 1883, Prague's National Theatre moved to its new house in 1983. Encased in glass flats, the theatre complex is the brightest spot in Europe, lit up at night and reflecting the artistic intention and glory of the artists who work inside the glass structure.

The present managing director is Jiří Pauer. The scene designer, Josef Svoboda, works regularly with the company. The artistic director of the drama section is Jaroslav Fixa. His dramaturges include Jan Císař, Jaroslav Král, and Radoslav Lošták. The theater also has a large staff of directors including Václav Hudeček, František Laurin, Miroslav Macháček, Jaromír Pleskot, and L'ubomír Vojdička.

The National also has opera and ballet sections. *Laterna Magika*, once connected with the Theatre Behind the Gate (*Divadlo za branou*), is now a part of the National, performing in the old space. *Magika*'s productions, which include a collage of live action and film clips, are a combination of Barnum and Bailey glitter and Social-Realistic clatter, but always well-executed. The theatre plays to packed houses with such productions as Anton Chekhov's *The Black Monk*, dramatized by Jiří Fried, directed by Evald Schorm, and with scene-design by Jindřich Smetana; *One Day in Prague*, (*Jednoho dne v Praze*) directed by Ladislav Helge, Eva Marie Bergerová, Ivan Balada, Raduš Cinčera, and Jan Kratochvil, with scene design by Miloslav Heřmánek; *The Magic Circus* (*Kouzelný Cirkus*), directed by Evald Schorm, Jiří Srnec, and Jan Svankmajer, with scene design by Josef Svoboda; Jiří Pauer's *Zvanivý Slimejš*, with a libretto by Míla Mellanová, directed by Břetislav Pojar, with scene design by Josef Svoboda.

The National boasts a roster of formidable talent: Blanka Bohdanová, Jana Boušková, Jana Březinová, Helga Čočková, Naděžda Gajerová, Marie Gláznová, Libuše Havelková, Jana Hlaváčová, Blažena Hohšová, Klára Jerneková, Eva Klenová, Jarmila Krulišová, Vlasta Matulová, Dana Medřická, Taťjana Medvecká, Jiřina Petrovická, Lída Plachá, Luba Skořepová, Zuzana Savrdová, Sylva Turhová, Jaroslava Tvrzníková, Marie Vášová, Bohumil Bezouška, Bohuslav

Čáp, Josef Čáp, Jiří Dohnal, Miroslav Doležal, František Filipovský, Rudolf Hrušínský, Josef Kemr, Emil Konečný, Petr Kostka, Radovan Lukovský, Ivan Luťanský, Jaroslav Mareš, Josef Mida, Luděk Munzar, Bořivaj Navrátil, Miloš Nesvadba, Josef Pehr, Václav Postránecky, Bedřich Prokoš, Vladimir Ráž, Martin Růžek, Čestmír Řanda, Soběslav Sejk, Josef Somr, Jiří Sovák, Milan Stehlík, Petr Svojtka, Petr Štěpánek, Jiří Štěpnička, Jiří Vala, Josef Velda, and Oldřich Vlček.

Unfortunately, even with such an array of talent, few productions during the past few years have been artistic successes. The following deserve special attention because they are proof that the company, given the opportunity, can attain heights of greatness. Ladislav Stroupežnický's *Naši Furianti* (*Our Freespenders*, 1979), directed by Miroslav Machaček, with scene design by Josef Svoboda; Karel Čapek's *Bílá Nemoc* (*White Illness*, 1980), directed by Machaček, with scene design by Svoboda; and William Shakespeare's *Hamlet*, directed by Machaček, with scene design by Svoboda. It may be that the National has become too large to pay attention to detail. Perhaps the new house will instill a new spirit in the management. The audiences deserve better fare.

EDWARD J. CZERWINSKI

NEW THEATRE
(Nová Scéna)
Kollárovo námeste 20
Bratislava 88014, Czechoslovakia

Founded in 1946, *Nová Scéna* is considered by many critics the best theatre in Czechoslovakia, due in part to its talented young directors. Under Karol Vlach's guidance, the theatre concentrated on developing young talent—actors, writers, technicians, scene designers, and so on, as well as striving for excellence. After Vlach's sudden death in August, 1982, the company vowed to continue his policy of presenting modern foreign works, as well as the classics.

Nová Scéna's Studio Theatre concentrates on a similar repertory. The poetry section (*Poetický Súbor*) attracts a young audience by presenting both established and avant-garde poets. The musical comedy section (*Spevohra*) also draws young people.

The directorial staff includes Oto Katuša, Peter Opálený, and Vladimír Strnisko. The chief dramaturge is Ondrej Šulaj. Each of the four sections has its own artistic director—Peter Opálený for the drama section—and its own dramaturges.

The acting ensemble consists of over fifty actors, with additional actors engaged on a short-term contractual basis, depending on the need for a special talent for a particular play. The permanent ensemble includes the following: Milan Lasica and Július Satinsky (both actors famous for their satirical sketches during the late sixties), Ivan Letko, Dušan Blašković, Ľubomir Roman, Zita Furková, Emil Horváth, Milan Kňažko, Zirzana Kronerová, Pavol Mikulík, Ivan

Krivosudský, Ján Kramár, Boris Farkaš, Viera Richterová, Viktor Blaho, Marián Zedniković, Augustin Herényi, Bohuslav Drozd, and others.

The most successful productions on the large stage during the past few years include Gorky's *The Barbarians* (1980), directed by Ondrej Šulaj; John Gay's *The Beggar's Opera* (1980), directed by Peter Opálený; and Shaw's *The Devil's Disciple* (1982), directed by Oto Katuša. The Studio Theatre's greatest success was Peter Shaffer's *Amadeus* (1982), directed by Vladimir Strnisko.

EDWARD J. CZERWINSKI

SEMAFOR THEATRE
(Semafor Divadlo)
Václavské nám. 28
Prague, Czechoslovakia

Founded in October 1959 by Jiří Suchy and Jiří Šlitr, the Semafor Theatre has concentrated on a repertory (skits and plays written by Suchý and Šlitr) consisting of a blend of satire and music. The Semafor was an outgrowth of Reduta, a small theatre inaugurated by Suchý and Ivan Vyskočil in 1957. Reduta became the prototype of the small theatre movement in Czechoslovakia.

From its inception, the Semafor was a political cabaret, much in the satirical style of the Voskovec and Werich ("V + W") theatre, the popular Czech satirists whose most important work dates to the late thirties.

In its early stages Semafor consisted mainly of musical entertainment presented in a tiny wine cellar in the center of Prague's Old City. Suchý and Šlitr wrote these musical skits and performed their own works. When the Semafor moved into its present location, the cabaret shows often alternated with full-length plays written by Suchý.

Semafor became the most popular theatre in Czechoslovakia in the sixties. The company, besides Suchý and Šlitr, included some of the finest musical comedy talents in Czechoslovakia. The songs from their productions became hit tunes; the topical humor was repeated throughout the country; and the satirical characters that appeared in the cabaret productions were identified with Semafor and became a part of the daily ritual during the Prague Spring and afterwards.

According to Miroslav Horniček, Semafor's resident critic, the theatre's philosophy consisted of responding "to its period. That means it should answer questions or formulate the questions. The questions of each period in time are quite real and urgent and are basically the same questions about being or not being. . . . The level on which answers are given is not important. It can be given by Shakespeare or by a cabaret." (Program notes to *Návštení den* [*Party Time*], 1967, n.p.)

Semafor's policy has not altered. The theatre is still popular and plays to full houses. Certainly, restraints have been placed on Semafor since 1970, but the authorities often turn a deaf ear to laughter which official censors consider to be a safeguard against open hostility.

Since Šlitr's death in 1969, Semafor has lost some of the magic and cama-raderie that were its staples. However, as if eager to continue a tradition, the company under Suchý strives to formulate "questions for the period," but lately these questions have become more existential and less topical.

This is not surprising when one becomes familiar with Suchý's artistic growth. Before founding Semafor, he was associated with Ivan Vyskočil and the Theatre on the Balustrade. Suchý collaborated on two plays with Vyskočil: *A Thousand Clarinets* (1958) and *Faust, Margaret, the Maid, and Me* (1959). Both plays had a satirical thrust and a playfulness that Suchý brought to his work at the Semafor.

Aside from its obvious meaning, the word "Semafor" is also an abbreviation in Czech for "seven small forms." The founders of the company had hoped that the theatre would develop along these lines. The company continues to experiment with these forms. According to Alena Urbanová, the Semafor offered the opportunity of "escape from the emptiness of big words to small, ordinary ones [which were] full of real life. From serious, celebrational lies to jokes that capture truth with the hook of absurdity . . . a theater that didn't programmatically insist on anything." (*Divadlo*, December, 1969, p. 29.) Semafor's policy was to avoid conventional dramatic and theatrical forms and emphasize a "new professionalism." In a personal interview, Suchý explained the term in the following way: "In the Semafor we ask for professionalism of work, not profes-sionally trained actors . . . because they are trained for a different type of theater and a different kind of acting." The policy of Semafor is to encourage self-creativity and to develop the performer's distinctive personality. The world of illusion is subjugated to the "entertaining" world of reality.

This policy is followed in promoting the talents of Milan Lasica and Julius Satinský, founders of Divadlo na korze (Theatre on the Promenade). These two writer-performers from Bratislava, Slovakia, can best be compared with Czech-oslovakia's most famous pair, Voskovec and Werich. In 1969 the pair was invited to perform at the Semafor. The entire theatrical community welcomed the union of the two Slovak satirists with the two Czech satirists at the popular Semafor Theatre, viewing it as marking a solidarity between the two ethnic groups, Slovaks and Czechs, against their Soviet guests.

It is difficult to classify Lasica and Satinský. Working under the formula name of L + S, they write their own material, act in their own productions, and help direct theatre operations, which until 1970 included the publication of an eight-page monthly broadside called *Infarkt* (*Heart Attack*).

Their most notable productions are *Soirée* and *Radostná správa* (*A Joyful Management*). They have also produced a number of foreign works, including Sławomir Mrożek's *Striptease*, *Charles*, and *On the Open Sea*, and Beckett's *Waiting for Godot*. Lasica's wife, Sora Kolinska, an excellent actress and singer, is also a member of the acting ensemble. Some of the satirical pieces written by L + S were published in a small volume entitled *Nečakanie na Godota* (*Not-waiting for Godot*, 1969).

According to Lasica, the material for these sketches is written specifically for the Promenade, where the small size of the audience dictates the subject matter and manner of presentation. The audience expects to be treated as part of a large family and often acts like one, sometimes contributing its own quips, more often expressing approval by prolonged applause. Both actors and viewers are repaid for their collaboration in terms of a theatrical experience that is at once entertaining, uplifting, and educational.

Lasica and Satinsky admit their debt to Sławomir Mrożek and the theatre of the absurd. But judging from their journal *Infarkt* and their two early productions, if a debt ever existed, it has been paid in full; writers in the future may very well owe much to them. Unfortunately, since 1970 *Infarkt* has ceased to exist, and the Promenade has had to make drastic changes in its policy.

In 1969, after Šlitr's death, Ferdinand Havlík took over as musical composer for Semafor. He has been with the company from the beginning in 1959, when he joined Šlitr and Suchý as musical director.

Presently, Semafor is made up of three creative groups: the first, headed by Jiří Suchý and Ferdinand Havlík; the second, by Miloslav Šimek and Luděk Sobota (after the death of Jiří Grossman in 1971); the third, by Jozef Dvořák. These artists are actors, singers, satirists, and masters-of-ceremony. Their function is to hold the production together.

Semafor's best productions during the past decade include *Kytice* (*Bouquet*, 1973), which ran until 1983, composed by Suchý and Havlík; *S pydlou v zadech* (*With a Knife in the Back*, 1981), composed by Pavel Fiala and acted by Dvořák's group; *Faust* (1982), composed by Suchý and Havlík; and Bohumil Hrabal's *Taneční hodiny* (*Dancing Hours*, 1984), acted by Dvořák's group.

Despite various hardships, Semafor continues to be the best theatre in Prague, true to the spirit of one of its founders, Jiří Šlitr.

EDWARD J. CZERWINSKI

SLOVAK NATIONAL THEATRE
(Slovenské Národné Divadlo)
Gorkého 4 Bratislava 81586, Czechoslovakia

The Slovak National Theatre in Bratislava was founded in 1920. The present managing director is Ján Kákoš. Like most National Theatres in Eastern Europe, the company consists of drama, opera, and ballet sections, each with its own artistic director. At present, Juraj Slezáček functions in that capacity of the drama section.

The directorial staff consists of five talented, young directors, who have helped shape the profile of the company: Pavol Haspra, Peter Mikulík, Miloš Pietor, Tibor Rakovský, and Karol Zachar. Anton Kret and Jan Sládeček are the company's dramaturges.

The company's acting style is eclectic, sometimes injected with Stanislavskian realism, sometimes with Brechtian coolness, depending on the play and the director. The productions are never heavy-handed, and the director's influence is always felt, even in the costuming and scene-design.

The company boasts some of the finest acting talent in Eastern Europe, including Magadalena Vášáryová, who was selected for the lead role in *Sophie's Choice*, only to be vetoed by the producers of the film who insisted on a known quantity to play Sophie. Other members of the ensemble are equally talented: Zdena Gruberová, Leopold Haverl, Oldřich Hlaváček, Martin Huba, Jozef Kroner, Juraj Kukura, Štefan Kvietik, Karol Machata, Ivan Rajniak, Jozef Šimonovič, Jozef Vaja, Gustáv Valach, Soňa Valentová, Judita Vargová, Emilia Vášáryová, and František Zvarík. Scores of younger and older talents are engaged on a contractual, short-term basis.

Some of the more successful productions during the past several years include Shakespeare's *Richard II* (1980), directed by Miloš Pietor; Gogol's *The Inspector-General* (1982), directed by Pietor, with scene design by L. Vychodil; and Gorky's *The Bourgeoisie* (1982), directed by Pavol Haspra, with scene design by V. Suchánek.

The company also has a chamber theatre, the Litte Theatre (*Malá Scéna*), which has had recent success with the following productions: Molière's *Tartuffe* (1979), directed by Pietor; Ivan Turgenev's *Month in the Country* (1980), directed by L. Vajdička; Jarosław Iwaszkiewicz's *Summer in Nohant* (1981), directed by Tibor Rakovský; and an adaptation of Voltaire's *Candide* (1982), directed by Peter Mikulík, with scene design by T. Berka.

EDWARD J. CZERWINSKI

THEATRE BEHIND THE GATE
(Divadlo za branou)
Národní tř. 40
Prague 1, Czechoslovakia

The Theatre Behind the Gate was founded by Otomar Krejča in 1965, after various arguments with and prolonged harassment by Prague's censors and cultural establishment. Krejča had long been associated with the Prague National Theatre and had developed an outstanding company of actors, writers, scene designers, and directors. When he set up the Theatre Behind the Gate, he literally moved his company from Prague's landmark theatre to a small theatre where he could have complete artistic control. Krejča was subsequently joined by Karel Kraus, one of the most learned theatre critics in Eastern Europe, and by Jozef Svoboda, who since the 1960s has become one of the most influential stage designers in Europe.

Krejča developed the concept of the dramatic workshop, in which the playwright was influenced by the director (Krejča) and by the dramaturge (Kraus). The finished product was a cooperative effort of everyone involved—dramatist, actors, scene designer, and so on—but with the director in control of all the elements. It was during these workshop sessions that such writing talents as

František Hrubín, Josef Topol, Milan Kundera, and František Pavliček were developed.

Krejča did not concentrate solely on native talent; in fact, his most daring production was Chekhov's *The Three Sisters* in 1965. A similar success with Chekhov was achieved in 1970 with *Ivanov*. It should be emphasized that Krejča's Chekhov came by way of the West and had little in common with Russian realism. It is not surprising then to note that during this period Krejča's charges were writing Chekhovian dramas—for example, Hrubín's *A Sunday in August* (1958) and Topol's *Their Day* (1962).

Because of the compact size of the Theatre Behind the Gate, Krejča had to compromise a bit. The new theatre was not heavily subsidized, and economic restrictions were imposed on productions. Although Krejča had more artistic freedom in the smaller theatre, he had to submit to the demands of reality. Physical limitations precluded plays with large casts, although actors were eager to work with him. Even Josef Svoboda could not overcome the handicap of a box-stage and a restricted budget. Nonetheless, Krejča opened his theatre in 1965 with Topol's two-character play, *Cat on the Rails*. The play received enthusiastic reviews. Topol's subsequent works met with equal success: *Nightingale for Supper* (1967) and *An Hour of Love* (1968).

The Theatre Behind the Gate was officially closed down in 1972. Members of the company continued to perform in private homes and still hope that the Czech bureaucracy will one day soften to permit the company to continue developing their art.

During Krejča's reign, the theatre produced seven premieres, all supervised and/or directed by Krejča. From the very beginning he opposed the "Stone Sentiment," the restrictive policies of the huge government-subsidized theatres: "I don't believe in a theatrical colossus, in a theater-factory, in a theater with several ensembles and buildings, with a dozen premieres each season, with a dozen performances a week. All of that contradicts the essence of theater. . . . It seems to me that today's theater ought to resemble a research institute for dramatic art rather than a production factory, a handcraft-workshop rather than an establishment for producing confectionary." (*Divadlo*, January, 1967, p. 35.) Breaking away from Prague's National Theatre, Krejča founded the Gate Theatre, located in Prague's Laterna Magika Theatre.

Although the theatre seats 450 comfortably, the same restrictions are found here as in all of Prague's small theatres: no fly-space, no wings, and stages with more breadth and hardly any depth. Krejča was frustrated even more because of the necessity of alternating performances with the Laterna Magika.

Krejča was a hard taskmaster and demanded total commitment from all his artists: his regular actors were forbidden to work in films; they were given one-year renewable contracts—but not tenure; and they were discouraged from "improvising." According to Krejča, "every theatrical work (perhaps more than any other form of art) resists its own totality, flees from its unity, and this constant breaking away can be corrected only by the organizational power of the director. Where this is lacking, the disintegration of productions and theaters is imminent." (*Divadlo*, March, 1970, p. 16.) Thus, in contrast to the actor-oriented Drama Club (Činoherni klub), the Gate Theatre is a completely director-oriented company.

Critics unanimously acknowledge that Krejča's best work went into two productions: Chekhov's *The Three Sisters* (1966) and Alfred de Musset's *Lorenzaccio* (1969). De Musset's play seems to comment upon the Soviet invasion. This story of a frustrated idealist in Renaissance Italy who is eventually humiliated and defeated by a decadent and malevolent world becomes a montage of Boschian and Grossian nightmarish images, reflected by mirrors that seem to swallow up both actors and audience. It is one world, one theatre. The production is proof of Krejča's often explicated theory that

art doesn't force its way, it infiltrates . . . it doesn't scream, it persuades in whispers. It works slowly, patiently, and persistently. It doesn't plead for freedom because it itself is free and radiates freedom. It expands and strengthens the realm of freedom in everyone who opens himself to it. And at the same time it immunizes him against coercion, fear, and falsehood. Against cant and demagoguery. Against closed mindedness and barbarism. Free art fills that space in each of us into which unfreedom might otherwise insinuate itself. (*Divadelní noviny*, 26 February 1969, pp. 1, 3.)

With such an artistic policy, it is little wonder that the present Gate Theatre is merely marking time.

Since 1972, Krejča has worked primarily in Belgium but has guest-directed throughout Europe. He has not directed in Prague since 1974, when he was invited to direct at the S. K. Neumann Theatre.

EDWARD J. CZERWINSKI

THEATRE ON THE BALUSTRADE
(Divadlo na Zabradli)
Anenské námesti 5
Prague, Czechoslovakia

The Theatre on the Balustrade was founded by Ivan Vyskočil, Jiří Suchý, and Jiří Šlitr in 1958, and largely developed by Jan Grossman, one of the finest critics and directors in Czechoslovakia, in 1963. The company gained widespread recognition concomitantly with the development of the talent of Vaclav Havel, Czechoslovakia's best postwar dramatist.

Havel began as a stagehand in Grossman's theatre and later became a dramaturge and resident playwright. His early collaboration with Vyskočil emphasized the extraliterary aspect of theatre: "Our theater will not be based on 'plays' (in other words, on a broad selection of dramatic literature), but, first of all, on questions, conflicts, and problems that are in need of urgent consideration." (Statement published in 1960 in the program to Vyskočil's *A Thousand Clarinets*.) After Grossman replaced Vyskočil in 1963, the dramatic text became more important and ideological concepts became less self-consciously pronounced. The cabaret-like atmosphere gave way to more traditional theatre, especially the full-length play. Foreign plays became a permanent part of the repertory, especially works by Beckett and Ionesco, Alfred Jarry's *Ubu Roi*, and an adaptation of Kafka's *The Trial*. But the most significant contribution of the Theatre on the Balustrade is the development of Havel as a dramatist.

Havel's first full-length play (he had earlier collaborated with Vyskočil and Miloš Macourek), which also inaugurated the Czech theatre of the absurd, was *The Garden Party* (1963). The work is a searing satire of bureaucracy and Socialism, but above all, it is a linguistic delight. Havel is a logophile and enjoys the game of words. In fact, his second full-length play, *The Memorandum* (1965), which most critics regard as a sequel to *The Garden Party*, concerns the introduction of a synthetic experimental language called Ptydepe to a large department in an obscure bureaucratic establishment. Havel uses language as a device to show man's alienation. It is significant that in his third and last play to be staged in Czechoslovakia, *The Increased Difficulty of Concentration* (1968), Havel shifted his emphasis from the world of manipulative bureaucracy to the mechanism and sterility of private life.

As Havel developed as a dramatist, so did Grossman as a director and mentor. There is little doubt that Vyskočil influenced the young Havel; there is less doubt that Grossman affected the mature Havel.

When the Balustrade was formed, the initial season included mime. Ladislav Fialka and his youthful troupe performed regularly until a rigid touring schedule precluded the group's participation in the theatre's regular repertory. However, the group still performs at the Balustrade whenever time permits.

The early efforts of the Balustrade were not a move toward polished, sophisticated works but rather toward seemingly imperfect forms. The Czech critic Eva Kozlanská rightly observed: "The postulate of seeking an adequate form for an urgent message doesn't apply, because more conspicuously than in any other art or genre the form here is itself the message—precisely in its lack of finish, incompletion, and . . . lack of finality." (*Divadlo*, March, 1970, p. 3.) This observation is especially true of Balustrade's first few years under Vyskočil. But even during this period the tendency was toward more conventional dramatic forms. The premiere production, *A Thousand Clarinets* (October 1958), was a combination of traditional drama with musical interludes. A parody of *Faust* during that first season had all the components of straight drama. The theatre's fifth production, *Autostop* (written by Vyskočil and Havel), during the 1960–1961 season gave evidence of a more unified and coherent dramatic form, although the play could not be considered a traditionally structured work. *Autostop* consisted of monologues, asides to the audience, and satirical sketches, with Vyskočil himself orchestrating the production. The set was made up of a bare stage with black drapes and minimal props. Vyskočil emphasized a Brechtian approach toward the acting: the actors were told not to play the characters but to act like the characters, even consciously commenting upon them.

Autostop marked the end of Vyskočil's association with the Balustrade, a period notable for experiments with actor-audience relationships. After his departure the Balustrade developed along different lines, toward a more conventionally ordered dramatic form and with a shift of emphasis from the personality of the performers toward the theme and ideas of the total presentation. According to Jarka Burian, "the mixture of absurdist and Epic elements found in *Autostop* developed into the single most distinctive theatrical feature of what came to be known as the Grossman-Havel era, from 1961–1968." ("Art and Relevance: The Small Theatres of Prague, 1958–1970," *Educational Theatre Journal* [23, Oct. 1971], p. 234.)

During this period the Balustrade became more concept- and theme-oriented. Grossman felt that the repertoire for a season should emerge "not from a list of original, interesting, or unproduced plays, but from an attempt to analyze contemporary problematic issues and typical conflicts and knots in which such problematics are snarled; only then should we search for material and methods of staging it." Vyskočil's "theatre of appeal" became for Grossman "a theater that elected a certain approach to reality, to the world in which we live and in which as its contemporaries we act—here and now for something and against something . . . a theatre that wants above all to pose questions to the spectator, often provocative and extreme ones, and it counts on a spectator who is inclined to reply to these questions." (*Divadlo*, January, 1967, p. 57.)

Because of the physical limitations of the Balustrade, a great deal of ingenuity went into scene design and staging. The auditorium consists of 220 seats closely spaced in a narrow orchestra and a small rear balcony. The stage is less than 20 feet wide and 25 feet deep with hardly any fly-space and with less than 4 feet of stage space to the sides. Although the acting was competent during the Grossman-Havel era, it would be far from accurate to term it an actor's theatre. The emphasis was on "socially oriented concepts encompassing a blend of the Absurd and Epic (the latter sans ideology), followed by the text, the director, and only then the staging and acting." (Burian, p. 236.)

After the departure of Havel and Grossman at the end of the 1967–1968 season, a third era began at the Balustrade with a less clear outline than the former two. Grossman's assistant, Jaroslav Gillar, became head of the theatre. His emphasis is on a more poetic and metaphysical repertoire with a stress on synthesis rather than on analysis as a fundamental production approach. His goal is to shape a "teatro mundi." The most notable productions during Gillar's directorship were Shakespeare's *Timon of Athens* (1969) and Milan Kundera's *Two Ears, Two Marriages* (1969). Most recent productions have included works of classical writers, Czech playwrights, and foreign authors.

Jan Grossman has recently (1983) returned to Prague and is engaged at the S. K. Neumann Theatre. The present artistic director is Jan Přeučil, who took over from Karel Vondrášek in 1982. Among the directors who have worked with the Balustrade are Jiří Krejčík, Vaclav Hudeček, Evalt Schorm, Jan Kačer,

Lucie Bělohradská. The managing director is Dr. Vladimír Vodička. The company's dramaturge is Otokar Roubínek.

The most successful productions during the past several years include Shakespeare's *Hamlet* (1978), directed by Evalt Schorm; Dostoevsky's *The Brothers Karamazov* (1979), directed by Schorm; Claude Conforte's *Marathon* (1980), directed by Schorm; Shakespeare's *Macbeth* (1981), directed by Schorm; Euripides' *Ephigenia in Aulis* (1984), directed by Jan Kačer; and Bohumil Hrabal's *Hlučná samota* (*Noisy Loneliness*, 1984), directed by Schorm.

Czechoslovakia's famous mime, Ladislav Fialka, and his company continue to perform at the Balustrade. Some of his most successful productions include *Etudes* (1960)—which has been performed over one thousand times; *Caprichos* (1971); *Lasky?* (*Love?*, 1974); *Finambules '77* (1977); and *The Nose* (1981), based on Gogol's short story.

EDWARD J. CZERWINSKI

Hungary

COMEDY or GAIETY THEATRE
(Vígszínház)
Rajk László u. l.
Budapest XIII, Hungary

The Comedy or Gaiety Theatre, located in Budapest, was established in 1896 and is the second oldest theatre in Hungary. The present administrative director or manager, István Horvai (b. 1922), received his training at the Leningrad Theatre Institute. Twice awarded the prestigious Kossuth Prize, Horvai was awarded the title of Merited Artist in 1974.

When it was first founded, the Comedy Theatre specialized in light pieces, mostly comedy and farces. At the end of the century the theatre branched out into contemporary Hungarian and foreign plays. In the early twentieth century, the Comedy's reputation was greatly augmented with its production of plays by Shaw, Chekhov, and O'Neill. Hungarian drama was also stressed: almost all the works by Sándor Bródy and Ferenc Molnár were premiered at the Comedy Theatre.

The theatre's structure was severely damaged during World War II. Reconstruction was completed in 1951, and the reborn Comedy Theatre once again became one of Budapest's most popular theatres. Since that time, the theatre has taken another direction, an emphasis on contemporary dramatists, such as Arthur Miller, Friedrich Dürrenmatt, Edward Albee, Joseph Heller, Aleksandr Vampilov, Witold Gombrowicz, Edward Bond, Harold Pinter, and Peter Hacks. Classical drama is less frequently produced, and when it is, the director's novel interpretation is usually the focus of the production. Thus, in recent years a new Chekhov cycle was presented under the direction of István Horvai, and Yuri Ljubimov guest-directed a stunning and controversial production of Dostoevsky's *Crime and Punishment*.

Today, contemporary Hungarian drama is the mainstay of the repertoire. The Comedy Theatre, as well as its chamber theatre, Pesti Színház (Pest Theatre), which has been in operation since 1967, premiered two of the greatest Hungarian successes in recent years: Károly Szakonyi's *Adáshiba* (*Operating Difficulties*) and István Örkény's *Macskajatek* (*Cat's Play*). In addition, a number of dramatists are in residence at the Comedy Theatre, including the prolific young writer, István Csurka, whose plays are usually directed by Horvai.

Flexibility is the main policy of the theatre's staff and company. The Comedy has no desire to become known as an avant-garde theatre; rather, it chooses to utilize the avant-garde in its productions. Thus, the Comedy has produced a number of rock musicals in recent years, in order "to attract a younger audience and to give young performers a chance to develop," according to István Horvai in a recent interview (1982). The following rock musicals have been among the most popular in recent years: an adaptation of Tibor Déry's novel, *Imaginary Report About an American Pop Festival*; the documentary montage *I Am Thirty*, produced for the thirtieth anniversary of Hungary's liberation; and an adaptation of Endre Fejes' novel, *Good Evening, Summer—Good Evening, Love*. The three productions were directed by László Marton.

Some of the more significant productions of the Comedy Theatre include Lajos Mesterházi's *Pesti emberek* (*People of Budapest*, 1958), directed by the dynamic and ubiquitous Károly Kazimir; Tolstoy-Piscator's *War and Peace* (1960), directed by István Kazán and Károly Kazimir; O'Neill's *Mourning Becomes Electra* (1963), directed by Zoltán Várkonyi; Chekhov's *Uncle Vanya* (1970), directed by István Horvai; István Csurka's *Eredeti színhely* (*Original Location*, 1976), directed by Horvai; Witold Gombrowicz's *Operetta* (1978), directed by Péter Valló; and Peter Shaffer's *Equus* (1980), directed by Dezsö Kapás.

The Comedy has some of the finest actors and actresses in Hungary. The company is made up of older and younger types who are given ample opportunity to develop their talents. Mária Sulyok is perhaps the most famous of the group: her roles include leads in Dürrenmatt's *The Visit*, Béla Orbán in Örkény's *Macskajatek*, and Mrs. Borkman in Ibsen's *John Gabriel Borkman*. Other equally talented artists include Éva Ruttkai, Erzsébet Kútvölgyi, Antal Páger, Iván Darvas, and Géza Tordy.

The Comedy has made frequent tours abroad, including guest appearances in Czechoslovakia (1964, 1968, and 1971), Yugoslavia (1968 and 1973), Romania (1973), Italy (1974 and 1980), Austria (1971 and 1974), Poland (1975 and 1979), Germany (1978), and the Soviet Union (1975 and 1980). Outstanding recent productions include Chekhov's *Platonov* (1981), directed by Horvai, with scene design by David Borovsky; István Örkény's *Scenario* (1982), directed by Peter Vallo, with scene design by Miklós Feher; and Shakespeare's *Midsummer Night's Dream* (1983), directed by László Morton, with scene design by Feher.

IVAN SANDERS and
EDWARD J. CZERWINSKI

NATIONAL THEATRE
(Nemzeti Színház)
Hevesi Sándor tér 4
1077 Budapest VII, Hungary

The National Theatre, located in Budapest, was established in 1837. It is the oldest Hungarian theatre. The present administrative director is Dezsö Malonyai, a former drama critic and editor. The goal of the National Theatre had traditionally been to present the best of classical and contemporary Hungarian drama, as well as the best in world drama. Malonyai is trying to add to the repertoire by including lesser known and rarely performed classical and modern plays.

The National Theatre welcomes the best talent available in Hungary and takes advantage of the talents of such outstanding directors as Tamás Major, Endre Marton, Gábor Székely, Gabor Zsámbéki, and Tomas Ascher. Each of these directors, considered among the finest in Eastern Europe, has influenced the artistic direction of the National Theatre.

Among the outstanding productions directed by Major are the following: Shakespeare's *Twelfth Night* (1947), *Macbeth* (1963), *Othello* (1967), *Romeo and Juliet* (1970), *Richard II* (1975), and *The Winter's Tale* (1978); Brecht's *The Good Woman of Setzuan* (1972); and Peter Bornemissza's *Magyar Elektra* (1964). Major's greatest success came with Imre Madach's *The Tragedy of Man* (1964). Under the influence of Jan Kott, Major began his experiments with Shakespeare, utilizing mixed media to contemporize plays, such as *Romeo and Juliet* (1971). Major is also a fine actor and appears frequently in films and on television. His greatest roles include Shylock (1942), Richard III (1955), and Puntillo (1977).

Unlike Major, Endre Marton, administrative director of the National from 1971 to 1978, has concentrated on contemporary drama, especially plays in which psychological realism is the chief ingredient. Among his best productions are the following: Peter Weiss' *Marat/Sade* (1966), Imre Madach's *Moses* (1967), and László Németh's *George VII* (1975). Marton had earlier made his reputation with his productions of Federico García Lorca's *The House of Bernarda Alba* (1955) and *Blood Wedding* (1957); Arthur Miller's *Death of a Salesman* (1959) and *The Crucible* (1961); and Eugene O'Neill's *Long Day's Journey into Night* (1963). Marton has also directed classical and contemporary Hungarian plays. His most controversial play remains Shakespeare's *King Lear* (1968), with sets by Prague's Jozef Svoboda. His productions are marked by an emphasis on group scenes and the concept of theatre within the theatre. His actors are encouraged to play down their characters, to search for subtlety. As a result, the actors in his plays have turned in some outstanding performances.

His pupil, Gábor Székely (b. 1944), made a remarkable debut at the National Theatre with Georg Büchner's *Danton's Death* in 1978. Earlier, Székely had worked in the theatre in Szolnok. His most outstanding production, which he repeated at the National Theatre in Prague, was Örkény's *Macskajatek* (*Cat's*

Play) in 1971. Székely became the administrative director of the National Theatre (1978–1982). He had the necessary taste, enthusiasm, and determination to shake up the establishment.

Like Székely, Gábor Zsámbéki (b. 1943) came to the National Theatre in 1978, after making a name for himself in provincial theatre. His most successful productions, prior to his coming to the National Theatre, were Shakespeare's *As You Like It* (1974), an adaptation of Heinrich von Kleist's *The Palm Sunday Horsedealer* (1975), and Andras Suto's *Captive Star* (1976). Zsámbéki often stresses the more controversial themes in the plays he directs. His productions are marked by an uncompromising approach to truth. Even the plays of Chekhov and Shakespeare become polemical in his hands.

In 1982, Székely and Zsámbéki took over the Studio Theater of the National and made it an independent theatre, József Katona Theatre, which most critics consider the best theatre in Hungary today.

Because of the talents of these five directors and others like them, the National Theatre has been able to attract the finest actors and actresses in Hungary. Among the best are Mari Töröcsik (*The Good Woman of Setzuan*) and György Kálmán (Fool in *Lear*, Baron in *The Lower Depths*, and Marat in *Marat/Sade*). Equally talented are Hilda Gobbi, Erzsi Máté, Margit Makay, Hédi Váradi, Gábor Agárdi, István Avar, Ferenc Kállai, and Imre Sinkovits. (Many critics consider Sinkovits to be Hungary's best actor).

The National Theatre often tours abroad: East Germany (1974), Romania and Yugoslavia (1975), and the Soviet Union (1977). The National received high praise from local critics in 1979 for its production of Mrożek's *Emigrés* and Arnold Wesker's *The Kitchen*. The best productions of recent years include Aleksandr Östrovsky's *A Lively Place* (1980), directed by Tomas Ascher, with scene design by Gyulla Pauer; Shakespeare's *Henry IV* (1980), directed by Zsámbéki, with scene design by Pauer; and Brecht's *The Threepenny Opera* (1981), directed by Yuri Ljubimov, with scene design by David Borovsky.

IVAN SANDERS and
EDWARD J. CZERWINSKI

THALIA
(Thália)
Nagymezó 22/24
Budapest, Hungary

Formerly known as the Jókai Theatre, the Thalia received its name in 1963, in memory of a company organized in 1904 by Sándor Hevesi, a Hungarian whose friends included Edward Gordon Craig and George Bernard Shaw. In 1961 Károly Kazimir joined the mismanaged theatre as director and recommended the talented actor Emil Keres to fill the post of administrative director or manager. In 1973, after years of revolutionizing Budapest's theatre world, Kazimir became manager of the Thalia, a post he had earlier declined.

According to *Film, Szinhž, Muszika* (the Hungarian weekly devoted to film, theatre, and music, Károly Kazimir has changed the profile of theatre in Hungary during the past twenty years. He initiated a revival of Greek tragedies, established the first arena theatre in Hungary (Koörzinház, in 1957), revived the Hungarian bourgeois playwrights Sándor Bródy and Ferenc Molnár, introduced the theories of Bertolt Brecht and Vsevolod Meyerhold, and premiered plays by such controversial Western writers as Samuel Beckett and Tennessee Williams. The Thalia today remains the most artistically—not politically—controversial theatre in Budapest, largely through Kazimir's artistic policies.

As artistic director of the Thalia, Kazimir made all artistic decisions, including play selection, and directed all productions, except those for which he invited guest directors or assigned to apprentices who worked under his supervision. It is the only theatre in Budapest where the director has such authority. Kazimir has produced classics as well as experimental modernists, both Hungarian and foreign, without neglecting Socialist message plays. Consequently, he has never had to justify his play selection on ideological grounds. Nor has he ever encountered censorship problems, except for a slightly postponed production of *Waiting for Godot* in 1965.

There are no stars in Thalia's company, except for Kazimir. His personality influences every aspect of the production, from play selection to costume design. At best, his style is eclectic: he borrows from everyone and is not afraid to admit his debt. His own tastes run to poetic drama, and he has directed several of his Thalia productions in other countries, most notably, István Örkény's *The Tot Family* (in Leningrad in 1970 and in Brussels in 1977) and John Milton's *Paradise Lost* in Helsinki in 1976. He received a special award from the government of Finland for his production *Kalevala*, which premiered in Budapest in 1968. His company has toured Finland, the Soviet Union, Austria, and Poland.

Born in 1928, Kazimir became a national figure with his experimental, non-realistic staging of Vsevolod Vishnevsky's *The Optimistic Tragedy* in 1957, a production which some critics feel "gave support to the ailing Kádár regime." (Personal interview with Adam Tarn [1974].) The next year, 1958, he repeated his success with Lajos Mesterhazi's *The People of Budapest*, using an open stage, which seemed revolutionary to the Hungarian public, nourished on Socialist Realism.

Kazimir's most successful productions include Isaac Babel's *Sunset* (1966), an adaptation of Mikhail Bulgakov's *A Theatrical Story* (1977), and premiere productions of plays by Sartre, Rolf Hochhuth, and Beckett. His favorite productions are collages of poems of Hungary's finest poets: Sándor Petöfi, Gyula Illyès, and Sándor Weöres. Kazimir has also adapted the works of foreign poets, including Polish Romantics, the Turkish *Karagöz*, and the Hindu Ramayana.

The Thalia has been awarded the Jászai Prize, the highest honor bestowed for Achievements in Theatre Arts. Kazimir is a bearer of the Kossuth Prize, distinction for merit in any field, and is also a member of the Communist party's Budapest Council.

Outstanding recent productions include Mikhail Bulgakov's *Master and Margarita* (1979), adapted by Kazimir and Janos Elbert, directed by Kazimir, with scene design by György Rajkai, Jr.; Fritz Höchwölder's *The Holy Experiment* (1982), directed by Kazimir, with scene design by Rajkai; and Hans Fallada's *Little Man, What Now?* (1982), adapted by Tankred Dorst, directed by István Iglódi, with scene design by Peter Makai.

EDWARD J. CZERWINSKI

THEATRE 25
(Huszonötödik Szinház)
Népköztársaság útia, Theatre 25
Budapest, Hungary

Theatre 25, located in Budapest, was founded in 1970. The main impetus was a combination of political and aesthetic ambitions. The founding group was composed of relatively young (in their thirties) artists from various disciplines: actors, reporters, directors, scene designers, and composers. The leading role of the group was assumed by Lázo Gyurkó (b. 1930), who later became Theatre 25's director. The premiere production, László Németh's *Mourning*, was directed by Károly Szigeti in the fall of 1970.

During the first five years plays were chosen with an eye to casting. The company consisted of only six professional actors. In 1974 two more actors joined the ensemble. During this period a studio stage was added to the theatre, where young actors were trained in the rudiments of diction, song, and dance. Most of these young talents made their debut within several months.

Theatre 25 was so named because it was the twenty-fifth theatre to be founded in Hungary after World War II. At the beginning the company staged its productions in the student clubs. Later, Theatre 25 found temporary quarters in the Journalist's Home. In 1977 the theatre was attached to the touring company Déryné; it was finally given permanent quarters in the restored King's Palace on the Buda side of Budapest.

After *Mourning*, the following productions were premiered: Plato's *The Defense of Socrates*, directed by Jenö Harvath in 1970; Kuan Han-Csing's *The Unjust Death of Tou O*, directed by a group of directors—Kati Berek, Eva Mezei, and Károly Szigeti in 1971; and Gyula Hernády's and Miklós Jancsó's *Healing Winds*, directed by Jancsó in 1971. It was during this period that an artistic policy was formulated: an ascetic approach to scene design and an equal emphasis on movement and text. The actors, dressed in work uniforms, were the most important element in each production. They mingled with the members of the audience, becoming quite familiar with some of them.

When the play began, it was the actor who dominated the stage with his rhythmic movements and voice. Like Jerzy Grotowski's Laboratory Theatre, Theatre 25 emphasizes the richness and complexity of the human voice. But unlike Grotowski's company, the actors in Theatre 25 are encouraged to emote realistically and to search for emotions that link them with their viewers. The two directors most responsible for this approach were the choreographer and director Károly Szigeti, and the film director Miklós Janscó. In 1973 István Iglódi (b. 1944), an actor from the National Theatre, made his debut as a director. His most outstanding production was *M.A.D.A.C.H.*, an adaptation of the works of Hungary's greatest poet-playwright, Imre Madach.

Theatre 25's repertoire has included the following: several plays by the theatre's director, László Gyurkó (*Electra, My Love* and *The Terrible Adventures and Noble Death of Don Quixote of La Mancha*), Herndy's *Phalanstery*, and Shakespeare's *King Lear*. Each of these productions emphasized and explored political problems, not for the purpose of agitation but rather for reflection. According to Gyurkó, "our purpose is to present in an artistic way our conception of the revolutionary world. For this reason, we must take into account the world in which we live, that is our social and political life." (Personal interview, 1981.)

With this in mind the company has toured various provinces, presenting its plays in workers' clubs, cultural houses, schools, and village squares. Its purpose is to improve the cultural and political life of its viewers, to make up for the lack of contact with people who live far from the focal points of government and society. "In improving the public, we improve ourselves," Gyurkó contends. "We invite amateurs to participate in our theatre in order to break down the elitist attitude of our professional theatres. We attached ourselves to the touring theatre (Déryné) and opened the People's Theatre (Népszinház) in order to achieve our goals." (Personal interview, 1981.)

In 1979, Gyurkó was replaced by László Vámos as Artistic Director. In 1982, he moved to the Nemzet Szinhaz, taking with him the best actors of Theatre 25. The touring theater (Déryné) became independent once more in 1982, under the rubric of "People's Theatre." In 1983, Jancsó, Gyurkó, and Hernády took over a provincial theatre, József Katona Theatre, in Kecskemét.

It should be added that the People's Theatre had an actress of star quality, Gabi Jobba, who appeared in almost all of the Theatre 25's repertoire. Unfortunately she committed suicide in 1983 at the age of thirty-six.

EDWARD J. CZERWINSKI

Poland

(Współczesny Teatr—Warszawa)
Ul. Mokotowska 13, Warsaw, Poland

In Polish theatrical life it is rare for one individual to remain with one institution for any long period. An individual associated with the Contemporary Theatre of Warsaw represents that rarity: not only did Erwin Axer retain his position as artistic director (1957–1981), but almost all of his staff and most of his actors continued to work with him for over a quarter of a century.

Axer (b. 1917), like many other Polish directors of his generation, came out of Leon Schiller's school. He graduated from the State Institute of Drama in Warsaw in 1939, shortly before the outbreak of World War II. He began his professional career as a director in the Polski Theatre in Lwów. Following the Nazi occupation of that city, he went to Warsaw. After the Warsaw Uprising he was deported to the Harz Mountains where he was put to work in a rock quarry. After the war ended, he returned to Poland and in 1946 took up work at the Kameralny Theatre in the Soldiers' Home in Łódź, as artistic director and later managing director of the theatre, which moved to Warsaw and changed its name to the Współczesny (Contemporary) Theatre in 1949. Between 1955 and 1957 Axer was the director of the Narodowy Theatre, which at the time was temporarily merged with the Contemporary Theatre.

Because of his long tenure with the Contemporary, Axer has been able to assemble a team of actors and artists whose artistic vision he has molded. Thus, he has created a theatre with a distinct shape and profile.

Above all, the Contemporary Theatre is a literary chamber theatre where the text is all important. The actors deliver the authors' words intensely, enriching them with nuances. Axer's theatre is midpoint between Konrad Swinarski's "total theatre" and Jerzy Grotowski's "poor theatre." In a sense, Axer's theatre is eclectic, selecting those aspects of contemporary theatrical vocabulary that will best present the sense of the particular work. It has been described as a "sceptical, cynical, thoughtful, doubtful, and intelligent" approach to theatre. The acting, like the rest of the production, is always in good taste and simple.

In keeping with the name of the theatre, the repertory is largely made up of contemporary plays. When classics are produced, the emphasis is on a new translation and a contemporary approach. Even during the Stalinist period, when contacts with the West were frowned upon, Axer insisted on presenting dramatists like Terence Rattigan, Tennessee Williams, Max Frisch, Samuel Beckett, Eugene Ionesco, Bertolt Brecht, Harold Pinter, and Edward Albee. He was also responsible for introducing some of the best Polish writers, like Sławomir Mrożek (especially *Tango*, 1964), Ernest Bryll (*Over Mountains, Over Clouds*), Tadeusz Różewicz, and Leon Kruczkowski.

Although the Contemporary Theatre is often referred to as Axer's Theatre, it would be unfair to suggest that he was solely responsible for its success. Much of the credit belongs to Jerzy Kreczmar, who has been Axer's literary advisor for almost a quarter of a century. The brilliant Polish critic Edward Csato (d. 1968) was also instrumental in guiding Axer.

But perhaps Adam Tarn (d. 1975, in Switzerland) deserves the greatest amount of credit for introducing young Polish dramatists and foreign writers to his friend, Erwin Axer. As founder and editor (until 1969) of *Dialog*, the Polish monthly devoted to the dramatic arts, Tarn was able to give Axer plays before they were published. An intellectual who spoke six languages fluently, Tarn was also a promoter of Beckett, Ionesco, Dürrenmatt, Frisch, and other foreign writers. It is not surprising that since Tarn's absence theatre is less exciting, not just at the Contemporary Theatre, but in all of Poland.

Since Axer's departure in 1981 and under the new artistic and managing director, Maciej Englert, the Contemporary seems to be undergoing a radical metamorphosis. Most of its best actors have left the company; those who have remained are young and inexperienced. Instead of developing a specific profile, Englert has opted to experiment, to allow his directors an opportunity to project an artistic profile for the theatre. He has managed to persuade one of Poland's best scene designers, Ewa Starowieyska, to remain with the company. His directors—Janusz Wiśniewski, Jerzy Kreczmar, and Krzysztof Zaleski—are among Poland's best-known artists. Wiśniewski's latest production, *The Battle of Carnival with Lent* (*Walka Karnawalu z Postem*, 1984), with music by Jerzy Satanowski, has created a great deal of controversy. Some critics accuse Wiśniewski of stealing from Tadeusz Kantor (it is rumored that Kantor is suing him for plagiarism) and repeating himself in each production.

It is an unfair assessment of his work. The world of mannequins has a long history in Poland, beginning with Witkacy (Stanisław Ignacy Witkiewicz), continuing with Józef Szajna (*Replika*, for example), and culminating in Janusz Warmiński's brilliant production of Bruno Jasieński's *The Ball of Mannequins* (*Bal manekina*) in the early seventies, and, of course, given world-wide fame with Tadeusz Kantor's *The Dead Class* (*Umarła klasa*) and *Wielopole, Wielopole*. If anyone should be credited with making the Polish tradition of mannequins an artistic metier, it is Janusz Warmiński and his staging of Jasieński's masterpiece. Warmiński never received the praise he rightly deserves.

Outstanding productions during the past few years include Max Frisch's *Triptychon* (1980), directed by Axer, with scene design by Starowieyska; Leon Schiller's *The Christmas Pageant* (*Pastorałka*, 1982), directed by Englert, with scene design by Starowieyska; Edward Bond's *Summer* (1982), directed by Englert, with scene design by Andrzej Przybył; Brecht's *Mahagony* (1982), directed and designed by Krzysztof Zaleski; and Alan Ayckbourn's *How the Other Half Loves* (1983), directed by Englert, with scene design by Marcin Stajewski.

EDWARD J. CZERWINSKI and
ALINA and ANDRZEJ MAKAREWICZ

CONTEMPORARY THEATRE OF WROCŁAW
(Współczesny Teatr—Wrocław)
Ul. Rzeźnicza Nr. 12, Wrocław, Poland

Kazimierz Braun established his young company of actors at the Contemporary Theatre (Wierciński Theatre) in Wrocław on January 1, 1975. He was then forty years of age and felt that the time had come to inaugurate a theatre that would be ''dedicated to contemporary works, and more specifically, to a repertory that was at once ideologically and literally avant-garde in thought as well as form.'' His emphasis has been to select the best works of new writers as well as those classical writers that could be considered to have a contemporary core, ''an intellectual basis that would challenge the audiences.''

Braun has published six books, in which he has developed his ideas about the theatre and about drama. They include *New Theater in the World: 1960–1970* (1975); *The Second Reform of the Theater?* (1979); and *Theater of Common Ownership* (1975). His publications expound his ideas regarding the place of theatre and drama in an ''intellectually oriented'' society.

Braun first came to prominence with his outdoor-indoor productions of Tadeusz Różewicz's works in Lublin, Poland. He considers the Polish playwright the best writer living in Eastern Europe. Braun's move to Wrocław in 1975 brought him closer to Różewicz, and since that time he has concentrated on staging, whenever the censor permits, all of Różewicz's latest works. These have included *Białe małżenstwo* (*White Marriage*, 1975), *Odejście głodomora* (*The Exit of the Starving Man*, 1978), *Stara kobieta wysiaduje* (*The Old Lady Broods*, 1975), and, most recently, his finest production, *Przyrost naturalny* (*Birth Rate*, 1980). It is in the last-named staging that Braun has incorporated his latest ideas: emphasizing themes that are current (the high birth rate, feeding the world, and so on); bringing the audience closer to the actors (the second act takes place upstage with the audience onstage); and utilizing every space of the theatre building (basement, loft, corridors—where movies are shown and sculptures are displayed). It was one of Poland's most controversial productions in 1980.

But it was the premiere of Braun's adaptation of Albert Camus' *The Plague* that brought attention to both Braun's innovative approach to theatre (which he tentatively calls spatial theatre) and to his critical attitude toward martial law. The play was banned after nine performances, and in September 1983 Braun was battling the authorities to allow the production to continue. The play, with cuts, entered the theatre's repertory in 1984.

In describing the production one is afraid to distort Braun's intent; undoubtedly, the work affects each person differently. For this reason, one tends to agree with Braun that no description of the production will adequately define it: "The production must be experienced," Braun insists. "A new theater quality has emerged. It is not the theater of Gombrowicz or Witkiewicz, nor is it the theater of Różewicz." (Braun, unpublished manuscript.)

Perhaps Braun's own statements regarding the meaning of *The Plague* (which were published in the official program) helped precipitate the heavy-handed response to his production: "The Plague is evil, evil outside us, as well as inside all of us. One must recognize it, label it, become aware of it. And take a stand against it; one must define oneself in regard to the plague."

Braun's dramatization employs all the devices of his new approach to theatre. Camus' *The Plague* is merely a metaphor. There are no rats: they have been transformed into four waiters. There is no play proper: two parts of the production take place in various areas of the theatre; the final scene is a play within a play and is enacted onstage. There is very little dialogue: most of the action is outlined in the text. And the audience is an integral part of the cast of characters.

The performance begins in the theatre, where the audience is divided into three groups: each group is led by a waiter-rat to separate areas of the building. The same scene is enacted before each of the three groups, that is, the actors perform the scene three different times. The three groups visit a hospital operating room, Grant's work room (he is referred to as an inner-emigré), and finally are silenced by Father Gustav, who delivers a blood-and-thunder sermon.

But it is after intermission that we experience the "new theatre"—Braun's theatre. The audience comes together in the auditorium to witness a new production, Molière's *The White-Haired Pedant*, a play within a play. Braun's addition to Camus' text astonishes the audience which has somberly gathered together to hear another sermon. Instead, they are served a delicious comedy, starring two lovely ladies, Armanda and Henrietta. Soon there is laughter in the theatre. When the audience has completely succumbed to Molière's wit, Braun slowly brings it back to the late twentieth century. As Armanda and Henrietta deliver their lines, each slowly becomes disoriented. The prompter's voice grows louder but to no avail. The plague has struck the theatre. New actresses are summoned. They, too, are overcome by the disease. As the plump promptress struggles into a tight costume, she also succumbs. Finally, the waiters assume the women's roles and take part in a dumb-show, destroying all the scenery on the stage in the process. Farce has given way to tragedy. Dr. Lambou enters, surveys the ruins, and stares at the audience: "People have gotten used to this; they've succumbed to the rhythm of the plague! And that, precisely, is the greatest misfortune.'' His admonition is an echo of the conversations heard on the streets of Warsaw and Wrocław.

If *The Plague* is permitted to continue, there is little doubt that most of the text will either be changed or removed altogether.

Among contemporary Polish dramatists Braun has directed and staged James Joyce's *Anna Livia*, adapted by Maciej Slomczyński (1976); and Witold Gombrowicz's *Operetta* (1977). He has also produced works by Helmut Kajzar, Sławomir Mrożek, Tymoteusz Karpowicz, and Bruno Jasieński.

Braun has managed to assemble some of Poland's finest actors in his company: Maria Zbyszewska, Gena Wydrych, Eugeniusz Kujawski, Zdzisław Kuźniar, Teresa Sawicka, Halina Rasiakówna, Grażyna Krukówna, Bogusław Kierc, Zbigniew Górski, Edwin Petrykat, and Jerzy Schejbal. His company is ranked among the most innovative groups in Europe. In 1977 it appeared with the Berliner Ensemble. Recent tours have included appearances in Greece, Spain, Germany, Czechoslovakia, and Yugoslavia.

Unfortunately, in September 1984, after being refused a passport to take part in Yugoslavia's BITEF, Braun was summarily dismissed from his position at the Contemporary Theatre. He now devotes his time to teaching.

EDWARD J. CZERWINSKI

CRACOW'S STARY THEATRE
(Stary Teatr im. Heleny Modrzejewskiej—Kraków)
Ul. Szczepańska 1, Cracow, Poland

The Stary Theatre is the oldest dramatic theatre in Poland, founded in 1865. With regard to its repertory, it is the youngest of all the theatres in Poland, always in the forefront of contemporary developments in the arts. The Stary Theatre is really an extension of the Cracow theatrical school, which was once defined by a theatre critic from the Cracow periodical, *Czas (Time)*, as ''always being interested in new trends.'' At the turn of the century the Stary Theatre produced the most avant-garde of all Polish plays, Stanisław Wyspiański's *The Wedding*. Today the theatre presents the plays directed by Andrzej Wajda, Jerzy Jarocki, Konrad Swinarski (who died in a tragic plane crash in 1975), and other brilliant contemporary directors.

The Stary Theatre is both a director- and an actor-oriented theatre. In addition to the above-mentioned directors, the Stary has also had the distinction of being run by some of the finest administrators in Poland, for example: Bronisław Dąbrowski, Władysław Krzemiński, Zygmunt Hubner, and at present Jan Paweł Gawlik. The recent roster of outstanding actors includes Tadeusz Łomnicki, Gustaw Holoubek, and Leszek Herdegen. Almost every important director has worked at the Stary, from Jerzy Grotowski to Tadeusz Kantor and Józef Szajna. The scene designers include Kantor and Szajna and the following outstanding artists: Andrzej Pronaszko, Wojciech Krakowski, and Krystyna Zachwatowicz.

Krzysztof Penderecki and Zygmunt Konieczny have composed music for various productions.

The list of critically acclaimed productions is endless. Perhaps the most striking credits belong to deceased director Konrad Swinarski. A director and scene designer by profession, Swinarski was greatly influenced by German expressionism early in his career. His productions were extremely rich, almost baroque and rococo. Beginning with George Lillo's *Arden of Feversham*, through the Polish classics (Zygmunt Krasiński's *The Undivine Comedy*, Juliusz Słowacki's *Fantazy*), Swinarski created works of monumental beauty, culminating in Adam Mickiewicz's *Dziady* (*Forefather's Eve*) in 1973. For the last-named production, Swinarski utilized every available space of the theatre, including the foyer and the staircase. Magnificent murals were constructed; the costumes were authentically reproduced, since the audience mingled among the actors; and the controversial nineteenth-century drama in verse took on apocalyptic as well as contemporary significance: it seemed to foreshadow the election of a Polish Pope. Swinarski spent several years with the Berliner Ensemble as Bertolt Brecht's assistant. Brecht's influence is evident in his work, but the Polish director brought his own genius into all of his work.

Andrzej Wajda has also been closely connected with the Stary Theatre. Although better known as a film director, Wajda began his association with the Stary in 1962 when he directed Wyspiański's *The Wedding*. Some critics found the work too static and devoid of life. In a way, it was Wajda's intention to exploit this aspect of the Polish classic. Ironically, the production seemed to be anti-Wajda: "I prize emotional qualities most of all," he has often said. "Intellectual films do not get across to the spectator, are really worthless. The means must be emotional in order to work, the heroes must move the public. My recipe is: lyrical heroes in dramatic situations." (Jan Styczyński, *The Artist and His Work*, Interpress Publishers, Warsaw, 1977.) After his debut, Wajda followed his philosophy to the letter. Among his most successful creative efforts at the Stary Theatre were Dostoyevsky's *The Possessed* (1970), successfully repeated at the Yale Repertory Theatre in 1974; and Wyspiański's *November Night* (1973).

The Stary Theatre received great acclaim on its recent tour of England in 1980 and to Argentina, Italy, and West Germany in 1982. Those who remembered that the great Polish actress, Helena Modrzejewska (Modjeska to the English-speaking world), was once connected with the Stary Theatre were not surprised at the high level of excellence of the productions.

Perhaps the greatest thrill for the company was performing in Rome in 1982, when Jerzy Stuhr was awarded the Italian Critics' Award for his performance in *Hamlet*. (He recited Hamlet's monologues in Italian.)

In 1980 Stanisław Radwan assumed duties as artistic and managing director of the Stary. His literary directors are Józef Opalski and Elżbieta Morawiec. Some of Poland's finest scene designers are presently connected with the company—Krystyna Zachwatowicz, Lidia i Jerzy Skarzyńscy, and Jan Polewka.

Outstanding productions during the past several years include Chekhov's *The*

Cherry Orchard (1975), directed by the brilliant director, Jerzy Jarocki, with scene design by Jerzy Juk-Kowarski, and music by Zygmunt Konieczny; Sławomir Mrożek's *Emigrés* (*Emigranci*, 1976), directed by Andrzej Wajda, with scene design by his wife, Krystyna Zachwatowicz; Dostoyevsky's *Nastasya Filipovna* (1977), directed by Wajda, with scene design by Zachwatowicz; Shakespeare's *Hamlet* (1981), directed by Wajda, with scene design by Lidia Minticz and Jerzy Skarzyński, and music by Stanisław Radwan; T. S. Eliot's *Murder in the Cathedral* (1982), directed by Jerzy Jarocki, with scene design by Jerzy Juk-Kowarski, and music by Radwan; and Pedro Calderón de la Barca's *Life Is a Dream* (1983), directed by Jerzy Jarocki, with scene design by Jerzy Juk-Kowarski, and music by Stanisław Radwan.

EDWARD J. CZERWINSKI and
ALINA and ANDRZEJ MAKAREWICZ

JERZY GROTOWSKI'S LABORATORY THEATRE
(Teatr Laboratorium Jerzego Grotowskiego)
Actors' Institute, Rynek 27, Wrocław, Poland

Jerzy Grotowski (b. 1933, in Rzeszów, Poland) studied acting and stage directing at the Cracow Academy of Drama from 1956 to 1964. Upon graduation, he began work at the Stary Theatre in Cracow, where he directed Ionesco's *The Chairs* and Chekhov's *Uncle Vanya*. In 1959 he became the manager and artistic director of the Theatre of the Thirteen Rows in Opole. In 1965 the theatre moved to Wrocław and assumed the name of Laboratory Theatre and Actor's Institute. During the course of his career, Grotowski also studied in Moscow, and early in his development recognized Stanislavsky as his mentor and guide. In fairness to both theoreticians of the theatre, it must be admitted that Grotowski continues where his mentor left off. The basis of Grotowski's theatre is his emphasis on physical movement, similar to Vsevolod Meyerhold's theory of biomechanics. But Grotowski's theatre does not stop there. In the past few years he has selected elements found in such varied groups and areas as the Peking Opera, the Indian Kathakali theatre, the Japanese Nō theatre, in addition to traditions existing in Poland, especially Juliusz Osterwa's Reduta Theatre—an emphasis on ensemble acting, a free and natural selection of artistic materials, a regimented priest-like life for the actors, and so on.

Grotowski proclaims a "poor theatre," free of traditional realistic decorations, costumes, lighting, music, and even the theatre space itself. It was an ascetic theatre, where only the human actor and his body exist. His theatre was an empty hall into which a maximum of thirty-four to forty people are admitted. The audience participates in a Mystery recalling the Middle Ages, a procession of flagellants, a ritual of a "Black Mass." It is Grotowski's intention to create his own kind of ritual, a liturgy free of all sacred, religious meaning. It is an attempt to utilize traditional sacred rituals, taken from various cultural milieus, and to create a completely secular experience. Grotowski selects archetypes and confronts them with contemporary reality. In the formative stage of his theatre, Grotowski attempted to bring the spectator into the State Mystery. The spectator was to participate in the Mystery, in much the same way as the actor. Later, Grotowski changed his views and allowed the spectator to be a mere witness to the Mystery.

From the beginning Grotowski selected materials already familiar to the audience. He drastically altered many of the classics and for this reason, he always insisted that the word *"według"* (according to or adapted from or, simply, after) be inserted with the title of the production. For example, *Cain według* Byron, *Mystery-Bouffe według* Vladimir Mayakovsky, *Sakuntala według* Kalidasa, *Forefather's Eve według* Adam Mickiewicz, *Kordian według* Juliusz Słowacki, *Acropolis według* Stanisław Wyspiański (with Józef Szajna's brilliant concept, placing the action in a concentration camp and a crematorium), and *The Tragic Affair of Doctor Faust według* Christopher Marlowe, which was shown in 1963 for members of the Congress of the International Theatre Institute and which brought fame to Grotowski's theatre.

Jerzy Grotowski is a unique phenomenon in the contemporary theatre: he cannot be called a director in the traditional sense of the word. He had little success at the beginning of his career. Only when he set up his own Laboratory Theatre did he find his metier, as a reformer of theatre and a theoretician. During this period various artists and groups influenced and helped shape his artistic credo. In the late fifties he visited China, and later he participated in theatrical seminars conducted by Jean Vilar at Avignon and Emil František Burian in Prague. It is to Grotowski's credit that he acknowledges all past influences: Charles Dullin's rhythm exercises, Françqis Delsarte's investigations into extroversive and introversive reactions, Stanislavsky's emphasis on "physical stimuli," Meyerhold's "biomechanical training," and Yevgeni Vakhtangov's attempts to combine external expression with Stanislavsky's method. In addition, as already mentioned, Grotowski was greatly attracted to the Oriental methods of acting, especially in the Chinese Opera, the Indian Kathakali, and the Japanese Nō theatre. He creatively transformed all of these elements in his Laboratory Theatre.

Shortly after his departure from the traditional theatre, Grotowski wrote an article entitled "Death and Reincarnation," in which he laid down the foundation of his new theatre: "The death of the theatre in its existing form seems to be inevitable. A neo-theatre will come into being as a new art, as a direct dialogue and a direct intellectual discourse between the audience and the actors." (August Grodzicki, *Polish Theatre Directors*, Interpress Publishers, Warsaw, 1979, p. 46.) In 1959, together with Ludwik Flaszen as literary director, Grotowski took over the direction of the Theatre of the Thirteen Rows. The inaugural performance of *Orphée* by Jean Cocteau was considered a failure; Grotowski felt the same about the second production, *Cain według* Byron, although it contained certain techniques that Grotowski would use in later productions. This was followed by Vladimir Mayakovsky's *Mystery-Bouffe*, staged in a cabaret style. This, too, was a failure. It was then that Grotowski fell back on his own experiences. At the end of 1960 he staged Kālidasā's *Sakuntala*, a production that marked a turning point in Grotowski's career. As Tadeusz Burzyński and Zbigniew Osiński report in *Grotowski's Laboratory* (1979, p. 46), the work helped define Grotowski's theories. Grotowski failed to point out that it was in this production that he was able to break the traditional stage auditorium arrangement, a development that was to become central in his Laboratory Theatre.

The acting exercises were also to become an integral part of Grotowski's new theatre. They were carried out systematically every day for four hours (exclusive of rehearsal time) and required a great deal of physical stamina. The exercises included gymnastics, acrobatics, movement, mimicry, and vocal training. Grotowski's actors thus achieved a consummate physical dexterity and excellent vocal techniques; they became the main exponents of his theatrical productions. Grotowski eschewed art for art's sake: these exercises were eventually to lead to new discoveries in acting.

For the most part, the subject matter for Grotowski's productions was provided by classical works. As Burzyński and Osiński explain in *Grotowski's Laboratory*, in 1968 Grotowski stated:

We always take on texts which have a well-established position in the tradition of literature, texts which have lost none of their vitality for us, not only for me and my colleagues but also for the majority of Poles, if not for all of them. I yielded first and foremost to the irresistible power of the tradition of Polish Romanticism. It was an art extremely tangible, direct and yet it had a metaphysical wing of its own: it tried to go beyond everyday life and situations in order to reveal a wide existentialist perspective of human life, that which may be called a quest for human destiny (p. 47).

Only certain carefully chosen elements of the texts were actually included in Grotowski's productions. Thus, the use of the word *"według"* became commonplace in every program and on every poster.

It was the production of Wyspiański's *Acropolis* that encompassed Grotowski's art. The work is an apotheosis of values created by mankind. As presented by Grotowski, in collaboration with Józef Szajna as co-director and stage designer, *Acropolis* became a "total cemetery" of civilization in the Auschwitz concentration camp, where Szajna had spent his formative years (from seventeen to twenty-two). Instead of apotheosis, Grotowski showed the death of culture and the annihilation of man. Figures did not emerge from the monuments of the past but from the dense smoke of the death chambers. As Burzyński and Osiński observe in *Grotowski's Laboratory*, two phrases were sinisterly repeated throughout the entire production: "our Acropolis" and "a cemetery of the tribes."

Acropolis was the culmination of Grotowski's explorations into new forms of theatre. From 1962, with the first adaptation of *Acropolis* (there were five subsequent versions), Grotowski felt secure in the direction he was heading, particularly in regard to aspects of the Laboratory Theatre: the relationship between the audience and the actors, the ties that bound them together in an act of

collective self-realization and understanding. The audience and actors participated in a ritual that had drawn out from the obscure past "important and secretive
concepts, lying deep at the very basis of our culture: myths, symbols and motives
which make up a total of collective experiences and mark out the primary and
elementary situations of mankind." The actors mixed with the audience but were
oblivious to their presence. The spectators were witnesses and observers. Thus,
a division was made: "Actors are in a way only shreds of human beings, people
from Auschwitz, dead people; whereas the audience consists of live people who
have come to the theatre after a good dinner in order to take part in a cultural
ceremony." (Grodzicki, p. 49.)

Grotowski began concentrating his entire attention on the art of acting. Grotowski's actors had achieved a virtuosity, but there was a danger that their
achievements could become superficial and banal, even artificial. Grotowski felt
it necessary to explore the inner depths and impulses of the actors, to have them
"confess" what their human selves were. He finally turned his attention to the
testing of the actors' abilities as creative artists.

When in 1965 Grotowski moved his Laboratory Theatre to Wrocław and
changed its name to the Institute of Research into Acting Methods, he had already
developed his theories to a point where he felt secure in expounding some of
his ideas. In his article, "Towards a Poor Theatre," he explained his ideas on
acting:

The method which we are developing is not a combination of techniques borrowed from
these sources (although we sometimes adapt elements for our use). We do not want to
teach the actor a predetermined set of skills or give him a "bag of tricks." Ours is not
a deductive method of collecting skills. Here everything is concentrated on the "ripening"
of the actor which is expressed by a tension towards the extreme, by a complete stripping
down, by the laying bare of one's own intimacy—all this without the least trace of egotism
or self-enjoyment. The actor makes a total gift of himself. This is a technique of the
"trance" and of the integration of all the actor's psychic and bodily powers which emerge
from the most intimate layers of his being and his instinct, spring forth in a sort of
"translumination." (Jerzy Grotowski, *Towards a Poor Theatre*, Simon and Schuster,
New York, 1968, p. 16.)

In his article, Grotowski, unwittingly perhaps, pointed in the direction he was
later to follow:

The education of an actor in our theatre is not a matter of teaching him something; we
attempt to eliminate his organism's resistance to this psychic process. The result is freedom
from the time-lapse between inner impulse and outer reaction. Impulse and action are
concurrent: the body vanishes, burns, and the spectator sees only a series of visible
impulses. (*Towards a Poor Theatre*, p. 16.)

He is only a step away from his recent explorations into paratheatrical projects.

The production of *The Constant Prince* by Pedro Calderón in Juliusz Słowacki's romantic rendering of the play, staged in two different adaptations in
1965, was at once a true representation of the poor theatre and of Grotowski's

acting theories. The Calderón/Słowacki/Grotowski tragedy was shown as a study of human constancy, of the sacrifice of a lay saint tortured to death in ecstasy. It was the poor theatre: a bolt of red woolen cloth and a royal crown were its only props, used by actors in different ways and taking on different meanings, performing different functions and changing into different symbols.

There is no music in the poor theatre, only the voices of actors singing, wailing, creating the murmur of the sea, mimicking sound effects. It is an orchestra of voices in different tonalities and of rich sounds, Don Fernando's ear-splitting cry in the final scene will always remain with those who saw the production.

Don Fernando was played by Ryszard Cieślak, who has been with Grotowski since Opole; he clearly illustrates Grotowski's acting method to perfection. Cieślak did not assume a role or act a part. His is a creative act of the actor who has reached the innermost layers of his self through a remarkable control of his body. Don Fernando and the actor literally made sacrifices of themselves. In Cieślak, Grotowski found his Nijinsky. No other actor in the company has been able to achieve his level of excellence, although some critics have hailed the talent of Maja Komorowska who left Grotowski's theatre after working with him for several years. Others of his company who have become theatre personalities include Antoni Jahokowski, Zygmunt Molik, Zbigniew Cynkutis, Rena Mirecka, and Elizabeth Albahaca.

Grotowski has influenced theatre all over the world, and it is impossible to say precisely how many companies pledge allegiance to him and his theories. A number of theatre people have come under his spell, including Peter Brook, Joe Chaikin, Andre Gregory, and the founders of the Kuku Ryku Theatre. Actors from all over the world come to him for guidance, for spiritual sustenance to continue their art. It is the actor who has been most influenced by Grotowski.

After *The Constant Prince* in 1965, Grotowski began to devote all his attention to the creative process as exemplified by the actor. *Apocalypsis Cum Figuris* (1969), which had been in preparation for three years, evolved from improvisations that enabled the actors to find their true selves. The text was then created, and the actors participated in the creative process. Material came from the Bible, and from the works of Dostoyevsky, T. S. Eliot, and Simone Weil. *Apocalypsis* was a lay Mystery play, a ritual touching upon archetypal motives but set firmly in the contemporary world. It was an ambiguous production that did not yield itself to facile intellectual analysis. Konstanty Puzyna, the Polish critic, tried to reduce the production to understandable terms:

It is a mystery play of the second, albeit unsuccessful, coming of Christ in the twentieth century of His going away. In the metaphors of the production God or Christ does not necessarily mean the Judaic-Christian God, but He may be associated with a subconscious yearning for love, truth, justice and a need for the redemption of one's sins—that is with archetypes. (Konstanty Puzyna, "The Return of Christ," *Teatr*, 1969, no. 19, p. 11.)

During the course of five years, however, *Apocalypsis* underwent a number of changes, some small, some of a more fundamental nature. As if contradicting

Puzyna, Małgorzata Dzieduszycka, in her book published in 1974, wrote the following:

Apocalypsis Cum Figuris is a show about man, not about God. It tells us how man creates his God and how he brings him down, and also that he needs and wants to create God, to produce sacred figures and images in order to destroy, ridicule and discredit, deride and anger them. All questions posed by the production concern man and only man, his conscious and unconscious being. They should not, therefore, provoke metaphysical considerations or lead to solutions referring to belief or disbelief. They revolve round the eternal striving of man for self-determination—a self-determination both in relation to himself and to others, and this is not the same as determination by others. (Małgorzata Dzieduszycka, *Apocalypsis cum figuris*, Wydawnictwo Literackie, 1974, pp. 61–62.)

Apocalypsis was a production that still remained, however fragilely, within the boundaries of theatre, namely the poor theatre. However, the character of acting in *Apocalypsis* was already a departure from the theatre and probed into the inner depth of the actor because he "revealed himself and disarmed himself" by throwing conventions away. This marked Grotowski's search beyond the theatre: the impasse had been reached.

Grotowski became aware of the new path he was to follow in 1970, after a performance of *The Constant Prince* in Iran, and after his visit to India and his participation in the Festival of Latin America in Colombia:

It was a moment of double meaning in my life. That which is the theatre, "technique" and methodology, is already over. Tending for years towards different horizons, it has eventually become determined in my inner-self. I did not enter the professional world in order to return to the amateur one but, it appears, that I did not do it in order to remain there. Everything that is a search in theatre, the seeking of new "techniques," even in the professional sense (but as we understood professionalism, i.e. as a vocation) has led me beyond the theatre, beyond "technique" and beyond professionalism. (Grodzicki, p. 54.)

The challenges referred to were his paratheatrical projects and experiments called *Holiday*, *Special Project*, and *Mountain Venture*, the last-named consisting of three parts: *Night Vigil*, *The Road*, and *The Mountain of Flame*. Grotowski prepared himself and his company for several years in the village of Brzezinka near Wrocław. Later, carefully selected visitors joined in their activities. Training sessions were held in Poland, the United States, Australia, Italy, and France. The laboratory has ceased to exist as a theatre, and only the institute remains. For the past few years it has carried on paratheatrical activities, in permanent or temporary groups, depending on what is needed. These activities may be of great help to professional actors; they touch the borderline of art and life and are a preparation for Grotowski's more important activities.

Like Peter Brook, with whom he has a constant dialogue, Grotowski continues to search. In the future, however, he will walk the path alone. In June 1983 he disbanded his group of actors and directors. The Laboratory Theatre no longer exists.

In 1984 Grotowski asked for and was granted political asylum in the United States. He now teaches and resides in California.

EDWARD J. CZERWINSKI

JÓZEF SZAJNA'S THEATRE STUDIO
(Teatr Studio Józefa Szajny)
Palace of Culture and Science, Warsaw, Poland

At seventeen, Józef Szajna (b. 1922) was taken to Auschwitz and later to Buchenwald, where he experienced the inferno of the concentration camp. Condemned to death after an unsuccessful attempt to escape from the camp and actually led with a group of prisoners to the place of execution, he was miraculously saved from death. His resurrection ("God added twenty years to my normal life") has become a parable of contemporary times in all of his productions: "I was released from the noose of death and that is why I know more than life." (Personal interview, 1976.)

Szajna, like Tadeusz Kantor with whom he is often compared, entered the theatre through the world of painting. After the war, Szajna studied at the Academy of Fine Arts in Warsaw and received his degree in graphics and stage design. In 1954 he became a lecturer at the academy, and since 1972 he has been a professor. He began his career in the theatre as a stage designer in Opole in 1953, the same city that also nurtured Grotowski a few years later. His collaboration with Krystyna Skuszanka and Jerzy Krasowski began at this time and continued when Skuszanka and Krasowski took over the direction of the Ludowy Theatre in Nowa Huta, just outside of Cracow. In this recently built town, the trio attempted to create an artistically ambitious theatre that would pave the way for art in a workers' environment. Szajna slowly began to outdistance the husband-and-wife team of directors in reputation. His revolutionary stage designs included the following productions: Carlo Gozzi's *Turandot*, John Steinbeck's *Of Mice and Men*, Franz Werfel's *Jacobowsky and the Colonel*, Jerzy Broszkiewicz's *The Names of Power*, Albert Camus' *State of Siege*, Shakespeare's *The Tempest*, *Twelfth Night*, and *A Midsummer Night's Dream*, and Friedrich Dürrenmatt's *Romulus the Great*. In these designs Szajna clearly influenced the artistic form of the productions; his surrealistic treatment of materials created a reality composed of his own logic. During this period, the most important of Szajna's designs was for *Acropolis* (1962) by Stanisław Wyspiański at Jerzy Grotowski's Theatre of Thirteen Rows in Opole. Szajna felt that this work was the most important development in his career.

Unlike Kantor, Szajna spent the war years in a death camp: his artistic statement is his life-statement. It is difficult to ascertain which artist (Szajna, Kantor, Grotowski, or any other in Poland) came to the source of his materials first. The boundaries are blurred; each seems to have influenced the other; each is a genius in his field; each has created a unique type of theatre. But for Szajna, today's artistic metaphors are just shadows of his experiences.

In 1963 Szajna became artistic director of the Ludowy Theatre in Nowa Huta. His first steps as a director were taken in this theatre:

In my work as director and designer, I think as a painter. I understand stage imagery as integrated elements of light, color, sound and space. This is connected with a new notion of theatrical space and props which may serve as decorations. For example, the torn mattresses in *The Inspector General* [Gogol] represented the apartments of provincial big-shots. Old tin toilet seats replaced armchairs, and a plastic goat, an intriguing piece of scenery, added yet another unexpected element to the chaotic arrangement of the stage space. (August Grodzicki, *Polish Theatre Directors*, Interpress Publishers, Warsaw, 1979, p. 156.)

The critics neither understood nor seemed eager to understand what Szajna was attempting to do. He was scorned by everyone. Szajna chose *Don Quixote* as his second vehicle. Visually sumptuous, the production was also scorned by the critics. Szajna decided to restrain himself in his third production, Kafka's *The Castle*. This was followed by Mayakovsky's *Mystery-Bouffe* and Tadeusz Hołuj's *The Empty Field*. The last-named production was shown at the Rassegna International di Teatri Stabili in Florence, Italy, in 1965. Like *Acropolis*, Hołuj's plays gave a gripping picture of Auschwitz through stunning metaphors, symbols, and visual associations. Live people, who looked more like wax dummies, rushed onto the stage to the deafening sounds of wheel barrows. In returning to the subject of death camps, Szajna had found his metier.

Szajna left Nowa Huta in 1966 and until 1971 had no theatre of his own. During this period, he directed and designed various productions in theatres throughout Poland. The most notable included Stanisław Ignacy Witkiewicz's *They* and *The New Deliverance* at Cracow's Stary Theatre and Witold Wandurski's *Death on a Pear-Tree* at the Ateneum Theatre in Warsaw. Szajna also worked abroad, most successfully in Nice, where he arranged a *Deballage*, and at the Playhouse in Sheffield, England, where he did the stage design for Shakespeare's *Macbeth*, directed by Colin George.

Szajna's art reached maturity in the early seventies, when he moved to Warsaw. His first major production, Goethe's *Faust*, was produced at the Polski Theatre. Szajna edited the text and allowed the stage design to carry the production. The actors were subordinated to the props and became props themselves. Goethe's *Faust* is an approval of life and an affirmation of man; Szajna's *Faust* portrays the defeat of man by a world that has outgrown him, a defeat of life that is nothing but a constant death.

Shortly thereafter, Szajna took over the management of the Studio Theatre. For his inaugural performance he chose to produce *Witkacy*, based on his own scenario; he also directed and designed it. The production was meant to show what his theatre was going to be like and to present his personal artistic credo. "You can kill an artist but you cannot kill art, for it is art which marks the progress of mankind with giant strides, although this is often difficult to perceive" (Grodzicki, pp. 157–58), Szajna explained to one critic. The production proved too heavy-handed, and three years later, Szajna presented a new version, *Witkacy II*. As usual, the stage was cluttered with dummies, prostheses, freakish creatures, giant puppets, and props of gigantic proportions. Szajna set in motion a gloomy, hideous world, stripped of any charm. His next work, *Gulgutiera* (1973), based on a script co-authored by Maria Czarnele and Szajna, seemed an extension of *Witkacy* and all of Szajna's previous works. The artist is the tragic hero in the production. Szajna's entire artistic property-room, a cemetery of inanimate objects, appears onstage. Those who have come to pronounce judgment on the artist exit, either spellbound or hurling abuse at him. He looks at them unperturbed: "Because I am immortal"—and convinced that such is the fate of true art.

During this period Szajna again returned to his original sources: in 1969 he created *Reminiscences*, a visual epitaph for Cracow artists who were murdered in Auschwitz. After its success at the Venice Biennale, *Reminiscences* was purchased by the Museum of Art at Recklinghausen, West Germany. In 1971 Szajna presented *Replika*, his second plastic-spatial composition at the Museum of Art in Gothensburg, Sweden. In 1972 he presented a second version of his work, *Replika II*, in which five actors participated. This was followed by *Replika III* and *Replika IV*, presented as theatrical productions in Warsaw, Europe, the United States, and almost every major city of the world.

The main idea of the work is contained in the title, *Replika*. In Polish the word means an answer, an answer by the artist who himself experienced the inferno of the concentration camps. But *Replika* also means a reproduction, a recreation of the world of annihilation. In short, Szajna has composed his requiem. From a refuse heap, a new generation emerges: "The offal of civilization—mannequins, wheels and shoes, bits of piping, newspapers, sacks, ropes, jute and plastic, all sprinkled with soil, comprising something of a vast rubbish heap"—lie scattered in the midst of the audience. Man emerges, but it is the puppets he plays with that are the symbols of life. A superman appears and becomes the leader of the group. He is destroyed by the power he has held over his victims. The game goes on. "What is it all about," Szajna asks, and then answers his own question: "About the agony of our world and about our great optimism. Because death is our time and time is our death. That is why art is at once an epitaph and an apotheosis." (Program for *Replika*, Slavic Cultural Center, Inc.)

This phoenix that encompasses both death and resurrection is grandly presented in *Dante*, undoubtedly Szajna's finest work. Ironically, *Dante*'s text is almost unimportant; words often merely repeat ideas, and other times they only accompany Krzysztof Penderecki's haunting music. Here, more than in any other of his productions, Szajna has attempted to make the entire theatre a stage. A ladder leads from the balcony to the stage, forming a cross on which the dregs of humanity sit. These form the real world. On the stage proper, Szajna projects his visions of hell and heaven. Visual compositions change before the spectators' eyes, and Dante is resurrected.

Following *Dante*, Szajna created a magnificent pictorial vision in *Cervantes* (1976). In this production a platform also projects into the auditorium. Suspended from the balcony at the end of the platform is a huge puppet with a death's head, lamps shining in its eye sockets, its arms made of chains, and its ladder-torso with a television set lodged in its belly. It is Szajna's vision of God, Devil, and Power. Before this surrealistic tribunal, Cervantes conducts a cruel examination of conscience, in which he is both judge and executioner. Cervantes' epitaph is also Szajna's: "Woe, woe to him whom human depravity has never stirred to revolt, who has never felt the urge to tilt at windmills." Cervantes is present in the play, but first and foremost, there is Szajna—Szajna who alone understands the convoluted metaphors and images that he spins around the heads of his audience.

One of Szajna's last projects as director of Teatr Studio was to be a production of *Melville*. As in the past, he was assisted in his work by a small group of actors who had remained with him for a number of years. They included Antoni Pszoniak, Irena Jun, Stanisław Brudny, Józef Wieczorek, Ewa Kozłowska, Helena Norwicz, and Tadeusz Włudarski.

Because of the recent turmoil in Poland, Szajna has announced his retirement and has resigned as director of Teatr Studio. The theatre world has taken the announcement with a grain of salt: Szajna, they feel, will go on fighting.

EDWARD J. CZERWINSKI

NEW THEATRE IN POZNAŃ
(Teatr Nowy w Poznaniu)
Ul. Dabrowskiego 5, Poznań, Poland

The New Theatre in Poznań celebrated its sixtieth anniversary in 1983. Founded in 1923 as an adjunct of the Great Opera and Theater, it soon became known as "The New Theatre of Helena Modrzejewska," in honor of the great Polish actress of international fame who became its patron before World War II. The first Artistic Director was Mieczysław Rudkowski. Emphasis was on "creating an outstanding theater, based on the most intensive collaborative work of all artists, of which each will be an equal force."

Some of Poland's greatest artists of the twentieth century participated in the work of the New Theatre. Among the most noted were the following: Jerzy Szyndler, Juliusz Osterwa of Reduta fame (a theatre which influenced Jerzy Grotowski's work), Irena Solska, Ludwik Solski, Maria Wiercińska, Stanisława Wysocka, Stefan Jaracz, Jerzy Leszcyzyński, Janina Zielińska, Józef Węgrzyn, Kazimierz Kamiński, Karol Adwentowicz, Aleksander Węgierko, Jacek Woszczerowicz (one of the greatest Richard III's of the twentieth century, according to Jan Kott), Jerzy Zawieyski (the Polish dramatist), Karol Benda, Kazimierz Korecki, and the greatest of Poland's comediennes, Mieczysława Ćwiklińska—in all, a magnificent panoply of Poland's theatre community.

The list of directors and scene designers is equally impressive: Leon Schiller,

Feliks Krassowski (scene designer), Edmund Wierciński, Emil Chaberski, and Teofil Trzciński. But the most important director was Edmund Wierciński, who produced one of the few prewar productions of Stanisław Ignacy Witkiewicz's plays. A proponent of the avant-garde, Wierciński spent a year in Russia and was associated with Stanislavsky, Meierhold, Tairov, and Evreinov. In Poland, he was part of Osterwa's Reduta Theatre. In 1927, he broke with Osterwa and came to Poznań. He directed Witkacy's *The Metaphysics of a Two-Headed Calf* in 1928. The production ran for five performances to empty houses. The critical and popular failure proved in the long run to be the New Theatre's most notable artistic success.

In 1972 the theatre was finally divided into two separate theatres—the Polish Theatre and the New Theatre. Izabella Cywińska became the managing and artistic director of the New Theatre in 1973. Her husband, Janusz Michałowski, became the theatre's foremost actor. In 1975 the team received critical acclaim for Suxovo-Kobylin's *The Death of Tarelkin*, directed by Cywińska at the Slavic Cultural Center in Port Jefferson, New York. The role of Tarelkin was performed by Michałowski in Polish while the other cast members performed in English. (Simultaneous translation was provided by the American actor Ferdinand Ruplin.)

Because the theatre emphasizes a political philosophy often at odds with the day-to-day workings of the government, it is little wonder that Cywińska was one of the first artists to be interned when martial law was declared on December 13, 1981. During her confinement in a barracks on the Soviet border, she allowed her hair to assume its present shade—iron grey—to match her current mood.

Politics aside, Cywińska is a superb artist. She has received scores of awards for best direction during the past ten years, among these that of the Festival of Polish Classics in Opole (1976), for Witkacy's *Oni* (*They*); the Theatre Festival in Kalisz (1981), where her husband won the Best Actor Award for his portrayal of Judas in Karol Hubert Rostworowski's *Judasz z Kariothu* (*Judas of Iscariot*); Poland's Theatre Festival in Wrocław for Teresa Lubkiewicz-Urbanowicz's *Wijuny* (*Centipedes*) in 1977, where her husband was again awarded Best Actor for his role of Cyranek in that play; the Festival in Kalisz in 1979 for Mayakovsky's *Banja* (*The Baths*), where her husband again was judged Best Actor; and various awards for Best Direction and Best Actor for Stefan Żeromski's *Turón* (1977), Gogol's *Revizor* (*The Inspector-General*) in 1980, Ibsen's *Enemy of the People* (1982), and Dürrenmatt's *The Visit* (1983).

Her greatest achievement, one for which she was ultimately interned during martial law, was *Oskarżony: Czerwiec, 1956* (*The Accused: June, 1956*), written by Cywińska and Włodzimierz Braniecki from documents of the trials and reports of witnesses regarding the Poznań riots of June, 1956. The production included poems by Stanisław Barańczak, Zbigniew Herbert, and Antoni Pawlak, with music by Andrzej Kurylewicz, performed by Stefania Woytowicz. It was co-directed by Cywińska and Michałowski, with scene design by Michał Kowarski and movement by Leszek Czarnota. Thanks to this production and Cywińska's insistence, a monument to those killed during the riots was finally erected. Of course the production was censored after December 13, 1981, but the staging with the actual photographs taken during the riots, long hidden in archives and once ordered destroyed, remains a part of the Polish tradition in the arts.

Cywińska's artistic policy involves nurturing young talent. The following outstanding directors are connected with the New Theatre: Kazimierz Wiśniak, Krzysztof Pankiewicz, Conrad Drzewiecki, Jerzy Satanowski, Jerzy Juk-Kowarski, and two new talents, Janusz Nyczek and Janusz Wiśniewski.

It is the latter's talent that is shaping the artistic policy of the New Theatre today. Wiśniewski acknowledges his debt to Kantor but feels his own productions are a "continuation of a tradition" and not a duplication of Kantor's work. He has gone farther than Kantor did in *The Dead Class* and *Wielopole, Wielopole*. He has gone back to Witkacy, who proclaimed "the end of civilization" by entitling his latest production *The End of Europe*.

But it is a joyful end: Songs, mime, dancing, laughter, and white-faced clowns mingle with dead soldiers, side-show freaks, prostheses (Szajna), old people, and agonized humanity. And Europe is linked with the new continent by the pathetic, ironic refrain—"America"—as if in that distant land of hope and glory a solution to Europe's destruction can be found. Of course, the refrain is also an indictment of the most powerful country in the world.

Wiśniewski's vision does not include hope, merely attitude—an attitude that can save man from self-destruction. The end must come (or is it already here?) but life will continue. Kiki the clown supplies the final question-answer: "America? America?"

Wiśniewski's production was awarded First Prize in Belgrade's BITEF—Festival of New Trends in Theatre—in October 1984. The ensemble was cited for outstanding performances by a group.

Michałowski, although the finest actor in the company, is not the only one who has won awards. Others include: Stefan Czyżewski for the role of Pobe-donosikov in Mayakovsky's *The Baths* (Festival of Theatres in Kalisz, 1979); Joanna Orzeszkowa for the role of Antolka in Lubkiewicz-Urbanowicz's *Centipedes* at the Polish Festival in Wrocław (1977); and Michał Grudziński for the role of Balandaszek in Witkacy's *They* at the Festival of Polish Classics in Opole in 1976.

The company includes some of Poland's best talent: Kazimiera Nogajówna, Wanda Ostrowska, Wiesław Komasa, Bożena Janiszewska, Jacek Różanski, Leszek Latocki, Paweł Hadyński, Marian Pogasz, Hanna Krupiana, Andrzej Saar, Tadeusz Drzewiecki, Sława Kwaśniewska, Jan Sterniński, Zbigniew Groschal, Marta Dobosz, Jerzy Stasiuk, Edmund Pietryk, Rajmund Jakubowicz, Bolosław Idziak, Waldemar Szczepaniak, Edward Warzecha, Żywila Pietrzak, Hanna Kulina, Wojciech Standello, Czesław Ciszewski, Barbara Drogorób, Eleanora Stachecka, Andrzej Laborek, and Marda Robaszkiewicz.

A Polish critic has called Cywińska's theatre "the only theater ensemble in Poland today." Perhaps her artistic successes will inspire other theatre companies to keep working, despite the artistic community's collective promise not to collaborate with the present government.

EDWARD J. CZERWINSKI

OLSZTYN PANTOMIME OF THE DEAF
(Pantomima Olsztyńska Głuchych)
House of Culture, U. Parkowa 1
Olsztyn 10233, Poland

Although Bohdan Głuszczak, the present artistic director of the Olsztyn Pantomime of the Deaf, took over the company of deaf people two years after its founding in 1959, he has left his mark on every aspect of each production and has become a spiritual father to every member of the company. The father of two children, he has adopted hundreds more through his work in this company. Today the Olsztyn Pantomime is considered the most disciplined and unique group of its kind in the world. The credit belongs to Głuszczak and to the Olsztyn town government which has financially supported the company since its founding in 1957.

In the spring of 1957, Tadeusz Ostaszkiewicz was invited by his brother Mirosław to watch a theatrical performance presented in the town Cultural Hall. Tadeusz invited some of his deaf friends who after several such visits decided to organize a company of their own. Within a few months the group presented a program made up largely of pantomimic sketches entitled "A Tourist in the Mountains," "In the Park," and several other etudes. The program ended with members of the group dancing the Polonaise. The program was presented in the rotunda of the Academy of the Deaf.

Unfortunately, there were no offers from impresarios or directors to continue their work. Once again Tadeusz began a campaign to attract a sponsor. It was found in the artistic director of the Town Cultural Committee, Witold Dowgird. The group was given space in the Cultural Hall and began to create its first professional program. The members of that group, who still work in various capacities with the company today, included Irka Walulewicz, Urszula Stahl, Teresa and Mietek Turzyńscy, Jurek Jabłoński, Heniek Michałowski, Walter Poszman, Leszek Michałowski, Halinka Gowkielewicz, and Tadeusz Ostaszkiewicz. Mirosław Ostaszkiewicz, who had learned the language of the deaf in order to communicate with his brother, became the translator for the group.

The first play selected by the company was Aleksander Fredro's "I Am a Murderer." After several months of rehearsal, the premiere of the one-act comedy was given in January 1958. Although the play met with enthusiastic praise from members of the town and friends of the family, it met with less success (finishing in third or last place) in the Festival of Deaf Groups, organized by the Olsztyn company. Groups from Warsaw and Wrocław took top honors. The problem, according to members of the jury, was that the play was presented in sign-language instead of pantomime. It was then that Głuszczak took over the directorship of the company. While he prepared his first production, Zygmunt Borejsza directed a program entitled "Colored Sketches," which was premiered in September 1959. A few months later the premiere of Głuszczak's *The Story of Harlequin* took place. It was made up of two sketches, "The Love of Don Perlimplin" and Federico García Lorca's "Umbrellas." In time these were followed by "The Silent Comedians," "The Great Kacper," and "Miniatures." During this period Głuszczak remained with a classical repertory; the sketches were a variation on themes written for Pierrot.

Głuszczak began to expand the repertory as the members became more proficient in mime. His first mime-drama was "The Order of Anna" by Anton Chekhov. It was followed by "Miniatures" and Franz Kafka's *The Trial*. Pierrot was thus joined by a nineteenth-century civil servant, a folk clown, and finally by a lonely contemporary man. In these sketches Głuszczak attempted to place less emphasis on the story line and developed gesture and movement, that is, pure pantomime with a system of signs. The anecdote was replaced by body movement and facial signs. "Miniatures" best exemplified the direction that the group would later take. Soon the repertory was augmented by the following: "Bird," "Window," "Bell," and finally fragments of Kafka's *The Trial*. In 1961 a documentary film was made of Głuszczak's company entitled "In the Circle of Silence." The film has received great acclaim and has been shown all over the world.

Głuszczak assumed duties as artistic director only after he was convinced that a high degree of professionalism could be attained from members of the group. His first question was: "Why do the deaf have this great desire to create theatre?" After spending several weeks with the company, he arrived at an answer: "In every man throughout his life there is a yearning and a dream to be something other than he is, something better and more beautiful. The dream can be realized in the theatre. In the case of the deaf, thanks to the art of pantomime, this dream is realized, this desire to leave 'the circle of silence.' " (Andrzej Hausbrandt, *Pantomima Olsztyńska*, Pagart, Warsaw, 1978, p. 20.) Głuszczak then realized that he could also fulfill his own dream: "I wanted to create a theatre for both the deaf and the hearing, because the normal theatre was closed to us. I wanted to play in that theatre," he "heard" Tadeusz Ostaszkiewicz say to him. "I want to hear the sound of applause." (Interview with Bohdan Głuszczak, Slavic Cultural Center, Inc., 1975.) Their dream was Głuszczak's dream.

Głuszczak set out to enlist the aid of Poland's best known artists—Mieczysława Ćwiklińska, the First Lady of the Polish theatre; Professor Bohdan Korzeniewski, one of Poland's leading theatrical directors; and Henryk Tomaszewski, director of the Wrocław Pantomime. Tomaszewski worked with Głuszczak and guided him through the early years of his directorship. Since 1969, the Olsztyn Pantomime Theatre (as the company prefers to be called) has twice won First Prize at the Festival of Polish Pantomime Groups held in Szczecin every year. Individuals from the company have won top prizes at most festivals, including First and Second Prizes for performers in "Miniatures," presented in Brno, Czechoslovakia. The winners were the husband-and-wife team, Jadwiga and Wiesław Jankowski.

Since 1970 Głuszczak has concentrated on mime-dramas, in much the same way that Tomaszewski has:

To find the subject for a pantomime scenario is perhaps the most difficult task that I have. It is an art which is governed by its own rules, but it is still the art of the theatre. It is not a ballet although it is the art of movement and composition. It is not drama although it is governed by the rules of dramaturgy. It is not its task to express literary matters, but rather to express the inexpressible and evanescent. It is the theatre of dreams—poetry. If we looked for a companion art to pantomime, it would be painting and sculpture. Mime sculptures air and paints in space: it represents everything on the stage. (Hausbrandt, p. 14.)

Głuszczak has been attempting to realize his own definition of pantomime during the past fifteen years. In 1971 he won worldwide acclaim with his production of *Caprichos*, inspired by the paintings of Francesco Goya. With music composed by Krzysztof Penderecki and scene design by Bożena and Eugieniusz Jankowski, *Caprichos* was Głuszczak's first experiment in constructing a new language for pantomime. It differed from the classic style found in Marcel Marceau's etudes or Tomaszewski's story-laden works, or Etienne Decroux's pantomime of improvisation. It is nearer the theatre of cruelty, with an emphasis on coarse and violent gesture.

Two years later, in 1973, Głuszczak stunned the world of pantomime with his production of *Apocalypsis*. "A Pantomime Spectacle in Five Parts," the production is enhanced by the presence of two magnificent artists, Jadwiga Jankowska, who has been with the company for over fifteen years, and Józef Kozłowski; their finely sculptured bodies made "loss of Eden" seem even more humanly tragic. With music by Penderecki and Henryk Mikołaj Górecki, *Apocalypsis* is regarded as the company's most effective work.

In 1975 the Olsztyn Pantomime Theatre was invited to the United States by the Slavic Cultural Center, located in Port Jefferson, New York. The premiere of their work *Szopka* (*A Mummer's Play* or *Christmas Pageant*) took place at the center on August 10, 1975. If *Apocalypsis* was the company's darkest production, *Szopka* proved to be the brightest. Composed of scenes from the birth of Christ, the members of the company "danced" to the folk music and religious hymns. It was difficult for the audience to believe that the members of the company could not "hear." Nor could their bodies feel the vibrations of the music. It was in truth the result of two years of training, during which time every movement was perfectly timed, and every gesture and nuance was studied to perfection. It was the genius and dedication of Bohdan Głuszczak that orchestrated the entire performance.

The company has toured both North and South America, Western and Eastern Europe, and is currently negotiating with countries of the Middle and Far East.

A return visit to the United States in 1986 will include two new works, *Galatea*, with a scenario and choreography by Głuszczak, directed by Głuszczak and Jerzy Obłamski, with scene design by Józef Zboromirski, and music by Czesław Niemen; and *Banquet* (*Bankiet*, 1983), based on a work by Witold Gombrowicz, with a scenario and choreography by Głuszczak, directed by Głuszczak and Jacek Wierzbicki, with scene design by Andrzej Markowicz, and music by Czesław Niemen.

EDWARD J. CZERWINSKI

RICHARD MISIEK'S INSTRUMENTAL THEATRE
(Rysard Misiek: Teatr Instrumentalny)
Plac Grunwaldzki 1
81-372 Gdynia/Gdansk, Poland

Richard Misiek's Instrumental Theatre is certainly the most unusual company in Eastern Europe today. Misiek, one of Poland's finest tenor-saxophonists, founded the company in 1971 as an affiliate of the Union of Student Theatres and the Polytechnic Institute in Wrocław. Since 1981, the company has been an adjunct of the Teatr Muzyczny (Musical Theatre) in Gdynia/Gdansk, under the direction of Poland's best musical-comedy director, Jerzy Gruza.

The company made its professional debut in 1978 at the Warsaw Autumn Festival. Since then, it has developed into what can be best described as Grotowski's Laboratory Theatre with music.

Misiek calls his talented actor-musicians "Musitors." His artistic philosophy stresses "pure form and a broad musical spectrum," based on the general principles expounded by Maurizio Kagel and Karl-Heinz Stockhausen. The chief aim is to create a complete form of "silent narrative." Misiek insists that music, sounds, and images can create moods, inspire deep feelings, and evoke catharsis better than words and texts: "Movement, gesture, and the entire body of a musician—made one with his instrument—together with the sounds of music—convey stage action, narrative, and plot." Costumes (or sometimes no clothes at all), stage-setting, and lighting complete the design.

Utilizing an idea, a title, or the spirit of an artistic work as the framework for a production, Misiek then relies on intuition and personal expression to develop his musical statement—his composition. He is as much a theoretician as Grotowski but his background is in philosophy (University of Wrocław) and in music (College of Music and the Performing Arts in Graz, Austria). Because of the nature of his theatre, his artists must possess special talents—in music and in mime-acting. "Musitors," of course, are a rare breed.

Nonetheless, Misiek continually searches for people endowed with the ideal combination of artistic gifts. He was fortunate enough to find the quintessential "musitor" in the person of Krzysztof Stopa, a young man with absolute pitch. Stopa is also a virtuoso of three instruments—violin, bass, and trombone. Because each production relies on a certain amount of flexibility, Stopa's performance is always "new." And because he is an excellent mime-actor, one sometimes forgets to concentrate on the music he is playing. Undoubtedly he will be compared to Laboratory Theatre's Ryszard Cieślak, but the comparison is unfair to both artists. Stopa has God-given talents in music. That he is able to affect audiences with his playing and mime-acting makes him truly an awesome talent. Stopa is the consummate artist.

He, however, is not the only outstanding artist in the company. Pianist Artur Dutkiewicz and clarinetist-saxophonist Waldemar Cibor also astound the viewer-listener with their acting and playing. Others in the company are: Jarosław Wrona; Jacek Birr; Lech Wieleba; Leszek Kuladowski; Antoni Śliwa; Aleksander Śliwa; Bogdan Czerniawski; Mariusz Przybylski; Andrzej Jastrzębski; Radosław Kusielczuk; Leszek Dranicki; the coloratura Olga Szwajgier, a young singer who has already made a mark in Europe; and the soprano Elżbieta Rubin.

The company is fortunate in having Zofia de Inez-Lewczuk as the scene designer. One of Poland's best, she has worked in various countries, including the United States, where she designed Kazimierz Braun's production of Różewicz's *White Marriage* at the Slavic Cultural Center in 1976.

Misiek has received a number of awards as a solo performer, including the Christopher Komeda Scholarship and a series of prizes in jazz music. He has toured a number of countries including West Germany and the Soviet Union. His work, *Defloration*, was awarded First Prize for composition at the Jazz Festival on the Oder in 1971; his audio-visual concert, *Amfregonia*, won First Prize for composition at the same festival. His other works premiered in Wrocław include *The Spirit Will Not Descend Without Song* (1975), *Portrait Preludes* (1976), and *The Ghost Sonata*, based on the spirit of Strindberg's text (1978).

But it is in Gdynia/Gdansk that Misiek has been able to devote all his efforts to his Instrumental Theatre. He has produced two outstanding productions in his new space: *The Trial—Broad Music in the Instrumental Theater for Franz Kafka* (1982) and *Dance of the Tenant* (1983). These two productions best express Misiek's credo that "musical instruments are main characters" and that words are best expressed by the viewer-listeners, "after being affected by the 'musitor.' "

Future tours include the following countries: West Germany, England, Austria, and the United States. The administrative director for the company is Józef Szostek.

EDWARD J. CZERWINSKI

TADEUSZ KANTOR'S CRICOT 2
(Cricot 2 Tadeusza Kantora)
Cricot 2, Ul. Szczepańska 2
Cracow, Poland

Known as Poland's perennial avant-gardist, Tadeusz Kantor (b. 1915) is the founder of the Theatre of Death. Brought to New York by Ellen Stewart to appear at La Mama in 1979, Kantor won the Obie for his brilliant production, *The Dead Class*. This work is the culmination of his life-long experimentation in theatre and the visual arts.

Kantor graduated from the Cracow Academy of Fine Arts in 1939, a few months before the outbreak of the war. His career began at the Independent Theatre in Cracow during the Nazi occupation. His first attempts at staging included Juliusz Słowacki's *Balladyna* and Stanisław Wyspiański's *The Return of Odysseus*. Based on abstract ideas and forms and revealing a fascination with objects which in the course of the action lose their practical purpose and become the matter of a separate reality, these plays contained the germ of Kantor's future work in the theatre. At every stage of his career, Kantor has proclaimed a new artistic manifesto and has given a new name to whatever he was doing. As a scene designer and painter, Kantor opposes any division between the genres.

After the war, Kantor created a number of avant-garde stage designs for various theatres (notably Cracow's Stary Theatre), the most interesting of which were those for productions of Jean Anouilh's *Antigone*, George Bernard Shaw's *St. Joan*, Shakespeare's *Hamlet*, and Eugene Ionesco's *Rhinoceros*. The most important stage of his development as a director came in 1955, when he founded Cricot 2. Together with a number of other painters, Kantor selected the name in honor of the famous Cricot Theatre which was developed by a group of avant-garde painters in the 1930s. The first play produced by the company was Kazimierz Mikulski's *The Circus*, followed by Stanisław Ignacy Witkiewicz's *The Cuttlefish* (1957). Since that time, Kantor has concentrated on the works of Witkiewicz and was instrumental in reviving the plays of the precursor of the theatre of the absurd, who committed suicide in 1939. At the beginning, performances were given in an artists' cafe in Cracow. The public, made up of mostly young students, came in from the streets.

Kantor referred to his production of *The Cuttlefish* as an abstract *commedia dell'arte*. His next production, Witkiewicz's *In a Small Country House* (1961), was an example of informal theatre. Kantor was one of the most radical exponents of informal art in Europe. He tried to destroy form and to leave both the matter and the action to random chance. The manifesto of the informal theatre was categorically stated: matter is not governed by the laws of construction. In his production, the actors were squeezed absurdly into a small wardrobe, making chaotic gestures and uttering broken fragments of sentences.

Kantor's international fame began with this production, albeit five years after he had first staged it. In 1966 Cricot 2 made a triumphal tour of Germany—Munich, Essen, Heidelberg, Baden-Baden, and Dusseldorf. In 1969 further accolades greeted him at the Premio Roma Festival of Modern Art. The performances of Cricot 2 at the Edinburgh Festival in the early seventies were recognized as the most important event of the festival. As a result, Kantor's theatre was invited to give several performances in London and Paris in 1974. In 1976 Kantor's *The Dead Class* was hailed as the production of the seventies at the

Festival of Theatres in Edinburgh and London. Its success in New York followed in April 1979.

The various stages in Kantor's development include the following: the informal theatre (*The Cuttlefish*), the zero theatre (Witkiewicz's *The Madman and the Nun*), the happening (Witkiewicz's *The Water Hen*, 1967), the "i" or impossible theatre (a new version of Witkiewicz's *In a Small Country House*), and *Manifesto 70*, to which Kantor attributed great importance. In an interview in 1970 with Elżbieta Morawiec in *Teatr* (the Polish weekly), Kantor made the following remarks:

Manifesto 70 is a continuation of the manifesto of the zero theatre, of the concepts on eliminating expression of their consequences. The elimination of expression must inevitably change the audience's reaction. I assume that a work can be created which is not intended for usual and traditional perception and yet it performs the role of a work of art because it simply exists without explaining itself—a work which has no form, no aesthetic qualities, no perfection, a work which is impossible, which conveys nothing and reflects nothing, which has no point of reference to reality, to the author, to the audience, a work which cannot be interpreted, which points nowhere, which has no purpose and no place, a work which is like life itself—transient, ephemeral, unstoppable, which simply is. By its very existence, this work places all the neighboring reality in an unreal, one might say, artistic situation.

Kantor demonstrated the principles laid down in the *Manifesto* at the Museum of Art in Oslo (in the realm of the fine arts) and at the Atelier des Recherches Theatrales ITI at Dourdan in France (in the realm of theatre). The latter performance lasted ten days and was held in various places. In 1973 Kantor produced Witkiewicz's *Lovelies and Dowdies* at Cricot 2. The production followed the principles set down in the *Manifesto*: it was only a step away from his Theatre of Death. The setting was a cloakroom; the actors played the cloakroom attendants, seating the audience and speaking with them. Kantor remained on stage during the entire performance. The play ended with an apocalyptic dance by the whole cast, reminiscent of the waltz in *The Dead Class*.

Kantor's *The Dead Class* (1975), which he refers to as a seance, is the crowning achievement of his career. The production is a dramatization of Kantor's own heart of darkness, although he utilizes themes, scenes, and ideas from Witkacy (Stanisław Ignacy Witkiewicz, *Tumor Mózgowicz*), Witold Gombrowicz (especially his ideas on education), and Bruno Schulz (*The Cinnamon Shops*, *The Pensioner*, and *A Treatise on Mannequins*). His ever-present death metaphor is a constant reminder of squandered life. The mannequins carried on the actors' backs represent that useless part of ourselves which all of us carry with us and with which we are identified. Kantor's presence onstage is a development of his theory of theatre, which he has labeled the theatre of death—the destruction of a myth. In destroying the myth of the avant-garde, Kantor has created today's avant-garde.

Kantor formulated his new program in a manifesto called *The Theatre of*

Death. Recalling the role life-like mannequins have played in his work, he supplied the following explanation:

The existence of these creatures, shaped like human beings in an illegal, almost impious manner, has been brought about by an heretical process and discloses the Dark, Nocturnal and Rebellious side of human activities. Crime and the Trace of Death are the source of awareness. It is a dim and incomprehensible feeling that, through this creature so like a live human being but deprived of awareness and destiny, Death and Nonentity are conveyed to us, and it is this creature that becomes the cause of transgression, repudiation and attraction, of accusation and fascination, all at the same time. . . . I do not think that a Dummy (or a Wax Figure) could replace a LIVE ACTOR, as Kleist and Craig wished. That would be too easy and too naive. I try to define the motives and the purpose of this strange creature which has suddenly appeared in my thoughts and concepts. Its appearance falls in with my steadily increasing conviction that *life* can be expressed in art only through the *absence of life*, by reference to DEATH, through *appearances*, through the VOID and the absence of a MESSAGE. In my theatre the dummy is to become a model through which a strong feeling of DEATH and a strong feeling of the condition of the Dead emanate. The model for a LIVE ACTOR. (August Grodzicki, *Polish Theatre Directors*, Interpress Publishers, Warsaw, 1979, p. 121.)

Kantor has often admitted that whenever he has an idea, he sits down with his group of actors and painters at the Krzysztofory Cellar and they "simply work it out." Although many artists and actors have remained with Kantor during the past thirty years, it is his vision and independent spirit that dominate his productions. His wife, Maria Stangret-Kantor, has subordinated her own artistic career so that her husband might be free of outside interferences. She is his agent, guardian angel, or hound of hell—depending on one's relation to her husband. In *The Dead Class*, she gives a superb performance as A Woman with a Mechanical Cradle. Other members of Kantor's family (for it is more than a company) include brothers, sisters, husbands, and wives: Wacław and Lesław Janicki, Teresa and Andrzej Welmiński, Jan Książek, Lila Krasicka, Celina Niedzwiedzka, Zbigniew Gostowski, Mira Rychlicka, Roman Siwulak, and Kazimierz Mikulski. Kantor, like Szajna, has also greatly influenced stage design in Poland.

When the Off-Broadway Obie was awarded to Kantor and *The Dead Class* in 1979, few critics guessed that Kantor would produce another work that could rival that production. On June 23, 1980, in Florence, Italy, Kantor premiered *Wielopole, Wielopole*. Two years later, in May 1982, Ellen Stewart again invited Kantor and Cricot 2, as a special twentieth-anniversary celebration of La Mama E.T.C. Once again, Kantor and his production received the Obie Award for the best play of the season.

A visually stunning production, *Wielopole, Wielopole*, nonetheless owes a great deal, not to Witkacy, Gombrowicz, Schulz, and the like, but to Kantor's contemporary, Tadeusz Różewicz, who in 1960 gave impetus to Poland's theatre of the absurd with his play, *Kartoteka* (*The Card File*). Kantor's production employs the same device—a hero who seems to be eavesdropping on his past life. Kantor is his own hero, and Wielopole is a tiny suburb of Cracow, where the director was born. But whereas Różewicz leaned heavily on humor and words, Kantor emphasizes music and mannequins. The result is tragic irony rarely experienced in the theatre.

This is not to suggest that Kantor's text lacks merit: it is simply secondary to the visual and aural images of the production. Kantor is constantly adding new material to the text and the staging; few sections have remained intact. He seems perpetually unsatisfied. To critics who have followed his career, Kantor's almost maniacal search for perfection seems to be part of an artist's awareness that time is swiftly passing. Some critics have gone so far as to predict that, like Szajna and Grotowski, Kantor is bidding farewell with *Wielopole, Wielopole*.

There is much in this outstanding work to substantiate this argument. Kantor's work is a personal journey through memory's vault. Even the repetition of the name of his birthplace—Wielopole—like an echo, conjures up remembrances of good and bad things past. The lulling sounds—the l's, the o's, the e's—emphasize childhood, a lullaby for the dead and the dying. Kantor sets the tone early in the production: ''It's not true that childhood's room remains sunny and bright in our memory.'' As if to underscore his theatre of death, he adds: ''It is a room dead and of the dead.''

Kantor forces each member of the audience to experience his life as he himself as the ever-present director recalls his past. We are present at the marriage ceremony of his parents, at which time the cast of characters is introduced, for example, ''That's her brother the Priest. We called him uncle. In a moment he will die.'' Kantor knows everything about these people. Like the stage manager in Thornton Wilder's *Our Town*, Kantor manipulates the audience through a process of ''unnatural selection,'' acting like God who is responsible for the fate of those he brings forth from his memory.

The five formal titles of the production seem deceptively simple: Marriage, Insults, Crucifixion, Adam Goes to the Front, and The Last Supper. The Christ-figure metaphor seems obvious, but Kantor's shocking images and juxtaposition of materials belie the simplicity of the text. The ''Dead'' Priest is a living presence, metamorphosed alternately into a relative, a religious figure, a contemporary political presence, and ultimately—Everyman. When the Priest holds out his hand to the Rabbi and they exit arm in arm, glancing over their shoulders before darkness descends, the message becomes clear: Man must hold out his hand to man before death comes. This is the meaning of salvation.

Wielopole, Wielopole was premiered in Kantor's new theatre in a nineteenth-century church on the Via Santa Maria, Florence, Italy. Kantor now has two centers, one in Cracow and the other in Florence.

Kantor and his productions of *The Dead Class* and *Wielopole, Wielopole* appeared at the Summer Olympics in Los Angeles during the summer of 1984.

EDWARD J. CZERWINSKI

TOMASZEWSKI'S MIME THEATRE
(Wrocławski Teatr Pantomimy Henryka Tomaszewskiego)
Aleja Dębowa 16, Wrocław, Poland

Variously known as the Wrocław Mime Theatre, the Mime Studio, and the Mime Theatre, Henryk Tomaszewski's group is an extension of himself. "Movement is an affirmation of life," he has written. "I take it as life, so it is a reflection of my own life, too. It broadens my own existence, gives it a more general sense, reduces it to its elements and, at the same time, sums it up." (Andrzej Hausbrandt, *Tomaszewski's Mime Theatre*, Interpress Publishers, Warsaw, 1975, p. 5.)

Tomaszewski's experiments in movement began in 1945 in Iwo Gall's Theatre Studio in Cracow. Gall was an avant-gardist whose main concern was to destroy the existing theatrical conventions. Tomaszewski studied with this outstanding innovator during the first years after the war, 1945–1947. His early training was not only in acting but also in ballet, under the tutelage of Feliks Parnell. Only after Tomaszewski's early success did Gall concede the importance of dance and movement in a new kind of theatre.

After a season with Parnell's Polish Ballet, Tomaszewski settled in Wrocław in 1949, a city with which he is associated today. He was first engaged as a ballet soloist; later he set up his own company, a theatre of dramatic dance. Several young dancers from the Wrocław Ballet joined Tomaszewski in his early experiments. These experiments were on the borderline of dance, mainly solo performances, but slowly he formulated the basic principles of his new art. In 1955, when the World Festival of Students and Youth burst upon Warsaw, the Polish organizers decided to enter Tomaszewski's group in the mime competition, since his was the only company experimenting in the art form in Poland. Tomaszewski appeared in a solo performance, *The Pianist*, a short etude that lasted less than fifteen minutes. He went on to win the festival's gold medal.

In 1956 Tomaszewski organized the Mime Studio in Wrocław. On November 4, 1956, four mime scenes written and directed by Tomaszewski were premiered at the Polski Theatre in Wrocław: *Sentenced to Live*, *The Hunchback of Notre Dame* (after Victor Hugo), *The Overcoat* (after Nikolai Gogol), and *The Tale of the Little Negro and the Golden Princess*. The costumes for the first program were designed by Jadwiga Przeradzka and the sets by Aleksander Jędrzejewski.

Tomaszewski underscored his credo during this early period: "Our Mime Theatre proposes to present realistic content using illusionistic means. Our themes come from literature and from life. It is from them that we try to draw humanistic inspiration." (Hausbrandt, p. 11.) His philosophy at that time echoed the essence of Socialist Realism, but this phase passed quickly away. In 1957 Tomaszewski went to the Festival of Mimes in Moscow and again won a gold medal. Armed with these impressive credentials, Tomaszewski expanded his first program, retaining *The Overcoat* and *The Hunchback of Notre Dame* and adding four new scenes: *En Passant*, *Nativity Play*, *Fortune-Telling*, and *Orpheus in Search of*

Eurydice. Tomaszewski conceived and directed the entire program. The first stage of his development comprised six such programs: *Program One* (1956), *Program Two* (1957), *Harlequin's Masks* (1959), *The Sorcerer's Apprentice* (1960), *The Cabinet of Curiosities* (1961), and *Entry into the Labyrinth* (1963). During this first period the number of mime scenes in each program grew from four to eight. It was a period of search and experimentation. Because his Wrocław Mime Theatre was heavily endowed by state and municipal subsidies, Tomaszewski concentrated on art and paid little attention to box office success.

The second stage of his development can be traced to 1964 when Tomaszewski began to limit the number of scenes in each program and to expand the contents of each scene. This second period included the following programs: *The Minotaur*, composed of five scenes, and *The Garden of Love*, containing only four scenes. The third stage was marked by monothematic, full-length productions, such as *Gilgamesh* (1969), *The Departure of Faust* (first version, 1970), *A November Night's Dream* (1971), and *The Menagerie of the Empress Phylissa* (1972). By this time Tomaszewski had developed what he was to term mimetic drama.

In the early seventies Tomaszewski came under fire from various critics. Up to this time he had been praised and admired for his efficiency, his ideas, his innovations, and his stage effects. When he began to reach out for greater thematic subjects, discarding sketches and etudes and concentrating more on the development of drama, critics were quick to react and demanded a return to familiar territory. Tomaszewski continued to go his own way.

Until 1962 Tomaszewski himself participated in all of his productions. He not only determined the form of each production but also imposed upon them his unique style of acting. According to the Polish critic Andrzej Hausbrandt, Tomaszewski "was the model, the measure and the brightest star of the theatre he had created. He was the actor whom the others tried to equal, by whose standards they judged themselves and were judged by the critics and the audience." (Hausbrandt, p. 12.)

This is not to say that Tomaszewski was alone, even at the beginning when he was laying the foundations of Polish mime. The emphasis was on teamwork. It is true that then as today he produced, choreographed, and rigorously and stubbornly implemented his own artistic credo. When he ceased to perform, the theatre survived because he had trained a whole group of mimes. The company included Janusz Pieczuro, Andrzej Szczużewski, Leszek Czarnota, Jerzy Kozłowski, Ewa Czękalska, Stanisław Brzożowski, Krystyna Maynowska, Pawel Rouba and, later, Stefan Niedziałkowski, Zdzisław Starczynowski, Danuta Kisiel-Drzewińska, and others.

Tomaszewski's main contribution to mime is his creation of an ensemble of actor-mimes. He consciously shaped his art as a collective phenomenon, a means of expression not only for himself but also for other artists. He was able to attract some of the finest artists to his theatre—set designers, musicians, and composers. Among the set designers who have collaborated on various of his productions are Krzysztof Pankiewicz, Kazimierz Wiśniak, Andrzej Majewski, Franciszek Starowieyski, Jadwiga Przeradzka, Aleksander Jędrzejewski, and Władysław Wigura. Among composers, Tomaszewski has drawn upon the talents of Chopin, Bach, Mozart, Moussorgsky, Karłowicz, and Berlioz, but he has also utilized a "montage of sound effects," created by specialists in Poland who regularly collaborate with him.

According to Tomaszewski, the function of theatre "cannot be reduced to offering answers to questions and solving people's doubts. Art justifies itself by the mere fact of its existence. It needs no other supports or arguments." (Hausbrandt, p. 15.) His credo is tantamount to an "art-for-art's-sake" system. However, Tomaszewski insists that even such art can appeal to man. Judging by his popularity in Poland and abroad, it would seem that Tomaszewski has been able to bring high art to the marketplace. In the past quarter of a century his company has appeared in Europe, Africa, Latin America, North America, and the Middle East and has given over two thousand performances abroad.

It is significant that both Tomaszewski's Mime Theatre and Jerzy Grotowski's Laboratory Theatre are located in Wrocław. There seems to be more than a passing similarity between Grotowski's "poor theatre" and Tomaszewski's "total theatre." Ironically, Grotowski's theatre eliminates everything from the stage except the actor, while Tomaszewski's Mime Theatre engages all possible means of expression—movement, sound, color, costumes, props, masks, lights, smoke, incense, and so on.

The two styles touch upon the primary and secondary elements in the structure of a theatre performance—the text and the human body. For Grotowski, it is the reaction of the body; for Tomaszewski, it is the movement. In addition, for Tomaszewski and his idea of spherical theatre, the central point of his theatre is people: "If I speak of a 'Spherical Theatre' with people as its hub, I do not, of course, have in mind seating the audience in the center of the stage or surrounding the spectators by a panoramic stage. The matter is more fundamental: to achieve a comprehensive attack by the theatre on people and to make people the central thing, the alpha and omega of all theatrical art." In February 1970 Grotowski seemed to echo Tomaszewski's ideas: "We are interested in people and only in people—working with people is the very nature of my work; my language comes to life only when I meet other people." For both artists, man is the sole point of reference—"both as the object and the subject of art, its destination and its road." (Hausbrandt, all p. 17.)

In 1970 Tomaszewski was awarded the Grand Prix at the Festival of Ballet in Paris. During the past few years, the company has traveled widely: Holland (1978), West Germany (1979, 1980, 1982, 1983, and 1984), Switzerland (1979, 1982), Japan (1983), and Hungary (1983).

Outstanding productions during the past few years include *The Battle* (*Spór*, 1978), with scene design by Kazimierz Wiśniak, and music by George Handel, Henry Purcell, and folk music; *Hamlet: Irony and Grief* (*Hamlet, ironia i żałoba*, 1979), with scene design by Wiśniak, and music by Gustaw Holst, Gabriel

Fauré, and Bogdan Dominik; *Knights of King Arthur* (*Rycerze króla Artura*, 1981), with scene design by Zofia de Ines Lewczuk, and music by Zbigniew Karnecki; and *The Prodigal Son* (*Syn marnotrawny*, 1983), with scene design by de Ines Lewczuk, and music by Bach, Debussy, Orlando Gibbons, Joaquino Rodrigo, Gerald Hoffnung, and Bogdan Dominik. All productions were conceived and directed by Tomaszewski.

EDWARD J. CZERWINSKI and
ALINA and ANDRZEJ MAKAREWICZ

UNIVERSAL THEATRE
(Teatr Powszechny)
Ul. Zamoyskiego 20, Warsaw, Poland

Considered by most critics the best theatre in Warsaw today, the Universal Theatre has the added distinction of being the first theatre to be reopened after the liberation of Warsaw in the autumn of 1944. The old building, located on the eastern bank of the Vistula River, was completely rebuilt in 1975, housing two spaces—a large auditorium and a chamber area.

Among the first managing and artistic directors were such Polish luminaries as Henryk Szletyński, Irena Babel, Tadeusz Każmierski, and Adam Hanuszkiewicz, a fine actor who in the 1970s became the director of the National (Narodowy) Theatre in Warsaw.

The repertoire during the postwar years included such interesting productions as Piscator's adaptation of Tolstoy's *War and Peace* (1957), directed by Irena Babel; Shakespeare's *The Tempest* (1959), directed by Krystyna Skuszanka, with scene design by Józef Szajna; and Stanisław Wyspiański's *The Wedding* (*Wesele*, 1964), directed by Adam Hanuszkiewicz.

The present managing and artistic director is Zygmunt Hübner, who, since assuming the position of artistic director in 1974 and managing director in 1977, has made the Universal the most popular theatre in Poland.

The premiere production after the opening of the new building was Stanisława Przybyszewka's *Danton's Affair* (*Sprawa Dantona*, 1975), directed by Andrzej Wajda, who in 1983 also directed the film version.

Some of Poland's finest actors have worked with Hübner, including Wojciech Pszoniak, Bronisław Pawlik, Władysław Kowalski, Elżbieta Kępińska, Edmund Fetting, Leszek Herdegen, Olgierd Łukaszewicz, Stanisław Żaczyk, Aniela Świderska, Joanna Żółkowska, Mirosława Dubrawska, Ewa Dałkowska, Gustaw Lutkiewicz, Marta Ławińska, Anna Seniuk, Roman Wilhelmi, Franciszek Pieczka, Andrzej Szalawski, Maciej Szary, Piotr Zaborowski, Kazimierz Kaczor, and Rafal Mickiewicz.

The past decade ranks among the finest hours in Polish theatre history: Gorky's *The Barbarians* (1976), directed by Aleksander Bardini, with scene design by Jan Banucha; Dale Wasserman's *One Flew Over the Cuckoo's Nest* (1977), directed by Hübner, with scene design by Kazimierz Wiśniak; Hübner's adaptation of Kazimierz Moczarski's novel, *Conversations with a Hangman* (*Rozmowy z katem*, 1977), directed by Andrzej Wajda, with scene design by Allan Starski; García Lorca's *The House of Bernarda Alba* (1978), directed by Janusz Wiśniewski, with scene design by Henryk Waniek; Janusz Głowacki's *Cinderella* (*Kopciuch*, 1980), directed by Kazimierz Kutz, with scene design by Jan Banucha; Marsha Norman's *Getting Out* (1982), directed by Hübner, with scene design by Paweł Dobrzycki; Andrzej Strzelecki's *The Clowns* (*Clowni*, 1983), directed by Andrzej Strzelecki, with scene design by Ewa Czerniecka-Strzelecka; Witold Gombrowicz's *Yvonne, the Princess of Burgundia* (*Iwona, Księżniczka Burgunda*, 1983); directed by Zygmunt Hübner, with scene design by Jan Banucha; and David Williamson's *The Department* (1984), directed by Piotr Cieślak, with scene design by Grzegorz Malecki.

With the cultural crackdown after the declaration of martial law in 1981, a number of the best actors parted company with the theatre. A dark shadow has fallen on Poland's theatres.

EDWARD J. CZERWINSKI

WARSAW MIME THEATRE
(Warszawski Teatr Pantomimy)
Warsaw Chamber Orchestra
Ul. Nowogrodzka 49, Warsaw, Poland

The Warsaw Mime Theatre is composed of five artists who create, choreograph, design, and direct their own productions as a unit without outside assistance. Founded in 1975 by four former members of Henryk Tomaszewski's Polish Mime Theatre, the group includes Andrzej Szczużewski, Stefan Niedziałkowski, Rajmund Klechot, and Zdzisław Starczynowski. The four men were subsequently joined by the prima ballerina of the Wrocław Opera, Jolanta Kruszewska. In 1979 Stefan Niedziałkowski broke from the group to form his own company in the United States. A female dancer was recently added to the group.

The main difference, besides size, that distinguishes the Warsaw group from Tomaszewski's Wrocław-based theatre is the emphasis on body as sculpture rather than on sexual-emotional response. The stress is on form and on individual creation, unlike the Tomaszewski experience, which develops Tomaszewski's own personal artistic vision and not the group's efforts.

The group hastens to explain that there is "no one director—we all share in the total creation. We employ mime, dance, music and poetry to recreate theater. We are not theater." (Program, Warsaw Mime Theatre, Slavic Cultural Center, Inc., 1976.)

The subtlety in differentiation from other groups sometimes borders on mystical interpretation. Even the Warsaw Mime Theatre's claim to the source of its inspiration—"nature, painting, sculpture and theatre"—is difficult to evaluate. Its desire, however, to break down "the barriers of cross-cultural and sociopolitical communication and to explore new horizons of international encounter and artistic exchange'' is a pragmatic goal. For these artists, ''nothing is more interesting for mankind than man himself.'' (Program.) Thus, a minimum of scenery and stage effects are employed. The emphasis is on body and movement to create evocative images.

The group has performed in every country of Eastern and Western Europe and on the North American continent. In their five appearances in the United States, the artists have performed three works and have traveled as far as Texas, Milwaukee, Chicago, North Carolina, Buffalo, and New York. Initially, the group was introduced to American audiences through the Slavic Cultural Center in Port Jefferson, New York, where they have premiered all their works.

Their productions include *The Mirror* (1975), *Beyond the Word* (1976), *Voice of Silence* (1978), and *Face to the Sky* (1979). The group designs its own costumes and scenery and utilizes music composed by Polish composers, like Augustyn Bloch and Krzysztof Penderecki. The women performers are in their mid-twenties and the men in their mid-thirties.

Since the declaration of martial law in December, 1981, a number of changes have taken place in the company. Of the original founders, only Zdzisław Starczynowski remains with the company, in the capacity of director and consultant. Klechot resides in Stony Brook, N.Y., with his American wife; Szczużewski works in France.

The company now performs in the Jewish Theatre in Warsaw. In 1984, the director of the Jewish Theatre, Szymion Szurmiej, in collaboration with Starczynowski and Andrzej Śmigielski, composed a new work for the new members of the company—*Guest Appearance in Lódź* (*Lódź na goscincu*, 1984), directed by Starczynowski and Jan Szurmiej, with scene design by Irena Skoczeń, and music by Marcin Błażewicz.

The new members of the company include Maciej Szczużewski, Andrzej Pankowski, Ryszard Kleczyński, Tomasz Witkowski, Ryszard Kluge, Jolanta Pankowska, Ewa Winneberg, Grażyna Chmielewska, Maria Werbik, Grzegorz Kulikowski, Janusz Porębski, Marek Derlaciński, Grzegorz Grzywacz, Zdzisław Tąpa, and Tomasz Tworkowski.

EDWARD J. CZERWINSKI

Romania

BACOVIA DRAMA THEATRE
(Teatrul Dramatic "Bacovia"-Bacău)
7 Strada Iernii, Bacău 5500, Romania

The Bacovia Drama Theatre, formerly located in Iasi and known as the People's Theatre, moved to Bacau on August 1, 1948. The founders were Ion Niculescu-Bruna, Vasile Cretzoiu, and Ernest Mafteu—actors who were later joined by Lory Cambos, Ion Buleandrea, and several other young artists from Bucharest. During the past five years several younger actors have joined the ensemble, including Liviu Manoliu, Diana Lupescu, Doina Iacob, Anca Alecsandra, and the brilliant director, Cristian Pepino.

Because of a population shift, the audiences of Bacău are largely composed of former farmers and workers. The personnel of the Bacovia found themselves with a problem that helped decide the philosophical basis of the theatre. At first the public was unresponsive. The actors and directors decided to include a mixture of classics and contemporary works in their repertory. In addition, it was decided to stress the visual aspects of each production and to contemporize not only language but the philosophic content of some plays as well. The finest example of all elements working in harmony was Federico García Lorca's *The Magnificent Shoemaker*. The production was ranked as one of the best plays of the 1958–1959 season. A good deal of the credit for its success lay in the colorful stage design by Toni Gheorghiu, one of Romania's finest artists.

Despite the fact that the Bacovia has a permanent roster of producers and directors, for example, I. G. Russu who is greatly responsible for the development of this theatre, its greatest successes have come from guest directors. The following directors have contributed outstanding work to the Bacovia: Mauriciu Seckler and his production of Brecht's *Mr. Puntila and His Hired Man, Matti*, in which he combined the Berliner Ensemble style of acting with a contemporary Romanian interpretation; Ion Olteanu's production of Friedrich Schiller's *Don Carlos*, enhanced by the magnificent performances of George Motoi and Ion

Buleandra; Georghe Harag's production of Steinbeck's *Of Mice and Men*; and Letitia Popa's electrifying production of Sławomir Mrożek's *Emigrés*.

The Bacovia Drama Theatre also promotes various festivals and forums devoted to improving the state of the arts and public perception regarding all phases of the theatre. It is one of the few opportunities in the world of theatre where critics are confronted by actors who have received good or bad reviews from the press. The colloquia have been hailed as a breakthrough in Romania where oftentimes artistic prejudice is dictated by a political stance.

The present artistic director is Stelian Preda. Under his leadership the company has dedicated itself to producing contemporary Romanian plays. The most successful during the past few years include Mihnea Gheorghiu's *The Head* (*Capul*, 1983), directed by Constantin Dinischietu, with scene design by Vasile Rotaru, and costumes by Gloria Iovan; and Dinu Sararu's *Love and Revolution* (*Dragostea și revoluția*, 1984), adapted from Sararu's novel by Virgil Stoenescu, directed by Constantin Dinischietu, and with scene design by Gloria Iovan.

ILEANA BERLOGEA and
JOSEPH J. NEUSCHATZ

C. I. NOTTARA THEATRE
(Teatrul "C. I. Nottara"—București)
Bdul. Magheru Nr. 20, Bucharest, Romania

The C. I. Nottara Theatre of Bucharest was inaugurated in 1946 as part of the Artistic Ensemble of the Army. The theatrical group became an independent entity in 1965. The theatre consists of a studio hall in addition to the regular theatre, which allows simultaneous productions of large-scale plays and those of limited scope and length.

During its first years the group's emphasis was on historical and sociorevolutionary dramas like *Richard III* by Shakespeare (with George Vraca, one of the last romantics of the Romanian theatre in the title role), *Vlaicu Voda* by Alexandru Davila, a historical drama in verse (with the same actor), *Despot Voda* by Vasile Alecsandri, and *The Fountain Ovejuna* by Lope de Vega.

During the past few years the following productions have received critical acclaim: *Hamlet* and *Timon of Athens* by Shakespeare, directed by Dinu Cernescu; *Flamand Visions* by Michel de Ghelderode, produced by the same director; and *The Tot Family* by István Örkény and *The Return of the Eldest Son* by Alexander Vampilov, both directed by Valeriu Paraschiv.

Liliana Tomescu, one of Romania's best actresses, received critical praise for her roles in *The Lark* by Jean Anouilh and *A Moon for the Misbegotten* by Eugene O'Neill. Other noted actors include George Constantin, Gilda Marinescu, Margareta Pogonat, Alexandru Repan, Ion Dichiseanu, Marga Barbu, Anda Caropol, Dorin Varga, Migri Avram Nocolau, and Eugenia Baduleascu.

The Nottara has also concentrated on contemporary Romanian plays, the most notable of which are *Suffering Without End*, *Paradise*, *I Was in Arcadia Too*, and *Petru Rares*, all directed by the then artistic director, Horia Lovinescu, who died in 1983. The Nottara's roster of directors includes some of Romania's best: Ion Sahighian, Alexandru Fintzi, Ion Olteanu, Dan Nasta, Sanda Manu, and George Rafael.

The theatre has toured extensively, including France (1969), Denmark (1970), Yugoslavia (1971), Czechoslovakia (1973), and Mexico (1978). Outstanding productions during the past few years include Dostoevsky's *The Karamazovs* (1981), adapted by Horia Lovinescu and Dan Micu, directed by Dan Micu, with scene design by Dragoş Georgescu; Maxim Gorky's *Children of the Sun* (1982), directed by Anca Ovanez-Doroşenco, with scene design by Gheorghe Doroşenco; and Horia Lovinescu's last play, *The Black and the Red* (1983), directed by Dan Micu, with scene design by Dragoş Georgescu.

ILEANA BERLOGEA and
JOSEPH J. NEUSCHATZ

COMEDY THEATRE OF BUCHAREST
(Teatrul de Comedie Bucureşti)
6 Strada Mandinesti, Bucharest, Romania

Inaugurated in 1961, the Comedy Theatre of Bucharest has established itself as Romania's best theatre for comedy. Initially led by Radu Beligan, Romania's best known actor-director, the company is now managed by Silviu Stanculescu. Among its young and talented actors are Grigore Vasiliu Birlic, Stefan Ciubotarasu, Mircea Constantinescu, Florin Scarlatescu, Marcela Rusu, Ion Lucian, Silvia Popovici, Nineta Gusti, Mircea Septilici, and Sanda Toma.

Beligan's main purpose in organizing the group was to develop an ensemble much like Chicago's Second City. The emphasis was on improvisation and adapting one's talents to fit the group. The theatre eventually became an experimental workshop for actors, producers, and directors.

Among the most notable past productions of the Comedy Theatre are *Schweyk in the Second World War* by Bertolt Brecht, *The Envelope* by Liviu Rebreanu, *The Bourgeois Gentleman* by Molière, and *The Three Sisters* by Anton Chekhov. David Esrig's production of Shakespeare's *Troilus and Cressida* received the greatest critical acclaim among the Comedy's repertory and won prizes for distinguished achievement in Paris (1965) and in Belgrade (1967).

The Comedy Theatre has placed great emphasis recently on contemporary Romanian plays. Among the most notable productions are *My Friend Pix* by V. E. Galan, *Pure Coincidence* by Paul Everac, and *The Big Tailor from Valahia* by Alexander Popescu.

During the eighties the company has emphasized foreign plays and classics but has not completely abandoned Romanian dramatists. Among the best productions of the past few years were Molière's *Don Juan* (1980), directed by Valeriu Moisescu, with scene design by Sanda Musatescu; Marin Sorescu's *Nerves Exist (Exista nervi*, 1981), directed by Florin Fatulescu, with scene design by Ion Popescu-Udrişte; Kōbō Abe's *The Ghosts of Kitahama* (1982), directed by Cátálina Buzoianu, with scene design by Ion Popescu-Udrişte; and Aleksandr Suxovo-Kobylin's *The Case* (1983), directed by Gheorghe Harag, one of Romania's finest directors, who works principally in Transylvania.

ILEANA BERLOGEA and
JOSEPH J. NEUSCHATZ

I. L. CARAGIALE NATIONAL THEATRE
(Teatrul National "I. L. Caragiale"—Bucureşti)
2 Bdul. Nicolae Balcescu, Bucharest, Romania

The I. L. Caragiale National Theatre is Romania's second oldest theatrical institution. Inaugurated in December 1852, the Caragiale was designated a national theatre in 1875. In 1877 the theatre obtained a charter similar to that of France's La Comèdie Française. The theatre has had an unbroken tradition since its inception, although temporary quarters had to be used after 1944 when a German air raid destroyed the main building. The present building on Nicolae Balcescu Avenue was occupied in 1973.

Almost every important Romanian actor has been associated with the Caragiale National Theatre since the nineteenth century. The following is a sampling of those who have appeared with the company: Matei Millo, C. I. Nottara, Aristizza Romanescu, Grigore Manolescu, Stefan Iulian, Petre Liciu, Nicolae Soreanu, G. Storin, Ion Talianu, Maria Filotti, Emil Botta, George Calboreanu, Sonia Cliceru, and George Vraca.

Each successor has tried to build upon the foundations set up by the first artistic director, Ion Luca Caragiale, for whom the theatre has been named. The Caragiale has always stressed ensemble acting and a predominantly Romanian repertory. Among the most notable productions of the past decade are Caragiale's *A Lost Letter*, Mihai Sebastian's *The Last Hour*, and foreign classics by Racine, Molière, Shakespeare, Pirandello, Shaw, Strindberg, and O'Neill. Among the most important directors who have worked with the company are Paul Gusty, Alexandru Davila, Soare Z. Soare, and Ion Sava.

Known for its ensemble work, the Caragiale has always been led by a strong-minded artist. Among its artistic directors who have shared in the success of the theatre are Alexandru Davila, Eliade Pompiliu, Victor Eftimiu, Camil Petrescu, Liviu Rebreanu, and Zaharia Stancu. The present artistic director is the noted actor Radu Beligan, president of the Romanian International Theatre Institute and past president of the World International Theatre Institute.

Under Beligan's leadership the company has alternated foreign plays and classics with contemporary Romanian plays. The best productions during the past several years include Samuel Beckett's *Waiting for Godot* (1980), directed by Grigore Gonţa, with scene design by Paul Bortnowski; Barbu Stefanescu-Delavrancea's *Hagi-Tudose* (1981), directed by Ion Cojar, with stage design by the talented painter, Constantin Piliuţa; Albert Camus' *Caligula* (1981), directed by Horea Popescu, with stage design by Paul Bortnowski, and costumes by Doina Lavinţa; Eduardo de Filippo's *Filumena Marturano* (1981), directed by Anca Ovanez-Doroşenco, with stage design by Gheorghe Doroşenco; Mircea Eliade's *Iphigenia* (1982), directed by Ion Cojar, with stage design by Mihai Tohan; and Mayakovsky's *The Bedbug* (1983), and Dale Wasserman's *One Flew Over the Cuckoo's Nest* (1983), both productions directed by Horea Popescu.

ILEANA BERLOGEA and
JOSEPH J. NEUSCHATZ

ION CREANGA THEATRE and LITTLE THEATRE
(Teatrul "Ion Creanga"—Bucureşti and Teatrul Mic)
1 Piata Amzei, Bucharest, Romania

In 1964 the Young Theatre of Bucharest split and formed two theatres: the Ion Creanga Theatre, which specialized in children's theatre; and the Little Theatre (Teatrul Mic), which concentrates on contemporary realistic and psychological dramas.

The Ion Creanga Theatre was officially inaugurated on May 25, 1965, with Ion Lucian's *The Disobedient Little Rooster*. Lucian directed his own works and developed a style for the Creanga Theatre, combining elements of both Romanian folklore and internationally known fairytale lore. It has become Romania's finest theatre for children, thanks largely to Lucian's efforts. Recently, Alecu Popovici, perhaps the most famous author of children's literature in Romania, became artistic director and has continued Lucian's work. The present artistic director is Emil Mandric, former director of the Youth Theatre in Piatra Neamţ.

Among the best of Creanga's productions are Letitia Popa's *The Naughtiness of Pacala*, Carlo Gozzi's *The Stag-King*, Lucian's *The Masked Snoaves*, Alecu Popovici's *The Unfinished Story*, and Vasile Alecsandri's *Sinziana and Pepelea*. The Ion Creanga Theatre has had numerous successes abroad: in Bulgaria (1968–1969), Yugoslavia (1969), Italy (1969), East Germany (1970), Canada (1972), Cuba (1972), the United States (1972), and France (1973).

Mandric has concentrated on a repertoire appealing to young people during the past several years. Outstanding productions of the past few years include Eugene Ionescu's *Images Are Images* (1982), directed by the talented actor, Ion Lucian, who helped adapt Ionescu's witty short stories for the stage, with scene design by Elena Simira-Munteanu; Colin Mortimer's *The Free Fall* (1983), directed by Cornel Todea; and Dumitru Radu Popescu's *The Eagles-Thieves* (1984), directed by Emil Mandric, one of Romania's best directors.

The Teatrul Mic was officially opened on December 23, 1964, with Lillian Hellman's *The Little Foxes*. Today it is considered Romania's finest theatre. Under the direction of Dinu Sararu, the theatre has concentrated on foreign plays and contemporary Romanian dramas. The following are some of the outstanding productions of this unusual theatre: Paul Zindel's *The Effects of Gamma Rays on Man-in-the-Moon Marigolds*, Sławomir Mrożek's *Emigres*, Arthur Miller's

Incident at Vichy, William Gibson's *The Miracle Worker* and *Two for the Seesaw*, and Alan Ayckbourn's *Absurd Person Singular*. Romanian dramatists who have received outstanding productions of their works include Marin Sorescu, Camil Petrescu, Mihail Sadoveanu, and Paul Everac.

Among Mic's actors, the following have given outstanding performances in various roles: Olga Tudorache, Ionescu Gion, Leopoldina Balanuta, Tatiana Iekel, Ion Marinescu, Victor Rebenguic, Octavian Cotescu, and Rodica Tupalaga.

The Teatrul Mic's directors are considered among the best in Romania and have produced some of Bucharest's best productions of the eighties, including Jean Paul Sartre's *The Devil and God* (1982), directed by Silviu Purcarete, with scene design by Adriana Leonescu; Shakespeare's *Richard III* (1983), also directed by Purcarete; and Mikhail Bulgakov's *The Master and Margarita* (1983) and Witold Gombrowicz's *Yvonne, the Princess of Burgundy* (1984), both directed by Cátálina Buzloianu.

The Little Theatre has a still smaller stage (Teatrul Foarte Mic), situated in the center of Bucharest. The Teatrul Foarte Mic is reserved for monodramas and intimate works. One of the best productions during the past few years was Robert Patrick's *Kennedy's Children* (1980), directed by Dragos Galgoțiu, with scene design by Andrei Both.

ILEANA BERLOGEA and
JOSEPH J. NEUSCHATZ

JEWISH STATE THEATRE OF BUCHAREST
(Teatrul Evreiesc de Stat, Bucureşti)
15 Strada Iuliu Barasch
Bucharest, Romania

The Jewish State Theatre was founded on August 1, 1948, in Bucharest. It was largely composed of actors from the postwar Ikuf Theatre. As a result of the success of the Jewish State Theatre, another Yiddish theatre was inaugurated in Iasi in 1976. Based on rich Jewish theatrical tradition, the repertory of the State Theatre includes works from past Yiddish writers as well as plays by contemporary writers. Musical productions alternate with dramatic plays.

The initial production of the group was Sholem Aleichem's *The First Prize Ticket*. Subsequent works included Nikolai Gogol's *The Inspector General*, Haim Sloves' *The Avengers*, Abraham Goldfaden's *The Two Kunilems*, and Schiller's *Intrigue and Love*.

Among the most notable directorial efforts were Mauriciu Seckler (with Brecht's *Mother Courage*), George Teodorescu (with Dürrenmatt's *Frank the Fifth* and Leonid Andreyev's *He Who Gets Slapped*), and Franz Auerbach (the present artistic director, with productions of Ibsen's works and original Romanian comedies and dramas). The most successful productions, however, have been those with roots in the classical Yiddish theatre, especially those of Goldfaden and adaptations of Sholem Aleichem. Mendele Moher Sfarim's *Benjamin the Third* (adapted by Bebe Bercovici and Ion Schwartz) was perhaps the most critically acclaimed of the theatre's productions.

In 1972 the Jewish State Theatre successfully toured the United States with Bebe Bercovici's *A String of Pearls* and Scholom Ansky's *The Dybbuk*. The theatre has also toured Israel and Germany with various musical productions.

The best productions of the eighties include Gogol's *The Diary of a Madman* (1981), directed by (and assuming the lead role) Bebe Bercovici, with scene design by Victor Cretulescu; Max Frisch's *Andorra* (1982), directed by Adrian Lupu, with scene design by Gheorghe and Carmen Rasovski; Osip Dimev's *The Singer of His Own Sorrows* (1982), directed by Adrian Lupu, with scene design by Doina Spiţer; and Dumitru Solomon's *Diogenes the Hound* (1983), directed by Gheorghe Todorescu, with scene design by Marie-Jeanne Lecca.

ILEANA BERLOGEA and
JOSEPH J. NEUSCHATZ

LUCIA STURDZA BULANDRA THEATRE
(Teatrul "Lucia Sturdza Bulandra"—Bucureşti)
Bdul. Schitu Magureanu, Nr. 1
Bucharest, Romania

The Lucia Sturdza Bulandra Theatre was inaugurated in September 1947, under the leadership of Romania's great actress, Lucia Sturdza Bulandra. At the beginning the theatre had only nine actors, including Beate Fredanov, Jules Cazaban, N. Sireteanu, and Sarah Manu. Later, other actors, producers, directors, and scene designers united in their efforts to create a repertory of high quality (involving mainly contemporary pieces and philosophical dramas), joined the group and helped create a theatre now known for its high degree of professionalism.

The initial production was *The Island*, an interesting metaphoric drama by Mihail Sebastian, developing the theme of a need for understanding among people of varied backgrounds. Other impressive contemporary Romanian works included *The Light from Ulmi* by Horia Lovinescu, *Three Generations* by Lucia Demetrius, *Passacaglia* by Titus Popovici, *Those Crazy Show-Offs* by Teodor Mazilu, and *Chitimia* by Ion Baiesu.

The Bulandra also concentrates on contemporary international dramas. Some of the more successful productions included *The Rainmaker* by Richard Nash, *A Streetcar Named Desire* and *The Glass Menagerie* by Tennessee Williams, *Look Back in Anger* by John Osborne, and *The Time of Your Life* by William Saroyan.

Until recently, the Bulandra was in the capable hands of Liviu Ciulei, actor, scene designer, and artistic director. He played a special role in the activities of this theatre. In 1956 he became the spiritual and artistic leader of his generation. His productions were best known for their seriousness of purpose and contemporaneity. Ciulei produced classical works and strove to find theatrical solutions for them. His most famous productions include *Danton's Death* and *Leonce and Lena* by Georg Büchner, *As You Like It* and *The Tempest* by Shakespeare, *Saint Joan* by George Bernard Shaw, *The Threepenny Opera* by Bertolt Brecht, and the Romanian plays *Passacaglia* and *The Strength and the Truth* by Popovici and *The Horia Trial* by Al Voitin.

The Bulandra is the best known of all Romanian theatres. It has made extensive tours abroad: Hungary (1960), USSR (1966), Italy (1969, 1970, 1971), France (1969), West Germany (1970–1971), Yugoslavia BITEF (Belgrade's International Theatre Festival) (1970), England (1971), Belgium (1971), Holland (1971–1972), East Germany (1972), and the United States (1979).

The present roster of actors includes Clody Bertola, Octavian Cotescu, Fory Etterle, Ileana Predescu, Victor Rebengiuc, Petre Gheorghiu, Valy Voiculescu-Pepino, Ion Besoiu, Gina Patrini, Gina Patrichi, Irina Petrescu, Lucia Mara, Stefan Banica, Violeta Andrei, Ion Caramitru, Mariana Mihutz, and Florian Pittis.

The present artistic director is Ion Besoiu. He has managed to continue Ciulei's innovations and has attracted young talent to the company. Some of the best productions of the eighties include Molière's *Tartuffe* (1982) and Mikhail Bulgakov's *Cabal of Hypocrites* (1982), both directed by the young director, Alexandru Tocilescu; and one of Romania's early classics, written in 1830, Iordache Golescu's *Barbu Vacarescul, the Traitor of the Country* (1983), directed by Tocilescu; and Jean-Paul Sartre's *No Exit* (1983), also directed by Tocilescu.

ILEANA BERLOGEA and
JOSEPH J. NEUSCHATZ

PIATRA NEAMT YOUTH THEATRE
(Teatrul Tineretului—Piatra Neamţ)
1 Piata Stefan cel Mare
Piatra Neamţ, 5600, Romania

Best known for its substantial but stable style and repertory, the Youth Theatre was inaugurated in August 1958 as a division of the Bacau Theatre and became an independent entity on July 2, 1961. The Piatra Neamt Youth Theatre was established in response to the industrial boom and the enormous increase of young workers in the area. The inception of this theatre coincides with the artistic debut of a group of new graduates from the I. L. Caragiale Institute for the Theatrical Arts and Cinematography. The actors included Leopoldina Balanuta, Florin Piersic, Cosma Brasoveanu, and George Motoi who arrived in Piatra Neamt to present their graduation productions. Among the plays were Molière's *Les fourberies de Scapin*, Shaw's *Pygmalion*, Aurel Baranga's *The Enraged Lamb*, and Nikolaj Pogodin's *The Kremlin Chimes*. The plays were directed by colleagues from the directing division of the Caragiale Institute.

The artistic quality of the work of these enthusiastic young people was reinforced by the dynamic energy of Ion Coman, the Youth Theatre's first artistic director. Only a handful of the original group of actors has remained with the company, but the Youth Theatre has become an experimental laboratory for artistic creativity, especially for young artists. Besides actors, producers and directors who graduate yearly from the institute gather around the Youth Theatre.

In 1961, when the Youth Theatre became an independent institution, Lucian Giurchescu produced and directed its initial production, Alecu Popovici's *The Boy from the Second Row*. The cast consisted of a new generation of graduates: Eugenia Dragomirescu, Virgil Orgasanu, Traian Stanescu, Radu Voicescu, Ion Bog, Iona Manolescu, Olga Bucataru, Mariana Buruiana, and Alexandru Dabija. A number of these artists rank among the finest talents in Romania today.

In 1965 Ion Cojar received the Award of the Year for his production of Ecaterina Oproiu's *I Am Not the Eiffel Tower*. In 1967 Alecu Popovici's *Outside Is a Painted Fence, Inside Is a Leopard* also received honors. In 1969 Magda Bordeianu, newly graduated, received an award as best director for her production of Paul Cornel Chitic's *Laonic's Personal Chronicle*.

Among the most important productions, the following deserve attention: Brecht's *The Good Woman of Setzuan*, produced by Andrei Serban—now one of the world's finest directors; Eduard Govali's *Youth Without Old Age*, produced by Catalina Buzoianu; and Shakespeare's *The Merry Wives of Windsor*, produced by Alexandru Tocilescu.

When the artistic director Emil Mandric moved to the Ion Crenga Theatre, Gheorge Bunghez took over. He has continued in the tradition established by his predecessors, that is, allowing young talent to take its first professional step. Two of the finest productions of recent years include Shakespeare's *Taming of the Shrew* (1980), directed by Iulina Vişa, with scene design by Judith Fekete-Kotlay; and Evgenij Schwartz's *The Dragon* (1981), directed by the talented young director, Victor Ivan Frunza.

ILEANA BERLOGEA and
JOSEPH J. NEUSCHATZ

TIRGU MURES NATIONAL THEATRE
(Teatrul National—Tirgu Mures)
2 Strada Retezatului
Tirgu Mures, 4300, Romania

The National Theatre in Tirgu Mures is the youngest of Romania's National Theatres. Inaugurated in 1949 as the Hungarian Theatre for the ethnic minority in that region, the theatre was elevated to the rank of a national theatre in November 1978, when Romanian was added to the productions. Today the theatre is recognized as one of the finest bilingual theatres in the world.

Under the direction of Kovacs Gijörgy, who has also received acclaim as an outstanding actor, the Tirgu Mures National Theatre is best remembered for *The Tot Family* and *Cat's Play* by István Örkény (the latter was successfully produced on Broadway in 1976), *The Lost Letter* by I. L. Caragiale, and *The Bourgeoisie* by Maxim Gorky. The theatre's roster of talent includes Andrassy Marton, Varadi Rudolf, and Lohinsky Lorand among the actors; and Tompa Miclosh, Delly Ferenz, and Szabo Ernö among the directors. The present artistic director is Romeo Pojan.

The most notable Hungarian productions in recent years include *A Love* by Berta Lájos and *The Strength and the Truth* by Titus Popovici, both directed by Harag Gheorghe; and *Two Hours of Peace*, by D. R. Popescu, directed by Kincses Elemer, a highly original production in which the subconscious thoughts of the characters in the play are transferred to the audience by means of plastic art.

The Romanian section of the theatre began as an experimental actors' laboratory but has evolved into a major producing unit, largely through the work of Gheorghe Harag, Dan Micu, George Teodorescu, Moni Ghelerter, Alexa Visarion, and other young directors. Among their most noteworthy productions the following have received most acclaim: *Those Sad Angels* and *The Midget from the Summer Garden* by D. R. Popescu; *Hope Does Not Die at Dawn* and *The Night of the Ham-Actors* by Romulus Gutga; *The Big Tailors from Valahia* by Alexandar Popescu; and *The Princess Turandot* by Carlo Gozzi. The focus of each director has been quite an individual one: Dan Micu has concentrated on the purity of neoclassical verse (for example, Racine's *Phaedra*); Alexa Visarion is more preoccupied with political statements (for example, *The Prosecutor* by Gheorge Djagarov); and Gheorghe Harag has developed teamwork among the actors, most notably in Aleksandr Suxovo-Kobylin's *The Death of Tarelkin*.

According to most Romanian critics, the Tirgu Mures National Theatre is one of the finest artistic ensembles in Romania today. It has received some of the finest awards meted out by both critics and governmental agencies. Perhaps the fact that it is situated away from the politically active capital has contributed to its ability to attract some of Romania's finest younger talent.

The best productions of the past few years include (in the Romanian Section) an adaptation of Dostoevsky's *The Brothers Karamazov* (1980), directed and with scene design by Constantin Codrescu; and Ion Drutza's *All We Hold Holy* (1982), directed by Andras Hunyadi; (in the Hungarian Section) Horia Lovinescu's *The Play of Life and Death in the Sand-Desert* (1982), and Joseph Katona's *Bank Ban* (1983), both directed by Kincses Elmer; and Romulus Guga's *The Bourgeois Twilight* (1983), directed by Dan Alexandrescu.

ILEANA BERLOGEA and
JOSEPH J. NEUSCHATZ

VASILE ALECSANDRI NATIONAL THEATRE
(Teatrul National "Vasile Alecsandri"—Iaşi)
18 9th of May Street
Iaşi 6600, Romania

The Vasile Alecsandri National Theatre is Romania's oldest national theatre. Founded in 1840 under the direction of Vasile Alecsandri, Costache Negruzzi, and Mihail Kogalniceanu, the Alecsandri Theatre has the longest continuing theatrical tradition in Romania. Although named the Vasile Alecsandri Theatre, it is also associated with one of Romania's greatest actors, Costache Caragiale, who was one of the first actors to appear on the Iași stage. The city of Iași already had something of a tradition in the performing arts before the inauguration of the Alecsandri Theatre: the first Romanian play was performed there in 1816. In 1835 Grigore Asachi founded the first conservatory dedicated to music and drama in the same city.

The Alecsandri Theatre early stressed comedy and romantic drama. At the end of the nineteenth century the theatre turned to realism and psychological dramas with social themes. Ibsen and Gorky became perennial staples in the repertory. Among the major Romanian dramatists, the most popular were Vasile Alecsandri, Barbu Delavrancea, Victor Ion Popa, Victor Eftimiu, Alexandru Davila, and I. L. Caragiale.

Most of Romania's best actors are associated with the Alecsandri Theatre: before World War I, Aglae Pruteanu and State Dragomir; and before World War II, Constantin Ramadan, Aurel Munteanu, Milutza Gheorghiu, Any Braesky, Margareta Baciu, Stefan Ciubotarasu, Costache Antoniu, and other students of Agatha Baresscu, one of Romania's greatest theatrical pedagogues, long associated with the Iasi Conservatory. Among the outstanding directors during this period were Aurel Ion Maican and Ion Sava, who usually collaborated with Romania's best scene designer, Theodor Kiriacoff Suruceanu.

After World War II the Alecsandri Theatre of Iași immediately went about its business of producing quality plays, this time emphasizing the classics. Young directors gathered around the theatre. Some of the finest productions of the past decade were directed by Romania's younger talents: Brecht's *Mother Courage* by Mauricui Seckus, Euripides' *The Trojan Women* by Anca Ovanez, Sophocles' *Philoctetes* by Aureliu Manea, and Molière's *The Imaginary Invalid* by Cátálina Buzoianu.

During the past few years the company has concentrated on both contemporary Romanian plays and foreign classics. Among the best productions during the past few years were Barbu Stefanescu Delavrancea's *The Sunset (Apús de Soare,* 1981), a Romanian historical drama, directed by Nicoleta Toia, with scene design by Constantin Russu; Dan Nasta's production of Schiller's *Don Carlos* (1981); Jarosław Iwaszkiewicz's *Summer in Nohant* (1981), directed by the Polish director, Jarosław Śletwinski; Vasile Alecsandri's *Chiritza in the Country (Chirița in provincie,* 1982), directed by Alexandru Dabija, with scene design by Laurențiu Dumitrașe; and Shakespeare's *As You Like It* (1983), directed by Nicoleta Toia.

ILEANA BERLOGEA and
JOSEPH J. NEUSCHATZ

Soviet Union

MALY THEATRE
(Maly Teatr SSSR)
(State Order of Lenin Academic Maly Theatre)
Ploščad' Sverdlova, Moscow, USSR

The Maly Theatre or Little Theatre dates from 1824. Long considered an actors' laboratory, it has produced some of the finest actors in Russia. Today its strength lies in the actors of the older generation—Igor Ilyinski, Boris Babochkin, M. I. Zharov, and M. I. Tsarev, among scores of others. The Maly has premiered two of Russia's first great plays: Aleksandr Griboyedov's *Woe from Wit* (*Gore ot uma*) and Nikolai Gogol's *The Inspector General* (*Revizor*). Russia's first great actor and founder of realism on the Russian stage, M. S. Schepkin, appeared in both productions as the governor in *The Inspector General* and as Famusov in *Woe from Wit*.

In the 1850s the Maly began its creative association with Aleksandr Ostrovsky, Russia's first popular dramatist. The Maly became known as the House of Ostrovsky. The actors developed a style that best suited Ostrovsky's plays; the collaboration lasted even after the dramatist's death. The Maly also produced world classic drama, especially Shakespeare, Lope de Vega, Hugo, Schiller, and Molière. Fortunately, the Maly had the actors to perform the great roles of world drama. The most brilliant was Pavel Mochalov, who relied heavily on an "internal" method to inspire a creative mood. Other great actors during this period included A. P. Lensky, Maria Yermolova, Prov Sadovsky, I. Samarin, and S. Schumsky.

The Maly suffered greatly during the early twentieth century and prior to the Revolution. Naturalism and an emphasis on stereotypes lowered the standards of the theatre. It was not until after the Revolution that the Maly was able to regain its former stature. Relying on Soviet plays to develop an audience, the Maly nonetheless did not forsake its classical repertory. Konstantin Trenyov's *Lyubov Yarovaya*, the Soviet warhorse, alternated with Schiller's *Don Carlos* and *Maria Stuart*. Soviet writers, like Leonid Leonov, Maxim Gorky, Boris

Romashov, and Vladimir Bill-Belotserkovsky mixed with Shakespeare, Augustin Scribe, Molière, and Carlo Goldoni.

Ostrovsky was resurrected from 1937 to 1944, when I. Y. Sudakov became artistic director. From 1944 to 1947 Prov Sadovsky, whose family had always been associated with the Maly, was named artistic director. He was followed by K. A. Zubov (1947–1956), M. I. Tsarev (1957–1963) and, finally, E. P. Simonov (from 1963). During their tenure the Maly suffered the consequences of political repression and party hostility: patriotic plays (for example, Aleksandr Korneichuk's *Front* and *Wings*) made up the repertory during the war; later "the cult of personality" and nonconflict themes became a staple of the theatre (for example, Vsevolod Vishnevsky's *The Unforgettable 1919*—a panegyric piece that literally enshrined the living Stalin).

After Stalin's death a number of promising young dramatists appeared on the scene: Victor Rozov (*Before Supper* [*Pered uzhinom*]), Vasili Aksyonov (an adaptation of his short story, *Colleagues* [*Kollegi*]), and G. Mdivani (*Your Uncle Misha* [*Vash djadja misha*]). But as in former times, the actors became a central feature of the Maly. Igor Ilyinski created his greatest characterization as Akim in Tolstoy's *The Power of Darkness* (*Vlast' t'my*, 1956); Babochkin directed and acted in Gorky's *Weekenders* (1964) and Ostrovsky's *Truth Is Good But Happiness Is Better* (1965). M. I. Tsarev directed and acted (together with Ilyinski) in Mikhail Lermontov's *Masquerade*, a production that leaned heavily on the Meyerhold tradition. L. V. Varpakhovsky, a Meyerhold disciple who had been incarcerated in one of Stalin's concentration camps, produced the play. It marked the beginning of the "Meyerhold spirit" at the Maly.

Since 1966, which marked the fiftieth anniversary of the October Revolution, a number of "personality" plays have been produced, including *John Reed* based on the American journalist's chronicle of the Revolution (*Ten Days That Shook the World*). In 1970 a play about Franklin D. Roosevelt was staged, *Man and the Globe* (with Yevgeny Velikhov playing Roosevelt). In 1973 B. I. Ravensky produced Tolstoy's *Tsar Fyodor Ivanovich*, stressing the tsar's reasonableness as a tragic flaw. In 1974 the Maly again revived Ostrovsky's *The Storm*, directed by Babochkin. In a way the Maly remains what it was when it was founded: an actor's theatre with a classical tradition.

After several months of battling the censors, the Maly was allowed to stage Ion Drutse's *The Birds of Our Youth* (*Ptitsy Nashei molodosti*, 1974), a drama that raises the argument that modernization should not take place at the expense of the past. Folk beliefs and the rich culture of Moldavia are emphasized, with the victory of the old over the new.

Following a trend, in 1980 the Maly staged an adaptation of Mikhail Alekseev's *The Unweeping Willow* (*Inushka neplakuchaya*, directed by V.I. Tyukin, with scene design by Yu. N. Ventsel), a "village" novel, a genre extremely popular with the Soviet public. The story is a familiar one: a brave, unsentimental peasant woman is left to guard the home front. She is the "unweeping willow," a stolid individual popular in Soviet literature. The production has become one of the most popular plays in Moscow and has marked a return to folk values in literature. Recent interesting productions include G. Mamlin's *The Bells* (*Kolokola*, 1982), directed by S. B. Dzhimbinovoj, with scene design by E. P. Zmojro; and Gogol's *The Inspector General* (*Revizor*, 1982), directed by E. Ya. Vesinka and Yu. M. Solomina, with scene design by E. I. Kumanjkov.

EDWARD J. CZERWINSKI

MAYAKOVSKY THEATRE
(Moskovskij Akademicheskij Teatr imeni Majakovskogo)
Ul. Herzena 19, Moscow, USSR

Formerly called the Moscow Theatre of Drama (1943–1954) and earlier the Moscow Theatre of the Revolution, the Mayakovsky Theatre is now formally called the Moscow Theatre Named in Honor of Vladimir Mayakovsky. It is aptly named because Mayakovsky was the Poet of the Revolution whose satirical pieces have remained a staple of the theatre's repertory. An outgrowth of the Theatre of Revolutionary Satire, the theatre was abbreviated to TEREVSAT. It was the first such theatre to be formed by a Soviet organization, the Moscow Department of People's Education (MONO). It was set up to provide "entertainment" for political meetings. These "entertainments" consisted of songs, dances, satirical sketches, and agit-prop materials, suited to the political questions dealt with at these meetings. The TEREVSAT was given a permanent home in the building formerly occupied by the Potopkhin's Operetta Theatre, located on Nikitsky Boulevard.

In the beginning the theatre was unable to function professionally. The members were political activists, not actors. It was not until 1923 when Meyerhold became artistic director that the theatre began to flourish. Professional actors rallied to Meyerhold's support. In fact, the entire roster of actors from the Nezlobinsk Theatre joined forces with the young company, including the young designer Victor Shestakov and the composer H. N. Popov, who later became musical director of the Mayakovsky Theatre.

Meyerhold introduced a repertory of new plays emphasizing contemporary themes and stylized staging: Aleksandr Ostrovsky's *Lucrative Post*, V. Volkenstein's *Spartak*, A. Faiko's *Lakes of Lule*, V. Kamensky's *Stepan Razin*, and Ernst Toller's *Man and the Masses* and *The Machine Wreckers* (imprisoned in Bavaria, the German expressionist sympathized with the Revolution). With the development of Soviet drama, Meyerhold added Boris Romashov's *The End of Krivorylsk* and *The Meringue Pie* to the Mayakovsky's repertory.

Meyerhold worked simultaneously in two theatres. In 1924 he left the Mayakovsky to work full time in his own theatre. His student, A. L. Gripich, became the new artistic director. Meyerhold's influence remained until 1930, when Alexei Popov became the artistic director and the theatre of revolution seemed to find its métier. New themes were explored; Soviet life was dissected in such productions as Anatoli Glebov's *Inga* (dealing with the new role of women in society), Nikolaj Pogodin's *Poem About an Ax* (dealing with the struggle against technical backwardness), Vsevolod Vishnevsky's *Battle in the West* (dealing with the working class in Western Europe), and N. Zarkhy's *Gay Street* (dealing with the working-class struggle in England).

When Popov left to become artistic director of the Theatre of the Red Army, the theatre once again lost its bearing. It was not until 1943 when Nikolai Okhlopkov became artistic director that the theatre began to blossom again.

The first thing that Okhlopkov did after the group returned from evacuation was to rename the theatre the Mayakovsky Theatre. At the same time he tried to synthesize all the influences that had acted upon him—Vsevolod Meyerhold, Eugenij Vakhtangov, and Konstantin Stanislavsky. His first notable production was a dramatization of Aleksandr Fadeyev's epic novel, *The Young Guard* (*Molodaya Gvardiya*). The set design by V. Ryndin (consisting of a huge red flag in the background, waving and variously lighted to fit the mood of the moment), effected a brilliant symbolic concept. Subsequent noteworthy productions included Gorky's *Mother* (*Mat'*), Aleksandr Shtein's *Hotel Astoria*, and Ostrovsky's *The Storm*. But the outstanding production during this period remains Shakespeare's *Hamlet*, also designed by Ryndin and directed by Okhlopkov. The symbolic setting (Denmark as a prison was suggested by prison bars behind an iron curtain) and the decision to alternate an experienced actor with an unknown youth (Samoilov) in the role of Hamlet created a disturbance that finally had to be quelled by the censor.

When Okhlopkov died in 1967, after scores of brilliantly conceived productions (Brecht's *Mother Courage and Her Children*, Alexey Arbuzov's *The Irkutsk Story* [*Irkutskaya istoriya*], and his greatest opus, Euripides' *Medea*), his dreams of creating a total theatre of the future died with him. His place was taken by Andrei Gorchakov who has maintained the tradition of a repertory consisting of contemporary and classical plays.

Gorchakov's more daring productions include Tennessee Williams' *A Streetcar Named Desire* (1970), Henry Borovik's *Three Minutes of Martin Crow* (1971), Aleksandr Ostrovsky's *It's All a Family Affair* (*Svoi lyudi—Sochtyomsya*, 1975), Edvard Radzinsky's *Conversations with Socrates* (*Besedy s Sokratom*, 1975), and Ignatij Dvoretsky's *The Farewell* (*Provody*, 1976). In 1979 the Mayakovsky scored a major triumph with the musical adaptation of Nikolai Leskov's *Lady Macbeth of the Mtsensk District* (*Ledi Makbet Mtsenskogo Uyezda*). Besides catchy tunes and a robust chorus line, the musical boasts the beauty and talent of Natalia Gundareva.

The Mayakovsky Theatre has more film and television stars on its roster than any other Soviet theatre. Even so, the theatre has often been singled out for its ensemble playing. Interesting productions during the past few years include Tennessee Williams' *A Streetcar Named Desire* (1980), directed by B. S. Kondratjev, with scene design by Yu. B. Bogoyavlenskij, and music by I. M. Meyerovicha; Williams' *Cat on a Hot Tin Roof* (1981), directed by A. A. Goncharova, with scene design by M. F. Kitaev, and music by I. M. Meyerovicha; and V. Arro's *Look, Who's Come!* (*Smotrite, kto prishol*, 1982), directed by B. A. Morozov, with scene design by A. A. Oparin.

EDWARD J. CZERWINSKI

MOSCOW ART THEATRE
(Moskovskij Xudozhestvennij Akademicheskij Teatr imeni Gorkogo)
(Moscow Art Academic Theatre, named after Gorky)
3 Proezd Xudožestvennogo Teatra, Moscow, USSR

In June 1897, at a historic eighteen-hour session at the Slavic Bazaar, a restaurant in Moscow, Konstantin Stanislavsky and Vladimir Nemirovich-Danchenko agreed to pool their acting companies and form the Moscow Art Theatre. Stanislavsky would train the actors and direct; Nemirovich-Dachenko would manage the theatre, serve as dramaturge, and also direct.

Both artists were disillusioned about the state of the theatre. According to Stanislavsky, they "thought the theatre's situation hopeless, for the brilliant traditions of the past had degenerated into a plain collection of easy technical devices. . . . The theatre was in the hands of dilettantes and bureaucrats." (Paul Gray, "Stanislavski and America: A critical chronology," *Tulane Drama Review* [vol. 9, no. 2, 1964, p. 21].) They intended both to change the art of acting by changing the current style of declamatory and melodramatic posturings and to replace the prevailing mode of drawing room and thesis plays. While selecting their company, they insisted on excluding male and female prima donnas ("She does not love art, but herself in art") and sought artists who lived for their craft ("He has ideals for which he is fighting"). (Gray, p. 22).

In October 1898, the Moscow Art Theatre opened with a disappointing production of Tolstoy's *Tsar Fyodor*. It was not until December 1898 that the company found its métier: Chekhov's *The Seagull* (*Chajka*), which had had a "respectable" premiere in 1896 at the Aleksandrinsky Theatre in Petersburg, was a "colossal" success. The seagull became the logo for the Moscow Art Theatre, and the style of acting ("inner technique") has remained the official artistic method of the Soviet Union to this day.

The company developed ensemble work to perfection. The audience was literally ignored, and the actors concentrated on their characters, bringing psychological depths to the surface and submerging their egos in the characters they were "becoming." The theatre was dedicated to the search for "truth in art," which subsequently developed into what became "Stanislavsky's method."

It is difficult to say what led to the Moscow Art Theatre's unusual success. Certainly, the actors in *The Seagull* (Vsevolod Meyerhold as Treplev, Olga Knipper as Arkadina, and Stanislavsky as Trigorin) had much to do with it. The fact that Théodule Ribot's *Psychologie des Sentiments* had been recently translated (1896) into Russian by F. Pavlenkov and that the company (including Chekhov) were debating the value of "emotional memory" undoubtedly contributed to the excitement of the production. Then, too, Stanislavsky was fortunate in having come across one of Russia's last great geniuses—Anton Chekhov.

Perhaps even a greater success than *The Seagull* came with Stanislavsky's *mise-en-scène* for Gorky's *The Lower Depths* in 1902. Again ensemble playing was emphasized; each detail of the production—actors, costumes, scene design, and so on—was scored as if part of a symphony. Stanislavsky was at the height of his creative powers. Two years later, after continuous attacks by the symbolist poet Valery Bryussov, Stanislavsky felt it artistically imperative to move away from naturalism and seek new theatrical forms. After staging numerous symbolist plays (Hauptmann, Ibsen, and Andreyev), the theatre managed to achieve a degree of success with Maurice Maeterlinck's *The Blue Bird* in 1908.

During this same period Stanislavsky invited Meyerhold back to the Moscow Art Theatre to experiment with new ideas of staging: "The time has come to stage the unreal" (Gray, p. 23), he wrote. But the Meyerhold Revolt, which began in 1902 when Meyerhold left the Moscow Art Theatre, simply exacerbated Stanislavsky's already growing disillusionment. In 1909, after several years of soul-searching, Stanislavsky wrote out the first sketch of his system. Preserved in the theatre's Museum, the forty-six page manuscript was never published but was consulted by members of the company.

Despite the skepticism of members of the company, including Nemirovich-Danchenko, Stanislavsky applied some of his techniques to his production of Ivan Turgenev's *A Month in the Country* in 1909. The success of the play heightened interest in Stanislavsky's system; everyone seemed to contribute something to it, even Maxim Gorky, who suggested to Stanislavsky the possibility of improvisations to develop character and plot spontaneity. In working out the exercises, the actors were taught the uses of the "magic if," of "drawing the circle" and of disciplined concentration. Many of these techniques evolved from Stanislavsky's experiments with yoga. The concept of "prana" was developed, helping the actor transfer his "inner feelings" or "radiance" to the audience. When Stanislavsky formed the First Studio in 1911, yoga became part of the teaching system. He chose Leopold Sulerzhitsky to direct the Studio. The first production was Herman Heyerman's *The Good Hope*, directed by Richard Boleslavsky, who was Gordon Craig's assistant in Moscow when Craig collaborated with Stanislavsky on *Hamlet*. This production, one of the Moscow Art Theatre's more controversial ones, represented a departure for Stanislavsky who by 1911 had decided "to break the chains binding his scenic imagination to naturalistic detail" (Gray, p. 25). He continued, however, to explore the areas of "emotional memory, especially those feelings which are beyond the reach of the conscious mind."

The First Studio gained prominence with Sulerzhitsky's production of Sushkevishch's adaptation of Charles Dickens' *The Cricket on the Hearth* in which Eugenij Vakhtangov, Richard Boleslavsky, and Michael Chekhov appeared. When Sulerzhitsky died in 1916, Vahktangov assumed leadership of the First Studio. At this time, Stanislavsky inaugurated the Second Studio, a school without any formal theatre affiliation, in which students were offered a three-year course of study. Stanislavsky worked closely with the students throughout his life.

During the October Revolution and during the Russian Civil War, the Moscow Art Theatre toured various areas of Russia. In 1919, when General Deniken's White Army had cut off the Moscow Art Theatre troupe which was touring in Southern Russia, several members of the company defected, including Boleslavsky and Maria Germanova, who together established a "Moscow Art Theatre" in Prague.

The following year, 1920, Vakhtangov, after disagreeing with Stanislavsky over the production of *The Festival of Peace*, set up the Third Studio of the Moscow Art Theatre. Vakhtangov continued to act and direct at the First Studio as well. The Third Studio's most successful production was Maeterlinck's *The Miracle of St. Anthony*, directed by Vakhtangov. Before he died in 1922 at the age of thirty-nine, Vakhtangov had managed "to translate Stanislavsky's teachings into highly stylized theatre" (Gray, p. 28), by imposing vivid imagery upon his productions and working through improvisational methodology. As Stanislavsky watched one of Vakhtangov's rehearsals of Carlo Gozzi's *Turandot*, he remarked that his "best pupil was dying."

Stanislavsky's last memorable production was his third staging of Gogol's *The Inspector General*, with Michael Chekhov portraying Khlestakov. It was during this time that the actor argued with Stanislavsky about "emotional memory." Stanislavsky insisted that the technique was useless for Chekhov with his "over-active imagination," but he felt that actors who were not so endowed needed it.

In 1923 the Moscow Art Theatre toured the United States, performing *The Lower Depths*, *The Three Sisters*, and *The Cherry Orchard*. Boleslavsky, who had emigrated to the states in 1922, met the company in New York. The company included Olga Knipper-Chekova, H. Ivan Moskvin, V. I. Kachalov, Leo and Barbara Bulgakov, Akim Tamiroff, Maria Ouspenskaya, and Stanislavsky. Some of them remained in the states, establishing the system in the United States.

Upon the main company's return, it presented its first Soviet play, Konstantin Trenyov's *Pugachev's Uprising*, which proved to be a dismal failure. It was followed by Mikhail Bulgakov's *The Days of the Turbins*, a successful production that was first banned by the censor, and then permitted to be performed after Stalin came to see the play and approved it. Later, the play was banned again, and Bulgakov was proclaimed a nonperson.

After 1927 the theatre produced a number of Soviet plays with blatantly political themes: Vsevolod Ivanov's *The Armored Train*, Aleksandr Afinogenov's *Fear*, Vladimir Kirshon's *Bread*, Gorky's *Yegor Bulyachyov*, and Konstantin Trenyov's *Lyubov Yarovaya*. Along with these Soviet plays, the theatre also successfully produced such plays as Beaumarchais' *The Marriage of Figaro*, Tolstoy's *Resurrection*, and Gogol's *Dead Souls* and *The Inspector General*.

During this period the theatre evolved a number of styles: naturalism (for example, Tolstoy's *The Power of Darkness*), psychological naturalism (Turgenev's *A Month in the Country*), stylization (the plays of Maeterlinck), its own style—psychological realism, and finally what it retains today—Socialist Realism.

After the death of Stanislavsky and Nemirovich-Danchenko, a number of equally talented individuals took control: the actor Ivan Moskvin and the artistic director N. P. Khmelov; and later, the actors Mikhail Kedrov, Viktor Stanitsyn, and Boris Livanov. Livanov's last directing and acting effort was a revival of Gorky's *Yegor Bulyachyov*, a superb triumph for the artist who died shortly afterwards in 1972. His post was assumed by Oleg Yefremov, the director of the Sovremennik (Contemporary) Theatre.

During the past ten years not one Moscow Art Theatre production has received critical acclaim. Even Anotoly Efros' production of Mikhail Roshchin's war play *Echelon* (*Eshelon*, 1975), drew harsh criticism: "He's not a director; he likes to pull strings—and we are not marionettes," one older actress exclaimed. (Related by Nikolaj Rzhevsky in a personal interview.)

One of the few productions which has not received as harsh criticism is Lev Ustinov's *An Island Split in Two* (*Ostrov popolam*, 1979). An almost embarrassing steal from the motion picture *Gulliver's Travels*, the fairytale relates the fate of the inhabitants of an island who have been doomed by a witch to live forever separated on one half of the island. Each side must sing its own song, unable to learn any other. As in all good fairytales, good triumphs, and the two halves learn to sing in harmony.

In 1983 the Moscow Art Theatre competed with the Maly Theatre to adapt a "village" novel for the stage. It chose Valentin Rasputin's *Last Days* (*Poslednye dni*). According to Nikolai Rzhevsky, this popular genre "represents an attempt to amalgamate the optimistic strain of socialist realism with a literary tradition that depends on psychological depth and moral honesty." (Personal interview, 1984.) *Last Days* has proved to be extremely popular with audiences.

Perhaps the Moscow Art Theatre has become too large (over 650 people, including technicians, actors, and musicians). Perhaps the new building to which it moved in 1973, with its huge auditorium seating over 1,350 and its modern electronic equipment that allows simultaneous translations into four languages, has destroyed tradition. On its seventy-fifth birthday, there were rumors that the theatre would move back to its old quarters. Unfortunately, both the old quarters and the new company have become museum pieces.

EDWARD J. CZERWINSKI

MOSCOW DRAMATIC THEATRE ON MALAYA BRONNAYA
(Moskovskij dramaticheskij teatr na Maloj Bronnoj)
Malaya Bronnaya 2, Moscow, USSR

Formerly the Studio of the Maly Theatre, the Moscow Dramatic Theatre was founded in 1922 by graduates of the Maly Theatre School. In its formative years the repertory was indistinguishable from that of its parent theatre, but in 1925–1926 the Studio, headed by F. N. Kaverin, produced *The Cinema Novel* by the German expressionist playwright, Georg Kaiser. In its use of mixed media, the play marked the beginning of a new wave at the small theatre. Style and technique were central in the Studio's productions, which included Shakespeare's *All's Well That Ends Well*, Voltaire's *The Savages*, Vasilij Shkvarkin's *The Pernicious Element*, and E. Vichuri's *Presidents and Bananas*. Because party pressure forced an emphasis on social content, the Dramatic Theatre had to play down form and style. An adaptation of Mikhail Sholokhov's *Virgin Soil Upturned* paved the way for further productions with social messages.

In 1946 the Studio became the Moscow Dramatic Theatre. Sudakov and Kaverin were among its outstanding directors. The Dramatic Theatre's artistic directors included S. A. Mayorov (1946–1957), Andrei Goncharov (1958–1967), and Anatoly Efros (from 1967, when he lost his position at the Moscow Lenin Komsomol Theatre). Efros has been a controversial figure throughout his tenure. His productions have always raised storms of controversy: Edvard Radzinsky's *Kalabashkin the Seducer*, Alexey Arbuzov's *The Happy Days of an Unhappy Man*, and, of course, Chekhov's *The Three Sisters*. The Chekhov play was removed from the repertory after a month because of its "inconsolable pessimism, somber hopelessness of life and distorted vision of the artist."

Efros has since returned to the Dramatic Theatre to direct Gogol's *Marriage*, Molière's *Don Juan*, Viktor Rozov's adaptation of Dostoevsky's *The Brothers Karamazov—Brother Alyosha* (1975).

In 1979, the Malaya scored two of its greatest triumphs with Radzinsky's *Don Juan Continued* and *Lunin, or the Death of Jacques, Written in the Presence of the Master*.

Don Juan was criticized for its staging, a semi-theatre-in-the-round. Moscow audiences are unaccustomed to the venturesomeness common in theatres in the West and even in Poland and Yugoslavia. On the other hand, it is hard to believe that the censor allowed the play to be produced. Efros was making a political statement, or so it would seem to a Western critic of Soviet drama. Radzinsky's two-character play involves role-reversal: Don Juan (now known as D. J.) becomes servant to Leporello's (now known as Leppo Karlovich Rello) master. It is the history of the bourgeoisie.

Radzinsky's *Lunin* is equally controversial, in that the drama presents a powerful picture of uncompromising faith in one's ideals. The time is the Decembrist uprising of 1825. The characters are Lunin and his beloved, a young Polish girl. Based on fact, the play centers around Lunin's recollections of things past, his carefree youth, his reckless growing up, and, finally, the present interrogation and his imprisonment. The play is in the form of a confession, similar to Diderot's *Jacques the Fatalist and His Master*. Radzinsky is proving to be a major force in Soviet literature.

During the 1982–1983 season, Efros staged Chekhov's *The Three Sisters (Tri-*

sestry) with a cast of young actors. Not so daring as the Ljubimov production at the Taganka, Efros' staging was nonetheless effective because of its emphasis on youth versus the older generation.

The Malaya, like the Taganka, has emphasized the development of younger dramatists, who today form the nucleus of a new wave of talent. Among the best of these dramatists are Ljudmila Petrushevskaya, Alexander Volodin, Semyon Zlotnikov, Edvard Radzinsky, and Mikhail Roshchin.

The present artistic director is Alesandr Dunaev, who seems to be following a daring path by associating with Efros. It is ironic that the Dramatic Theatre on Malaya Bronnaya is housed in the building that was once the famous State Yiddish Theatre. Liquidated under Stalin, the theatre will always be remembered: the building contains frescoes painted by Marc Chagall.

Some of the more interesting productions during the past few years include Tennessee Williams' *Summer and Smoke* (1980), directed by A. V. Efros, with scene design by D. A. Krymov (with an exciting performance by O. M. Yakovleva in the role of Alma) and Shelagh Delaney's *A Taste of Honey* (1981), directed by A. S. Spivaka, with scene design by D. A. Krymov.

EDWARD J. CZERWINSKI

MOSCOW KOMSOMOL THEATRE
(Teatr Imeni Leninskogo Komsomola)
(The Moscow Theatre Named in Honor of the Leninsky Komsomol)
Ul. Chekhova 6, Moscow, USSR

Founded in 1928 as a Theatre of Young Workers, the Moscow Komsomol Theatre has always concentrated on plays and performances for young people. In its formative years the productions were both written and improvised; proletarian themes were the main staples of the repertory. In 1933 after the theatre was reorganized under the auspices of the Moscow Art Theatre, I. Y. Sudakov became its director. During his tenure the theatre was united with the Simonov Theatre Studio. Plays of the younger generation were produced, for example, Alexej Arbuzov's *Distant Road*.

The artistic director of the Komsomol Theatre, of course, influenced the repertory. The directors included I. N. Bersenev (1938–1951), S. V. Giatsintova (1951–1963), Anatoly Efros (1963–1967), and Mark Zakharov (1967 to the present). Zakharov is largely responsible for the theatre's recent popularity.

Bersenev alternated plays with contemporary youth themes with classics, such as Tolstoy's *The Living Corpse* (*Zhivoj trup*), Ibsen's *A Doll's House*, and Edmond Rostand's *Cyrano de Bergerac*. On the other hand, during Giatsintova's tenure the emphasis again was on plays for young people. Interestingly, she managed to produce Elmer Rice's *Street Scene* in 1959. But it was not until Efros took over in 1963 that the theatre became truly cosmopolitan.

Efros produced plays with themes that were never seen in the Soviet theatres. These included Viktor Rozov's *On the Wedding Day*, Alexey Arbuzov's *My*

Poor Marat, Edvard Radzinsky's *A Movie Is Being Shot* and *One Hundred and Four Pages of Love*, I. A. Volchek's *A Legal Chronicle*, and Aleksandr Volodin's *Attractions*. Although the plays cannot be compared with the daring experiments in Poland and Czechoslovakia, they nonetheless were a departure from the boring divorced-from-life dramas that permeated the Soviet theatres in the fifties.

Not surprisingly, Efros was severely reprimanded by the censors for deviating from the doctrine of Socialist Realism, with its emphasis on the positive hero and the leading role of the party. When he produced Bulgakov's *Molière*, he was chastized for "consistently developing one theme dear to him—a talent's crown of thorns." He was relieved as artistic director and transferred to the Moscow Gogol Theatre and later to the Moscow Soviet Theatre on Malaya Bronnaya. Zakharov then took over the directorship of the theatre.

The theatre's recent renaissance can be credited to Zakharov who has stressed mixed media in his productions—music, plastic arts, and youthful themes that appeal to young people. The following are some of Zakharov's most successful productions: A. Makarenko's *The Colonists* (1973), Aleksandr Ostrovsky's *The Bride Without a Dowry* (1974), *Till*, an adaptation by G. Gorin of the classic *Till Eulenspiegel* (1974), and, more recently, Mikhail Shatrov's *Blue Horses on Red Grass* (A Revolutionary Etude). A great deal of credit for these productions goes to the scene designers—V. Lalevich and N. Sosunov (*My Poor Marat, The Seagull*, and *On the Wedding Day*); V. Durggen and A. Chernova (*Molière*); and E. Sternberg (*Rock-and-Roll at Dawn*). The Moscow Komsomol Theatre has become one of Moscow's most popular theatres.

In 1982 the Komsomol scored its greatest success with the contemporary operetta *Juno and Avos*, a sentimental tale of unrealized love between a Russian and an American, who becomes California's first nun. Based on a true event, the text by the poet Andrej Voznesensky and the music by Alexander Rybnikov are an interesting blend of Russian folk and American rock.

EDWARD J. CZERWINSKI

PUSHKIN DRAMA THEATRE
(Leningradskij gosudarstvennij dramaticheskij teatr imeni Pushkina)
(The Leningrad State Academic Theatre of Drama)
Ploshchad Ostrovskova, Leningrad, USSR

Formerly one of the imperial theatres, the Alexandrinsky Theatre was renamed the State Academic Theatre (Alexander S. Pushkin) in 1937. Prior to the Revolution, the theatre was considered one of the more experimental of the official theatres. Vsevolod Meyerhold, for example, produced three plays during his formative years: Molière's *Don Juan* (1910), E. Znosko-Borovsky's *The Transfigured Prince* (1910), and Mikhail Lermontov's *Masquerade* (1917). Immediately after the Revolution (1917–1923), the repertory consisted largely of classics (Ibsen, Schiller, and so on), except for a production of Anatolij Lunacharsky's *Faust and the City* (1920).

After 1924 Soviet plays became a common staple of the once classical repertory. For the next seven years over twenty contemporary (Soviet and Western) plays were produced, including Lunacharsky's *Poison*, Boris Romashov's *The End of Krivorylsk*, E. Yanovsky's *Wrath*, Vsevolod Ivanov's *The Armored Train*, Jack London's *Wolf-Spirit*, Somerset Maugham's *Rain*, and two plays by Walter Hasenclever, *The Businessman* and *The Napoleonic Invasion*. It was during this time that the theatre changed its name.

Prior to World War II the Pushkin Theatre, like most Soviet theatres, was forced to conform to the policies of Socialist Realism. The repertory consisted largely of Soviet plays or works that adhered to the official line: glorifying the leading role of the party, nonconflict themes, and criticism of "self" or the country's "enemies," mainly the West. Among the less offensive productions were Gorky's *Enemies*, Aleksandr Korneichuk's *The Wreck of the Squadron*, Aleksandr Afinogenov's *Fear*, and Konstantin Trenyov's *On the Banks of the Neva*. Trenyov's work was interesting for its idealized depiction of Lenin. During the war the theatre was evacuated to Novosibirsk in Siberia. Naturally enough, the repertory consisted of plays with patriotic themes, such as Aleksandr Korneichuk's *Front*, Konstantin Simonov's *The Russian People* (*Russkye ljudi*), and Leonid Leonov's *Invasion* (*Nashestvye*). The theatre moved back to Leningrad in 1944. For the next ten years, except for occasional productions of Russian classics, the repertory consisted of "nonconflict dramas." During this Stalinist period even *Hamlet* was banned, as were *Othello* and *Romeo and Juliet*.

In 1955 the Pushkin Theatre began to show signs of life with the premiere of Vsevolod Vishnevsky's *The Optimistic Tragedy* (*Optimisticheskaya tragedia*), directed by the talented Georgij Tovstonogov. Shortly thereafter, with Stalin's death, the theatre became less oppressed. Mikhail Bulgakov's *Flight* (*Beg*), with Nikolai Cherkassov in the leading role, signaled the beginning of the thaw.

Even contemporary plays found a place once again in the theatre's repertory. Miller's *Death of a Salesman* and Brecht's *The Good Woman of Setzuan* were given excellent productions. Georgij Tovstonogov's best work included premieres of Chekhov's *The Three Sisters* (*Tri sestry*), Aleksandr Griboyedov's *Woe from Wit* (*Gore ot uma*), and Gorky's *Smug Citizens* (*Meshchane*).

During the past ten years Tovstonogov has been largely responsible for making the Pushkin Theatre the center of high art. He either directed or produced the following productions: Aleksandr Vampilov's *Provincial Anecdotes* (*Provintsialnye anekdoty*), (directed); A. Tsagareli's *Khanuma*, a Georgian vaudeville (produced); Aurel Baranga's *Public Opinion*, a Romanian revue (produced); Viktor Rozov's *Situation* (*Polozhenie*) (directed); and Tolstoy's *The Story of a Horse* (*Khostolmir*) (directed).

The Pushkin's artistic policies have been dictated by a number of directors, including Georgij Tovstonogov, I. O. Gorbachev, A. F. Borisov, Y. V. Tolubeyev, and B. A. Fokeyev. As with all Soviet ensembles, it is difficult to outline a programmatic statement for any group, since the voice of art is supposedly the voice of the party. Nonetheless, individuals manage to be heard without saying a word: Tovstonogov makes such statements in each of his productions. His work is characterized by deep social consciousness, an inner harmony, and an adherence to artistic form.

EDWARD J. CZERWINSKI

SOVREMENNIK (CONTEMPORARY) THEATRE
(Sovremennik Teatr)
Čhistye Prudy 16, Moscow, USSR

Founded in 1956 by Oleg Yefremov and graduates of the Moscow Art Theatre Institute, the Sovremennik has emphasized a contemporary Soviet repertory and has occasionally included Western dramas. The plays have dealt with themes of the younger generation. Young Soviet authors have been nurtured by Yefremov, who in 1971 gave up his post to assume the role of artistic director at the Moscow Art Theatre where he received his early training.

Among Soviet authors who have developed their craft at the Sovremennik are A. Volodin (*Two Flowers*, 1959; *My Older Sister*, 1962 and the controversial play, *The Appointment*, 1963); V. Tendryakov (*Without a Cross*, 1963); Viktor Rozov (*Alive Forever*, 1961 and *On the Wedding Day*, 1964); and Vasili Aksyonov (*Always on Sale*, 1965). Among contemporary foreign dramatists, the following have been produced: William Gibson (*Two for the Seesaw*, 1962); John Osborne (*Look Back in Anger*, 1965); and Edward Albee (his dramatization of Carson McCuller's novel, *The Ballad of the Sad Café*, 1967). Among Yefremov's most successful productions are the adaptation of Ivan Goncharov's *An Ordinary Story* (1966); and his trilogy, produced in 1967, that explored the nature of the Revolution and its aftermath—*The Decembrists* (Leonid Zorin), *The Populists* (A. Svobodin), and *The Bolsheviks* (Mikhail Shatrov).

The Sovremennik attempted many productions that never reached the boards, including, in the early sixties, Aleksandr Solzhenitsyn's *The Love-Girl and the Innocent*. The play and its author were subsequently banned. Many productions were produced after great difficulty, including Evegenij Schwartz's *The Emperor Has No Clothes* (1973), Shatrov's *Tomorrow's Weather* (1974), and Chingiz Aitmanov and Kaltai Mukhamedzhanov's *The Ascent of Mount Fuji* (1974). The last-named had its U.S. premiere in 1975, produced by the Arena Theatre in Washington, D.C. Shakespeare's *Macbeth*, directed by the Latvian director Jonas Jonasis, failed to impress the censors, especially since Jonasis insisted that the Three Witches should appear in the nude.

In 1975 the English director Peter James was invited to direct *Twelfth Night*, which reached the boards in spite of scenes with partial nudity. In the same year the Soviet director Galina Volchok directed *Eshelon* (*Echelon*) by Mikhail Roschin. The production was far more successful than the Moscow Art Theatre's more realistic presentation of the play which was produced simultaneously.

In 1982 Galina Volchok, in competition with Anatoly Efros at the Malaya Bronnaya and Yuri Ljubimov at the Taganka, staged a rather shrill production of Chekhov's *The Three Sisters*, in which the acting seemed more compatible with the American Lee Strasberg's method than with the Russian Stanislavsky's system. Nonetheless, the staging received good reviews and has been popular with audiences.

The following are among the company's artists: L. Tolmachova, A. Pokrovskaya, and Galina Volchok—the outstanding and controversial director; Y. Yevstigneyev, I. Kvasha, M. Kazakov, and Oleg Tabakov—who took over as artistic director in 1972. Among the Sovremennik's best scene designers were P. Kirillova, S. Barkhin, M. Anikst, D. Borovsky, B. Blanc, B. Messerer, M. Kunin, and M. Ivnitsky.

Outstanding productions of recent years include Ibsen's *Enemy of the People* (1974), directed by I. S. Ungurijanu, with scene design by M. F. Kitajev; Mikhail Bulgakov's *Cabal of Hypocrites* (*Kabala svjatosh*, 1981), directed by I. Kvasha, with scene design by B. Birger and P. Sapegin; and Chekhov's *Three Sisters (Tri sestry*, 1982), directed by G. Volchok, with scene design by P. Kirillova and V. Zajtseva.

EDWARD J. CZERWINSKI

TAGANKA THEATRE
(Teatr dramy i komedii na Taganke)
Moscow Theatre of Drama and Comedy
Taganskaja ploščad' (square), Moscow, USSR

Considered the Soviet Union's finest theatre, the Taganka was founded in 1964 by Yuri Lyubimov. Originally intended as an experimental theatre attached to the Vakhtangov Theatre, the Taganka was to incorporate the theories of Bertolt Brecht, Vsevolod Meyerhold, and Evgenij Vakhtangov. The initial production, Brecht's *The Good Woman of Setzuan*, utilized the various contributions of the three theoreticians.

But it was obvious during the following year that the Taganka was more than a mere duplication of past achievements. Lyubimov's staging of John Reed's *Ten Days That Shook the World*, a play that was banned during the Stalinist era, indicated the direction the Taganka was to follow. Lyubimov experimented in mixed media, adding music, choreography, pantomime, and film projections. In order to neutralize the censors, he included a quotation from the writings of Krupskaya, Lenin's wife: "John Reed's book is a kind of epic poem." Still, the text was censored, and a number of leading revolutionaries, including Leon Trotsky, were omitted from the play.

Subsequent plays ran into similar difficulty, supposedly because of their "modern treatment." Each had to be rewritten to conform to the censor's vision of literature. These included Vladimir Mayakovsky's *Listen!* (1967), based on the poems that stressed Mayakovsky's attacks on bureaucracy; Brecht's *The Life of Galileo* (1967); Andrej Voznesensky's *Watch Your Faces* (banned after two performances); Serġej Esenin's *Pugachov*; Molière's *Tartuffe* (1969), which heavily emphasized the hypocrisy in society; Boris Vasiliev's anti-Nazi play, *The Dawns Are Quiet Here* (1971); *Anti-Worlds* (1974), based on Voznesensky's poems; and Evgenij Evtushenko's *Under the Skin of the Statue of Liberty* (1975).

More recently, Lyubimov has come under attack from the city administration for his production of *Hamlet*, which included Hamlet in a sweater, playing a guitar, and singing a poem on Hamlet from Pasternak's banned novel, *Doctor Zhivago*. The dramatization of Mikhail Bulgakov's satirical novel, *The Master and Margarita*, was finally staged on April 6, 1977. Earlier in 1975 Lyubimov took further chances by allowing Anatoly Efros to direct *The Cherry Orchard*. Efros is currently director of the theatre after Lyubimov's departure to the West.

On July 28, 1980, the Taganka became the center of another type of controversy when over twenty thousand people gathered around the theatre in Taganka Square to honor the memory of Vladimir Vysotsky, the popular balladeer and actor, who died on July 26. There is little doubt that the Taganka has become a symbol of freedom in the arts in the Soviet Union.

In 1981–82 Chekhov's *The Three Sisters* was staged by three of the finest directors in the Soviet Union: Anatoly Efros at the Malaya Bronnaya Theatre, Galina Volchok at the Contemporary Theatre, and, perhaps the most daring of the three, Yury Ljubimov at the Taganka. The production was a multimedia event: stage-left was a soldiers' barracks room with iron cots, stage-right was a lectern from which actors delivered introspective soliloquies, the backdrops were covered with frescoes reminiscent of Andrej Rublev (one was actually opened out to the streets of Moscow), and the recorded voices of past great actors often began the more famous soliloquies.

For theatricality and originality, *The Three Sisters* was rivaled only by Ljubimov's 1983 production of Pushkin's *Boris Godunov*. Ljubimov sought to achieve textual coherence by simple staging—an iron staff, a metaphor for political power, and a wooden table, which becomes simultaneously a field of battle and, in the end, Boris' coffin. But the message is clear: Boris' tragedy is everyman's tragedy. The play has been removed from the repertory, and the director of the Taganka has been asked to resign. Ljubimov's plans to stage *Vladimir Vysotsky* will never be realized; he decided to remain in the West in 1983.

Ljubimov, the doyen of Soviet directors, made the Taganka the center of quality theatre in the Soviet Union. In the summer of 1983 he was invited to London to direct his adaptation of Dostoevsky's *Crime and Punishment*. The highly acclaimed production was criticized in the Soviet Union because Ljubimov portrayed Raskolnikov as a morally reprehensible character rather than as a victim of the corrupt tsarist government. In 1978 Ljubimov was refused permission to direct *The Queen of Spades* at the Paris Opera. Other invitations to direct abroad have also been viewed negatively by Soviet authorities. According to John Nordheimer in an article in the *New York Times* (Sept. 13, 1983, p. C-17), Ljubimov was greatly dissatisfied with the attitude of the Soviet censors: ''I am 65 years old and I simply don't have the time to wait until these government officials finally arrive at an understanding of a culture that will be worthy of my native land.''

Interesting productions during Ljubimov's tenure included Yuri Karyakina's adaptation of Dostoevsky's *Crime and Punishment* (*Prestuplenie i nakazanie*, 1979), directed by Ljubimov, with scene design by D. Borovsky; Chekhov's *The Three Sisters* (*Tri sestry*, 1981), directed by Ljubimov, with scene design by Yu. Kononenko, and music by E. Denisov; and *Five Stories by Isaac Babel* (*Pjat rasskazov I. Babelja*, 1981), directed by E. Kucher, with scene design by B. Karafelov.

EDWARD J. CZERWINSKI

Yugoslavia

ATELIER 212
(Atelier 212)
Ul. Lole Ribara 21
Belgrade, Yugoslavia

Atelier 212, located in the center of Belgrade, was founded in 1956 by Mira Trailović, one of the most dynamic and innovative theatrical personalities in Eastern Europe. Together with Jovan Ćirilov, her dramaturge and literary advisor, Trailović has developed a company of actors, dramatists, and directors that ranks among the best in Europe.

Employing over one hundred people, thirty of whom are actors, Trailović has concentrated exclusively on avant-garde theatre. In September 1967 she and Ćirilov inaugurated Belgrade's International Experimental Theatre Festival. Practically every important major theatrical company in the world has appeared at one of the festivals since its inception, including La Mama, Peter Brook's company, Józef Szajna, Tadeusz Kantor, Jerzy Grotowski, Otomar Krejča, Eugenio Barba's company, Peter Schumann, Robert Wilson, and the Living Theatre.

Atelier 212 is made up of two theatres: the Great Stage (seating four hundred) and the Theatre in the Cellar (seating one hundred). Except for a summer vacation, the repertory company operates throughout the year, concentrating on new world dramatists, as well as young Yugoslav playwrights. With the help of Borislav Mihajlović and Borka Paćićević, who joined the company as dramaturges in the early seventies, Atelier 212 has nurtured some of the best writing talent in Yugoslavia, the most outstanding of which is Aleksandar Popović.

Popović is the only Yugoslav dramatist who has ever had four plays running in repertory during a single season. The plays were *Piggy Trot* (*Krmeči kas*, 1966), *The Damascus Sword* (*Sablja dimiskija*, 1967), *Bora the Tailor* (*Razvojni put Bore Snajdera*, 1968), and *Deadly Motorism* (*Smrtonosna motoristika*, 1968). When Atelier 212 made its guest appearance at Lincoln Center in 1968, through the auspices of William Jovanovich of Harcourt Brace Jovanovich, *Bora the*

Tailor was presented and received favorable reviews from most of the New York critics.

Popović is probably the best example of Atelier 212's policy of nurturing native talent. The Serbian dramatist is probably the most produced contemporary playwright in Yugoslavia, but he is also the most controversial figure in theatrical circles. Self-educated, Popović has fought hard for recognition, often with Trailović and Ćirilov. In the late sixties, he set up his own theatre company and produced his play, *Second Door Left* (*Druga vrata levo*). He directed the American premiere of the play at La Mama Theatre in 1969. It was the first Yugoslav play to employ total nudity on the stage.

Popović's plays rely heavily on Serbian language and culture; they are difficult to translate into another culture. Trailović realized that Popović was a Serbian phenomenon and allowed him to develop without restraints. Father of four girls, Popović was greatly influenced by his wife, Danica, who has of late become a theatrical personality through stage appearances in her husband's works.

For a number of years Popović was identified solely with Atelier 212. The company developed as he developed. It was during this time that Trailović formulated her philosophy to present only avant-garde theatre, for Popović had proved that there was an audience prepared to accept the most unexpected, even bizarre, works of artists.

Significantly, Beckett's *Waiting for Godot* was Atelier 212's first production, and it has remained in the repertory to the present day. The following writers have been added to the repertory: Jean-Paul Sartre, William Faulkner, Eugene Ionesco, Sławomir Mrożek, Harold Pinter, Tadeusz Różewicz, Adamov, James Joyce, Alfred Jarry, T. S. Eliot, Jean Genet, Witold Gombrowicz, Mikhail Bulgakov, and Peter Weiss. Among Yugoslav dramatists, besides Popović, Atelier 212 has produced works by Miodrag Pavlović, Bora Ćosić, Dušan Kovačević, and Danilo Kiš. Some of Yugoslavia's best directors have worked with the company, including the film director Radoš Novaković, Bojan Stupica, and from the younger generation, Ljubomir Draškić, Zoran Ratković, Ljubiša Ristić, Arsa Jovanović, Paolo Magelli, and the well-known film director, Saša Petrović.

During the first phase of its development, Atelier 212 was located in a makeshift building that seated 212 spectators. The present building was designed by Bojan Stupica (1910–1970), one of Yugoslavia's best directors, who was also the theatre's first theorist. The name Atelier 212 originated with its first site. In 1964 Trailović became director of the theatre and helped shape its present artistic policy.

Trailović continues to search for new talent, although she prefers writers from other genres who have little experience as dramatists but who are known artists in other areas of literature. She has directed a number of contemporary plays, among them, Edward Albee's *Who's Afraid of Virginia Woolf?*, Sartre's *No Exit*, Ionesco's *The Chairs*, Eliot's *The Cocktail Party*, Rado-Ragni-McDermott's *Hair*, Tom Stoppard's *Jumpers*, and Witkacy's *Mother*.

Although Atelier 212 has a comparatively small group of actors (thirty),

Trailović invites actors from other theatres in order to give variety to her repertoire. The style she and Atelier's other directors have developed has often been described as grotesque, with an emphasis on realism which the actor's presence brings to the play.

Atelier 212 has achieved a prominent position among theatres in Eastern Europe through its sponsorship of BITEF, the International Theatre Festival. Since 1967 the festival has hosted practically every significant theatrical group in the world. During its first three seasons, such outstanding groups as the following appeared: Jerzy Grotowski's Laboratory Theatre; Jan Grossman and Otomar Krejča from Prague; Józef Szajna from Poland; Luca Ronconi, Richard Schechner, Peter Schumann, Victor Garcia, and Georgij Tovstonogov from the Soviet Union; and the Royal Court Company. A special theme is usually emphasized: the classics in our times, free forms, space beyond the stage, new experience, the actual text, post-avant-garde, and between myth and reality. Among the more outstanding recent productions presented at Belgrade's International Experimental Theatre Festival (BITEF) were Tadeusz Kantor's *The Dead Class* (1977), Yuri Ljubimov's *Hamlet* (1976), Robert Wilson's *A Letter for Queen Victoria* (1974) and *Einstein on the Beach* (1976), Andrei Serban's *Greek Trilogy* (1975), Ingmar Bergman's *To Damascus* (1974), Pina Bausch's *Macbeth* (1979), Peter Stein's *Class Enemy* (1981), Jerzy Jarocki's *On Foot* (1981), Alexander Lang's *Danton's Death* (1982), and Janusz Wiśniewski's *The End of Europe* (1983). Three unusual approaches to Shakespeare's *Midsummer Night's Dream* (Peter Brook, Lindsay Kemp, and Robert Ciulli) received high praise during the past ten years.

The company's actors and actresses include the following: Zoran Radmilović, Ružica Sokić, Danilo Stajković, Mira Vanjac, Dragan Nikolić, Bora Todorović, and Jelisaveta Sablić.

Atelier 212 is constantly invited to tour abroad. Among the countries visited have been the following: the United States (Lincoln Center, New York), France, the Soviet Union, Italy, Iran, Mexico, Venezuela, Poland, Czechoslovakia, Hungary, Romania, Sweden, Bulgaria, West Germany, and Switzerland.

EDWARD J. CZERWINSKI

CHAMBER THEATRE '55
(Kamerni Teatar '55)
(formerly Male Pozorište—The Little Theatre)
Ul. Maršala Tita 56/II
71000 Sarajevo, Yugoslavia

Male Pozorište, The Little Theatre, was founded March 7, 1955, when the political climate became favorable to departure from Socialist Realism. The Little Theatre, because of continuous confusion with other "little theatres," finally changed its name in 1971 to Kamerni Teatar '55 (the Chamber Theatre '55). The driving force behind this excellent theatre was Jurislav Korenić (1915–1974).

The present managing director is Slavko Šantić, who is filled with an energy and enthusiasm that spills over into every area of the Chamber Theatre's activities—from selecting guest artists to supervising clean-up details after a performance. Because of his love of theatre, especially the avant-garde and new trends, and because of his sympathetic but no-nonsense bearing, Šantić has been able to continue developing an excellent ensemble, despite present economic difficulties. He has been ably assisted by the theatre's dramaturge, Slavko Milanović, a young man with an excellent command of English.

An amphitheater with about 150 permanent seats, the theatre's acting space resembles the cramped quarters often found in New York's off-off-Broadway theatres. Miraculously, the space is always ample and used by each guest director as an experimental challenge. The theatre has no problems in obtaining the services of some of the best young directors in Yugoslavia, and in Eastern Europe. Judging by the present quality of performance and production (1983–1984), the Chamber Theatre's reputation is justly deserved. One is tempted to call it the finest ensemble group in Yugoslavia. Perhaps because it is far from Belgrade, it seldom is given the publicity accorded theatres in the capital city, such as Atelier 212 or Zagreb's ITD. Nevertheless, it has an impressive history.

Like Poland, Yugoslavia began to shake off its traditional image of staging "tractor dramas" in 1955–1956. It is interesting to note that the Chamber Theatre was in the forefront of the avant-garde, together with Atelier 212's Mira Trailović. The Chamber Theatre's first production was Herman Wouk's *The Caine Mutiny Court Martial* in 1955, and its emphasis since has been on modern trends in drama and developing young dramatists in Yugoslavia. Like most avant-garde theatres, the emphasis is on youth.

However, the two pillars of the Chamber Theatre's ensemble are two older character actors who are as professional as any in the world. Ines Fančović and Milenko Vidović are two favorites of Yugoslav audiences, since both regularly appear in movies and on television. These two actors can best be compared to two American actors, Bea Arthur and Spencer Tracy. They have been with the company for over twenty-five years and are actors from whom the others learn their trade.

The formative years of this ensemble were marked by a heavy dose of foreign plays, from George Büchner's *Danton's Death* (1957) to Bertolt Brecht's *The Threepenny Opera* (1960). These were followed by a number of American plays, including Edward Albee's *A Delicate Balance* (1968), Paul Zindel's *The Effect of Gamma Rays on Man-in-the-Moon Marigolds* (1973), and one of the theatre's most popular comedies, Murray Schisgal's *Luv*, which had an off and on run of over five years from 1967 to 1972.

Some of the most successful productions during the past ten years have included the following: Ivo Brešan's *The Unforgettable Production of Hamlet in the Village of Mrdusa Donja* (*Nezapamčena predstava Hamleta u selu Mrduša Donja*, 1972); Samuel Beckett's *Endgame* (1973); Rudi Šeligo's *Beautiful Vida* (*Lepa Vida*, 1980); Dušan Jovanović's *The Karamazovs* (1981); Goran Stefanovski's *Proud Flesh* (*Divo meso*, 1981) and his *Hi-Fi* (1982); Sławomir Mrożek's *Tango* (1982); Franc Ksaver Krec's *Neither Fish nor Meat* (*Niti riba niti mesa*, 1982, directed by the talented Egon Savin); and Vlado Gačina and Mirko Ljubojević's *Honda Blues* (1983).

The company regularly tours the provinces and has successfully toured in Italy, Hungary, Guatemala, Mexico, and the Soviet Union.

Young Yugoslav writers are now a prime concern of the theatre. During the formative years established Yugoslav dramatists such as Miroslav Krleža and Miodrag Žalica were regularly produced. Today the repertory includes a majority of young Yugoslav writers such as Nikola Koljević, Safet Plakalo, Borislav Pekić, Božidar Ljumović-Zuba, Velimir Stojanović, Matjaž Kmecl, Bratislav Petković, Vojin Kajganić, Rudi Šeligo, Goran Stefanovski, Dušan Jovanović, and Milica Novković.

The Chamber Theatre has a policy of inviting guest directors from all parts of Yugoslavia as well as from other countries. Poland's Tadeusz Minc repeated his successful Warsaw production of Tadeusz Różewicz's *White Marriage* in 1979. He was first invited to direct Sławomir Mrożek's *Emigrés* in 1976 and Witold Gombrowicz's *The Ritual* in 1977. He returned again in 1982 to direct Velimir Stojanović's *Fruit Day* (*Vočni dan*).

Some of Yugoslavia's finest directors have been invited as guest directors: Marko Fotez, Josip Lešić, Žarko Petan, Katarina Dorić, Milan Kosovac, and Zvone Šedlbauer.

Scene designers have also been eager to experiment with the theatre's minuscule acting area. The following have had success with their work: Ivica Bilek (Ilf and Petrov's *The Golden Calf*), Vlado Dobrović (*The House of Bernarda Alba*), Vlada Lalicki (*A Delicate Balance*), Strahinja Petrović (Dostoevsky's *The Idiot*), Matjaž Vipotnik (Pinter's *The Birthday Party*), and, of course, the remarkably serviceable set created for the latest production, *Quarantine*, by Miroslav Bilać and by his costume designer, Ozrenka Mujezinović.

Actors are also invited to appear in certain roles. The list includes the Metropolitan Opera coloratura, Gertruda Munitić, as Viola in Shakespeare's *Twelfth Night*; Ratko Petković; Rudi Alvadj; Maja Dimitrijević; Vlajko Šparavalo; Drakče Popović; Boris Smoje; Ismet Pašić; Dušica Manzalović; Sabina Kajanac; Saša Vojtov; Zoran Rankić; Mile Pani; and Luka Delić.

The present members of the ensemble include the following: Faruk Sofić, Jasa Beri, Jasna Diklić, Žana Jovančić, Firdaus Nebi, Vlado Gačina, Ravijojla Jovancić, Vesna Mašić, Vera Milovanović, Hranislav Rašić, Zijah Sokolović, Dara Stojilković, Aleksandar Vojtov, Zvonko Zrnčić, Miralem Zupčević, and, of course, Milenko Vidović.

Past actors of the company include such Yugoslav notables as Uroš Kravljača, Nada Djurevska, Zoran Bečić, Aleksandar Mičić, Vera Pregarc, Marija Aljinović, Olivera Kostić, Zvonko Marković, and Branko Rabat.

In addition to founding the Festival of Small and Experimental Theatres in 1967, the Chamber Theatre '55 was responsible for setting up the first drama studio in Bosnia-Herzegovina in 1967, which is now a bona-fide department of the University of Sarajevo.

It is with one of their most recent productions that the Chamber Theatre has paved the way for other groups to follow. Živojin Pavlović's *Karantina* (*Quarantine*, 1983), directed by Egon Savin, is a remarkable work from various points of view. The production marks a return to naturalism; but, unlike the style of the fifties, it has an entirely different emphasis. The style is greatly influenced by television and the "living-room" atmosphere that the theatre and stage suggest. The audience in the amphitheatre is part of a closely knit family. One cannot help murmuring comments into a neighbor's ear as the action progresses and audience involvement is generated. It soon becomes a family affair, much like television viewing at home.

And yet it is far from family entertainment. The Chamber Theatre caters to adult fare. In *Quarantine*, the following scenes are graphically and realistically enacted: a young man urinates into a bowl and soaks a rag in the urine in order to disinfect objects around him; the same young man takes off his pants and performs a sexual act on the upper torso of an older woman; another young man rapes a woman as the lights slightly dim; another young lady defecates into a bowl, which in turn is emptied in full view of the audience into a chest; and, finally, a young lady commits suicide, her blood splattering bright red on the window separating the acting area and the sound-booth. It should be kept in mind that members of the audience are only inches from the action.

Certainly film techniques are employed in this production, but more significantly, one senses the influence of the "television family" in his living-room. This aspect of the production deserves attention: it very well may be the direction of future theatre—chamber audiences, television-like sets, and most importantly, a realism that reflects today's family fare on television. Audiences today have been educated by what they see on the screen: the theatre carries the process one step further, that is, what "seems" on television becomes "actual" on the stage. The audience is forced to react in the theatre because it is happening "next" to them. At home, they can leave the room: in the Chamber Theatre, they are forced to stay and suffer.

Most of the credit for this new trend in theatre goes to Egon Savin, who, at twenty-eight, promises to become one of Yugoslavia's major directorial talents.

EDWARD J. CZERWINSKI

THE CROATIAN NATIONAL THEATRE
(Hrvatsko Narodno Kazalište)
Trg Maršala Tita 15
Zagreb, Yugoslavia

Like most venerable institutions, the Croatian National Theatre has a profile that is readily recognizable and difficult to change. Since it is a government-subsidized organization, it must serve the people. The general policy, therefore, is to produce national and international classics for general consumption, that is, to educate the young and satisfy the tastes of the older generation. The Chamber Theatre, the second stage of the National, leans toward intimate works and is somewhat experimental in nature. Modern writers, both local and foreign, are often produced in the small theatre.

The Croatian National Theatre, whose roots go back to 1860, settled into the present building—a smaller, but no less opulent, version of the Opera House in Vienna—with the intention of developing a Croatian Theatre whose main purpose was to stage world classics. In its present format, the theatre produces operas, ballets, and dramas in repertory. The Chamber Theatre is solely used for dramatic performances.

The present managing director is Vjekoslav Vidošević. He is responsible for the drama section of the National Theatre, a company that totals over one hundred artists and technicians.

Almost every major Croatian actor has appeared on this stage. From past generations, the most notable are the following: Zinka Kunc-Milanov (the glory of the Metropolitan in the forties, as was Milka Trnina before her), Maja Strozzi, Tito Strozzi, Vila Mosinger, Milan Orlović, Ivona Petri, Vika Podgorska, Irma Pollak, Arnošt Grund, Ervina Dragman, Ruža Cvjetičanin, Sofija Borštnik, and Bianka Dežman.

The actors that make up part of the present company include Boris Buzančić, Zlatko Crnković, Saša Dabetić, Ivka Dabetić, Mira Furlan, Eliza Gerner, Dragan Milivojević, Mustafa Nadarević, Božidar Orešković, Neva Rošić-Lonza, Zvonimir Zoričić, Mira Župan, and Koraljka Hrs.

Past and present directors include some of Yugoslavia's most prominent artists: Georgij Paro, Kosta Spaić, Božidar Violić, Irica Kunčević, Petar Sarčević, Mladen Skiljan, and Vjekoslav Vidošević.

The company tours Yugoslavia regularly and has visited Italy, West Germany, Austria, and the Soviet Union.

The theatre was not in operation from 1967 to 1969, during which time the building was completely renovated and its facilities modernized. The staging facilities are among the best in Europe and certainly comparable to those of any Broadway house. The revolving stage offers limitless opportunities to the director, and scene and costume designers, but is a challenge to the lighting designer and crew, as lighting instruments are rather primitive and highly inadequate.

The most notable productions during the past fifteen years include: Ibsen's *Peer Gynt*; Ranko Marinković's *Cyclops* (*Ciklop*) and *The Desert* (*Pustinja*); Ivo Vojnović's *The Dubrovnik Trilogy* (*Dubrovačka trilogia*); Marin Držić's *Uncle Maroje* (*Dundo Maroje*); Sartre's *No Exit*; Miroslav Krleža's *Golgotha* (*Golgota*), *Silesia* (*Galicija*), and *Banquet in Blitva* (*Banket u Blitvi*); Maxim Gorky's *The Lower Depths*; and Gogol's *The Inspector-General*.

Three productions received highly favorable reviews during the past two seasons: Radovan Ivšić's *Ajaxaja, or The Power of Words* (*Aiaxaia ili moći reči*, 1983); Molière's *The Misanthrope* (1983); and Rostand's *Cyrano de Bergerac* (1983).

The management foresees no future changes in policy for the Chamber Theatre, except a greater emphasis on experimentation. On the other hand, the National's production of *Ajaxaja* suggests a change in programming, if not in policy itself. The text of this futuristic drama is based on the story of Ajax, a hero from Greek mythology, and Xaja, a woman from a distant future, and the battle waged between the so-called "protectors" of the word—tradition in literature and in the arts—and the boorish "motorcycle riders" of the future-present, who destroy each other in the climactic scene. Their remains are viewed by a child on a skateboard who declares: "In my view, the battle wasn't bloody enough. I'd have one even more gory."

The play is in defense of words, which according to Ivšić are losing their meaning in all areas of life—not only in literature and in the theatre. The director, a character in the play, appropriately has the same name as the director of the production, Vlado Habunek.

The production is quite bold in execution and is the most ambitious the National has attempted. It marks the return of the artistic team of Radovan Ivšić, a writer who lives in Paris, and Vlado Habunek, a director who has worked in most major theatres in the world, including Covent Garden and Lincoln Center. Their collaborative efforts on Ivšić's play *Gordogan* (in 1979 at the ITD Theatre in Zagreb) received unanimous praise. To give the production an international flavor, the National invited the French scene and costume designer, Pierre Faucheux, to join Ivšić and Habunek.

Ajaxaja is quite a departure for the staid National. The futuristic effects, the electronic music, the sci-fi costumes and decor, bring the theatre into the twentieth century. The emphasis on youth and the future is in keeping with the artistic policy of the National—to educate audiences and to give them what they want. *Ajaxaja* has proved to be one of the most popular productions in recent years. Children are being urged to attend. Their verdict—*fino!*(great)—indicates that the National's ensemble is heading in the right direction.

EDWARD J. CZERWINSKI
(with Vesna Cvjetković-Kurelec)

ETC. THEATRE
(Teatar ITD)
Ul. Savska 25
Zagreb, Yugoslavia

The Etc. Theatre was founded in 1966 at the Student Center of the University of Zagreb. The company has two stages: the first, with a proscenium stage, seats 224 spectators; the second, an amphitheater, seats 100. The young company, eschewing censorship and administrative machinations, concentrates on contemporary works.

The premiere production, directed by Tomislav Durbešić, was Eugene Ionesco's *The Balcony*. Although no artistic policy evolved during its formative years, the company, made up of young actors and directors, searched for "truth and meaning" in experimental works. Rather than develop an acting style and artistic policy, the company, with the help of leading theatrical people, decided to concentrate on a "theme" rather than emphasize styles of acting or directorial approaches.

One of its most successful "themes" was a cycle of Shakespeare's plays during the 1971–1972 season. After that season it was decided to concentrate on contemporary drama, especially works by new writers. During the past ten years the following works have been produced: seven plays of Ionesco (including *The Lesson* and *Macbeth*), three by Harold Pinter (including *No Man's Land* and *Old Times*), and plays by Samuel Beckett, Edward Bond, Albert Camus, Günter Grass, Peter Handke, Peter Nickols, and Tom Stoppard. Yugoslav dramatists have also been successfully produced, especially plays by Miroslav Krleža, Jovan Hristić, Ivan Brešan, and the younger generation of Yugoslav writers.

Guest directors have included Kosta Spaić, Georgij Paro, Božidar Violić, and Dino Radojević. Several younger directors made their debut with the Etc., including Petar Veček and Miro Medjomorec. Some of Yugoslavia's best scene designers and composers have worked with the company. The theatre's policy attracts some of the best Yugoslav talent because each artist is signed to a contract of only two seasons with a specified repertoire. Because of this arrangement, artists are able to freelance, especially in films and television.

The theatre has received numerous awards and tours regularly. It is considered one of Yugoslav's finest theatres, second only to Atelier 212 in its influence on contemporary Yugoslav drama.

In 1977, Slobodan Sembera assumed duties as Managing Director. He immediately formed a Program Committee, made up of twenty-five members from various areas of life, including artists, writers, painters, and working-people. He then selected a new group of actors, many of whom are with the company today: Izet Hajdarhodžić, Ivica Vidović, Ratko Buljan, Miljenka Androić, Nataša Maričić, Vera Zima, Maria Sekeles, Žarko Savić, Drago Ljubjazarov, Željko Mavrović, and Pero Juričić.

A number of recent productions have received excellent reviews and have been popular with the public. They are still playing in repertory in 1984: Tom Stoppard's *Travesties* (1980), directed by Menad Puhovski; Milan Kundera's *Jacques the Fatalist and His Master* (1980), directed by Miro Medjimorec; Sławomir Mrożek's *On Foot* (1982), directed by Miro Medjimorec; Sidney Kingsley's adaptation of Arthur Koestler's *Darkness at Noon* (1983), directed by Slobodan Praljak; and the company's greatest success, an adaptation of Tom Stoppard's *Hamlet* (*The Fifteen Minute Hamlet*) by Zlatko Bourek, a puppet-theatre *Hamlet* (1982), a production which tells the tale of Hamlet in forty-five minutes.

The theatre has toured all over the world, including Latin America, West and East Europe, and the United States, and has received a number of awards, including Yugoslavia's prestigious "Sterijno Pozorje" award in Novi Sad, for its production of Ivo Brešan's *The Unforgettable Production of Hamlet in the Village of Mrduša Donja* (*Nezapamćena predstava* Hamleta *u selu Mrduša Donja*).

EDWARD J. CZERWINSKI

GAVELLA DRAMA THEATRE
(Dramsko Kazalište Gavella)
Ul. Frankopanska 10
Zagreb, Yugoslavia

The Gavella Drama Theatre was founded in 1953 by a group of young actors and directors. The theatre was formerly an appendage of the Academy of Theatre Arts, which was founded in 1950. The group's protector was Yugoslavia's foremost director, Branko Gavella (1885–1962), founder of the modern Yugoslav theatre and mentor of an entire generation of Yugoslav directors. In 1970 the theatre's name was changed from Zagrebačko Dramsko Kazalište (the Zagreb Drama Theatre) to the Gavella Drama Theatre, an honor reserved for only the greatest Yugoslav artists.

Under Gavella's direction, during the fifties the company developed a realistic style of acting, while stage design tended toward expressionistic rendering. Gavella always placed the text in primary position. His most successful productions include Miroslav Krleža's *Golgotha* (1954), Shakespeare's *As You Like It* (1955), and Graham Greene's *The Living-Room* (1959).

Gavella's protégé and eventual successor, Kosta Spaić, worked with Gavella, often imposing his views on various productions. Spaić laid less stress on expressionistic design and moved in the direction of more literal interpretations. His theories were best realized in the following productions: García Lorca's *Blood Wedding* (1954), Ionesco's *The Chairs* (1958), Molière's *The Misanthrope* (1960), Ibsen's *An Enemy of the People* (1967), and Marin Držić's *The Miser* (1974).

During the same period another of Gavella's proteges, Dino Radojević, added psychological probing to Gavella's expressionistic tendencies. Radojević's most significant productions, in which his artistic theories were developed, include Arthur Miller's *The Crucible* (1954), Tennessee Williams' *Cat on a Hot Tin Roof* (1956), Sophocles' *Oedipus Rex* (1963), August Strindberg's *The Dance of Death* (1965), Luigi Pirandello's *Six Characters in Search of an Author* (1965), Bertolt Brecht's *The Life of Galileo* (1969), and Miroslav Krleža's *Kraljevo* (1970).

In the sixties Georgij Paro and Božidar Violić, two of Yugoslavia's finest directors of the younger generation, joined the Zagreb Drama Theatre. Among Violić's best productions were Gogol's *The Marriage* (1960), Dostoevsky's *Crime and Punishment* (1968), Peter Weiss' *Herr Mockinpott* (1969), Georg Büchner's *The Death of Danton* (1969), and Pedro Calderon de la Barca's *Life Is a Dream* (1974). It was he who changed the direction of the company: the grotesque elements of a play were interlaced with metaphysical underpinnings.

Paro's artistic theories were best expressed in the following productions: Henrik Ibsen's *Ghosts* (1963), Harold Pinter's *The Collection* and *The Lover* (1964), and Shakespeare's *Macbeth* (1972).

In 1972 Kresimir Zidarić became artistic director. He managed to attract a number of other fine directors to his theatre, among them, Bogdan Jerković, who often directs abroad (Poland, Italy, and Germany). Jerković is attracted to the Gavella Drama Theatre because it offers him an opportunity "to experiment and to develop my ideas freely, without the constraints of an artistic policy. Violić's company is eclectic. What is important today is what matters—not what someone developed years ago."

The company consists of forty actors and forty-five people on the technical staff. The theater is located in a former movie-house, Helios, built in 1914. The company often performs abroad and regularly tours various provinces in Yugoslavia.

The present artistic director, Petar Veček, assumed his duties in 1983. The following directors form part of the company: Dino Radojević and Želimir Mesarić. Zvonimir Mrkonjić, the company's dramaturge, has been with the Gavella since 1968.

Among past productions which received favorable notices are the following: Edward Bond's *Saved* (1971), directed by Vanča Kljaković; Peter Weiss' *Hölderlin* (1973), directed by Kosta Spaić; Marin Držić's *The Miser* (1974), directed by Spaić; Ivo Vojnović's *Masquerades and Attics* (1976), directed by Ivica Kunčević; August Strindberg's *The Ghost Sonata* (1977), directed by Želimir Mesarić; Shakespeare's *Twelfth Night* (1978), directed by Dino Radojević; Chekhov's *Ivanov* (1978), directed by Kunčević; and Vaclav Havel's *Audience* and *Versinage* (1980), directed by Božidar Violić. The most recent successes include Fabijan Sovagović's *The Falcon Did Not Love Him* (*Sokol ga nije volio*, 1982), directed by Violić, and Nikolaj Erdman's *Mandate* (1983), directed by Mesarić.

Mandate is by far the company's finest ensemble work. The Gogolian comedy provides ample opportunity for every member of the cast of twenty-five actors to use both skill and imagination. This brilliant satire on Communism depends on broad comedy and sight-gags. The scene design (Marin Gozze) and costumes (Jasna Novak)—mostly shades of grey with dabs of red here and there (on the shoe-heels of the hero, on belts, ties, flowers, and hats)—provide the necessary touches of humor (red) and political realism (grey).

The fact that *Mandate* could be produced in a Communist country like Yugoslavia speaks highly of the system, its sophistication and lack of paranoia. In none of the other Slavic and Eastern European countries could Erdman's words be uttered: "Who are you—Bolsheviks or some other gangsters?" The production deserves to be seen all over the world.

EDWARD J. CZERWINSKI and
ZVONIMIR MRKONJIĆ

SLOVENIAN NATIONAL DRAMA THEATRE OF LJUBLJANA
(Drama Slovensko narodno gledališče v Ljubljana
Erjačeva 1, 6100 Ljubljana, Yugoslavia

The Slovenian National Drama Theatre (usually called Drama SNG in Ljubljana) was founded on October 24, 1867, as the Drama Circle. After World War I, the name was changed to the National Theatre in Ljubljana; after World War II, it was temporarily referred to as the Slovenian National Theatre on Liberated Territory. On October 17, 1945, it acquired its present name.

In 1983 Igor Lampret became artistic director. Three dramaturges assist him in shaping the repertory: Janez Negro, Nina Kovič, and Boris A. Novak. The theatre has no permanent directors. Each is selected for a specific project. During the past several seasons, the following directors have worked with the company: Mile Korun, Zvone Šedlbauer, Jože Babič, Georgij Paro, France Jamnik, Janez Pipan, Miran Herzog, Dušan Mlakar, and Peter Lotschak.

The present company consists of forty-four actors and actresses, many of whom have been with the theatre for over ten years. They include Marija Benko, Janez Albrecht, Marijana Brecelj, Miha Baloh, Ivo Ban, Štefka Drole, Danilo Benedičič, Lenka Ferenčak, Vika Gril, Polde Bibič, Angelca Hlebce, Barbara and Katja Levstik, Mihaela Majcen, Tone Homar, Boris Juh, Igo Samobar, Dare and Aleš Valič, Vojko Zidar, and Iva Zupančič.

The Slovenian Drama Theatre considers itself a classical repertory theatre. It is made up of two stages: a larger area with 460 seats and a smaller space with 100 seats. The company regularly tours Slovenia, as well as the other republics of Yugoslavia. The repertory usually consists of a Slovenian classic, such as Ivan Cankar's Servants (Hlapci [Slugie]), a Slovenian contemporary play, for example, Emil Filipčič's Altamira; a foreign classic, for example, Mikhail Bulgakov's Cabal of Hypocrites or Sheridan's School for Scandal; and a foreign contemporary play, such as Sławomir Mrożek's On Foot.

During the past ten years, the company has had a number of fine productions such as Georg Büchner's Woyzeck (1972), John Arden's Live Like Pigs (1976), Fyodor Gladkov's Cement (1976), Edward Bond's The Sea (1979), Shakespeare's Measure for Measure (1980), Ivan Cankar's Servants (Hlapci [Slugie], 1980), Carlo Goldoni's The Servant of Two Masters (1980), Drago Jančar's The Dissident Arnož and His Kind (Disident Arnož in Njegovi, 1982), Aleksandr Ostrovsky's The Storm (1982), Dominik Smole's Golden Slippers (Zlata ceveljcka, 1983), and one of its most popular productions, Tone Partlič's My Father,

The Socialist Kulak (*Moj tata, socialistični kulak*). Besides touring Yugoslavia, the company has also performed in Austria, Italy, and the Soviet Union.

Scene and costume designers are also invited to participate in specific productions. The scene designers most often associated with the company are Meta Hočevar, Niko Matul, Sveta Jovanović, and Zlatko Kauzlarić-Atač; the company's costume designers include Mija Jarc, Alenka Bartl, and Marija Vidan.

Future plans include a more political orientation, with respect to repertory, and more tours abroad.

EDWARD J. CZERWINSKI and
MOJCA KRANJC

THE SLOVENIAN YOUTH THEATRE
(Slovensko Mladinsko Gledališče)
Trg. VII Kongresa 1
61000 Ljubljana, Yugoslavia

The present artistic director of the Slovenian Youth Theatre is Dušan Jovanovič, probably Slovenia's finest contemporary dramatist. The theatre's dramaturge is Marko Slodnjak, who also doubles as voice-coach. The director Janez Pipan is part of the theatre's artistic committee and often replaces Jovanović, who regularly travels abroad. Petar Jović handles administrative duties.

Sponsored by the City of Ljubljana, the theatre was founded in 1955 by Balbina Battelino-Baranović, who became its general manager. Those who followed Battelino-Baranović—the poet Tone Pavček, the director Dušan Mlakar, the dramatist Dominik Smole, and from 1979 the director and dramatist Dušan Jovanović—have attempted to implement Battelino-Baranović's program, that is, to provide theatre for young people and to open a polemic with them regarding new movements and trends in theatre. Young dramatists are often produced and encouraged to contribute to the work of the ensemble and to make contact with audiences frequenting the Youth Theatre.

The present company is made up of these actors: Radko Polič, Željko Hrs, Niko Goršič, Sandi Pavlin, Pavle Rakovec, Pavel Ravnohrib, Miloš Battelino, Marko Mlačnik, Jožef Ropoše, Majolka Suklje, Mina Jeraj, Milena Grm, Marinka Štern, Olga Grad, Draga Potočnjak, Damjana Černe, and Jadranka Tomažič. Almost every important Slovenian director has directed the company: Mile Korun, Miran Herzog, Zvone Šedlbauer, Dušan Mlakar, Dušan Jovanović, and, from other areas of Yugoslavia, Ljubiša Ristić and Mira Erceg. Costume and scene designers who regularly work with the company include Niko Matul, Meta Hočevar, Matjaž Vipotnik, Doris Kristić, and Kostja Gatnik.

The most significant productions during the past years include Rostand's *Cyrano de Bergerac*, directed by Miran Herzog (1975); Dušan Jovanović's *Sacrifices a la BOOM-BOOM* (*Žrtve mode bum-bum*), directed by Jovanović (1975); Evgenij Švartz' *The Dragon*, directed by Mile Korun (1976); Svetlana Makarovič's *Dream of a Green Night* (*San zelenoj noći*), directed by Jovanović (1978); Ljubiša

Ristić's *Mass in A Minor* (*Missa in A Minor*), directed by Ristić (1980); Nigel Williams' *Class Enemy*, directed by Vito Taufer (1982); and Emil Filipčič's *Prisoners of Freedom* (*Ujetniki svobode*), directed by Janez Pipan (1982).

The Slovenian Youth Theatre tours Yugoslavia regularly and has been invited to a number of international festivals. The company has also taken part in some Yugoslav festivals like Sterijno Pozorje, in 1981 and 1983; the Sarajevo Festival of Chamber and Experimental Theatres, in 1983; and at BITEF, the International Festival in Belgrade, in 1981, where Ristić's *Mass in A Minor* received the Best Production Award. In 1983, Emil Filipčič's *Prisoners of Freedom* was similarly honored.

EDWARD J. CZERWINSKI
(with Marko Slodnjak)

YUGOSLAV DRAMA THEATRE
(Jugoslovensko Dramsko Pozorište)
Ul. Maršala Tita 50
Belgrade, Yugoslavia

The Yugoslav Drama Theatre was founded in 1947 by a group of artists from various disciplines in the theatre. The purpose was to utilize the best theatrical traditions of those countries which then made up Yugoslavia. The theatre opened on April 3, 1948, with the premiere of Ivan Cankar's *Kralj Betajnove* (*King Betajnove*), under the direction of Bojan Stupica, who next to Branko Gavella, was then Yugoslavia's best director. Although the theatre critic Eli Finci performed administrative duties, Stupica controlled all artistic aspects of the theatre, including hiring the actors and directing major productions. After Stupica joined Trailović in setting up Atelier 212 in 1956, a number of outstanding directors, e.g., Milan Dedinac, Miroslav Belović, Milan Dijaković, and Velibor Gligorić, subsequently assumed the role of Artistic Director. Gligorić remained with the Drama Theatre until 1971, when Peter Volk took over. He was replaced by Janez Šenk in 1983.

During its formative years (1948–1953), the company concentrated on a classical repertory. Milan Dedinac, the poet and translator, acting as dramaturge and artistic advisor, shaped the profile of the theatre's repertoire. Shakespeare was the most performed dramatist during this period, although the repertory included a variety of plays, from Aeschylus and Sophocles (*Prometheus Bound* and *Antigone*, respectively) to Ibsen (*John Gabriel Borkman*) and Strindberg (*Miss Julie*). One of the greatest artistic successes was a work by Yugoslavia's own sixteenth-century poet-playwright, Marin Držić. The play, a precursor of Shakespeare's comedies, is *Dundo Maroje* (*Uncle Maroje*), in an adaptation by Marko Fotez and directed by Bojan Stupica.

The company developed a style that was best suited to a classical repertory. Movement and diction were stressed, and the actors were considered some of the finest in Yugoslavia. In the late fifties, however, the company did an about-face: contemporary plays predominated the repertoire. Sean O'Casey (*The Plow and the Stars*), Jean-Paul Sartre (*The Condemned of Altona* and *Dirty Hands*), Eugene O'Neill (*Long Day's Journey into Night*), Albert Camus (*Caligula*), John Whiting (*The Devils*), and Sławomir Mrożek (*Tango*) replaced the classics. A new repertoire brought a change in acting styles, which can be best described as neo-Studio. Abjuring Stanislavsky, the company leans more on Western trends, especially those of Lee Strasberg. The director chiefly responsible for developing the new acting style is Miroslav Belović, who is best known for his productions of the prolific twentieth-century Yugoslav dramatists Miroslav Krleža and Branislav Nušić.

Since 1969 a Chamber Theatre (Bojan Stupica Theatre) has opened with a concentration on experimental works. The following are among the premieres in this experimental theatre: Erdman's *The Suicide*, Paul Zindel's *The Effect of Gamma Rays on Man-in-the-Moon Marigolds*, and David Mercer's *Flint*. In 1977 the theatre scored a great success with Sławomir Mrożek's *The Hunchback*.

The company consists of fifty-four actors. The theatre is unique in Yugoslavia in that over 30 percent of its performances are staged in smaller theatres. The company has also had numerous tours abroad, including the Theatre of Nations in Paris in 1954, their first guest appearance. The company has since toured the Soviet Union (1956, 1965, and 1978), Austria (1956 and 1969), Hungary (1956), Poland (1959, 1964, and 1983), Bulgaria (1960 and every year since), Italy (1969 and 1981), and Romania (1970).

The present dramaturges include Dusan Č. Jovanović, Mile Petrović, and Vencislav Radovanović. The resident director is Dimitrije Jovanović. The theatre historian is Ružica Djordjević-Masnikosa.

The present company includes the following actors: Maja Dimitrijević, Radmila Andrić, Bosilka Boci, Olga Savić, Svetlana Bojković, Branka Petrić, Djurdja Cvetić, Dubravka Perić, Rada Djurićin, Stojan Dečermić, Marko Todorović, Mihailo Janketić, Predrag Laković, Miodrag Radovanović, Slavko Simić, Nikola Simić, Gojko Šantić, Tanasije Uzunović, Milan Gutović, Mihajlo Kostič, Bronislav Lečić, and Ivan Bekjarev.

The most significant productions of recent years include Shakespeare's *Othello* (1977), directed by Stevo Žigon, who also played Iago; Isaac Babel's *Sunset* (1979), directed by Jerzy Jarocki, with music by Radwan and designed by Kowarski; Sam Shepard's *The Buried Child* (1980), directed by Edward Hastings; Jovan Sterija Popović's *Simeon the Foundling* (1981), directed by Dejan Mijać; Dragan Tomić's *Crossroads* (*Raskršče*, 1981), directed by Stevo Žigon; Chekhov's *The Three Sisters* (1981), directed by the Soviet director, Georgij Tovstonogov; Slobodan Šnajder's *The Croatian Faust* (*Hrvatski Faust*, 1982), directed by Slobodan Unkovski; Dušan Kovačević's *The Balkan Spy* (*Balkanski špijun*, 1983), directed by Dušan Jovanovic; Edward Bond's *Summer* (1983), directed by Dimitrije Jovanović; and Ireneusz Iredyński's *The Terrorists*, directed by Jan Bratkowski.

The theatre also has an intimate drawing-room space, set up in 1978, where experimental and chamber works are performed, as well as monodramas, for a limited audience of one hundred. Some of the more outstanding works produced in this space were: Erica Jong's *Fear of Flying* (1979), adapted, directed, and performed by Rada Djuricin; Sartre's *No Exit* (1981), directed by Ivana Vujić; and *Sofia Tolstoy's Diaries* (1982), adapted and directed by Miroslav Belović, performed by Maja Dimitrijević.

EDWARD J. CZERWINSKI

LATIN AMERICA

George Woodyard, Area Editor

Introduction

Theatre in the Western Hemisphere was a well-developed artistic form before the Spanish arrived in the late fifteenth century, and it has grown and advanced steadily throughout the years. Until recently, the normal aesthetic tendencies paralleled the dominant modes in Europe at any particular point in time, with a few notable exceptions which incorporated indigenous themes and characteristics. The impetus of the 1950s, however, brought a new character to the Latin American theatre. Building on the successes of the experimental and independent theatre movements of the 1930s and 1940s, especially in Mexico and Argentina, the theatre movement of the post-World War II period brought marked changes with a new consciousness of style and identity. For virtually the first time since the period of the Spanish conquest, the theatre of Latin America became an independent art form. In its new state it transcended national boundaries in order to speak with multiple voices about a wide range of themes, concerns, and interests.

In this fertile thirty-year period, the theatre has taken wing. New companies have been formed, new buildings have been built, and more people have been trained in theatrical arts. The theatre in Latin America is a nationalistic art that often acquires transcendence. Even though the lines of communication with New York, Paris, and Madrid remain strong, the capitals of Latin America are interconnected by the theatre, and it is not uncommon for Argentine plays to appear on Mexican stages or for Chilean plays to be staged in Costa Rica. The first Latin American theatre festival was held in Manizales, Colombia, in 1968, an event that is significant for several reasons. It marked the beginning of an epoch in which the community of Latin American theatre artists pooled their resources and reached out to share with others their rich heritages and traditions as well as their techniques and crafts. Although the Manizales Festival was discontinued because of political and economic problems, other festivals have sprung up to replace it in Buenos Aires, Caracas, Havana, and even the United States. Since the 1970s the Ateneo de Caracas has promoted a variety of theatre activities and publications through its Centro Latinoamericano de Creación e Investigación

(CELCIT), which is gradually establishing a network of cooperating units throughout the Americas.

Major dramatists continue to write in Latin America while new experiments are underway. In the years immediately following World War II, the influences of European existentialism and the theatre of the absurd were keenly felt throughout Latin America, but those aesthetics have been replaced by Brechtian tendencies and others that reflect more precisely a Latin American reality. The enormous political, social, and economic difficulties that beset the countries of Latin America have tended to manifest themselves through a committed theatre. Almost all countries have experienced some degree of censorship, but signs of protest can often be seen through an allegorical or symbolic veneer when the political climate will not tolerate a more overt form of protest. Many theatre groups throughout Latin America have developed a style of staging and performance appropriate to the spartan economic conditions under which they work. Thus, the vicissitudes of harsh political climates and depressing economic conditions encourage them to concentrate on the development of subtleties in their art and techniques instead of relying on elaborate staging or extravagant costuming.

In several areas of Latin America, the *creación colectiva* has become a dominant mode. Oftentimes, these collaborative efforts involve an entire company from the initial conception of the idea through the long and arduous process of the research and development of the play. Especially in Colombia and Cuba, the working relationships formed within the theatre groups enable them to translate the concerns and aspirations of the people into an artistic and aesthetic experience on the stage. Many of the most representative plays of recent years have emerged through this process, such as *Los novios* (*The Engaged Couple*) (Teatro Escambray, Cuba) or *I Took Panama* (TPB, Colombia). The collective process works to mold the group into a tightly knit unit since all participate in the total process, in contrast with the traditional approach of performing a play written by an external author.

The essays that follow give a panoramic view of the theatre in twelve Latin American countries in the past several years. While this picture may be far from complete, it establishes a good foundation for those interested in pursuing the subject through further reading or investigation. The theatre in the 1980s has reached an unparalleled level of maturity and development. Latin American plays are now regularly seen on the stages of principal cities throughout the world (New York, Berlin, Madrid, and London). Their distribution and popularity abroad can generally be attributed to the high quality of the initial efforts of theatre companies on the home front.

GEORGE WOODYARD

Argentina

INTRODUCTION

By the dawn of the twentieth century Buenos Aires and its sister city, Montevideo, were establishing new standards for theatre productivity in the hemisphere. The rich tradition of a popular rural drama associated with the circus led to the development of a popular theatre style in the capitals. The first decade of the century, the so-called Golden Decade, was dominated by Florencio Sánchez whose portrayal of earthy characters and social problems with an innate tenderness earned him respect and popularity. A stream of followers set the tone for a psychological theatre, Argentine in nature but with a European overlay, that was to flourish until the 1930s.

In Buenos Aires—which in theatrical terms means all of Argentina, since the whole country looks toward the capital—there was once an "independent" theatre movement, so-called because it tried to free itself from the demands of the commercial theatre which at that time catered to the general public. The person responsible for this movement was Leónidas Barletta, who founded his Teatro del Pueblo in 1929. It was a reaction, and as such, along with indisputable successes, there were many exaggerations, and the theatre became immensely difficult for the popular taste. Nevertheless, its proponents revolutionized the theatrical scene, and with their motto of advancing without haste and without pause, like the star (as Goethe put it), they contributed to Buenos Aires' position today as the most important theatrical city in the Spanish-speaking world.

Later, there was a period of calm, since the objectives had been achieved. Nevertheless, in the mid-1960s, some groups felt commercial theatre did not respond to the demands of a spectator who had not only come of age but had also evolved sufficiently to accept plays that could only be presented in unconventional places. If one were to make a comparison with the United States, this movement would be defined as "Off-Broadway." Even so, in Argentina the difference between "legitimate theatre" and other theatres does not exist, for all theatre is viewed as legitimate.

The four theatre companies described in the following pages detail the history of the major professional theatres in Buenos Aires. A recent phenomenon that cannot be described accurately as a theatre company but that is of enormous importance within the development of the most recent Argentine theatre is the Teatro Abierto (Open Theatre). Conceived in 1981 by Osvaldo Dragún, one of Argentina's leading contemporary playwrights and directors, Teatro Abierto consisted of a program of twenty-one one-act plays written especially for a special season by as many authors. When teamed with twenty directors (one play had to be canceled) in a program that offered three plays each night for a week, with a repeating schedule in the following weeks, Teatro Abierto swept the city with enthusiasm. In spite of financial problems, political hostility, and a suspicious fire that totally destroyed the Teatro del Picadero, Teatro Abierto finished a successful season that was repeated with new plays in 1982, 1983 and 1984. The vitality and dynamism of this theatrical experiment have contributed to a new wave of interest in Argentine theatre.

ARGENTINE NATIONAL THEATRE
(Comedia Nacional Argentina)
Liberated 815, Buenos Aires, Argentina

It is impossible to refer to the Argentine National Theatre without describing, even in synthesized form, the history of the Cervantes Theatre, a place where the company has carried out its activities since it was established in 1933. The Cervantes will never be moved to another site because it is a national institution. It was inaugurated on September 5, 1921, and as the historian Juan José de Urquiza said, "In addition to its material value it represents the sublime charm of María Guerrero and Fernando Díaz de Mendoza, who bequeathed us a synthesis of the national ancestral mansion." (Juan José de Urquiza, *El Cervantes en la historia del teatro argentino* [Buenos Aires: Ediciones Culturales Argentinas, 1968], p. 120.).

Guerrero and Díaz, famous actors in Spain, ran a great risk in touring Argentina in 1897, since theirs was a cultured theatre, and the spectators of that period were accustomed to the so-called Spanish *género chico* played by low-grade actors. On the other hand, they chose to present Lope de Vega's *La dama boba* (*The Foolish Lady*), a work considered now to be excessively ingenuous for Argentine tastes at the end of the century. Its success was smashing, and from then on they played several seasons in Buenos Aires until they finally settled there.

Both María Guerrero and Fernando Díaz de Mendoza, her husband in real life, felt a great affection for Argentina and its public. In 1918 they publicly launched the idea of constructing a palatial theatre for performances by the world's outstanding actors, to be available for Argentine companies. The vicissitudes that beset the project were many, but the two were determined to carry through without concern for costs. They insisted on building the theatre in colonial Spanish style: from Valencia importing tiles and damask; from Tarragona the red flagstone for the floor, which would serve as background for the colored border of the small enamel mosaics; from Ronda the doors of the boxes, copied by skilled carpenters from an ancient sacristy; from Seville the seats, the inlaid gilt secretaries for the antechambers to the boxes, along with mirrors, benches, grill-work, ironwork, and tiles; from Lucena candles, lamps, lanterns of old design, and southern handiwork; from Barcelona the huge painting al fresco for the ceiling of the theatre; from Madrid the tapestries, the coat-of-arms cover, draperies, and the main stage curtain. In short, they attempted to bring the best of Spain to Buenos Aires. Proof of their success is that throughout nearly sixty years all foreign artists who have worked the house extol its magnificence to the point that it can be considered among the most sumptuous in the world.

Although the first performance was apotheosic—artistic success was always required—the economy began to fail, and in 1926 the theatre had to be auctioned, since debts had reached the equivalent of several million dollars. In this climate of tragedy, the critic Enrique García Velloso mobilized the state to acquire the theatre, which it did by means of the Argentine National Bank.

In 1933 the Law of Intellectual Property was passed; Article 69 created the Teatro Nacional de Comedia. Until then, the only official theatre in the country had been the Teatro Colón, which was used for music and opera and did not belong to the state but rather to the city of Buenos Aires. This move was designed to give the greatest recognition to national drama, to conserve the basic repertory of Argentine dramaturgy, to regulate the artistic process of the theatre in all its aspects, and to stimulate the appearance of new values appropriate to the evolution and exaltation of the vernacular scene. So it was that in 1936 the curtain went up for the first time on an official new company, which (with the interval of a fire described later) has continued its activity for more than half a century. At the head of the company was the director, Antonio Cunill Cabanellas, a Catalonian who was at the same time director of the Conservatory of Dramatic Art. In Argentina there is an official drama school where a five-year course of studies leads to the title of "national actor." The tuition and the whole program of courses are absolutely free, as is all official instruction in Argentina, whatever the level—primary, secondary, or university.

Cunill Cabanellas has taught several generations of Argentine actors, and his activity in the new Teatro Nacional de Comedia has left an unforgettable impression. The first work presented was *Locos de verano* (*Summer Madmen*) by Gregorio de Laferrère, perhaps the most important dramatist Argentina has had. Later came in *La divisa punzó* (*The Red Badge*) by Paul Groussac; *En familia* (*As a Family*) by Florencio Sánchez; *La conquista* (*The Conquest*) by César Iglesias Paz; *Calandria* (*The Lark*) by Martiniano Leguizamón; *Facundo* (*Facundo*) by David Peña; *La novia de los forasteros* (*The Strangers' Sweetheart*) by Pedro E. Pico; *La casa de los Batallán* (*The House of the Batalláns*) by Alberto Vaccarezza; *El puñal de los troveros* (*The Dagger of the Troubadors*) by Belisario Roldán; *Mamá Culepina* (*Mother Culepina*) by Enrique García Velloso; *Martín Fierro* by José Hernández, in an adaptation by José González

Castillo; *El Sergento Palma* (*Sergeant Palma*) by Martín Coronado; *Los mira-soles* (*The Sunflowers*) by Julio Sánchez Gardel; *El halcón* (*The Falcon*) by José León Pagano; *Los conquistadores del desierto* (*The Desert Conquerors*) by En-rique García Velloso; *Una mujer desconocida* (*An Unknown Woman*) by Pedro Benjamín Aquino; and *Marco Severi* by Roberto J. Payró.

This was the Argentine repertory until 1947. These works alternated with *La discreta enamorada* (*The Discreet Lover*) by Lope de Vega; *Cyrano de Bergerac* by Edmond Rostand; *El hombre de mundo* (*The Man of the World*) by Ventura de la Vega; *The Merchant of Venice* by William Shakespeare; and *Los intereses creados* (*Created Interests*) by Jacinto Benavente. The principal philosophy was, and continues to be, to offer Argentine plays with Argentine directors, actors, technicians, and scene designers. This was much easier in the earlier epoch than it is now, since foreign plays have invaded Argentina's theatre fare at a time when the national authors have not produced anything to merit special attention. Another of the group's concerns has been to present plays that are in a sense archaeological. Since they belong to the cultural heritage of the country, they should be known, even though their commercial potential is dubious. Schools are invited to bring students free of charge, and for that reason the house is filled almost every day with children.

It was also resolved to open the theatre doors to the new authors, and contests were held which permitted up to two unpublished plays to premiere per season. Among the new authors, Horacio Rega Molina, Belisario García Villar, Tulio Carella, and Graciela Teissaire stand out. After Cunill Cabanellas, the directors were Armando Discépolo, Elías Alippi, and Enrique de Rosas. This takes us up to 1947. From then until 1955—the Peronista period—Claudio Martínez Paiva, Eduardo Suárez Danero, Roberto A. Vagni, José María Fernández Unsain, Al-berto Vaccarezza, and Pedro Aleandro were at the head. During that period of time there was no Argentine play of importance, but one could see and appreciate, among other plays, *Six Characters in Search of an Author* by Luigi Pirandello, *The Taming of the Shrew* by William Shakespeare, and *The Knights of the Round Table* by Jean Cocteau.

The name of the Comedia Nacional Argentina (Argentina National Theatre) was officially conferred on August 14, 1956, although the troupe had been unofficially known by that name for several years. The law establishing the Argentine National Theatre states that the company

aspires to be a new moment in our theatre history, with its own style and broad cultural projections. Its aspirations have not been limited to conceiving of the bright new institution as merely an official company; on the contrary, it is seen as an organic attempt capable of promoting not only the renovation of dramatic literature, but also of theatre art, as well as an esthetic phenomenon in which authors, actors, technicians and the public participate.

Orestes Caviglia was named director and defined the complex as "a society of persons of the profession." He indicated that a laboratory workshop "will be joined to the regular Company, which in addition to courses in plastic and rhythmic exercise, improvisation, diction, and choral recitation, will mold the unique style of the house, the distinguishing tone of the company. It will be a channel of vocations, but not an instrument of vanities."

For that reason, stars have never acted in the Argentine National Theatre. Instead, attempts have been made to form companies of inured actors, to which, little by little, graduates from the Conservatory of Dramatic Art can be incorporated. In theory, it is not a system like the one of the Comédie Française with "sociétaires" and "pensionaires," but in practice the membership of the Comedia changes very little.

The new authorities invited foreign companies; in July 1957 came the Compagnia deix giovani—Giorgio de Lullo, Rosana Falk, Annamaría Guarnieri, and Romolo Valli—and Jean Vilar with the Théâtre National Populaire (TNP). In June 1959 they presented the Comédie Française, and in 1961 Jean-Louis Barrault with Madeleine Renaud.

In its new period the Argentine National Theatre presented, among other Argentine plays: *Facundo en la ciudadela* (*Facundo in the Citadel*) by Vicente Barbieri; *El pan de la locura* (*The Bread of Madness*) by Carlos Gorostiza; *El escarabajo* (*The Beetle*) by Pablo Palant; and *Las aguas del mundo* (*The Waters of the World*) by Samuel Eichelbaum. The foreign plays include *Man and Superman* by George Bernard Shaw, *Murder in the Cathedral* by T. S. Eliot, and *La casa de Bernarda Alba* (*The House of Bernarda Alba*) by Federico García Lorca.

But in 1960 a difficult situation arose. The new authorities—this time civilian ones—asked for the resignation of Orestes Caviglia, and the whole company resigned in mass, solidly behind him. Although it was never said clearly, the authorities attributed leftist ideas to the director, which for the brand-new director of culture, Héctor Blas González, was nearly a crime. The Argentine National Theatre floundered for a couple of years, under the direction of Narciso Ibañez Menta and Omar del Carlo, until July 10, 1961, when a catastrophe occurred— the Teatro Cervantes burned, at the very time Jean-Louis Barrault was performing there. It was a national misfortune, and the company had to relocate in the Teatro Municipal San Martín until 1968, when it opened the doors of the reconstructed theatre. In those seven years, the company rambled through several locales, under the direction of the actress Luisa Vehil, followed by Juan José de Urquiza, Nestor Suárez Aboy, and Rodolfo Graziano, the present director. During that period several important Argentine works were seen, such as *Capocómico* (*Head Clown*) by Sergio de Cecco and *Ollantay* (*Ollantay*) by Ricardo Rojas, in a version by Rubén Vela. Since national authors had begun to desert, foreign plays were more numerous, including *The Three Sisters* and *The Cherry Orchard* by Chekhov; *The Intellectual Ladies* by Molière; and *The Cap of Bells* by Pirandello.

From 1968 to 1977 the trajectory of the Argentine National Theatre was routine, primarily because of the mediocrity of those in charge of staging the plays, which divided between Argentine reruns and an occasional title of importance such as Michel de Ghelderode's *Barabbas*. That year Rodolfo Graziano was named director—an important event. Graziano was known as the *metteur-en-scène* of the Taller de Garibaldi, a company cited separately in this section for its originality and creativity. The season began with *The Importance of Being Earnest* by Oscar Wilde, followed by Carlo Goldoni's *The Fan*, *Martín Fierro* by José Hernández, *Oedipus Rex* by Sophocles, and *Un sombrero de paja de Italia* (*An Italian Straw Hat*) by Eugène Labiche. Graziano brought the public back to a theatre that had been nearly abandoned by spectators because of the poor quality of previous seasons. At the same time, he has succeeded in getting more tax dollars for the Argentine National Theatre, even though the prices of its shows are considerably lower than those of the commercial theatres.

GARIBALDI WORKSHOP
(Taller de Garibaldi)
Rocha 907, Buenos Aires, Argentina

Perhaps it is noteworthy that one of the principal companies in Argentina carries the name Taller de Garibaldi (Garibaldi Workshop). This demands an explanation, since it has to do with a troupe assembled in an old carpentry shop in the area of the Boca, one of the most picturesque parts of Buenos Aires, near the port, where a great number of Italian immigrants settled at the beginning of the century. The Boca is famous for its pizzerias, bars, ships, and the Boca Juniors Athletic Club, Argentina's most popular football team. In a country that has won two world championships this is no small matter.

The workshop is so named because it stands on the corner of Garibaldi and Rocha streets, one block from the river. It was previously an old carpentry shop in the neighborhood, until Rodolfo Graziano discovered it and determined to convert it into a theatre. Its structure is unconventional. There is a great hall on which a grill identical to those in the general stores in the country exhibits pictures and writings, generally of the most modern stamp. The theatre itself is small, and the stage is circular. The seats are wooden and terribly uncomfortable, but the public does not seem to mind, as the theatre is always full. A ladder leads to the upstairs, which is cleverly used in all productions. A lot of people go to the Garibaldi Workshop simply for its atmosphere, which is Bohemian and sophisticated at the same time.

The company was established in 1974, and although it may be difficult to imagine after the description given here, it opened with Goethe's *Faust*, directed by Rodolfo Graziano with one of the country's best young actors, Juan Carlos Puppo, in the principal role. The show was splendid, full of imagination and poetry, and for that reason a second production was warmly awaited. All the suggestiveness of Jean Giraudoux was translated with mystery and fantasy by the same director, who brought to the stage *Ondine*, in a creative interpretation by Lidia Argibay. In both plays Graziano took advantage of the distribution of the house with abundant talent and imagination, and after only two shows the

Workshop became one of the favorite companies of the Argentine public. Throughout 1975 *Ondine* alternated with *Faust*.

The next year, Buenos Aires witnessed the most intelligent and amusing version possible in Spanish of Molière's *The Bourgeois Gentleman*. Here the eloquence of the director Graziano (the only director in the group) reached new heights, and the show was a smash. All Argentine critics agreed that the Garibaldi Workshop performed only excellent works. This judgment was reconfirmed in 1977 with Shakespeare's *A Midsummer Night's Dream*, where the grace and poetry of the text were translated with the usual exceptional talent.

Unfortunately, Graziano was so successful the authorities called on him to direct the Argentine National Theatre. Since he was constitutionally unable to delegate his work to subordinates, lack of time kept him from continuing to head the Taller. In 1978 Shakespeare's *Romeo and Juliet* played there, and it was evident that Graziano could not direct simultaneously in the Cervantes and in the Garibaldi Workshop. From that time, with a parenthesis in which he put on Michel de Ghelderode's *Escorial*, the company has been in recess. Nevertheless, the group may decide to proceed with the work that has made it the most provocative group in all of Buenos Aires.

PAYRÓ THEATRE GROUP
(Equipo Teatro Payró)
San Martín 766, Buenos Aires, Argentina

The Payró Theatre Group has two dimensions: on the one hand, it pays homage to Roberto J. Payró, an important man of letters in Argentine culture; on the other, it works as a team, eliminating the traditional impresario, who has omnipotent power in the commercial theatres to make or to break. The founders of this theatre complex were Jaime Kogan, who continues at the helm today, Felisa Yeny, Berta Dresler, Francisco Díaz, Jorge Alberti, and others. They were young, some of them coming from university environments, and sincerely interested in the theatre, although for the most part they were without academic preparation. They probably had no specific philosophy, but their inclination was toward a theatre unconventional in formation and structure. The theatre was officially founded in 1967, when the country was governed by a military dictatorship. The dictatorship began in 1930 when the Army, under the command of General José Félix Uriburu, defeated the constitutional government of Irigoyen. The government had fallen into the worst kind of corruption, and Irigoyen, nearly eighty years old, had become senile, manipulated by unscrupulous politicians. At that moment a reactionary mentality took over and imposed censorship on theatrical performances—although it would be fair to say that it did not concern itself much with the theatre.

The Payró's first presentation was *Viet-Rock* by Megan Terry, directed by Jaime Kogan. The play ran for two years and achieved a very respectable 409 performances in a house with 135 seats. The Payró's public is different from the commercial theatre public, since it consists for the most part of radicalized youth, highly intellectual and very enthusiastic. Nevertheless, over a period of time the theatre became more bourgeois, and today its premieres attract all segments of Buenos Aires society, although the directors have not changed.

When *Viet-Rock* ended its run, the company produced *Historia tendenciosa de la clase media argentina (The Tendentious History of the Argentine Middle Class)* by Ricardo Monti, a young Argentine author who had become known earlier through a work called *Una noche con el señor Magnus y sus hijos (A Night with Mr. Magnus and His Children)*. Monti is an adherent of the theatre of the absurd, which means that his plays depend more on performance than on text. "Middle-class" in English does not capture all the nuances of "clase media" in Spanish, since in Argentina the concept embraces a much broader spectrum than in the Anglo-Saxon countries. Monti's play is quite esoteric, as is all of his theatre, and although he may intend it as social criticism, it is difficult to understand. Nevertheless, it was very successful and ran for 319 performances during 1970 and 1971.

The company's next work, *El señor Galíndez (Mr. Galíndez)* by Eduardo Pavlovsky, was more political. Pavlovsky, also a psychoanalyst, is responsible for, if not the introduction, the divulgation of the most modern, vanguard theatre in Buenos Aires. This work premiered in 1973, when the political situation in Argentina had changed a great deal. After several years of military rule, General Juan Domingo Perón had returned to the government. While the first Peronist regime, starting in 1946, had imposed extreme censorship and had forced those who did not relate to the governing party to leave the country, the third Perón presidency started off more liberally. Since military regulation prevented Perón's election directly, a subterfuge was invented to elect the dentist Héctor José Cámpora, who conducted the campaign with the motto of "Cámpora to the government, Perón to power." Scarcely two months had passed after Cámpora acceded to the presidency when Perón ordered him to renounce in order to present himself as a candidate.

But Cámpora had the support of the most radicalized groups of Peronismo, who would then be expelled from the movement by Perón himself. In theatrical terms this was translated into a series of works in which subversion against the constituted authorities was openly exalted. *El señor Galíndez* was by no means of this nature, but it focused on a very sad theme for the Argentine Republic— that of police torture. Pavlovsky did not locate his play in a specific place, but it was evident it referred to his country. The play is sensational, and was received with enthusiasm by both the public and the critics, especially since it dealt with a theme that had been taboo. It was presented 816 times, and it represented Argentina in the 1976 International Theatre Festival in Nancy, afterwards continuing a tour through Spain, France, and Italy. In the following year, the play was taken to the II International Theatre Festival in Caracas, with subsequent performances in Ecuador, Panama, Costa Rica, and Colombia.

Liberalization ended in 1977 after the defeat of the government of María Estela

Martínez de Perón, who upon Juan Perón's death assumed the presidency. The military returned to power and censorship was and continues to be very severe. As a result, no play with a political content could be offered. *El señor Galíndez* was banned, and Eduardo Pavlovsky sought exile in Spain.

But the Payró group was not bothered, although it has imposed a prudent self-censorship. In 1977 it premiered another play by Ricardo Monti, *Visita* (*The Visit*), which ran for two years with 280 performances. Like the other works directed by Jaime Kogan, more values derive from the performance than from the text. Reaction to the play was extraordinarily favorable, with critics even coming from Montevideo. The play is decidedly surrealistic, and Kogan, who is very effective in that vein, infused it with an attractive element of fantasy. *Visita* also received foreign acclaim, being taken to the IV World Session of the Teatro de las Naciones in 1978 in Caracas.

With so favorable a reception, in 1978 the group inaugurated its second theatre, the Teatro Planeta. It was an opportune time to try out another major work. Through the years the Payró had been accepted by the "establishment," and it was in line with the more commercial theatres. Its ticket sellers, who before had met the public dressed in blue jeans and T-shirts, now dressed like the dandies of Saville Row. People who would never have attended the theatre before rushed to appreciate the works of the group.

For the inauguration of the second theatre, the group chose a major play, Shakespeare's *Julius Caesar*, adapted by Máximo Soto, a feature film writer, who found considerable fault with the original. The directing—as usual by Jaime Kogan—was provocative and intelligent, and well-known professional actors were used such as Víctor Laplace.

In 1977 the Payró won the Carlos Arniches Prize in Madrid, awarded to Ricardo Monti for his *Visita*. It also received the Juana Sujo Prize in Venezuela the same year for the best performance of a foreign play. Kogan won the Molière Prize for his direction of *Visita* in 1977.

REPERTORY GROUP
(Grupo de Repertorio)
Las Heras 4015, Buenos Aires, Argentina

The Repertory Group was established in 1974 and continues to work with its initial fervor. Its founders were Agustín Alezzo, director and creator of the company, and actors Norberto Díaz, Miguel Moyano, Angela Ragno, Boris Rubaja, Edgardo Moreira, Patricia Calderón, Luisa Kulliok, Lidia Catalano, Raquel Merediz, Julio Ordano, Carlos Sproviero, Jorge Vera Ocampo, and Graciela Wesker. Alezzo is an important director in Buenos Aires, known for his rigorous criteria for selecting plays, the seriousness of his work, and his professional skill.

The Repertory Group was formed in order to present Argentine and international plays which could not be incorporated easily into the repertory of a commercial theatre. The actors were expected to grow and develop through constant group practice to form a true theatrical company. Many of the actors are well-known figures who have worked in successful plays.

In the initial years (1974–1978), the company concentrated on the development of theatre directors, for few schools in Buenos Aires turn out directors. In this period the company presented plays directed by eleven individuals who were making their first efforts, including Aída Bortnik, Hugo Urquijo, Horacio Agustoni, Julio Ordano, Luis Gutman, Oscar Cruz, Beatriz Seibel, Beatriz Matar, Julio Baccaro, and Laura Yussen. Some of them (Baccarro, Urquijo, and Cruz) have distinguished themselves, going on to direct important commercial plays.

Some plays were directed to the general public, while others were experimental, especially those by Argentine authors. Among them is *Juegos a la hora de la siesta* (*Games at Siesta Time*) by Roma Mahieu, a Polish writer residing in Argentina; the work deals with the problem of what would happen if children ruled the world. The play was a tremendous success, but after a run of nearly two years the government banned the production, at which point Roma Mahieu left the country for Paris. Also noteworthy are *Vida y milagros* (*Life and Miracles*) by Horacio Agustoni; *Las romerías* (*The Pilgrimages*) by Carlos Mauricio Pacheco, an Argentine author from the early twentieth century; *El rincón de los encuentros* (*Rendezvous Corner*) by Julio Ordano; *Cosméticos* (*Cosmetics*) by Bernardo Carey; *Locas por el biógrafo* (*Mad Women by the Biographer*) by Carlo Adami; *Vecindades* (*Neighborhoods*) by Maximo Soto; and *Malacara* (*White-face Roan*) by Sara Strasberg, a children's play.

These plays present varied themes. While the play by Soto is incomprehensible, the one by Adami is a nostalgic fresco about the film world of the 1930s. In each of the works presented by the theatre, nearly two hundred people collaborated, including actors, directors, scene and costume designers, musicians, and choreographers. Among the actors were Hedy Crilla, Federico Luppi, Nelly Prono, Chela Ruiz, Selva Alemán, Franklin Caicedo, Carlos Moreno, Beatriz Matar, and Elita Aizenberg. Some of them, such as Federico Luppi, have achieved stardom and status as public idols.

Of the more than twenty-five plays presented during 1974 to 1978, a few, like Colin Higgins' *Harold and Maude*, were repeated in successive seasons, primarily because of the excellent interpretation of Hedy Crilla. Modern North American theatre was represented by Israel Horowitz (*The First*), Leonard Melfi (*The Birdbath*), and several plays by Thornton Wilder; the English theatre by Harold Pinter (*The Caretaker*) and Simon Gray (*Butley*); and the German by Peter Handke (*The Minor Wants to Be Guardian*) and Frank Wedekind (*The Awakening of Spring*). This eclectic group has also ventured into Irish theatre via Synge, Russian theatre via Chekhov, and Spanish theatre via García Lorca.

The Repertory Group is directed by Agustín Alezzo with Norberto Díaz, Angela Ragno, Boris Rubaja, Miguel Moyano, Edgardo Moreira, Lizardo Laphitz, and Ezequiel Obarrio as actors. Of the stable companies, it is one of the most prestigious.

JAIME POTENZE
(Translated and revised by George Woodyard)

Brazil

INTRODUCTION

Together with Argentina and Mexico, Brazil has the greatest number of professional theatrical activities in Latin America. It therefore comes as a surprise that Brazil has so few permanent theatre companies with permanent or long-term casts. Between the 1920s and the 1950s, many fairly stable companies existed in the country, and all of them centered around a leading actor or actress (or both). Itália Fausta, Leopoldo Fores, Jayme Costa, Procópio Ferreira, Dulcina, and Odilon are perhaps the most famous. But even during that period the company was made up of a small nucleus which would be permanent, plus the extra actors needed to complete the cast of a particular play, some of whom might "usually" be called upon by this or that impresario.

During that same period one may find the classic example of the fate of most permanent casts in Brazil. In 1939 perhaps the most historical of all theatre groups in Brazil, Os Comediantes, was founded. Its first production reached the stage two years later, and in 1943 it presented Nelson Rodrigues' *O Vestido de Noiva* (*The Wedding Gown*), directed by the refugee Polish director Zbigniew Ziembinski. This marked the birth of modern Brazilian theatre. Despite the group's great success, in four short years it disintegrated. A theatre that reached a very restricted public did not permit a large professional and permanent cast. This has been the pattern of many a successful amateur group turned professional.

The most significant attempt to establish a permanent professional company in Brazil was the Teatro Brasileiro de Comédia (TBC) in São Paulo, which theoretically lasted from 1948 to 1968, but preserved its full permanent structure only until the early 1960s. Its contemporary in Rio was Os Artistas Unidos, which lasted about ten years but never had a permanent cast. After the TBC, the Teatro de Arena and Teatro Oficina made serious attempts in São Paulo, while in Rio there appeared, in succession, three companies with small permanent casts and extra actors appearing for each production: Companhia Tonia-Celli-Autran, Teatro Cacilda Becker, and Teatro dos Sete. The core of each company was made up of actors and directors who had earlier been with the TBC. This is also true of the Companhia Sérgio Cardoso-Nídia Lícia in São Paulo.

All of these groups were much smaller than the TBC and by the end of the 1960s had disappeared. None of them ever worked on a repertory basis in the city in which it was permanently based. All of them, however, took two to four of their plays on tour in some of the main capital cities, playing each for a few days, obviously with considerable substitutions in the casts of the earlier productions.

Since the early 1950s, the Serviço Nacional de Teatro, the federal agency for the support of theatre, has made several attempts to establish a permanent company. All attempts have been short-lived and only once, in the late 1950s, was a cast assembled for a season of three plays. A new attempt is now being made, but only one production has reached the stage.

Only Rio de Janeiro and São Paulo have permanent companies that are fully professional, even though some professional activity is evident in Belo Horizonte, Porto Alegre, Salvador, and Recife. Briefly in the late 1960s, the state of Paraná actually started a permanent company, state-operated, but it is no longer important.

There are sixty-eight fully registered "companies" or "producers" in Rio de Janeiro and eighty-one in São Paulo. A few of these are now defunct or in abeyance; many produce only occasionally. Only those groups with regular productions are listed here.

ARTISTIC AND CULTURAL SOCIETY THEATRE GROUP
(Grupo Teatral da Sociedade Artística e Cultural)
Rua Tabaiares 36
Santo André, S.P. 09000, Brazil

This group, the most stable in São Paulo, has been working for about ten years and, in spite of occasional financial strictures, has maintained a surprisingly high level of quality. The director, Antonio A. Petrin, is responsible for this continuity. Among the productions that have been well received are Antonio Callado's *Cidade Assassinada* (*Dead City*), Beaumarchais' *The Marriage of Figaro*, Molière's *Georges Dandin*, the prize-winning Brazilian play by Marcílio de Morães, *Mumu, a Vaca Metafísica* (*Moo-Moo the Metaphysical Cow*), and Osman Lins' *A Guerra do Cansa-Cavalo* (*The War of the Horse Tamer*).

ASDRÚBAL BROUGHT THE TROMBONE
(Asdrúbal Trouxe o Trombone)
Av. Rio Branco 156/1266
Rio de Janeiro, R.J. 20040, Brazil

This young company, with the incredible name of "Asdrúbal Brought the Trombone," was founded in July 1975 and has achieved three considerable hits with Alfred Jarry's *Ubu Roi*, Nikolai Gogol's *The Inspector General*, and especially the collectively written text, *Tráte-me Leão* (*Deal with Me, Lion*), which had long and triumphant runs in both São Paulo and Rio, where it originated. In a series of flashes that gave a varied and rich impression of the outlook and problems of adolescence and youth, it includes some good talents within its numbers. It is to be hoped that it will be able to hold out as a permanent company for some time to come. Hamilton Vaz Pereira is the director of the company.

BRAZILIAN DRAMATIC COMPANY
(Companhia Dramática Brasileira)
Subordinated to the Serviço Nacional de Teatro
Av. Rio Branco 179
Rio de Janeiro, R.J. 20040, Brazil

Theoretically, the Brazilian Dramatic Company stages the winning entry of the annual playwriting contest sponsored by the parent organization. Actually, this has happened only twice: in 1966, for the regular full-length play contest, and in 1978, when it staged the winning entry for puppet plays, *Sonhos de um Coração Brejeiro Naufragado de Ilusão* (*Dreams of a Roguish Heart Shipwrecked by Illusion*). *Sonhos* used both actors and puppets (of the "mamulengo" type) and traveled widely, not only in Brazil but also in several Latin American countries and the United States. Future plans are for the production of Brazilian plays as well as regular production of the contest winners. Beatriz Vega is the production manager.

DINO PRODUCTIONS, INC.
(Dino Produções Ltda.)
Rua Ayres Saldanha 130/802
Rio de Janeiro, R.J. 22060, Brazil

João Bethencourt, playwright and director of Dino Productions, produces exclusively his own plays or foreign plays that he translates. The company has been in existence for approximately ten years, with several long runs to its credit. One of Bethencourt's plays, *The Day the Pope Was Kidnapped*, has been produced in several countries. Dino has no permanent cast, as director Bethencourt tends to call certain actors rather regularly.

DOLORES COSTA BARROS PRODUCTIONS
(Dolores Costa Barros Produções)
Rua Pompeu Loureiro 27/804
Rio de Janeiro, R.J. 22061, Brazil

Dolores Costa is by far the longest lived producing unit in Brazil. Dercy Gonçalves has been a great favorite as a popular comedienne for decades. Dozens and dozens of plays have been produced, and even when they are by well-known authors, they are thoroughly altered to suit the actress. For many years Gonçalves worked in "revues" (vaudeville/burlesque). Her personal style otherwise has nothing to do with the development of Brazilian theatre.

EMERIC AND PERDIGÃO
(Emeric e Perdigão) (now associated with Paulo Autran)
Rua Capt. Antônio Rosas 376/91
São Paulo, S.P. 01443, Brazil

This group presented Tennessee Williams' *Cat on a Hot Tin Roof* in 1979 in São Paulo and in 1980 in Rio. It has also produced William Douglas Home's *The Secretary Bird* (via Marc-Gilbert Sauvajon's adaptation *Canard à l'Orange*) with Paulo Autran in the main part. Autran's own producing unit, presently in abeyance, has been responsible for a series of very successful productions, including *Oedipus Rex*, Arthur Miller's *After the Fall*, Dale Wasserman's *Man of La Mancha*, Molière's *The Bourgeois Gentleman*, and Shakespeare's *Coriolanus*. One of the country's outstanding actors, Autran has toured most of the country with his major productions. The producer for the unit is Aldo dos Santos Perdigão.

FERNANDO TORRES DIVERSIONS
(Fernando Torres Diversões)
Rua Frei Leandro 29
Rio de Janeiro, R.J., Brazil

Both Fernando Torres and his wife, Fernanda Montenegro, were members of the Teatro dos Sete. This group started at the very end of the 1950s, with every intention of becoming a permanent company. The other members were Gianni Ratto (director and set designer); Luciana Petrucelli (costumes); Sérgio Britto and Italo Rossi, actors; and Alfredo Souto de Almeida, who had directed several plays for amateurs but who left the group before it actually started operating. *O Mambembe* by Artur de Azevedo, *A Flea in Her Ear* by Georges Feydeau, and *Festival de Comédia* (with one-acters by Cervantes, Molière, and Martins Penna) were some of their most outstanding successes. When the group broke up in the mid-1960s, Torres and his wife set up their own producing unit and have worked constantly since. Their favorite Brazilian author is Millôr Fernandes (*A Mulher de Todos Nós* [*Everyone's Woman*], *O Homem do Princípio ao Fim* [*The Man from Start to Finish*], *Computa, Computador, Computa* [*Compute, Computer, Compute*], and *E . . .*) [*And . . .*]. They have staged Harold Pinter's *The Homecoming*, Eugene O'Neill's *More Stately Mansions*, and Samuel Beckett's *Happy Days*, and plan to continue to alternate Brazilian plays with good international texts.

IPANEMA THEATRE
(Teatro Ipanema)
Rua Prudente de Morães 824
Rio de Janeiro, R.J. 22420, Brazil

Ivan de Albuquerque and Rubens Correa, actors and directors (Albuquerque being more outstanding as director, Correa as actor), opened their own theatre in the late 1960s with a remarkable production of Chekhov's *The Cherry Orchard*, but perhaps their most extraordinary production was that of Fernando Arrabal's *The Architect and the Emperor of Assyria*, directed by Albuquerque and with Rubens Correa and José Wilker in the cast and a simple, imaginative, and impressive set by Arlindo Rodrigues. Several plays by new Brazilian authors, such as José Vicente, José Wilker, and Isabel Câmara, and extensive experimentation with scenic space and concepts of staging marked the Teatro Ipanema as an important landmark. Then, for a few years, the company went into abeyance and the theatre was rented out to other theatrical groups and, often, for purely musical shows. The group resumed activity with a tremendous failure in 1978. Finally, in 1979, it presented *Prometheus Bound* by Aeschylus, a production that was well received by the critics as a serious and difficult job.

The Ipanema Theatre's 1981 production of Manuel Puig's *The Kiss of the Spider Woman* (*O Beijo da Mulher Aranha*), with Rubens Correa and José de Araujo, ran for a year in Rio de Janeiro, eight months in São Paulo, and returned to Rio in 1983 for a month before touring Brazil and playing a limited season in Lisbon.

OFFICE THEATRE
(Teatro Oficina)
Rua Jaceguay 520
São Paulo, S.P. 01315, Brazil

Throughout the 1960s the Office Theatre was the most important group in São Paulo and for a good many years had a permanent nucleus and several actors who usually worked with the group. Among their first important productions was Clifford Odets' *Awake and Sing*, but the play that "made" the company was Maxim Gorky's *The Petit-Bourgeois*, an exceptionally fine production. After that, they did another and less successful Gorky, *The Enemies*, and then went on to a long period of sometimes brilliant and sometimes uneven formal experimentation. The most significant productions of that period were Brecht's *The Life of Galileo* and *In the Jungle of the Cities* and the remarkable staging of *O Rei da Vela* (*The Candle King*) by Oswald de Andrade, a play that had been written in 1929 by one of the most original minds of Brazil's modernist movement, which up to then had either been ignored or considered unstageable. The formal inventiveness was undoubtedly responsible for the success achieved by the production. After the second Gorky, the group, for a number of reasons, some of them political, started to come apart. Their farewell performance was a dubious collage entitled *Gracias, Señor*. Since then, José Celso Martínez Correa, the heart and soul of the project, has spent a number of years away from Brazil, mostly in Portugal and Mozambique. He has returned to Brazil and has announced that the Office Theatre will be resumed, with considerable alterations in its structure and type of repertoire.

OTHON BASTOS ARTISTIC PRODUCTIONS
(Othon Bastos Produções Artísticas)
Rua D. Alice c.22
São Paulo, S.P. 04544, Brazil

Having started his career in Bahia, Othon Bastos has been working in São Paulo for about ten years. He appeared with the regular groups of the 1960s and, with their disintegration, became his own producer. Basically, Bastos' productions are dedicated to Brazilian authors and to committed plays. The author his group has staged most frequently has been Gianfrancesco Guarnieri, who spent his formative years with the Teatro de Arena. Among his plays done by the Othon Bastos (actor) group are *Castro Alves Pede Passagem* (*Castro Alves Requests Passage*) and *Um Grito Parado no Ar* (*A Scream Silenced in the Air*), both of which were very successful. Another considerable success was achieved with *Caminho de Volta* (*The Return Road*) by Consuelo de Castro. Recently, the group has had considerable success (in Rio and São Paulo) with Augusto Boal's *Murro em Ponta de Faca* (*A Blow by Knife's Edge*) about Brazilian political exiles.

PAU BRASIL THEATRE GROUP
(Grupo de Teatro Pau Brasil)
Teatro São Paulo
Rua Albuquerque Lins 171
São Paulo, S.P. 01230, Brazil

This group has presented only one production, *Macunaíma* (1979), after the book of the same title by Mário de Andrade. The adaptation of the text carries the name of Jacques Thieraut, but most of it was completed after much collective experimentation. Working with mostly inexperienced actors for nearly one year, and helped by visual elements and costumes by Naum Alves de Souza, the perfect solution to the needs of Antunes Filho's direction, it was immensely successful. The group plans to do similar work based on Guimarães Rosa's *Grande Sertão: Veredas*, and it is hoped that this highly experimental group will be able to keep up the job it began so well.

PAULO GOULART ARTISTIC PRODUCTIONS, INC.
(Paulo Goulart Produções Artísticas Ltda.)
Teatro Paiol, Rua Amaral Gurgel 164
São Paulo, S.P. 01221, Brazil

While this is not a permanent company, Paulo Goulart, his wife, Nicette Bruno, and their two daughters are stage and television actor/actresses, and, on occasion, form a somewhat permanent nucleus. Goulart has been producing for about fifteen years. Among his productions (many of them directed by Antonio Abujamra, who sometimes co-produces with him) are Gorky's *The Last Ones*, Joe Orton's *Loot*, Paul Zindel's *The Effect of Gamma Rays on Man-in-the-Moon Marigolds*, and several comedies by the Brazilian Sérgio Jockyman, such as *Lá (There)*, *Boa Tarde, Excelência (Good Evening, Your Excellency)*, and *13*. These are just a few among many productions, and the Goularts, as a family, are among the most constant workers in Brazilian theatre.

RUTH ESCOBAR THEATRE
(Teatro Ruth Escobar)
Rua dos Ingleses 107
São Paulo, S.P. 01329, Brazil

Portuguese-born Ruth Escobar has been an extremely dynamic producer in São Paulo. Besides actual productions, she has organized Latin American and international theatre and dance festivals, as well as conferences and seminars. She has been producing for over ten years. Early in her career she produced Friedrich Dürrenmatt's *The Marriage of Mr. Mississippi*, which had no great success but pointed the way to her continuous interest in ambitious, large, and risky productions. The high points of her career were reached with two productions for which she brought the Spanish director Víctor García to Brazil: Fernando Arrabal's *Cementerio de automóviles (The Automobile Cemetery)* and Jean Genet's *Le Balcon (The Balcony)*, both well-deserved successes. She has not been equally successful on other occasions, including her recent, visually attractive production of Fernando Arrabal's *Tower of Babel*, when the directorial inexperience of C. Ripper, an excellent set designer, left the text's faults wide open. At present Escobar is not producing, but she will no doubt turn up with a new ambitious project in the near future.

SESI POPULAR THEATRE
(Teatro Popular do SESI)
Av. Paulista 1313
São Paulo, S.P. 01311, Brazil

The only permanent feature of the SESI is the director, Osmar Rodriguez Cruz, who selects his casts among professional actors and has had some plays run over a period of two or more years. Since the whole project is planned as an activity of the social services industry, no admission is charged and tickets are given away to workers as well as to all comers. After a very successful run of *O Poeta da Villa e Seus Amores* (*The Town Poet and His Loves*) by Plínio Marcos, about the life of a famous composer of the 1930s, Noel Rosa, the group has recently launched a new production of Nelson Rodrigues' 1952 play *A Falecida* (*The Diseased Woman*). Now housed in its own magnificent new theatre, the SESI's activities are likely to continue for a long time.

STAGE ARTISTIC PRODUCTIONS
(Platéia Produções Artísticas Ltda.)
Rua Tomé de Souza 1671
São Paulo, S.P. 05079, Brazil

Having achieved incredible popularity in television, always playing ingenues in the soap operas which are so successful with Brazilian audiences, Regina Duarte has returned to the theatre, where she has had a not very remarkable early career, as her own producer. Her first production was *Reveillon* (*Midnight Supper*) by Flávio Márcio, a very promising young Brazilian author who unfortunately died recently. It achieved both critical applause and public acclaim. Her second production, *Concerto para Piano No. 1*, by João Ribeiro Chaves Netto was feeble both as text and as production, but her third production, *O Santo Inquérito* (*The Holy Inquisition*) by Dias Gomes (an old play that earlier had not been well received) was again triumphantly successful. In a situation that permits her to dictate her own terms to the television network for which she works, Duarte has moved to more mature texts on video and plans to continue her theatre work.

TAC ARTISTIC PRODUCTIONS, INC.
(TAC Produções Artísticas Ltda.)
Rua Fonte da Saudade 47/cobertura
Rio de Janeiro, R.J. 22471, Brazil

Tônia Carrero, one of the best known actresses in the country, after leaving the Teatro Brasileiro de Comédia was one of the founding members of TAC, along with Adolfo Celi and Paulo Autran. This group maintained a regular nucleus of actors for several years, breaking up in the late 1960s. On her own, Carrero has produced with regularity. Her most outstanding acting during that period was Plínio Marcos' *Navalha na Carne* (*Knife in the Flesh*), directed by Fauzi Arap. Among her most recent successes is the long-running Somerset Maugham's *The Constant Wife*, a tremendous box office hit, despite a somewhat dubious direction by Cecil Thiré, Carrero's son. Between productions, Carrero works for other producers, as happened in the case of Edward Albee's *Who's Afraid of Virginia Woolf?*

TEREZA RAQUEL ARTISTIC PRODUCTIONS, INC.
(Tereza Raquel Produções Artísticas Ltda.)
Rua Siqueira Campos 143/51
Rio de Janeiro, R.J. 11031, Brazil

Tereza Raquel, one of the foremost actresses in Brazil, produces intermittently and, in between, works as an actress for other producers. Her most outstanding productions have been Witold Gombrowicz's *Mother*, for which she brought to Brazil the French director Claude Rógy; Sławomir Mrożek's *Tango*, directed by the Brazilian Amir Haddad; Chekhov's *The Seagull*, under the direction of the Argentinian Jorge Lavelli; and, most recently, Tennessee Williams' *Cat on a Hot Tin Roof*, directed by the Brazilian Paulo José. Raquel produces only the plays she deems worthy of grand-scale production.

THEATRE OF THE FOUR
(Teatro dos Quatro)
Sérgio Brito Produções Artísticas Ltda.
Rua Marquês de São Vicente 52
Rio de Janeiro, R.J., Brazil

Actor-director Sérgio Britto, individually or with three associates, has been producing regularly for about eight years. In 1978 the Theatre of the Four opened its own theatre with a much praised production of *Summerfolk* by Maxim Gorky, winning several prizes. Its second production at that same theatre, *Papa Highirti*, by Oduvaldo Vianna Filho, had been banned for several years. During 1982 and 1983 Fernanda Montenegro starred in a popular production of Rainer Werner Fassbinder's *Petra von Kant*. Earlier productions include Beckett's *Endgame*, a Feydeau, a new musical by the well-known popular composer Chico Buarque de Holanda, *A Opera dos Malandros* (*The Work of the Scoundrels*), based on John Gay's *The Beggar's Opera* and another musical, *O Rei de Ramos* (*The King of Boughs*), by Dias Gomes (book) and Chico Buarque de Holanda and Francis Hime. Here, again, we have a case of no permanent cast but a number of actors who appear with some regularity in Brito's productions.

BARBARA HELIODORA

Chile

INTRODUCTION

The development of the modern theatre in Chile dates from the early 1940s when the Teatro Experimental de la Universidad de Chile and later the Teatro de la Universidad Católica were first established. These two theatre groups are still in existence, both now forty years old. In terms of longevity of theatre companies—which are notoriously transitory—these groups clearly represent stability and endurance in a country that has been rocked by gigantic social and political changes over the years.

In the 1940s and 1950s a multitude of small groups emerged which contributed to the artistic and cultural process. Groups such as the Teatro Libre, Atelier 212, ICTUS (considered later on), Taller de Arte Dramático, and the Sociedad de Arte Escénico, whose mission was or still is to form actors and mount plays, are the offspring of the university theatres, in many cases born under their protective care. As a result, by the 1960s the national scene was populated with groups, directors, dramatists, and actors in continual movement. In short, the original objective of the university theatres had been achieved: a theatrical environment had been established in Chile.

Similarly, the State Technical University and the University of Concepción (in the south of Chile) founded schools and theatres of distinction in the same years. The work done by TEKNOS (of the Technical University) was outstanding until it disappeared by administrative decree in 1977. It specialized in the production of classical works (Shakespeare's *The Taming of the Shrew*, Ben Jonson's *Volpone*, Beaumarchais' *The Marriage of Figaro*), but from a Chilean and very current point of view, vitalizing the productions by incorporating Brechtian or Sartrian methods.

During the post-Allende period (1973 to the present), the theatre has survived in spite of severe hardships and economic deprivation. Although many talented and artistic Chileans now live in exile, the theatre continues to grow and prosper, making a national statement in a variety of appropriate forms. The recent incursion of established novelists, such as José Donoso (*Sueños de mala muerte*

[*Second Class Dreams*]), and Antonio Skármeta (*Ardiente paciencia* [*Burning Patience*]), into the realm of theatre indicates the attractiveness of the art form and its vitality within a Chilean milieu.

CATHOLIC UNIVERSITY THEATRE
(Teatro de La Universidad Católica)
Diagonal Oriente 3.300
Nuñoa, Santiago, Chile

The Catholic University Theatre was originally called the Teatro de Ensayo of the Catholic University. Its first performance was *Auto sacramental: El peregrino* (*Sacramental Play: The Pilgrim*) by Josef Valdivieso on October 17, 1943. The group was created by Pedro Mortheiru and Fernando Debesa, architecture students of the university. Until a few years ago it functioned in its original locale, the Camilo Henríquez Theatre. Among the important persons who created the Catholic University Theatre or worked with it over a period of time are Eugenio Dittborn, Ana González, Justo Ugarte, Fernando Colina, Elena Moreno, Héctor Noguera, Jaime Celedón, Violeta Vidaurre, Rafael Benavente, Sara Astica, and Jorge Alvarez.

In the beginning, the Catholic University Theatre sprang directly from the idea of a theatre that would correspond to the Teatro Experimental of the University of Chile, but with a Catholic character. This last feature, which came to be counterproductive for some, was discarded, and the Catholic University Theatre has shown, through the years, broad professional and ideological criteria. Following in the footsteps of the University of Chile, this group also began to perform first-class works, forming actors and directors, diffusing culture to various points in Chile, and performing—often before any other Latin American country—works that were at that very moment being presented in Europe and the United States. Its principal directors—Eugenio Dittborn, Fernando Colina, and Raúl Osorio—have shown professionalism, a zest for diffusion and study, and especially an interest in fulfilling a social function through performances. The theatre of the Catholic University has performed classical works (Carlo Goldoni, Molière, Honoré de Balzac, Cervantes, and Tirso de Molina), Chilean works (Sergio Vodanović, Luis Alberto Heiremans, Egon Wolff, Santiago del Campo, and Acevedo Hernández), and contemporaries (J. B. Priestley, Jean Giraudoux, Eugene O'Neill, and Jean Anouilh).

In addition, for many years the theatre of the Catholic University has been publishing its journal, *Apuntes*, which includes theatre items of importance to directors, actors, scenographers, and professors. A few years ago, this institution returned to the production of classical works. In 1978 it attempted to continue performing contemporary Chilean plays, but one day before the opening of Marco Antonio de la Parra's *Lo crudo, lo cocido, lo podrido* (*The Raw, the Cooked, the Rotten*), the work was prohibited by order of the university authorities. Raúl Osorio staged an interesting and professional production of *Hamlet*. Later productions include *Parejas de trapo* (*Rag Couples*) by Egon Wolff, *El gran teatro del mundo* (*The Great Theatres of the World*) by Calderón, *A Doll's House* by Ibsen, and *Faust* by Goethe.

ICTUS
Teatro la Comedia, Merced 249
Santiago, Chile

Created by a group of people working in the Catholic University, ICTUS came to life in 1961. Among the founders were Germán Béker, Paz Irarrázaval, Aníbal Reyna, Julio Jung, Mónica Echeverría, Jorge Díaz, Carla Cristi, and Jaime Celedón. At first, ICTUS mounted plays by contemporary authors, especially Europeans and North Americans, following its principles of commenting on contemporary mankind, creating vanguard theatre, and performing works of artistic rigor. ICTUS staged such plays as *Murder in the Cathedral* by T. S. Eliot, *The Lark* by Jean Anouilh, *The Caretaker* by Harold Pinter, and *The Visit of the Old Lady* by Friedrich Dürrenmatt.

At the same time, the group made known a Chilean writer, who later emigrated to Spain and renovated the themes and forms of Chilean theatre. The author was Jorge Díaz; the plays presented were *El cepillo de dientes* (*The Toothbrush*), *Réquiem por un girasol* (*Requiem for a Sunflower*), *El velero en la botella* (*The Ship in the Bottle*), *El lugar donde mueren los mamíferos* (*The Place Where the Mammals Die*), *Introducción al elefante y otras zoologías* (*Introduction to the Elephant and Other Creatures*), and *El nudo ciego* (*The Blind Knot*). Around 1968 ICTUS began to vary its style and to perform works in which the participation of the actor and director would have more influence on the product created than in traditional production. Thus, there began a questioning of the actors' work, which finally arrived at the formula for collective creation, a style still in vogue today in Chile. Works such as *Hablemos a calzón quitado* (*Let's Talk Honestly*) and especially *Cuestionemos la cuestión* (*Let's Question the Question*) are a point of departure for breaking down the traditional separations among author, director, and actor, in order to enter into a collaborative process. Along this line, the first great work by ICTUS was *Tres noches de un sábado* (*Three Nights of One Saturday*), a combination of two known authors and the ideas of a company actor for one of the three sketches that compose the work. For the first time it could be seen that, in a professional way, ICTUS' theatre was more theatrical than literary, more spontaneous than polished. At times speeches that were deficient or without a clear conflict were sustained marvelously on stage by the force of the characters and the atmosphere created by the actors.

With this play, the company produced a work created by both the professional author and the group, where ideas were questioned and stage possibilities were discussed. The group sought to create a theatre that would offer great vitality and an interior electrifying force for the present day, even though it might be short-lived. Along this line it has created *Nadie sabe para quién se enoja* (*No

One Knows for Whom to Be Angry), Pedro, Juan y Diego (Pedro, Juan and Diego), and *Cuántos años tiene un día (How Many Years in a Day).* The last two were developed with the Chilean playwrights David Benavente and Sergio Vodanović, respectively. Their theatre also is strongly Chilean, preoccupied with certain national problems. The last two works deal with the unemployment problems of construction workers (and of all workers in general). In the second play, the difficulties of achieving authentic culture in Chile today are shown by means of some television reporters who are harassed by the authorities. In both plays, the movement on stage, the silences, the characters' attitudes, their evasiveness, and their imagination, while incomprehensible in a reading, can only be appreciated with the staging. *Cuántos años tiene un día (How Many Years in a Day)* was presented in the Caracas Festival of 1978 and in the Encuentro de Teatro de las Américas in the United States in 1979. Also from 1979 is *Lindo país esquina con vista al mar (Pretty Country Corner View to the Sea),* followed in 1981 by *La mar estaba serena (The Sea Was Calm)* and in 1982 by *Sueños de mala muerte (Second Class Dreams),* developed by the group in collaboration with José Donoso. Its principal members today are Nissim Sharim, Claudio di Girólamo, Delfina Guzmán, Cristián García Huidobro, Maité Fernández, and Sergio Freitas.

IMAGE GROUP
(Grupo Imagen)
Teatro Bulnes, Avenida Bulnes 188
Santiago, Chile

The Image Group was created in 1974 in order to revitalize the decadent Chilean theatrical atmosphere of those years. The group initiated its presentations with the premiere of *The Day They Released Joss* by Hugo Claus, followed by *My Beloved Idiot* by Charles Boyer. These foreign works were not being done in Chile at that time. In this same line they gave an impeccable performance some time later of Marcel Pagnol's *Topaze* and a pair of works by the contemporary Jewish author Victor Häim, *The Visitor* and *The Widow.* But their most interesting effort was to rescue from obscurity some Chilean authors practically unknown until then. The first works of this type were *Te llamabas Rosicler (You Were Called Rosicler)* by Luis Rivano and *Las tres mil palomas y el loro (Three Thousand Doves and the Parrot).* Afterwards, they staged *El último tren (The Last Train),* a collective work, and *Lo crudo, lo cocido, lo podrido (The Raw, the Cooked, the Rotten)* by Marco Antonio de la Parra, which won the TOLA (Theatre of Latin America) festival prize of 1979. More recently, the group staged *Viva Somoza (Long Live Somoza)* in 1981.

The Image Group, especially through its performances of *Te llamabas Rosicler (You Were Called Rosicler)* and *El último tren (The Last Train),* has developed a theatre of popular, simple, and profoundly Chilean themes, achieving realism and at times almost melodrama, the latter sought as a valid and still viable aesthetic option. Its themes are based on contemporary Chile—its people, daily conflicts, and popular language. In short, the group has salvaged a type of theatre which speaks much more to the average national spectator—emotive and simple. It is a theatre that deals with current themes, but whose universality makes them always current. Throughout the years, the group has shown a necessary continuity, which it is hoped will endure. It is currently producing another realistic Chilean work developed with the dramatist Juan Radrigán, also discovered by the group's members. Among those who make up the company are Gustavo Meza, Jael Unger, Tennyson Ferrada (Chile's poet laureate), Coca Guazzini, and Juan Cuevas.

NATIONAL THEATRE
(Teatro Nacional)
Morandé 25, Santiago, Chile

The National Theatre was earlier known as the Teatro Experimental of the University of Chile. Founded in June 1941 by a group of students from the country's most important university, it was directed by Pedro de la Barra (d. 1977), one of Chile's most creative and serious theatre personalities. The creation of the Teatro Experimental indicated a complete reversal in Chilean theatre, which had been repeating outdated commercial trends of theatre of "great figures." Its fundamental purpose was to renovate old theatre styles in Chile, to terminate the "divo" or star system by which the star performed for his or her personal glory, and to impose a directing and acting focus on the written work—in short, to create a spectacle of cultural and artistic significance at the highest possible level.

To accomplish this purpose, the theories of Konstantin Stanislavsky, Erwin Piscator, André Antoine, and Jacques Copeau were brought to Chile for the first time. The entire approach to drama was renovated: scenography was no longer thrown together at the last minute with paper and cardboard; depth and realism were achieved with curtains and sets. Lights were used with dramatic intent. Character became more important than the actor. The group rehearsed for months, with a great sense of responsibility, in order to present a first-rate performance. They were striving for a serious professionalism and were also learning techniques of acting and direction, which would overcome old improvisations.

Among the founders of the Teatro Experimental were Pedro de la Barra, José Ricardo Morales, Bélgica Castro, Roberto Parada, María Maluenda, Rubén Sotoconil, Héctor González, Domingo Piga, and Pedro Orthus. The functions began in 1941 with *La guardia cuidadosa* (*The Careful Guard*) by Cervantes, *Ligazón* (*The Bond*) by Ramón del Valle Inclán, *Egloga séptima* (*Seventh Eclogue*) by Juan del Encina, and *El mancebo que casó con mujer brava* (*The Young Man Who Married an Ill-tempered Woman*) by Alejandro Casona. Through the years, the Teatro Experimental—later called Instituto Teatral de la Universidad de Chile (ITUCH)—has presented classical works (Shakespeare, Lope de Vega, Tirso de

Molina, and Goethe), Chilean works (Daniel Barros Grez, Enrique Bunster, María Asunción Requena, Isidora Aguirre, and Luis Alberto Heiremans), and contemporary European works (Luigi Pirandello, Federico García Lorca, and Anton Chekhov). These works were made known throughout the country by a series of tours, recitals, and presentations, which were commonly offered during certain periods of the year.

The theatre of the University of Chile, through its presentations abroad and its training of actors, scenographers, dramatists, and directors, built up over several decades a reputation that brought recognition in the Spanish-speaking world as an example worthy of imitation. Its basic policies in these years can be characterized briefly as follows: (1) *Diffusion of classical and modern theatre.* Until then, there was no continuity in developing a serious sample of universal classics and current dramas. (2) *Formation of a theatre school.* This encompasses an optimal scenic production, professionalism of the actor, integration of theatre roles, adoption of a point of view for the performance, and so on. (3) *Creation of a theatrical environment.* The impetus for the creation of other schools, groups, and companies, which would promote theatre of a high cultural level, resulted in the emergence of important groups and personnel for Chilean theatre. (4) *Presentation of new values.* This would encourage dramatic creativity and new dramatists under the auspices of an Annual Contest for Theatrical Works, in order to draw out many silent dramatists, who could not otherwise produce their works. For all of these reasons, ITUCH was the great renovator of the Chilean theatre. No change exists nowadays in its bases, and the plays mounted are, in general, mediocre. The founders and their successors are either dead or in exile; in addition, the government-imposed administration limits the group's activities.

JUAN ANDRÉS PIÑA
(Translated and revised by George Woodyard)

Colombia

INTRODUCTION

It is awkward to talk about theatre "companies" in Colombia, as the term nowadays carries a contemptuous connotation. The word "company" used to refer to commercial Spanish troupes which began visiting this country in the eighteenth century. Their repertory and technique were so low grade that the term became discredited during the second half of that century.

Since at least 1957, Colombian theatre troupes have tended to call themselves simply "theatre groups," a term implying a noncommercial position. This new attitude is also a reaction against Colombia's chief dramatic figure before 1957, the playwright and "impresario" Luis Enrique Osorio. He used the word "company" for his old-fashioned theatre, following closely the Spanish model of a frivolous theatre. Paradoxically, he continually referred to the need to create a national theatre, but the forms he gave it can hardly be said to be original. The date 1957, therefore, marks a change in attitude toward Colombian theatre, as the traditional concept was officially rejected by the chairman of the First National Theatre Festival held in Bogotá that year. Impresarios tended to disappear in the theatre in favor of groups functioning as cooperatives in which there is no patron and the whole group autonomously manages its own investments and profits.

Consequently, professional theatre has a very specific meaning in Colombia as the vast majority of actors, directors, and playwrights do not make their living from the theatre, although a "maestro," that is, a theatre professional, has vast experience and knowledge of dramatic art. Until now, Colombia has never worried about financing a national theatre company. Hence, commercial theatre is practically nonexistent today, except perhaps for some of what we call café-theatre, which is done mainly by television actors with television commercial standards.

Colombia's latest dramatic productions reflect the powerful hold of the country's political ideology. All too often characterization and plot are dehumanized. Moreover, nothing is heard anymore about building a national theatre, but rather about establishing a class theatre whose class is even obscure. There is a repetition of stagings, versions, themes, and techniques, and an avowed attitude of non-dialogue with "bourgeois" standards, which sometimes seems to be a simple and naive prejudice against the opposition. This situation has led other groups into a tiresome and poor imitation of what the leaders keep doing. These trends do not augur well for the future of creativity in Colombian drama. The country needs a frank and brave recognition of these discomforting facts, as well as an open attitude toward whatever opposing theatrical forces still exist.

BOGOTÁ POPULAR THEATRE
(Teatro Popular de Bogotá)
Carrera 5 14-71
Bogotá, D.E., Colombia

The idea of the Bogotá Popular Theatre was conceived as far back as 1964, when Jorge Alí Triana, its present director, and some other members of the first Teatro Popular de Bogotá obtained a grant to continue their dramatic studies at the Art Institute in Prague, Czechoslovakia. Upon their return, they initiated their theatrical activities in 1968 at a restaurant in the center of the old city, with a number of plays within the classical European tradition. Many of the initial actors were already professional, and thus the Bogotá Popular Theatre achieved a considerable reputation in those first years. The group presented some very fine productions, such as Carlo Goldoni's *The Landlady* or Calderón de la Barca's *La vida es sueño* (*Life Is a Dream*). The latter was an original television production filmed at the old salt mines of Zipaquirá. Television shows afforded the economic support for further productions, since they were of notably better quality than the majority of Colombian television theatre shows at the time. In 1969 the Argentinian actress Fanny Mickey, who had retired after several years at the Teatro Experimental de Cali, decided to join the newly established Bogotá Popular Theatre. Her experienced vision and her public relations ability helped the new institution gain moral and economic support from a vast and enthusiastic audience. Since 1969, the group has been established in the Teatro Odéon, an old movie-house that was turned into a theatre by the University of America Theatre Group in 1965. (Fanny Mickey, for unknown reasons, resigned around 1973 and founded the first café-theatre to exist in the capital.) Luis Alberto García, actor, director, and playwright, who had previously managed the Theatre Group of the University of America, joined the Bogotá Popular Theatre, serving as both actor and author of several of its most successful national productions. The history of the group, however, is characterized by two rather distinct periods: 1968 to 1973, and 1973 to the present. During the first period its tendency was mainly that of a classic repertory group in a time when the rest of Colombian theatre groups were involved in experimentation. This produced problems with the other groups, which had adopted a radical political view, especially at the International Theatre Festival at Manizales. Paradoxically, the group carried on the vanguardist drama of the moment through its classic repertory. This program was bound to invite strong confrontation with the dogmatic National Theatre Corporation (founded in 1970), which attempted to dictate an overall policy for Colombian drama.

This confrontation led to the company's second period of production in which it came into closer contact with other Colombian theatrical tendencies. To the first period belong such plays as García Lorca's *El amor de don Perlimplín y Belisa en su jardín* (*The Love of Don Perlimplín and Belisa in Their Garden*), Cervantes' *La cueva de Salamanca* (*The Cave of Salamanca*), Nikolai Gogol's *The Inspector General*, Machiavelli's *The Mandrake*, Sławomir Mrożek's *Karol*, and Plautus' *The Pot*. The second period begins with an original production of the group's first Latin American play, *Delito, condena, y ejecución de una gallina* (*Crime, Sentence and Execution of a Chicken*) by the Guatemalan Manuel José Arce, followed by a collective staging of *Toma tu lanza, Sintana* (*Take Your Lance, Sintana*) in 1972, a play intended as children's theatre. This play about Colombian Indian tribes proved to be a clear approach to other contemporary experimental productions.

Since this last production the Bogotá Popular Theatre has continued to adhere to the general tendencies stipulated by the Colombian Theatre Corporation. Characteristic plays of this period are *I Took Panama* and *La primera independencia* (*The First Independence*, 1977). The texts of these plays—again collective productions—belong to Luis Alberto García and deal with Colombian history in a sometimes excessively caricaturesque and dehumanized way. Nevertheless, the Colombian Theatre Corporation has chosen the Bogotá Popular Theatre to participate at several international festivals outside Colombia. At the Caracas International Festival in Venezuela in 1972, the company won a Juana Sujo Award. Although the critics consider its treatment of Colombian history and characters to be superficial, the Bogotá Popular Theatre is still a leading theatre group in Colombia today.

CALI EXPERIMENTAL THEATRE
(Teatro Experimental de Cali)
Calle 7 8-61, Cali, Colombia

The Cali Experimental Theatre (TEC) is Colombia's first modern theatre group. Enrique Buenaventura, its leading personality, acquired some theatrical experience with visiting troupes as early as the late 1940s. After working in Buenos Aires and Chile in the 1950s, he returned to Cali, his hometown, around 1957, where he worked as a teacher in the new Departmental Theatre School of Cali. The rise of the Cali Experimental Theatre dates from 1959, when the Third National Theatre Festival was held at the Teatro Colón, the official theatre of Bogotá since 1892. The company won first place with its production of Sophocles' *Oedipus Rex*, but it was perhaps the production of *A la diestra de Dios Padre* (*On the Right-hand Side of God the Father*), Buenaventura's dramatic version of a story by the Colombian novelist Tomás Carrasquilla, that brought the Cali Experimental Theatre its greatest recognition. The play is based on traditional folk tales treated in a professional and original manner. In 1960 the group participated in the Festival des Nations in Paris, where for the first time it won an international award for a Colombian theatre group.

The Cali Experimental Theatre remained the leading Colombian theatre group for many years because of its mature position with a theatre school, producing enough professional actors to maintain an excellent level of production. We can, therefore, divide the history of the company into two distinct periods: one in which the Departmental Theatre School was producing professional actors for it; and one in which the new Cali Experimental Theatre had to depend on its old actors or accept new ones without necessary training. This situation has led to two different levels of production, both within the new Cali Experimental Theatre as a group, as well as in Buenaventura's own production as a playwright. The first period coincides with the Bogotá Popular Theatre's classical period of productions of European or North American plays, with some isolated exceptions of a few national plays, all of which were written by Buenaventura himself.

To the first period belong the main productions of García Lorca's *La casa de Bernarda Alba* (*The House of Bernarda Alba*), Molière's *The Affected Ladies*, Buenaventura's *Un réquiem por el Padre Las Casas* (*A Requiem for Father Las Casas*), Fernando de Rojas' *La Celestina* (*The Go Between*), and Arthur Miller's *A View from the Bridge*, among many others. This last important production, directed by Pedro I. Martínez in 1965, provoked the first deep crisis within the company. The group's excessive attention to commercial productions led to economic breakdown. Fanny Mickey left for her native Argentina, and when she returned to Colombia in 1969 she joined the Bogotá Popular Theatre. Nonetheless, the Cali Experimental Theatre continued its intense dramatic activity, notably with the production of *Ubu Roi* by Alfred Jarry, which anticipated the future theatrical compromise of the group.

In 1966 the newly founded La Casa de la Cultura Theatre in Bogotá attempted to initiate an interesting dramatic experience by interchanging directors with the Cali Theatre. Buenaventura came personally to Bogotá to direct Shakespeare's *Macbeth* with the cast of La Casa de la Cultura Theatre. Santiago García traveled to Cali where he directed the cast of the TEC in Buenaventura's *La trampa* (*The Trap*). This play, finely written and finely played, contributed to the crisis, for the institutional Armed Forces of Colombia termed it "subversive," even though it treated the distant subject of Ubico's dictatorship in Nicaragua.

Other political happenings coincided. In 1968 the expulsion of Buenaventura and his staff of teachers from the Departmental Theatre School, including Helio Fernández, Luis Fernando Pérez, and Fernando González Cajiao, resulted in the loss of the TEC's financial support by the authorities—but not its audience. At this time a new concept of the theatre developed within the group. Instead of compromising with the traditional authorities of the establishment, the group assumed a more compromising attitude toward its popular audience, which naturally led to more overt opposition to the establishment. This position of protest is evident both in Buenaventura's productions as a playwright, and in the plays staged by the company since then.

The first production by this new Cali Experimental Theatre in 1968 was *Los inocentes* (*The Innocents*), an adaptation by Buenaventura of Emmanuel Robles' *Montserrat*. Although it kept some of the external form of its classic period (that is, the traditional treatment of plot, character, and theme), the group dealt mainly with the problems of political independence in nineteenth-century Latin America. Staged in the traditionally professional manner, the play won for Iván Montoya a first prize for acting in the National Theatre Festival in Bogotá. With this and later successful productions, the group accumulated sufficient capital to buy its own center in Cali in 1970. The next productions showed clearly that Buenaventura and the group were struggling to develop new ways to approach Colombian theatre more in line with the national reality. *Papeles del infierno* (*Papers from Hell*), written by Buenaventura and staged by Danilo Tenorio in 1969, consists of a series of sketches dealing with the general theme of "la violencia" in Colombia, a period of nondeclared civil war that cost thousands of lives among the poor and defenseless peasants of the country. Although this national theme had been anticipated by the writings of Gustavo Andrade Rivera or Fanny Buitrago, the TEC's approach was a new theatrical experience that led to a new technique. Buenaventura also adapted Ramón del Valle Inclán's novel on colonialism, *Tirano Banderas* (*Tyrant Banderas*), for staging by Alberto Castilla at the Study Theatre of the National University. The production of Peter Weiss' *Song of the Lusitanian Bogey*, directed by Helio Fernández, belongs to this tendency toward political compromise.

Perhaps the most significant production, begun in 1969 and revised a thousand times, is *Soldados* (*Soldiers*), a play by Carlos José Reyes based on texts by the Colombian novelist Alvaro Cepeda Zamudio. The production technique was definitely new at the TEC: no set, only three actors at the beginning, perhaps a fourth later on; the simplest possible costumes and props, used to symbolize a river, a village, a brothel, a train, and a barracks. This dramatic technique was also foretold by the productions of *Macbeth*, where actors also functioned as a set to build Macbeth's castle, and *The Seven Capital Sins* by Bertolt Brecht, produced earlier by the TEC. *Soldados* assimilated the theories in vogue at the time, such as Antonin Artaud's theatre of cruelty or, especially, Jerzy Grotowski's poor theatre. A notion of the Japanese and Chinese theatres was also evident and was acknowledged by Buenaventura himself.

At that time, the Cali Experimental Theatre did not have a stable place for rehearsals or its productions. As a result, it took to the streets or to an occasional theatre house, a creative approach to a difficult situation. The techniques developed by the company were soon recognized and imitated all over the country (and perhaps Latin America). In the following years, the group won international recognition at San Francisco, Nancy, Mexico, and Caracas. This, then, is the company's second period to which belong lesser productions such as *La denuncia* (*The Denunciation*), *Seis horas en la vida de Frank Kulak* (*Six Hours in the*

Life of Frank Kulak), and *El convertible rojo* (*The Red Convertible*), all by Buenaventura.

DON ELOY LITTLE THEATRE
(Teatrino Don Eloy)
Academia de Arte del Sur Don Eloy, Calle 20 Sur 10-B-36
Bogotá, Colombia

Critics, especially the Colombian Theatre Corporation, rarely pay any attention to the Don Eloy Little Theatre, perhaps because it has prolonged an outdated theatrical tradition. Nonetheless, it deserves recognition. Its theatrical philosophy differs notably from that of the other, better known Colombian theatre groups, as it has been capable of maintaining an independent attitude and a faithful audience since at least 1963. The Don Eloy is, in fact, the oldest existing theatre group in Bogotá, as well as the first to have a school in this city.

Its founder and actual director is Sofía de Moreno, whose background is very different from that of the other directors treated here. She is the last of the pupils of the late Luis Enrique Osorio (although she has abandoned some of his dramatic concepts), and she and her husband, Angel Alberto Moreno, worked with Osorio's company in the 1940s and 1950s. The two Morenos have been principally concerned with producing Colombian playwrights, since Sofía herself is a playwright.

The Don Eloy is really the name for the place where the Art Academy of the South functions as a theatre. The Art Academy is at the same time a children's theatre school from which the Don Eloy, much like the old Cali Experimental Theatre, receives its actors, generally children. The financial support Sofía gets is nonexistent, probably because of her avowed modesty. She has called important people to work for her, but economic difficulties prevent the academy from giving an overall general training to the children, except in the areas of music, dance, theatre history, and actual practice for theatre productions and television shows. In some of these productions, the Don Eloy has attained a certain professionalism that must be recognized and, if possible, supported.

The history of the Don Eloy Little Theatre has been rather uniform since its foundation in 1963, when it acquired its actual locale—Sofía's house—through the private initiative of the two Morenos. Its emphasis is on children's theatre, although it has occasionally produced some adult plays, all of them written by Colombian playwrights. The academy and the Don Eloy are financed by student tuitions, with some profits from annual regular performances at Teatro Colón or Teatro Municipal in Bogotá. The Don Eloy is also responsible for a one-half hour television program every week, which has brought some economic relief.

Among its successful productions presented in Bogotá and environs are the folk plays by Ciro Mendia; *José Dolorcitos*, *Rin Ron Abuelo* (*Rin Ron Grandfather*), *Las brujas modernas* (*The Modern Witches*), and *El culpable* (*The Guilty*), all by Sofía de Moreno; and *El globo* (*The Balloon*) and *La comadreja*

(*The Weasel*) by Fernando González Cajiao. Through these productions Sofía has sought to lead the children away from foreign influences. She still has a long way to go in establishing enough personal independence of thought and action to allow her to be entirely free of these same influences. Nonetheless, the production of her musical play, *Rin Ron Abuelo* (*Rin Ron Grandfather*), which revitalizes Rafael Pombo's children's characters and tales, has established the Don Eloy as an agent of renewal for Colombian drama.

LA CANDELARIA THEATRE
(Teatro La Candelaria)
Calle 12 2–59, Bogotá, Colombia

La Candelaria traces its origins to the now defunct Teatro El Buho (1957–1961), the first experimental theatre in Bogotá. Santiago García got his start in theatre there. Together with Carlos José Reyes, in 1966 he founded the La Casa de la Cultura Theatre on an independent basis. This theatre group started working with some of the actors of the previous Study Theatre of the National University in Bogotá, most of whom had scant theatrical training. Its professional quality, therefore, was not at the level of the Cali Experimental Theatre (TEC) during its first period. Nonetheless, many of the actors of La Candelaria have acquired professional status.

The history of La Candelaria is also easily divided into two periods: in the first one (1966–1972), the group was called Casa de la Cultura; and in the second (1972 to the present), La Candelaria. Although many of its original members have changed, the director, Santiago García, gives a certain consistency to the group.

La Candelaria, in its Casa de la Cultura period, did not develop a definitely classical repertory, as was the case with the Bogotá Popular Theatre and the Cali. Rather, it continued the experimental line of El Buho and the Study Theatre. At the latter, Santiago García had already directed an ambitious production of *Galilei* (*The Life of Galileo*) by Brecht, in an attempt to emulate the TEC. La Casa de la Cultura commanded neither strong financial support nor a faithful audience that would allow it to stage large productions with a professional group of actors. Its first productions were *Soldados* (*Soldiers*) by Carlos José Reyes and *The Zoo Story* by Edward Albee.

The first large-scale production that brought La Candelaria closer to the TEC was Peter Weiss' *Marat/Sade* in 1966, in its first Spanish translation, which was done by Fernando González Cajiao. Next followed Shakespeare's *Macbeth*, a production that showed a lack of professionalism, and then *The Marriage* by Witold Gombrowicz, *The Good Woman of Setzuan* by Brecht, *Metamorfosis* by Carlos José Reyes on Kafka, *The Seagull* by Chekhov, *The Bathhouse* by Vladimir Mayakovsky, and *The Surrounded Corpse* by Kateb Yacine, among many others. Finally, there was the production of the *Oresteia* by Aeschylus, which failed to create the enthusiasm García had expected among its audience of workers. Rarely do Colombian plays appear in the repertory, except for the productions by Carlos José Reyes, which he personally staged.

Around 1971 a crisis resulted over the repertory of La Casa de la Cultura Theatre: the plays were intended mainly for people knowledgeable about European dramatic trends and history, but did not attract the popular audience of workers Santiago García had anticipated. Unfortunately García never dared to mount a production by a national playwright, which would have given him some hints about how to attract a popular audience. National themes were forwarded indirectly, so that a new attitude toward the creation of a compromising theatre made itself indispensable with less force than at the Cali Experimental Theatre.

This change in attitude occurred at the same time Santiago García and his collaborators realized the need for a stable theatre location. (The Bogotá had already acquired a stable center around 1969, and the Cali around 1970.) García took advantage of the City Council's desire to establish a series of cultural centers in the old quarter of the city called La Candelaria. He obtained a loan to purchase an old house, which he adapted as the Teatro La Candelaria. La Candelaria is finally the property of the whole group, but as an institution, it is incapable of supporting its actors on a stable economic basis, even with help from official institutions.

Naturally, a new production policy was soon the result of all of these changes: collective productions were in vogue and were useful for La Candelaria, as they allowed the actors to study and present national themes and characters to attract a popular audience. The first production of this type was *Nosotros los comunes* (*We, the Common People*), a play based on the commoners' revolution of the late eighteenth century, shortly before Colombian independence. The subject had been treated by several Colombian dramatists, but it got a very special interpretation at La Candelaria. This first production was historically inaccurate, presenting the peasants' historical fight against the Spanish forces without showing the antagonist on stage. The play became a series of political speeches without real conflict, characterization, or plot. La Candelaria merely adopted the prevalent tendency of the times.

The tendency of La Candelaria coincides basically with that of the Cali Experimental Theatre and the Bogotá Popular Theatre; the group has received international recognition in San Francisco, Mexico, Nancy, Paris, Italy, New York, and Caracas through prizes bestowed by the National Theatre Corporation. The words used to describe the Cali and the Colombian theatre in general may also be applied to La Candelaria, although it has made an original contribution and does not seem worried about precious repetition. La Candelaria must be considered a fundamental group for understanding Colombia's present dramatic development.

FERNANDO GONZÁLEZ CAJIAO
(Edited by George Woodyard)

Costa Rica

INTRODUCTION

The Costa Rican theatre movement came of age in the 1970s. While there was some theatrical activity in the country since the nineteenth century and both religious and secular pieces of merit were produced, only recently did it achieve permanence and professionalism. These characteristics, as we shall see, are closely linked to the formation in 1970 of a Ministry of Culture and in 1971 of a National Theatre Company, organizations that have attempted to establish art throughout the nation.

During the period of Spanish colonization, Costa Rica was unable to retain the indigenous ritual tradition that survived—although in mutilated form—in Guatemala and Nicaragua. Rather, the interest in theatre in Costa Rica was awakened through the influence of sixteenth-century European drama. Construction of the Teatro Mora in 1850 stimulated interest in theatre productions, especially lyric ones, and some traveling companies stopped over in the capital. Performances were not regularly scheduled, however, until after 1897, with the opening of the National Theatre—an expansive architectural work imitating Italian constructions.

In the 1920s and 1930s, especially during the postwar years, several lyric and dramatic companies from Spain and the Americas considered this theatre an obligatory stop on their tours. The novelty and color of foreign productions awakened the interest of the intellectual classes, which gave rise to some costumbristic comedies with obvious French and Italian influence. These first national playwrights attracted attention, and several movie theatres were taken over for productions by such authors as Carlos Gagini, Eduardo Calsamiglia, José Marín Canas, Alfredo Castro Fernández, José Fabio Garnier, and Raúl Salazar. But these periods of spendor lacked continuity and generally vanished at the first sign of national economic, political, or social pressures.

In fact, the national theatre movement began to take on an organic structure only after 1950, when the visit of famous Spanish companies (for example, the Lope de Vega and María Guerrero) stimulated local artists to experiment on stage and to rescue some national theatre manuscripts which had not appeared on the boards. This pioneer effort had an amateurish character and counted on little governmental support, but it was different from preceding activity in that, for the first time, a theatre season was opened with some hope of continuity. The groups were elitist, but over a period of time, they were to give a stamp of maturity to the theatre movement.

The first step in this process was the creation in 1951 of the Teatro Universitario (TU), a group developed around three Spanish actors from the Compañía Lope de Vega who decided to remain in San José and who were soon contracted by the University of Costa Rica. The pioneer artists of the new Costa Rican theatre and the first stable company (the TU) coalesced around these professionals (Pilar Bienet, Conchita Montijano, and José Carlos Rivera). In 1951 they staged Cervantes' *Entremeses* and later many other important works from the world repertoire. This first team of theatre people, who performed all functions from stagehand to stage manager, consisted of Jorge Charpentier, Anna Poltronieri, Daniel Gallegos, José Tassies, Norma Orozco, Fernando del Castillo, Eugenio Fonseca, Luis Castro, Oscar Bakit, Alfredo Sancho, Nelson Brenes, Nury Raventós, and Lucio Ranucci, as well as their relatives and friends who cooperated in these first ventures.

After this amateur thrust, carried out in the university, the company launched a successful program of universal works, such as *Topaze* by Marcel Pagnol, *Debora* by Alfredo Sancho, *Prohibido suicidarse en primavera* (*Suicide Forbidden in Springtime*) and *La sirena varada* (*The Beached Mermaid*) by Alejandro Casona, *Ninotchska* by Marc-Gilbert Sauvajon, *The Importance of Being Earnest* by Oscar Wilde, and *Ghosts* by Henrik Ibsen. The distinctive efforts of this university group, which caught on rapidly in this context, stimulated the parallel formation of another important group on the national theatre scene: the Arlequín, a group of amateurs who premiered in 1955 with José Quintero's *Mañanitas de sol* (*Sunny Mornings*) and Noel Coward's *Ways and Means*. Some individuals relevant to later developments were involved in this private company, such as Guido Sáenz, Jean Moulaert, Lenín Garrido, José Trejos, and Kitico Moreno.

Between 1950 and 1970, these two companies were the mainspring of all dramatic activity in the country. They are mentioned here because without their contribution theatre developments in the 1970s cannot be understood or reviewed. Between the two groups, they staged more than two hundred plays and created enough interest and activity for the following movement to incubate.

On May 8, 1970, the federal government created the Ministry of Culture, Youth, and Sports, an entity expected to coordinate the areas mentioned in the title, but because of the composition of the board, it was in the first sector that it produced a true revolution. Alberto Cañas, an experienced dramatist, critic, and theatre promoter, was appointed minister, and Guido Sáenz, a talented actor, vice-minister. This combination soon resulted in an event of maximum importance in the history of Costa Rican drama—the formation of a National Theatre Company.

The event was formalized on January 1, 1971. The administrative structure, as well as the goals, follow somewhat the pattern of the prestigious Tyrone Guthrie, although later some preference was given to restricting the repertory in order to undertake greater efforts to spread theatre to all sectors of the country. In June of that year, under the direction of the Spaniard Esteban Polls, the group staged Cervantes' *Juego de pícaros, damas y cornudos* (*Game of Rogues, Ladies, and Cuckolds*). Since then the country has enjoyed a fixed annual season, which embraces the participation not only of the three groups mentioned but also of many others carrying out parallel programs. With the stimulus provided by the National Company, theatre is reaching rural areas which had never before been blessed with dramatic productions. In 1971 too, the Compañía Nacional itself inaugurated a basic program called the "summer season," which consisted of a continuous run of national and foreign works, at popular prices, outdoors, in places easily accessible.

The integration of theatre into sectors of the population coincided with the arrival in the country of a great number of foreign artists—some exiled, others under special contract—who brought a high professional quality to productions. These artists came especially from Spain, Argentina, Chile, and Uruguay. So it is that the theatre in the 1970s, from whatever vantage point one adopts, reached its highest levels of achievement, with an average attendance of nearly thirty thousand spectators per title. Thus, what was earlier an elitist activity has become a massive cultural phenomenon in proportion to the limited total population (2.3 million). No one group can claim credit for this achievement; rather, the perfect correlation of political and cultural factors provided the framework. In addition to the four most prominent groups discussed here, Costa Rica has many other groups and theatre companies. Some of them are as prominent as the Moderno Teatro de Muñecos, which won prizes in Puerto Rico, and the Teatro Carpa, which currently is trying to popularize theatre with tours throughout the country.

ANGEL THEATRE
(Teatro del Angel)
Cuesta de Moras, San José, Costa Rica

This theatre group originated outside the country but has been completely installed in San José since September 19, 1974. The group was created in Santiago, Chile, by actors Bélgica Castro, Alejandro Sieveking, Lucho Barahona, and Dionisio Echeverría, and architect Luz María Sotomayor in 1971. It is maintained in Costa Rica by the first four named, who rent a centrally located theatre and who offer an annual season. It is a private theatre, self-financed, which obligates the group to a varied repertory for its large productions, and a theatre of minimal cost and wide acceptance for its public.

Since its arrival in the capital, the group has imposed a work schedule and a professional quality that were not always present. The extremely careful productions, the advance preparation of programs, the tentative schedules, the zealous maintenance of the house—in short, all the details characterizing a professional theatre with a long tradition—were transmitted by this company to other groups. Its billing has changed twenty times in the last six years, and among the important productions were Ibsen's *Ghosts* (1976), Ramón del Valle Inclán's *Los cuernos de don Friolera* (*The Cuckolding of Don Friolera*, 1977), George Bernard Shaw's *Mrs. Warren's Profession* (1977), and a minor piece which has turned out to be a huge box office success in the country, *Hablemos a calzón quitado* (*Let's Talk Honestly*) by Guillermo Gentile, which premiered in 1976 and has returned four times. The Angel has contributed a great deal to the professionalization of the art. Its work and its assimilation into the environment have contributed to the improvement of theatre in every respect.

Far-seeing and rigorous as it is in its tasks, in 1980 the Angel produced Goethe's *Faust*, Fernando de Rojas' *La Celestina* (*The Go Between*), and Luigi Pirandello's *Six Characters in Search of an Author*. In 1981 the most important production was *The Elephant Man* by Bernard Pomerance, directed by Sieveking. Their best works in 1982 were *Orquesta de señoritas* (*Young Ladies' Orchestra*) by Jean Anouilh, also directed by Sieveking, as well as his own folkloric Chilean play, *Animas de día claro* (*Souls of a Clear Day*). Since the group is small and consists essentially of three multitalented artists (Sieveking, Castro, and Barahona), it contracts invited actors and utilizes, to the fullest extent, its small theatre with 180 seats, which works with a small cast.

HARLEQUIN THEATRE
(Teatro Arlequín)
(defunct)

This group, a supporter and pioneer of dramatic art, became a private cultural association in 1956. In that year it established its own house with its own name and undertook an intensive effort which ended in June 1978, when a deficient administration led to its dissolution. This misfortune notwithstanding, the Harlequin had by then established the base for all later development of dramatic art in the country and during its long trajectory had performed more than one hundred titles from the national and universal repertory.

Among its directors were Jean Moulaert, Daniel Gallegos, and Lenín Garrido, all of whom sought to popularize the best of contemporary theatre, Costa Rican plays, and classical theatre. The group generally worked through a system of contracted artists, and its fundamental concern was always to maintain a live program of theatre for that select but reduced public which existed. The small theatre it occupied is presently rented to a group of youngsters who call themselves Teatro Tiempo.

The Harlequin's list of productions is enormous and difficult to reconstruct, since it spans about thirty years. Nevertheless, it is possible to single out such plays as *El cepillo de dientes* (*The Toothbrush*, 1972) by Jorge Díaz, directed by Nicolás Belucci; Edward Albee's *A Delicate Balance* (1973), directed by

Lenín Garrido; Paul Zindel's *The Effect of Gamma Rays on Man-in-the-Moon Marigolds* (1975), directed by Jean Moulaert; Ricardo Talesnik's *La fiaca* (*The Lazy One*, 1973), directed by Carlos Catania; and Peter Shaffer's *Equus* (1976), directed by Lenín Garrido. Among the enthusiastic supporters of the Harlequin are José Trejos, Irma de Field, Guido Sáenz, Haydeé de Lév, Anabelle de Garrido, Daniel Gallegos, and those already mentioned. This group had to grapple with the problem of continuity through all the theatre's crises and serve as a training center for almost all the actors who are the stars of today's theatre.

NATIONAL THEATRE COMPANY
(Compañía Nacional de Teatro)
Ministerio de Cultura, Juventud y Deportes
Apartado 10227, San José, Costa Rica

This group has played a pivotal role in the development of Costa Rican theatre. Its philosophy can be synthesized in the express wish to embrace an ever larger public, to bring down the cost of productions, to take theatre throughout the country, and to utilize the stage as an instrument of acculturation. In order to achieve these goals, the company instituted the open air summer season. In cooperation with other groups, it created a stable company with an annual repertory; it initiated tours to the provinces; and it offered performances in schools, colleges, and industry. Since it enjoyed an economic subsidy from the government, the price of a ticket was put within reach of all sectors of the society ($1.25 in 1980). It is an unusual situation indeed when the theatre is cheaper than the movies.

The most important directors have been the founder, Esteban Polls, and, later, Alfredo Catania, Oscar Castillo, Daniel Gallegos, and Mimi Prado. From 1971 to the present the company has mounted over thirty shows, a number of them by national playwrights. Their productions have been critical successes both within and without the country. Among the plays that have brought the greatest success are *Puerto Limón* by Joaquín Gutiérrez, which won the prize for best foreign company in the Cervantes Festival in Mexico in 1975, *Arturo Ui* by Brecht in 1977, under the direction of Atahualpa del Cioppo, and *The Crucible* by Arthur Miller, under the direction of Daniel Gallegos in 1978.

The major productions of 1979 were Ibsen's *An Enemy of the People*, in a version by Arthur Miller; *Murámonos Federico* (*Let Us Die, Federico*), an adaptation of Joaquín Gutiérrez's novel directed by Alejandro Sieveking, and Atahualpa del Cioppo's rendition of Lope de Vega's *Fuenteovejuna* (*The Sheep Well*). In 1981 the National Company mounted the world premiere of Mario Vargas Llosa's *La señorita de Tacna* (*The Young Lady from Tacna*), as well as a controversial production of Ramón del Valle Inclán's *Divinas palabras* (*Divine Words*).

This group can claim credit for having increased the number of theatre spectators from thirty-five hundred in 1971 to nearly forty thousand, who now regularly attend in a given season. The creation of a stable company (with corresponding remuneration for full-time commitment) introduced the "profession" of actor to the country. As a result, everyone involved in the theatre stood to gain, and acting achieved professional rank and prestige.

UNIVERSITY THEATRE
(Teatro Universitario)
Universidad de Costa Rica
Apartado 92, Ciudad Universitaria, San José, Costa Rica

The University Theatre, the initiator of the total artistic process that culminated in the 1970s, is also the theatre group with the most fragmented history in Costa Rica. While it is still active and influential, it has experienced long periods of recession, dissolution, and total changes in its composition and orientation. The year 1969 is a good estimate of its period of consolidation, when the University of Costa Rica, to which it belongs, formally opened a program in dramatic arts. From the classrooms there came forth prospective librettists, set designers, and directors, who made their first attempts in this group.

At the beginning of the decade, the group divided its activities between professional and student productions, leaving the professional to the actor/professors and the student to the apprentices, with the result that its program was in constant change. Every year the present director, Juan Katevas (a Chilean), in coordination with the professors of the Department of Theatre, sought to establish a varied program that would include at least one national work, one Latin American play, and two classics, one ancient and one contemporary. Thus, during the last few years, the group has managed to achieve good theatrical fare with the implicit training of new talent. The 1979 program is a good example of the line the University Theatre has followed. It included three short works: George Bernard Shaw's *Augustus Does His Bit*, Eugene O'Neill's *Before Breakfast*, and Luigi Pirandello's *The Man with the Flower in His Mouth*; Bertolt Brecht's *The Guns of Carrar*; Carlo Goldoni's *La locandiera* (*The Innkeeper*), and two Costa Rican children's plays.

The group now has both consistency and a permanent base. It performs in its own theatre in the University of Costa Rica and strives for both didactic and social action works, according to the director Katevas. Since the group was established in 1951, it has mounted more than one hundred shows, and across its stage have passed excellent directors and the most important names from the world theatre.

Among its best productions are *The Chairs* by Eugene Ionesco (1971), directed by Lenín Garrido; *Danse Macabre* by August Strindberg (1971), directed by Daniel Gallegos; and *Death of a Salesman* by Arthur Miller (1974), directed by Júver Salcedo. Among the persons who gave impetus and direction to the University Theatre are the dramatist Daniel Gallegos; the actors Carlos and Alfredo Catania and Anna Poltronieri; and the present dean of the Faculty of Fine Arts,

Alberto Cañas. The group maintains a fixed repertory that especially attracts the university population, composed of more than thirty thousand people. In 1980 it successfully staged *OK* by Isaac Chocrón, *Ni mi casa es ya mi casa* (*Not Even My House Is My Home Now*) by Alberto Cañas, *No hay isla feliz* (*No Happy Island*) by Sebastián Salazar Bondy, and *The Mandrake* by Machiavelli. Under the direction of Luis Carlos Vásquez, the group mounted García Lorca's *La zapatera prodigiosa* (*The Shoemaker's Prodigious Wife*) in 1981. In 1982 the award for best production of the year went to *No se paga, no se paga* (*It Doesn't Pay, It Doesn't Pay*), a satirical work by Dario Fo under the direction of Juan Fernando Cerdas.

CARLOS MORALES
(Translated by George Woodyard)

Cuba

INTRODUCTION

To refer to the development of theatre and to the work of theatre groups in Cuba after 1959 is to refer to the Revolution itself and to its transcendental importance in the country's artistic development. This date, more than any other, establishes a dividing line that delimits perfectly two opposing stages: as Alejo Carpentier expressed so well, for Cuba's artists the "age of solitude" came to an end, and the "age of solidarity" began.

With the triumph of the Revolution, the dreams and efforts of many serious artists began to materialize, and for the first time the people had access to culture, which had been the exclusive privilege of the bourgeoisie. In the specific case of the theatre, the art reached new stages of development in regard to the number of groups and spectators.

This new reality facilitated and stimulated the work of actors, directors, and scenographers, who could devote themselves completely to their work without economic worries. The Revolution, through the National Council for Culture, assured employment for theatre people by creating dramatic collectives not only in Havana, but also in the several capitals of the provinces. In the first years of the 1960s, collectives were established in Oriente, Camagüey, Las Villas, Matanzas, and Pinar del Río. At the same time, various groups emerged—the Conjunto Dramático Nacional, the Grupo Rita Montaner, the National Theatre of Guiñol, the Provincial Brigade Francisco Covarrubias, the Group Milanés—all of which joined other already-existing groups, such as the Teatro Estudio, created in 1958.

Numerous theatres and playhouses were opened throughout the country, as existing ones were being renovated. Regions that had not known the art of theatre could now enjoy it, and the theatre began to function as a phenomenon of national interest. Simultaneously, the national theatre workshops were organized to supply costumes and sets for the groups.

The Casa de las Américas has played an important role in the development of the work of these groups by establishing contact with the theatre movement in other parts of the island. The literary contests established in 1960 permitted the groups to enrich their repertory with dramatic works from all over Latin America. In 1961, under the auspices of the Casa de las Américas, the I Latin American Theatre Festival was organized. This event was held until 1966, enabling the Cuban public to make a positive and useful contact with the theatre work of sister countries. In addition, representatives from the Americas as well as from the theatre worlds of Europe, Asia, and Africa attended the Encuentros de Teatristas. These colloquia provided the opportunity for people from diverse regions to become acquainted and to discuss, in a fraternal atmosphere, many aspects of theatre problems: repertory, content, form, and public.

During this developmental period, the collaboration of Latin American artists, principally from the independent theatres of Uruguay and Argentina, cannot be overlooked. Invaluable assistance was offered in the creation of the provincial groups by Jaime Sventisky, Adolfo Gutkin, Pablo Verbitsky, Alberto Panelo, and Isabel Herrera, while Ugo Ulive, Juan Larco, Néstor Raimondi, and Amanecer Dotta were working with the Havana-based groups. Luisa Josefina Hernández and Osvaldo Dragún collaborated in the organization of the Seminario de Dramaturgia (1961–1965), and Manuel Galich joined the Department of Theatre of the Casa de las Américas, a position he held until his death (1984).

Cuba has about fifty-three professional groups, located in various provinces, although Havana, of course, has the greatest concentration. The Ministry of Culture is seeking to extend and strengthen the theatre movement in Cuba's fourteen provinces and in the municipality of Isla de la Juventud.

Special attention has been given to children's theatre, following the precepts of José Martí for whom "nothing is more important than a child." More than one-half of Cuba's existing theatre groups are devoted to children's theatre. In most cases, they have their own theatre, but a considerable number of performances are given outside the theatre itself: in schools, hospitals, day care centers, rural communities, and suburban neighborhoods. In addition, several national meetings concerning children's theatre—events of confrontation, balance, and evaluation of the proceedings—are held regularly. A notable step has been the opening of a school in Lenin Park, which groups from all over the country attend. They take classes and seminars there; at the same time they offer activities as part of their practical training.

Cuban theatre has acquired characteristics of movement and growth through the Revolution. In this sense, the contribution of the so-called Teatro Nuevo has been decisive. Under this designation are the Grupo de Teatro Escambray, Cabildo Teatral Santiago, Grupo Cayajabos, Colectivo Teatral Granma, Grupo Cubano de Acero, Teatro Juvenil Pinos Nuevos, Teatrova, Teatro de Participación Popular, Cabildo Teatral Guantánamo, and La Yaya.

What distinguishes these groups from the other companies? Some of the traits of the Teatro Nuevo are the search for new scenic spaces (a street, a school, a dairy, or a factory shop), the public as a collaborative and participating force, a new language capable of effectively expressing the problems of the public and of contributing to solve them, the new interpersonal relationships of the group, as well as its relations with the community, the systematic study of concrete zones of reality, and the treatment of present and historical themes.

All of these groups elaborate their own texts, as a result of the close contact of their work with the aesthetic and ideological necessities of a new public. The consequence has been the discovery of renewed sources for national dramaturgy. Is Cuba facing the application of known methods of collective creation? If one considers examples such as the Libre Teatro Libre or La Candelaria, where the text emerges from the collective effort without any individual author being identified, the answer is no. With these groups, the works are with few exceptions registered in the name of one author. Nevertheless, behind them is a collective labor, with respect to the research, interviews, collection of materials, and even modifications in the text.

Hence, new writers have emerged, who work for their own particular group. In this way, some actors and directors have made inroads for the first time into the area of dramaturgy. The titles range from efforts with merely good intentions to more mature works. Among them are such successful works as *La vitrina* (*The Showcase*), *La emboscada* (*The Ambush*), *Autolimitación* (*Self-Limitation*), and *Ramona* which have enriched Cuba's theatrical literature.

With the creation of the Ministry of Culture, new possibilities have opened for Cuban theatre. And although it is still premature to speak of accomplishments, change is evident, and an interest in finding solutions to difficulties has been shown. La Casa de las Américas, for its part, initiated a closer and more fruitful approach to representative groups of the continent: the presentations in Cuba of La Candelaria from Colombia and of Aleph from Chile are the first indications. A long road is open for Cuban theatre, a road that will not be free of obstacles, any more than it has been in the past.

BERTOLT BRECHT POLITICAL THEATRE GROUP
(Grupo Teatro Político Bertolt Brecht)
Calle 13, esquina I, Vedado
Ciudad de La Habana, Cuba

The Bertolt Brecht Political Theatre Group created at the beginning of the 1970s, follows an established line: in its repertory, co-productions with Socialist countries occupy a fundamental place. In general, texts with a marked social content predominate, although it would be well to clarify that the existence of a group designated as "political" does not imply that the others are any less so. The list of their productions to date includes works by their German namesake: Bertolt Brecht's *Los días de la comuna* (*The Days of the Commune*, 1972) and *La panadería* (*The Bakery*, 1973); Soviet plays: Vsevolod Vishnevsky's *La tragedia optimista* (*The Optimistic Tragedy*, 1975), B. Vasilyev's *Los amaneceres son aquí apacibles* (*The Dawns Are Quiet Here*), and Nikolai Pogodin's *El carillón del Kremlin* (*Kremlin Chimes*, 1977); and Cuban authors: Paco Alfonso's *Cañaveral* (1974) and Raúl Macías's *Brigada 2506* (*Brigade 2506*, 1974). The group has carried on regular extension work with A. Guelman's *El premio* (*The Prize*), which it has presented with notable success in various work centers in Havana as well as in the interior. With José Brene's *El ingenioso criollo don Matías Pérez* (*The Ingenious Creole Don Matías Pérez*, 1978), the group seems to have opened a new orientation by integrating this comedy about a popular Cuban character of the nineteenth century into its repertory. Recent productions include Abraham Rodríguez's *Andoba* (*Scum*, 1979) and his *El escache* (*Worthless*, 1980), Juan Carlos Tabío and Tomás Gutiérrez Alea's *La permuta* (*The Exchange*, 1980), Rodolfo Pérez Valero and Antonio Veloso's *Crimen en noche de máscaras* (*Crime on a Masked Night*, 1981), and Yulky Cary's *Rampa arriba, rampa abajo* (*Up Ramp, Down Ramp*, 1981).

MUSICAL THEATRE OF HAVANA
(Teatro Musical de La Habana)
Consulado esquina Virtudes
Centro Habana, Ciudad de La Habana, Cuba

The Musical Theatre of Havana, which opened its doors at the end of 1978, was a revival of a similar experiment which operated with the same name several years before. This is evident in the first production mounted, Héctor Quintero's *Lo musical* (*The Musical*), the last work performed by the previous group. The productions of the new group to date are *Mi bella dama* (*My Fair Lady*, 1981), *En el viejo varietés* (*In the Old Varieties*, 1982), and Pablo Cabrera's *La verdadera historia de Pedro Navajas* (*The True Story of Pedro Navajas*, 1983). This artistic group has enormous possibilities, given the idiosyncrasies of the Cuban people, and it is initiating refreshing perspectives.

RITA MONTANER GROUP
(Grupo Rita Montaner)
Línea No. 504, entre E y D
Vedado, Ciudad de La Habana, Cuba

The Rita Montaner Group, which is housed in the Teatro El Sótano, has a record of sixteen years of uninterrupted work. Its initial orientation was toward comedy and vaudeville in the style of *Ese lunar* (*That Mole*) and Jean Anouilh's *The Waltz of the Toreadors*, but gradually it has been enriched with works from the Socialist sphere: V. P. Katayev's *La cuadratura del círculo* (*Squaring the Circle*, 1968) and Joseph Topol's *La gata sobre los rieles* (*The Cat on the Tracks*, 1969); classical texts: Molière's *Amphytrion* (1970) and Calderón de la Barca's *La dama duende* (*The Phantom Lady*, 1972); Cuban works: Ignacio Gutiérrez's *Llévame a la pelota* (*Take Me on a Useless Journey*, 1970) and also his *Los chapuzones* (*The Ducklings*, 1972); and plays by Latin American authors, such as Isidora Aguirre, René Marqués, and Pablo Neruda. Recently, the group presented Carlos Torrens's *Aquí en el barrio* (*Here in the Neighborhood*, 1981), Molière's *The Bourgeois Gentleman* (1982), and Pirandello's *Esta noche se improvisa la comedia* (*Tonight We Improvise*, 1983). The company has been interested in theatre for children, and in this sense it was one of the first groups from the capital to take to the plazas and the streets. Lenin Park was one of the first sites chosen for its Sunday performances.

STUDIO THEATRE
(Teatro Estudio)
Calzada No. 657, entre A y B
Vedado, Ciudad de La Habana, Cuba

The Studio Theatre has the longest and richest trajectory of the groups studied here. The majority of Cuba's most prestigious directors, actors, designers, light technicians, and musicians have been trained in this practical academy. The repertory of the group is characterized by stylistic and thematic variety, and includes titles that signal key moments in Cuba's theatre: from the introduction of Brecht's techniques to the staging of the classics, passing through the European vanguard and the most recent Cuban dramaturgy. The group's most recent productions constitute an eloquent index of these trends: next to *El becerro de oro* (*The Golden Calf*, 1967) by the nineteenth-century Cuban writer Joaquín Lorenzo Luaces, we find the original and dynamic production of *Don Gil de las calzas verdes* (*Don Gil of the Green Breeches*, 1969) by Tirso de Molina, the innovative spectacle *Los diez días que estremecieron al mundo* (*Ten Days That Shook the World*, 1977) in the version by the Moscow group Taganka and *Santa Juana de América* (*Saint Joan of America*, 1978) by the Argentine Andrés Lizárraga. More recently, the Studio Theatre has mounted Federico García Lorca's *Bodas de sangre* (*Blood Wedding*, 1979), *Ni un sí ni un no* (*Neither Yes nor No*) by Abelardo Estorino (1980), *Aire frío* (*Cold Air*) by Virgilio Piñera (1981), and José Brene's *Santa Camila de La Habana* (*Saint Camille of Havana*, 1982). The group's permanent home, the Hubert de Blanck Theatre, stands out today as one of the sites to which the public from the capital can go without being disappointed.

CARLOS ESPINOSA DOMÍNGUEZ
(Translated by George Woodyard)

Ecuador

INTRODUCTION

There is no commercial theatre in Ecuador as it is known in the United States. Few gain a livelihood from this occupation; all theatre practitioners have to supplement their meager income with other jobs. Although most groups charge admission, which varies from the equivalent of US $1.00 to $5.00, they usually receive some kind of subsidy, be it from an educational institution, a social organization, or a government entity. The most encouraging support comes from the well-established Casa de la Cultura Ecuatoriana. This institution has a state budget and is charged with promoting a wide variety of cultural activities. The central Casa is in Quito, the capital, and there are branches—of lesser means and facilities—in most of the provinces. Under its present national director, Edmundo Ribadeneira, it has helped the theatre a good deal in the last few years. Since the opening in March 1977 of Casa de la Cultura's Prometeo Playhouse (with seating for 270 spectators and enough technical equipment, not to mention its attractive circular design), several companies have presented their work there without incurring any expense, and rather have kept, as an additional incentive, the entire box office receipts. Casa de la Cultura is building another playhouse, with a 1,500 seating capacity, which is scheduled to open in 1985. Other adequate locales in Quito, where most of the Ecuadorian theatrical activity takes place, are the old but graceful Teatro Sucre and the modern theatre-in-the-round, Quitumbe. Central University's new Theatre Arts School (Antonio Ordónez, director) has had its own playhouse since 1980, which still needs some finishing touches. There are several reclaimed (Patio de Comedias, in Quito, for instance) and provisional locales in both the capital and provinces.

Among the Quito theatre groups are Mojiganga, Teatro Experimental Ecuatoriano, Clan de Teatro, and Patio de Comedias. Mojiganga was founded in 1977 by a young Belgian named Carlos Theus, who was an actor for Teatro Ensayo in 1975. The group has focused on the satiric, "juglaresco," and on children's theatre, and has made a serious attempt to form a mobile type of theatre with a repertory suitable for young and popular audiences. Some of its adult programs were Peter Weiss' *Señor Mockinpott* (1978), Dario Fo's *El milagro de los inocentes* (*The Miracle of the Innocents*, 1979), translated by Theus himself, Enrique Buenaventura's *La orgía* (*The Orgy*, 1980), and Angelo Beollo's *Bilora* (1981). Fo's piece was an exercise in the *commedia dell' arte* style, adapted to the Ecuadorian milieu, with actors interchanging parts from one performance to the next. Unfortunately for Quito theatregoers, this excellent company has been inactive since Theus returned to Belgium in August 1981.

Teatro Experimental Ecuatoriano, also sometimes called Taller Experimental Ecuatoriano, has been run by Víctor Eduardo Almeida who is also the author of *Oratorio para una muñeca* (*Oratory for a Doll*, 1978). Its activity has been sporadic.

Clan de Teatro, directed by Carlos Martínez, had a very successful production with *La loca estrella* (*The Mad Star*) by Pedro Saad Herrería in 1977. In April 1979 Clan reappeared with a play for children staged in Teatro Prometeo, entitled *El espantapájaros que fue rey* (*The Scarecrow Who Was King*), with the participation of Toty Rodríguez, a seasoned actress. Both Saad Herrería and Rodríguez are working now in the radio, television, and movie industries, and for all practical purposes the Clan de Teatro has ceased to exist.

Patio de Comedias (18 de Septiembre 457, Quito) is an active group and has been led by Raúl Guarderas since 1980. The locale is an interesting courtyard, adapted for the stage, with a seating capacity of two hundred. The repertory has consisted of Chekhov and Strindberg.

The main port of Ecuador, Guayaquil, has experienced a theatre awakening in recent years. The main company, El Juglar (Boyacá 1616 y Clemente Ballén, Guayaquil, Ecuador), began in 1978 under the leadership of Ernesto Suárez of Argentina and the sponsorship of the Centro Municipal de Cultura. In 1980 it produced *Lágrimas y risas* (*Tears and Laughter*), which was a historical collage from *Edipo Rey* (*Oedipus Rex*), *Fuenteovejuna* (*The Sheep Well*), and *Huasipungo* (*Huasipungo*), and in 1981 Agustín Cuzzani's *El centroforward murió al amanecer* (*The Center Forward Died at Dawn*), as well as the pivotal (in terms of public acceptance and recognition of the group's work) *Guayaquil Superstar*, followed by *Banda de pueblo* (*Town Band*), an adaptation of a short story by José de la Cuadra. These and other stagings by the ensemble have been *creaciones colectivas* closely orchestrated by Ernesto Suárez.

El Juglar's members earn a living from the box office receipts and by giving theatre classes in local schools. They have also devoted considerable effort to children's theatre and to the formation of new groups. Every year Centro Municipal de Cultura organizes a Muestra Estudiantil de Teatro, which is the only regular activity resembling a theatre festival in Ecuador. The other groups active in Guayaquil are Vanguardia (Iván Argudo), Saltimbanqui, La Pirueta, La Cucaracha (street theatre), and Grupo de la Península (with headquarters in the peninsula Santa Elena). Guayaquil also has a locale for vaudeville—Candilejas—which replaced Humoresque. Cecil Vilar and Enrique Pacheco have entertained middle and upper class ''guayaquileños'' with risqué stories of old times in both theatres. *Aquellos viejos tiempos* (*Those Old Times*) was Humoresque's most roaring success.

Elsewhere in Ecuador the theatre rests on the enthusiasm of young people, mostly college and high school students, with variable support from educational institutions and the local branches of the Casa de la Cultura. In 1977 the theatre journal *La Ultima Rueda* (*The Last Wheel*), published by the Escuela de Teatro of the Universidad Central in Quito, included in its Nos. 4-5 issue a survey of theatrical activity in five provinces. Among the groups interviewed is the Teatro de la Universidad Técnica Luis Vargas Torres of Esmeraldas. Established in 1968, the group stages an average of two productions and some eighty performances a year under its director Hugo Arias Bone. It has practiced the *creación colectiva* since the beginning, although a notable exception to this tendency was the staging of Jorge E. Adoum's *El sol bajo las patas de los caballos* (*The Sun under the Horses' Hooves*, 1977).

CLAM
Alejandro Calisto 139, Luluncoto
Quito, Ecuador

Carlos Villalba is one of the most energetic theatre figures in Ecuador. He was a student of Fabio Pacchioni in the mid-1960s and a member of the original Teatro Ensayo. He was an actor for several companies until 1976 when, as a literature instructor at Colegio Luciano Andrade Marín, he started a student group known as CLAM (for the school's initials). Those young actors and actresses eventually became university students, but remained active in the theatre under the same director and with the same acronym. The problem was that Villalba kept training actors at the Colegio Andrade Marín, who then became known as GECLAM (Grupo Estudiantil of CLAM). In 1980 the indefatigable Villalba started also to work for an agency of the Ministry of Education, where he structured yet another collective: Grupo de Teatro del INACAPED (Instituto Nacional de Capacitación y Perfeccionamiento Docente). As a result, Carlos Villalba enjoys a dual institutional sponsorship which has made it possible for him and his groups to offer some convincing productions. CLAM's most outstanding productions have been *Una casa en Lota Alto* (*A House in Lota Alto*, 1979) by Víctor Torres; *Huasipungo* (*Huasipungo*, 1981) by Jorge Icaza in Marco Ordóñez's adaptation; *Los inocentes* (*The Innocents*, 1983) by Enrique Buenaventura (based on Emmanuel Robles' *Montserrat*); and its greatest hit to date, *Monte calvo* (*Bald Mountain*, 1980), by Jairo Aníbal Niño. With the INACAPED ensemble, notable productions included Demetrio Aguilera-Malta's *Infierno negro* (*Black Hell*, 1980), Hugo Salazar Tamariz's *En tiempos de la colonia* (*In Colonial Times*, 1981), Jorge Dávila Vásquez's *Con gusto a muerte* (*With a Taste of Death*, 1982), and Eliécer Cárdenas' *Polvo y ceniza* (*Dust and Ashes*, 1983)—all plays by Ecuadorian authors. Carlos Villalba is the vice-president of the Asociación de Trabajadores del Teatro. His groups have participated in local and national "muestras" and have won several awards.

CUATRO CLAVOS
Alianza Francesa, Quito, Ecuador

Cuatro Clavos' director Diego Pérez became known in Quito's theatre circles in 1976, when he founded the Teatro de la Alianza Francesa (TAF). A former member of the Ballet Experimental Moderno, Pérez provided TAF with leadership as director, actor, and occasionally as playwright until 1979, when the group disbanded. Working in a refurbished locale under an overpass of Eloy Alfaro Street, the company's activities were impressive: in 1978 it performed six times a week for an aggregate audience of seventeen thousand and a total of twenty-nine different plays (in the Chekhov/Ibsen category), and organized a festival of chamber theatre.

Since its inception in 1979, Cuatro Clavos has performed in the TAF, with the full support of that institution. In 1981 its main production was Brecht's *El proceso de Juana de Arco* (*The Trial of Joan of Arc*) and in 1982 García Lorca's *Bodas de sangre* (*Blood Wedding*). Diego Pérez has ventured recently into the movies as an actor, and his wife, Rosita, Cuatro Clavos' main actress, as a producer.

MALA HIERBA
Tamayo 1024 y Lizardo García
Quito, Ecuador

Mala Hierba was started in 1979 by two Argentinians, one Spaniard, and several Ecuadorians. So far its productions have been very professional: *Robinson Crusoe* (1981), adapted from a text by Jerome Savary (from France's Magic Circus) and directed by Charo Francés, and Dario Fo's *Mujeres* (*Women*, 1982), under the direction of Arístides Vargas. Mala Hierba organized a seminar on actor training in May 1982 and formed another group called Taller de la Feroviaria Alta, which has adopted the collective creation method.

OLLANTAY
Teatro Popular de La Tola
Quito, Ecuador

First organized in 1971 by a handful of students of the Polytechnic Institute of Quito, Ollantay has been the most radical (technically and politically) experiment in Ecuadorian theatre in recent years. Although most of the founding members were bona fide engineering students, they had little support from their school, and since 1976 their connection with it has been nonexistent. The group's director is Carlos Villarreal, who is also the president of the Ecuadorian Association of Theatre Workers, founded in 1979. Ollantay has admittedly borrowed ideas and techniques from the three "Bs" (Brecht, Augusto Boal, and Enrique Buenaventura) in order to raise the political and social consciousness of workers, its target audience. Its main technical guidance has been Buenaventura's method of collective creation. It has staged plays by Brecht, as well as an adaptation of *Las dos caras del patroncito* (*The Two-Faced Boss*, 1974) by the American Luis Valdez, and has created its own pieces: *S + S = 41* (1973), *Cuánto nos cuesta el petróleo* (*How Much Does the Oil Cost?*, 1975), *América guerrera, América heroica* (*Fighting America, Heroic America*, 1977), and *Las aventuras del payaso Paco* (*The Adventures of Paco the Clown*, 1982). It has performed in many places: school auditoriums, union halls, plazas, streets, and sometimes on a conventional stage. Recently, the Ollantay diversified its activities to include puppet and music shows. Its current center of operations is Teatro Popular in barrio La Tola.

POPULAR THEATRE WORKSHOP
(Taller de Teatro, Popular)
% Escuela de Teatro, Universidad Central
Quito, Ecuador

Formed in 1977, the Popular Theatre Workshop enjoys a reputation as one of the more professional groups in Quito. Ilonka Vargas, who teaches dramatic arts at the Central University, is one of its actresses and directors; Jorge Guerra is one of its most notable actors, and he has also directed. In the first two years, the group staged six plays, including Ricardo Talesnik's *La enorme pereza de Néstor González* (*La fiaca*) [*The Great Idleness of Néstor González* (*The Lazy One*), 1977] and Enrique Buenaventura's *A la diestra de Dios Padre* (*On the Right-hand Side of God the Father*, 1979), both directed by María Escudero, who is no longer with the company. It was staged in Quito's most technically equipped playhouse, Teatro Prometeo. Both plays were adapted for the national audience by young and promising writers: Abdón Ubidia and Raúl Pérez Torres, respectively. In 1980 the Taller staged Osvaldo Dragún's *Historias para ser contadas* (*Stories to Be Told*) and Ramón Rodríguez Bowen's *Muñeca de trapo* (*Rag Doll*), under the direction of Vargas. Abdón Ubidia wrote a monologue, *La consumación* (*The Consummation*) in which José Guerra starred in 1981.

REHEARSAL THEATRE
(Teatro Ensayo)
Avenida 6 de Diciembre, intersección Orellana
Quito, Ecuador

Founded in 1964 by the Italian Fabio Pacchioni, who was in Ecuador under contract with UNESCO, Rehearsal Theatre is the oldest and one of the best known Ecuadorian ensembles. It was formed as a direct result of a theatre seminar given by Pacchioni in the Casa de la Cultura, the local sponsoring institution. Its first public performance was given on August 24, 1964, with a pair of playlets by Miguel de Cervantes and Lope de Rueda. The company was well received by a wide-ranging audience, which was perhaps symptomatic of a change of direction in the scant theatrical activity in Quito. It was not a simple coincidence that not long afterward, while Rehearsal Theatre gained importance, other groups like Francisco Tobar García's Teatro Independiente, which had entertained a small, well-educated, and conservative audience for several years, started to decline.

During the following three years, Pacchioni's troupe performed in Casa de la Cultura's Aula Benjamín Carrión, as well as in Teatro Sucre, and also traveled to other cities and rural villages. The repertory consisted mostly of national plays, such as Demetrio Aguilera Malta's *El tigre* (*The Tiger*, 1965), José Martínez Queirolo's *Réquiem por la lluvia* (*Requiem for the Rain*) and *Montesco y su señora* (*Montesco and His Wife*, 1965), Simón Corral's *El cuento de don Mateo* (*The Story of Don Mateo*, 1967), and César Dávila Andrade's *Boletín y elegía de las mitas* (*Bulletin and Elegy of Indian Forced Labor*, 1967).

Antonio Ordóñez, Rehearsal Theatre's present director, was one of its founding members. In 1966 he was working very closely with Pacchioni, and by 1968 he was pretty much in charge. Since then he has directed most of the group's productions as well. Among them are Buenaventura's *A la diestra de Dios Padre* (On The Right-hand Side of God the Father, 1968), Gerhart Hauptmann's *The Weavers* (1969), Jorge Díaz's *Topografía de un desnudo* (*Topography of a Nude Man*, 1969), Andrés Lizárraga's *Santa Juana de América* (*Saint Joan of America*, 1973), João Cabral de Melo-Neto's *Vida y muerte severina* (*Harsh Life and Death*, 1977), Jorge Icaza's *Huasipungo* (adapted by Marco Ordóñez, 1972, which was a fairly good success), and Molière's *Tartuffe* (1980). Occasionally, Víctor Hugo Gallegos, Moshen Yassen, Isabel Casanova, and Ramón Serrano have also directed for the group.

In 1972 Rehearsal Theatre disassociated itself from the Casa de la Cultura and became independent, although recently it has drawn some financial support from Quito's Central University, where Ordóñez teaches dramatic arts. The group has participated in international theatre events, such as a Latin American festival in San Francisco, California (1972), and the II International Festival of Caracas, Venezuela (1974). Besides financial problems, which are common to all Ecuadorian groups, Rehearsal Theatre has suffered from a serious actor turnover, to the point that only two or three members, including Ordóñez, have been with the group for several years. The company's activities are not as intense as before. It stages an average of only two plays a year and does not have a regular performing place. But Ordóñez is determined to continue his long struggle to improve Ecuadorian theatre and will not give up that fight easily.

REHEARSAL THEATRE OF THE CATHOLIC UNIVERSITY
(Teatro Ensayo de La Universidad Católica)
Apartado Postal 2184, Quito, Ecuador

The Rehearsal Theatre of Catholic University's first production was Jorge Díaz's *Réquiem por un girasol* (*Requiem for a Sunflower*, 1971), which a few months later was performed in the IV International Festival of Manizales, Colombia. Another of Díaz's plays, *El cepillo de dientes* (*The Toothbrush*), was staged in 1973. *El cruce sobre el Niágara* (*The Crossing of the Niagara*, 1976) by Alonso Alegría was very successful, as was an adaptation of Gabriel García Márquez's *El coronel no tiene quien le escriba* (*No One Writes to the Colonel*, 1978). The company has produced the following plays by Ecuadorian authors: *Los unos versus los otros* (*Some Versus Others*, 1971) by José Martínez Queirolo, *Con gusto a muerte* (*With a Taste of Death*, 1977) by Jorge Dávila Vásquez, and *Gabriel García Moreno* (1980), an adaptation of a play by Alvaro San Félix. In 1979 the ensemble staged several Renaissance "entremeses." Of its two better known directors, José Ignacio Donoso and Francisco Febres Cordero, Cordero is no longer with the company. Vicky Frey and Víctor Carvajal, a Chilean, are now directing for the group. Marta Rojas has given fine performances. Rehearsal Theatre has its own café-theatre, with a seating capacity of ninety, where it usually performs one play a year; it enjoys the full sponsorship of Quito's Catholic University. The company has not made an effort to reach out to a public different from the white-collar, student audience that gathers in its own locale. Its productions have been generally of good quality.

GERARDO LUZURIAGA

Mexico

INTRODUCTION

For the past twenty-five years, theatre in Mexico has constituted a struggle between the symbolic and the specific. Here we are speaking of theatre in the sense of actual production, not as literature. Until now, the written history of Mexican theatre has emphasized its literature more than its dramatic representations. A small but substantial booklet by the Centro de Estudios Literarios of the Universidad Nacional Autónoma de Mexico about national drama production from 1950 to 1975 indicates with panoramic clarity the tendencies and attitudes of recent Mexican dramatists. Antonio Magaña Esquivel in his *Cincuentenario del teatro experimental* (*Revista Mexicana de Cultura*, May 27, 1979) carefully registers the groups and tendencies that surfaced outside of, or in addition to, the commercial productions in Mexico during a fifty-year period.

The many contemporary influences of production techniques have been of more interest to young Mexican directors than to the dramatists. The crisis of aesthetic values springs precisely from the incorporation of these influences into Mexican theatre, while in dramatic composition the tendencies are perfectly marked. A cursory analysis of the tendencies in Mexican dramatic literature of the last fifty years indicates that the incorporation of styles and novelties has come about more slowly in literary production than in stage production.

There have been two currents in the experimental (nonprofessional) Mexican theatre during the last twenty-five years: one approaches the literal interpretation of the text (and generally obeys the author's indications); the other attempts to transform the text completely either by dramatic devices (achieving a partial or total substitution of the work) or by the work's complete "re-creation" or "re-invention."

Among the followers of the antiliteral conception of the theatre are Abraham Oceransky (imbued with suggestive techniques of improvisation) and, especially, Julio Castillo. The latter has adopted a style that corresponds to his spontaneously imaginative showings, a procedure that has permitted him to update such difficult works as Fernando Arrabal's *The Automobile Graveyard*, Maurice Maeterlinck's

The Bluebird, Heinrich von Kleist's *The Prince of Homburg*, and Aristophanes' *The Insects*, while also mounting strictly Mexican musical comedies, vaudeville, and spectacles inspired by Mexican show business figures (homages to José Alfredo Jimenez and Agustín Lara). Other directors, such as Salvador Flores, Germán Castillo, and Luis de Tavira, frequently adopt this imaginative, poetic, and barely discursive mode of theatre as well. There are dramatic situations in the productions of these directors in which the cathartic results acquire an exceptional dimension.

Vis-à-vis these phenomena, one must consider that, in Mexico, theatrical tradition imposes the styles of romantic and modernist theatre. In fact, commercial theatre has dictated box-like sets, overt acting styles, ad-libs, disguises, inferior equipment, gestures, grimaces, and truculent glances that have endured to the present period. Influenced by Spanish theatre at the beginning of the century, commercial Mexican theatre, to suit its spectators, does not offer contradictions or challenges about reality but rather the "pleasure of escapism." Only in these instances of commercial Mexican theatre have the organizational forms and concepts of the traditional company survived. While refined or experimental theatre productions rest exclusively in the hands of the director, in the commercial theatre the notion of "company" is related directly to an economic investment, an "easy" play, accessible to a popular audience and a group of actors who, after achieving success, will survive in later works and productions.

In this way, one can understand the challenge which nonliteral theatre represents. The directors present the public (principally the intellectual or enlightened petit bourgeoisie) a new access to art and culture, transposing (and sometimes surpassing) the simple experience of going to the theatre to observe, from a distance, a series of happenings with which the spectator has no cultural, political, or social relationship. The commercial theatre (sexist, antisensual, noncathartic) does not confront the audience symbolically, metaphorically, or even realistically with plausible situations. In these circumstances, some nonliteral theatre directors battle with the text; others, following the line of Poesía en Voz Alta, take the content, the meaning, and, at times, the form and spirit of the text to actualize them.

A young director of university extraction, Ignacio Merino Lanzilotti has found his own synthesized formula: through personal research and with the application of an original, technical work, he and his actors have brought to the theatre Mexican myths from before and after the Conquest. At the same time, he has turned to the popular revues of the 1930s and 1940s to design spectacles in which the problems, expressions, and manners of the Mexican urban middle class emerge in a new way. Violent aspects, historically accurate, as well as metaphors about Latin American revolutions, have emerged in productions such as Lanzilotti's *Las tandas del Tlancualejo* (*The Shows of the Tlancualejo*) and Pablo Neruda's *Fulgor y muerte de Joaquín Murieta* (*Brilliance and Death of Joaquín Murieta*, cantata with text). In a very personal manner, Merino Lanzilotti possesses that continental restlessness (Santiago García and Enrique Buenaventura) that defends a theatre which not only "represents" but also confronts a collective reality—and which achieves that reality collectively.

The current that interprets a dramatic work according to the author's indications is composed of no less talented directors. Some of them, such as Marta Luna, Raúl Fermeño, and Ludwig Margules, have observed, analyzed, and studied the different tendencies and "schools" of the present theatre in depth. Their capacity for dramatic manipulation, therefore, is formed principally by a kind of "technical facility," which allows them to resolve the works dramatically through a general conception of a panoramic vision of each play. For example, Marta Luna was responsible for the production of Brecht's *The Threepenny Opera* which came to Mexico City audiences as a challenge of expressionist staging, with songs and ballets composed professionally by Mexico's best choreographer, Guillermina Bravo, and with a skillful set design by Alejandro Luna. While the actors had their limitations in gestures and style, the production turned out to be a superb interpretation of Brecht and of expressionistic theatre. Ludwig Margules presented Chekhov's *Uncle Vanya*, pushing histrionics to the maximum and searching for a movement/scenography synthesis that would give the pleasing and interesting sensation of a photographic ensemble. In this same rigorous line are found the productions of Adam Guevara and Ignacio Sotelo. Likewise, José Caballero has produced August Strindberg's *The Pelican*, Shelley's *Oedipus Tyrannus*, Georg Kaiser's *October Day*, and Ferdinand Bruckner's *The Malady of Youth*.

Salvador Garcini's recently discovered capacity for directing in this style resulted in a notable production of Jean Genet's *The Maids*, a production that respected Genet's intentions. In the same manner, the works of Rafael López Miarnau have been outstanding for several years. This enterprising director considers commercial aspects as well as the intellectual and cultural requirements which every accessible and attractive production demands. López Miarnau has known, above all, how to choose selectively: he has brought to the stage works that are representative of universal theatre, provided them with dramatic dignity, and offered them as a contribution of his actors. This professional honesty has removed him from the vanguard/tradition quarrel. In the works of López Miarnau, the actor has very clearly designated parameters within which he can construct his character. The public can perceive the characteristics of this personage with the necessary depth. In this way, the actor must prove that he is up to the quality of the character, the author, and the director. In addition, López Miarnau's productions are completely professional in regard to set design and costumes, as well as production and sound teams.

Manuel Montoro maintains the most accomplished and interesting level of this literal, refined, mature, and basically difficult theatre. This Spanish-born director initiated his work and studies in Spain and France and renewed the university theatre atmosphere in Xalapa, during his stay of several years in that provincial capital. In Mexico City he has organized a group of excellent actors who do not exactly form a company but who have been responsible for key moments in Mexican theatre: Harold Pinter's *Old Times* (with Claudio Obregón, Ana Ofelia Murguía, and Mabel Martín), Sławomir Mrożek's *The Emigrants* (with Claudio Obregón and Salvador Sánchez), Samuel Beckett's *Happy Days* (with Beatriz Sheridan), Montoro's *Fuentevaqueros* (a collage of pieces by Federico García Lorca, with the previous actors and Martha Verduzco, Manuel Ojeda, and Rosenda Monteros), and *Acreedores* (*The Creditors*, with Claudio Obregón, Salvador Sánchez, and Ofelia Murguía).

Manuel Montoro does not conceive of a theatrical solution exclusively as an imaginative device. He studies in depth the cultural, historical, and social world which the work proposes, extracting from the analysis the psychological possibility of each character. The technique emerges, therefore, as a unique formula free of truculence, exaggeration, or elements foreign to the work. The actors' movements on stage have a close relation to the knowledge that they themselves have acquired from the literary world, through their own studies and discussions about the work. The scenographer (almost always Guillermo Barclay) reaches a design following similar procedures, confronted with the "spatial reality" the work suggests. Every play staged by Montoro obliges the spectator to capture from the first moment a spatial-intellectual atmosphere which, in turn, forces him to concentrate on what the author wants to express. This does not mean that the actor becomes a mere vehicle, since among the attributes and obligations of the director, one finds the task of incorporating everything consciously into a whole. Under these circumstances, it is obvious that Manuel Montoro, in this stage of his professional career, prefers to work with experienced, mature, and responsible actors. At the same time Montoro has maintained sufficient perception to balance out presentations of "difficult" avant-garde works, and works rooted in the sensibilities of a wide but inexperienced public.

The most interesting part of Mexican theatre production (its aesthetic, vanguard, experimental, universal aspects) is the responsibility of artists, who individually propose fresh, new theatrical experiments and productions. Theatre activity in Mexico is impressive for its intensity and diversity.

ALBERTO DALLAL

CADAC
Centro de Arte Dramático, A.C.
Centenario 26, Coyoacán 21, Mexico, D.F.

Héctor Azar, the creator and organizer of CADAC (Centro de Arte Dramático, A.C.), has worked tirelessly as playwright and director. Driven by the idea and the practice of theatre as didactic and aesthetic action, in 1958 he reorganized theatre activities in a university atmosphere. Later he did the same with official theatre until he created his own center. The breadth of Azar's vision (he has also written about dramatic space) indicates the search for a "total theatre" in the Wagnerian manner and proposes a redefinition of production. His productions of Georges Neveux's *Julieta o la clave de los sueños* (*Juliet, or the Dream Key*),

Dumas père's *Kean* (adaptation of Jean-Paul Sartre), and Alfonso Reyes' *Ifigenia cruel* (*Ifigenia the Cruel*) reveal a particular consciousness of what theatre is, as well as playwriting: "a complex situation in which all artistic experiences concur," "the language which the artist offers the public that attends a performance as a meeting place to discover persons, facts, climates, images, colors, emotions, abstractions." (Héctor Azar, *Zoon Theatrykon* [teoría CADAC], Universidad Nacional Autónoma de México, México, 1977.) According to Azar, theatre is a platform on which the vital elements of human nature come to rest and from which they are subsequently launched in an effort to fulfill and bring about this ideal of humanity: love with both its positive and negative consequences. In Azar's productions, there is a kind of plastic-poetic "visualization" of the text, a reinterpretation of the dramatist's objectives in the direction of the "message," through which he obliges the spectator to reread the text in its altered form, or reinvent it according to the director's rules.

ALBERTO DALLAL

POETRY ALOUD
(Poesía en Voz Alta)
(defunct)

Artists of many schools and levels of dedication have converged in Poetry Aloud: writers (Octavio Paz, Juan José Arreola, Diego de Meza, Elena Garro, Carlos Fuentes, and Jaime García Terrés), scholars (Antonio Alatorre and Margit Frenk), young directors (Héctor Mendoza and José Luis Ibáñez), painters (Juan Soriano and Leonora Carrington), and others. Supported by the Universidad Nacional, between 1956 and 1963 they presented various programs in which the dramatic dimension was established through the incorporation of sensorial and poetic elements that transcended not only the text—be it by the Arcipreste de Hita, Octavio Paz, or other Spanish and Spanish-American dramatists—but also the traditional resources of production. Through their voices and their bodies actors working outside conventional boundaries alluded to the spectators' most basic sensibilities: shouting, songs, voices, modern dances, and colorful clothing.

Like a great metaphor collectively created, each work of Poetry Aloud expanded the panorama of refined theatre in Mexico, which at that time was severely reduced. Surely the participants underwent a kind of "revelation" in regard to the different paths a production can assume, since many of them have formed the vanguard of the experimental theatre for the last two decades: Héctor Mendoza, José Luis Ibáñez, Juan José Gurrola, and Juan Ibáñez emerged as talented directors, and, among others, Rosenda Monteros, Ana Ofelia Murguía, Carlos Fernández, Beatriz Sheridan, Tara Parra, Pilar, and Pina Pellicer have persisted in Mexican theatre with quality acting.

Poetry Aloud constituted an entire movement, bringing together representatives from diverse artistic activities, and represented a landmark in the development of Mexican theatre. One could not speak of a precise "socializing" production method, but rather of a requirement that the production disentangle the text, and also its freshest, most current, and impressive meanings. The participation of Paz, Fuentes, and Arreola, and the later conceptions, manifested implicitly or explicitly by Héctor Mendoza and José Luis Ibáñez, indicate a fundamental condition: the vast knowledge of authors, works, and literary currents (including philosophic thought) of the corresponding era *before* they determine the dramatic solutions which always (in spite of a certain degree of permissible textual and spatial "poetization") would obey the text before fully interpreting it. The dramatic experience was a re-creation that emerged from the very soul of the work and permitted the inclusion of many other elements: games, presences, talent, improvisation, hoaxes, organization of effects, and messages.

ALBERTO DALLAL

UNIVERSITY THEATRE OF UNAM
(Teatro de la Universidad Nacional Autónoma de México)
Difusión Cultural, UNAM
Ciudad Universitaria, México, D. F.

Although one cannot talk in the strictest sense of a stable theatre at the University Theatre of UNAM, neither can one deny the constant and important presence of the university in the theatre of the country. For several decades the flagship Mexican university has fostered and brought together the concerns of many theatre people, either as a breeding ground for future artists, as a field for dramatic experimentation, or most especially as a catalyst which in its time has modified the aesthetic conceptions of many directors. Under its influence these directors constituted a vigorous vanguard that transformed the previously routine staging techniques of the classics and even some modern plays and converted them into something fresh and challenging. If over time these innovative routes have been traversed too much by the masters and their imitators and have been converted, by the same token, into another routine, this is a common phenomenon of all the vanguard movements that at certain moments seem to close in upon themselves. Later, other talents arise to take a new step forward. In general terms this does not invalidate one of the most imaginative generations that Mexico has enjoyed in its theatre during the last quarter-century. Theatre artists of the rank of Héctor Mendoza, Juan Ibáñez, Héctor Azar, Juan José Gurrola, José Luis Ibáñez, and Julio Castillo, among others, were formed in and offered their best work to the support of this movement, although some later followed other paths and others who continued, along with their disciples, carried it to very controversial extremes.

The UNAM, of course, does not offer just this path, although the Centro Universitario de Teatro, founded under the aegis of the vanguard and therefore with very well-defined aesthetic orientations, seems to lean toward exploring the possibilities of the body as an expressive device, carried to its extreme consequences. The Department of Dramatic Literature and Theatre of the Faculty of Philosophy and Letters nevertheless prepares its students within a stricter theoretical orientation. Since the students of the two centers work on productions under the direction of a professor, the university student has dual options as to which direction to follow. This same plurality can be seen in some of the more professional productions, although with a university basis, which are offered on its stages. Along with productions that still correspond to the old vanguard (an interesting paradox!) which subordinate the text to the luster of a formal spectacle, one can see productions that take control of the text and eviscerate it, appropriating spaces and blocking, as in the case of the exceptional stage productions of Ludwig Margules, the most demanding of the UNAM directors.

This experimental work, appropriate for a university theatre, extends to its own scenic space. Architect and set designer Alejandro Luna has constructed buildings with limited seating in which the possibilities of the stage seem to multiply without any limitation other than the creator's imagination. Opening, closing, or emphasizing real and potential depths permits the exploration of theatrical areas in ways impossible to achieve with more conventional spaces. The only question one can put to the theatres of the Centro Cultural Universitario regards their enforced elitism, since they attract very small audiences and they are located in an area difficult to reach. But the search for a new location is a challenge which the university is beginning to confront with some success, since it owns some beautiful old colonial buildings that were part of the legacy of this first American university located in the historic center of the city. In these buildings, as in the Casa del Lago located in Chapultepec Park, the company can offer professional productions to a more popular public and thus fulfill its third function (after teaching and experimentation), which is cultural diffusion.

The University Theatre's recent works include *La dama duende* (*The Ghost Lady*) by Pedro Calderón de la Barca, under the direction of Néstor López Aldeco; *La dama boba* (*The Foolish Lady*) by Lope de Vega, adapted and directed by Héctor Mendoza; *Como han de ser los amigos* (*The Way Friends Should Be*) by Tirso de Molina, directed by Alejandro Aura; *King Lear* by Shakespeare, directed by Salvador Garcini; *Historia de la aviación* (*History of Aviation*), a spectacle put on by Héctor Mendoza; *Leoncio y Lena* (*Leoncio and Lena*) by Georg Büchner, directed by Luis de Tavira; *Miscast* by Salvador Elizondo, directed by Juan José Gurrola; Guillermo Sheridan's pastoral play *El medallón de los Mantelillos* (*The Medallion of the Mantelillos*), directed by José Caballero; *Muerte de amor* (*Death of Love*) by Luis González de Alba, directed by Ernesto Bañuelos; *Armas blancas* (*White Weapons*) by Víctor Hugo Rascón Banda, directed by Julio Castillo; *Uncle Vanya* by Anton Chekhov, directed by Ludwig Margules; *El destierro* (*Exile*), Juan Tovar's play about the personality of the Mexican politician and philosopher José Vasconcelos, directed by José Caballero; *De la vida de las marionetas* (*On the Life of Marionettes*) by Ingmar Bergman, directed by Ludwig Margules; and *Humboldt y Bolívar* (*Humboldt and Bolívar*) by Claus

Hammel, with the Uruguayan group in exile, El Galpón (The Shed), directed by Rubén Yañez.

OLGA HARMONY

VERACRUZ UNIVERSITY THEATRE
(Teatro de la Universidad Veracruzana)
Maestra Marta Luna
Universidad Veracruzana, Xalapa, Veracruz, Mexico

Although several provincial Mexican universities have recently made efforts to sponsor more or less stable companies, the University of Veracruz holds first place in this enterprise, not only because of the quality of most of its productions but also because it has sustained a continuous level of activity over a thirty-year period. If at first the actors were enthusiastic amateurs, they have become more professional in the exercise of their theatrical activity. Those who joined later have become some of the best actors and actresses on the Mexican stage. The initial Taller de Nuevo Teatro, established by Dagoberto Guillaumín, developed through the enthusiasm and help of various playwrights, directors, scenographers, and actors until they formed what is now the official company of the Veracruz University Theatre. It would be lengthy and of little interest to review here the rich and complex trajectory, full of vicissitudes, of the Veracruz theatre, but it is important to point out that such important theatre people as Emilio Carballido, Seki Sano, Luisa Josefina Hernández, Manuel Montoro, Guillermo Barclay, Marco Antonio Montero, Claudio Obregón, María Rojo, and Ana Ofelia Murguía have participated.

In addition to providing for performances by groups of theatre students in liberal arts, the Veracruz University maintains two companies which were formally organized through the intense work of theatre artists from Xalapa. One company located in Xalapa is the result of thirty years of experience and constitutes the oldest of the stable companies, not only in regard to university theatre but also to professional theatre, in the entire country. During long periods, this company, currently under the artistic direction of Marta Luna, was the only one that existed in Mexico. For that reason, above and beyond the qualitative unevenness that can be observed in its evolution, the theatrical title company of the Veracruz University has won the respect of other national theatre artists.

The second company, of more recent origin but also established with previous experiences in the institution, is the official company of the Teatro Milán, under the direction of Manuel Montoro who, in collaboration with scenographer Guillermo Barclay, participated in one of the most brilliant periods in Xalapa theatre. For that reason and for the excellence of subsequent productions, he was charged with the task of developing this company which has proved to be the most important of the stable companies in the country. It has attained this status not because of the number of permanent actors (its first production, Sławomir Mrożek's *Emigrants*, involved only two brilliant actors), but because of the homogeneous quality it has managed to maintain throughout every season. The company functions under the command of a director—in this case and for many reasons a true *regisseur*—who has impeccable talent and solid preparation, as well as strong aesthetic points of view around which he has gathered important artists, some of whom already worked with him in the Xalapa period. Having begun several years ago with the play by Mrożek, which constituted a major event in Mexican theatrical life, Montoro has continued through nine seasons in the Teatro Milán with pieces that are very dissimilar but that have a perceptible continuity. The Teatro Milán demonstrates that a stable locale and a single directorship—or at least a single intention in the theatre orientation—are superb conditions for any company. Although the stage is rather small and lacks certain technical equipment, Barclay's talent has brought to it truly memorable set designs for Montoro's skillful productions, which at times involve many characters. All of this demonstrates the importance of fostering stable companies with a single locale, under the auspices of cultural institutions.

The Official Company of the Teatro Milán has also been active in Mexico City. Under the direction of its head, Manuel Montoro, it recently performed *Emigrants* by Sławomir Mrożek, *The Creditors* by August Strindberg, *It Was a Love Story* by Gilbert Leautier, *Sacco and Vanzetti* by Mino Roli, *The Misunderstanding* by Albert Camus, *Medea* by Euripides, and *The Last Ones* by Maxim Gorky.

In Veracruz, the Official Company of the University of Veracruz has presented *The Witches of Salem* by Arthur Miller, directed by Raúl Zermeño, *The Lower Depths* by Maxim Gorky, directed by Julio Castillo, and *Felicidad (Happiness)* by Emilio Carballido, directed by Dagoberto Guillaumín. Under the direction of Marta Luna, leader of the company, it has also performed *To The Green Cockatoo* by Arthur Schnitzler, *El baile de los montañeses (The Dance of the Mountaineers)* by Víctor Hugo Rascón Banda, *Con algo de música (With a Bit of Music)* by Jaime Cortés, *Atlántida (Atlantis)* by Oscar Villegas, *Pastorela (Pastoral)* by Willebaldo López, *Yvonne, princesa de Borgoña (Yvonne, Princess of Burgundy)* by Witold Gombrowicz, *Rashomon* by Rynosowoke Aputagawa, and *Electra* by Sophocles. Attempting an interdisciplinary collaboration, Manuel Montoro directed a production of Igor Stravinsky's *Story of a Soldier*, with the participation of the Symphonic Orchestra of Xalapa.

OLGA HARMONY
(Translated by George Woodyard)

Paraguay

INTRODUCTION

To a foreign observer the theatre in contemporary Paraguay might appear to have little variety and dynamism. This phenomenon of slow development with sharp and sudden interruptions (triggered by forty revolutions, the Chaco War, and the War of 1947) has characterized the present century in Paraguay.

All theatrical activity is concentrated in the capital, Asunción. Until 1980, in fact, all theatrical activity was centered exclusively in the Municipal Theatre, the only place equipped with appropriate technical apparatus, with the result that possibilities for performance were limited and the economic bases for the subsistence of the different companies were very weak. Today, however, with the emergence of two new theatres, the Teatro de las Américas and the Arlequín, possibilities for both the public and the companies have expanded.

In 1960, Paraguay began to establish modern lines of communication (such as improved roads and the President Stroessner International Airport) with its neighbors, Brazil and Argentina. The resulting commercial and tourist traffic also produced a greater traffic of ideas. With knowledge of the artistic experiences in neighboring countries and, through them, the world, Paraguay was finally able to end its historic isolation. The appearance of new social sectors and, consequently, new educational and cultural appetites, determined the growth and development of various theatrical groups. Among these groups two types can be clearly differentiated: comic theatre of a commercial tendency and a theatre of art.

Comic theatre companies base their repertoire on everyday life situations, giving them a superficial view. They perform at the Municipal Theatre. The companies of the theatre of art use the two new theatres already mentioned, in addition to other occasional places. Their repertoire consists of comedies and dramas of universal authors.

Two currents are evident in the companies of artistic theatre: (1) the traditional which is based on a technique of performance and a repertory of universal works within the line of "high comedy" and presents works with a profound sense of artistic dignity; and (2) the so-called independent or experimental which is based on more modern techniques (Stanislavsky, Grotowski, Buenaventura) and presents work that deals with the social reality or with conflicting topics on the human condition.

Although obvious advances have taken place in Paraguayan theatre, certain factors are currently impeding the normal growth of the theatre and limiting its expansion. Paraguay is the only country in South America without a state organism designed to support these activities. The state does not invest a cent in cultural activities. The Municipal Theatre was constructed a century ago. Moreover, the large theatre building constructed by Marshall López around 1860, whose construction was interrupted by The War of the Triple Alliance, was not finished according to the original plans and was converted into the center of a tax collection agency. Theatre groups must hand over more than 20 percent of their net income in different kinds of taxes. In addition, they must present the texts of their works with the complete cast of actors to City Hall according to censorship regulations established in 1974.

In the context of the historical development of Paraguayan theatre, the decade of the 1970s marks a notable and sustained increase in activity, quantitatively as well as qualitatively, constituting a stage, that, hypothetically, can be considered as one of basic consolidation. An index of this activity is the proliferation of groups at different levels (professional, experimental, student, and amateur), the appearance of new authors, and more demand in audiences.

The theatre today has become a relevant aspect of national life as a vehicle for the aspirations of different emerging social sectors. Within the framework of the present socioeconomic development, characterized by the establishment of huge foreign enterprises and by the construction of the colossal power plant at Itaipú, increased audiences offer new challenges to artists in the theatrical medium.

ASSEMBLY
(Aty Ñe'e)
Casilla 72
Asunción, Paraguay

Established in 1975, Assembly is made up of a group of young actors committed to the investigation of a popular theatrical language. They have presented works such as *Velada* (*The Vigil*) by the national authors Alcibíades González del Valle and Tony Carmona, *Mascarada en Río Revuelto* (*Masquerade in Churning River*), *Noche de pesca* (*Fishing Night*), based on Bertolt Brecht's text, and other plays.

ASUNCIÓN PLAYERS
(Comedia Asunceña)
Casilla 72
Asunción, Paraguay

The Asunción Players (1969) is a troupe formed by actors from the Municipal School of Dramatic Art, the only such school in the country. The group was founded and directed by the veteran actor and director Manuel Argüello. He has earned the support of both the general public and the critics with works such as *The Fox and Grapes* by the Brazilian Guilherme Figueiredo, *El médico a palos* (*Doctor by Force*), an original version of Molière's play, *Our Town* by Thornton Wilder, and *A View from the Bridge* by Arthur Miller.

ERNESTO BÁEZ COMPANY
(Elenco Ernesto Báez)
Teatro Municipal, Asunción, Paraguay

Paraguay's outstanding company of comic theatre is one directed by the author, director, actor, and producer Ernesto Báez. In general, his plays are presented in *yopará*, a mixture of Guaraní and Spanish. He has successfully presented such plays as *El comisario de Valle Lorito* (*The Commissioner from Lorito Valley*) of comic character and both *La madama* (*Madame*) and *Magdalena Servín* of dramatic character. His company dates from the fifties and marks an entire epoch in the public taste for his populist orientation, with characters based on clearly recognizable types.

FREE STUDIO THEATRE
(Teatro Estudio Libre)
Misión de Amistad, 12 de Octubre y Ave. Gral. Santos
Asunción, Paraguay

The Free Studio Theatre belongs to the groups of independents formed after their counterparts in Argentina. It appeared in 1970, was founded and directed by Rudi Torga, and was installed in the locale of the Misión de Amistad in a highly populated section of the capital. The group has offered annually such works as *Barranca abajo* (*Down the Cliff*) of the Uruguayan Florencio Sánchez, *El centroforward murió al amanecer* (*The Center Forward Died at Dawn*) of the Argentinian Agustín Cuzzani, *Mbocaya Ha'eno* (*Solitary Coconut Palm*) by Néstor Romero Valdovinos, a precise portrait of political caudillos and the agrarian country life, and finally *A la diestra de Dios Padre* (*At the Right-hand Side of God the Father*) by the Colombian Enrique Buenaventura. This group regularly offers plays in two- or three-week runs. With institutional support, this company has been able to maintain a stable cast and a healthy repertory of the best national and Latin American titles, directed toward the popular sector.

HARLEQUIN THEATRE
(Arlequín Teatro)
De Gaulle y Quesada, Asunción, Paraguay

A theatre whose owner is also an actor, Harlequin Theatre produces the majority of Paraguay's theatre presentations. Such was the case, for example, of the play by the national author Josefina Kostianovsky *Que nos queremos tanto* (*We Love Each Other So Much*) and *La casa de Bernarda Alba* (*The House of Bernarda Alba*) of Federico García Lorca, for which very well-known figures were hired to stimulate the performance. The latter production set a record of public attendance, with more than twelve thousand persons in a two-month run.

HÉCTOR DE LOS RÍOS COMPANY
(Compañía Héctor de los Ríos)
Estrella y 15 de Agosto, Asunción, Paraguay

Héctor de los Ríos is properly called a theatrical *"trashumante"* (vagabond). Since childhood he has acted with his siblings and relatives in front of South American audiences. Having settled in Paraguay, he resumed his theatrical activities in 1959 after several years of interruption. As the head of his company, he has offered high-quality productions that consist almost exclusively of international works such as Friedrich Dürrenmatt's *The Physicist* and John Osborne's *Look Back in Anger*, both in the Theatre of the Paraguayan-American Cultural Center (CCPA), after they were banned in the Municipal Theatre. More recently, he presented *In the Middle of the Road* by Peter Ustinov in La Farándula, a dinner theatre rented by the group for weekends, to alternate with musical shows and functions by other groups. In the words of the present director, Edda de los Ríos (who is also his daughter and a talented actress), she hopes "to contribute to the formation of audiences and actors through a theatrical work conscious of the limitations of the environment." Since the "acting profession" as such does not exist in any practical sense, this group works constantly with new figures, with a repertory that ranges from simple local sketches to the most demanding works of an international repertoire (*Sarah Bernhardt* by John Murray, *El hilo rojo* [*The Red Thread*] by Henry Denker, and *Same Time Next Year* by Bernard Slade, all presented at the Theatre of the Americas of the CCPA).

PARAGUAYAN THEATRE COMPANY
(Compañía del Ateneo Paraguayo)
Nuestra Señora de La Asunción y Humaita
Asunción, Paraguay

One of the oldest theatre companies in Paraguay is the Ateneo Paraguayo, founded in 1941. It is presently under the direction of María Elena Sachero, an outstanding actress, and Mario Prono, a long-time actor. Banned from the Municipal Theatre for several years, its presentations have become more sporadic of late. Its repertoire consists of heterodoxical works ranging from the Paraguayan musical comedy *zarzuela* (such as *María Pacurí*, *La tejedora de ñandutí* [*The Lace Maker*], both by Frutos Pane and Moreno González), to detective works and substantial plays, such as *Antigone* by Jean Anouilh, *The Heiress* by Ruth and Augustus Goetz, and *Interrogante* (*Interrogator*) by the prolific national author Mario Halley Mora. All were presented with great interpretative skill and considerable response from the public and critics. In the words of its directors, the objective of the group is "to form actors and give good works to the public, without being avant-garde."

PEOPLE'S THEATRE
(Gente de Teatro)
Arlequín Teatro
Quesada y de Gaulle
Asunción, Paraguay

The People's Theatre (1971), which split off from the Compañía del Ateneo Paraguayo de Teatro, is one of Paraguay's most outstanding groups of its class for its consistent repertory, frequency of productions (about fifteen per year), high interpretive quality, and sizable audience its performances attract. Formed by a group of young actors, Gustavo Calderini, Carla Fabri, Clotilde Cabral, and José Luis Ardissone, it has presented a number of successful productions, such as *Jaque a la reina* (*Check the Queen*) by Santillán and Peyrou at the Municipal Theatre and Arlequín Teatro, as well as *La nona* (*The Grandmother*) by Roberto Cossa, and *Requiem for a Woman* by Faulkner-Camus in the CCPA. To date it has not included national works in its repertory.

PIRIRI THEATRE
(Piriri Teatro)
De Gaulle y Quesada, Asunción, Paraguay

The Piriri Theatre was founded in 1980. Its repertory is oriented toward children with works based on local issues and legends such as *Una hora al revés* (*A Backwards Hour*) and *El pícaro sueño* (*The Rogue's Dream*). It attained great success with the musical comedy *Abran cancha que aquí viene Don Quijote de la Mancha* (*Open the Court, Here Comes Don Quixote*) by the Argentinian author Adela Basch.

UNIVERSITY THEATRE GROUP
(Grupo de Teatro Universitario)
Casilla 72, Asunción, Paraguay

Created in 1980, this troupe has chosen mostly a classical repertoire to offer to youngsters of schools and universities in the capital and neighboring cities.

It has presented plays like *La guarda cuidadosa* (*The Careful Guard*) by Cervantes, *Egloga* (*Eclogue*) by Juan de la Encina, *Las preciosas ridículas* (*The Ridiculous Women*) by Molière, and *Historia de un número* (*Story of a Number*) by the national author Josefina Plá.

ANTONIO PECCI
(Edited and translated by Carlota Villagra
and George Woodyard)

Puerto Rico

INTRODUCTION

Puerto Rican theatre has developed steadily since the 1930s, registering many achievements, especially after 1940, when Emilio S. Belaval—author, director, and empresario—challenged the native theatre artists to forge an authentic Puerto Rican theatre. These achievements are the fruit of years of struggle and effort by theatre groups, which have managed to overcome the many economic, cultural, and spiritual limitations imposed by the island throughout those years. Because of space limitations, this study will focus on three groups—Producciones Cisne, Teatro del Sesenta, and Taller de Histriónes—for the period 1960 to the present.

Each of these groups has its own style and theatrical preferences. Their combined histories give a varied and nearly complete view of Puerto Rican theatre. They have not only produced a professional theatre of high quality, but have also served as advanced workshops, in which the great majority of Puerto Rico's present theatre artists acquired their experience and training. Although Producciones Cisne, Teatro del Sesenta, and Taller de Histriones are incorporated, they are called groups here rather than companies, since they do not perform commercial theatre and have not abandoned their workshop structure.

ACTORS' WORKSHOP
(Taller de Histriones)
University of Puerto Rico
Departmento de Drama
Río Piedras, Puerto Rico 00931

The Actors' Workshop was founded at the request of the pantomime students of the University of Puerto Rico Drama Department. Professor Gilda Navarra compromised with the students to develop a practical workshop, in which they could adapt what they learned to the Latin American actor's temperament. "Histrion" is the Greek word for actor, but the group's members are not exactly actors, since they do not use words. Yet they are not exactly mimes either, since they do not follow a rigid pantomimic style. Rather, for each production they develop a peculiar form of movement, in which traditional forms blend with those newly discovered through improvisation.

The Actors' Workshop does not have a board of directors. According to Gilda Navarra, it is a big family; all production aspects and problems are discussed in weekly meetings, and decisions are made by the group. The members have accepted Navarra's leadership in recognition of her talent and experience. Navarra has been a dancer most of her life; she studied with the American Ballet of New York and founded the Ballet de San Juan in Puerto Rico with her sister, Ana García. As a dancer, she is known as a Spanish specialist; she lived many years in Spain, where she studied and worked with Pilar López. By the early 1960s the Institute of Puerto Rican Culture (ICP) granted her a scholarship to study pantomime in Paris with Jack Leqoc, Etienne Decroux, and Wolfgang Merril. When she returned to Puerto Rico in 1964, she devoted herself mainly to teaching pantomime in the university's Drama Department.

The Actors' Workshop's first works were produced by other groups: by Teatro del Sesenta from 1971 to 1973; and by Producciones Cisne from 1974 to 1976. It was not until 1977, with *Abelardo and Eloísa* that the group began production. The group is a workshop—an instrument of search and experimentation. Each production is worked on for a whole year through a process of improvisation and tightly scheduled daily rehearsals. Workloads are divided for the productions, and although Navarra is responsible for the economic aspects, the whole group feels responsible for contributing to the production's success.

According to Navarra, *Ocho mujeres* (*Eight Women*, 1974), a work based on García Lorca's *La casa de Bernarda Alba* (*The House of Bernarda Alba*), was the production that gave the group a greater cohesiveness. After that, the group knew it could survive and make a significant contribution to the Puerto Rican theatre. *Ocho mujeres* was the group's first work for the Puerto Rican Theatre Festival. It was also performed in 1976 for the Music and Theatre Festival at Coro, Venezuela, and in 1980 at the Latin American Popular Theatre Festival in New York. Other works performed by the group include the group's creations *Asíntota* (*Asymptote*, 1976), *La mujer del abanico* (*The Woman with the Fan*, 1981), and *La tocata para percusión* (*The Toccata for Percussion*, 1982).

The group's members have always looked for quality and excellence in their development as performers. Membership requirements are three years of pantomime, outstanding participation in the class, and strong determination to follow the discipline imposed by the workshop. Four members have pursued further training in pantomime in Europe: Rafael Fuentes, Luis Oliva, Ricardo Molina, and Ana Mía Erica Reyes.

A remarkable aspect of the group's labor has been the attempt to integrate other forms of art, such as music and painting, into its works. In 1975, with *Eleuterio el coquí* (*Eleuterio the Frog*), it began to integrate live music into the productions. In the most recent production, *Antibón, Ogún y Erzulí*, based on a series of Afro-Caribbean myths, the group worked closely with Puerto Rican painter Antonio Martorel, who actually painted the costumes and make-up on the performers' bodies. The Actors' Workshop has many plans, but its main objective is to preserve the discipline and group cohesion that enables it to do its best work.

CISNE PRODUCTIONS
(Producciónes Cisne)
P.O. Box 21644, University Street
Río Piedras, Puerto Rico 00931

Moved by the urgency of carrying the best drama to every corner of the island, three women with theatrical interests conceived of Cisne Productions in 1963. Josie Pérez (president), an actress with a solid national reputation, has a varied background in professional acting. She attended the American Academy of Dramatic Arts, the New School for Social Research (New York), Columbia University, and the Actors' Laboratory in Los Angeles. In Mexico, Pérez studied under Seki Sano, a famous member of Konstantin Stanislavsky's staff. Myrna Casas (production director and treasurer), a renowned playwright, is a graduate of the University of Puerto Rico's (UPR's) Drama Department, with an M.A. from Boston University and a Ph.D. from New York University. Casas is a former director of the UPR Drama Department. Gilda Navarra (executive secretary) is a former dancer, presently professor of pantomime in the UPR Drama Department, and serves as the group's counselor in scenic movement and choreography. The name Cisne Productions captures the group's objective: to be, as the Cygnus constellation, a guide for those artists who search for excellence. The name was also inspired by Luis Llorens Torres' verses, in which Puerto Rico is seen as an ugly duckling transformed into a beautiful swan only when its authentic and traditional values are recognized. Cisne Productions has sought to extol the island's cultural values through its theatrical efforts.

From 1963 to 1966 the group produced several plays, among them Myrna Casas' *Eugenia Victoria Herrera* (1963). In 1966 the Instituto de Cultura Puertorriqueña sponsored an illustrated lecture on Puerto Rican theatre, with short representations of selected scenes from plays produced by the group that transversed the island. That same year Cisne was invited to the International Theatre Festival sponsored by the Instituto and has since produced a play every year for this festival. The group has also produced independently of the festival. To date, its most successful productions have been William Gibson's *The Miracle Worker* and Eduardo de Filippo's *Filumena Marturano*. In both plays, Josie Pérez has demonstrated that she is one of Puerto Rico's most sensitive and talented actresses. In 1972 the group opened the First Mayagüez Theatre Festival with *The Trojan Women*, and in 1976 it produced for the Puerto Rican Theatre Festival *Eleuterio el coquí* (*Eleuterio the Frog*), a dramatization of Tomás Blanco's short story by Taller de Histriones, and Myrna Casas' *Tres y cuarenta años después*

(*Three and Forty Years Later*). In the 1980–1981 season it presented *Mariana Pineda*.

Cisne's first performance outside Puerto Rico was in 1971, when the Ministerio de Educación y Patronato Pro Cultura of El Salvador invited the group to the Second International Music Festival, where they presented Walter Béneke's *Funeral Home*. In 1976 the Patronato Pro Cultura renewed the invitation, this time to present *The Miracle Worker* and Antonio Gala's *Anillos para una dama* (*Rings for a Lady*) at the Teatro Nacional de El Salvador. The next year, Cisne Productions toured various Latin American countries. Two plays were presented in Costa Rica under the sponsorship of the Junta del Teatro Nacional: *Anillos para una dama* and Antonio Buero Vallejo's *La doble historia del Dr. Valmy* (*The Double Story of Dr. Valmy*). *Anillos para una dama* was presented again at the Teatro Nacional in Nicaragua, and under Fundarte's sponsorship in Venezuela. Doña Emma Balaguer invited the group to perform this play at the Teatro Nacional of Santo Domingo. Cisne Productions returned to Santo Domingo in 1979, by invitation of the Patronato del Teatro Nacional, with *Filumena Marturano*. In 1980 the group performed in the United States in Houston and Boston, and in 1981 in Miami.

The following group of artists has worked continuously with Cisne in the last years: José Reymundí (leading actor), Santiago García Ortega, Ernesto Concepción, Elsa Román, Esther Mari (character actors), Nina Leget and Carmen H. Bouet (scenery designers), Gloria Sáez (costume designer), and Jesús García del Toro (stage manager). Since 1973 Cisne Productions has maintained a workshop for amateur actors in Hato Rey, located in the same building used as office and rehearsal space. In this workshop, beginning actors receive acting classes from Myrna Casas, diction from Josie Pérez, pantomime from Gilda Navarra, and make-up from Carmen Correa. These amateur actors often get their first opportunities in the group's productions. Furthermore, Cisne has, on two occasions, obtained grants for graduate studies in theatre for its young theatre artists.

For the group's members, theatre is not only an art but also a form of communication. Through theatre, they are able to communicate the most subtle ideas in vivid and immediate ways. Cisne Productions' objective is to communicate the best ideas of the most profound playwrights and to carry a message of fraternal love and collaboration in extolling the highest ideals that, like the stars in the sky, guide human beings in their pursuit of excellence.

THEATRE OF THE SIXTIES
(Teatro del Sesenta)
P.O. Box 5122, Puerta de Tierra Station
San Juan, Puerto Rico 00906

During the 1960s Puerto Rican university students, wishing to make a significant contribution to the island's cultural development, began to join forces in several creative workshops. At one of those evenings of coffee and conversation, the members of Guajana (one of the creative workshops) challenged a group of theatre students (Dean Zayas, Carlos Nieves, Miguel Angel Suárez, and Ligia Rolón) to make a concrete contribution to Puerto Rican theatre. In this way, the Theatre of the Sixties was born. Almost immediately, the young theatre artists elected a board of directors, planned their first production—a double program with Eugene Ionesco's *The Lesson* and Edward Albee's *The Zoo Story*—and wrote their first manifesto (1963), in which they stated their principal purpose was to experiment with theatrical forms and trends virtually unknown in the native theatre milieu. From 1963 to 1966 the group devoted itself to following this objective. Nevertheless, its first big success was a realistic psychological drama, Arthur Miller's *A View from the Bridge* (1967). After this production, in the same year, the group was invited to the First Vanguard Theatre Festival, sponsored by the Ateneo Puertorriqueño, where it presented Osvaldo Dragún's *Milagro en el mercado viejo* (*Miracle in the Old Market*), and to the International Theatre Festival (ICP), where it presented Tennessee Williams' *A Streetcar Named Desire*.

From 1967 to 1974 the group produced mainly social and psychological plays, without abandoning experimental styles. The group's national renown, however, was definitely established with two great successes in a realistic mode: Paul Zindel's *The Effect of Gamma Rays on Man-in-the-Moon Marigolds* (1971) and John Herbert's *Fortune and Men's Eyes* (1971). Both productions combined a highly talented cast with one of Puerto Rico's most sensitive directors, Dean Zayas. A graduate of the University of Puerto Rico Drama Department, Zayas studied at New York University and later obtained an M.A. from Yale. He has worked as an actor in the island theatre festivals as well as with Miriam Colón's company in New York. Until 1974, when he left the group, Zayas was the president of Theatre of the Sixties except for the year 1971, when Fernando Luis Aguilú replaced him.

In 1972 the group acquired its own theatre, which its members named the Sylvia Rexach in honor of this Puerto Rican composer of popular music. The scarcity of auditoria has been a major obstacle in the evolution and expansion of the Puerto Rican theatre. For this reason several groups, like Coop-Arte and COPEI (Corporación de Imagen y Escena), tried unsuccessfully in the 1960s to support their own theatres. To this point, Theatre of the Sixties has been the only group to have succeeded.

The group has taken part in almost every theatrical encounter celebrated on the island. In 1971 at the Festival de Teatro Latinoamericano it presented *El herrero y el diablo* (*The Blacksmith and the Devil*), Carlos Ferrari's adaptation of Juan Carlos Gené's play. In 1973 the group presented for the I Muestra Mundial de Teatro Experimental another adaptation by Ferrari, Friedrich Dürrenmatt's *The Trial about the Donkey's Shadow*. In 1976 the Theatre of the Sixties presented for the I Muestra Nacional de Teatro a dramatization of Pedro Juan Soto's *Spik*, a collection of short stories. Contact with Brechtian theatre throughout Latin America encouraged the group to experiment with this style;

added to Ferrari's association, the group produced *Puerto Rico Fuá* (*Puerto Rico Hurrah!*) in 1974, its most successful and controversial play. The group was invited to present this play at the International Theatre Festival of Caracas in 1974 and at the International Theatre Festival in Nancy, France, in 1975. In 1979 the group traveled to Cuba and presented another work by Ferrari: *1898* (el último año de la desgracia colonial, y el primero de lo mismo) (the last year of the colonial disgrace, and the first year of the same) at the Festival de la Juventud y los Estudiantes.

Carlos Ferrari, playwright and the group's artistic director during the 1970s, is a product of the independent theatre movement that developed in Argentina during the 1950s. In the mid-1960s he attended a television directing course given by the Radio Corporation of America in New York. After six years, he moved to Puerto Rico and began his successful association with the Theatre of the Sixties with such plays as *Puerto Rico Fuá*, *Los Titingós de Juan Bobo*, and *Amor en el caserío* (*Love in the Village*). Ferrari was part of the group's board of directors from 1974 to 1979. At present he is separated from the group, but he still writes and directs for his own group—Nuestro Teatro—which is established at a theatre in Santurce.

Since the group settled in the Sylvia Rexach, the Theatre of the Sixties has done its best to give seminars and workshops for amateur theatre artists. While the group does not give regular classes, it has helped many young theatre artists to continue their undergraduate and graduate studies in theatre in Puerto Rico as well as abroad. Since there is no star system, work is handled collectively. Hence, a member may do everything from working the box office to acting. Moreover, the group's members do not charge for their work; if the production has been a success, however, the members receive a bonus. From 1974 to 1977 the Theatre of the Sixties received economic aid from the Instituto de Cultura Puertorriqueña; at this point, its income derives mainly from box office receipts and stage rental to other companies. Recently, the group's members completed a massive campaign to obtain the $150,000 needed to buy the Sylvia Rexach. Many of the popular television artists, among them Johanna Rasaly, have joined efforts to help them. Two recent important events have encouraged the group: the successful presentation of *El gran Pinche* (*The Great Pinche*) by Florita Garay, a former member of the group, and the overwhelming success of *La verdadera historia de Pedro Navaja* (*The True Story of Pedro Navaja*), an adaptation of Brecht's *The Threepenny Opera*.

The Theatre of the Sixties' philosophy has varied through the years. In its early vanguard period, its main purpose was to experiment with new forms and trends, and to use theatre as a means of expressing the nonconformity characteristic of youth during the 1960s. Later, as the group matured and began to search the depths of the human soul, it produced sociopsychological dramas. Theatre was then mirror-like in that the audience saw a portrayal of their own anguish and fears. After contact with other Latin American theatre, the group adopted a Brechtian style. At this point, theatre has become an instrument of analysis and protest, a way of expressing the island's political and social situation. The first successful attempt at this theatrical style in Puerto Rico has, perhaps, been the group's staging of Ferrari's scripts and *La verdadera historia de Pedro Navaja*. The group's greatest desire is to keep the Sylvia Rexach running and to strengthen the group's relationship with its audience.

CARMEN J. RODRÍGUEZ
(Edited by George Woodyard)

Uruguay

INTRODUCTION

A number of different permanent theatre activities coexist in Uruguay: (1) official theatre (represented by the professional Comedia Nacional); (2) independent theatre (amateur groups); (3) experimental theatre (vocational groups with sporadic activity); and (4) commercial theatre (controlled by producers of extravaganzas). The activity of the first two has an aesthetic rigor from its conception to its staging. The experimental theatre fulfills objectives common to other countries (theatre of the absurd and dramatic experiences), while the commercial theatre normally presents foreign plays (comedies, vaudeville, and farces), which satisfy a certain sector of the public. In terms of their representative quality—temporal durability, public response, and definition of artistic obligations—it is appropriate to mention the work carried out by three companies, which fit into the categories of official and independent theatre.

ALLIANCE THEATRE
(Teatro Alianza)
Alianza Cultural Uruguay–USA
Paraguay No. 1217
Montevideo, Uruguay

The group began a systematic and continuous activity upon completion of its building in the Uruguay-U.S. Cultural Alliance in Montevideo in 1975. The theatre space is flexible to the demands of the program: theatre in the round, proscenium stage, movie theatre, or television studio. The Alliance's Office of Cultural Activities decided to repeat in Uruguay the experience of transforming theatre space in ways that are now customary in the United States, France, England, Poland, and Italy, among others, considering the multi-spectacles that have received glowing reviews and subsequent spectator support.

From 1975 (*Charlie, Your Own Thing*, a musical comedy based on Shakespeare's *Twelfth Night* by Hally Hester y Apolinar) to date, the Alliance Theatre has been producing plays within the strictest criteria of workshop presentation—set design, sketches, costumes, sound, props, direction (shared at times), and individual and group acting supervision—all the product of an excellent workshop in full development.

In August 1977 the group performed Voltaire's *Candide*, a performance in which the visual aspects, the scenic dynamics, and the colorful contrast of clothing, lights, and sound made the workshop's collective creation stand out. That year a workshop for authors was established, with the dual purpose of offering the national writer a live and continuous experience before the stage, as well as the infrastructural elements needed.

In 1979 an excellent beginning was made in color television, with the presentation of Tennessee Williams' *This Property Is Condemned*. The videotape is available to the public in the Artigas Washington Library (a branch of the Uruguay-U.S. Cultural Alliance), and a copy was sent to Washington. The response to this experience was so positive that it will probably permit the inclusion of this program, with new titles, as a normal exchange activity with other alliances in Latin America. Most recently, the group presented the world premiere of *Pater Noster* (1979), a work by the Uruguayan author Jacobo Langsner, one of the most representative authors of national dramatic literature. In 1980 the group staged Colin Higgins' *Harold and Maude* and restaged *Pater Noster* in its 1981 season.

In short, the workshop's efforts create an authentic climate of collaboration among the actor, the author, and the other arts, which corresponds on an artistic level to the sensitivity of the directors—Elena Zuasti and Enrique Mrak. The negative aspects of personal or individual stardom have been excluded, with the intention of elevating the cultural aspects of the presentation.

MONTEVIDEO ARENA THEATRE
(Teatro Circular de Montevideo)
Avda. Rondeau No. 1388
Montevideo, Uruguay

The work of Uruguay's independent companies—noncommercial theatre—dates to the late nineteenth century with its sporadic presentations of amateur groups. A more systematic work, which adhered to certain aesthetic norms and a cohesive philosophy, was pioneered by the dramatic presentations of the Teatro del Pueblo (1937–1955). The Montevideo Arena Theatre has continued an important and enthusiastic activity to the present, and is known for its high-quality productions.

Established in December 1954, the Arena initiated theatre-in-the-round in Uruguay—in opposition to classic frontal theatre. Its programming spans the entire year, presenting on the average three new plays, with daily performances simultaneously in two theatres. The group maintains its own School of Dramatic Art for the training and preparation of actors. Since 1970, it has regularly sponsored a seminar for playwriting, as well as annual contests for Uruguayan authors. Its repertory includes the most important universal and national titles, and its work is accompanied by a permanent nucleus of spectators, who function as its exclusive source of revenue.

The group's artistic work won high praise from the Critics' Circle of Montevideo in 1967, and subsequently the Florencio Prize (a small statue of Florencio Sánchez) in 1968 and 1970 (the last year in which it was given) for the staging of Chekhov's *The Cherry Orchard* in 1968, Alfred de Musset's *Lorenzaccio* in 1970, and Carlo Goldoni's *The Servant of Two Masters*. The group received favorable reviews for its participation in the III International Theatre Festival in Caracas in May 1976, with its versions of *Lorenzaccio*, Chekhov's *The Three Sisters*, and *El asesino anda solo* (*The Assassin Walks Alone*) by the Uruguayan author Juan Graña. After the III Festival, the group began a successful tour through Colombia, Costa Rica, Guatemala, and Panama in 1976, and performed in Asunción, Paraguay, the following August.

In December 1979 the group celebrated twenty-five years of uninterrupted activity. The 1980 season featured *La farsa del palito* (*The Farce of the Stick* by Juan Graña, Uruguay), *Mariana Pineda* (by García Lorca), and *The Emigrants* (by Sławomir Mrożek). In 1981 and 1982 the group presented *Los engañados* (*The Deceived* by Lope de Rueda), *Vivir para atrás* (*Live for the Past* by Juan Graña), and *Doña Ramona* (by Víctor M. Leites).

NATIONAL THEATRE
(Comedia Nacional)
Teatro Solís
Buenos Aires esq. Bartolomé Mitre
Montevideo, Uruguay

The National Theatre of Uruguay was founded in October 1947, as the culmination of a crisis produced by the lack of artistic quality (performance and repertoire) in Montevideo's commercial houses. Simultaneously, there existed concern with upgrading the work of national authors who found it impossible, because of the aforementioned superstructure, to perform their works. To date, the national company has mounted professionally 230 plays by universal authors, classic and modern, and 61 plays by national playwrights.

Aware of the precarious nature of the medium with respect to the formation of actors, and conscious of the need to restructure the cast and to integrate other members, in 1949 the company began to create auxiliary services with definite programs, such as the Municipal School of Dramatic Art. This institute, for many years under the direction of the eminent Spanish actress Margarita Xirgú, was designed to systematize pedagogical training in the dramatic arts. The National Theatre also carried on successful activities outside Uruguay—in Buenos Aires (1948, 1956, and 1970); Viña del Mar, Chile (1955); Mar del Plata,

Argentina (1957); the Theatre Festival of the Nations (Théâtre des Nations, Paris, 1963); and Rome (1963).

Its outstanding productions in recent years have been the following: 1979, *El león ciego* (*The Blind Lion* by Ernesto Herrera), *The Merchant of Venice* (Shakespeare), *The Visit of the Old Lady* (Friedrich Dürrenmatt), and *Hedda Gabler* (Ibsen); 1980, *La Celestina* (*The Go Between*, Fernando de Rojas), *El burlador de Sevilla* (*The Seducer of Seville* by Tirso de Molina), and *El huésped vacío* (*The Empty Guest* by Ricardo Prieto); 1981, plays by two Uruguayans, *Los cuentos del final* (*The Stories of the End* by Carlos Manuel Varela) and *La planta* (*The Plant* by Jacobo Langsner); and 1982, *Matar el tiempo* (*Killing Time* by Carlos Gorostiza, Argentina), *Palabras en la arena* (*Words in the Sand* by Carlos M. Varela), *La nona* (*Grandma* by Roberto Cossa, Argentina), and *La casa de Bernarda Alba* (*The House of Bernarda Alba* by García Lorca).

WALTER RELA
(Translated by George Woodyard)

Venezuela

INTRODUCTION

Professional theatre artists in Venezuela are determined to overcome difficulties, even though at this point theatre work does not guarantee remuneration. Only in the last few years has it become apparent that the Venezuelan theatre may become more like that in countries with a more solid theatrical tradition.

Pioneers of forty years ago had a basically artistic and political vision of theatrical art. These circumstances were reflected as much in the repertories of theatre groups as in the ethical attitude of the participants vis-à-vis political and social pressures. Venezuela's political instability until the middle-1960s, not as dramatic as that in other countries of the continent but equally determinative, had a permanent influence. The nation has needed time to overcome its dictatorships, which limited its development of a national culture.

This situation was particularly alarming in the 1950s. The theatre movement which had just begun at the end of the previous decade had to face an intransigent dictatorship, which, although it did not eliminate theatre activity, severely impaired it. The most important theatre companies of the period—Máscaras, El Duende, and Compás—were able to survive because their participants were always militant about art and politics. Nevertheless, the political situation hampered the development of a serious and ambitious theatre.

Despite its wealth, Venezuela has few stable companies. First, the country needed to attain political stability before certain companies could be formed. In the 1960s the instability of theatre groups continued, for two reasons. First, new theatrical ideas had been discovered which were much richer than those that had filtered in during the dictatorship of the 1950s. The acceleration in information created confusion in the new generations, which began to experiment loosely, bringing a modicum of anarchy to the national theatre movement. Second, in those same years the political situation in the country continued to hamper the theatre, since the national crisis produced by the guerrilla movement did not facilitate the interpersonal agreements necessary for theatre companies to become stabilized.

Venezuelan theatre professionals are now receiving a salary for their work as a result of the economic boom of the country. The population's greater buying power has stimulated interest in the theatre. Some producers have been able to exploit this tendency: for the first time in forty years a theatre that is decidedly commercial has been promoted.

Venezuelan theatre companies receive subsidies from governmental organizations charged with cultural promotion. They could not survive without this support since the theatre public continues to be small. Nevertheless, the work of these Venezuelan theatre people is extremely rigorous and serious. These two traits define its professional level.

The New Group is the most famous Venezuelan Theatre company. For several years the group has had a second theatre: the Juana Sujo. The Rajatablas is the best known alternative for "experimentalist" theatre in Caracas. Both companies are pillars of national theatre culture. In recent years new attempts have been made in Caracas to form other theatrical companies, but by and large they have failed, primarily because of the shortage of theatres to guarantee a stable base of operations, the difficulty in securing adequate subventions, and the lack of a coherent philosophy.

The Teatro Tilingo (a children's Theatre Group) maintains an important activity in the field of children's theatre. Its work is constantly improving. In 1979, it won the National Critics' Prize and the Municipal Theatre Prize for its free interpretation of *A Midsummer Night's Dream*, under the direction of Clara Rosa Otero de Altamirano, who also did the adaptation. In 1979 she created the International Contest for Children's Theatre, in conjunction with the International Year of the Child and with direct support from the Cultural Affairs Office of the Ministry of Foreign Relations.

NEW GROUP
(El Nuevo Grupo)
Teatro Alberto de Paz y Mateos
Apartado 10213, Caracas, Venezuela

In 1967 the Venezuelan theatre companies took a new and definitive step. In September of that year the New Group began work in the Teatro Alberto de Paz y Mateos. The theatre is named for a Spanish director who arrived in the late 1940s and taught some of Venezuela's most important theatrical figures. He died at the very time the New Group was initiating its activities.

The New Group is the most important theatre company in Venezuela, and has three of the five best national playwrights: Isaac Chocrón, José Ignacio Cabrujas, and Román Chalbaud. The New Group appeared on the scene when the excesses of the experimental theatre had nearly decimated the dramatic author. The company therefore proposed to develop a high-quality textual theatre, which explains why the principal organizers are three playwrights. The approximately one hundred plays performed so far by the company are evidence of its conscientious effort to influence national theatre. Through this work the New Group succeeded in establishing itself. The country considers it a key factor in the national culture, since it knew how to interpret the process of Venezuelan theatre and presented a valid response.

Its multiple productions reflect an immense variety of authors, who were perhaps selected in an eclectic form but who always vindicated the dramatist. Its inauguration on September 15, 1967, included a play by Arnold Wesker (*Roots*), *Tric-trac* by Isaac Chocrón, and *Fiésole* by José Ignacio Cabrujas. Murray Schisgal, Edward Albee, Harold Pinter, Molière, Paul Claudel, Bertolt Brecht, Fritz Hochwalder, Shakespeare, Eugene Ionesco, Anton Chekhov, Roger Vitrac, Eugene O'Neill, Joe Orton, Carlo Goldoni, and Jean Genet are some of the foreign authors. On behalf of national playwrights, the New Group also maintains a contest for the promotion of young writers, later producing the prize-winning plays. This activity is unique in the country. The group has also given special attention to children's theatre.

Although the New Group does not have an exclusive team of collaborators, it is the home of the most important figures in national theatre and has won many prizes. The nation's most important theatrical figures are members of the group: directors such as Ugo Ulive (who won a prize for best director in 1978 and 1979), Armando Gota, and Antonio Costante; actors and actresses such as María Cristina Lozada, Rafael Briceño (who marked forty years of professional activity in 1980), Amalia Pérez Díaz, Pilar Romero, Fausto Verdial, Manola García Maldona, and Herminia Valdés; scene designers such as José Luis Gómez Fra (who won a prize for best set design in 1978) and John Lange; costume designers such as Elías Martinello (who won a prize for costume design in 1978); producers such as Elías Pérez Borjas, Eva Ivanyi, and Esther Bustamante.

The New Group has had exceptional moments. *La revolución* by Isaac Chocrón, premiered in 1971, directed by Román Chalbaud, and acted by Rafael Briceño and José Ignacio Cabrujas, is a key text in Venezuelan literature and theatre. It was still being performed in short seasons in 1977 and 1981. *Acto cultural* (*Cultural Act*) and *El día que me quieras* (*On the Day That You Love Me*), written and directed by José Ignacio Cabrujas, brought wide national acclaim. Besides, *Acto cultural* had an excellent critical reception in the IV World Session of Théâtre des Nations, held in Caracas in 1978. Plays by Pinter and Genet directed by Ulive, a Fernando Arrabal play presented by Gota, *Vida con mamá* (*Life with Mama*) by the Venezuelan writer Elisa Lerner under the direction of Antonio Costante, and plays by young writers such as Edilio Peña continue to be points of reference. *Prueba de fuego* (*Trial by Fire*) by Ugo Ulive opened in 1981, and 1982 saw productions by Román Chalbaud, *Todo bicho de uña* (*Every Beast of Hoof and Claw*), as well as by Emilio Carballido (Mexico), *Mimí y Fifí en el Orinoco* (*Mimi and Fifi on the Orinoco*).

The most recent success was *Humboldt y Bonpand, taxidermistas* (*Humboldt and Bonpand, Taxidermists*) by the young writer Ibsen Martínez, under the direction of the new director Enrique Porte, who will surely be the best director of the current decade. In 1980 Chocrón premiered one of the finest and most complex plays of recent years, *Mesopotamia*, under the direction of the impeccable Ugo Ulive.

Chocrón, Cabrujas, and Chalbaud differ considerably among themselves as playwrights, but in spite of these differences they manage to give the country a rigorous, superior theatre, promoting the best national values. Nowadays the New Group is a point of reference in Latin America, and its objective of reinstating the dramatic author in large part explains its success. In 1977 the Circle of Theatre Critics of Venezuela (CRITVEN) gave the group its special annual prize for invaluable contributions to the Venezuelan theatre in its ten years of activities.

RAJATABLA GROUP
(Grupo Rajatabla)
Ateneo de Caracas, Apdo. 662
Caracas, Venezuela

Near the end of the 1960s, the Ateneo of Caracas, which has always promoted national theatre in its several decades of existence, began to reorient its activity. Chilean-born Horacio Peterson had consolidated this activity with great merit and success since the 1950s. In 1970, after a tour through Latin America which included the University Theatre Festival of Manizales (Colombia), Carlos Giménez, director and founder of the group El Juglar of Córdoba (Argentina), arrived in Caracas. Giménez replaced Peterson in the Ateneo and created a group which in ten years would become one of the most important theatre companies in the country. In 1981, on the fiftieth anniversary of the Ateneo, the federal government began construction of a new building, which allows the Ateneo to have two theatres: the Rajatabla under Carlos Giménez, and another located in the new seven-story building.

The Rajatabla Group initiated an "experimentalist" work equivalent to that of the previous period, but with greater care for detail and form. In that way it achieved a professional character superior to the amateur tone which the "experimentalist" theatre had shown in Venezuela. To begin with, it achieved a controversial success with *La orgía* by the Colombian Enrique Buenaventura. After the play was suspended, it was taken to the Manizales Festival in September 1970, to protest its banning in Venezuela.

Rajatabla is a polemical group in the Venezuelan theatre. Its emphasis is on foreign tours, it has a marked individuality, and it announces its opinions with evident correctness. To this one must add the benefit of promotional support given by the newspaper *El Nacional*, whose owners are closely linked with the Ateneo of Caracas.

Until 1976 the group was only minimally successful in achieving the director's goals. The plays produced until that year showed that the group was working with caution and immaturity. There were no significant titles in the repertory, although they had been attractive to the public. Near the end of 1976 the group performed *Divinas palabras* (*Divine Words*) by Ramón del Valle Inclán. From that time, the group began a feverish round of activities, which coincided with the work of Giménez and the Ateneo of Caracas in various international theatre festivals in Caracas. The coverage the Venezuelan theatre received and the increase in visits by foreign groups stimulated Giménez to dig into his work.

In that same year Rajatabla premiered *El juego* (*The Game*) by the young writer Mariela Romero and under the direction of Armando Gota, who was invited for the production. The critics unanimously recognized the artistic quality of the production, which was an expression of the new wave the group was beginning to exhibit. Gota won the National Critics Prize as best director of the year.

The years 1977 and 1978 were decisive for this company. Their productions of *El señor presidente* (*Mr. President*) by Miguel Angel Asturias and *El menú* (*The Menu*) by Enrique Buenaventura (under the title *El candidato*) show that the group has achieved a mature form of expression. In both plays the company was able to define a formal, serious, and coherent language. In those years the group performed in the most important festivals in Europe, where it got a warm, well-deserved critical reception. *El héroe nacional* (a free version of *Stranitsky the National Hero* by Friedrich Dürrenmatt) and *La muerte de García Lorca* (*The Death of García Lorca*) by José Antonio Rial (born in Spain) are other important productions that merit international recognition. The company's 1982 premiere of *Bolívar*, also by Rial, coincided with the centennial observations in honor of the national hero.

UNIVERSITY THEATRE OF CARABOBO
(Teatro Universitario de Carabobo)
Dirección de Cultura, Universidad de Carabobo
Valencia, Venezuela

Theatre activity in the interior of Venezuela is mostly the work of amateurs. The exception is the University Theatre of Carabobo, located in Valencia, ninety miles west of Caracas. Its solid professional level and its daring aesthetic posture derive from the rich, personal temperament of its director, Miguel Torrence. The group has been in existence for more than ten years. Even though its crew of actors, who for the most part are university students, is not stable, Torrence, inspired by a creative and political obsession, has mounted some notable productions, including works by Alfred Jarry, Bertolt Brecht, August Strindberg, and Enrique Buenaventura.

Torrence is perhaps one of the most imaginative of Venezuela's directors. As do few others, he assumes great risks with boldness and personally adapts the expressive language of his company to the national dynamics. His work represents a break with traditional patterns in Venezuelan theatre. The experimental work of the University Theatre, whether one mentions *The Pelican* or *The Trial of Lucullus*, transcends a political and artistic compromise in order to bring together the content of universal theatre and Venezuelan idiosyncrasies. This objective, even when not fully coherent, has placed this theatre group in the vanguard of experimental theatre and has differentiated it from the "experimentalist" currents.

LEONARDO AZPARREN GIMÉNEZ
(Translated by George Woodyard)

THE MIDDLE EAST

Iran

Seasonal festival farces, some predating the Arab conquest (mid-seventeenth century), as well as shadow plays and puppet theatres were current in Iran before the sixteenth century, when Shi'ite Islam became the state religion. Storytellers (*Naqqal*) have recounted tales of epic legends or popular picaresque romances in teahouses and public squares since the days of ancient Iran. Jesters were important in the courts of kings and were the first to enact topical playlets.

By the seventeenth century troupes of musicians and dancers were singing and performing comic and amorous sketches in the houses and courtyards of the rich. Bawdy women appeared on stage. Acrobats and conjurers were also popular.

By the eighteenth century the Shi'ite clergy prohibited such levity. The female roles were thereafter taken by young boys. However, troupes still performed on the occasions of marriages, births, and circumcisions. In the second half of the century, improvised comedies made their appearance denigrating the rich, the state, and the society and its injustices.

The first theatre for popular comedies opened in Tehran in about 1917. The stage was a square surrounded by the audience, before the arena became three-sided against a backdrop, under Western influence. Europeans became the butt of jokes and women reappeared on stage. Periodically, the theatres were burned by religious groups, always to reopen. The trend was toward basically historical, pseudo-epic, or moral comedies. Generally, women who appeared on the stage were considered disreputable.

The first comedies written for the Persian stage appeared in Turkish, translated into Persian during the nineteenth century. These were followed by comedies based on the older Persian improvised skits, denouncing the corrupt officialdom of the absolute ruler, the exactions by dignitaries, and the sheepishness of the people.

As monarchs and educated Persians began to travel in Europe, a theatre hall was built in Tehran, and adaptations of French plays were performed for several years, chiefly for members of the court. These were mostly translations of Molière in which the characters were Persianized. This theatre, which was located in the first Iranian polytechnic institution, had a short life.

Theatres in the Western style were established in the twentieth century: the National Theatre in Tehran (Teatr-e Melli) in 1911 and the Iranian Comedy Theatre (Komedi-e Iran) a few years later. Their repertory consisted of foreign plays, translated into Persian, and original Persian comedies and tragedies. These theatres were an inspiration to nascent playwrights.

During the reign of Reza Shah (1925–1941), the writing of drama suffered a mild setback when sociopolitical allusions in plays were censored. During this period men and women were seated separately in the theatres, according to Muslim custom. Outside Tehran, only in the cities of Rasht in the north and Isfahan were there theatrical activities.

After the Allied Occupation of Iran in 1941, the theatre revived. The middle class and intellectuals comprised most of the audience. After 1948 censorship was reestablished more firmly, and playwrights began to use symbolic language to avoid it, as earlier generations of Persians had used similar devices in their poetry.

In the late 1950s the National Arts Group was formed (Goruh-e Honar-e Melli), in which stage directors, writers, and actors collaborated. Many Persian literary works were adapted for the stage, including national legends as well as classical and contemporary literature. In 1958 a Dramatic Arts Center was established in connection with the Ministry of Culture and Arts. The School of Dramatic Arts was then established at Tehran University. A new theatre, sponsored by the government, was erected in Tehran and called "Teatr-e 25 Shahrivar." In the provinces only the theatre in Isfahan was worthy of mention.

The 1960s and early 1970s could be considered the best years for the writing of dramas, which for political reasons were seldom produced. From 1966 on, national radio and television began to program plays, both traditional and popular, and contemporary plays, both foreign and Persian.

In 1967 the Festival of Arts in Shiraz was established with the support of the broadcast media companies. For eleven years until 1977, Shiraz became a meeting ground of East and West, old and new, in the fields of theatre, dance, ballet, and music. There were productions by Shuji Terayama, Peter Brook, Robert Wilson, Jerzy Grotowski, Andre Sherban, and other contemporary directors. By contrast, traditional groups from Asia and Africa interspersed the programs. In 1969 a theatrical workshop in Tehran (Kargah-e Nemayesh) was developed from the activities of the Festival of Arts and television. The group attracted many directors, actors, scenic designers, and playwrights, to produce foreign and local plays and to encourage new talents, until the Revolution of 1978 put a stop to these endeavors.

The ritual drama of Iran deserves separate consideration because it is the only indigenous drama in the world of Islam. This is the dramatic representation of the passion and death of Imam Hussein, the grandson of the Prophet Muhammad, who was murdered, together with his sons and supporters, on the plain of Kerbela in the year A.D. 680 by his religious and political opponents. The renditions of this story fascinated many men of letters and the theatre of the West, such as Matthew Arnold, Count de Gobineau, Ernest Renan, Peter Brook, and Jerzy Grotowski.

The Kerbela tragedy further divided the world of Islam between the Shi'ites and the Sunnites. At the beginning of the sixteenth century Shi'ite Islam became the state religion of Iran, giving impetus to the annual mourning observance of Hussein's death. In these observances, all classes of society participated. Two major features of these rituals are as follows. First, there were processions interspersed with floats, in which the themes of the tragedy were shown as living tableaux. Great throngs of people joined these marches, flagellating themselves with chains and knives, beating their chests with fists and stones, wailing, and crying. Second, recitations were held about the passion, suffering, and death of Hussein and many Shi'ite martyrs, in courtyards, private houses, or specially built edifices called Husseiniyeh. Emotional participation of the audience was characteristic of these gatherings, called Rowzeh-khani, for active involvement in the sufferings of the martyrs was believed to pave the way to salvation for believers, with Hussein acting as intercessor.

In the middle of the eighteenth century, these two rituals fused, giving birth to the drama called Ta'ziyeh. In the beginning, the Ta'ziyehs were a part of the parades. Subsequently, they were performed at street intersections, in public squares, and then in the courtyards of private houses. Finally, special edifices were constructed for them called Takiyeh. The most famous was Takiyeh Dowlat, built in the 1870s, the royal theatre in Tehran. According to many Western travelers, its dazzling splendor and intensity of dramatic action overshadowed even the operas of the Western capitals. Takiyeh Dowlat's high activity lasted for over twenty-five years.

The genius of a Ta'ziyeh drama is that it combines immediacy and flexibility with universality. Uniting rural folk art with urban, royal entertainment, it admits no barriers between the archetype and the human, the wealthy and the poor, the sophisticated and the simple, the spectator and the actor. Each participates with and enriches the other.

The performance takes place on the stark, curtainless stage, which is situated in the middle of the audience. To indicate a change of place, the actors jump off the central stage and circumambulate it. The action extends from the central platform outward into the circular arena, facilitating audience participation. The protagonists sing their parts, while the antagonists recite. The good people are dressed in green and white, and the villains wear predominantly red. The roles of women are played by boys. The director is always on stage, prompting the professional actors, who are assisted in the minor parts by members of the village or town.

Plays can last from two to four hours, at the spontaneous discretion of the director and his troupe. Drums and trumpets initiate certain sections. From the middle of the nineteenth century on, the performance of Ta'ziyeh has not been restricted to the month of mourning for Hussein and his companions, called Muharram. Roughly speaking, there are about 250 plays devoted to various episodes of the Shi'ite martyrology.

In the latter part of the twentieth century, as the result of Westernization, this dramatic form persists only in rural areas and was performed in villages. In *Parabola*, Vol. IV, No. 2 (New York: May, 1979), Peter Brook recently spoke about Ta'ziyeh:

I saw in a remote Iranian village one of the strangest things I have ever seen in theater: a group of four hundred villagers, the entire population of the place, sitting under a tree and passing from roars of laughter to outright sobbing—although they knew perfectly well the end of the story—as they saw Hussein in danger of being killed, and then fooling his enemies, and then being martyred. And when he was martyred the theater form became a truth—there was no difference between past and present. An event that was told as a remembered happening in history, thirteen hundred years ago, actually became a reality at that moment. Nobody could draw the line between the different orders of reality. It was an incarnation: at that particular moment he was being martyred again in front of those villagers.

PETER J. CHELKOWSKI

Israel

INTRODUCTION

The history of Hebrew theatre is unique because its most significant company was established abroad before moving to Palestine. In 1918 the Habima, which began as a Hebrew drama studio, was established by Nahum Zemach in Moscow. Eight years later, the company left Moscow to tour the world, finally settling in Palestine in 1932. In *The Hebrew Theatre: Its First Fifty Years* (New York: KTAV Publishing House, 1969), Mendel Kohansky calls attention to a landmark in the history of Hebrew theatre which occurred in 1961 when the Habima produced Nissim Aloni's *The Emperor's Clothes*, the "first major play by an Israeli author which dealt with universal problems in the modern idiom" (p. 280).

Quality theatre companies in Israel gradually evolved from student and amateur groups. In 1890 the students of the Laemel Trade School produced Moshe Leib Lillienblum's *Zerubabel* (*The Return to Zion*), which was the first Palestine theatre performance in Hebrew. An amateur theatre group called the Lovers of the Hebrew Theatre and based in Jaffa presented Karl Gutzkov's *Uriel Acosta* as its first production in 1904 and continued to function until 1914. In 1926 Moshe Halevy founded Ohel, the Workers' Theatre of Palestine; in 1944 a group of actors and directors, who were headed by Yosef Millo, founded the Cameri Theatre of Tel-Aviv; in 1958 a group of young actors organized the Zavit, presenting Jean-Paul Sartre's *No Exit* as their first production; and in 1961 the Haifa Municipal Theatre was established as a public corporation through the initiative of the late Mayor Abba Khoushy and the City Council of Haifa (Kohansky, pp. 279-80).

Many Israeli theatre companies are presently producing the best of classical and modern drama, national and foreign plays. The Israel Centre of the International Theatre Institute assists the theatregoing public in developing an understanding of the various activities of those theatre groups.

COLBY H. KULLMAN

CAMERI THEATRE OF TEL-AVIV
101 Dizengoff Street
P.O. Box 3014, Tel-Aviv, Israel

The Cameri Theatre of Tel-Aviv is the municipal theatre of Tel-Aviv, the largest city in Israel. The company has performed continuously since its founding in 1944 by a group of actors and directors, headed by the director and actor Yosef Millo and the actor Avraham Ben-Yosef. The theatre was established to perform plays in the Western European style, a contrast to the Eastern European style of other Israeli theatres in those days. Searching for "pure" theatre, Millo wanted to return to the sources of the theatre and offer the public an alternative to the realistic bourgeois theatre of the Habima and Ohel. Since 1944 the company has produced over 250 plays.

Among the Cameri's many successful productions are Brandon Thomas' *Charlie's Aunt* (1946), George Kaufman and Moss Hart's *You Can't Take It with You* (1947), Moshe Shamir's *He Went Through the Fields* (1948), Nathan Shaham's *They'll Arrive Tomorrow* (1950), George Bernard Shaw's *Pygmalion* (1954), Yigal Mossinson's *Casablan* (1954), Henrik Ibsen's *A Doll's House* (1959) and *Hedda Gabler* (1966), and Noel Coward's *Hay Fever* (1967). One of the company's most recent successes was the 1983 production of Peter Shaffer's *Amadeus* (Hebrew version by Dan Miron), which starred Oded Teomi as Antonio Salieri and Michael Warshaviak as Mozart.

The Cameri appeared in Paris in 1956 and 1965 at the Théâtre des Nations. In 1967 it appeared in London at the World Theatre Season and in Montreal at the EXPO. In 1980 the company won first prize at the Edinburgh Fringe Festival when it performed a play of Cameri 2. Cameri 2 presents its works in the smaller auditorium of the Tzavta Club of Tel-Aviv, which holds 350 people. It houses three or four plays each season, mainly new Israeli work.

The Cameri presents between five hundred and six hundred performances every year. Two-thirds of these appear on the main stage and Cameri 2 auditorium, and the final one-third are presented on tour in Jerusalem, Haifa, and regional centers. Of the Cameri's budget, 55 percent is covered by ticket sales. The remaining 45 percent comes from subsidies from the Ministry of Education and Municipality of Tel-Aviv.

A recent development by the Cameri and the Habima is "Word for Word," a new dimension in culture which supplies theatregoers with simultaneous English dialogue translation, making it possible for non-Hebrew speakers to enjoy Israeli theatrical productions.

Cameri is directed by five people, headed by the Director General Uri Ofer. There are forty-five of Israel's finest actors and actresses in the company, and plays are directed by Israeli as well as by visiting foreign directors (mostly from Great Britain).

COLBY H. KULLMAN
(Adapted from materials provided by
The Cameri Theatre of Tel-Aviv.
Thanks to Rina Mendelsohn.)

THE HABIMA: ISRAEL'S NATIONAL THEATRE
Tel-Aviv, Israel

The history and development of the Habima Theatre in many respects parallels those of the Zionist movement. The Habima (literally meaning the Stage) was founded in Moscow during the 1917 Revolution by a small group of Zionist teachers: Nachum Zemach, Menachem Gnessin, and Hanna Rovina. The theatre was established several months prior to the Balfour Declaration, which affirmed the Jewish people's right to establish a Jewish National Home in Palestine. Prior to the Habima, there had been naive attempts to establish Hebrew dramatic groups in Palestine (the Lovers of the Hebrew Stage) and in Eastern Europe, all abortive and short-lived. Indeed, the Habima's greatest contribution was its success in establishing a permanent Hebrew art theatre.

The theatre's history can be divided into four distinct historical eras; the Moscow period (1917–1926); the transitional era (1926–1931), during which the theatre toured Europe, the United States, and Palestine; the Palestinian era (1931–1948); and the Israeli era (1949–present). These different historical and political settings affected the theatre's ideology and repertoire.

The Habima's ideology in Russia, which reflected the rationale for its formation, consisted of five values: a distinctively Hebrew theatre, biblical and historical theatre, moral-educational theatre, high-level art theatre, and national theatre in Palestine.

The commitment to perform exclusively in Hebrew was the central value. It should be noted that Hebrew was not a spoken language until the nineteenth century, when it was revived by the Haskala (Enlightenment) movement and the Zionist movement. Rather, it was considered an ancient scholarly language, used by a small minority of religious scholars, intellectuals, and militant Zionists. Indeed, there was no need, so to speak, for a Hebrew theatre in Russia, especially not in Moscow. First, the city did not have a large Jewish population, and of this population few spoke Hebrew. Second, Hebrew was not the mother tongue of many of the actors (who spoke either Yiddish and/or Russian). Third, both Hebrew and Zionism were illegal in Russia in the 1920s and brought persecution by the regime and the Jewish Communists.

The Habima's survival in Moscow was a "miracle," made possible by the benevolent and enlightened policy of the regime toward the Russian theatre in the 1920s. Furthermore, the Habima was recognized as an official Soviet state theatre in November 1919, one year after its first public performance (October 8, 1918). This official support meant a yearly subsidy of 100,000 rubles and, more importantly, the social and moral support of the Russian cultural elite, including Maxim Gorky, Konstantin Stanislavsky, and Eugene Vakhtangov.

The motivation of the founding members derived by no means from their wish to become professional actors. For the founders, the theatre was a calling rather than an occupation; they conceived of themselves as contemporary prophets, emissaries of the Zionist philosophy employing artistic rather than political means.

The actors' commitment to the Hebrew language provided the psychological and pragmatic motivation to establish a theatre, an enterprise strongly linked to language and history.

For nine years, the Habima was affiliated with the Moscow Art Theatre, directed by Stanislavsky, as one of its many studios. Thus, the theatre's artistic ideology, which was a product of this affiliation, stressed the following values: the theatre as a collective enterprise; repertory theatre; ensemble acting rather than the star system; long periods of rehearsals and thorough study of each play and each part; rotation of parts among the actors in successive performances; and the belief that all theatre arts should complement each other in order to unify the style of the production as a whole. The strong emphasis upon systematic professional training and upon high-level artistic standards separated the Habima from most Yiddish-speaking theatres at the time, especially the wandering troupes.

The Habima's organizational creed was an outgrowth of the Bolshevik Revolution's egalitarian spirit, which stressed that man fulfills himself only by serving society and that the collective is always more important than its individual members. Accordingly, the Habima was established as an actors' collective with the actors as owners and directors of the theatre. The actors' collectivism had one major postulate: the moral value of the group and its primacy over the interests of the individual actors. Thus, equality and fraternity were among the group's chief moral beliefs. Organized as an actors' cooperative, the company required all actors to take an active part in the general meetings of the collective, where all issues (artistic, administrative, and financial) were discussed and determined by a majority vote. All actors, regardless of talent, importance, or popularity, had equal rights and received equal pay. The Habima collectivist structure lasted half a century; in 1968 the actors' collective was dissolved and the Habima became Israel's state theatre.

Because the Habima was founded before the existence of native drama in Hebrew, it was forced to translate all its plays into Hebrew. In Moscow, the theatre believed it should confine itself to biblical and historical plays giving voice to the awakening of Zionism and to the renaissance of the Jewish national consciousness. Accordingly, five of the six plays presented in Russia were specifically Jewish: biblical, messianic, and national. The Habima presented *The Eternal Jew* (1919), *The Dybbuk* (1922), *The Golem* (1925), and others. *The Eternal Jew* was based on the ancient legend that the Jewish Messiah was born on the day of the Temple's destruction. This tragedy described the lamentation of the Jews over their lost country but stressed the prophetic revelation that a child born during the catastrophe would be the Savior and would restore the departed glory of the Jews.

The Habima's most important production to date is S. Ansky's *The Dybbuk*, directed by Vakhtangov which opened January 31, 1922. This production exemplified Vakhtangov's doctrine of theatricality, according to which every play must be given a special form and must be viewed from a contemporary standpoint. He saw the play as a struggle for freedom from the old religious order and as the erection of a tombstone for the old Jewish life. The Habima's production of *The Dybbuk* was a milestone in the history of the modern theatre; it announced the end of Stanislavsky's naturalism and instead launched the doctrine of theatricality and expressionism. While it was the theatre's third production, it became the emblem of the Habima in the same way that Chekhov's *The Seagull* was the emblem for the Moscow Art Theatre. Since its premiere, it has been presented over a thousand times; despite the fact that the Habima has produced more than 350 plays, the theatre and the play are still synonymous.

The Habima left Russia on January 26, 1926, never to return. From 1926 to February 1931, it toured Europe, the United States, and Palestine. These tours had two missions: national and artistic. The theatre aimed not only to spread the Zionist philosophy and Hebrew language but also to show its innovative artistic work. These tours became national holidays for Jewish communities all over Europe, especially in Eastern Europe where they suffered from active anti-Semitism.

The Habima production tours were highly acclaimed by directors, drama critics, and audiences, but they were a financial failure. In June 1927, as a result of conflicts over the theatre's artistic and administrative direction, the Habima split into two groups: the minority, headed by Nachum Zemach (the founder), which stayed on in New York; and the majority, which left for Berlin and from there for Palestine.

In August 1929, eighteen months after it had arrived in Palestine, the Habima left again for Europe, although it was clear that the theatre would eventually settle in Palestine. The second tour lasted eighteen months and included eight countries: Germany, Poland, Belgium, Switzerland, Denmark, Sweden, Italy, and England. The most urgent problem was to prepare a new, appropriate repertoire. Thus, the Habima presented four new plays, three of which had a Jewish theme: Sholem Aleichem's *The Treasure*, Calderón de la Barca's *David's Crown*, and Karl Gutzkow's *Uriel Acosta*. The fourth, Shakespeare's *Twelfth Night* (1930), was the first foreign play and light comedy in the theatre's repertoire. It was a deviation from the group's original ideology and marked the beginning of a new trend in the repertoire: an attempt to maintain a balance between specifically Jewish and non-Jewish plays.

The Habima established its home in Tel-Aviv, Palestine, in February 1931. From then until 1948, the theatre mounted seventy-nine new productions, forty-four of which were specifically Jewish and thirty-five of which were non-Jewish universal plays. It averaged four productions per season, two of which were Jewish. The category of Jewish plays was varied from the point of view of locale and plot, ranging from the biblical era to modern Jewish history. The Habima wanted to emphasize genuinely Palestinian plays that would reflect the new Jewish spirit, but no one wrote such plays. Because the modern Jewish settlement in Palestine (ruled until 1948 by the British Mandatory regime) was of comparatively recent origin, a native Hebrew drama had not yet developed.

Indeed, in this period Yiddish plays constituted the largest (over 20 percent) category in the repertoire. Most of these plays were shtetl plays, warmly human comedies (or melodramas) depicting Jewish life in Eastern Europe. The successes of Sholem Aleichem's *It Is Hard to Be a Jew* (1936) and *Tevye the Dairyman* (1943) and Jacob Gordin's *Mirele Efros* (1939) were symptomatic of the period. Sentimental Jewish plays were popular with the audience, which in the 1920s and 1930s consisted predominantly of immigrants from Eastern Europe.

In the 1930s the Habima presented several modern Jewish plays, originally written in German (such as *Professor Mannheim* and *The Jew Suess*). Many of these were morality plays with a message: only in their national and historical homeland would the Jews escape anti-Semitism and live normal, happy lives. As for the Habima's few Hebrew plays (the best of which was Aaron Ashman's *This Earth* in 1942), they all presented romanticized reality and were strictly reportage propaganda plays, glorifying the pioneering experience in Palestine.

The Habima's non-Jewish plays were classical, modern, and contemporary. The classical plays included works by Sophocles, Shakespeare (*The Merchant of Venice* and *Hamlet*), Molière (*Tartuffe* and *The Imaginary Invalid*), and others. The modern classics included plays by Chekhov, Ibsen, and Shaw. Most of the plays were drawn from the European repertoire, with a few from the American. In these years, the Habima's artistic style was, for the most part, Russian expressionism. Most of the productions were directed by the company's two resident directors: Zvi Friedland and Baruch Chemerinsky. The Habima also worked with directors of world fame: Alexander Granovsky (*Uriel Acosta*, 1930), Michael Chekhov (*Twelfth Night*, 1930), Leopold Lindtberg (*Green Fields*, 1935), Leopold Jessner (*The Merchant of Venice*, 1936), and Tyrone Guthrie (*Oedipus Rex*, 1947).

In 1948, with the establishment of the independent state of Israel, the Habima began a new era. From 1948 to 1968 (when the organizational structure of the theatre changed), the Habima presented 146 new plays, of which the vast majority (107 plays) were non-Jewish and only one-fourth (39 plays) were distinctively Jewish. The increase in the number of productions was a result of the growth of Israeli society, from six hundred thousand Jews in 1948 to over 3 million in 1968. In addition to the decrease in the proportion of Jewish plays, their content also changed. In the post-state era there was a decline in the number of biblical, shtetl, and historical plays (dealing with Jewish life in the Diaspora) and a dramatic increase in the number of Israeli-Hebrew plays. Furthermore, there was a significant decrease in the number of Yiddish plays and an increase in the number of English (British and American) plays.

In the post-state era, the Habima presented over thirty Israeli plays, written for the most part by young Israeli playwrights (Igal Mossinson, Moshe Shamir, Aaron Megged, Hanoch Bar-Tov, and others). These plays concerned three major topics: the importance of collective life for Israeli society (kibbutz plays), the Holocaust, and the absorption of immigrants. The other Israeli plays included several comedies and satires on contemporary Israeli society, modern biblical dramas, and children's plays.

The kibbutz plays were ideologically and socially the most important Hebrew plays. *In the Wastes of the Negev*, which premiered in 1949, is one of the most important and most popular Israeli plays. It focused on the heroic stand of the Jewish settlements in the Negev against the Egyptian army during the 1948 War of Independence. The play concerned a current event, one that had taken place only nine months before the play opened. The kibbutz plays were agit-prop dramas stressing that abandoning the kibbutz (and the country) was dangerous to the security of Israel and that collective life was superior to life in the city. These plays presented the plot and characters in elementary, black-and-white fashion, with a typical happy ending. They were sincere and naive, and appealed to the audience because they dealt with current Israeli issues and events.

Of the Holocaust plays, three were noteworthy: the American play, *The Diary of Anne Frank* (1957) by Frances Goodrich, and the Israeli dramas, *Hanna Szenes* (1958) by Aaron Megged and *The Children of Shadow* (1962) by Karl Wittlinger. *The Children of Shadow*, the first Israeli play on the Holocaust, was the story of the continuous struggle of many Israeli youngsters to forget their past and to become healthy *sabras* (native-born Israelis). The play maintained that renewed contact with the past might relieve the guilt of forgetfulness and estrangement.

One of the most significant changes in the composition of the Habima troupe occurred in 1953, when it accepted into its ranks many young Israeli actors. These actors represented the new heroes of the country: they had been born or raised in Palestine and therefore spoke Hebrew with no accent, in a clear Israeli diction. Furthermore, because they fought in the War of Independence, they were extremely popular with the country's younger generation. The younger actors' approach was more natural and realistic, and they asserted themselves with a style of acting that was natural, immediate, and direct.

In October 1958, the Habima was officially recognized as Israel's National Theatre. This recognition, however, did not bring about any change in the theatre's organization or operation. In addition to the honor of being the National Theatre, the new status meant a yearly subsidy of nearly 10 percent of the annual budget. A major change occurred in December 1968 when, as a result of a series of financial and artistic crises, the actors decided to dissolve the cooperative. The Habima became a publicly owned theatre, and the Israeli government took over the administration of the theatre. The troupe kept its old name—the National Theatre Habima—and the actors' ensemble was not affected. Thus, after fifty-one years of existence as an actors' collective, the Habima became a state theatre, with a board of trustees, general director, and artistic director appointed by the government. The yearly subsidy at present amounts to over one-half of the theatre's annual budget.

The Habima's current problem is to find and establish a specific and definite artistic identity, a problem that is related to its conception of the function of National Theatre in Israel in the 1980s. Until 1948 the Habima was the major cultural institution; at present it faces severe competition from Israel's three municipal theatres in Tel-Aviv, Haifa, and Beer-Sheva. Seen from an historical perspective, the fact that the Habima is still a thriving and vital institution is the best indication of its ability to adapt to changing demands, new artistic values, and new audiences. The Habima's ability to deal with continuous changes in Israel's demographic, political, and social settings is the crucial test of its sustained vitality.

EMANUEL LEVY

HAIFA MUNICIPAL THEATRE
50, Pevsner Street
P.O. Box 5270, Haifa, Israel

The Haifa Municipal Theatre (HMT) was founded on January 29, 1961, through the initiative of the late Mayor Abba Khoushy and the City Council, as a public corporation with half its shares in the hands of City Hall and the other half in the hands of Friends of the Haifa Theatre Organization.

The Haifa Theatre's first artistic director was Yosef Millo, who founded the Tel-Aviv Cameri Theatre and has mounted numerous Israeli and European productions, both classical and modern, at the HMT. His aim was to make the HMT a repertory theatre that would stress quality productions and sponsor educational programs. Among the company's many early successes were Shakespeare's *The Taming of the Shrew* (1961, starring Hayim Topol), Eugene Ionesco's *Rhinoceros* (1962), Carlo Goldoni's *The Servant of Two Masters* (1964), Shlomo Sheva's *Days of Gold* (1965), and Shakespeare's *Richard III*. Millo left the company in 1967.

The group of young actors who took over after Millo's departure had a different conception. Led by Oded Kotler, actor and director, they set out to make the Haifa Municipal Theatre into a unique theatre through the use of original Israeli material. They have, at last, achieved this goal, for under their influence the original Israeli play holds a top place in the public's preference and the critics' praise.

The main stage of the theatre house, which belongs to the Haifa Municipality, has 850 seats and all the stage and lighting facilities of a modern theatre. The company employs about forty actors and actresses every year, and about sixty other workers "behind the scenes." Its activities are divided according to the following plan: (1) the main stage, for large productions which present the best of the world repertory; (2) Stage 2, with a "chamber" character, showing mostly original work; and (3) Stage 3, for young groups and experimental projects. Stage 3's core is the "Project Group," a team of ten actors led by Director Nola Chilton, who also perform in development towns, plants, and neighborhoods, seeking to bring the theatre closer to audiences that have had little previous exposure to this medium. During the 1977–1978 season, the group stayed for a whole year in Kiryat Shemona, where it assisted local drama groups, performed, and engaged in a wide range of social activities.

The HMT's season opens in September and ends in July. During a season, ten plays are usually produced on the company's three stages. HMT has a large subscription program, with subscribers during the 1979–1980 season numbering over eighteen thousand. The following season, the company achieved a national record for subscribers. About 60 percent of the budget comes through public channels and 40 percent through box office income. As of the 1980–1981 season, the HMT had given eighty-four thousand performances throughout the country and produced over 130 plays for over 5.3 million spectators.

Among the numerous awards received by the company are the Meskin Prize to Nola Chilton for directing and the Margalit Prize to Ruth Segal, for her performance in Sean O'Casey's *The Plough and the Stars*, and to Michael Kfir, for his performance in Tennessee Williams' *A Streetcar Named Desire* and his monodrama *The Discourse*.

During the 1980–1981 season, the Haifa Project in Haifa's Neevé Yosef area was established under the direction of Hagit Rahavi. The group's members perform for the community and work with its inhabitants in youth groups, kindergartens, drama groups for adults, and separate groups for mothers, the aged, and so on.

The company has transformed the HMT's building into a center of cultural activities by supporting an active youth club, a wide range of cultural events, exhibitions, films, and "Theatre Days" for teachers and students. In June 1980 Jane Fonda appeared on three occasions on behalf of the Haifa Municipal Theatre to advance special projects by the theatre in development towns and underprivileged areas. In October 1980 members of the Tony Award-winning Actors Theatre of Louisville (Kentucky) arrived as guests of the HMT.

By presenting the best plays by outstanding artists from Israel and abroad, the HMT has become one of the world's outstanding theatre companies.

COLBY H. KULLMAN
(Adapted from materials provided by
the Haifa Municipal Theatre.
Thanks to Amalia Pelled.)

SCANDINAVIA

Carla Waal, Area Editor

Denmark

INTRODUCTION

Dance has always been an integral part of theatrical life in Denmark. It has a rich history at the Danish Royal Theatre, which pays homage to the nineteenth-century choreographer August Bournonville by keeping his ballets in their repertory. It is sometimes difficult to draw the line between theatre and dance in Denmark, as exemplified by the Billedstofteatret which combines theatre, sculpture, and dance.

Danish dance has attained international recognition. Also familiar to international visitors is the Pantomime Theatre in Tivoli Gardens in Copenhagen. The colorful Chinese building, which was opened in 1874, the staging conventions which can be traced to the eighteenth century, and the characters such as Harlequin and Pierrot have delighted audiences through the years.

Theatre historians Lise-Lone and Frederick Marker have described the historical background of Danish theatre in medieval religious drama, such as the miracle plays of Duke Knud and Saint Dorothea; a morality play of Virtues and Vices staged in Copenhagen in 1634; school dramas which served as exercises in rhetoric; and opulent entertainment provided for Renaissance court celebrations. English, German, and Dutch traveling troupes found their way to the Danish court in the sixteenth and seventeenth centuries, while a French troupe took up residence in the capital in the late seventeenth century. René Montaigu, who joined the troupe later, is now honored as the founder of Denmark's first national theatre in 1722.

Associated with that first Danish theatre are the witty, rollicking comedies of Ludvig Holberg. The repertory of original Danish drama encompasses works in many genres, including, in the nineteenth century, the romantic tragedies of Adam Oehlenschläger, the vaudevilles of Johan Ludvig Heiberg, and the naturalistic modern plays of Edvard Brandes, while the diversity of twentieth-century drama is highlighted by the plays of Kaj Munk, Kjeld Abell, Klaus Rifbjerg, and Ernst Bruun Olsen. The repertory of Danish theatres has always reflected trends and innovations in world drama, through productions of Shakespeare, Ibsen, Brecht, Miller, Camus, and others. Some private theatres have been very successful with productions of foreign plays, as was the Dagmar Theatre with August Strindberg's *The Dance of Death* in 1920, Riddersalen with productions of Brecht in the 1930s, and the Fiol Theatre with plays by Harold Pinter, Samuel Beckett, and Edward Albee in the 1960s.

Whereas Max Reinhardt was the most influential foreign theatre artist in the early part of this century, in recent years Jerzy Grotowski has probably exercised the greatest influence, especially upon the internationally acclaimed Odin ensemble in Holstebro. Not only major theatre artists, but also political developments and world events have profoundly affected Danish theatre since the 1960s. Some ensembles see theatre as a political force that can raise the consciousness of audience members by presenting documentary and debate plays dealing with controversial topics, such as the Vietnam War and nonproliferation of nuclear weapons. This approach has provoked heated discussions about the role of theatre in society and the relationship of government authorities to theatres seeking financial subsidy.

Since the mid-sixties many alternative collective theatre groups have been formed. Critics of such groups admire their ethical commitment and vitality but find fault with the artistic professionalism of their productions. The opposing argument is that established theatres have artistic polish but a repertory that is not always interesting and stimulating. Reforms of legislation regulating theatre have decentralized and reorganized theatrical activity throughout the country. Many small groups, as well as amateur theatre, have been encouraged.

Tours are also being encouraged, though not on the same scale as the traveling theatres of Norway and Sweden. Touring in Denmark since 1976 has been coordinated largely by the Danish Theatre (Det Danske Teater). In 1980–1981 sixty ensembles of all sizes advertised about 185 different productions which could tour. Many of them were for children and young people, and some sought out special audiences that might gather for purposes other than viewing theatre. Of course, theatre outside of Copenhagen is performed not just on tours, but also at the large regional theatres of Odense, Aalborg, and Aarhus, where repertory is varied and production standards are excellent.

According to Frederick J. Marker and Lise-Lone Marker (*TDR*, T95), Danish theatre today is characterized by a great variety of forms, by audience development campaigns, and by competition for talent. Developments in the eighties will be affected by the relationship of art and politics and the influence of courageous, independent artists.

CARLA WAAL

Legislation

The Danish regional theatres in Aarhus, Odense, and Aalborg were established legally during a sweeping reform authorized by the passing of the theatre law of 1963. According to this law, the Danish government would pay half of the deficit for the theatres' production costs and three-fourths of the costs of operating the theatre facilities, as well as funding repairs, improvements and technical installations. Each municipality would provide the remaining financial support.

In a revision of that law in 1970, in connection with a reorganization of the municipalities, these regional theatres were placed under the new provincial administrative units and economic responsibility was transferred from the municipality to the province. The law stated "that the regional theatres should contribute to meeting the need for theatre in that region by performing a varied repertory, consisting of older as well as more recent dramatic works with special consideration of the works of Danish dramatists." This law meant that, for the first time in Danish theatre history, a decision had been made directly obligating the national government and the provinces to sponsor purposeful, concrete artistic activity.

To assure the fulfillment of its intent, the theatre law stipulated that the regional theatre would be run as a company or independent institution. The board of directors would include representatives of the appropriate provincial government and concerned citizens, thereby counteracting any private financial interests in the theatre's leadership and operations.

The law also indicated that without the approval of the minister for cultural affairs the head of the theatre could not be restricted in his or her right to decide freely and independently on repertory, hiring, and other artistic matters. As a safeguard, however, the law required the appointment of an advisory panel for every regional theatre. The panel would consist of the chief administrator and representatives of all groups of the theatre's employees, who also have two representatives on the board of directors. The driving force behind the formation of these laws and their acceptance was to a high degree the Social-Democratic party and its spokesman on cultural matters, the late Niels Matthiasen. Matthiasen, who later became minister for cultural affairs, gave invaluable support to the theatre and the rest of Danish cultural life.

But many worthwhile initiatives had preceded this significant advance in Danish theatre legislation, especially the great effort of Arthur Ilfeldt to establish contact among the regional theatres in Aarhus, Odense, and Aalborg. In 1953 he arranged an agreement among these three theatres—an agreement to "stick together" in the future and in negotiations with the authorities. Thus, the Regional Theatres' Cooperative Council was formed, which, through overtures to the government, sought to improve economic conditions for the theatres through an effective arrangement for subsidies, in which both state and municipality would participate. The council pointed out the cultural value of maintaining the regional theatres, which serve as wide a spectrum of the population as possible. Since the regional theatres are the only producers of regular theatre outside the capital of Copenhagen and are centrally located, they provide theatre for Denmark's three largest provincial cities and surrounding areas.

With this initiative as a precedent, in 1954 the government established a theatre commission, which was assigned to investigate Denmark's theatre situation as a whole and to report what measures should be taken to improve Danish theatre. In their report the regional theatres received endorsement in regard to solving their special problems. This led in 1955 to a temporary plan of subsidization with public funds to meet the deficits. At the end of the 1950s it was possible to establish salary guidelines for actors, and somewhat later comparable guidelines for technical and administrative personnel. Reasonable salaries and living conditions were obtained for those on whom the continuance of theatre depended.

The theatre legislation of 1963 and 1970 significantly increased the expectations of artistic achievement in the provinces, which resulted in an increasing need for subsidies. At the Aarhus Theatre, for example, the subsidy in 1950 was 200,000 Danish crowns, increasing to 30 million crowns in 1981. In addition, a nationwide subscription plan, which went into effect in 1975, has greatly expanded the potential audience of the regional theatres.

Inspired by what for Danish theatre was an epoch-making development in 1977, the Greater Copenhagen Regional Theatre was established as an independent institution. At present it consists of thirteen Copenhagen theatres that joined together in economic cooperation with an obligation to perform a varied repertory, depending on the size of the participating theatre, its artistic position, and the composition of its audience. The managing board's eleven members represent the municipalities and provinces, as well as interested citizens, theatre administrators, and theatre employees.

The regional theatres were established by law, and barely twenty years of operation have demonstrated the foresightedness of the state and provinces in realizing this project. These twenty years have also witnessed a new and steadily growing influx of adults and children to the productions of the regional theatres.

JØRGEN HEINER
(Translated by Carla Waal)

AARHUS THEATRE
(Aarhus Teater)
Skolegade 9
8000 Aarhus C, Denmark

Under the leadership of director Jacob Kielland and his predecessor, Henrik Bering Liisberg, the Aarhus Theatre has been a successful regional theatre. The largest of the three "old" regional theatres and at the same time Denmark's largest acting stage, it receives an annual subsidy (1980–1981) of over 30 million Danish crowns, and at the same time has an average attendance of 86 percent, which means a sale of about two hundred thousand tickets per season from September to June.

The Aarhus Theatre was inaugurated in 1900 and was designed in typical Art Nouveau style by the architect Hack Kampmann. By international standards, it is one of the best European buildings from the turn of the century—a distinctive architectural work that distinguished itself from other opera and theatre architecture of that period because of the imaginative execution and use of beautiful materials, fashioned in consultation with the best artists of the times. The auditorium is in tones of gold, green, and bronze, accented by rich gold ornamentation and stucco work, along with illumination made effective by the use of chandelier prisms of varying size. The exterior is distinguished by the frieze with the Holberg motif, ornamentation, and a number of stained-glass pictures.

Through the years the building has undergone significant architectural changes to keep pace with theatrical developments. On the whole, the changes have taken into consideration the building's originality and appearance. In 1955 a large hall (Scala) used for concerts and movies was added in a harmonious way; during the day it is used for children's plays. A Studio Stage was constructed in the basement of the theatre in 1968. Technical improvements and renovations of the facilities in the 1960s and 1970s have made the theatre more functional and up to date. By carrying through a renovation of 24 million Danish crowns in the 1981–1982 season, the Aarhus Theatre is now able to utilize six playing spaces of various sizes: Main Stage (706 seats), Studio (150 to 200 seats), Scala I (370 seats), Scala 2 (175 seats), Stiklingen (75 seats), and the Salon (50 seats). Aarhus has the country's best equipped theatre facility, a center of energy unmatched in Denmark. This theatre will more abundantly fulfill the theatre's demand for diversity.

The Aarhus Theatre employs 170 artistic, technical, and administrative people, 35 of whom make up the acting company (on long-term contracts) supplemented with guest artists. They and visiting directors—Danish and foreign—are responsible for around fourteen productions per year. The theatre has been very pleased with foreign directors, including Michael Blakemore, Arnold Wesker, Jane Howell, Gordon March, Kevin Robinson, Bob Fosse's assistant Gene Foote, and the Rumanians Lucian Giurchescu and Stefan Lenkisch. In addition, many of the best directors in Danish theatre have worked with the broad and varied repertory.

This repertory is determined by the head of the theatre, Jacob Kielland, in consultation with a three-man dramaturgical and repertory committee, consisting of Kielland and representatives from the artistic, technical, and administrative personnel. Since 1973 the public has been offered an extremely varied and inclusive repertory, consisting of works by modern dramatists like Harold Pinter, Bertolt Brecht, Arnold Wesker, Howard Brenton, Arthur Miller, Edward Albee, Edward Bond, Alan Ayckbourn, Stephen Poliakoff, Odön von Horváth, Jean Genet, Dario Fo, Kjeld Abell, and Nordahl Grieg, and classics by Shakespeare, Chekhov, Ibsen, Holberg, Calderón, Farquhar, Gorky, and Strindberg.

True to tradition, the season opens each year with a musical comedy, varying from older works to the newest, but with the emphasis on integration of the genre in which music, text, and movement form a unified whole. In this genre the theatre has presented outstanding productions.

In addition to the repertory mentioned above, younger Danish dramatists have an unusually strong position in the program since Aarhus Theatre is the first and, until now, the only theatre in Denmark to be a workshop employing resident dramatists. One of its artistically significant works is Sten Kåløe's drama *Alpha and Omega*, a psychological fantasy-play based on the life of the painter Edvard Munch. A number of other Danish dramatists have also found their way to theatre through this regional theatre's initiative.

The renovation and expansion of the Aarhus Theatre pose renewed demands for untraditional ideas and creative imagination in content, theatre form, and administrative structure for the Danish regional theatre of the future and for the continued pleasure of its audience.

JØRGEN HEINER
(Translated by Carla Waal)

CAFÉ THEATRE
(Café Teater)
Skindergade Nr. 3
1150 Copenhagen K, Denmark

A link between experimental and established theatre; a workshop where visions can take shape; a theatre for close and meaningful contact between actors and audience; a center for activity offering experiences that are both artistically entertaining and informative; an open house where one can work independently or seek support—these phrases suggest the uniqueness of one of Copenhagen's smallest and most active theatres.

With institutionalized theatre in danger of dying out under the umbrella of bureaucracy, the Café Theatre along with a couple of other small theatres represents what is left of free initiative. They all are government supported to some extent, but in contrast to the fully subsidized, established theatres, they dare to take chances.

Opening in 1972 with a production of Klaus Rifbjerg's *Developments*, this was just another "little theatre" where four young people decided to establish a more solid foundation for the work they had been trying since the start of the 1960s. The Café Theatre has developed into an intimate theatre with three playing areas, seating sixty, eighty, and one hundred spectators, respectively. It is an intimate theatre, which produces its own shows and at the same time provides space for foreign guest artists and groups and individuals with good ideas but no place to try them. In short, it is a theatre for actors.

The form and the name come from Paris, where the founders got their inspiration from seeing theatre and from themselves presenting Danish drama in French. The Danish form of café theatre no longer has much in common with the Parisian form. Instead of cabaret-style shows, there are experiments of every kind intended to combine an experience of theatre at close range and interaction with other people—either fellow audience members or the performers who stay after the show, not just to talk but because of a fundamental belief: If one has had an experience that provokes comment or questions, one should not just be ushered out into the night but should be permitted some outlet for these thoughts.

This openness also applies to the newest activity: A drama school where someone interested in theatre can explore his or her means of expression, learning how the actor works with himself or herself. About a dozen actors and artists from Copenhagen theatres are the teachers. They contribute to a demythologizing of the world of theatre. This is one of the ideas behind the school, whose approximately two hundred students either are simply interested in theatre or are using the school as preparation before auditioning for the more official theatre schools.

That the openness surrounding this experience of theatre is also an inspiration in the opposite direction—from audience to stage—can be confirmed by many of the performers. The open attitude is also evident in the work process. It leads to training and mutual understanding where different groups of skilled workers are drawn into the process on an equal footing. Through an overlapping of the theatre's separate functions, all elements are involved in independent work.

Since the open theatre functions both in producing its own shows and enabling new ideas from outside to be born, it is sometimes difficult to find a clear direction in the repertory.

At what other theatre have twenty-five spectators at a time been treated like refugees in their own land—with a body search, confiscation of valuables, distribution of an identity card and ration stamps, and psychic torment from a numerically superior group of actors (Brecht's *Refugee Dialogues*)? And what other theatre would next present the Danish premiere of Racine's tragedy *Andromaque* as total theatre, but otherwise in a strictly classical interpretation . . . or a poetic cabaret of Jacques Prévert's songs and texts . . . or forty-five minutes of lunatic ravings in a production on the topic of homosexuality built on a pastiche of Russian drama from the turn of the century (Copi's *Happy Days in Siberia*)?

What other theatre dares, without funds, to schedule over twenty new productions in the course of a season so that a newspaper critic must ask in desperation if they might set up a cot since he has to spend most of the season there? He does not want to miss anything, for "if just every fourth production succeeds, they have given more than any of the established theatres have dared to offer." In 1981 the Café Theatre was awarded the new "Initiative Prize" by a group of newspaper critics.

And what other theatre tackles production of new scripts in Danish and gives space and help to other groups, while at the same time undertaking tours to other countries to present Danish drama in translation?

There is, nevertheless, a sense of purpose behind this broad repertory, which is chosen by a seven-person council (the theatre's management plus two members selected by the company for one season at a time). The basic purpose of most of the productions, without offering ready solutions, is to call attention to the individual's situation in relationship to society and its institutionalized machinery. The repertory council will wholeheartedly and with enthusiasm consider any idea that seems to have some merit, feeling it would be a shame to turn down anything just because it did not fit into some predetermined scheme. When a production reflects everyday life, provides food for thought and discussion, and is professional, there is a place for it at the Café Theatre, provided the schedule permits—and scheduling is becoming the theatre's biggest problem.

In recent years the Café Theatre has become almost the only place where theatre people are free to try ideas on their own terms. Demands for the facilities have occasionally made it necessary to do a production elsewhere, as in the spring of 1980 when this "little" theatre cooperated with one of the "big" established theatres in presenting a timely Swedish play by Anders Ehnmark and Per Olov Enquist, *The Man on the Sidewalk*, in matinee performances on the big stage of the Folk Theatre. This was another experiment, which was well received in theatre circles and beyond.

Among the many groups that formed in Copenhagen in the mid-sixties, the Café Theatre is the only one that has survived with its original members unchanged. The transition from a touring enterprise via modest café theatre to intimate theatre with multiple productions has probably been so painless because its internal structure gives each individual the greatest possible freedom of expression, and because there has been constant inspiration from the many innovative artists who use the building.

Some changes have taken place in the internal structure of the theatre. No longer a four-person operation based on volunteer help, it is now a self-sufficient institution with a management consisting of the founders: Sejer Andersen (actor and leader of the drama school), Erling Larsen (administrator), Niels Skjoldager (actor), and Lisa Thorslunde (actress), plus Søren Glad (technician) since 1975.

Daily business matters are handled by the administrator and a secretary. Decisions regarding the day-by-day management are taken up at a weekly personnel meeting where the entire staff of employees (who all receive equal pay) and the regular volunteer helpers meet and organize the work. More far-reaching artistic decisions—and those that involve the theatre's financial obligations—are taken up at management meetings twice a month. The Café Theatre personnel are convinced that this organizational plan without a traditional director of theatre—and still not completely a collective—has helped the theatre survive and obtain Ministry for Cultural Affairs approval for a subsidy which increased steadily from 10,000 crowns in 1971–1972 to 550,000 crowns in 1980–1981. Since the subsidy barely covers the expenses of operating the building and of publicity, the theatre is also dependent on box office receipts and increased support from private foundations.

What will be the next stage of development? The facilities in Skindergade, where the theatre rents five out of seven stories of an eighteenth-century building, cannot contain any more activities. Sometimes one end of the café is used for a children's play in the afternoon; in the evening the chairs are turned around and an adult production is given at the other end of the room. There is talk of finding a place with three hundred seats, as a supplement to the three stages in

Skindergade. There cannot be more seats, for then the intimacy would be destroyed, and there cannot be fewer, for any new theatre must not economically burden the theatre in Skindergade which still is the most important. It is there that plans are being made for the coming seasons, plans that aim to involve those workers who have long functioned as assistants for the ideas of others and who now are "ripe" to try their own experiments. They plan a collective performance blending cabaret and commedia dell'arte, illustrating the dilemma of the average citizen confronted with the power structure of society.

"It will get on the boards," the group says, "and we shall learn something from trying."

ERLING LARSEN
(Translated by Carla Waal)

DANISH ROYAL THEATRE
(Det Kongelige Teater)
Kongens Nytorv
1050 Copenhagen K, Denmark

The Danish Royal Theatre in Copenhagen, which in age and importance ranks among the great classical theatres of Europe, was founded in 1748. Far older, however, is the theatrical heritage from which the Danish national theatre sprang. A succession of itinerant German, Dutch, and French acting troupes provided entertainment for the Danish court throughout the seventeenth century. By 1722 René Montaigu, a French actor and former court theatre director, had organized a company of Danish actors to form the first popular national theatre in Scandinavia. The life of Montaigu's small playhouse in Lille Grønnegade (Little Green Street) was brief, but by the time of its demise in 1727 its real purpose had been achieved. Ludvig Holberg had created for it a body of native comedies of international stature. The desire for a permanent national theatre in the Danish capital had found expression and was not ultimately to be denied.

The first Royal Theatre, designed by the court architect Niels (or Nicolai) Eigtved, opened its doors to the young King Frederick V and his subjects on December 18, 1748. Eigtved's elegant and harmonious rococo palace, which accommodated 782 spectators in three tiers of boxes and a pit, was equipped with the latest in modern stage machinery and appliances by Jacopo (or Jacob) Fabris, a noted Venetian designer and technician. The financing of this venture was precarious, however, and by 1750 control of the debt-ridden playhouse on Kongens Nytorv had passed out of the hands of the actors, to whom a royal patent had been granted, and was entrusted to the none-too-willing Copenhagen city fathers. It was, in fact, not until 1772 that the Danish "Royal" Theatre finally came under the direct administration and economic patronage of the monarchy.

By that date Eigtved's hastily constructed building had been declared structurally unsound, and Caspar Frederik Harsdorff, the leading architect of his day, was commissioned to undertake a radical rebuilding of the theatre. This operation altered its appearance and enlarged its capacity to 1,192 seats. Harsdorff's playhouse, which reopened for performances on January 29, 1774, was evidently more solidly built than its predecessor, for it was to remain in service for the next one hundred years.

This second Royal Theatre was thus the theatre of Denmark's so-called Golden Age—those middle decades of the nineteenth century when a new constellation of native playwrights, led by Adam Oehlenschläger and Johan Ludvig Heiberg, joined forces with an exceptional company of gifted actors and actresses to create the most luminous period in Danish theatrical history. Architecturally as well as intellectually, the playhouse on Kongens Nytorv dominated the daily life of the Danish capital, and the cultural giants of the age gathered in the stalls each evening. Hans Christian Andersen's lodgings were always located within easy walking distance of the playhouse; Oehlenschläger was there every evening; the great sculptor Bertil Thorvaldsen died in the theatre; and the solitary Søren Kierkegaard was a habitual playgoer. "In Denmark there is but one city and one theatre," the renowned philosopher was prompted to observe in 1848—and his comment illustrates succinctly the central place which the Royal Theatre occupied in nineteenth-century Danish culture and society.

By 1870, as the winds of theatrical change began to blow vigorously across the entire face of Europe, the need for a larger and more up-to-date Royal Theatre was recognized, and an architectural competition was proclaimed by the Danish Parliament. The winning design, by Vilhelm Dahlerup and Ove Petersen, provided for a spacious new playhouse that could seat roughly 1,400 spectators. More essential, however, was its capacity to accommodate under one roof the three allied art forms that have comprised the repertory of the Royal Theatre almost from its inception: drama, opera, and the flourishing Danish ballet that had acquired its unique character from choreographers Vincenzo Galeotti and August Bournonville in the early years of the nineteenth century.

The third Royal Theatre—the structure that still stands on Kongens Nytorv today—held its gala opening performance on October 15, 1874. The bronze statues of Oehlenschläger and Holberg outside the main entrance and the venerable Horatian motto "Ei blot til Lyst" (Not only to please) inscribed in bold letters above the proscenium reaffirmed the theatre's indissoluble links with the traditions of the past. At the same time, however, the pioneering naturalistic productions of both Ibsen and Holberg directed by William Bloch during the closing decades of the century quickly thrust the Danish national stage into the vanguard of the new modernism.

The Old Stage, as Dahlerup and Petersen's playhouse has come to be called, has undergone very few structural alterations since Bloch's day. The most radical such change took place in 1930, when the last vestiges of boxes were eliminated in the auditorium and the raked stage floor was made flat to accommodate a newly installed turntable stage. An adjacent concert hall and theatre seating about one thousand spectators—the so-called New Stage—began to be utilized on a trial basis in the early thirties. This became a permanent—if rather inadequate— second stage of the Royal Theatre in 1957. A small studio theatre (Comediehuset) was added to the operation in 1970. This was supplanted by a somewhat larger, two-hundred-seat chamber stage (Graabrødrescenen) in 1981. In all, over seven hundred performances are given on these three stages during a normal nine-month season.

Quite recently, the forces of major change that seem to stir at least once a century on Kongens Nytorv have once again begun to make themselves felt. An architectural competition to elicit an acceptable design project for a new Royal Theatre completed its first phase in 1978. The eventual outcome of this competition will presumably be a modern new theatre for dramatic productions, incorporating both a flexible and fairly intimate main auditorium (750 to 900 seats) and a 175-seat experimental facility. For the time being, however, only the Old Stage will be completely renovated, at a cost of some $24 million, to become (once construction is finished in 1986) the home of the Royal Theatre's flourishing ballet and opera companies.

The severest challenge any such building project must meet is that created by the great range and variety of the Royal Theatre's artistic program. As a "pure" repertory theatre, the playbill for each of its stages changes daily. Nor is it unusual to find ten or more different productions being played in rotation during a single week. Typical statistics for one season will help to bring the extent of this company's commitment to the repertory system into sharper focus. During the thirty-nine-week regular season from September 1, 1978, to May 31, 1979, it presented a total of forty-six different plays, operas, and ballets in repertory. Fifteen different plays were acted, ranging from works by Henrik Ibsen, August Strindberg, John Millington Synge, Sean O'Casey, and Jean Giraudoux to Danish classics by Johan Ludvig Heiberg, Ludvig Holberg, and Jens Christian Hostrup. The sixteen operas performed during the season included major new productions of Monteverdi, Beethoven, and Verdi and revivals of works by such diverse composers as Gluck, Rossini, Puccini, Donizetti, Carl Nielsen, Wagner, and Richard Strauss. Slightly less than one-half of the forty-six works presented were either new to the company or else were being staged in a new *mise-en-scène*. As a result, a total of 2,475 rehearsals was needed for the preparation of such a season.

Clearly, a repertory system of such dimensions as this presupposes a firm and enlightened policy of state subsidy. Total operating expenses for the 1978–1979 season amounted to slightly more than $20 million, by far the largest portion of which covered the salaries of the theatre's seven-hundred-member staff. Income during the same period—even with a solid overall average attendance of over 67 percent—amounted to less than $2 million. However, a deficit of this kind is planned for and absorbed in the national budget—for the Danish Royal Theatre is seen as a truly national theatre, charged by the Theatre Legislation of 1935 with a cultural mandate which, through its radio broadcasts, television transmissions, and nationwide tours, embraces the entire country. In 1978 the Ministry for Cultural Affairs, under whose jurisdiction the institution now operates, again appointed a committee charged with the task of defining the objectives of the Royal Theatre and proposing future legislation to support its activity. Particular attention was devoted "to the question of what more can be done to offer a broader spectrum of the population access to the theatre's productions." The commission's final report in April 1979, bore a title which, in itself, announces the governing artistic mission of Scandinavia's oldest national theatre: "The Royal Theatre: A Future as the Entire Nation's Theatre."

Henrik Bering Liisberg assumed the post of *teaterchef*—the theatre's chief administrative officer—in 1980.

LISE-LONE MARKER

FOLK THEATRE
(Folketeatret)
Nørre Voldgade 50
1358 Copenhagen K, Denmark

The curtain for the first performance at the Folk Theatre in Copenhagen went up on September 18, 1857, after a group of interested citizens had received permission from King Frederick VII to engage in theatrical activity. The Folk Theatre is, therefore, the oldest privately founded theatre in the Danish capital. Only one institution is older, the Royal Theatre. While the Royal Theatre operates today in a building erected in 1874, the Folk Theatre is still located in its original facilities, Copenhagen's oldest continuously active theatre building.

The theatre does not have the same form of organization it had upon its founding. It is no longer a joint stock company, but is part of the Greater Copenhagen Regional Theatre (Den Storkøbenhavnske Landsdelsscene), and thereby receives a certain amount of its budget in the form of public subsidy. This imposes no restrictions on the choice of repertory or cast, which the theatre makes autonomously.

The Folk Theatre does not have a permanent artistic ensemble, although certain actors and actresses appear there frequently. The theatre contracts individual actors for each separate production. Thirty-four full-time employees make up the technical and administrative personnel. The present company under the leadership of Preben Harris as artistic director has delineated a distinctive artistic policy, making this one of Denmark's foremost theatres.

In 1964 with a group of young actors Preben Harris founded the experimental and intimate stage Svalegangen in Aarhus. Several of the actors involved in starting Svalegangen went with Harris when he later became head of the Gladsaxe Theatre in one of the northern suburbs of Copenhagen. In 1971 he took over the leadership of the Folk Theatre at Nørregade 39 in the heart of Copenhagen.

Experimental drama, which was emphasized in Aarhus, has continued in Copenhagen on the intimate stage of the Folk Theatre, the Hippodrome, with space for seventy spectators placed in three rows around a central playing area. Classics by authors like Strindberg and Gogol are presented on this stage, and plays by relevant but seldom-performed dramatists such as Odön von Horváth, are introduced. The mainstay of the Hippodrome's repertory is modern Danish drama, which the theatre aims to develop and support through, for example, commissioning plays by younger Danish playwrights, including such well-known figures as Benny Andersen, Sven Holm, Klaus Rifbjerg, Tove Ditlevsen, Leif Petersen, Erik Knudsen, Tage Skou-Hansen, and Ulla Ryum. The 1980–1981 season included, besides von Horváth's *Don Juan Returns Home from the War*, a new play by Ulla Ryum on a day in the life of the poet Johan Herman Wessel, and a new musical adaptation of Jules Verne's *Around the World in 80 Days*.

The main stage of the Folk Theatre is a traditional house seating 933 spectators. The auditorium still has its original interior with the original decor. Danish plays are presented here as well. For example, Sven Holm was commissioned to write for the main stage a play on the idealistic preacher and missionary Hans Egede. In the 1980–1981 season there was a production of *The Mailman from Arles*, based on the paintings of Van Gogh; this play is by Denmark's greatest living dramatist, Ernst Bruun Olsen, who also directed the production.

In addition to Danish plays, the Folk Theatre produces classical plays from the international repertory in appropriate period style. Such well-known playwrights as Shakespeare, Chekhov, Shaw, and Molière are represented. Modern classics like Miller's *Death of a Salesman* are also part of the main stage repertory.

Social criticism in dramatic form is well represented at the Folk Theatre. It is noteworthy that no other Danish theatre has performed so many plays by Bertolt Brecht. This resulted in a visit in September 1980 by Brecht's own Berliner Ensemble, which performed *The Caucasian Chalk Circle* and *Galileo* at the Folk Theatre with overwhelming success. In October 1980 the Folk Theatre met with an equally enthusiastic public reception for its performance of *The Imaginary Invalid* in Berlin.

The Folk Theatre also has a little cabaret stage with seating for fifty in its restaurant, the Snoreloftet, which is located on the balcony level and is decorated with props from past productions. Here in the morning "Blue Lessons" are presented to school classes. A Blue Lesson is a collage of texts—sketches, poems, songs, and monologues—by or about a particular Danish author, performed by a musician and five actors. During the years Blue Lessons have focused on Jens August Schade, Johannes V. Jensen, Poul Henningsen, and Klaus Rifbjerg, to name just a few.

In the evening, when the performance on the main stage is over, the lights go on at 11:00 P.M. for cabaret and musical entertainment in the Snoreloftet. Young and unknown actors perform here as a way to try their talents, alternating with well-known musical "veterans."

The Hippodrome also has special morning performances for teenagers, the regular productions of the Young Stage. The greatest success in this series has been a production of Englishman Barrie Keefe's *Whoom*. Both the Blue Lessons and the Young Stage are designed to stimulate young people's interest in theatre and dramatic art.

Even the Rehearsal Hall of the Folk Theatre has many different functions besides its regular use for rehearsals, notably, symphony orchestra rehearsals, chamber music performances, jazz, art exhibits, cabarets, poetry readings, theatrical performances, and many other special events. When not in use by the Folk Theatre, the locale may be borrowed by groups of young artists who have no other place in which to exhibit their art. The Rehearsal Hall can really be considered the Folk Theatre's fourth stage. Obviously, the Folk Theatre is a center for artistic activity almost around the clock.

The Folk Theatre has been an institution in Danish theatre life for over one hundred years. Symbolic of its rich traditions is the classical family Christmas comedy, *The Parsonage at Nøddebo*, adapted by Elith Reumert from the story by Bishop C. I. Scharling. Written expressly for this theatre, the play had its premiere in 1888 and is still played before Christmas each year with undiminished popularity. The leading role of the student Nicolai is one of the best known in Danish comic tradition. Many great character actors played Nicolai in their youth.

Through the years the various boards and artistic directors have had their own particular emphasis with regard to repertory and artistic intent. Yet all have had one thing in common—they have put equal emphasis on the significance of both parts of the name. The Folk Theatre is dedicated to serving the people of Copenhagen and the art of theatre.

OTTO BÜHRING
(Translated by Carla Waal)

ODIN THEATRE
(Odin Teatret)
Nordisk Teaterlaboratorium for Skuespillerkunst, Box 118
7500 Holstebro, Denmark

Named for the Norse god of war, victory, wisdom, poetry, and magic, the Odin Theatre has been a source of inspiration and a catalyst for theatre in Scandinavia and internationally, including the Third World. The theatre has developed a unique form of theatrical and pedagogic activity through its productions, publications, films, seminars, and sponsorship of guest artists from Europe, Asia, and South America. A "theatre laboratory for the art of the actor," the Odin Theatre has reevaluated and continued to develop theatrical means of expression by working with the creative growth of individual actors within the framework of a performance, using systematic training and relating to earlier conventions. The theatre's research may be said to have continued traditions from the work of Konstantin Stanislavsky, Vsevolod Meyerhold, Etienne Decroux, and Jerzy Grotowski.

The history of the Odin Theatre may be divided into three completed phases:

founding in Oslo (1964–1966), establishment in Holstebro (1966–1974), and years of pilgrimage on "new paths" (1974–1980).

The Odin Theatre was founded in Oslo in 1964 by Eugenio Barba and five aspiring Norwegian actors who had been denied admission to the government theatre school. Originally, their idea was simply to create a repertory theatre with regular performances, based on dramatic texts. The young Norwegians would be trained as actors, with Barba as their director.

In cooperation with the Norwegian author Jens Bjørneboe, whose work was inspired by Brecht, they prepared a free adaptation of the preliminary text for his play *The Bird Lovers*. Working under miserable financial circumstances, they rehearsed in an air raid shelter. The title became *Ornitofilerne*, and the basic theme—the sentimental postwar German indignation over the Italians' eating of small song birds—was given a simple, serious treatment.

Ornitofilerne was ready in the summer of 1965. Its tour included Jylland in Denmark, where Holstebro, a provincial town with about twenty-five thousand inhabitants and a Social-Democratic mayor, Kaj K. Nielsen, offered the ensemble shelter on an old farm. A cow barn and pigsty could be rebuilt. The authorities would add heat and electricity, plus a basic subsidy of 60,000 Danish crowns. The rest was up to the ensemble.

Not all the Norwegian actors wanted to move to Denmark, but from that pioneer period two members remain: Torgeir Wethal and Else Marie Laukvik. During the second phase new co-workers joined the group, and its aims were redefined. Linguistic difficulties made it impossible to try for repertory drama based on written texts. The facilities suggested other activities, such as a series of large inter-Scandinavian seminars with outstanding guest teachers, including Jerzy Grotowski, Dario Fo, Etienne Decroux, Jean Louis Barrault, and Luca Ronconi. Guest artists often performed during the seminars and afterward toured Scandinavia.

Two acting spaces were prepared: a "black hall" and a "white hall," both neutral or "open" spaces of about 150 square meters. The halls had reasonable height and flat wooden floors, and could be arranged according to the demands of each performance, placing spectators in the proper relationship to the action.

Productions were suitable for touring, since this was a form of theatre that did not demand a great deal of equipment. Instead, there was close contact with the audience, which was limited to sixty to one hundred members. With the visions of Gordon Craig, Adolphe Appia, Jacques Copeau, and later of Jerzy Grotowski and Peter Brook as models, in this type of performance the actor is central.

Since 1966 the ensemble has included actors with different languages, at first Scandinavian and later from all of Western Europe. They had to learn to communicate with each other and to perform for any audience. They wanted to come into contact with all types of people and share a learning process with their audience. "A theatre for illiterates," one dramatist called them.

After a trial period, students are accepted for training. Eventually, they may have a role in a production, given after a period of preparation that may last several years. Students are also trained to teach, using their individual potential and interests. Since 1966 much of Odin Theatre's activity has been pedagogic in a broad sense, leading toward new means of expression and new initiatives for a contemporary living theatre.

Since 1970, the Odin Theatre has been legally recognized as an alternative theatre school because of its experimental activity and research. The municipality of Holstebro still provides free facilities, electricity, heat, subsidies, and occasionally special grants for seminars and publications. Starting in 1980, the Odin has also qualified for state support, since it provides local theatrical activity, including tours and children's shows.

The Odin Theatre's productions can be played almost anywhere, from international festivals to humble locales where the audience may never have seen any type of theatrical performance. The work is based on the theory that an actor can communicate despite language barriers, usually working from literary models and myths. For the performer discipline is of primary importance.

All visionary explosions must be mastered: the actor must *ride on the tiger*, he must not let himself be devoured by it. The physical exteriorization of the emotions must be canalized, controlled, and thus become a wave of explicit signs. It must not be allowed to get the upper hand and plunge the actor into confused actions which ape suffering. (Eugenio Barba, "Waiting for the Revolution," in Barba, *The Floating Islands: Reflections with Odin Teatret*, ed. Ferdinando Taviani [Holstebro, 1979], p. 34.)

Kaspariana (1967) evolved from a synopsis by Danish author Ole Sarvig. The basic fable was the true story of Kasper Hauser, who suddenly appeared in Nürnberg in 1828—without parents, a past, education, or identity—and needed to be taught and "civilized."

Ferai (1969) was developed from a manuscript by Danish author Peter Seeberg, who combined the Greek myth of Alcestis with the Danish saga about King Frode Fredegod. Especially relevant because of events in Czechoslovakia in 1968, *Ferai* was played 220 times in twelve different countries, signifying an international breakthrough for the Odin Theatre.

My Father's House (1972) was a collage based on the ensemble's encounter with the authorship of Dostoevsky, the actors' interpretations of personal visions being unified artistically under Barba's direction.

Come! And the Day Will Be Ours (1978), also a kind of personal collage performance, takes as its starting point General George Custer's order before the battle at Little Big Horn and as its theme the suppression of other people and their cultures by the "White Man's" civilizaton.

Brecht's Ashes (1980) is an attempt at a living dialogue with Brecht, starting from his life and works, but focusing on contemporary dialectic and problems, with great significance for theatrical art, debate, and pedagogy.

Since 1974, the beginning of the third phase, the Odin Theatre has spent most of its time on a journey of discovery. Those who remained with the ensemble after *My Father's House* settled down in a village in southern Italy, Carpignano (Apulia). In this voluntary exile they responded to new surroundings and human challenges. (The Odin Theatre continued to offer short courses in Holstebro, but the publications, seminars, and guest appearances were discontinued.)

Early each morning the actors began training for their new production (*Come! And the Day Will Be Ours*), but they noticed that the local citizens of Carpignano—mostly women, children, and old people—wanted some contact with their new neighbors. The Odin Theatre decided to make a "folk" production, including clowns, for children of all ages. In exchange, the villagers would also prepare performances, and a kind of "barter" system was set up across linguistic and cultural barriers.

Eugenio Barba has since formulated his thoughts about what he calls "The Third Theatre"—a form of human communication using theatrical means of expression and related to so-called underdeveloped minorities which have been crushed or trampled by modern civilization. All such ethnic minorities have a culture that may remain only in the memory of its old people, but they feel a need to express themselves and maintain their roots and identity.

The Odin Theatre has continued on new paths with its productions: a children's play, *Johan Sebastian Bach*; a dance program, *The Book of Dances*; a procession, *Anabasis* (1977); and *Millionen* (1979), which in a lightly ironic form deals with the company's travels and the new impressions and skills they brought home with them.

The new experiences have developed into research activity conducted by the International School of Theatre Anthropology (ISTA). The Odin Theatre is again offering seminars, sharing anthropological discoveries and its study of the basic laws of the actor's experience of the body and its expressiveness. In the fall of 1980 ISTA presented demonstrations in Germany, Denmark, Norway, and Sweden. ISTA's staff consists of actors from Asia and of university scholars, mostly from Western Europe.

The leader of the Odin Theatre is still Eugenio Barba, who was born in 1936 in Apulia, Italy, and trained at Grotowski's Laboratory. Its members, after a four-year apprenticeship, become shareholders. About half of the total budget (which was 2.9 million Danish crowns in 1979–1980) is provided by public subsidies, but its artistic decisions are autonomous. The theatre has great ambitions—to cross linguistic and geographical boundaries through theatrical communication and to express new ideas and visions through production, pedagogy, and research:

Our profession gives us the possibility of changing ourselves and thereby of changing society. One must not ask: what does the theatre signify for the people? . . . But rather: what does the theatre signify for me? The answer, converted into action without regard and without compromise, will be revolution in the theatre. (Barba, *Floating Islands*, p. 36.)

CHRISTIAN LUDVIGSEN
(Translated by Carla Waal)

SOLVOGNEN COMPANY
(Solvognen)
Den Grå Hal
Christiania, Copenhagen, Denmark

The Solvognen (Sun Chariot) Company is probably the Danish theatre group that has most clearly tried to carry out the ideals of the student rebellion of 1968. In the early 1970s the group became known for anticapitalistic and anti-imperialistic street happenings and, since 1976, for large total-theatre performances.

Solvognen originated in 1969 as a light-and-sound-group, working concerts and its own shows, using silhouettes, masks, puppets, mime, and projections. The first happenings took place in 1972, timed with the plebiscite on Denmark's participation in the European Economic Community and Vietnam demonstrations.

Inspired by Wounded Knee, Solvognen in 1973 staged an event in which cavalrymen led Indians in chains through the streets to the City Hall Square. A Nixon-figure gave a speech condemning the Indians' ingratitude and with a smoke bomb signaled for the shooting of the Indians. When the smoke cleared, the Indians lay dead—smeared with blood and animal entrails—and a girls' band marched over their corpses playing "Stars and Stripes Forever." The theme was put into perspective that evening when the company presented a play on how the Danish government treats the "Danish Indians"—the Greenlanders.

For a North Atlantic Treaty Organization (NATO) meeting in 1973, Solvognen organized its own army. Passersby witnessing the brutal seizure of supposed Communists believed that the short-haired members of Solvognen were genuine NATO soldiers, and were horrified that such a thing could happen in Denmark. The action culminated with the false army seizing the television station and demanding time to warn of the Communist danger.

Later that year NATO maneuvers were held in Denmark. Solvognen forces took part (uninvited), interrupting the exercise with angels of peace and a funeral procession led by Death with a scythe.

One of the most famous happenings was the "Army of Christmas Men," who the week before Christmas 1974 did "good deeds." The point was to show the Christmas Man as a paradox in a capitalistic society. The first three days the 150 Christmas Men behaved nicely, singing for old people, arranging a big show in the City Hall Square, and presenting a porcelain Christmas plate to the police. A large self-propelled Christmas Goose paraded with them through town.

At a press conference on the fourth day the group showed its true colors: "From now on the Christmas Man's costume is red, because he is fighting for a socialist upheaval of society." The men stormed the General Motors factory, where all workers had been given notice. Those captured cooperated with the Christmas Men, agreeing to protest the closing of the factory. The manager called the police, and the Christmas Men were thrown out.

To point out that workers must determine production, the Christmas Men assembled in front of the Labor Court and began to tear down the building with cranes, bulldozers, air hammers, and other tools. They were hastily removed by police.

Next, the Christmas Men went to large department stores, where they gave items from the shelves to the customers, symbolically returning goods to the people. When the police arrested the actors, they encountered crying children, unable to understand why the good Christmas Men must go to jail.

In a final attempt to do good, the Christmas Men went to a major bank and asked for a large interest-free loan, to be used to put unemployed construction workers back to work. The bank could not approve the application, and the Christmas Men had to report their failure. With a big parade they wished everyone "Merry Christmas" and left town.

Some months later the happening had an epilogue which received almost greater press coverage than the event itself: the National Art Fund's literary council awarded Solvognen a prize of 20,000 crowns for "purposeful and artistically valuable broadening of the concept of literature." Many right-wing politicians protested, but the amount was eventually paid.

Every year on July 4 Danish-Americans hold a celebration at Rebild. The festival in 1976 drew more than twenty-five thousand spectators, and speakers included the queen, the prime minister, and the American ambassador. As television transmission to the United States began, Solvognen started its performance with a procession of oppressed peoples: Indians, blacks, Greenlanders, and poor whites. Flags from Vietnam, Cambodia, Angola, and Cuba were carried and four hundred white doves were set free. There was a huge bloodbath as police fought the actors, since participants wore bags of animal blood. Along the road leading from Rebild were people in Ku Klux Klan costumes and bloody Indian puppets hanging from trees.

The resultant court case developed into a media event in which Solvognen presented documentary evidence of police brutality.

In 1971 old barracks in Copenhagen were occupied by squatters who proclaimed the free city of Christiania. Despite the authorities' efforts to clear the area, Christiania has survived and given shelter to from six to eight thousand people. The buildings, formerly in ruins, were repaired, and the Gray Hall, a warehouse, became a theatre. From the beginning the Solvognen Company was associated with Christiania, where many of its members lived.

In 1975 Solvognen used the Gray Hall for a total theatre performance, *Elfin Hill* (the title taken from a beloved romantic play by Johan Ludvig Heiberg from 1828). *Elfin Hill* depicts two strategies for changing society: one, the cultural revolution of changing consciousness; the other, class struggle. The two strategies were represented by lovers: the elfin girl and the laborer. The problem posed was very much Christiania's own—the alternative society's possible alliance with the working class.

The performance was influenced by Solvognen's street theatre experiences. Light, colors, scene design, drama, and music worked together in what was then—for the left wing—unfamiliar imaginative and spectacular staging.

In 1977 Solvognen performed two productions simultaneously: *The Merchant's Life* in the Gray Hall and *Soldier Comrades* in a circus tent.

The Merchant's Life treats middle-class ideology and the threat of fascism. A small, independent merchant's livelihood is threatened by a big supermarket company. He must close and go to the Welfare Office; humiliated by his plight, he commits suicide. The rise of a fascist party and a strike at a big newspaper are also shown (both had parallels in the contemporary Danish political situation). The play ends with police storming the newspaper and a general strike. *The Merchant's Life* was arranged on many simultaneous stages set up around the hall. Artistically, it was noteworthy for its many-faceted scenic fantasy. Politically, it was interesting that Solvognen positioned itself with the small businessman, whom many political theatre groups treated with contempt.

Soldier Comrades is a musical about the innocent participation of two young draftees in a fascist organization's murder of a cabinet officer, resulting in a military coup.

The Free City of Christiania has had a steadily growing narcotics problem. In late 1979 the residents successfully got rid of the dealers of hard drugs. The Solvognen Company contributed to the ongoing campaign with a total theatre performance: *The White Castle* (1980). In this play the morphine and heroin trade is linked to the nuclear power industry. Solvognen again used large visual effects, such as a gigantic pinball machine where the balls were replaced by people on roller skates.

Solvognen's women's group on several occasions—such as women's festivals—has performed debate plays, dealing with the sexual and political suppression of women, women's roles, lesbian problems, and international sisterhood.

Individual members of Solvognen have always been anonymous, not only because they reject the star system but also because anonymity offers protection from reprisals. A core group of ten to fifteen members plans the individual activities which afterward are open to other participants.

The work is usually collective, without any designation of author, director, actor, or technician. For street theatre vigorous training programs and strict discipline are required.

Although the Solvognen Company doubtlessly supports a socialistic overturning of society, it does not endorse any specific political direction or party. Some members say they want a society where goods are divided equally and individuals are free to develop, but not at the expense of others.

The Solvognen Company has been mostly self-financed. In addition to the admission income from stationary performances, where ticket prices have been kept low, there has been income from recordings, books, and films based on its productions and happenings. Street theatre has always been financed by the participants.

In addition to the award from the National Art Fund, the group received 80,000 crowns from the Ministry for Cultural Affairs after the success of *Elfin Hill*.

At Solvognen's street happenings passersby automatically become spectators—willingly or not. This audience has a significantly broader social composition than the traditional theatre audience. The Solvognen's actions are perhaps not universally regarded as theatre; it depends on one's definition.

The audience which comes to the Gray Hall is quite different from both the street audience and the traditional theatre audience. They are mostly young, more or less leftist, and belong to the lower income group. The Solvognen's performances in the Gray Hall are planned for them, in part laying the groundwork for political discussion within leftist circles.

The Solvognen Company has always consciously made use of the mass media's interest in the unusual, informing journalists about "surprise" events in advance. And if one compares the number of newspaper articles and letters from readers to the relatively small number of events and performances the group has produced, there is no doubt that the Solvognen Company has won greater attention for its art than any other theatre in Denmark.

STIG JARL JENSEN
(Translated by Carla Waal)

Finland

INTRODUCTION

The oldest forms of theatrical activities in Finland were quest rituals and ceremonies which could go on for days. In the Middle Ages Christian legends were performed dramatically, and theatrical events had their part in school education. In the seventeenth century the nation's strong religiosity opposed all original Finnish theatre for more than a hundred years.

In the late eighteenth century Swedish and German touring companies invaded the country. There was no Finnish court theatre because there never was a Finnish king. Dreams of an independent theatre culture to replace foreign touring companies found a firm base in the national awakening of the nineteenth century.

The people had two languages: Finnish and Swedish. The Swedish-speaking minority continued to keep connections with its former mother country, but they also took part in the national movement. One of its aims was to strengthen the position of the Finnish language. The campaign for the independence and maturity of Finnish was supported by an expanding group of intellectuals, university teachers, politicians, and artists.

Many did not believe that the Finnish language was capable of transmitting high dramatic poetry. Theatre was also hampered by a lack of both actors and audience. Nevertheless, the first leader and founder of the Finnish theatre, Dr. Kaarlo Bergbom (1843–1906), succeeded in creating a theatre policy and a repertory that not only brought enough subscribers to support the group and follow its work with excitement, but also attracted the most promising writers and made them contributors of the new theatre.

From the start the theatre was considered to be of social significance and close to the people, though its point of departure was to promote general culture rather than to entertain the lower classes. There was a tremendous interest in amateur acting in those days, backed by the growing working-class movement especially and a number of other idealistic organizations. They were seen as a means of bringing together people who were seeking a new way of life in the increasingly industrialized, urban world.

At the beginning of the twentieth century some drama societies became independent and began to reach out for more ambitious professional performances. The artistic and social status of the theatre was now clearly visible. In several towns a bourgeois and a workers' theatre existed side by side; the differences were not so distinct in the repertory or the artistic and professional aims as in the make-up of the audience, whose political affinities usually dictated which theatre they attended. The most important workers' theatre grew up in Tampere.

The theatres were dependent on the economic support given by the government and the local authorities. As their number increased, they encountered severe financial difficulties. They were forced to take this situation into consideration in their repertory policy and to give far too many premieres in order to tempt audiences with something new.

After the civil war, in the twenties the workers' theatres were in great difficulties because the authorities wanted to cut down the support granted state theatres. Ever stronger grew the voices that spoke for combining the professional or semiprofessional workers' theatre and the bourgeois theatre of the same town. This change took place mostly after World War II, when because of increasing economic pressures permanent theatres were ready for amalgamation.

Today there are forty-two state-subsidized professional theatres in Finland, thirty of which are Finnish-language theatres in a fixed place, four are fixed Swedish-language, and eight are mobile professional group theatres. A theatre based on a permanent ensemble is a constant feature of Finnish culture.

The fixed theatres usually have a theatre building that contains a main stage as well as a studio. Of the fixed theatres fifteen are completely owned by the local authorities or their equivalent. The professional group theatres were started chiefly at the beginning of the 1970s, with the aim of discovering new audiences through such means as touring companies and a new kind of performance aesthetics. The amateur acting tradition also continues to be strong, and every year a special Amateur Theatre Festival gathers together the best performances.

Developing regional theatres has been a major objective of Finnish theatre policy for more than a decade. Traditionally the art of the theatre has been considered to be close to the people, and therefore it is felt that it should be available to the entire nation. The regular professional theatres, however, cannot reach everyone. Since most theatres are located in the large and medium-size cities, the rural population and those in remote districts (development areas) have only limited opportunities to go to the theatre.

Regional theatres seek to level out the differences in location, education, and wealth that affect the theatregoing of those who live outside urban centers. To extend and diversify the composition of audiences, a regional theatre regularly goes on tour, arranges for audiences to be transported to the theatre, and develops various forms of cooperation with the population, writers, amateur theatres, and other forms of cultural activity within its region.

Regional theatre was run on an experimental basis from 1969 to 1970. During that period a number of theatres received special state aid for regional work. In

1978 the Ministry of Education terminated the experiment and made the theatres of Joensuu, Kajaani, and Rovaniemi permanent regional theatres for the development areas of north and east Finland. This decision did not, however, mean that the regional theatre became statutory, but was made permanent administratively.

In 1980 an appropriation of 5.7 million Finnish marks was set aside for regional theatre, state aid equivalent to 50 percent of the approved net expenses of each regional theatre. Two new theatres were added in 1980, both Swedish-language. They are the Åbo Svenska Teater, centered in Turku, and the Wasa Teater in Vaasa. Their audiences include the Swedish-speaking minority living in the southwestern archipelago, to which access is difficult, and the west coast of Finland.

To support regional activities, an advisory committee has been set up for all the regional theatres. The municipalities of each region appoint representatives to this committee. In addition, the regional theatres have a network of representatives covering the field who act as contacts between their municipality and the theatre, arrange local visits, and endeavor to get the municipalities to budget appropriations to cover visits by the regional theatre.

Finnish theatre policy is to keep prices so low that nobody need stay away from the theatre for financial reasons. The price of theatre tickets is kept at the level of cinema tickets and is much less than that of many sports events.

All professional theatres in Finland are subsidized by the community. Financial aid is divided between the state and the local authorities. Together this works out, according to statistics for 1979, at about US $9.00 (38 Finnish marks) on the average of aid for each ticket sold. Total public aid for theatres in 1979 amounted to approximately 76 million Finnish marks. Theatre support has become an increasing strain on the resources of local authorities. The professional group theatres get the least local aid because in theory their field of operation covers the whole country. Even this does not make their state aid above the average.

State aid comes from the proceeds of the state monopoly lotteries, from which fixed appropriations are paid to science, the arts, and sports. The theatres are not too keen on this procedure because it puts their operations at the mercy of the nation's desire to gamble and because the amount of funds thus accumulated may be affected by a deterioration of general economic conditions.

Among the worst threats to art maintained by community funds is that the representatives of the financing authorities consider themselves entitled to dictate what art produces. Conflicts sometimes arise between representatives of the local authorities and the theatre workers, mainly concerning repertory and personnel policy. From the standpoint of theatre work, the best results seem to be obtained when the representatives of society—the theatre committee or board—decide on the general outlines and main principles for the repertory and leave the detailed decisions to the theatre professionals. It is especially important that concepts of the need for artistic and professional ambition be preserved and emphasized within the theatre.

In the 1978–1979 season 1,591 people did their main work in the professional theatre. Of these 1,319 worked in fixed Finnish theatres, 177 in Swedish, and 95 in group theatres. The largest professional groups are the technicians (603) and the actors (597). The theatres engage no full-time playwrights. Theatre engagements are generally for two years, after which they can either be renewed or discontinued. The trend toward continued employment with normal terms of notice has increased, however, and the threat of discontinuance has been considered a disturbing influence on artistic work. Finnish theatre artists currently have a strong professional identity and a feeling of collectivity. This feeling is backed by strong organization of different groups, the oldest and largest of which, the Finnish Actors' Union, was established in 1913.

Theatre has supported the Finnish cultural identity with a strong domestic repertory. The share of Finnish plays in the total repertory is about one-half. In the 1978–1979 season forty-nine new plays by Finnish authors were produced.

The interest in folk traditions and folklore has led many playwrights to seek their themes in this field. Especially popular in recent years have been plays describing the lives of people important in the cultural development of the country. In the 1960s the epic play form, with brief scenes and often with music, proved suitable for dealing with topical problems (for example, *The Lapua Opera* [*Lapualaisooppera*] by Arvo Salo and Kaj Chydenius). The form was gradually exhausted, however, and no form of equal force has been discovered.

A strong line in the theatre's repertory comes from the works of women dramatists like Minna Canth, Maria Jotuni, Hella Wuolijoki, and Eeva-Liisa Manner. Their works sharply delineate the woman's position under the pressure of her environment and her own expectations, her economic, intellectual, and moral defenselessness.

A glance at the foreign repertory of the Finnish theatre reveals the need for new stimuli in topical drama and for a renewal of connections with classical drama. Most of the foreign plays come from English-speaking countries, Germany, and the Soviet Union. In the 1978–1979 season there were twenty-four American plays, seventeen English, seventeen Soviet Union, sixteen French, and fourteen German and Swedish plays.

While an attempt is being made to absorb and adopt influences from various quarters, the Finnish theatre's basic strength has continued to lie in realism. Only quite recently have there been symptoms of a new theatre aesthetics, characterized by strong visual associativeness and the use of the stage as a co-actor instead of merely a setting. Kalle Holmberg, Ralf Långbacka, Jouko Turkka, Jotaarkka Pennanen, Kaisa Korhonen, and Arto af Hällström are all interesting and original directors. Each has found a personal language of the theatre either through a vibrating sense of rhythm, a deep and shocking emotion, or a profound dialectical analysis.

The number of theatregoers in Finland is constantly increasing. The total number in the 1978–1979 season was about 2.5 million. The largest percentage of the audiences come to block-booking performances: either an employer or some organization books a performance and sells or distributes the tickets to employees or members. There are no permanent advance-booking societies in Finland except for those that book for the first nights; they do so mostly because of social position or from upper middle-class family tradition. In Finland, as in many other countries, the educational level of theatregoers is considerably above the average. The mobile group theatres have been successful in reaching people of lower educational and social status. The same development seems likely for the regional theatres.

Attention has also recently been given to children's theatre. Some of the free theatre groups play mainly for child audiences. Although some prejudices concerning the importance of these activities remain, it is acknowledged that an awareness of theatre's special features must be created at an early age.

The overall picture of theatre life in Finland would be incomplete without at least a mention of the outdoor summer theatre. Many professional theatres arrange their summer theatre performances outdoors. The summer theatre is also the highlight of amateur activity; there is no corner of Finland where local amateur groups do not perform in summer. The audiences differ considerably from winter audiences in professional theatres. The situation is less formal, and a well-acted summer folk play may for many a spectator open the first gate to the world of the theatre.

IRMELI NIEMI

FINNISH NATIONAL THEATRE
(Suomen Kansallisteatteri)
Läntinen Teatterikuja 1 B
00100 Helsinki 10, Finland

The origins of the Finnish National Theatre are both distinctly individual and tied up with the development of Finnish culture in general. Finland has never had a court theatre, nor have theatres been established at the bidding of the mighty. National idealism, the increased number of Finnish-speaking educated people, and keen amateur activities are the forces that created the Finnish theatre, which was the country's first permanent professional theatre and direct predecessor of the present National Theatre.

The Finnish Theatre succeeded in giving its opening production in Pori, an Ostrobothnian coastal town, in 1872, chiefly as a result of the work of one man, Dr. Kaarlo Bergbom, who then was less than thirty years old. It was his idea, and he brought it into being. Earlier generations had, of course, expressed their hopes, had written about a Finnish theatre, and had given occasional productions.

Three other vital conditions for establishing a Finnish-language professional theatre already existed—the writers, the actors, and the audience.

The Finnish Theatre at first had two divisions—one for the spoken word and the other for opera—but the second was discontinued seven years later as too expensive. Until the turn of the century the theatre toured Finland extensively in line with the belief that the elevating and civilizing influence of theatre should be diffused throughout the nation. When the theatre was established, there were fourteen actors, who put on thirty-six premieres during the season. The legendary first home of the theatre in Helsinki was the old, wooden Arkadia Theatre, designed by architect Carl Ludvig Engel, creator of the empire-style center of Helsinki. In 1902 the theatre moved to its present home, a gray granite building in the national romantic style, designed by Onni Tarjanne. It was then given its present name, the Finnish National Theatre.

Kaarlo Bergbom's period as manager of the Finnish Theatre was a time of pioneer work, of fresh triumphs, and an intimate atmosphere. Known as "the Doctor's time," this period spanned three decades until 1905. After more than ten years with rapid changes in management, in 1916 Eino Kalima, a young critic and director who had studied in Stanislavsky's theatre in Moscow, became manager of the National Theatre and remained in this post for over three decades.

Kalima was succeeded in 1950 by Professor Arvi Kivimaa, writer and poet. Kivimaa was an ardent and valuable participant in international activities of the International Theatre Institute. In 1974 he was followed by the present manager, Kai Savola, who had previously led the Tampere Workers' Theatre.

Today the National Theatre plays on three stages: the "big stage," the "small stage" opened in 1952, and an intimate, experimental theatre called Willensauna, which was started at the beginning of Kai Savola's managership. At the moment there are forty-two actors, and each stage gives an average of four or five premieres per season.

From the first, Kaarlo Bergbom clearly indicated the main lines of the repertory which he considered it the duty of the leading national theatre to follow: Finnish drama, the great classics, and topical new plays. Naturally, the relative proportions of these categories of the repertory have varied with the passage of time.

The foundations of the domestic repertory were brilliantly created before the first Finnish-language theatre was established. As far back as the 1860s, the main plays of Aleksis Kivi had appeared: the comedy *The Heath Cobblers* and the tragedy *Kullervo*, both keystones of Finnish dramatic literature. Along with Kivi's other dramatic works, these plays have repeatedly appeared in the theatre's repertory during its over one hundred years of existence. The theatre has therefore earned the right to call itself Aleksis Kivi's house.

In its early years the theatre had another great dramatist at its disposal, Minna Canth, who—following Ibsen—radically attacked social injustice. The plays of another talented woman dramatist, Maria Jotuni, were first produced at the National Theatre and have stayed in its repertory. Jotuni's comedies, characterized by their broad human register and new style of dialogue, were brought into the repertory during the Eino Kalima period in the 1920s. In the forties, one of the National Theatre's playwrights was Mika Waltari. The themes of his many versatile comedies interestingly foreshadowed the key themes of the fifties.

The younger generation, encouraged to write for the theatre in the fifties and sixties during Arvi Kivimaa's managership, introduced a new concept of drama, freed from the illusion of reality and often with highly individual, poetic dialogue. The most distinguished writers in this genre are Paavo Haavikko, Eeva-Liisa Manner, and Juhani Peltonen. Veijo Meri, master of the short story, dealt with the irrationality of war in connection with the events of the Winter War in a play called *Private Jokinen's Marriage Leave*, recalling the spirit of Brecht's Schweyk. Since then the proportion of Finnish drama in the repertory has strikingly decreased.

Right from the start the theatre's repertory ventured to include great works of world drama, such as Molière's *The Miser* and Shakespeare's *Romeo and Juliet*. Juliet was radiantly played by a young natural talent who would later win international fame, Ida Aalberg, the first and unforgettable interpreter of great women's roles from Schiller, Ibsen, and others. This actress made a number of tours in all the Scandinavian countries, St. Petersburg, and Berlin, where she played Juliet with the famous Joseph Kainz as Romeo.

Other memorable Shakespeare performances were the King Lear of the talented, profound character actor Yrjö Tuominen, and the Antony and Cleopatra of Joel Rinne and Ella Eronen, two of the theatre's foremost actors.

Finnish actors were surprisingly at home in Molière's comedies of character. The first link in a long tradition was Adolf Lindfors, a talented comedian and interpreter of the French repertory from Kaarlo Bergbom's time, who won fame in the part of Harpagon. His tradition was continued in the 1940s by Uuno Laakso, an original and very human comedian, who had the rare opportunity at the end of the fifties to play Harpagon in Paris.

Henrik Ibsen has been performed frequently at this theatre, at first as a controversial topical writer and later as a dramatist of modern classics. All his plays from *A Doll House* onwards have been played while still new. *John Gabriel Borkman* was actually played here, for the first time, in 1897. In a fine production by Eino Kalima in the thirties of *The Wild Duck*, the actors included Henny Waljus as Hedvig and the talented, intelligent, and versatile Joel Rinne, who recently celebrated his sixtieth year on the stage, as Hjalmar Ekdal.

The other great Scandinavian dramatist, August Strindberg, has been given somewhat less prominence in the National Theatre's repertory. Perhaps the greatest artistic triumphs among Strindberg productions have been Pekka Alpo's direction of the intimate chamber play *Storm Weather* in the thirties and the poetic *A Dream Play*, fitting in with the modernism of the fifties, directed by Arvi Kivimaa. In both plays the main roles were taken by Ruth Snellman, daughter of the composer Jean Sibelius, and Joel Rinne, who played together successfully from the twenties until the sixties.

The plays of Luigi Pirandello, George Bernard Shaw, Karel Ĉapek, Jules Romain, Romain Rolland, Frantizek Langer, Franz Werfel, Eugene O'Neill, and Elmer Rice were brought fresh to the repertory of the National Theatre during Eino Kalima's time. Contacts with new European drama were equally vital during Arvi Kivimaa's time, when the post-World War II playwrights came into the limelight. Jean Anouilh, Jean-Paul Sartre, Samuel Beckett, and Eugene Ionesco were presented to the Finnish theatre public soon after their world-renowned first performances. At this time the choice of repertory was in close touch with the pulse of the times.

In his first year as manager (1916), Eino Kalima introduced a playwright who has become almost a household god in this theatre—Anton Chekhov. The first production was *Uncle Vanya*; no new Chekhov plays were seen until thirty years later, but then with splendid success. In a series that remains unforgettable in Finnish theatre history, all the great plays by this Russian master of character-ization were produced. Young, enthusiastic actors played the leading roles in *The Three Sisters, The Sea Gull, Uncle Vanya*, and *The Cherry Orchard. The Sea Gull* toured in Paris, Moscow, and Berlin, winning undisputed success for its authentic Chekhov style. Many talented Finnish actors who have won their laurels in a variety of parts gave of their best in Chekhov roles. It can safely be said that with the Chekhov productions by Kalima, the Finnish theatre has been able to add something original, individual, and of high quality to the overall picture of European theatre.

In accordance with its proper task, the National Theatre has rarely attempted extreme experimentation. Changes in means of expression and responses to new artistic demands have occurred through evolution, not through sudden and ex-plosive changes in style. Eino Kalima's prolonged, quiet work towards an in-timate, inner line cleansed of false pathos was an example of this far-reaching and profound style. Direct contact with the avant-garde drama of the fifties naturally placed new stylistic demands on the performers and changed the the-atre's style considerably. It was the assistant manager at that time, Jack Witikka, who brought the theatre up to date.

Naturally this—like most other national theatres—has had its ups and downs. Nevertheless, the vitality and effectiveness of the Finnish National Theatre has largely depended on the fact that from the start it has had at its disposal the best actors in Finland.

KATRI VELTHEIM

HELSINKI CITY THEATRE
(Helsingin Kaupunginteatteri)
Ensi Linja 2
00530 Helsinki 53, Finland

The Helsinki City Theatre was founded in 1965 by changing the name and the administration of what had been known as the Helsinki Popular Theatre-

Workers' Theatre (Helsingin Kansanteatteri-Työväenteatteri). In 1967 the theatre moved from its temporary, leased facilities to a brand-new building of its own. In this splendid new building, housing two stages, the Helsinki City Theatre has experienced both ups and downs. It has suffered all the ailments of this type of established theatre, while also succeeding in breaking down enough prejudices to make itself known as one of the leading cultural establishments of the country.

The Helsinki City Theatre has had its share of difficulties. The leading performers of this large establishment say that each successful performance is the result of a struggle, inherent in the nature of things in this type of large theatre. Having gotten through its infant years, the Helsinki City Theatre in the late seventies developed into a far more interesting establishment than anyone could have imagined. This theatre, sometimes detrimentally referred to as "a theatre of the city officials," was producing plays that excited spectators and actors alike. The theatre as a whole did not indiscriminately generate this feeling of excitement, however. It was reserved for certain individual achievements of both actors and directors, achievements characterized by a rare fervor and honesty.

Significant changes began in 1975, when Paavo Liski began a term as head of the theatre, with Jouko Turkka as assistant director. Ralf Långbacka was appointed the next manager, beginning in August 1983. Previous administrators were Sakari Puurunen (1965–1970) and Timo Tiusanen, with Artistic Director Eugen Terttula (1970–1975). In the 1979–1980 season the personnel consisted of 168 persons, 47 of whom made up the acting company.

In his capacity as stage director, Jouko Turkka has waged an incessant war on the rigidity of "a theatre of the city officials," and both his dramatizations of Finnish novels and his actual productions have become true hallmarks of Finnish theatre. Turkka has made the Helsinki City Theatre into an important arbiter of Finnish drama. His special field has been the production of well-known Finnish plays. Particularly noteworthy is his inherently sexual interpretation of a Finnish classic, *The Heath Cobblers*, by Aleksis Kivi. Important contemporary Finnish novels have also been transformed into living theatre on the stage of the City Theatre, for example, *Sinnä näkijä missä tekijä (There You See, Where You Do)* by Hannu Salama. This performance brought a new form of expression to the Finnish stage: in simultaneous action it pictured the development, struggles, and conflicts of the Finnish working-class movement.

Turkka's productions are a source of continuous public debate and discussion. Conservatives are generally upset by the sharply analytical way in which he comes to grips with life. He also tends to upset those who want their theatre to be a pleasant evening's entertainment. Turkka's theatre does not seek to please. Often it clearly intends to be deliberately unpleasant—to affect the audience, to shock them even, and at the same time to broaden their outlook on life, people, society, the present, and the future. With Turkka, the status of the Helsinki City Theatre has risen. Visiting directors have been among the foremost in the country. At its best, the repertory maintains a high and demanding level.

The classics have received a face-lift at the City Theatre. Examples are *Othello*, which was interpreted by Arto af Hällström, a talented young man straight from the theatre school; the same young director's production of Molière's *The Misanthrope*; the same playwright's *Don Juan*, in a production directed by Antti Einari Halonen, in which several expressions of fascism are presented; and Chekhov's *The Sea Gull*, directed by Ralf Långbacka, currently professor of the arts.

Today's audience has grown to appreciate the City Theatre; performances are usually sold out in advance. This big theatre of the "establishment" has reached out to people, speaking on today's issues in the language of the theatre, whether through a new contemporary production or a classic.

The artistic profile of the theatre is not quite as uncomplicated as it may sound. It also has a "lighter" side. From the very beginning the Helsinki City Theatre was duty-bound to include musical theatre productions in its repertory, thus upholding a tradition established by its predecessor, the Helsinki Popular Theatre-Workers' Theatre. The popular musical *Showboat* ran for well over a year. One can only surmise what influence such productions may have on the development of the theatre.

The Helsinki City Theatre is an eminent example of how a strong artistic personality can transform a theatre grown to factory-like dimensions, with an assembly line of productions, into a workshop of passionate creativity and new ideas. Today there is a high percentage of domestic productions, and these productions are made to relate to the world at large and to the basic questions of all creative work. In this sense the Helsinki City Theatre has been able to convince people that the theatre has more than a chance in the competition with mass entertainment.

JUKKA KAJAVA

KAJAANI CITY THEATRE
(Kajaanin Kaupunginteatteri)
Kauppakatu 14
87100 Kajaani 10, Finland

The region covered by the Kajaani City Theatre is the sparsely populated province of Oulu with over 400,000 inhabitants. The bulk of the theatre's regional work is centered in its home district, Kainuu. During the 1970s the theatre developed from a small, half-professional, half-amateur theatre to a medium-size municipal professional theatre, recognized throughout Finland for its artistic achievements.

The history of the Kajaani Theatre is quite typical, with an important part played by the workers' amateur theatre becoming established and gradually turning professional. Its earliest predecessor, the Kajaani Play Society, was founded in 1906. It continued as the Workers' Theatre until 1969, when the name was changed to the Kajaani City Theatre. It became a completely municipal theatre in 1978 at the same time as it was made a regional theatre.

In its hometown the theatre plays in the former city hall, built in 1907, with seats for 230. At the start of the seventies there were only seven full-time employees, not all of whom had professional training. The year 1973 was an important turning point in the theatre's artistic development, for in that year Kari Selinheimo became theatre manager and a stage director with bold vision, Kaija Viinikainen, joined the theatre. The theatre also began its regional theatre experiment, with conscious repertory and staff planning and a stepped-up touring program. Within four years the number of spectators doubled, as did the staff.

Today the Kajaani City Theatre is considered a medium-size theatre in Finland. In relation to the size of the theatre, the staff of thirty-seven is strongly weighted toward artistic planning. There are four directors, a scene designer, a dramaturge, a costume designer (there are only five costume designers in all Finland), and fifteen actors. The staff is not yet large enough to serve both home and regional audiences, but growth has been rapid and objectives have been clearly set.

By strengthening its material resources, the Kajaani City Theatre has been able to establish its own cultural objectives and repertory policy. The repertory has been built up with an eye to the special needs of different population groups, such as children and young people, farmers, workers—and the unemployed. The repertory has been diversified and fairly reflects the ideas of different social groups in its national content.

The repertory of recent years clearly reveals certain main groups: drama of national and regional significance (*Kalevala*; Eino Leino, *Simo Hurtta*; Aku-Kimmo Ripatti, *Black Goose, Fly This Way*; Matti Pulkkinen-MarjaLauri, *The Nesting-Tree Wept*), children's and young people's theatre (Uspensky, *Uncle Fedya, the Cat and the Dog*), classics of world literature (Shakespeare, Ibsen, Gogol, Ostrovsky, Brecht), and topical foreign plays (Dario Fo, several Soviet plays).

National and regional drama are played a great deal at the Kajaani Theatre, as well as elsewhere in Finland, in order to foster the growth of the spectator's sense of identity. Thus, an important task of a theatre performance is to show a constructive connection between the world of the spectator and the world of drama. The theatre's repertory has included a number of regional plays dealing with the special problems, social and individual, of its own district.

Ambitious artistic goals have also been set. Copying everyday life on stage through expression and interpretation has been opposed. Instead, the theatre tries to convey immediate reality by emphasizing the inner meanings of the text by stripping down and stylizing situations. An example is Pirkko Saisio's *On the Edge of the World*. Performed in several theatres, this play depicts the rapid social changes taking place in the countryside and the bitter conflicts these changes cause in the people living there. The interpretations seen elsewhere have followed the unsurprising logic of the folk play, giving a naturalistic picture of the milieu and the people. The Kajaani production, on the other hand, was located in a suggestive environment, characterization was strongly stylized, and the production as a whole was illogical but rich in associations.

Interpretations of the classics have also been bold and have broken with accustomed traditions. Kaija Viinikainen's direction of Gogol's *The Inspector General* was one of Finland's major theatrical events in the 1978–1979 season. It was a dynamic production, surprisingly combining the means of expression of cabaret, circus, and cinema. In all the theatre's productions the artistic components—directing, design, costume, music, and acting—combine to create an overall effect originating from a democratic and collective work process.

About one-third of a season's performances are given outside the theatre's hometown. On tour, difficulties are often encountered because of poorly equipped places of performance. Much attention has been given to planning new schools and other public premises, or restoring old ones, with an eye to the requirements of the theatre. A narrow, low box stage often presents artistic difficulties. For this reason Alexandr Ostrovsky's *Bankruptcy* when on tour was played in different parts of big halls, partly in the midst of the audience.

An average of two hundred people see each of the Kajaani City Theatre's performances. The annual number of spectators divides into roughly equal halves between those who come to the Kajaani theatre house and those who see performances on tour. Many people are brought by bus from various parts of the region to Kajaani. It is important that children and those of school age experience the theatre for the first time in an environment that is close and familiar to them. For this reason performances in schools have been very popular.

Kajaani Theatre has also suffered from the conflicts that are most commonly connected with the administration of municipal theatres in Finland. These conflicts reveal the strong desire of various political interests to run the theatre. The repertory of the Kajaani Theatre has been criticized as one-sided and too left wing. Resolution of disputes has not been left at the theatre's own municipal administration level, but has been carried right to the top decision-making level in the city.

This reflects, on the one hand, the theatre's status as a socially significant form of art, and, on the other hand, the difficulty of bringing the ideas of those responsible for the theatre's artistic nature in line with the ideas of the political decision-makers of the city with responsibility for large appropriations, and with the often varying political views of the municipalities in the region. The government has not intervened in these disputes. A key problem for Kajaani has been the extent of the theatre's regional activities. The theatre itself considers it important to achieve cultural equality for the whole broad area of the Oulu Province and wishes to extend its influence as far as possible within the limits of its resources. But the decision of the city of Kajaani has restricted tours, at the theatre's own financial risk, to the ten municipalities of Kainuu. The city, in fact, pays a subsidy on each entrance ticket that is one-third larger than that paid by the state. Regional theatre in Kajaani and elsewhere so far has shown that by continuing to develop along the same line and by emphasizing the artistic side, a new and living response and interest will be won from its audiences.

Today the Kajaani City Theatre is led by Hannu Tyhtilä.

IRMELI NIEMI

KOM THEATRE
(KOM Teatteri)
Yrjönkatu 31
00100 Helsinki 10, Finland

The Finnish theatre world was shaken at the end of the sixties by a movement that originated in response to the sluggishness of the big established theatres. It began at the student theatres and the drama school, and eventually gave birth to a number of small groups that called themselves free theatres.

The activities of these theatres were based on common aims and work methods that were decided upon together. Artists were no longer controlled by an external administration or a board of laymen elected according to the relative importance of political parties. The chief aims of these groups were (and still are) to fill certain social vacuums. The theatre was taken to places where it had never been seen before: to Finnish frontier areas and to villages and schools in remote regions. The groups especially tried to play for children. Artistic and creative freedom sprang from the need to produce theatre about things felt to be of primary importance. A sense of social inequality and criticism of the bourgeois world-view very soon led these groups to topical cabaret performances—prepared quickly, performed with consuming fire, and as quickly left behind.

Under extremely difficult financial circumstances, these groups toured the length and breadth of Finland in old faded buses. They worked summer and winter. The young actors did ardent pioneer work at the cost of their health and family lives. After ten years, most of these groups stayed in one location for part of the year—in Helsinki, Tampere, Vantaa. But they still went on tour for part of each year as well. Tours have been increasingly directed to the neighboring country of Sweden, to take theatre in the Finnish language to the areas where Finnish immigrants live. Seven of the small theatres organized an association called the Theatre Centre.

The KOM Theatre, a member of the Theatre Centre, began in 1969 as an offshoot of one of the larger established theatres, the Swedish Theatre in Helsinki, playing independently on its own small stage. But very quickly the aims of this small group and the parent theatre ran into conflict, and the KOM separated to become a wholly independent theatre.

At first the KOM was a typical example of a small group without its own stage. Its only premises were a small office and rehearsal room. Performances were prepared for touring, and scenery was designed so that it could be loaded on top of a bus. Its only permanent playing space was a summer stage in the historical fortress of Suomenlinna. Soon this summer stage saw productions breaking with the whole tradition of Finnish summer theatre. They were written especially for this theatre, with subjects from Finnish history, treated critically and often in the form of satire, and audiences crowded into the fortress even in the rain.

Throughout the seventies the KOM repertory included, on the one hand, strongly national plays (often taking a theme from folk tradition), and, on the other hand, new interpretations of the great classics of world literature. But the search for national identity has not meant that the theatre has limited itself to the old folk-play tradition. Tradition has been linked with the present, the world of the *Kalevala* has been seen through the eyes of the present decade, and the style of performance has come from the rich resources of the stylized musical theatre.

These new folk plays have thrown light on Finnish people who have been shaken from their roots by social development, thrown into the cities to join the unemployed, or forced through the powerful polarization of society to a harsh loss and reevaluation of their identity. Pentti Saaritsa's *Northern Darkness*, Matti Rossi's *The Wooden Bird Carver*, Pirkko Kurikka's *Kullervo* on a *Kalevala* theme, and Aku-Kimmo Ripatti's *Tar Goose* were productions that all won praise and recognition both at home and abroad. Toward the end of the seventies the theatre became increasingly experimental; a bold emphasis on artistic merit kept alive a theatre that by financial standards should already have died.

Its boldness, originality, and artistic triumphs brought the KOM Theatre to the front rank in Finland. It was a trendsetter, specializing increasingly in musical theatre, using its own composers and orchestra as an organic part of its art. The KOM players also made history in the Peacock Theatre of the Helsinki amusement park, where they played Vsevelod Vishnevsky's *The Optimistic Tragedy* as a sharp and sinewy study of heroism, with the simplest of decor. Other successful classics were Brecht's *The Rifles of Frau Carrar* and *The Threepenny Opera*, which ran for three years.

The renting of its own premises was a decisive step forward in the brief history of the KOM Theatre. In 1979 the theatre took over an old cinema, which it has been renewing and shaping as serviceable theatre premises. After obtaining its own premises, the theatre divided its repertory into two main lines: small-scale touring plays and larger plays for the permanent stage. Tours have often been made with one- or two-actor productions. The productions for the home stage take advantage of the theatre's total capacity. Milestones in the theatre's artistic development have been new interpretations of such classics as Chekhov's *The Three Sisters*, Miller's *Death of a Salesman*, and Shakespeare's *The Tempest*, with new music. The national classic, *Here Under the Northern Star*, a trilogy by Väinö Linna, has also been played.

The starting point in doing the classics has been their reevaluation from today's perspective. Thus, for example, *The Three Sisters* seeks answers to the weariness and passivity of frustrated man today. *The Tempest* is seen as a study of the prospects of humanity seeking itself in the face of global destruction. *Death of a Salesman* shows the forces driving a man to drop out from a society with restrictive norms.

Characteristic of the KOM ensemble's artistic work, both in these great classics and in their own small-scale new plays, has been its emphasis on grasping the fundamental social situation through keenly pointed acting. The company has sought man with a capital M, whether it has created a song or a parody about him.

Workers at the KOM Theatre have sought their own artistic identity through self-awareness and have geared it to what happens on the stage. Work has been done with a burning heart, with belief in their own aims. This, in turn, has required several critical artistic seminars in which previous work has been evaluated and guidelines for the future have been set.

The KOM has been a working collective, seeking opportunities to express dynamically the phenomena of art and society. Its aim has been unceasing questioning—directed both inwardly and outwardly—and movement over a broad geographical, social, and intellectual field. Very often this aim has been achieved. The theatre has created its own broad-based audience, consisting largely of people whose interest has not been aroused by the big established theatres, which are indifferent and do not raise questions. These people come again and again to the KOM Theatre with new expectations and new questions.

The KOM has also enlarged its field across the arts. It has been a pioneer of Finnish cultural policy in arranging evening programs, thematic evenings, discussions, seminars, concerts, international solidarity activities, and so on.

The KOM Theatre is administered democratically, with the workers themselves deciding questions of repertory, staff, and salaries. Outstanding for their leadership of the company have been Kaj Chydenius, serving as artistic director from 1977 to 1979, and Pekka Milonoff working as co-director with Chydenius from 1979 to 1981.

The KOM Theatre began a two-year period of collaboration with the Helsinki Little Theatre in September 1981. The administration and finances of the theatres remained separate, but the theatres exchanged directors, actors, scene designers, and musicians, and they arranged for training and production projects involving members of both companies. The director Kaisa Korhonen was engaged as artistic director of the Little Theatre, and Kalle Holmberg, also a director, was appointed to head the KOM Theatre. To coordinate the artistic cooperation of the two theatres a committee was formed with Professor of the Arts Ralf Långbacka as chairman.

KIRSIKKA SIIKALA

SWEDISH THEATRE IN HELSINKI
(Svenska Teatern i Helsingfors)
Skillnaden, 00130 Helsinki 13, Finland

The Swedish Theatre in Helsinki has written into its statutes a cognomen that might strike the uninitiated as unusual. The theatre calls itself Finland's Swedish National Theatre—and thereby hangs a tale.

Finland has no court theatre tradition, since its court resided in Stockholm or St. Petersburg. From the middle of the twelfth century until 1809 Finland was a part of Sweden, later becoming a grand duchy under Russian supremacy. During the greater part of the autonomous period that followed and that was concluded with the declaration of independence in 1917, Swedish maintained its position as the language of culture and the bureaucracy, and, to a large extent, of commerce and industry as well. In the quite democratic electoral reform of 1906, the Swedish-speaking element of the population (then about one-eighth of the total) was relegated officially to a minority status. In the Constitution of 1919 the new republic declared itself a bilingual nation, where the two groups in the population were to have their cultural needs fully met on an equal basis.

From the end of the eighteenth century the Swedish-speaking bourgeois elite was large enough to make it worthwhile for touring theatre companies to travel to or through Finland. This occurred irregularly, performances being given mainly in Swedish and German. When a company did arrive, it meant business. For example, J. A. Schultz's German-speaking troupe brought on its tours to Finland during the 1820s and 1830s a repertory of six hundred plays and forty operas.

Efforts to enrich the repertory with indigenous texts in Swedish were made from the 1840s. They were met in general with great enthusiasm by the public, and they contributed support to the plans for a new and modern theatre building. The theatre would be located in Helsinki, which in 1812 was established as the capital instead of Åbo (Turku), which the tsar saw as incurably devoted to the old mother country.

In the fall of 1860 productions could begin in the city's first stone theatre building, the New Theatre, which stood in a prominent place in the center of the city. After a destructive fire some years later, renovations included a new interior—a beautiful, intimate baroque auditorium designed by Nicolas Benois, architect for the imperial theatres in St. Petersburg. This auditorium was preserved even during the thorough modernization of the theatre in the 1930s.

The Swedish Theatre considers that it was founded in 1860, when the new building was dedicated to "The True, the Good and the Beautiful; to Literature, Song and the Fatherland." In other words the new temple of Thalia was dedicated to serve many noble purposes, the Fatherland not the least of these. The national awakening in Finland was a cultural awakening, with theatre an important instrument. Even if the mainstream of nationalism was Finnish both ethnically and linguistically, the Swedish theatre, with Swedish as its stage language, also cherished patriotic ideals.

The repertory long remained the tried-and-true mixture of French and German plays, but there were intermittent efforts to cultivate indigenous drama. The most significant result came early: J. J. Wecksell's *Daniel Hjort* in 1862, a Hamlet-like story rooted firmly in Finland's history, deservedly considered the most noteworthy play in Swedish dramatic literature before Strindberg.

Not until a quarter-century later was the ensemble publicized as the Swedish Theatre. This occurred during Harald Molander's term as head of the theatre from 1886 to 1893, when he let loose a flood of the new Scandinavian literature known as the "modern breakthrough."

At intervals between 1894 and 1909 August Arppe served as chief administrator of the theatre and in other leading functions. He was the first Finn in this position. During this period there took place an extended and sometimes acrimonious debate as to what should be the theatre's linguistic norm. Traditionally on stage High Swedish, as cultivated in Sweden, had been spoken; Finno-Swedish speech had been relegated to bit parts or comic servants, as in the genres of classical drama reflecting a class society.

The concept of Swedish-language theatre performed by Finno-Swedish talent had been proposed as early as the mid-nineteenth century but then mostly as a pious hope for the future. By the turn of the century the situation changed. A company based in Åbo, the Swedish Domestic Theatre (Svenska Inhemska Teatern), had performed publicly in 1894. Qualitatively, the group left something to be desired, but a start had been made. In 1902 the Finnish-language theatre erected a national romantic granite palace in the center of Helsinki; the Finnish National Theatre had become a reality. To create a theatre for the Finno-Swedish idiom became a possibility at about the same time that many began to realize it was seriously needed.

In 1899 the Folk Theatre (Folkteatern) was established. It presented Finnish artists in a popular repertory suited for that segment of the city's Swedish-speaking audience which did not regard the ensemble's norms of articulation as a major problem. In 1907 the Folk Theatre moved its performances to the Swedish Theatre; in 1913 the two companies merged, maintaining two divisions—one using High-Swedish and the other Finno-Swedish. This arrangement was not favorable for the Finno-Swedish; to its lot fell folk plays and petit-bourgeois comedies, while the High-Swedish ensemble took charge of the more brilliant part of the repertory—literary drama and elegant comedies.

During these years as well as earlier, a number of talented actors from Sweden went through an apprenticeship at the Swedish Theatre. Two such actors were Lars Hanson and Mauritz Stiller, who before his film career directed productions and created twenty-four roles in Helsinki. After their journeyman period these performers usually moved back to Sweden.

The supporters of indigenous theatre and those endorsing High-Swedish for the stage engaged in a feud that culminated in a final clash in 1915. The result was a meager but definitive victory for indigenous principles. The Swedish Theatre had been nationalized.

One of the activists in the movement for indigenous theatre was Nicken Rönngren. He had been engaged in 1908 as an instructor in elocution at the theatre's newly founded acting school, a school that was really his handiwork. Its aim was twofold: to polish Finno-Swedish for stage use and to create general Finno-Swedish standards of pronunciation. It was a question of providing for the formation of a permanent ensemble with artistic continuity.

And continuity there was. Rönngren headed the theatre from 1919 until 1954. He became a prominent figure in Finnish theatre, and during his regime he secured the Swedish Theatre's position as a major stage. Its repertory was eclectic, as is often the case with theatres striving to function as major national stages. As a result of traditions from the High-Swedish period, as well as the rather upper-middle-class profile of its board of directors, a sophisticated comedy style has been one of the theatre's distinguishing features. The classical tradition—native, Swedish, and foreign—has also been an integral part of the theatre's endeavors. During the greater part of its existence and most recently in the 1960s, the theatre was also one of the nation's most important musical stages.

Having its own drama school has significantly influenced the theatre's artistic level and continuity; the majority of its foremost artists have been products of this training program. (Today training of Swedish-speaking actors takes place at Finland's Theatre Academy.) One of the Swedish Theatre's most enduring popular favorites, Nanny Westerlund, was first seen in student performances in 1911. Along with May Pihlgren, who joined the theatre in 1924 and is highly regarded for her many refined poetical characterizations, Westerlund was still performing in 1981 in Joseph Kesselring's *Arsenic and Old Lace*. Eric Lindström has been the foremost artist in the history of the Swedish Theatre. From 1926 to 1972 he created a number of the most demanding roles in world drama. Because of his Hamlet at Kronborg in 1947 and other characterizations, he came to be considered one of the most prominent Scandinavian actors.

Rönngren was succeeded as head of the theatre in 1954 by the actor Runar Schauman, who was in turn succeeded in 1963 by Carl Öhman, who still leads the theatre. Öhman has been active in national and Scandinavian theatre politics. Among the theatre's artistic leaders should be mentioned the director Ralf Långbacka (1965–1967) and director-author Bengt Ahlfors (1975–1979). Lars Svedberg, a director and actor, served as artistic director from 1980 to 1982, being succeeded in the fall of 1982 by Jack Witikka.

With close to one hundred employees, the Swedish Theatre is the fourth in size among the country's theatres. Subsidies in 1981 consisted of state support for 40 percent and municipal support for 34 percent of the theatre's income.

In addition to its main stage, the Swedish Theatre has a small, flexible foyerstage which is used for experimentation. The theatre also tours to some extent in the Swedish-speaking region around Helsinki. Tours to other Nordic countries have long been on the theatre's agenda. This kind of interaction has in recent years been complemented by the engagement of guest directors from the Finnish-language theatre. These contacts have enhanced and diversified the theatre's artistic identity.

CLAS ZILLIACUS
(Translated by Carla Waal)

TAMPERE WORKERS' THEATRE
(Tampereen Työväen Teatteri)
Keskustori 12
33100 Tampere 10, Finland

The Tampere Workers' Theatre deserves recognition as a symbol of the workers' theatre movement in Finland as well as for its high artistic standards.

In the mid-nineteenth century the labor movement in Finland was motivated by a desire for progress and education. Entertainment committees planned activities such as reading, choral singing, and play production. By the turn of the century some dramatic societies evolved into workers' theatres, the one in Helsinki being established in 1899 and the one in Tampere in 1901. For many years the permanent workers' theatres operated primarily on an amateur basis, with perhaps one director and a few actors and actresses being engaged permanently, while the amateurs received training and experience by working on productions. By 1919 there were 137 active dramatic societies affiliated with various labor associations, and in 1920 a Union of Workers' Theatres was established with headquarters in Tampere.

By the 1920s actors at workers' theatres were usually employed on a professional basis. During the 1930s the tendency was for workers' theatres to merge with bourgeois theatres in their districts. Some of the workers resisted this trend, since it seemed to counteract their educational goals. There were practical and financial reasons for the mergers, and the number of workers' theatres was gradually reduced. In the 1940s many theatres were brought under municipal control. Because some workers' theatres stopped operating and many were merged with other theatres, the number of workers' theatres decreased until finally the Tampere Workers' Theatre stands alone as the last professional workers' theatre in Finland.

The history of the Tampere Workers' Theatre is typical of the movement. In 1886 the Tampere Workers' Association was founded and by 1890 had its own building. Various trades—tailors, shoemakers, machine and metal workers, for example—had their own dramatic societies. Some of the actors and actresses who performed with these societies eventually worked in the Tampere Workers' Theatre after its founding in 1901. The first performance was on September 27 of that year; the play was *Anna Liisa* by Minna Canth.

The year 1905 was a turning point in the history of Finnish theatre and of the labor movement. Just before a general strike, on October 28, the workers' association took over the theatre and proclaimed its constitution; just after the strike, on November 11, a new building was inaugurated. Heikki Tiitola had designed the theatre in 1900, but performances were given on a tiny stage of an old wooden building until the auditorium and stage were ready in 1905. That was also the year the actress Tilda Vuori joined the staff of the theatre; within a year she became its director. Despite the difficulties of producing plays when workers had only a few hours in the evening to rehearse, Tilda Vuori and her colleagues were courageous and enthusiastic. Her term as head of the theatre lasted until 1917, when the civil war closed the theatre and dispersed the staff.

In April 1919 Kosti Elo became the next director of the theatre, but operations did not begin until fall. In 1920 many of the amateurs gave up their other jobs and became full-time actors, and were joined by some professional actors brought in from elsewhere. A new wing, including workshops and dressing rooms, was put into use in 1924. During Kosti Elo's term of leadership, which lasted until

1943, the repertory was challenging and varied. He was noted as an interpreter of expressionist plays.

Plays by Finnish dramatists were stressed by the next head of the theatre, Eino Salmelainen, an art critic and theatre director. Salmelainen's innovative staging methods and choice of repertory led to even greater artistic achievements.

Eugen Terttula was next to head the theatre, beginning in 1964. During this time the Cellar Theatre was opened, in space formerly used by the Workers' Association for wrestling. An intimate theatre with 118 seats, the space has proved flexible and popular. During Terttula's term, productions of the plays of Bertolt Brecht won recognition.

Kai Savola, a dramaturge, was appointed to head the theatre in 1968. He chose interesting plays so appealing to the public that impressive attendance records were set.

In 1973 the actor Lasse Pöysti became artistic director, a position he was to hold until January 1981. Supported by an excellent artistic and technical staff, he led an enlargement of the facilities in 1976. This involved restoring the original shape of the auditorium and providing extra space at the sides of the stage. He also led the celebration of the Tampere Workers' Theatre's seventy-fifth anniversary. To observe that milestone Pöysti played Gert in Strindberg's *Master Olof* and dramatized, with the author Väinö Linna, Part Three of the novel *Here Under the Northern Star*. Lasse Pöysti paid tribute to the spirit of past generations of theatre artists, while working to present a vital repertory that would preserve close ties with the working class by reflecting their situation.

The history and problems of the working class have always been foremost concerns of the Tampere Workers' Theatre, but that interest has not limited the variety of its offerings. At first there were not many plays available conveying working-class ideology. From 1901 to 1917 entertainment dominated the playbill with musical dramas, German farces, and Finnish folklore in the spotlight. More compatible with the philosophy of the theatre were productions of *Children of Destiny* by Minna Canth and Tolstoy's *The Living Corpse* and *Resurrection*.

In the 1920s farces and operettas were frequently played, but this period became known as "the reformation" because workers' theatres began performing expressionist plays, such as Georg Kaiser's *Gas* and Ernst Toller's *The Machine Wreckers*. An emphasis on popular appeal in the late twenties gradually gave way to more challenging choices and a larger proportion of serious plays by the mid-thirties. Among the popular plays in that decade were *The Women of Niskavuori* and *Burning Country* by Hella Wuolijoki; the theatre even became known as "The Wuolijoki Theatre." Although some professional theatres ceased functioning after war broke out in 1939, the Tampere Workers' Theatre went on uninterrupted.

One of the most popular foreign playwrights in the 1950s was Jean Anouilh. Bertolt Brecht was represented by *Mother Courage* and Albert Camus by *Les Justes*. Finnish dramatists included Mika Waltari, Kyllikki Mäntylä, and Leena Härmä. The theatre reached another turning point by 1961, when efforts were channeled toward more serious plays with social relevance. Brecht's *The Three-penny Opera* (1960), *The Good Woman of Setzuan* (1961), and *The Caucasian Chalk Circle* (1962) were representative of the more challenging repertory. In 1961 the most important event was a dramatization of Part Two of *Here Under the Northern Star* by Linna. The avant-garde and the theatre of the absurd had a place throughout the 1960s, as did Finnish drama such as the first production in the Cellar Theatre, *New Year's Night* by Eeva-Liisa Manner. *Burnt Orange* by Manner was one of the most popular works in the repertory for years.

Classics of the international stage were done in the 1970s, such as John Millington Synge's *The Playboy of the Western World*, Georg Büchner's *Woyzeck*, and Shakespeare's *The Tempest*. Plays by Carlo Goldoni, Nikolai Gogol, Maxim Gorky, and Federico García Lorca were also performed. One of the theatre's greatest successes was Teuvo Pakkala's adaptation of *The Lumberjacks*, which met the demand for interesting plays based on folklore. During the seventies a number of plays were staged depicting the working class, including Arnold Wesker's *The Wedding Feast* and Raimo J. Kinnunen's *Violent Blood*. The history of the labor movement in Finland and the life of one working-class family were seen in the very successful *Rantanen and Family* by Hella Wuolijoki and Mikko Majanlahti. The range and diversity of the repertory during the 1970s are evidence of the theatre's vigor and artistry.

There are some unanswered questions about the future of the Tampere Workers' Theatre. Plans for a new building are ready, but details of financing remain to be worked out. Once a cooperative plan involving the national government, the city of Tampere, and the theatre itself is underway, completion of the new structure will require about three years. A competition for a new design was won by Marjatta and Martti Jaatinen. All seats will have equally good sight lines, and the stage will be adaptable to five different shapes—by moving wagons in the auditorium, platforms, wings, and a sliding floor, and by raising or lowering sections of the stage floor hydraulically. During the 1980–1981 season the staff of the theatre included seventy persons, of whom twenty-nine formed the acting company. When new facilities are completed, plans are to increase the acting company to forty, out of a permanent staff of 103 and approximately twenty-four part-time employees, led by Mikko Majanlahti, who became artistic director in 1981.

The future status of the theatre also awaits a decision. At present both this theatre and the Tampere Theatre operate independently, receiving the same appropriation from the municipality and offering stimulating competition for each other. It has been proposed that when the new building is completed, the Tampere Workers' Theatre might be made a state theatre with full government support and a status resembling that of the National Theatre in Helsinki. The Tampere Workers' Theatre would aim to remain true to the cultural tradition of the workers' movement, which is its heritage from the past, while realizing the potential of theatre art to contribute to social progress, which is the hope of the future.

CARLA WAAL

Iceland

INTRODUCTION

Icelandic drama and theatre are little known outside the boundaries of the isolated volcanic island, but an impressively large number of the Icelandic people find their way to the theatre each season.

Icelandic drama and theatre, according to historian and director Sveinn Einarsson, may have its roots in pagan rituals, folk dances, and games at the annual national assembly. In the early eighteenth century there was a dramatic celebration at the Cathedral School of Skálholt, and later Sigurdur Pétursson wrote plays comparable to those of Ludvig Holberg and Molière for student performances. Students were also on stage at the Grammar School in Reykjavik, doing Icelandic plays in the second half of the nineteenth century, as part of the national movement toward cultural independence. Einarsson notes three important dates in the history of Icelandic theatre: 1851, the first public performance in Icelandic with tickets sold; 1897, the founding of the Reykjavik Theatre Company; and 1950, the opening of the National Theatre.

Amateur theatre not only formed the basis of today's professionalism, but it is still flourishing. Many amateur groups perform plays, usually led by a professional guest director. One such amateur club, in Akureyri, has become a professional theatre.

Since the performances by Danish actors in the nineteenth century, foreign influence has been important. Icelandic dramatists and theatre artists have brought back ideas and craftsmanship from travel and study abroad. Plays by foreign dramatists have been prominent in the repertory; of these, Ibsen has been especially popular. Icelandic drama of great variety has also been performed—some based on history and folklore, and others on current political issues. Although Halldór Laxness, a Nobel Prize winner in 1955, stands out as the most honored Icelandic author, there have been many other interesting native dramatists. In fact, the dominant characteristic of the past twenty years in Icelandic theatre has been the emphasis on and growing popularity of new Icelandic drama.

CARLA WAAL

NATIONAL THEATRE OF ICELAND
(Thjódleikhúsid)
Hverfisgötu 19, 101 Reykjavik, Iceland

The National Theatre of Iceland was founded in 1950, but its history can be traced much further back. The idea of a national theatre was proposed by the painter and theatre champion Sigurdur Gudmundsson in the 1860s. To observe the thirtieth anniversary of the theatre in 1980, a play by Gudmundsson was produced. Actually, the author left *The Shepherdess and the Outlaws* unfinished at the time of his premature death in 1874. It was edited and completed by the novelist-essayist-playwright Thorgeir Thorgeirsson, directed by Thórhildur Thorleifsdóttir, and designed by Sigurjón Jóhansson. Well received by the public, *The Shepherdess and the Outlaws* is a significant addition to the classical heritage of Icelandic drama.

Gudmundsson influenced the playwright Indridi Einarsson, who in 1907 launched a campaign for a national theatre. Support for the idea grew until, in 1922, the Icelandic Parliament passed a bill authorizing the establishment of a national theatre. Building and operating costs were to be guaranteed by the revenue from a special entertainment tax; however, that money was needed for other purposes during the 1930s. In 1945 work was resumed on the theatre, which had been designed by Gudjón Samúelsson. Gudlaugur Rósinkranz was appointed as the first general manager of the theatre.

The program to inaugurate the theatre on April 20, 1950, began with Indridi Einarsson's *New Year's Eve* (1871), followed by Jóhann Sigurjónsson's *Eyvind of the Mountains* (1911) and a dramatization of a Halldór Laxness novel, *The Iceland Bell*. True to its mission, the National Theatre has frequently revived the "classics" of the Icelandic stage and has produced many new plays by Icelandic dramatists. Among the classics in the repertory have been the plays of Sigurdur Pétursson, Matthias Jochumsson, Indridi Einarsson, Einar H. Kvaran, Gudmundur Kamban, Jóhann Sigurjónsson, and Davíd Stefánsson.

The 1979–1980 season was somewhat dominated by the success of *The Shepherdess and the Outlaws* and another Icelandic play, *A Brief Respite*. Written by Gudmundur Steinsson, *A Brief Respite* ran throughout the season, totaling eighty performances and thus becoming the longest running Icelandic play in the history of the Icelandic theatre. Only *Fiddler On the Roof* had enjoyed a longer run, having been performed ninety-two times during the 1968–1969 and 1969–1970 seasons. *A Brief Respite*, directed by Stefán Baldursson and designed by Thórunn S. Thorgrímsdóttir, won international acclaim. Critics in Scandinavia praised it, as did critics from all over the world when it was performed at the

International Theatre Institute Festival in Belgrade, Yugoslavia. The National Theatre also toured the production to Finland, Sweden, Denmark, and Germany.

Previously, another production that won international acclaim was *The Man* (*Inuk*), created by Haraldur Olafsson and a group of actors in 1974. Showing both the ancient life of Eskimos and how modern civilization affects them, *The Man* was developed with the help of an anthropologist and the group's own observations on a trip to Greenland. Dressed in white anoraks, the five actors performed old mimes, sang to the accompaniment of drums, and showed scenes of hunting and the family, in a form that was part ritual and part entertainment. Its universality was evident in its acceptance on the stages of twenty foreign countries.

The diversity of the theatre's repertory is illustrated by other productions from the 1979–1980 season. Two other Icelandic plays were *What Did the Angels Say?* by the poet Nína Björk Árnadóttir, and *Within a Safe City*, the last play from the pen of Jökull Jakobsson, whose death in 1978 at the age of forty-five was a major loss for Icelandic theatre. *What Did the Angels Say?* was directed by Stefán Baldursson and *Within a Safe City* by Sveinn Einarsson, who has been head of the theatre since 1972. In addition to Icelandic works, the theatre presented *Summerfolk* by Maxim Gorky, the opera *Orfeus and Eurydice* by Gluck (directed by Kenneth Tillson and designed by Alistair Powell), and a production done in Kabuki fashion. *Cherry Blossoms on Northern Mountain*, which presented two traditional Japanese Kabuki plays, was a surprise hit; it was directed and designed by Haukur J. Gunnarsson.

On the average there are fifteen new productions each season, all done in Icelandic. Plays run in repertory so that there is usually a choice of five to seven different productions at a time. Not all the performances are done in Reykjavik. Every year plays are taken to many different parts of Iceland, and in recent years some plays have had their premiere outside of Reykjavik. In addition to tours of the major productions, a number of smaller productions have been done in schools and other institutions in and around Reykjavik, as group projects independent of the main company.

The permanent company consists of thirty-two actors, two directors, and two designers. The number of freelance actors, directors, designers, singers, and dancers engaged by the theatre varies from season to season but averages around forty.

There is great emphasis on presenting theatre for children. Each year there is a special children's play at the National Theatre, sometimes with children in the cast, sometimes developed in rehearsal with the author. Lower admission prices are usually charged for these productions, and all the children in Reykjavik have the opportunity to see them. In 1979–1980 the children's play was *The Innocents*, written by Gudrún Helgadóttir, directed by Brynja Benediktsdóttir, and designed by Gylfi Gíslason. In *The Innocents*, children's parts were played by adults, and vice versa.

Although the emphasis is on drama, the National Theatre also produces operas, operettas, and musicals. *Rigoletto*, done in 1951, was the first operatic production, and since then there have been one or two operas or musicals per year. An opera company was founded in 1983 to perform at another theatre, but the National Theatre is known for its successful productions of, for example, *Carmen* and the world premiere of Jón Ásgeirsson's comic opera *The Lay of Thrym*.

Dance has always been part of the National's offerings, and in 1952 the theatre opened its own ballet school. In 1973 the Icelandic Dance Company was formed. Although it has only ten members, with the help of guest performers and pupils from the school it has had success in staging classics like *Coppelia* and *The Nutcracker* and in establishing its identity. The first ballet director of the company was Alan Carter; other choreographers have been Ingibjörg Björnsdóttir, Unnur Gudjónsdóttir, and Marjo Kuusela.

Being able to choose from the varied repertory of both the Reykjavik Theatre Company and the National Theatre, theatregoers of all social classes come in record numbers, some using season tickets. At the National Theatre they can see productions on the main stage or at the "Theatre Downstairs," a space that is used as a restaurant and for avant-garde and cabaret programs. The peak year at the National Theatre was 1975–1976 when there were 394 performances and attendance was 134,090. During the 1980–1981 season the attendance was 85,427, the lowest in years. Attendance began rising again significantly during the 1981–1982 season.

The schedule for the 1980–1981 season included productions of *Night and Day* by Tom Stoppard, *Death of a Salesman* by Arthur Miller, *La Bohème* by Giacomo Puccini, a new full-length Icelandic ballet choreographed by Jochen Ulrich, *Oliver Twist* in a new dramatization by Árni Ibsen, *Tracks in the Snows of Time* by Icelander Valgardur Egilsson, the musical *Strider*, plus works by Pavel Kohout, Václav Havel, and James Saunders. The 1981–1982 repertory included *Hotel Paradiso* by Georges Feydeau, *Tales from the Vienna Woods* by Odön von Horváth, *Amadeus* by Peter Shaffer, *The Love Story of the Century* by Märta Tikkanen, and works by Icelandic authors Halldór Laxness, Bríet Hédinsdóttir, and Steinunn Jóhannesdóttir. There have been a number of guest troupes in recent years as well, such as the Swedish Theatre of Helsinki, the Théâtre de Chapeau Rouge of Avignon, and the Peking Opera Troupe of Wuhan.

ÁRNI IBSEN and
CARLA WAAL

REYKJAVIK THEATRE COMPANY
(Leikfélag Reykjavíkur)
Idno, Vonarstræti 3, P. O. Box 208
121 Reykjavik, Iceland

The Reykjavik Theatre Company (RTC) has operated continuously ever since its founding on January 11, 1897, first as the capital's only stage and after 1950 as the nation's second largest theatre. Its management has always been structured democratically, so that in recent discussions in Scandinavia about greater participation in management by actors and other personnel, the organization of this company has been regarded as a model. To become a member of the company one must work as an actor or on the artistic staff for at least two years. As a member one is entitled to vote on artistic and financial matters at the company's annual general meeting. The executive committee, with three members, is elected at the general meeting; a member can remain on the committee no longer than three years. This committee appoints the artistic director, with the appointment first approved at a general meeting. The artistic director then appoints a manager, and the two of them are responsible for the day-by-day management of the theatre. The repertory is chosen by a board of directors consisting of the company's executive committee, the artistic director, and a representative of the city council. In the near future the RTC's work will continue at the new Reykjavik City Theatre. The administration is set up so that a majority of the board of directors will always consist of representatives from the theatre's personnel, but this means that the company is held responsible not just for the theatre's artistic profile but for its finances as well.

In cooperation with representatives from various craft unions, a group of fourteen actors founded the Reykjavik Theatre Company in 1897. They were not trained actors but experienced amateurs who eventually succeeded in establishing quite a strong ensemble under the leadership of the authors Indridi Einarsson and Einar H. Kvaran. The early productions were usually Danish vaudevilles, but as time went by in the first decade these were replaced by plays by such authors as Henrik Ibsen, Bjørnstjerne Bjørnson, Ludvig Holberg, Molière, Alexandre Dumas, Friedrich Schiller, and later George Bernard Shaw. After a period of experimentation the theatre was receptive to new Icelandic drama; the years 1907–1920 are recognized as the Icelandic period in the theatre's history. The plays of Indridi Einarsson, Einar H. Kvaran, and Matthías Jochumsson are considered minor classics. It was not until Jóhann Sigurjónsson wrote his plays that Icelandic drama achieved some recognition beyond Iceland. His most famous play, *Eyvind of the Mountains*, had its world premiere in 1911, and *The Wish* three years later, both directed by Jens B. Waage. Sigurjónsson used material from Icelandic folk sagas for his plays. Gudmundur Kamban, another great dramatist, wrote *We Murderers*, produced in 1920, the first successful play in the realistic-bourgeois genre in Icelandic literature.

After 1924 the theatre's activity was marked by new impulses from abroad. Indridi Waage, a director inspired by Max Reinhardt, introduced authors like August Strindberg, John Galsworthy, Luigi Pirandello, and Shakespeare, and directed successful dramatizations of Icelandic novels. Haraldur Björnsson and Lárus Pálsson, both educated in Copenhagen, along with Indridi Waage, worked as leading directors and actors in the 1940s. Under their leadership the ensemble presented a series of fine productions, both classics and works by young authors who were concerned about postwar problems. In this period Pálsson directed such plays as *Volpone, The Inspector General*, and *The Merchant of Venice*, and himself played Peer Gynt and Hamlet, but the theatre's greatest success was his production of Davíd Stefánsson's *The Golden Gate* in 1941, which the theatre did on tour in Finland right after the close of World War II.

When the National Theatre of Iceland opened in 1950, most of the Reykjavik Theatre Company's ensemble went to the new theatre. Many believed that this meant the end of the RTC's function. Luckily, there was some opposition by theatre historian Lárus Sigurbjörnsson and others. With the actors Thorsteinn Ö. Stephensen and Brynjólfur Jóhannesson of the older generation and a group of young and enthusiastic actors, Sigurbjörnsson believed that RTC could offer the National Theatre some healthy competition. This proved to be true. RTC's choice of plays and its productions, done mostly by the Danish-born director Gunnar R. Hansen, were encouraged by both critics and public. After the war American and English plays were given at the theatre; its productions of *The Glass Menagerie* and *All My Sons* were great successes. The same was true of the Chinese drama *Pi-pa-ki* and Gudmundur Kamban's *Marble* (1950). The Icelandic theatre audience was unacquainted with the theatre of the absurd until RTC produced Samuel Beckett's *Waiting for Godot* and plays by Eugene Ionesco in 1960.

The theatre's maturity appeared in full bloom in Gísli Halldórsson's production of Jökull Jakobsson's *Hard A-Port* in 1962, one of the greatest successes in Icelandic theatre history and the beginning of a new epoch in RTC's work. Before 1962 the theatre had introduced authors like Halldór Laxness, Jónas Árnason, and Agnar Thórdarson, but not until *Hard A-Port* was there talk of the intimate cooperation between authors and theatre people which since then has characterized RTC. This tendency was further strengthened by the Artistic Director Sveinn Einarsson. Jakobsson wrote a series of plays that were actually completed at rehearsal (*Dominoes* [1971–1972] and *Candle Glimmer*), and the theatre created dramatizations of some of Laxness' novels (*Christianity at the Glacier* and *The Atomic Station* [1971–1972]) that proved to be extremely popular. Something similar may be said of Árnason's plays of a later date—*You Remember Jörund* and *Shield Rock*. The latter is the theatre's greatest popular success to date. After having won first prize in a competition sponsored by the RTC in connection with its seventy-fifth anniversary, Birgir Sigurdsson wrote three significant plays, all of which had their premieres at this theatre—*Peter and Runa* (1973), *The Seal Has Man's Eyes* (1974), and *Rose, the Poet* (1977). The theatre introduced many other new authors in the 1970s, of whom Kjartan Ragnarsson is considered one of the most promising. An actor in the company, he has directed his own plays *The Workshop* (1975) and *The Happy Quiverful* (1977), as well as his dramatization of Thórbergur Thórdarson's autobiographical novel *The Genius* (1979–1980), which is without doubt one of the theatre's most important productions in recent years.

Besides offering both direct and indirect encouragement to Icelandic authors to write for the theatre, the RTC is known for its ensemble art, for members of the group are trained to work closely together. Since 1960 Gísli Halldórsson, Jón Sigurbjörnsson, Helgi Skúlason, and Sveinn Einarsson have been responsible for most productions, but lately the group has been expanded with directors like Gudrún Ásmundsdóttir, Pétur Einarsson, Steindór Hjörleifsson, and Thorsteinn Gunnarsson. The theatre's leading designer has been Steinthór Sigurdsson.

Radical changes in the theatre's form of administration and management have occurred since 1963 when the first artistic director, Sveinn Einarsson, was named. He was entrusted with the task of reorganizing the theatre's internal structure so that somewhat later permanent positions could be offered to a group of actors. Vigdís Finnbogadóttir succeeded Einarsson in 1972. In September 1980 Stefán Baldursson and Thorsteinn Gunnarsson were appointed co-artistic directors. In addition to providing artistic leadership, they participate in production work. In 1983 Baldursson became the sole artistic director. Gudmundur Pálsson was the manager for years, succeeded in 1975 by Tómas Zoëga.

In 1980–1981 there were thirty-four actors, half of whom were given permanent appointments; four musicians; and forty-two other employees, of whom eighteen have permanent positions. Approximately 52 percent of the theatre's expenses are covered by public subsidy, most of which comes from the city.

Each year the Reykjavik Theatre Company schedules at least seven new productions in repertory besides several from the previous season. The emphasis is on Icelandic drama, contemporary plays from abroad, and classics. Outstanding productions of the classics in the 1970s include *The Wild Duck, The Dance of Death, The Sea Gull, The Cherry Orchard*, and *Macbeth*. There have been productions of plays by authors like Edward Bond, Sean O'Casey, Edward Albee, Sławomir Mrożnek, Lillian Hellman, Alan Ayckbourn, and Fernando Arrabal, and musical productions of such different works as *Jesus Christ Superstar* and *L'Histoire du Soldat*. In 1980–1981 the theatre performed S. L. Coburn's *The Gin Game*, Sam Shepard's *Buried Child, The Taming of the Shrew*, a new Icelandic rock musical called *Grettir*, Kjartan Ragnarsson's *The Genius*, and a children's play done in the schools.

If we consider Icelandic theatre life as a whole, the RTC plays a major role. In 1979–1980 there were 230 performances for sixty thousand patrons. Working conditions are crowded. Performances are still given in a building from 1897 with only 230 seats; it is necessary to rent a movie theatre with about 800 seats for larger productions. Vigdís Finnbogadóttir convinced the city government that a new theatre building was of the utmost importance for the theatre's continued work. In 1976 construction began on the new building, to be financed jointly by the RTC and the city. The new Reykjavik City Theatre should be completed in 1986; it will provide the setting for the RTC's future efforts.

STEFÁN BALDURSSON and
THORSTEINN GUNNARSSON
(Translated by Carla Waal)

Norway

INTRODUCTION

The sagas tell of entertainment provided to Viking audiences by the Norse equivalent of the *jongleurs*, and later records provide evidence of church drama featuring the Three Wise Men and of plays coached by schoolmasters. Since Norway never had a court theatre, its dramatic entertainment was provided by touring companies from Germany and Denmark in the seventeenth century, and from Sweden and Denmark in the nineteenth century, according to theatre historian and archivist Øyvind Anker. From about 1780 to 1830 amateur dramatic societies flourished, providing exclusive entertainment for upper class audiences, often featuring talented actors and beautiful costumes. An early effort to run a truly Norwegian theatre was made by the entrepreneur Johan Peter Strömberg, when he opened his theatre in January 1827. Although he did not last long as manager, the theatre he started evolved into the Christiania Theatre, which functioned until the National Theatre opened at the end of the century.

Ludvig Holberg's interest in drama was nurtured during his childhood and youth in Norway. Not only Holberg, but also many other Norwegian poets and playwrights found their way to Copenhagen for their education and to pursue a career. Theatre in Norway in the nineteenth century struggled vigorously to free itself from the dominance of the Danish language and Danish performers. The national romantic movement inspired the founding of the Norwegian Theatre in Bergen in 1850, and thus the career of the young stage manager and playwright Henrik Ibsen was launched. Ibsen contributed a further chapter to theatre history with his management of the Christiania Norwegian Theatre from 1857 to 1862. The capable theatre manager, critic, dramatist, and poet Bjørnstjerne Bjørnson also began his theatrical career in Bergen. Among Norway's most outstanding theatre artists, his son Bjørn Bjørnson deserves recognition for bringing the methods of modern directing from the continent to Norway as well as for leading the drive to found the National Theatre.

Although Norwegian theatre has always paid homage, through frequent productions, to its master dramatists—Holberg, Bjørnson, and Ibsen—there has been richly varied drama written by a new generation of dramatists: Jens Bjørneboe, Georg Johannesen, Finn Carling, Peder W. Cappelen, Tor Åge Bringsværd, Edvard Hoem, Klaus Hagerup, Arne Skouen, Bjørg Vik, and others. Along with the fresh approaches and material used by these dramatists, there has been a range of production styles. Audiences have seen not only the realistic mode associated with Ibsen's later plays, but also current political issues treated boldly, new approaches to the classics, and in general a reemphasis on theatricality. Some of the new drama and experimental production styles have been seen on the studio stages. This trend has been exemplified at all the major theatres, where a second stage allows for intimate or provocative productions and tends to attract a new and younger audience. There are also independent groups, such as the Grenland Friteater of Porsgrunn, which work with original material and new performance modes reflecting international influences.

One manifestation of cultural policy is the effort to reach new audiences, including children and teenagers, partly by attracting new social groups to established theatres, partly by bringing theatre to where people work and live. In Oslo, for example, the Torshov Company of the National Theatre performs in a former library for its working-class neighbors. Bringing theatre to the people may require an arduous journey by bus or boat. The State Traveling Theatre, with a full-time company of forty, has a long tradition of forging ahead through all types of weather. The regional Sogn and Fjordane Theatre in Førde, led by Anne Gullestad, brings shows to remote communities, sometimes giving performances on a boat.

A trend typical of Norwegian theatre in the 1970s and early 1980s was toward more democratic decision-making processes. Whether members of a theatre company, the board of directors, or the artistic director should determine policy and decide personnel matters has been an issue of lively debate and legal challenge, as are the implications for the performing arts of the regulations established in the Act on Worker Protection and Working Environment (1977). Hålogaland Regional Theatre in North Norway has been a prime example of collective management and of creating drama that reflects the life and meets the needs of the people of its region. Actually, the desire of all the regional companies, including those at Førde, Molde, Skien, and Mo i Rana, is to fulfill a unique mission for their area of this long and rugged land. The high costs of touring threaten the fulfillment of their mission, just as financial considerations affect artistic decisions at all theatres that receive financing from national and local budgets and yet must consider the box office appeal of their repertory.

The trend toward commercialism, the role of unions, the cultural policy of the Ministry of Education and Culture, trends in the public's use of leisure time, and artistic innovations are the factors that will determine the survival and vitality of Norwegian theatre.

CARLA WAAL

NATIONAL STAGE
(Den Nationale Scene)
Engen 1, P. O. Box 78
5001 Bergen, Norway

The National Stage in Bergen opened under its original name of the Norwegian Theatre on January 2, 1850, thanks to the initiative of the famous violinist Ole Bull (1810–1880). This was the first completely Norwegian theatre, Norway's true "mother stage." Ole Bull engaged Henrik Ibsen (1828–1906) as the theatre's full-time stage manager and literary consultant. Ibsen was also expected to write a new play for the theatre every year. The theatre is significant both artistically and nationalistically. It fostered an impressive succession of Norwegian actors, including the talented Johannes Brun and Lucie Wolf; it stimulated Norwegian drama, including playwrights like Ibsen and Bjørnson; it established Norwegian as a natural stage language, as Danish had been previously.

After a brief period of inactivity from 1863 to 1876, the theatre—renamed the National Stage—has been active without interruption for more than a hundred years. Most of the great Norwegian actors and actresses made their debut on this stage—Bernt Johannessen, Sofie Reimers, Johanne Dybwad, Egil Eide, Halfdan Christensen, Stub Wiberg, and Ingolf Schanche. Under the leadership of Gunnar Heiberg (1857–1929) from 1884 to 1888 and Hans Jacob Nilsen (1896–1957) from 1934–1939, the theatre won national and international recognition for its bold experiments and vigorous artistic achievement. The author and playwright Nordahl Grieg was closely associated with the theatre in the years 1934–1939, and wrote—to some extent on commission—several important plays taking a clear stand against advancing Nazism and antihumanism. German, Czechoslovakian, Swedish, and other contemporary drama expressing opposition to political oppression and dictatorship also left their mark on the theatre in this period, something that echoed over all of Scandinavia.

Originally the theatre operated in a structure built around 1800—the country's first true theatre building. In 1909, the building housing the National Stage was constructed on a hill in the center of the city. It was destroyed during a bombing raid in 1944. Since then the building has been enlarged and modernized several times in the 1960s and 1970s, and in 1982 an extra playing space with 250 seats was added. There are already a main stage with 470 seats and the "Little Stage" with 100 seats. Attendance at the theatre varied in the 1970s from about 150,000 to 257,000 per year. Included in these figures is an average attendance of approximately 50,000 at children's plays.

The theatre usually presents fifteen productions per year with 450 to 500 performances, including some given on tour away from Bergen. In 1979 the permanently employed personnel totaled 131, of whom 34 were in the acting ensemble. The head of the theatre from 1976 to 1982 was Sven Henning. In 1982 Kjetil Bang-Hansen became artistic director of the National Stage, followed by Tom Remlov in 1986.

Since 1975 the theatre has been owned cooperatively by the national government, the district of Hordaland, and the city of Bergen. These agencies also
cover the theatre's major operating expenses in the proportion of 60 percent, 27
percent, and 13 percent. In 1980 the total expenses were 22,712,690 Norwegian
crowns, of which public subsidies paid 19,777,000 crowns. Attendance at the
theatre in recent years has represented slightly less than 15 percent of the total
attendance at theatres throughout Norway. Ticket prices are kept low to encourage
the public to attend more frequently. Sociological studies still indicate that those
who attend the theatre do not represent a balanced cross-section of the population;
the major portion of the audience is the better educated and more prosperous
segment of society.

In the 1960s there were in-depth sociological investigations of the theatre's
audience, along with economic studies of its finances. The history of the theatre
has also been studied; three volumes have been published covering the period
1876–1976, including a complete overview of the repertory. The history of Ole
Bull's theatre from 1850 to 1863 is also described in several books.

The National Stage has supported the establishment of a theatre museum and
archive, both of which are now affiliated with the Theatre Institute of the University of Bergen, but as a separate entity. The theatre museum was opened in
its new, specially designed facilities in May 1980, by His Majesty King Olav.
In its valuable collection the museum has many interesting items of Henrik
Ibsen's, including two of his paintings.

Ibsen was the Norwegian dramatist most often performed during the years
1876–1976, with 20 different plays, 107 productions, and 1,621 performances.
Next came Ludvig Holberg with 15 plays, 55 productions, and 1,150 performances. And third was Bjørnstjerne Bjørnson with 23 plays, 86 different productions, and 750 performances. A significant number of the productions at the
National Stage each year—about 30 percent—are still Norwegian plays.

The repertory of the Little Stage consists primarily of modern plays, experimental pieces, absurdist theatre, and new Norwegian and foreign plays. The
audience attracted to these offerings tends to be university students and other
young people.

ARNLJOT STRØMME SVENDSEN
(Translated by Carla Waal)

NATIONAL THEATRE
(Nationaltheatret)
Stortingsgaten 15
Oslo 1, Norway

The National Theatre, built in 1899 with a stage and architecture in keeping
with the bourgeois traditions of the nineteenth century, is Norway's largest
theatre. In its present form the theatre has three permanent stages: the main

stage, an intimate theatre in the original building, and the theatre at Torshov, which is a small, modern theatre built in a suburb in the autumn of 1977.

The theatre tours to the provinces in cooperation with the State Touring Theatre (Riksteatret). A visiting ensemble started in 1969 performs in schools, clubs, and other locales in and around Oslo.

In every way the National Theatre is in a transitional phase. The main stage suffered severe damage in a fire in October, 1980. The renovated stage has more up-to-date and efficient equipment and, above all, more space in the wings, thus ensuring greater technical potential.

The intimate "upstairs" stage, called the Amfiscenen, formerly a mini-theatre seating 130 on three sides, opened on September 1, 1980, as a circular amphi-theatre accommodating 230.

The opening season in the renovated Amfiscenen demonstrated the flexibility and potential of the new playing space with four successful productions in different genres: Ibsen's *Love's Comedy* in the guise of a newly composed musical, *Antigone* by Sophocles, *Protest/Attest* by the Czech authors Pavel Ko-hout and Václac Havel, and Brecht's *Fear and Misery in the Third Reich*.

The National Theatre acquired a new artistic director, Toralv Maurstad, upon the retirement in the summer of 1978 of Arild Brinchmann after a term of eleven years. Both have a well-established reputation in the Norwegian theatre world, Brinchmann as a director for stage and television and as head of the TV-theatre where he pursued a radical policy in the choice of repertory, and Maurstad as an actor, director, and head of the Oslo New Theatre for eleven years. Kjetil Bang-Hansen was chosen to take Maurstad's place as head of the theatre in 1986.

Over the years the National Theatre has been led by a number of eminent personalities. The first of these, and the moving force in the project to build the theatre, was Bjørn Bjørnson, son of the poet and author Bjørnstjerne Bjørnson. Bjørn Bjørnson was himself an actor, having in his younger days studied at the theatre of the Duke of Saxe-Meiningen. He became one of Norway's great theatre personalities, as actor, director, and manager. Bjørnson gathered around him a number of talented actors and actresses from the old Christiania Theatre. With outstanding performers like Johanne Dybwad, Ragna Wettergreen, and Halfdan Christensen, the first two decades in the life of the National Theatre represent a veritable Golden Age in the history of Norwegian theatre art.

As its name indicates, the National Theatre has certain obligations, but opinion as to how these are to be met has varied somewhat over the years. One of its main tasks is to maintain Norwegian dramatic traditions as well as to promote contemporary Norwegian drama.

Not surprisingly, Ibsen's plays have figured prominently in the theatre's rep-ertory. With the exception of *The Feast at Solhaug*, every one of his twenty-two plays has been presented, most of them in a variety of productions.

Ibsen's most popular play in Norway is *Peer Gynt*, chosen for the opening of the renovated main stage in 1985. It was performed for the first time at the Christiania Theatre in 1876 and subsequently transferred to the National Theatre, where it remained in the repertory—though in an abbreviated version—until 1936. In that year a new production, directed by Halfdan Christensen and with Alfred Maurstad in the role of Peer, was staged. It proved a success, both artistically and at the box office. *Peer Gynt* is regarded primarily as a national drama, and the leading role is assumed to satirize and portray the Norwegian character. Alfred Maurstad infused the part with a freshness and fidelity that are remembered to this day. Twenty years later he directed the play with his son Toralv Maurstad in the role of young Peer and himself as the aging hero.

A major production of *Peer Gynt* was directed by Edith Roger in 1975. She stuck faithfully to the text, and the result was a performance lasting over three hours and with three different actors in the title role. Edith Roger, who has been affiliated with the National Theatre since 1967, is widely regarded as one of Norway's leading directors. With her ballet training and her highly sensitive approach to the language and to the means of expression available to the actor, she combines a unique range of talent. Other Ibsen plays she has directed include *A Doll House, Brand*, and, more recently, the musical version of *Love's Comedy*.

Other memorable performances of Ibsen's plays in recent years include *The Wild Duck, Ghosts*, and *Hedda Gabler*. The Ibsen jubilee in 1978, celebrating the 150th anniversary of his birth, witnessed a spate of performances, including new productions of *The Lady from the Sea, The League of Youth*, and *Brand*. In recent years marked efforts have been made to renew the Ibsenian tradition, both at the National Theatre and at other Norwegian theatres. It goes without saying that this tradition has proved most viable and enduring at the country's leading theatre.

Ibsen has also exercised an influence on the choice of repertory generally, insofar as the ensemble has shown a special flair for the psychological-realistic style of acting. Playwrights such as Strindberg, Shaw, O'Neill, and Albee have consequently found a ready niche in the repertory, for example, with productions of *The Father, Joan of Arc, Desire Under the Elms*, and *Who's Afraid of Virginia Woolf?*, respectively. Among other productions especially remembered in recent years are *A Midsummer Night's Dream*, Ariano Svassuna's *The Dog's Testament*, and Peter Weiss' *Marat/Sade*.

One of the most important events in the theatre's history during the last decade has been its transition from a semiprivate shareholding company to the status of a real national theatre enjoying full financial support from state and municipality, on the basis of 60 percent and 40 percent, respectively, of the total grants received. The new form of organization was accompanied by a more expansive and open theatre policy.

The establishment of the "Visiting Theatre" may be regarded as an expression of the youth revolt of the 1960s, with performances of plays such as *The Black Cat* and *Commuters*, written by actors in the group. Unlike the other Scandinavian countries, where groups broke away from the major theatres to form their own free ensembles, in Norway the political theatre of protest made its first impact within an institutional theatre.

A number of Norway's most talented actors and directors, as well as a large number of young artists, joined the theatre in the 1960s, making a special contribution to its artistic activity and subsequently giving the Norwegian theatre as a whole a new lease on life.

GERD STAHL

NORWEGIAN THEATRE
(Det Norske Teatret)
Postboks 1278 Vika
Oslo 1, Norway

After four hundred years of union with Denmark, Norway during the nineteenth century experienced strong currents moving to liberate its art and culture from Danish influence. Prominent figures like the violinist Ole Bull and dramatists like Bjørnstjerne Bjørnson and Henrik Ibsen were leaders in the movement to establish an independent theatre with Norwegian as the stage language.

Besides the struggle for Norwegian pronunciation and orthography, a distinct form of the language later called "New Norwegian" was constructed by synthesizing dialect forms from rural areas. Eventually, supporters of New Norwegian demanded equal status with the language of urban culture in literature, the schools, broadcasting, and so on. The relationship between these two variants of the language is still an unresolved problem.

The idea of a separate theatre for the New Norwegian language occurred early, associated with the tradition from Bull and Bjørnson, even though they had not promoted New Norwegian but simply a "Norwegianized" Dano-Norwegian. The National Theatre, founded in 1899, used the language of the urban culture almost exclusively.

The Norwegian Theatre had humble beginnings. While it was greeted with much good-will, it also encountered strong opposition expressed through demonstrations during performances and polemics in the press. The theatre opened in 1913 with a group of amateur actors who the previous year had toured with folk dances, folk music, and plays. The leader was Hulda Garborg, author, journalist, and wife of Arne Garborg, who was then the leading New Norwegian author. His play *The Teacher* has been performed regularly at the Norwegian Theatre as a symbol of enduring tradition. Rasmus Rasmussen, a professional actor and tour manager, became the first administrative head of the theatre.

Touring has always been important for the Norwegian Theatre, which has to some extent functioned as a theatre for the entire country. Its repertory was based on material from rural life, sagas, and folklore. Because of the special nature of its repertory, its working-class audience, and the New Norwegian movement's traditional connections with the left, there was a tendency to regard the Norwegian Theatre as a "folk theatre," contrasted to the more bourgeois and conservative National Theatre. As both theatres developed, the differences—both political and artistic—became less and less noticeable.

In order to fulfill its linguistic mission effectively, a foremost task for the Norwegian Theatre was to develop more professional standards. The actors quickly gained skill in portraying types and situations within the limited repertory, but often failed with plays presenting other character types and milieus or deviating from strict realism. The supporters of New Norwegian believed it should be possible to present all drama in that language and that authors writing in New Norwegian need not limit themselves to rural life, sagas, or folklore.

Managing directors were engaged who were not primarily supporters of New Norwegian, but instead knew how to develop the ensemble's artistic potential through choice of repertory and intensive work. Hiring Agnes Mowinckel to direct plays in the 1920s represented an important step in that direction; she was a distinctive and colorful personality in Norwegian theatre for years. Mowinckel and the administrators Hans Jacob Nilsen and Knut Hergel continued the improvement in the 1930s, and gradually it became clear what an excellent acting company the Norwegian Theatre had developed. There were artists who had strongly individual qualities and yet were able to fit into an ensemble style. They included Ingjald Haaland, Edvard Drabløs, Lars Tvinde, Johan Norlund, Ragnhild Hald, Lydia Opøien, Tordis Maurstad, and Astrid Sommer. Most remained permanently affiliated with this theatre throughout their careers. Many of the foremost actors before World War II continued to make vital contributions after the war.

One individual who has left a significant mark on the Norwegian Theatre is scene designer Arne Walentin. He helped give the theatre a new style through his simple and imaginative scenic designs. From his debut in the mid-thirties until the present, he has created scenery and costumes for many widely differing productions. His foremost quality is a sense for the artistic stage picture, created through simple and well-planned means. In particular he has utilized projections artistically.

The 1930s were decisive for the Norwegian Theatre. During those years the repertory was renewed, with an orientation toward new European and American drama. Under Knut Hergel, for example, the Danish poet-pastor Kaj Munk's religiously and politically controversial plays assumed a central position. The theatre joined the growing politicization of Norwegian theatre from the mid-thirties until the German occupation in the spring of 1940 with plays by Friedrich Wolf, Karel Čapek, and others.

The Norwegian Theatre also continued to present realistic plays—Norwegian and foreign—which treated people and situations in a country setting or in the folk life of the city. The mood and characterizations in these productions had an authenticity and closeness to reality, but also a touch of poetry. This style has often been considered most characteristic of the Norwegian Theatre. Olav Duun's novel, *Fellow Human Beings*, which the author dramatized in collaboration with Knut Hergel, belonged in this category. It was a great success in 1938 and has been revived at regular intervals. Oskar Braaten, who headed the Norwegian Theatre for a while, wrote plays set in Oslo's East Side, which also were suited to the performance style of the New Norwegian stage.

Despite considerable artistic growth, the Norwegian Theatre did not fulfill the original expectations that it would promote extensive production of New Norwegian drama. Of course, there were performances of a number of plays by New Norwegian authors, but only a few were especially original or spirited. The three outstanding playwrights of this period—Jo Ørjesæter, Tarjei Vesaas, and Aslaug Vaa—all had plays produced at the Norwegian Theatre before and after World War II. Their works show a fresh creativity that tends toward the symbolic and poetic.

The Norwegian Theatre's special position and development are typified by its relationship to Ibsen's drama. For the centennial of the playwright's birth in 1928, his son was asked for permission to perform *The Feast at Solhaug* in New Norwegian, but Sigurd Ibsen refused. Eventually in 1948 the theatre performed an Ibsen play in New Norwegian—*Peer Gynt* as directed by Hans Jacob Nilsen, with designs by Arne Walentin and music by Harald Sæverud. The production was widely debated and highly praised, not just because of the translation but also because it broke with the national romantic tradition.

Many years went by before the Norwegian Theatre presented one of Ibsen's contemporary plays. It was one thing to play *Peer Gynt* with its country setting in New Norwegian; it was quite another to present his contemporary dramas with their bourgeois city settings. Tormod Skagestad, director, playwright, and head of the theatre from 1960 to 1979, set himself the goal of performing most of Ibsen's contemporary social plays in New Norwegian, starting with *Ghosts* in 1964. In 1962 Skagestad had produced a new version of *Peer Gynt*, in which the action represented a projection of the inner conflicts of the central character. This production was taken to the Théâtre des Nations in Paris, where Arne Walentin won an international prize for his stage design, which was even more simplified and abstract than previously. In 1967 the Norwegian Theatre toured Eastern Europe, with a guest appearance of *A Doll House* at the Moscow Art Theatre as the high point.

Central to Skagestad's work as head of the theatre was his dramatization of Sigrid Undset's trilogy from the Middle Ages, *Kristin Lavransdatter*, which under his direction and with Walentin's sets became beautiful performances rich in atmosphere.

Certain types of foreign drama have proved especially well suited to the Norwegian Theatre. As early as 1945 a production of *Antigone* proved how well the style and poetic language of the Greek tragedies were suited to New Norwegian translation. Later, *King Oedipus, Medea,* and *The Oresteia* were produced. The Norwegian Theatre has staged many outstanding Strindberg productions, including *The Dance of Death, Miss Julie, The Ghost Sonata, The Father, A Dream Play,* and *To Damascus.* The Brechtian style has been well done in *Mother Courage, The Caucasian Chalk Circle*, and *Saint Joan of the Stockyards*. During the past thirty years musicals have been produced regularly as a kind of continuation of the folk comedy tradition from the theatre's early years.

For quite a long time there was prejudice against the Norwegian Theatre, stemming from general opposition to the New Norwegian language. Some considered it a socially less genteel theatre, but such prejudices seem to have completely disappeared.

The Norwegian Theatre has operated in four different locales. A building at Stortingsgaten 16, used from 1945 to 1985, seated about six hundred people. In 1970 the theatre obtained a studio theatre, Scene 2, with room for one hundred spectators.

In the fall of 1985 the Norwegian Theatre moved into the most modern theatre building in Northern Europe, with a main theatre seating approximately eight hundred persons, and a studio theatre with two hundred seats. The architects, Tom Thoresen and Ole Fredrik Stoveland, have designed the main playing space so that stage and auditorium function together flexibly. Although seating is permanent, there is the capacity to change from proscenium theatre through a number of variations to arena theatre. The studio space has ideal flexibility, with the audience seated on movable platforms.

Svein Erik Brodal, administrative and artistic director of the theatre, has the important task of coordinating the move to the new building and planning an integrated repertory. The Norwegian Theatre can be said to have reached its goal: to become a New Norwegian national theatre.

TRINE NAESS
(Translated by Carla Waal)

OSLO NEW THEATRE
(Oslo Nye Teater)
Rosenkrantzgate 10
Oslo 1, Norway

Norwegian men of letters led the way when a fund was started for the establishment of the Oslo New Theatre. The aim of the theatre was to present modern Norwegian drama. The opening performances consisted of Knut Hamsun's trilogy: *At the Gates of the Kingdom, The Game of Life*, and *Dusk*. These were followed by a number of exciting productions of contemporary drama.

The theatre, completed in 1929, was equipped with a stage which at the time was extremely modern, including an elevator stage similar to the one in the Théâtre Pigalle in Paris. A scenic artist by the name of Alexy Zaitzow, reared in the tradition of Russian expressionism, set his seal on the external decor, while adventurous directors and prominent actors recruited from the National Theatre created an era of excitement.

The rich promise of the 1920s gave way to the paucity of the 1930s, when financial straits compelled the theatre to turn to box office successes. The sure-fire modern naturalistic style of acting continued to be a hallmark of this theatre.

Lillebil Ibsen, daughter of the director and theatre manager Gyda Christensen, and the wife of Henrik Ibsen's grandson, was launched on a career which in many ways paralleled that of the theatre. During the German occupation, when the repertory was necessarily restricted by the censorship in force, performances of Ibsen's plays were allowed, and the theatre scored notable successes with *The Wild Duck, The Lady from the Sea*, and *Hedda Gabler*.

During the postwar period financial stability was ensured, thanks to Lillebil Ibsen's prowess as a comedienne. At the same time the manager of the theatre in those days, the International Theatre Institute (ITI) president Axel Otto Normann, introduced the plays of Beckett and Ionesco to Norway.

In 1959 the municipality of Oslo started making financial contributions to the running of the theatre. At the same time an attempt was made to define the true role of the Oslo New Theatre in the theatrical life of the capital. The theatre began emphasizing comedy, partly because of the need for substantial box office revenue. Interpreting the concept of comedy in its widest sense, the theatre also performs plays by Shakespeare and Molière, departing from the traditional line whenever the personnel in the ensemble permit. This was the case in the 1970s with O'Neill's *A Moon for the Misbegotten*, starring Liv Ullmann, and a dramatic version of Hamsun's *Mysteries*.

The theatre's subsidiary facility, Centralteatret, has a sort of thrust stage and seating for some three hundred persons. The repertory aims essentially to appeal to young people, alternating between classical plays presented in extroverted and lighthearted productions and musicals in rock style.

In the normal course of events the theatre presents two productions annually for children, with the permanent ensemble giving matinee performances.

The Oslo New Theatre also has a separate ensemble, with its own premises accommodating two hundred where puppet plays are shown. Continuously active since 1952, the puppet group has acquired considerable technique in a number of styles, *inter alia* by cooperating with directors grounded in different traditions. In some cases original plays are also written for this ensemble.

The Oslo New Theatre also administers the capital's revue theatre, Chat Noir, with its venerable traditions. Whenever capacity allows, the Oslo New Theatre stages its own productions there or rents the premises to other producers, preferably in order to present revues.

The theatre employs some 150 people, among whom are 30 actors, 6 musicians, and 6 puppeteers on year-long contracts.

In recent years the Oslo New Theatre has endeavored to revert to its original aim, namely, to promote modern Norwegian drama by active cooperation with authors. Productions in the early 1980s included several new comedies by Norwegian authors, as well as plays by Shaw, Peter Nichols, and Jean-Claude Grumberg. On the smaller stage, there were productions of *The Merchant of*

Venice, Measure for Measure, Il Campiello by Carlo Goldoni, and original
musical comedies.

BARTHOLD HALLE

ROGALAND THEATRE
(Rogaland Teater)
Kannikgt. 2,
4000 Stavanger, Norway

During the latter half of the 1970s, the Rogaland Theatre, although the smallest
and youngest of the six large public theatre companies in Norway, gained both
national and international prominence. With an impressive record of high-quality
productions, it won a reputation as the foremost place for innovation in the
Norwegian theatre for a whole generation.

From a very modest and rather difficult beginning in 1947, the Rogaland
Theatre has grown into what is today a well-established company. In the 1979–
1980 season it employed one hundred people, thirty of whom were actors. It is
housed in the nearly one hundred-year-old theatre building in the city of Stavanger, which today is the center for production and exploration of oil on the
continental shelf off the southern coast of Norway. The company performs in
two auditoriums and also tours the county of Rogaland and visits schools and
other institutions. Every year five or six productions are performed in the Main
House, three or four in the Studio, plus one or two children's shows, and a
couple of community events. The productions on tour are normally produced
especially for this purpose and then are brought back for a run at the theatre. In
1979 the company staged twelve productions altogether, giving a total of 483
performances with an attendance of just under one hundred thousand. The budget
for that year was 12 million Norwegian crowns, with a 90 percent subsidy from
state and local authorities.

Both because of the high level of public funding and the strong trend toward
decentralization in Norway, there is no appreciable difference between the theatres in the capital of Oslo and their counterparts in the provinces. Most of the
country's leading artists have at one time or another been resident or regular
visitors to the Rogaland Theatre, and directors and designers of international
repute, such as the Dane Sam Besekow and the Pole Kyrstyna Skuszanka, are
as easily attracted to Stavanger as to Oslo. As the only theatre in the region, its
repertory over these past thirty-odd years has been a mixture of modern and
classical, national and foreign, entertainment and drama, and the theatre has
functioned much the same as a state-subsidized theatre anywhere.

Through its first decade the Rogaland Theatre was run by a series of actor-
managers and very much on a shoestring. Apart from furnishing the theatre with
more or less truthful anecdotes of its suitably shaky and romantic beginnings,
the importance of this period was the survival and acceptance of a permanent

theatre company in the city of Stavanger. This was the capital of a notoriously puritan part of Norway and a major supplier of emigrant religious dissenters to the United States of America over the past hundred years.

From 1960 to 1970 the theatre was run by the writer and director Bjørn Endreson, under whom a great many stars of the Norwegian theatre served their apprenticeship, among them Liv Ullmann. Endreson also founded the renowned Rogaland Children's Theatre, an amateur organization that operates in association with the theatre and stages at least one semiprofessional production a year, with children between five and eighteen years of age making up the cast.

From 1970 to 1976 the theatre was run by an actor-director, Arne Thomas Olsen. In consolidating the theatre financially, he created an exemplary balance between the serious and the popular in the repertory, and he also brought both Norwegian and international stars to work in Stavanger. This resulted in memorable productions of *Uncle Vanya, The Lower Depths*, and Edward Bond's *The Sea*, among others.

But it was under the artistic leadership of Kjetil Bang-Hansen and with the company he assembled that the Rogaland Theatre gained its particular prominence. Several of the productions during his period as artistic director received unanimous critical acclaim, as a result of which the theatre was invited to international festivals in Yugoslavia, the United States, and Norway itself. At the same time it attracted large audiences, bringing the company nearer to fulfilling its required function as both entertainer and pioneer.

Bang-Hansen's basic policy was to make full use of the resident permanent ensemble, without resorting to guest artists other than directors and designers, and at the same time without imposing a rigid mode of presentation. Furthermore, the policy was reflected in the internal organization of the theatre. A consultative committee of elected representatives and others played a vital role in the creation of the company's artistic profile, albeit without the director for one moment eschewing his ultimate artistic responsibility.

This policy created a commitment among the company, which in turn gradually produced a more distinctive style. The 1978 production of *Peer Gynt*, which also visited the BITEF Festival in Belgrade, was the first to point in such a direction. Later, it was developed through such diverse productions as Peder W. Cappelen's *King Sverre* (a contemporary Norwegian verse play), García Lorca's *Yerma* (the New Theatre Festival, Baltimore, 1979), Tolstoy's *Strider, The Story of a Horse* (the Bergen Festival, 1980), Pavel Kohout's *Cirkus!* (1980), and Shakespeare's *Coriolanus*.

Any style in the transient art of the theatre would tend to defy labeling. Suffice it to say, therefore, that the products of the collaboration between Bang-Hansen and his resident head designer, Helge Hoff Monsen, were characterized by a poetic quality, which became progressively more committed and at the same time both blatantly naive and carefully orchestrated. Through their leadership the company made unique contributions to contemporary Norwegian theatre, which is still struggling under the weight of a realistic Ibsenite tradition.

As an extension of this "style," a tangible and pronounced feature of the company's work over these six years was a concerted effort to emphasize the "theatricality" of any given production. This resulted from a realization of the need for the theatre in contemporary society to refine and develop what distinguishes it from television and films. For the productions in the flexible Studio, for example, this led to attempts at total theatre, with a complete change of the whole environment for each play. Thus, for the acclaimed production of *Yerma*, the room was turned into a horseshoe-shaped bullring, with the floor covered in a three-inch layer of sand. For the classical Norwegian comedy *Three Couples* by Alexander L. Kielland, the entire basement area of the theatre, including the Studio, was transformed, and the audience was taken on a guided tour through a replica of Victorian Stavanger in the course of the performance.

In the selection of plays, the characteristics and composition of the ensemble were balanced against a wish to give the repertory a unifying idea. But this idea was never an academic or exclusive one and was often restricted to a simple "dialectic" between the Main House and the Studio. For Bang-Hansen's final season this resulted in a repertory in which Chekhov's *The Sea Gull* was set against Miller's *A View from the Bridge*, a company version of Molière/Dunlop/Dale's comedy *Scapino* against the European premiere of W. Mastrosimone's *Extremities*, John Arden's modern classic *Sergeant Musgrave's Dance* against Euripides/Sartre's *The Trojan Women*, with the Norwegian premiere of George Farquhar's *The Beaux' Stratagem* bringing the season to a colorful and light-hearted climax.

In 1982 the actor Alf Nordvang succeeded Bang-Hansen as artistic director. The future will be shaped by his policy, but since the Rogaland Theatre is the only professional company in the region, any long-term plans will more than anything be determined by requirements attached to public funding. In the immediate future, however, the company will be able to explore the uses of new technical equipment, such as a supermodern fly tower, and expand the range of its work slightly. A third playing space is being opened, intended for more informal events. At the start of the 1980s both financial and artistic resources were concentrated on certain productions or historical periods each year. The hit of the 1980–1981 season was the first Norwegian revival for nearly fifty years of Shakespeare's political tragedy *Coriolanus*, and in 1981–1982 it was the tandem productions of *Sergeant Musgrave's Dance* and *The Trojan Women*. It seems clear that the new artistic director will continue this policy.

TOM REMLOV

TRØNDELAG THEATRE
(Trøndelag Teater)
Kalvskinnet, P.O. Box 4540
7001 Trondheim, Norway

"We congratulate the National Theatre on their new modern Amfiscene and Rogaland Theatre on their nearly finished scene tower, and we are keeping our fingers crossed for the new building of the Norwegian Theatre. Next in line has to be the new house of the Trøndelag Theatre."

With these words Ola B. Johannesen wished the audience welcome to the forty-fourth season of the Trøndelag Theatre. At the same time he described his impatience with the national and municipal bureaucracy, in light of the Trøndelag's efforts to meet the public's demand for realism and reliability in 1980 with a stage constructed according to seventeenth-century principles. Since then scenic design has developed from a two-dimensional pictorial art into an art of spatial organization in three dimensions and with demands that Norway's oldest "playable" theatre building no longer can satisfy. The state custodian of antiquities declared in 1969 that the building should be preserved unchanged; one day the house will serve as a theatre museum.

Finished in 1816, the baroque building has housed all four regular theatre companies one usually considers in the history of Trondheim: the Public Theatre (Det Offentlige Teater), 1816–1829, the Norwegian Theatre (Det Norske Teater), 1861–1865, Trondheim's National Stage (Trondhjems Nationale Scene), 1911–1927, and the present Trøndelag Theatre, from 1937 on. The first company was established in a boom period of cultural development, and the second and third in periods of strong nationalism and demands for uniting cultural institutions. The fourth was founded in the midst of the economic depression. The building was already there, ready for use and with a distinctive atmosphere.

After energetic preliminary work by the first managing director, Henry Gleditsch, Trøndelag Theatre opened in 1937. It was understood that as a provincial theatre, the only one in the region, the Trøndelag Theatre had to play all kinds of works in order to satisfy the taxpayers' different tastes. Classical drama and contemporary plays in various genres constituted the core of the repertory, supported by comedies and farces. Even during the first season, however, the theatre gave a Christmas performance for children and a musical comedy and revue in the spring, genres that would obtain a permanent place in the repertory. In addition, the ensemble went on tour early in the summer to fulfill their obligations to the region, even though the theatre did not yet receive grants from localities other than Trondheim. National grants were received during the second season.

In 1942 Henry Gleditsch was shot by the Germans in revenge for sabotage by members of the resistance movement, and the theatre was taken over by the Nazis. It was reopened in 1945 with Georg Løkkeberg as managing director. He was followed by Alfred Maurstad in 1948, who was succeeded by Nils Reinhardt Christensen in 1950. From 1951 Victor Huseby was in command, from 1967 Erik Pierstorff, from 1970 Arne Aas, and from 1973 Kjell Stormoen. The present director, Ola B. Johannesen, took over in 1979.

Trøndelag Theatre still presents a diverse repertory, the spectrum of genres having widened through the years. The theatre has been obliged to respond to changes in public taste created by the media and by socioeconomic changes in Norwegian society after World War II. Youth problems, women's lib, social criticism, and theatre for children are concerns to which the theatre must respond in its repertory policy. For example, among the seventeen productions in 1979 were plays by Agatha Christie, John Steinbeck, Bjørnstjerne Bjørnson, Dario Fo, William Shakespeare, one Norwegian writer making his first appearance, and two plays for children. In addition, the theatre booked two puppet shows.

Taking into account the obvious production limits and various segments of the public, one must conclude that the theatre has not acquired a style or profile of its own which could be attained only by concentration on particular dramatists or works. The demand for versatility, together with constantly low funds, has reduced the staff's ability to experiment but has not prevented it from introducing several plays and playwrights. The theatre has staged the first performances in Norway of works by Jean-Paul Sartre, Irving Berlin, John Osborne, Siegfried Lenz, and Norway's own Johan Falkberget.

In spite of the baroque surroundings, the staff has at times been aggressively unconventional in its artistic attitude. The inauguration of the Theatre Attic (Teaterloftet) in 1969, under the leadership of Erik Pierstorff, has given the theatre opportunities for some experiments within modern dramatic genres. Since 1976 this secondary stage has also been the setting for a theatre week for amateurs under the direction of the Trøndelag Theatre. Six or seven groups from Trondheim and the region give performances, receive awards, and have some instruction in different theatre techniques.

The decade of the 1980s has meant changes and innovations for Trøndelag Theatre. In spite of strikes, lack of space, and lack of funds after national and municipal grants dried up, activity has been stepped up, partly to achieve a necessary increase of income, but also in order to broaden the general repertory and vary the tasks of the ensemble.

Three events in 1979 are noteworthy: the establishing of a record for Trøndelag Theatre with 112 performances of Dario Fo's *Vi betale itj* (*We're Not Paying*); the theatre's backing of local writers, in recognition of the serious lack of contemporary Norwegian works for the stage; and, perhaps the most unorthodox project, a café-theatre at one of the restaurants of Trondheim. The café-theatre was a great success and will surely continue as a permanent part of the theatre's activities.

The theatre has two stages. The main stage serves an audience of 350 persons, and the Theatre Attic can stow 70 spectators under the roof. The total seating capacity was utilized at a rate of 70 percent in 1979. When the theatre completed a new rehearsal hall in 1980, it was able to retain its increased level of activity.

In the autumn of 1979 a dramaturge was permanently appointed to Trøndelag Theatre and proved of great assistance to the newly established repertory board. Following the strike from March to April 1979, a board for appointments and dismissals was also set up.

In 1980 the theatre had ninety-eight employees, twenty-nine of whom were actors. Remarkably, the actors' share of the whole staff was reduced during the 1970s from 34 percent to about 28.5 percent. The number of actors remained fairly stable. Increasing demands on the theatre as an independent economic and administrative unit, together with more rigid rules for working hours, have necessitated more administrative machinery.

These nearly one hundred artistic and nonartistic employees perform their daily work in a restored and well-equipped theatre building to the accompaniment of traffic noise, streetcar bells, and ambulance sirens down Prince's Street, constantly distracting audiences and reminding everyone that construction plans for a new theatre building move silently in the bureaucracy.

SVEIN GLADSØ

Sweden

INTRODUCTION

Sweden shares with the other Scandinavian countries a heritage from the Middle Ages, when liturgical plays, especially at Christmas and Easter, were performed by priests and acolytes, and later by teachers and students. School drama in both Latin and the vernacular reflected an admiration for classical genres, and from the academic environment the first national historical plays appeared, establishing the genre that would be enriched by August Strindberg and Lars Forssell in the nineteenth and twentieth centuries. The Renaissance was a time of splendid court entertainments, with magnificent masques and ballets produced to entertain and honor Queen Christina.

Traveling troupes, especially Italian and French, visited Sweden often in the seventeenth and eighteenth centuries, and were sometimes invited to take up residence at court. Admiration for French culture was especially evident at the court of Lovisa Ulrika at Drottningholm and during the reign of Gustav III. An ardent participant in all phases of theatrical activity, Gustav III supported the renovation and construction of theatre buildings, performances at Gripsholm and Drottningholm, the training of Swedish actors by a French troupe, and the development of Swedish drama based on national themes. The Royal Swedish Dramatic Theatre, founded in 1788, and the charming theatre at Drottningholm, with its summer opera productions, remind us of Gustav III's patronage, but represent only part of the varied and vigorous theatrical activity in Sweden today.

Swedish theatre builds upon tradition while aiming to keep theatre relevant to the needs of society. Whereas the Royal Swedish Dramatic Theatre, the Opera in Stockholm, and the Swedish National Theatre Center with tours throughout the country are national theatres, there are many others—city and municipal, regional, private, and free groups for theatre, music and dance. Since sociological studies show that the majority of theatregoers come from that level of society with the best education and financial means, efforts have been made to reach people who do not habitually attend theatre or who do not live where they have easy access to performances. The average annual attendance figure for the country is 4.5 million, of which one-third is at performances by free groups.

In recent years the small free groups have made the most vigorous efforts to reach new audiences. TURteatern, one of the first, has worked closely with the public in Kärrtorp. The Music Theatre Group October has had unusual status as the municipal theatre of Södertälje since 1978, while touring as a free group for part of each year. October contributes to the community by playing in schools, offering courses for teenagers, and studying the situation of immigrants. One of their productions, *The People of Södertälje* (1980) by Björn Runeborg, featured Finnish, Assyrian, and Swedish families depicted in part by amateur actors, all speaking their native languages.

Group theatres have also tried to reach young audiences. The Pocket Theatre, which began playing in the streets in 1968 with two actors and a prop box, specialized in children's theatre and school performances. In the late 1960s groups decided to base their repertory on the reality of children's experiences. Disturbing subject matter and the Socialist political tendency of the new plays aroused controversy, but the value of the new drama was verified through pre- and post-performance research and interaction with children. Suzanne Osten, a member of the original Pocket Theatre and artistic director of Unga Klara Children's Theatre, has led the revitalization of children's theatre. *Medea's Children*, which she and Per Lysander developed on the theme of divorce, exemplifies the new trends. Although many productions are done simply, there have also been beautiful and imaginative uses of scenic and lighting resources and unique combinations of live actors and marionettes, as at Michael Meschke's world-famous Marionette Theatre.

The establishment of regional theatres in the 1970s was another important development. Regional theatres, such as the Norrbotten Theatre based in Luleå, have attempted to become acquainted with the people in their region, to understand their experiences and problems, and to establish an identity as theatres that reflect and deal with these problems. The regional theatre in Dalarna, for example, has worked with groups of retired workers in developing plays on labor and unemployment.

During the 1970s many ensembles developed their own scripts. However, the typical repertory has been drawn from the works of major foreign playwrights, such as Shakespeare, Molière, and Brecht, and of Swedish dramatists. The plays of August Strindberg have dominated the repertory of the twentieth century, inspiring significant stagings by directors such as Olof Molander, Alf Sjöberg, and Ingmar Bergman. A resurgence of interest in Strindberg's dramas and fresh interpretations were highlighted during the International Strindberg Festival in 1981. The choice of repertory is a matter of concern. There is always a need for new creative contributions by Swedish playwrights, who are paid an excellent basic fee plus increments for a long run. As ticket prices increase and box office receipts play a more decisive role in each theatre's survival, there is less opportunity for experimentation and a danger of commercialization.

The survival of regional and group theatres and the vitality of large institutional theatres are being threatened. A change of government in 1982 raised questions about a possible change in cultural policy. Events resulting from the "manifesto" at the Gothenburg City Theatre turned the spotlight on democratic planning of repertory, artistic freedom, and political influence. Economic trends, public interest, cultural policy, demand for democratization, and innovative artistic ideas will all be factors determining the stability and influence of Swedish theatre in the 1980s.

CARLA WAAL

GOTHENBURG CITY THEATRE
(Göteborgs Stadsteater)
Götaplatsen, P.O. Box 5094
S-402 22 Gothenburg, Sweden

The two major national stages in Sweden, the Royal Opera and the Royal Dramatic Theatre, were established in the capital city of Stockholm in the eighteenth century. It was not until the early 1900s, however, that the idea of a local, municipal theatre began to develop in the second largest Swedish city, Gothenburg. A provisional stage, the Lorensberg Theatre, was founded in 1916, essentially financed by generous contributions from local private donors. After a few seasons, the Gothenburg City Council approved for the Lorensberg company a municipal subsidy that was subsequently augmented with annual grants from the national government. With the joint support of the local authorities and the state and under the inspired leadership of the creative designer-director team of Knut Ström and Per Lindberg, theatre life in Gothenburg began to blossom in the 1920s. Soon there developed a growing need for larger and better facilities. In 1934 a magnificent, brand-new theatre building was inaugurated, to which the entire Lorensberg company was moved. This was the official establishment of the Gothenburg City Theatre, which became the first professional stage in Sweden to embody the concept of a municipal theatre. With its two stage areas— one large main stage and one intimate studio stage—and with its excellent technical equipment, designed by Ström, the Gothenburg City Theatre has remained one of the most modern and innovative theatres in Europe.

Ever since its inception in the 1930s, the Gothenburg City Theatre has distinguished itself within Swedish theatre life in two particular areas. First, this theatre company stressed excellence in ensemble acting from the very beginning. The device of featuring one or two "stars" to "carry" a production—a tradition that was often practiced on the national stage and in many other theatre centers in the world—was never adopted in Gothenburg. Instead, the emphasis was on the perfect interaction of the entire cast as a group of equals. The directors worked as diligently on the crowd scenes and with individual minor characters as with the portrayers of the principal parts. Several generations of theatre reviewers have borne witness that the consistently outstanding ensemble work has become a true trademark of the Gothenburg company. This concern for the collective effort has made the Gothenburg City Theatre both a uniquely inspired and an inspiring dramatic form.

Another distinctive tradition which the Gothenburg theatre established in the 1930s and subsequently maintained is that of often being the first stage in the country to produce dramatic works, domestic and foreign, of a topical and sometimes quite controversial nature. Particularly in the years before and during World War II, the production policies of the Gothenburg City Theatre represented a critical front against Nazi terrorism in Europe. Under the uncompromising management of Torsten Hammarén, the City Theatre presented a repertory that scoffed at the official neutrality demonstrated by the major stages in the capital city. The municipal stage in Gothenburg came to reflect a local climate of independence during the politically precarious years of the 1930s and 1940s, and the audiences soon learned to respect and appreciate this alertness and intrepidity in their theatre. Among the most memorable productions of original Swedish dramas were Pär Lagerkvist's *The Hangman* in 1935 and the dramatization of Vilhelm Moberg's resistance novel, *Ride This Night!*, in 1942. During the war years the theatre also produced Franz Werfel's anti-Nazi play *Jacobowsky and the Colonel*; John Steinbeck's drama about the occupation of Norway, *The Moon Is Down*; and Kaj Munk's *Niels Ebbesen*, as a tribute to Munk, a Danish pastor and playwright who was murdered by the Nazis. In all of Scandinavia, the new City Theatre in Gothenburg acquired a reputation as a fearless and outspoken commentator on the times.

During the postwar seasons of 1946–1950, young Ingmar Bergman was employed as a director in Gothenburg. He was responsible for several spirited productions at the City Theatre, including the presentations of some of his own dramas. In the 1950s, the repertory in Gothenburg generally displayed a strong interest in modern international drama. Many French, English, and American plays were produced, and Bertolt Brecht's drama *The Caucasian Chalk Circle*, written during his exile from Germany, received its first Swedish performance on the Gothenburg stage in 1951. Quite typical of the tendency of the City Theatre to be the first to discover and import new trends in the theatre abroad was the production of John Osborne's *Look Back in Anger*, which had its Swedish opening night in Gothenburg not long after the premiere in London in 1956.

In 1962 Mats Johansson became the artistic and managing director of the Gothenburg City Theatre, a position from which he resigned in 1982. Under his leadership in the 1960s and 1970s, the Gothenburg stage again emerged as an innovative forerunner in Swedish theatre life. One of the most stimulating new lines of development to emanate from the Gothenburg theatre in the 1960s was the creation of a ''group theatre,'' functioning within the boundaries of the established company. The general philosophy behind the group theatre idea was to allow a dramatic production to take shape through the close collaboration of a small group of writers, actors, and theatre technicians with mutual artistic, social, and political frames of reference. The source material tended to be of a topical, documentary nature, dealing with the issues of the day and frequently containing pointed social criticism. In Gothenburg, an autonomous little team of mostly younger theatre workers requested and received special permission from the theatre director to invent, produce, and perform their own dramatic material. This experiment yielded several "homemade" productions of high artistic calibre. The group theatre emerged as a viable alternative to the traditional production team with a cast of actors dealing with their assigned roles from a finished manuscript and with one director in charge. A very representative product of the experimental "group theatre" activities was the so-called Gothenburg Trilogy (1967–1968) of three original social plays—*The Raft, The Home*, and *The Sandbox*—created by a collective effort with Kent Andersson and Bengt Bratt as the principal writers. The trilogy already belongs to Swedish theatre history and has been performed on many stages in Scandinavia.

Uno Myggan Ericsson served as artistic and administrative director of the theatre until July 1983, when Gunilla Bergh took over the artistic leadership.

The Gothenburg City Theatre has about 250 employees and performs on two active repertory stages within the main theatre building in the center of the city. In addition, a separate stage, managed by a group theatre faction, has been successfully operating for a few years in one of the Gothenburg suburbs in a commendable effort to seek out new audiences by bringing theatre performances to the sometimes culturally deficient city outskirts. Financial arrangements for municipal theatres were finally prescribed by law in the 1960s. The basic stipulation was that the state government would contribute 55 percent of the salaries at the Swedish city theatres, while the local authorities would be responsible for all other expenditures.

The Gothenburg City Theatre is committed to maintaining a productive working climate of creative dramatic experimentation and living up to its long-standing reputation as an artistically committed and socially involved major theatre institution.

BIRGITTA DAHLGREN KNUTTGEN

MALMÖ CITY THEATRE
(Malmö Stadsteatern)
Helmfeltsgatan 4, P.O. Box 17520
S-200 10 Malmö, Sweden

The Malmö City Theatre was inaugurated on September 23, 1944. With Europe in blackout, the new theatre radiated light and hope—not just for peace but for a new age of culture and democracy, humanity and humanism. The concept of a people's theatre was integral to the new building, which, with its large stage and 1,700-seat auditorium, presented a challenge and a problem.

Malmö had been discussing its need for a new theatre since the beginning of the century. The city's historic theatre from 1809, too small and technically antiquated for permanent operation, was used only for touring productions. In an old circus building, the Hippodrome, operetta had its home and a strong hold on its audience. The Hippodrome was converted to a church, and its tradition was transferred to the new city theatre along with a number of popular actors. Malmö is a city of laborers—an early stronghold of the social-democratic movement—but its theatre tradition has been dominated by operetta.

An architectural competition for a new theatre was announced, and, in 1937, two prize-winning proposals were combined. Three architects can be credited with the theatre complex: Sigurd Lewerentz (first prize) with Erik Lallerstedt and Daniel Helldén (who shared the second prize). The fundamental concept was the folk theatre, which had been championed by the director Per Lindberg. He vigorously proposed a number of characteristics for the Malmö City Theatre, his spiritual child: no proscenium arch but an open, flexible relationship between stage and house; a semicircular variation of the Elizabethan thrust stage; and a large auditorium where all seats are equally good.

Lindberg died a few months before the theatre was dedicated. Sandro Malmquist, who shared Lindberg's belief in folk theatre, became the first artistic director. He directed the opening production, *A Midsummer Night's Dream*, utilizing the theatre's technical resources to construct the magical forest on a turntable and to raise the rustics swiftly on an elevator from the pit.

The former head of the Hippodrome, Oscar Winge, an outstanding character actor, was responsible primarily for carrying on the operetta tradition. The first season three operettas were produced in rapid succession, and in 1946 the first opera, Tchaikowsky's *Eugene Onegin*, was performed in cooperation with the Malmö Symphony Orchestra.

How to fill the large theatre—with art on stage and an audience in the house—became the leading question in an endless debate. Artistic ambitions were set against economic limits, a repertory theatre built on Shakespeare-Strindberg-Brecht against musical theatre, which drew crowds but was expensive.

Operetta often dominated, and artistic ambition was relegated to the chamber stage, Intiman (the Intimate Theatre). Originally intended for rehearsal, it was equipped as an alternative theatre with 204 seats. Here psychologically subtle naturalism was achieved in productions of Ibsen, Strindberg, and Chekhov. Gradually, experimentation also took place: in the fifties the director Yngve Nordwall turned the Intiman into an exciting forum for theatre of the absurd, especially Ionesco. Under Malmquist's successor, Stig Torsslow (1947–1950), Jean-Paul Sartre, Jean Anouilh, Eugene O'Neill, García Lorca, Tennessee Williams, and others were on the Intiman's schedule.

In 1950 Lars-Levi Laestadius became head of the theatre. After directing a couple of ambitious failures on the main stage, he withdrew to the Intiman, where he triumphed with productions of dramatists like Ibsen, Chekhov, Jean Giraudoux, Max Frisch, and Friedrich Dürrenmatt. He allowed operettas and musical plays to dominate the main stage—until he found the solution that would give the artistic alternative a decent chance there also.

The solution was Ingmar Bergman. He had created a sensation when in 1944, at the age of twenty-six, he became head of the little city theatre in Helsingborg. At the same time the government withdrew its support of the Helsingborg Theatre and gave it to Malmö. During two years in Helsingborg Bergman directed nine productions of such artistic merit that the theatre regained its government subsidy. He was succeeded in 1979 by Holger Reenberg, who in turn was succeeded by Claes Sylwander in 1983.

Bergman's six years in Malmö (1952–1958) became the theatre's great epoch, and perhaps also Bergman's great period in the theatre (coinciding with his definitive breakthrough in film). Bergman established a brilliant ensemble in Malmö, actors who would win world renown through his films: Naima Wifstrand, Gertrud Fridh, Ingrid Thulin, Harriet Andersson, Bibi Andersson, Gunnel Lindblom, Benkt-Åke Benktsson, Max von Sydow, Toivo Pawlo, Georg Arlin, Oscar Ljung, Åke Fridell, and so on. He polished their ensemble playing with intense intimate productions like Molière's *Don Juan*, Pirandello's *Six Characters in Search of an Author*, Kafka's *The Castle* and some of his own plays, including *Wood Painting* (filmed as *The Seventh Seal*).

But it was on the main stage that Bergman triumphed—first with two of Strindberg's plays: *The Crown Bride* (1952) and *The Ghost Sonata*. He brought the early interior scenes of *The Crown Bride* onto the forestage and in the final act—the big clash between the two feuding factions—used the full effect of the space: it became a huge, dark, frozen field of ice where spotlights followed the surging test of strength. In *The Ghost Sonata* he took a similar approach but with sensitive restraint. The action opened up gradually to spaciousness, naturalism dissolved in stylization, hate in reconciliation.

Cat on a Hot Tin Roof had bold dimensions and intensive compression in scenes between Max von Sydow (Brick) and Benkt-Åke Benktsson (Big Daddy). Bergman's skill in blocking—placing actors where they can be seen and heard to advantage—developed as he wrestled with the huge Malmö stage. This was evident in Strindberg's *Erik XIV*, which alternated rhythmically between intimacy and expansiveness with Toivo Pawlo's brilliantly mad autocrat always in focus. In *Peer Gynt*, in a colossal five-hour performance, Max von Sydow wandered through fantastic environments—the Norwegian wedding farm, the hall of the Mountain King, the Arabian desert, the madhouse in Cairo—all in a sequence of scenes rich in dramatic meaning and fantasy.

The high point was Molière's *The Misanthrope* (1957). Scene designer Kerstin Hedeby transformed the forestage into a baroque salon that almost seemed to encompass the audience. The lighting and acting increased the closeness and intensity. The classical Alexandrine verse was charged with modern relevance in the interplay between Gertrud Fridh's mockingly beautiful and isolated Célimène and her aggressively serious admirer, portrayed by Max von Sydow as one of the angry young men just then conquering the theatre world. With Hedeby, Bergman went on to a beautiful interpretation of Goethe's *Faust*, with Max von

Sydow in the title role made up like Mephistopheles' (Toivo Pawlo's) twin brother. Gunnel Lindblom's Gretchen reached tragic stature when in prison she confused the Tempter's figure with her lover's.

Perhaps the theatre has never been so close to the original vision of folk theatre as in Bergman's two musical productions, *The Merry Widow* and the nineteenth-century Swedish classic, *The People of Värmland*, his last production in Malmö. The Royal Dramatic Theatre in Stockholm was beckoning—and the theatre was once again faced with its basic problem. Gösta Folke, who headed the theatre from 1960 to 1976, tried to solve the problem with *My Fair Lady*, which ran for two seasons and set attendance records. In 1963 he staged an interesting version of Shakespeare's *The Tempest*. The great Danish designer Helge Refn created a sculpted ocean wave or shell that permitted action on various levels. Refn also was to make remarkable use of space in Brecht's *Schweyk in the Second World War* (1966; directed by Lennart Olsson) and *Mother Courage* (1968; directed by Jan Lewin), but unfortunately they stand out as isolated efforts.

Lennart Olsson had great success with a vital and committed production of Arnold Wesker's *Chips with Everything*; it was invited to the Théâtre des Nations in Paris in 1964. Jan Lewin's version of Weiss' *Marat/Sade* also used the open stage space in a memorable way, as was true of Pierre Fränckel's production of a modern Swedish classic which takes place in a mental hospital, *The State of Affairs* by Kent Andersson and Bengt Bratt. Fränckel has done several distinctive productions, such as Fernando Arrabal's anti-Franco play, *And They Put Handcuffs on the Flowers*, which aroused a raging debate for its alleged indecency, and an unconventional new version of *The Merry Widow* for the theatre's twenty-fifth anniversary. In 1978 Fränckel wrote the libretto for a musical based on the Viking novel *The Red Serpent* by Frans Gunnar Bengtsson. With music by Bengt-Arne Wallin, the production was one of the theatre's great successes.

From the end of the 1940s opera was regularly produced in cooperation with the Malmö Symphony—at first one production per year, later two. Opera production reached a high standard in the 1960s with Folke Abenius as director. The ballet had included ambitious works in its repertory, classical ballet as well as new choreography.

It was difficult for the Malmö City Theatre to find a successor to Gösta Folke. The interests of the musical ensemble clashed with those of the dramatic ensemble, and heady demands for democratization with the views of local politicians. This led to vigorous conflicts, and Rolf Rembe, whom the company wanted as sucessor to Folke, decided to resign after three years. He was succeeded in 1979 by Holger Reenberg, a dancer, choreographer, and previously head of programming for the theatre.

In 1979–1980 the theatre presented 819 performances on its various stages (including the New Theatre which was inaugurated in 1965). Total attendance was 276,218. The theatre received 17 million crowns from the national government; 23.8 million crowns from the city of Malmö; and 6.4 million crowns in ticket sales.

The theatre's personnel in 1980–1981 totaled four hundred, including about fifty actors, twenty-five singers, a chorus of forty, and a ballet corps of forty-six. The Malmö Symphony Orchestra, with which the theatre works, has seventy-six musicians.

HENRIK SJÖGREN
(Translated by Carla Waal)

ROYAL DRAMATIC THEATRE
(Kungliga Dramatiska Teatern)
Nybrogatan 2, P.O. Box 5037
S–102 41 Stockholm, Sweden

Founded in 1788, the Royal Dramatic Theatre was the culmination of Gustav III's ambitions to establish a national stage. "Dramaten," as it was eventually called, was the result of a conscious effort by an enlightened, artistic, and nationalistic king to encourage the Swedish language on stage and the growth of native drama. Gustav III had previously granted the privilege of starting a national theatre to A. F. Ristell, who failed after one season. The king then asked Gustav Mauritz Armfelt to draw up statutes for the Royal Dramatic Theatre of Sweden.

Like the Comédie Française, the theatre in Stockholm was an independent "republic," where an actors' association decided the repertory and a board was responsible for economic and administrative details. Salaries were shares of box office receipts. A secretary from the Royal Spectacles Society was director of the board. The theatre was susceptible to political squabbles involving the actors, the board, and the king—via the Royal Spectacles Society.

Dramaten was not an immediate success because of internal strife, the inadequacy of the Bollhus stage, lack of public support, and competition from established troupes. War and the untimely death of Gustav III in 1792 put a damper on efforts to build a new stage, but in November 1793 the theatre took over a palace named Makalös—referred to as the Arsenal.

Type-casting was common, but drastic changes created a situation in which the actors had to learn to be far more flexible. In 1799 Gustav IV Adolf canceled all theatre privileges in Stockholm except for the Opera and Royal Dramatic Theatre. In 1806 the king closed the Opera. Some of its activities were transferred to Dramaten, where the repertory included dramas, comedies, popular operas, and opera-comiques. Yet, the company was limited to eighteen men and twelve women. They performed against painted backdrops depicting both exteriors and interiors, standing in an arc in front of the prompt box, with extras in semicircles along the walls.

After 1809 the Swedish Riksdag (Parliament), together with the king, determined the theatre's subsidies. By 1813 these subsidies were incorporated into a modest fund for Dramaten and the reestablished Opera. With the Royal Dramatic a state-run institution, its head had to plead for funds. Parliament was often split in its decision, with the farmers voting against an increase on grounds that the theatre was frequented only by upper-class, urban audiences.

In 1825 the Arsenal burned during a performance, claiming two lives. For the next thirty-eight years, Dramaten played at the Opera. An attempt to change the salary system to fixed wages led to a strike among the actors. In 1832 a repertory committee was formed, to which the actors elected three representatives. The more prominent actors maintained the right to star performances, for which the public paid to see its favorite performer in a leading role. Despite some status and popularity, actors were exposed to humiliations and could be thrown into prison for minor offenses such as temperamental outbursts.

The Royal Dramatic braved new repertory trends, presenting plays by Schiller, Franz Grillparzer, Adam Oehlenschläger, and Victor Hugo. A new generation of actors reached stardom with an emotionally expressive style directly related to the new drama. That the old decors were discarded seems fitting.

By mid-nineteenth century history plays featuring Sweden's past rulers could be seen at the Royal Dramatic. The upsurge of interest in history as well as in Shakespeare's plays was a consequence of a cultural romantic movement eager to revive the past as myth and folklore. The theatre may have adopted the history play as its trademark partly because its new head was G. O. Hyltén-Cavallius, founder of the Artists' Guild, a group whose programs featured folk history and historical heroes.

Under Hyltén-Cavallius' successor, E. von Stedinck, the national stage entered an illustrious era of transition between romanticism and realism. Much credit goes to August Bournonville, advisor for three years in the 1860s. Bournonville possessed many of the qualities that infused new life into Dramaten in the twentieth century, when Olof Molander and Ingmar Bergman were directors. All three men believed in discipline, and shared a commitment and enthusiasm for the profession, as well as a vision or charisma that gave their instruction a concrete, yet magical, touch.

In 1863 Dramaten took over Edvard Stiernström's Mindre Teatern. Bournonville and his protegé Ludvig Josephson opposed the move. Their fears were not unfounded: to pay for the purchase, Dramaten catered to popular taste and focused on boulevard comedies and lighter dramas, while increasing performances from 200 to 450 a year, done with only twenty-one men and twelve women. Only after the emergence of Ibsen's modern realistic drama did Dramaten present a more serious repertory. In the 1880s, Ibsen's plays and thesis dramas by Swedish playwrights Ann-Charlotte Leffler and Alfhild Agrell were performed. The company learned precise repartée and superb ensemble acting. By the mid-1890s this forte was threatened, as impressive guest performers, including the company of the Duke of Saxe-Meiningen, Sarah Bernhardt, Eleanora Duse, and Constant Coquelin, accustomed Stockholm audiences to great solo performances.

In 1888 the Riksdag discontinued the subsidies to the Opera and Dramaten, stripping the stages of their royal insignia and letting private ownership take over. The artists formed an association, once again sharing box office receipts.

With no guaranteed income other than the rent for the king's boxes, the uncertainty of Dramaten's future was increased by competition from independent theatres.

Among the sins of omission in the repertory during the nineteenth century, few are more noticeable than the neglect of August Strindberg. With Emil Grandison as director-in-residence at the turn of the century, Strindberg finally found a sympathetic interpreter of his dramas. The world premiere of *To Damascus* I (1900) marked not only a triumph for Strindberg but also new hope for Dramaten. With Harriet Bosse as the Lady, the production used a subdued and intimate style.

The present theatre at Nybroplan was ready in 1908, opening with Strindberg's *Master Olof*, and the theatre was again "royal" in name. The Riksdag decided the budget and granted subsidies, but the financial basis of the theatre was a private, independent share company. The management was free to choose productions and set artistic policy. Since the mid-1960s such matters have been worked out in close cooperation with the resident actors, now numbering seventy-five.

Although Strindberg's drama helped launch the Royal Dramatic Theatre into the twentieth century, the basically conservative stage continued to feature star actors in French boulevard comedies. Some improvements occurred under Karl Michaelson and Tor Hedberg, but the truly innovative period began in the 1920s, when two directorial giants, Olof Molander and Per Lindberg, joined its staff. Continental artistic impulses were seen in Stockholm in Max Reinhardt's Strindberg productions, Lindberg and Sandro Malmquist's *Life Is a Dream*, and Molander's expressionistic *Phèdre*.

The Club Theatre, a subscription membership for experimental Saturday matinees, had a membership of five thousand. Although the Club Theatre lasted only a few seasons, the concept of an experimental stage at Dramaten had taken root and still survives.

Through his stagings of Shakespeare, Strindberg, and O'Neill in the 1930s and 1940s, Olof Molander wrote theatre history that gave a new profile to the Royal Dramatic Theatre. Molander emphasized ensemble acting, meticulous character analysis, and faithfulness to the written text. So strong was his impact that it took Ingmar Bergman years to overcome a hesitation to present his own version of *A Dream Play* (1970) and *To Damascus* (1974) on Molander's old territory.

Starting in 1963, Bergman assumed administrative responsibility for Dramaten. Following the "folk theatre" debate in the 1930s, Molander had sent Dramaten on tour in the provinces. In the 1960s debate about elitist versus democratic art, Bergman promoted high-quality performances for children and high school students. Both men deliberately overspent their budget and were "forced" to resign when the government could not subsidize Dramaten's vision of itself as a truly national theatre.

After World War II Dramaten made an artistic comeback in 1945 with O'Neill's

All God's Chillun Got Wings on its new studio stage, followed two years later by Molander's remarkable staging of *The Iceman Cometh*. Dramaten became known internationally for its O'Neill productions, culminating with *Long Day's Journey into Night* (1956). Directed by Bengt Ekerot, the production was long considered the most overwhelming, flawless stage event in the theatre's postwar history.

Negotiations leading to the world premiere of *Long Day's Journey* were carried on by Karl Ragner Gierow. During Gierow's tenure (1951–1963), director Alf Sjöberg added to his impressive Shakespeare productions the first staging of two nineteenth-century works by C.J.L. Almqvist, *Amorina* (1951) and *The Queen's Jewels* (1957).

One result of the social and political debate of the 1960s was the use of the studio by small groups of actors for projects of their own. One such production was *NJA* (1968), a docu-drama in Brechtian style based on interviews with workers at the Norrbotten Iron Works.

The democratization of theatre in Sweden is a complex matter involving much more than Dramaten policies. The government's decision in the 1970s to boost decentralization by subsidizing all professional theatre groups has not led Dramaten to fall back on its reputation as Sweden's classical stage. It has developed a lively workshop with performances at both the theatre-in-the-round Målarsalen and the Nybro Pavilion. Because of budget cuts mandated by the government, Dramaten may close its smaller stages and produce fewer experimental productions in the 1980s. Lasse Pöysti succeeded Jan-Olof Stranderg as administrative head in 1981. Lars Löfgren took over the position in 1985.

The Royal Dramatic Theatre developed from a court theatre into a traditional bourgeois stage in the nineteenth century and continued to grow into a modern democratic institution in a culture-conscious welfare society. Dramaten has a record of artistic excellence and social responsibility with which few national theatres in the world could compete.

BIRGITTA STEENE

STOCKHOLM CITY THEATRE
(Stockholm Stadsteater)
Wallingatan 21, Box 45102
S-104 30 Stockholm, Sweden

When the Stockholm City Theatre was founded in 1960, Stockholm was the last major city in Sweden to receive a civic theatre. Since the founding of the first such theatre in Gothenburg, civic theatres had opened their doors in six other cities (Norrköping-Linköping, Uppsala, Borås, Hälsingborg, and Malmö). But Stockholm, the natural hub of Swedish theatrical activity since the late 1700s, already housed Sweden's two largest companies (the Royal Opera and the Royal Dramatic Theatre) and was therefore considered to be ''well provided for.'' The fact that other cities needed new theatres more than Stockholm, however, did not remove the need in Stockholm for an alternative to the Royal Dramatic Theatre. The Stockholm City Theatre immediately filled a long-felt need, charting a strong, individual course that is now as indispensable to Swedish cultural life as the more established courses steered by the Opera and the Dramatic Theatre.

The Stockholm City Theatre is organized as a civic corporation with a board of directors named by the municipality of Stockholm. Artistic policy, however, is completely under the aegis of the theatre's managing director. As is the rule in Sweden's civic theatres, the state pays a subsidy of 55 percent of the theatre's salary expenses, while the municipality must make up the remainder of the budget in communal subsidies and ticket sales. For purposes of comparison, the 1968–1969 budget showed 3.9 million Swedish crowns received from the state, 5.7 million from Stockholm, and 1.3 million from ticket sales. The comparable figures for 1979–1980 show state support of 14 million Swedish crowns and 17 million from Stockholm.

The Stockholm City Theatre is the fourth largest theatre in Sweden in terms of budget (after the Opera, the Dramatic Theatre, and Malmö City Theatre). The theatre has 320 employees, including an acting ensemble of eighty, and four stages. The theatre mounts twenty to twenty-five productions a year, which are given a combined total of approximately one thousand performances for around three hundred thousand visitors in several locations. A separate Children's Theatre stage at Sveavägen 59 opened in 1981. The artistically independent Marionette Theatre, under the direction of Michael Meschke, was sponsored by the Stockholm City Theatre until 1981.

From the first, playing on two stages, the Stockholm City Theatre has continued to expand and enthusiastically meet new challenges. Trends begun under managing director Lars-Levi Laestadius (1960–1965) were intensified and consistently explored under Frank Sundström (1965–1969). The sixties were years of strong polarization into political versus nonpolitical theatre. In the late sixties, the Stockholm City Theatre had its own political group theatre led by actor Hans Bendrik and director Jan Bergqvist. In these years dramatists started developing scripts in improvised group work with actors. The decade was also marked by a considerable influx of contemporary Anglo-Saxon drama. Director Sten Lonnert, who was involved in the Bendrik-Bergqvist cooperative venture, was instrumental in bringing a number of modern American plays to the Stockholm City Theatre, for example, Jack Gelber, *The Connection* (1963); Kenneth Brown, *The Brig* (1965); Megan Terry, *Keep Tightly Closed in a Cool Dry Place* (1966); and, also by Terry, *Viet-Rock* (1967). From England he brought Ann Jellicoe's *The Sport of My Mad Mother* (1963) and *The Knack* (1966), and David Rudkin's *Afore Night Come* (1965). A particularly fortuitous circumstance was Arnold Wesker's settling in Sweden, where he worked on the Socialist farce *The Wedding Feast* (1974).

In the 1970s the Stockholm City Theatre continued to develop as a politically aware theatre with uncompromising standards. The managing director for the crucial second decade was the able, forceful Finnish-Swedish director Vivica Bandler (1969–1979), who was replaced by the current director, Lars Edström, in 1979. Under Bandler's strong leadership, the theatre solidified its stand as the foremost stage for introducing new Swedish playwrights and continued its previous—often experimental—approach to the classics. One prominent Swedish playwright produced at the Stockholm City Theatre is Lars Forssell, represented by *Christina Alexandra*, a play about the seventeenth-century Swedish Queen Christina, and the satirical pastiche *At the Hare and Hawk*, based on the songs of Carl Michael Bellman (1740–1795). Bandler worked for "the ideal people's theatre," striving for quality productions with box office appeal. The work in collective dramaturgy continued but with a new twist: the team of Suzanne Osten and Margareta Garpe humorously tackled the question of women's liberation in *Gee, Girls—Freedom Is Near!* (1974).

Since its opening, the Stockholm City Theatre has appealed to a particular audience. It tends to be young, socially and politically aware, and culturally rather sophisticated. Many of the theatre's political messages are therefore "preached to converts." On the other hand, conservative theatregoers need not avoid the City Theatre, as its productions are of the highest artistic quality.

If there is any discernible trend in the Stockholm City Theatre's aesthetic policy, it is safe to say that this is toward continued experimentation in *mise-en-scène*, sponsoring of new Swedish talent, emphasis on ensemble expression (more so here than at other Stockholm theatres, as the City Theatre is more politically militant), and emphasis on provocative and entertaining theatre.

The unorthodox approach that characterizes much of the City Theatre repertory has resulted in some spectacular successes over the years, as well as in a number of flops. Some of the most ambitious undertakings have turned out to be the most critically and financially successful. The uncut five-hour version of Jean Genet's *The Screens*, directed by Per-Verner Carlsson in the spring of 1964, was a gamble that paid off. The imported French guest director Yves Bureau directed a much-acclaimed *L'avare* (*The Miser*) in 1976. But the 1967 *Hamlet* with matinee idol Jarl Kulle (Sweden's Professor Higgins) in the title role and in a new translation proved unexpectedly boring. *Parisian Life* by Göran O. Eriksson (1975), an attempt to develop political theatre out of operetta, was an interesting concept that died on stage. (The action centers on an operatic company trying to rehearse an Offenbach operetta right after the 1871 Paris Commune.) The critics felt that Offenbach—intended as a foil for the serious message— came off as more theatrically satisfying than the frame story.

Other notable productions have included, not surprisingly, several plays by Brecht. Brecht's call for theatre to both "entertain and illuminate" could be quoted as the motto for the Stockholm City Theatre, particularly during the last decade. A *Caucasian Chalk Circle* of barbaric splendor (director: Hans Dahlin, 1963) has been followed by *The Good Woman of Setzuan* and *Saint Joan of the Stockyards* (both directed by Johan Bergenstråhle) and Peter Palitzsch's production of *Arturo Ui*. Other playwrights of political bent who have been championed at the City

Theatre include Michel de Ghelderode and Dario Fo, who was introduced to Swedish audiences at the Stockholm City Theatre as early as 1962.

On the other hand, certain playwrights are not performed at the Stockholm City Theatre. Lighter contemporary comedy of the Neil Simon type, salon comedy, operetta, or traditional musicals are not found in the City Theatre season. In American theatre terms, the repertory at the Stockholm City Theatre probably best resembles a cross between an Off-Off-Broadway Theatre and the drama department of a politically activist school. One might define the City Theatre repertory negatively by saying that whatever is performed there would never be seen in an American community theatre. On the other hand, the "heavier" classical repertory is not often found at the City Theatre, being considered the province of the Royal Dramatic Theatre. This includes top-ranked modern serious plays, like those by Peter Weiss, as well as the works of Shakespeare, Molière, Ibsen, Strindberg, and Chekhov. A certain overlap is, of course, inevitable: the City Theatre has its share of "classics," while the Royal Dramatic Theatre's smaller stages have mounted many contemporary, even improvisational, pieces of political thrust. But on the whole, the Stockholm City Theatre is still more truly "popular"—in program policy, repertory, and audience.

In this context, it is worth noting that the City Theatre has had the daring to produce some "period" plays which other theatres would not touch. The City Theatre produced Strindberg's seldom-seen drama of folk magic, sin, and redemption, *The Crown Bride*, in the mid-1960s. *Lars Anders, Jan Anders, and Their Children*, a folk comedy from 1894, was revived in the late 1970s and proved to be both effective theatre and a commentary on the cultural and social currents of the turn of the century. (This simple play, with its family feud plot and musical interludes, was an enduring favorite among Swedish Americans, and played in Swedish ethnic theatre groups all over the United States in the 1920s and 1930s.) One of the most successful plays ever at the City Theatre was a dramatization in 1970 of Per-Anders Fogelström's *Do You Remember That Town?*, a moving chronicle of working-class Stockholm that touched the hearts of thousands. It exemplified the best of Stockholm City Theatre's offerings: an imaginative, carefully crafted ensemble production of material by a modern Swedish author on a local and "popular" theme. The theatre may wish to be remembered for its avant-garde political message plays; Stockholmers will remember it for showing them their roots. As long as the Stockholm City Theatre continues to experiment and at the same time touch base with its audiences, the outlook for the 1980s is bright.

ANNE-CHARLOTTE HANES HARVEY

SWEDISH NATIONAL THEATRE CENTER
(Riksteatern)
Råsundavägen 150
S-171 30 Solna, Sweden

The Swedish National Theatre Center is a unique organization dedicated to increasing interest in the theatre, ensuring that it can be seen wherever people live. Since its founding in 1934, the center's work has been both innovative and influential. It is now the largest theatre in the country with the greatest amount of activity, in terms of both number of performances and geographical coverage. It has often led the way with new forms of audience contact and theatre activity, such as providing performances for schools. The Theatre Center's work has several facets: *creating* its own productions; *distributing* its own shows and those produced by other Swedish and foreign companies; *publishing* magazines (*Teatern* and *Entré*), books on theatre, and play scripts for amateur groups; and *consulting* on children's theatre, amateur theatre, and technical theatre. The consulting work ranges from leading training courses for amateur theatre groups to conferring on plans for renovating or building theatres.

Shortly after the social-democratic government took office in 1932, the cabinet minister Arthur Engberg formulated a directive that emphasized the right of people living away from large cities to have access to theatre. With decentralization as the goal, a new perspective was opened and a period of expansion began for Swedish theatre. According to Gösta M. Bergman, who served as head of the National Theatre Center from 1934 to 1957, "the walls around certain isolated cultural centers began to be broken down." (*Svensk teater* [Stockholm: Almqvist & Wiksell, 1970], p. 31.) In some ways this was a continuation of the principles in practice in the 1920s, when the Skådebanen organization sent productions on tours and provided subscription plans attractive to the working class, and when entertainment became more widely available at the folk park theatres and on radio. Engberg's original idea was to create mobility and flexibility for the Opera, the Royal Dramatic Theatre, and other state-supported theatres so that they could tour; he also wanted to encourage amateur dramatic activity. From the initial conception of its task solely as distribution, the idea evolved that this could also be a producing organization. Quite early in its history it engaged the outstanding directors Per Lindberg (whose productions included *The Threepenny Opera, Peer Gynt*, and *Hamlet*) and Olof Molander (who directed plays by Maxwell Anderson, William Saroyan, and Ragnar Josephson). *The Threepenny Opera* was the first play by Brecht ever to be seen in the provinces. During the war the Theatre Center made courageous political statements through its choice of repertory. It sponsored performances by actors who had escaped from the Nazis in Norway and now called themselves the Free Norwegian Stage. During the war, the Theatre Center presented performances for fifty-five to sixty-five thousand military personnel each year.

Since World War II there have been dynamic changes in the activities of the Swedish National Theatre Center. New subscription plans have been devised, there has been much visitation of schools, and there is greater geographical coverage and contact with new audiences. To stimulate interest there are open rehearsals, and after performances audiences may sometimes stay for a discussion with the director and cast. Now that the Theatre Center uses the Södra Theatre, its own productions may be seen in Stockholm and not just on tour.

Throughout its history the Theatre Center has always exemplified democracy in action as it has encouraged contact with the public through its organizational structure. Since 1974 the national cultural policy has emphasized decentralization, a principle already integral to the Theatre Center. However, since 1974 organizational units away from the capital have assumed increasing responsibility. There are now about 150 local theatre associations and 10 county theatre associations that work with theatre consultants and interested citizens to plan for the performances given by ensembles of the Theatre Center. Representatives from the local and county associations meet every three years in a congress in order to make major decisions about policy and repertory. This continues the tradition begun by the first congress in 1934, at which there were representatives of forty-two local organizations. There is also a board with twenty-three members, twelve of whom are appointed by the Congress. The artistic director of the Theatre Center attends, and there are other board members appointed by such organizations as the National Board of Education, the County Council Association, and the Theatre Center staff. In addition to the personnel which produces dramatic and musical productions, the Theatre Center has several special ensembles, including two renowned dance companies, the Cramér Ballet and the Cullberg Ballet, and two ensembles that have their residence away from the capital and tour in their region: the Växjö Ensemble and the Örebro Ensemble. In addition, there are two groups that meet special needs: the Silent Theatre, which performs in sign language, and the Pioneer Theatre, which produces shows especially for prisons and hospitals.

Approximately 450 permanent employees perform the wide range of administrative and artistic work of the Swedish National Theatre Center. Mats Johansson succeeded Hans Ullberg as administrative head of the center in 1983. About 80 percent of expenses are paid by the national government, which in 1977, for example, provided a subsidy of 58 million Swedish crowns. The subsidy not only covers production and traveling costs, but also helps to guarantee that ticket prices will remain reasonable. The Theatre Center sells a performance to a community for a package price; the local theatre association is then responsible for advertising and selling tickets. The administrative offices, storage space, technical workshops, and eight large rehearsal halls are located at Film City in Solna (Stockholm). In Stockholm performances are given on the two stages of the Södra Theatre, which may also be used for guest performances sponsored by the Theatre Center or be rented by other producers. Built in 1853, the Södra is Stockholm's oldest theatre building. On tour productions are presented in many types of locations—school assembly halls, civic centers, factories, libraries, and hospitals. Certain large productions tour only where there is a proscenium stage with adequate space; others are designed to be performed anywhere.

The number of performances presented by the Swedish National Theatre Center has increased impressively since the 469 that were given in the 1934–1935 season. The average number of performances per year is now more than four thousand, which means that twenty to twenty-five performances are given each day of the season in that many different locations. The number of people who saw a Theatre Center production in 1935 was 137,000; now each season the audience numbers over 1 million. There are about 130 different programs in each season, of which perhaps 100 are the Theatre Center's own shows. The others may be sent out from national or city theatres or may be foreign troupes, such as a Nō company from Japan, Laterna Magica from Poland, or the Royal Shakespeare Company from England. Productions are seen in more than five hundred locations throughout the country. Comedies, such as *Cactus Flower*, and musicals, such as *Fiddler on the Roof*, are most popular with the public. Each year the center produces two musicals of its own and distributes other musical and operatic productions. Among the foreign playwrights whose work has been shown are Shakespeare, Edward Albee, Fernando Arrabal, Samuel Beckett, Georg Büchner, Anton Chekhov, Eugene O'Neill, Harold Pinter, and William Wycherley. Swedish dramatists represented have included Kent Andersson and Bengt Bratt and, of course, Strindberg. About 40 percent of the repertory is planned for children and young people, and there are special productions for migrant groups, particularly Finnish-speaking audiences.

For employees of the Swedish National Theatre Center, travel is an integral part of their lives. In the 1980–1981 season the productions being taken to the people included a one-man show of African material, Nikolai Gogol's *The Inspector General*, and Ludvig Holberg's *Erasmus Montanus*. True to its origin as part of the popular movement, the Theatre Center strives to bring the producer of good theatre ever closer to the individual audience member and to develop the audience of the future.

CARLA WAAL

THEATRE 9
(Teater 9)
S:t Eriksplan 2
S-113 20 Stockholm, Sweden

Theatre 9 is not the most typical Swedish theatre, but it may be one of the most interesting from an international perspective. With roots in a very Swedish and Northern European political and artistic situation, Theatre 9 is a link between Swedish and foreign theatre, between political and experimental traditions in contemporary theatre.

Theatre 9 belongs to the first generation of the Swedish group theatre movement, which started around 1968. It is the only group that has consistently worked at an international level while maintaining close contacts with younger group theatres of the late 1970s, a new movement strongly influenced by the Odin Theatre of Denmark and the "third theatre" movement, and sometimes violently rejected by the generation of 1968. Theatre 9 has its own theatre in Stockholm but also tours in Sweden and abroad with works for both children and adults.

It has visited festivals in Wroclaw, Caracas, and Freiburg, and has toured five European countries and Venezuela.

Until the 1960s Swedish theatre was synonymous with the institutional theatres supported by state and cities. Private "commercial" theatre hardly existed outside Stockholm. In the 1960s many young theatre workers started to form their own free groups instead of trying to win access to official theatres. There was growing dissatisfaction with "bourgeois" theatre and a longing to reach new audiences with a new theatre or sometimes with new messages in a new socio-theatrical form. Many free-group members were radical students, but some were young actors from the big theatres and state schools, dissatisfied with the conservative repertory, the naturalistic tradition, and the hierarchic organization. There were notable impulses from the Living Theatre, La Mama, and Bread and Puppet Theatre, all of which appeared in Sweden from 1965 to 1970. Jerzy Grotowski also came as a teacher and with his group. But the most decisive influence was Bertolt Brecht and his theories. Still more important were the social and political forces behind the leftist movement of a whole generation. The hunger for change was born out of an increase in education and information. In the case of Sweden it developed from the combination of a continuous economic boom and sudden exposure to problems of the Third World, including the international reaction against U.S. warfare in Indochina and a renaissance of Marxist philosophy. The new theatre movement wanted to change not only the theatre, but the world as well. How to achieve this has been disputed and modified since then.

Most Swedish groups today belong to Teatercentrum, the umbrella organization founded in 1969. After the pioneer years (1965–1972) many small or less stable groups disappeared. Some important artists in the movement returned to the big theatres, continuing to develop at least some of the exploits of the free groups. Around 1977–1978 a new wave appeared with a number of groups influenced by what can roughly be described as the Artaud/Grotowski tradition but also by the ecological movement and the interest in old forms of folk art, jugglery, and street theatre. Among them were young people active in the contemporary counterparts to the rebellions of the 1960s, creating street theatre or working in more limited, experimental forms.

Theatre 9 was founded in 1968 by two student theatres. They broke all ties with the university and opened their doors to anyone interested in creating alternative theatre on a collective basis. The first production toured Sweden outside traditional theatre venues, playing in schools, libraries, prisons, and so on. Theatre 9's first theatre opened in March 1969. The foyer had an art gallery and coffee machine; "backstage," one room served as dressing room, office, archive, and meeting place. At first, over sixty members worked at Regeringsgatan 9, from which address the group took its name. In 1971 the group moved to a former cinema built in 1911, with offices in an eighteenth-century inn, and was condensed into its present size of thirteen members and two associates.

The group started developing its working principles with the production of

Vsevolod Vishnevsky's *The Optimistic Tragedy* (1973), a complex and controversial play about conflicts between Bolshevism and anarchism during the Russian Revolution. This was a significant choice, vital to the development of the movement out of which Theatre 9 and many other new theatres were born. The staging combined an almost cinematographic use of light, space, and rhythm, with strong pathos in acting, rarely seen then in the pseudo-Brechtian theatre of many free groups. This new approach had been prepared for in some of the early Theatre 9 productions, of plays by Oscar Panizza, Frank Wedekind, Alfred Jarry, Brecht, and Latin American authors. In 1974 Theatre 9 created *Deadly Knowledge*—a production about the dangers of nuclear power—combining elements of the visual arts, nonmatrixed performances, and didactic political cabaret theatre. This work was invited to festivals in Poland and Venezuela, the beginning of Theatre 9's international adventures.

Theatre 9 has brought a number of foreign theatres to Sweden including Kathakali, the Odin Theatre, Temps Fort Theatre of France, many Polish and Latin American groups, and women's theatres from Britain and the United States. The Comuna Baires from Argentina (today based in Milan) collaborates with Theatre 9 as well as with Teatr 77 of Lodz, Poland. Both Comuna Baires and Teatr 77 visited Stockholm in 1977. That year they, along with other groups and individuals from several countries, founded the International Federation of Independent Theatre (IFIT), which organized the 1978 Wroclaw Open Theatre Festival. In 1979 Theatre 9 and IFIT hosted the first International Festival of Independent Theatre in Stockholm. Thirteen groups from six countries gave seminars and over fifty performances, mainly on the two stages of the present Theatre 9. In August 1982 Theatre 9 hosted another international festival for "free" theatre. Since Swedish theatre life tends to a certain provincialism, initiatives of this kind are vitalizing.

Working within IFIT, Theatre 9 has embarked on a series of joint productions with theatres from other countries. The first such performance was *Crossroads*, performed with Teatr 77 in Polish, English, and Swedish on the theme of the "welfare state" from Swedish and Polish perspectives with critical comment on the respective systems. *Crossroads* premiered in Stockholm and Lodz in 1978 and has been seen in Olesnica, Wroclaw, Cracow, Szczeczin, Freiburg, and Milan. In 1980 Theatre 9, Teatr 77, and Comuna Baires with groups from Denmark, Hungary, and Czechoslovakia worked on *Together*, a project based on an allegory about the state of the world and man by the seventeenth-century writer Komensky (Comenius). *Together* is a theatrical work, an appeal for peace and an anthropological research project. These appear to be the first joint works by theatres from different cultures and political systems. They demand a new dramaturgy plus living and working together in close contact with local communities in participating countries.

In Theatre 9's own work, *Babylon* (1977) meant a new kind of performance: it started in the realm of myths and reached through contemporary political and cultural problems to visions of the future. The first part, based on Icelandic Edda poems, survives in a children's play performed in Sweden, Poland, Switzerland, Germany, and Italy. *Aftermath* (1979) was a harsh analysis of the development of the New Left, a semirealistic "well-made play" with sequences of introspective poetry or theatrical grotesque. The same year *Barbarity* by Roberto Merino harked back to Latin American experiences and commented on ideas of French new philosophy. *Prometheus Bound* (1979) was developed partly through experimental musical principles and partly through improvisations which (without changing the basic myth) transposed this oldest of tragedies to multiple levels of archetypic, contemporary, and visionary experiences.

This working process continued with Strindberg's *A Dream Play*. Ten actors (of whom two directed the performance) and two scenographers used Strindberg's full text to compose a three-and-a-half-hour "orchestration" with ten actors. The result is both a true version of the text, which is rather obscure and seldom performed in its entirety, and ten new "dramas," composed individually for each actor/actress by him/herself and the directors. *A Dream Play* was invited to West Germany in 1981.

In 1980 the group prepared a new version of *Prometheus* as part of a larger cycle of performances built on myths told to children. The second work was an adaptation of Goethe's *Iphigenia in Tauris*, which had its premiere in 1982.

Theatre 9 has had a remarkably homogeneous development in its personnel; the members have worked together for all or most of their professional careers. As a result, Theatre 9 has developed its own performing style and working methods, consciously eclectic and integrating theatre, music, and visual art, profiting from but not copying theatrical and pedagogical "trends" of the past decade. With Comuna Baires and Teatr 77 the group has developed a coherent anthropological view of theatre as social meeting-place and tool for change, a "mini-medium" with more intense possibilities for individual contacts with the spectator than the larger media. Theatre 9 has consciously combined the two opposed but interdependent traditions inherited from the 1960s and from all revolutionary periods of the arts in our time: never-ending experimentation and deep social and political commitment.

STEFAN JOHANSSON